BIG ENGLISH

2ND EDITION
Teacher's Edition

6

CONTENTS

Welcome to Big English!	iii
Component Walk-through	iv
Big English Course Pedagogy	vi
Unit Walk-through	xii
Big English Lesson Flow	xvi
Time Guidelines	xviii
Scope and Sequence	T2
Welcome to Class!	a
1 All About School	4
2 Amazing Young People	16
3 Dilemmas	28
Checkpoint, Units 1–3	40
4 Dreams for the Future	44
5 If I Could Fly…	56
6 The Coolest School Subjects	68
Checkpoint, Units 4–6	80
7 Mysteries!	84
8 Why Is It Famous?	96
9 That's Entertainment!	108
Checkpoint, Units 7–9	120
Cutouts for Checkpoints	T124
Stickers	T125
Cambridge Young Learners English: Flyers Practice Paper	T126
Game Bank	T136
Audio Scripts	T138
Workbook Answer Key	T154
Wordlist	T162
International Phonetic Alphabet	T166

Welcome to Big English!

This new edition of Big English builds on the firm foundations and big ideas of the first edition, but brings a whole host of new features and components to help young learners make progress and communicate confidently.

Why Big English?

Learning happens in context, not in isolation.
We believe that learners are best motivated by intriguing content that is relevant to their lives and puts English in the context of the world that surrounds them.

Three big ideas that build on established and proven methodologies.
Three of the central bases for the Big English program philosophy are: 21st century skills, Content and Language Integrated Learning (CLIL), and Assessment for Learning (AfL) techniques.

Multiple experiences all in one book.
Kids learn best when they engage with the language in a variety of ways. Big English provides multiple and varied opportunities for success, including singing, role-playing, watching videos, reading fiction and nonfiction texts, project work, and conducting research.

It's a digital world.
Today's students are digital natives who have never known a world without computers and the internet. Big English comes with new digital learning tools, the use of which reflect learners' reality and expectations.

So what's new in Big English?

New components and features to engage your learners.

- A completely new digital offering which includes teacher digital resources with the Teacher Presentation Tool, and student digital resources with assignable interactive activities.
- New content including welcome units to bridge any gaps between the levels and serve as a quick review to the previous level, giving the students the foundations and confidence to start the next level.
- New Content Connection and Culture Connection pages.
- Additional Big TV videos supported by a video workbook.
- Big English has a fresh new look with a simplified design which helps learners to focus on content and the activities. Plus we have great new signposting to help you really get the most of all the Big components.
- A refreshed approach to Assessment for Learning with students and teachers given plenty of opportunities to review their progress in both the Student's Book and the Workbook.

Global Scale of English

At the start of every unit you also get an overview of the GSE reading, listening, speaking, and writing objectives covered by the content of that unit. End of unit *I can* statements directly relate to the vocabulary, grammar, and skill descriptors within the Global Scale of English. They appear in the review sections of the Student's Book and are also highlighted in the unit openers of the Teacher's Edition.

The Global Scale of English (GSE) is a standardized, granular scale which measures English language proficiency. Unlike some other frameworks which describe attainment in broad bands, the GSE identifies what a learner can do at each point on the scale across speaking, listening, reading, and writing skills. The scale is designed to motivate learners by giving more granular insight into learning progress.

The badging on the back of your coursebook shows the range of objectives that are covered within the content. Knowing this range helps you select materials with the right level of support and challenge for your students to help them progress. It does not mean that students need to have mastered all objectives below the range before starting the course, or that they will all be at the top of the range by the end.

For more information about how using the GSE can support your planning and teaching, your assessment of your learners, and in selecting or creating additional materials to supplement your core program, please go to www.english.com/gse.

COMPONENT
Walk-through

1 PLAN ❭ **2 TEACH** ❭ **3 PRACTICE** ❭ **4 ASSESS**

1 PLAN: Before class

Teacher's Edition
The Teacher's Edition is the place where you can find everything you need to know to teach with Big English. It includes comprehensive and easy to follow visuals of Big English lesson flows, activities and ideas, and supporting material such as a Game Bank, audio scripts, and full assessment support including Cambridge English Young Learners practice materials.

NEW Teacher Presentation Tool
Step-by-step lesson flows follow the same learning path as those in the Teacher's Edition.

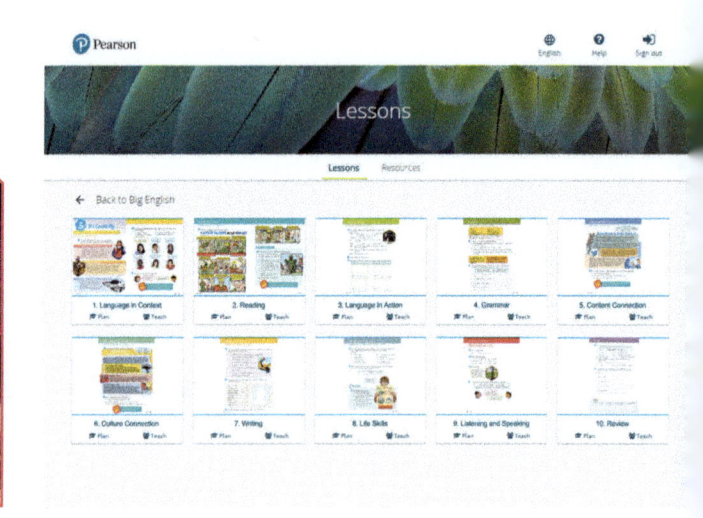

4 ASSESS: After class

Assessment Pack
Comprehensive suite of assessment materials including Diagnostic Pre-Tests, Practice Tests, Unit Tests, Mastery Tests (every three units), Final Exams, and materials for oral assessment.

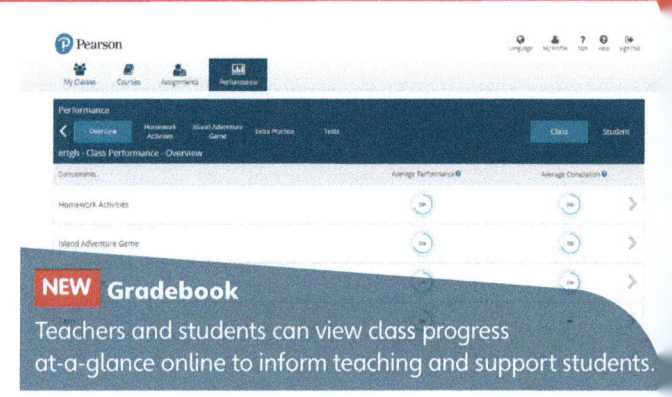

NEW Gradebook
Teachers and students can view class progress at-a-glance online to inform teaching and support students.

iv

2 TEACH: In class

Student's Book

NEW Welcome Unit
Students review key language at the start of the school year.

Workbook

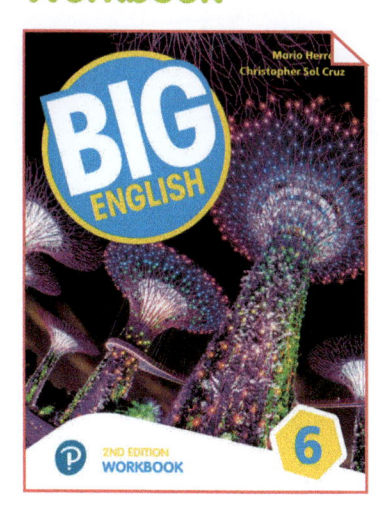

NEW Teacher Presentation Tool

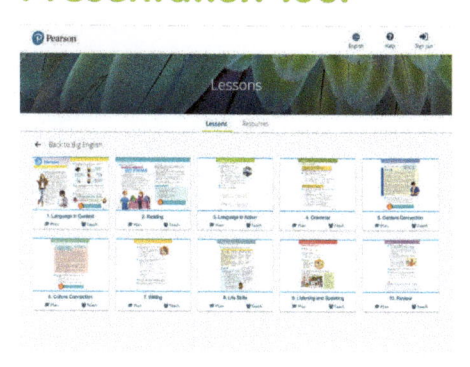

Audio CDs, Documentary and Dramatic videos

Flashcards

backpack

Posters

NEW Big TV videos and Video Workbook

3 PRACTICE: Out of class

Workbook
Workbook activities correlate exactly with the learning objectives in the Student's Book. These activities are flexible and they can be carried out in class or set as homework.

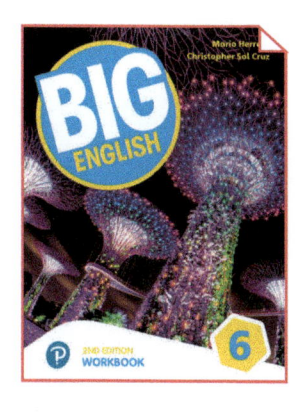

NEW Student digital resources
Interactive digital activities can be assigned for individual practice in the student digital resources.

v

BIG ENGLISH
Course Pedagogy

Big English is based on a number of pedagogical approaches which are critical to effective learning. These are all explained below, along with examples of how to deliver successful lessons using the course.

21st Century Skills

What are 21st century skills?

21st century skills are the skills and competencies that learners need to be successful in the increasingly complex life and work environment of today's rapidly changing, digital world. These skills include critical thinking, communication, collaboration, creativity and innovation, and social and cross-cultural interaction.

Big English combines rich, real-life content, a variety of tasks, and specific teaching guidance to ensure ample coverage of these skills.

Why are 21st century skills important?

It is important that students are encouraged and motivated to think deeply about issues, to develop critical thinking skills, and to solve problems creatively. These skills, paired with a communicative approach, provide a foundation that learners can build on throughout their studies.

How do I use 21st century skills whilst teaching with Big English?

21st century skills are embedded throughout Big English. You will find clearly sign-posted sections in the teaching notes to show you how to best enhance 21st century skills on a regular basis.

A key element of our approach to support critical thinking is the regular *Think BIG* feature which is included in all units and which is integrated across all components. The *Think BIG* feature offers young learners the opportunity to discuss, analyze, collaborate, and be creative. The Teacher's Edition includes detailed guidance on how to manage the *Think BIG* questions, as well as set up other communicative, collaborative, or creative tasks, such as projects.

An important method to embedding this approach into your teaching is questioning. In order to develop analytical skills, questions in class should be, as much as possible, open-ended. For example, rather than "Do you want to be a doctor?", you can ask "What do you want to be?" and, critically, "Why?". Even if the students cannot answer open-ended questions fully in English, any attempt should be praised.

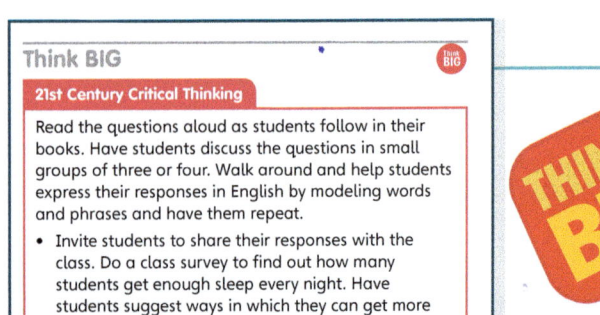

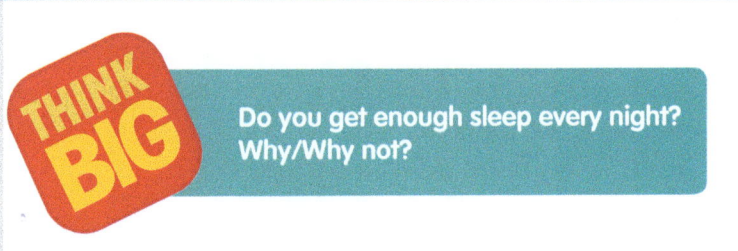

Think BIG

21st Century Critical Thinking

Read the questions aloud as students follow in their books. Have students discuss the questions in small groups of three or four. Walk around and help students express their responses in English by modeling words and phrases and have them repeat.

- Invite students to share their responses with the class. Do a class survey to find out how many students get enough sleep every night. Have students suggest ways in which they can get more quality sleep.

THINK BIG: Do you get enough sleep every night? Why/Why not?

Content and Language Integrated Learning (CLIL)

What is CLIL?
Content and Language Integrated Learning (CLIL) is an approach where the students are learning a subject, for example math, science, or art through the medium of English. This helps deepen their understanding of both the curriculum material and the English language. This enhanced comprehension places them far beyond where they would be by studying only non-academic, everyday English.

The CLIL lessons in Big English help increase learners' motivation and confidence in their acquisition of key language and expand their content knowledge.

Why is CLIL important?
Learning other subjects through English gives students a reason to learn – to understand and discuss the subject matter. This is motivating for young learners.

By teaching relevant subjects that reflect the world around them, for example science, students are likely to become more engaged and curious about the world in general, and about the English they need to describe it.

CLIL also includes learning about other cultures, which provides insights into how people around the world have similarities and differences and helps to develop open, global citizens.

How do I use CLIL whilst teaching with Big English?
CLIL lessons appear in every unit of Big English. The learning objective of these Content Connection and Culture Connection lessons are clearly signposted on the Student's Book page. This is shared with the class at the start of each lesson.

Key content words can be pre-taught prior to listening or reading the presentation text. These are extra words that might be useful when discussing the text rather than being key vocabulary items.

Subject material is presented through listening and/or reading activities, which is followed by spoken and/or written practice of the content, including using some of the key vocabulary.

Workbook practice activities are provided for these lessons which can be carried out in or out of class, and which further reinforce the concepts and key language.

There is always a *Think BIG* feature included in these lessons – a question or activity which encourages learners to think deeply about the content.

Each unit also includes an engaging video for either the Content Connection or Culture Connection lesson which brings the subject to life. To support the teacher, there is a Video Guide which contains pre-, while, and post-watching activities.

Content Connection | Science and Technology

I will learn about predictions for the future.

🎧 59 Listen and read. How will we be learning new skills in the future?

CONTENT WORDS
futurist   microscopic   nanotechnology
revolutionize   wireless

The Next Big Thing
Experts' Predictions for the Future

Futurists are people whose job is to look ahead and help us plan for the future. Futurists can't say what the future will definitely be like, but they use their knowledge to say what will probably happen and what we can prepare ourselves for. How will we be learning fifty years from now?

Nanotechnology
Nanotechnology is the science of incredibly small things. As a unit of measure, a nanometer is one billionth of a meter! When something is nano-sized, it's so small, it's invisible! With nanotechnology, we'll have microscopic computerized robots called nanobots. Because nanobots can be built into almost anything – even appliances – household chores will be easier. Nanobots could also be used to travel through your body and treat problems and disease without expensive and painful operations.

Brain-to-Computer Communication
How about this for an amazing prediction? One day, everyone and everything will be linked through wireless technology. Nanocomputers will be in your system, so your brain, just like a computer, will be able to receive downloads and uploads. Would you like to learn a new language or how to tango? As soon as you think the thought, your brain will download the new language or the dance steps, and you'll be learning them instantly!

Assessment for Learning

What is Assessment for Learning?

As opposed to traditional, summative assessment tools that measure what has been learned, formative assessment or Assessment for Learning takes a different approach. It is based on three key principles: having students participate in setting learning objectives, performing ongoing assessment, and helping students to learn how to set their own goals and self-assess.

Using this approach, the ongoing assessment that a teacher makes informs the teaching of the next lesson or module to ensure all students, whatever their starting point, make clear progress.

Why is Assessment for Learning important?

When Assessment for Learning strategies are integrated in the lesson, students take an active role in their own learning and seek out help they need to meet their goals.

Assessment for Learning can include a variety of activities, for example classroom discussions, peer or group work, homework, and traditional quizzes. The important thing to remember about formative assessment is that the method of assessment is not what makes it useful, but the way in which the results are used. Formative assessment is most successful when results are analyzed to determine the current state of student understanding. Results are folded into the classroom experience as teachers take specific actions to improve any deficiencies or correct misunderstandings.

Another key aspect of formative assessment is sharing clear targets with the class. Discussing learning objectives at the start of the lesson helps students to focus. Reviewing these objectives at the end starts to develop self-awareness of the progress they are making, and what they need to do to improve.

Performing ongoing assessment means that gaps in learning are filled early, so that every child reaches their full potential.

Training young learners to set their own goals and be aware of progress develops reflective learners, which is a quality of paramount importance for their later studies.

How do I use Assessment for Learning whilst teaching with Big English?

Assessment for Learning techniques are embedded in all lessons in Big English. Lesson objectives are given on every page in the Student's Book, focusing learners on the learning goal at the start and end of every lesson.

A self-assessment feature is built into each Review lesson at the end of each unit. This requires students to think about the key learning objectives of the unit, and to what extent they have met them. This raises awareness about their own progress. It is also a useful tool for the teacher to gauge who has any learning gaps that need to be filled.

In addition to that, every Checkpoint section (after every three units) contains both self-assessment and peer assessment, further developing awareness of the students' own progress.

The Teacher's Edition is a rich resource for embedding Assessment for Learning into your lessons, and follows a clearly signposted process through all teaching notes.

INVOLVE
This feature provides opportunities to engage students in the learning objective and help them to develop self-awareness of their English progress.

MONITOR
This feature creates opportunities to assess how well students are learning the material and identify gaps to inform teaching.

ASSIST
This feature provides guidance to immediately resolve a gap in learning that has been identified. For example, through presenting the material in another context.

CHALLENGE
This feature goes beyond the page by getting students to personalize, analyze, and apply the language. This is often a more productive task requiring greater fluency. It can be given to a group of students or a whole class.

This process aims to help teachers to see which students need more of a challenge and which ones need remediation in order to keep all learners progressing appropriately.

Systematic Vocabulary Development

What is systematic vocabulary development?

Systematic vocabulary development means explicitly presenting the key vocabulary in multiple contexts from real world examples to classroom situations so that students understand all aspects of a target word or phrase; giving students multiple opportunities to encounter the word, to make it memorable and meaningful.

Why is systematic vocabulary development important?

Presenting and practicing vocabulary in a systematic way gives students exposure to the right amount of new vocabulary in any one lesson, preventing overload. Knowing a small number of words at a time, and knowing them well engenders motivation in learners.

Careful scaffolding through visuals and audio support means that young learners feel secure and confident in the early stages of learning.

How do I teach vocabulary in a systematic way with Big English?

In Big English, the Vocabulary lessons always start with sharing the lesson objective with the class and reminding students what they already know about the topic.

New vocabulary is practiced using a variety of skills – through listening, speaking, reading, and writing in the Student's Book and Workbook. Engaging practice activities are carefully scaffolded to ensure that children feel secure in learning the target words. Activity types include games, matching, personalization, critical thinking, etc.

Extra practice is provided in the Workbook, a flexible component which gives students an opportunity to reinforce the new language in class or at home.

Key vocabulary is also recycled throughout the unit in the Story and Review lessons and the Checkpoint sections, providing a wealth of practice. This results in increased exposure to the target language, developing familiarity and mastery of the language.

Explicit vocabulary presentation	Scaffolded vocabulary practice	Vocabulary practice through other contexts and activities	Memory and understanding of the vocabulary reviewed
Vocabulary presented with visuals and audio	Vocabulary practiced through a variety of activities	Vocabulary reviewed in other lessons	Vocabulary reviewed again at the end of the unit

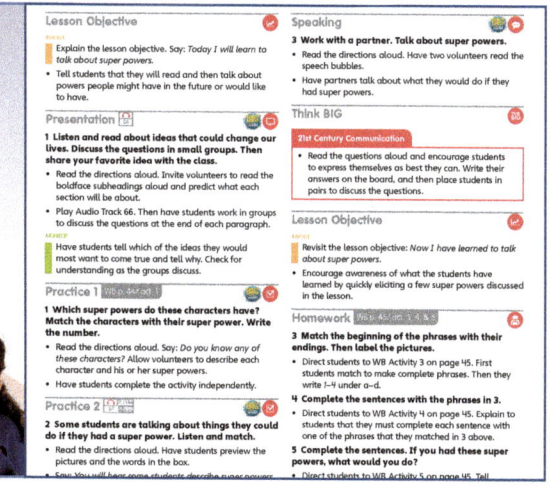

Grammar Instruction

Why is grammar instruction important?

It is not always appropriate to present new grammar structures to learners as a set of rules that require analysis and manipulation. Instead, they should be made aware of these structures by teaching them as chunks of grammar which they see and hear again and again until they start using them in a natural way. As children begin to think more analytically, they are able to remember and apply rules to language structures.

The careful scaffolding through charts, visuals, and audio support in the grammar presentation and practice stages means that young learners feel secure and confident in the early stages of learning. This should give them a solid foundation on which to build further English language learning.

How do I teach grammar with Big English?

In addition to the four skills and vocabulary development, Big English recognizes that learners need systematic and repeated exposure over time to language structures if they are to make the new language their own. As with other lessons, the Grammar and the Language in Action lessons always start with sharing the learning objective with the class and reminding students what they already know about the topic.

Big English gives students the opportunity to consider structures in such devices as grammar boxes in their books. But Big English never abandons the necessity of presenting language structures in meaningful contexts, and highlights differences and similarities in language use to encourage students to work out the grammatical principle. This makes the grammatical rule more meaningful and memorable.

The Workbook also provides a variety of extra grammar practice activities to help students understand and eventually produce the target grammar.

Big English contains a wealth of recycling of structures throughout the course. This results in increased exposure to the target language, developing familiarity and mastery of the language. Students gain further opportunities to review the structures in the Review lessons at the end of each unit, as well as the Checkpoint sections that feature after every three units. This is crucial to mastering the target language.

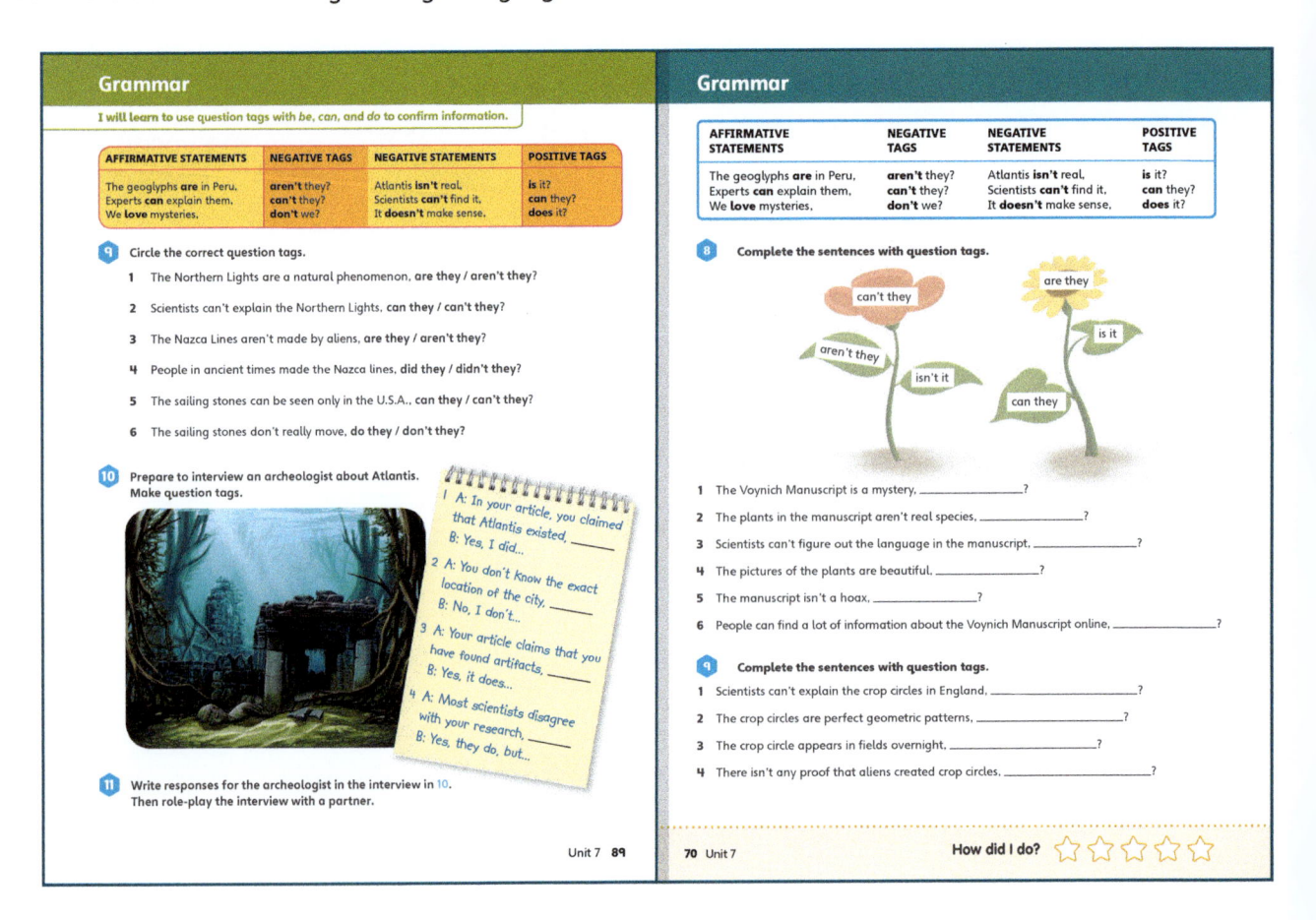

🔵 Systematic Phonics Development

What is systematic phonics development?

This approach to phonics development means an explicit and focused presentation of a small number of letter-sound correlations at any one time. The teacher follows a carefully planned sequence of sounds, and students build up to producing whole words by first listening to the separate key sounds, blending them, and finally attempting to produce a whole word which contains the target sound.

Why is systematic phonics development important?

Presenting the sounds of English in a systematic way means that all children will feel secure in what they need to do in these lessons. Students are given plenty of auditory support which acts as exposure to the spoken language. This is especially important for children with little exposure to English outside of class.

Having plenty of opportunities for practice, either receptively or productively, builds confidence in understanding spoken English. This will, in turn, build confidence in and mastery of using those sounds while speaking.

How do I teach phonics in a systematic way with Big English?

In this new edition, Big English now contains a dedicated Listening and Speaking section within each unit. The Listening and Speaking lessons always start with sharing the learning objective with the class and reminding students what they already know about the topic.

Each Listening and Speaking lesson follows a highly-structured sequence. The target sounds are presented with clear audio and illustrations. This is followed by an opportunity to listen and blend the target sounds in complete words. The target sounds are then practiced in context, through an engaging chant.

The Teacher's Edition contains comprehensive and highly supportive teaching notes. Target sounds are presented with audio to support teachers with the modeling of the sounds.

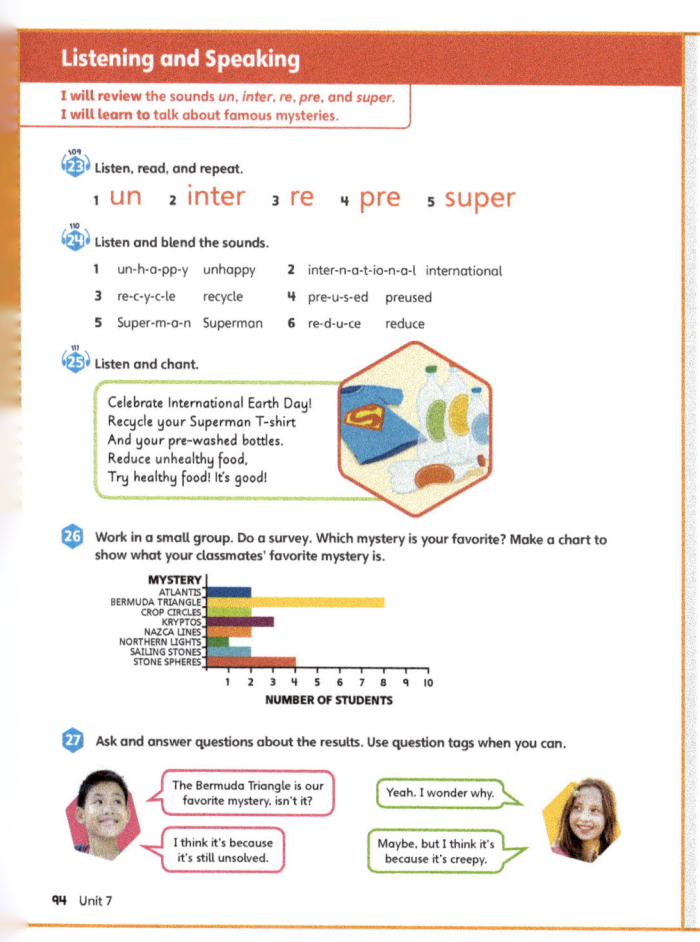

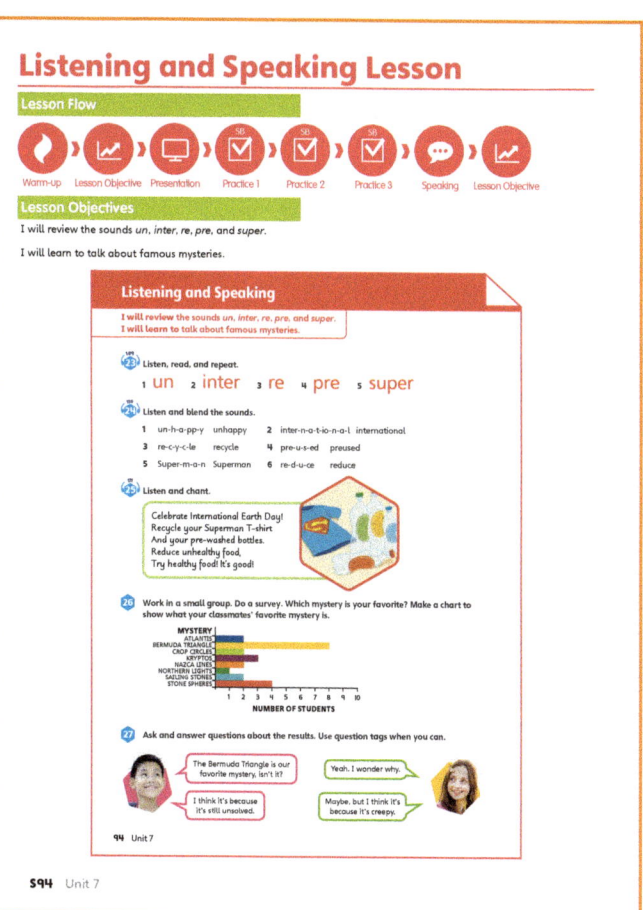

xi

UNIT Walk-through

Language in Context Lesson

Theme-based units encourage deeper understanding of concepts and language.

Learning objectives on the page help to focus learners and make them aware of the progress they're making.

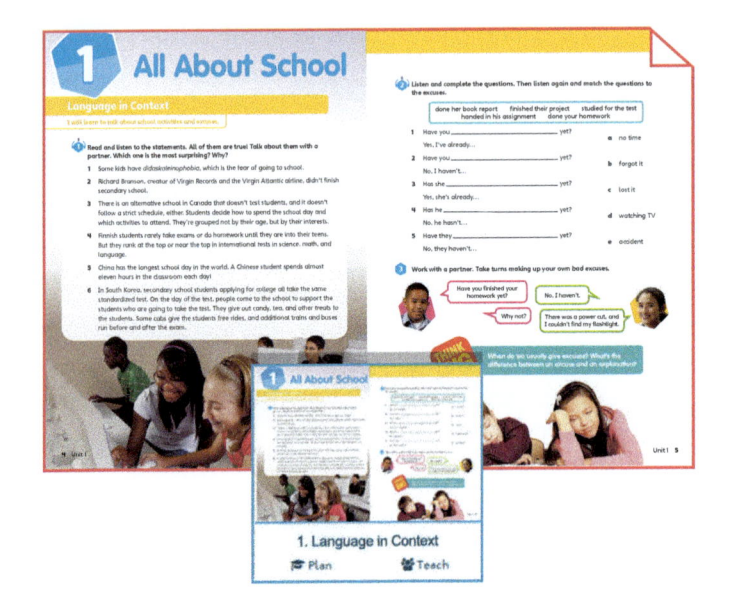

Key unit vocabulary is presented in context. The vocabulary is practiced in a kinesthetic way, through games and similar engaging activities.

Think BIG questions prompt students to use critical thinking skills, personalize language, collaborate, and use key vocabulary in context.

Reading Lesson

Comprehension strategies and critical thinking are developed through frequent reading practice.

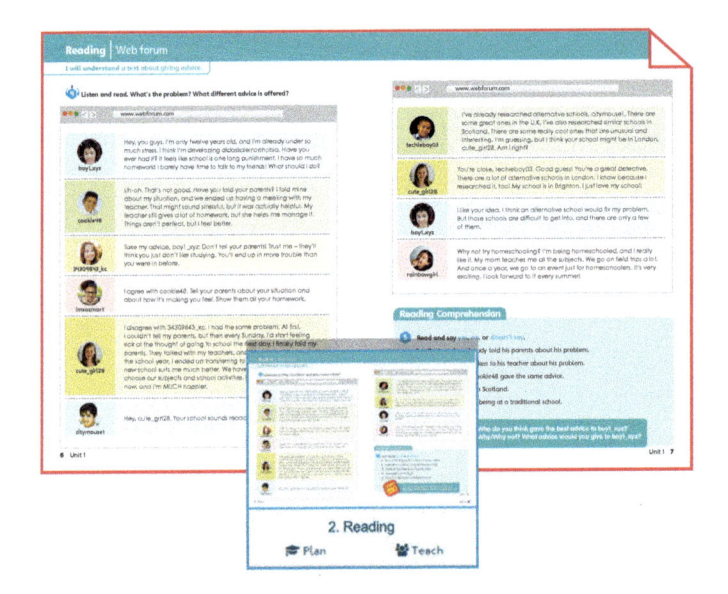

Target vocabulary is practiced through engaging reading texts.

xii

Language in Action and Grammar Lessons

A dialog is presented and practiced to increase students' communicative competence.

Following an **integrated approach**, students read, listen, speak, and write all in one lesson.

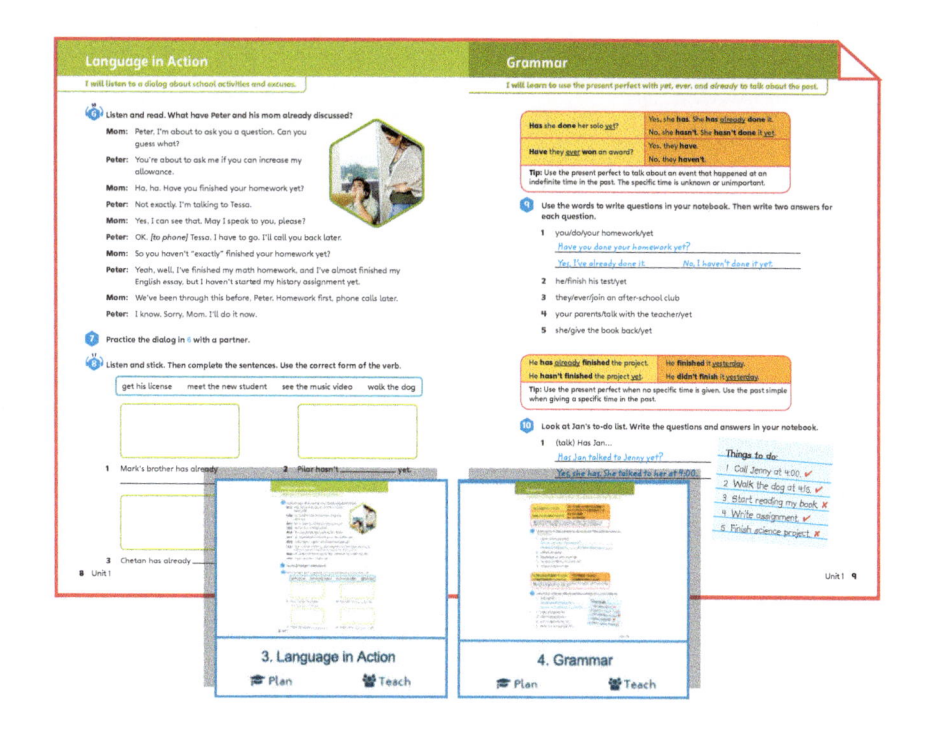

Grammar is taught in context and supported by clear grammar charts.

Content Connection and Culture Connection Lessons

In Content Connection lessons, students encounter texts from academic areas such as social studies, science, and math. Content vocabulary is clearly signposted.

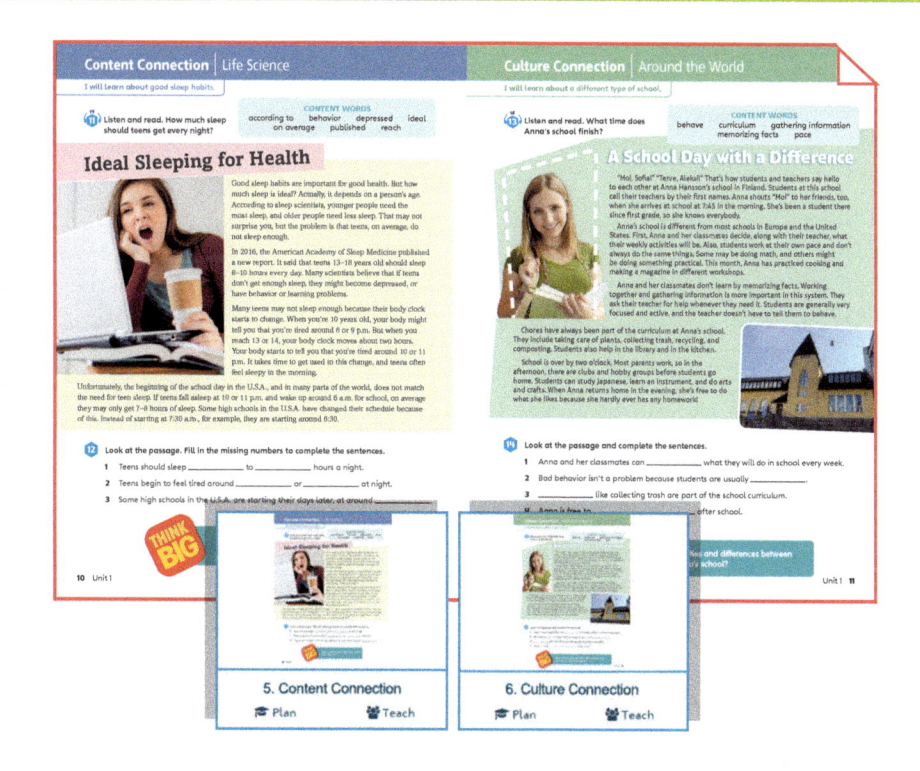

In Culture Connection lessons, students learn about other cultures and countries.

Video enriches the learning experience, reinforcing target language and bringing culture lessons to life.

xiii

Writing and Life Skills Lessons

The Writing lessons feature an **integrated skills** approach. Students are given a model to read, listen to, and discuss, before writing their own text.

Students gain experience of different text types that they will encounter later in their education.

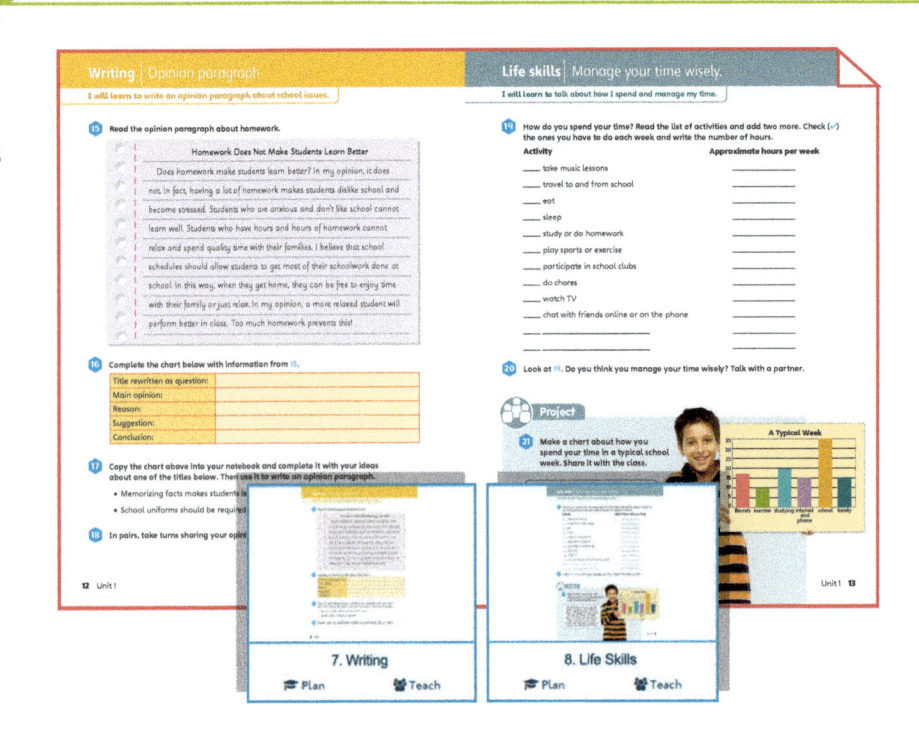

Students reflect on a life skill related to the theme of the unit and apply this in a collaborative project.

Projects promote collaboration and creativity.

Listening and Speaking and Review Lessons

th The sounds of English are presented in a systematic, supported way.

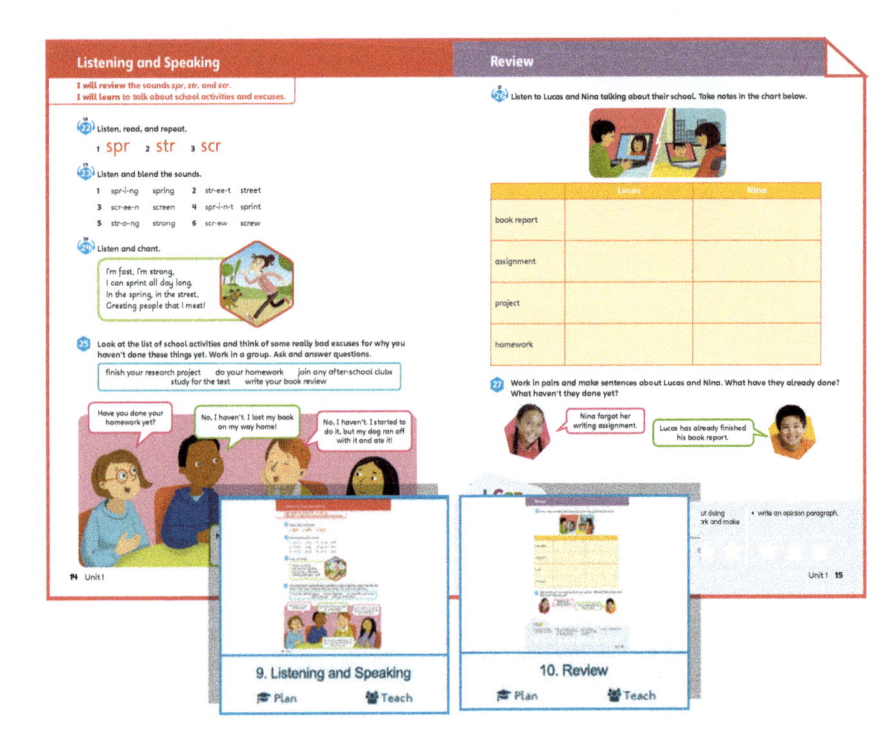

Vocabulary and grammar from the unit is practiced again in the context of game-style activities, language exercises, and through a dramatic video.

Self-assessment activities and *I can* statements aligned to the GSE allow students to reflect on their progress.

xiv

Checkpoint

There are four Checkpoint lessons after every third unit.

Students reflect on what they know and don't know from the unit.

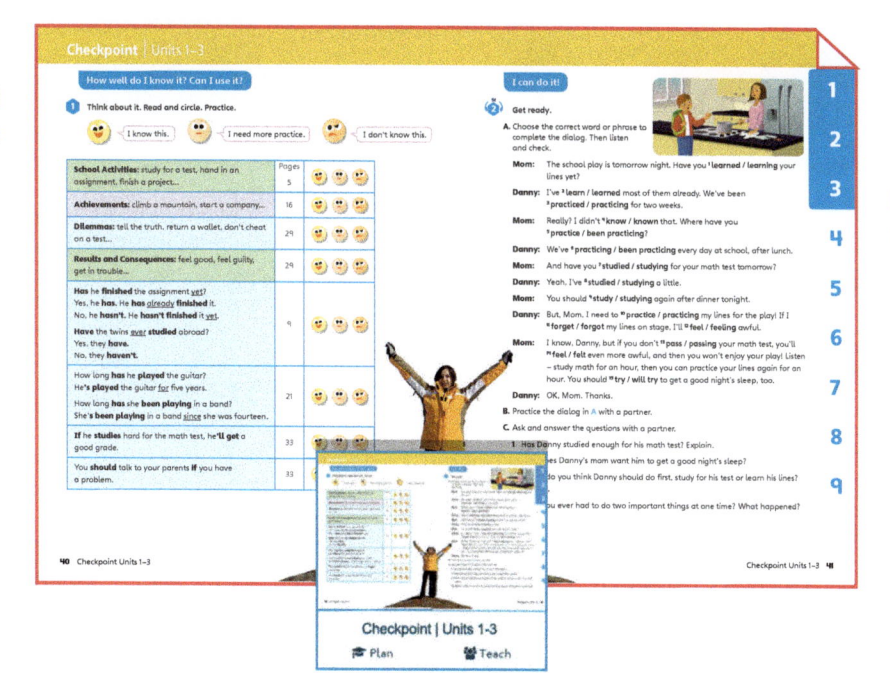

The *Get ready* task helps identify gaps in learners' knowledge of the key language points so that teachers can provide a review as needed.

Vocabulary from the unit is practiced again in the context of an activity using cut-out cards.

Target grammar is recycled in the context of a dialog.

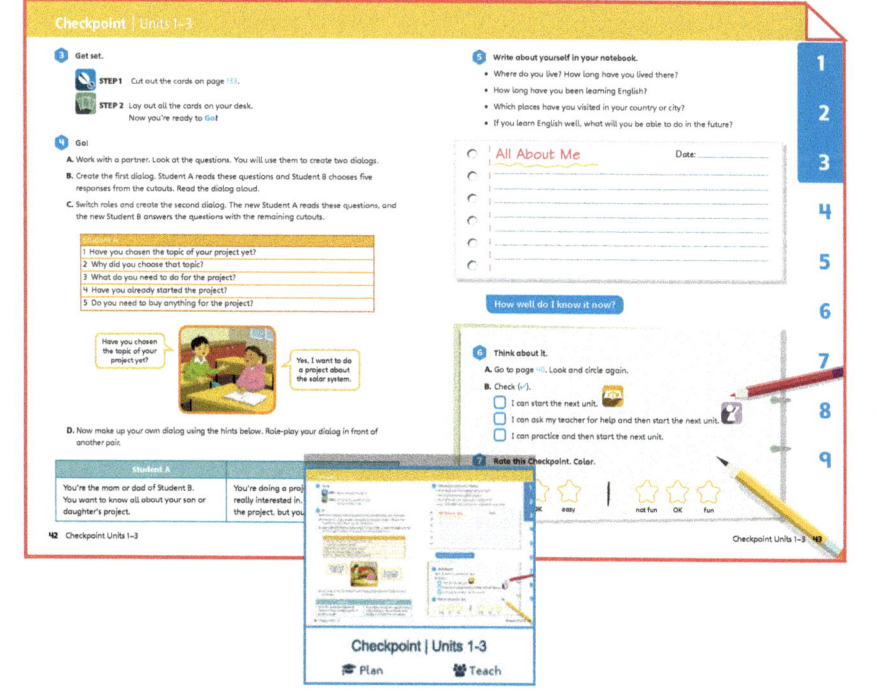

Students use the language they know to carry out a mini-portfolio task.

The *How well do I know it now?* feature prompts further self-assessment which raises students' awareness of the progress they're making.

xv

BIG ENGLISH
Lesson Flow

The lesson flows in Big English show a suggested sequence through the various resources in the course. These lesson flows are exactly the same in the print Teacher's Edition and the digital Teacher Presentation Tool, allowing teachers to move seamlessly between them as they wish.

Warm-up
This is an activity which either recycles previously learned target vocabulary or grammar in a fun or game-like way, or activates prior knowledge on a topic to get young learners into the right frame of mind at the start of a lesson.

TE

Lesson Objective
This is a stage where the teacher and students can discuss and focus on what their learning objective for the lesson is.

SB **TE**

Homework
Most lessons end with a suggested homework from the Workbook either as a print or interactive digital exercise. Alternatively, all digital exercises can be assigned as homework too.

WB **SB**

Lesson Objective
The lesson objective is reviewed at the end of each lesson. This is to raise awareness of what the students have learned, and to give them a sense of achievement and progress.

SB **TE**

SB Student's Book   **WB** Workbook   **TE** Teacher's Edition

xvi

In the Teacher's Edition the lesson flows appear at the start of each lesson and tell the teacher how many activities are included and what their purpose is, for example, presentation or practice. The teaching notes follow this sequence of activities, providing guidance every step of the way as well as extra activities and ideas.

The Big English Teacher Presentation Tool gives you access to all the support of the lesson flows and teaching notes as well as:

- all the material you need for an activity in one place;
- interactive activities to carry out in class that you can use as an alternative to, or extension of, the print Student's Book or Workbook activities;
- supporting material to carry out some of the activities in the Teacher's Edition.

You can use the Teacher Presentation Tool on your projector or IWB to present the material from the course where each unit is broken down into individual lessons that mirror the structure of the print course.

Lesson flows in Big English are designed around the specific lessons, but they share common stages.

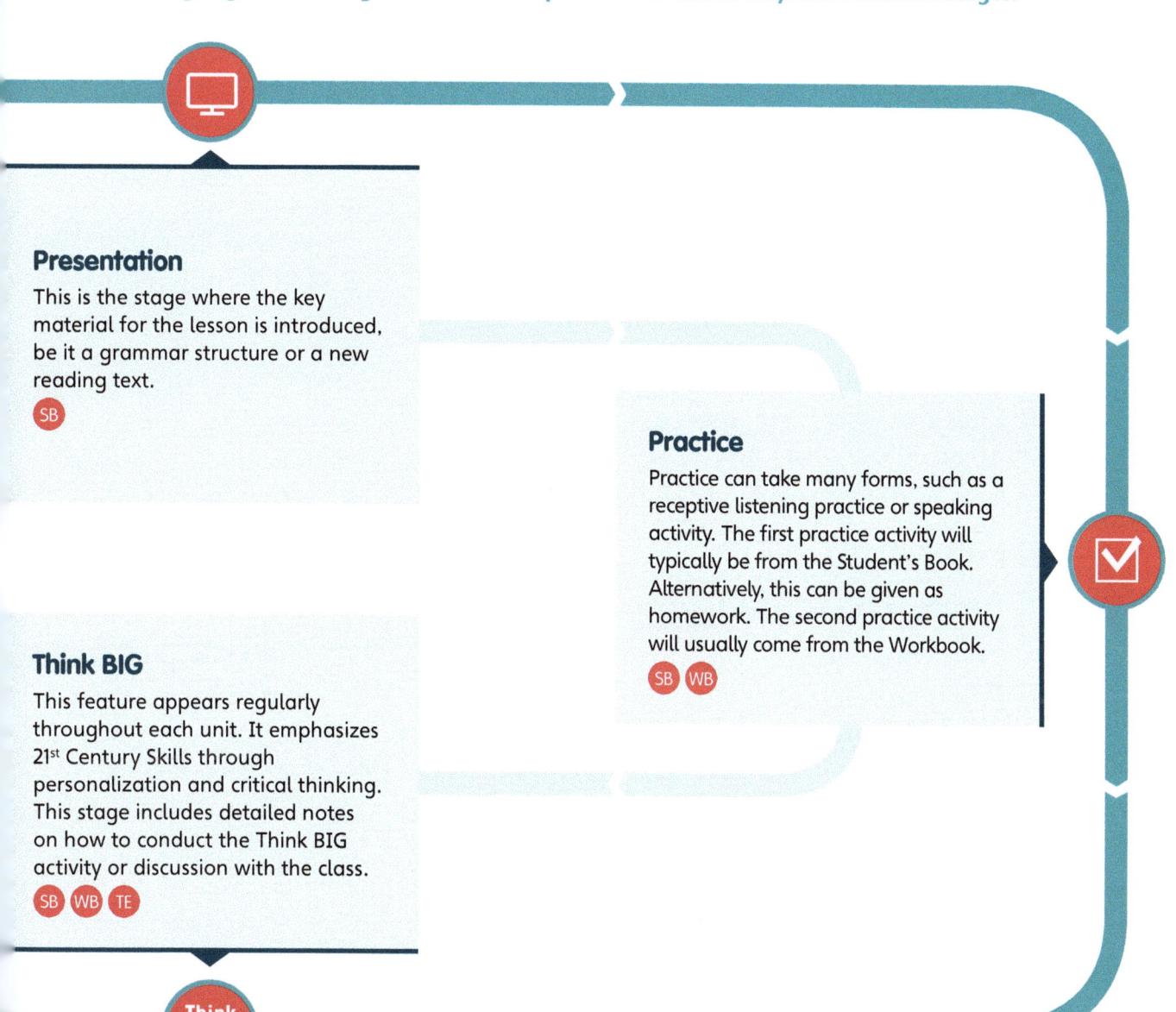

Presentation
This is the stage where the key material for the lesson is introduced, be it a grammar structure or a new reading text.
SB

Practice
Practice can take many forms, such as a receptive listening practice or speaking activity. The first practice activity will typically be from the Student's Book. Alternatively, this can be given as homework. The second practice activity will usually come from the Workbook.
SB WB

Think BIG
This feature appears regularly throughout each unit. It emphasizes 21st Century Skills through personalization and critical thinking. This stage includes detailed notes on how to conduct the Think BIG activity or discussion with the class.
SB WB TE

xvii

TIME Guidelines

		Week 1	Week 2
5–6 hours per week	Teacher digital resources	Teacher Presentation Tool	
	Student's Book		
	Workbook	Corresponding pages of the Workbook	
	Teacher's Edition	Corresponding pages of the Teacher's Edition	
	Extra print resources	Cutouts and Stickers in the Student's Book • Flashcards • Posters • Assessment Pack	
	Extra digital resources	Flashcards • Wordlists • Posters • Assessment Pack • Audio, etc.	
7–8 hours per week	Extra print resources	Extra grammar practice in the Workbook • Extra application and practice activities in the Teacher's Edition • Cambridge English Young Learners practice tests in the Student's Book and Teacher's Edition	
	Extra digital resources	Teacher Presentation Tool • Student digital resources • Games • Documentary and Dramatic videos and corresponding Video Guides	
8+ hours per week	Extra print resources	Big TV Video Workbook	
	Extra digital resources	Big TV videos and Teacher Notes	

xviii

Week 3	Week 4	Week 5 (every third unit)

Teacher Presentation Tool

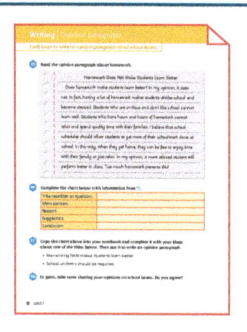

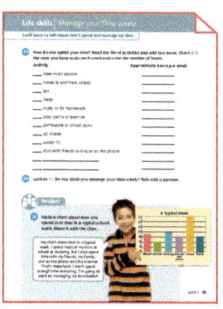

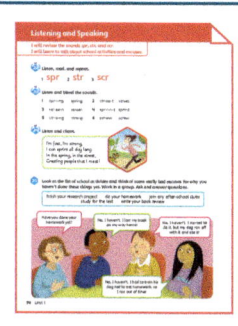

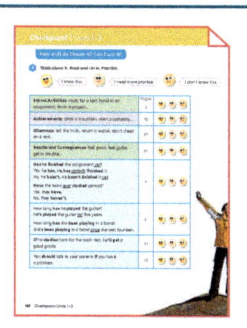

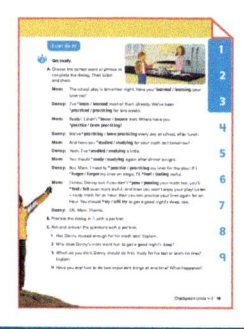

Corresponding pages of the Workbook

Corresponding pages of the Teacher's Edition

Cutouts and Stickers in the Student's Book • Flashcards • Posters • Assessment Pack

Flashcards • Wordlists • Posters • Assessment Pack • Audio, etc.

Extra grammar practice in the Workbook • Extra application and practice activities in the Teacher's Edition • Cambridge English Young Learners practice tests in the Student's Book and Teacher's Edition

Teacher Presentation Tool • Student digital resources • Games • Documentary and Dramatic videos and corresponding Video Guides

Big TV Video Workbook

Big TV videos and Teacher Notes

xix

Contents

Unit	Vocabulary	Structures
Welcome to Class! pp. a–d	**School Life:** advice, assignment, English, essay, field trip, history, homework, math, schedule, test	**Have** you **ever been** late for school? Yes, I **have.**/No, I **haven't**. You **should** always listen to the teacher. You **shouldn't** leave your homework until the last minute.
1 All About School pp. 4–15	**School Activities:** do a book report, do homework, finish a project, hand in an assignment, study for a test	**Has** she **done** her homework **yet**? Yes, she **has**. She **has** already **done** it./No, she **hasn't**. She **hasn't done** it **yet**. **Have** you **ever hosted** an exchange student? Yes, I **have.**/No, I **haven't**. He **has** already **studied** for the test./He **hasn't studied** for the test **yet**. He **studied** yesterday./He **didn't study** yesterday.
2 Amazing Young People pp. 16–27	**Achievements:** become a doctor, climb a mountain, invent something, meet a world leader, play an instrument, start a company, win a tournament, write and publish a book	How long **have** you **lived** here? I**'ve lived** here **for** five years./I**'ve lived** here **since** I was six. How long **has** she **been singing**? She**'s been singing** since she was four./She**'s been singing for** 10 years.
3 Dilemmas pp. 28–39	**Dilemmas:** (cheat/don't cheat) in a test, (return/don't return) a wallet, (tell/don't tell) the truth **Results and Consequences:** be upset with, feel good, feel guilty, get into trouble	If you **tell** your parents you forgot, they**'ll be** upset. You **should tell** your parents **if** you have a problem.
Checkpoint Units 1–3 pp. 40–43		
4 Dreams for the Future pp. 44–55	**Dreams:** be famous, earn a good salary, live in another country, raise a family, run my own business, speak a foreign language, take adventurous vacations, work in my dream job, work in the music industry	Where **will** you **be living** fifty years from now? In fifty years, I**'ll** probably **be living** in France. I definitely **won't be living** with my parents. **Will** you **be raising** a family? Yes, definitely./No, probably not. I'll probably…/I definitely **won't**…
5 If I Could Fly… pp. 56–67	**Super Powers:** become invisible, fly, have superhuman strength, read people's minds, run at lightning speed, travel through time	If **I were** you, **I'd choose** something else. If you **could fly**, where **would** you **go**? If **I could fly**, **I'd go** to the moon.
6 The Coolest School Subjects pp. 68–79	**Areas of Study:** art, English, literature, math, music, P.E., science (biology), social studies **Things We Learn About in School:** artists, democracy, exercise, grammar, legends, mammals, murals, myths, plants, playwrights, prime numbers, sports, vocabulary	My teacher gives **more** homework **than** your teacher. There are **fewer** playwrights in the U.S.A **than** in the U.K. I do **less** exercise **than** my sister. My brother has **the most** homework of anyone I know. Jenny has **the fewest** cards. She has **the least** space.
Checkpoint Units 4–6 pp. 80–83		
7 Mysteries! pp. 84–95	**Mysteries:** Atlantis, Aurora Borealis (Northern Lights), Bermuda Triangle, crop circles, Great Pyramids, Kryptos, Nazca Lines, sailing stones **Mystery-Related Words:** explanation, phenomenon, proof, scientific, theory, unsolved	The geoglyphs **are** in Peru, **aren't** they? Astronauts **aren't** going to Pluto, **are** they? Experts **can** explain the aurora borealis, **can't** they? Scientists **can't** explain crop circles, **can** they? We **love** mysteries, **don't** we? It **didn't** make sense, **did** it?
8 Why Is It Famous? pp. 96–107	**Famous Places:** Big Ben, City of Petra, Christ the Redeemer statue, Easter Island, Forbidden City, Great Sphinx of Giza, Great Wall of China, Machu Picchu, Pyramid of Kukulcán, St. Basil's Cathedral, Statue of Liberty, Stonehenge, Sydney Opera House, Taj Mahal, Temple of Borobudur **Structures:** cathedral, mausoleum, monument, palace, pyramid, statue, temple, tower	Stonehenge **was constructed** more than 4,000 years ago. Louis XIV was a French king **who ruled** for 72 years. The Statue of Liberty is a landmark **that has become** a symbol of welcome.
9 That's Entertainment! pp. 108–119	**Entertainment:** book signing, comic book exhibit, concert, festival, movie premiere	Sara said, "The sequel **isn't** as good as the first movie." She said (that) the sequel **wasn't** as good as the first movie. Paul said, "I**'m going** to the concert." He said (that) he **was going** to the concert.
Checkpoint Units 7–9 pp. 120–123		

Cambridge Young Learners English: Flyers Practice Paper pp. 124–132 **Cutouts** pp. 133–138

CLIL: Content and Culture	Writing	Life Skills/Project	Listening and Speaking	I can…
Life Science: Ideal sleeping for health according to, behavior, depressed, ideal, on average, published, reach **Around the World: A school day with a difference** behave, curriculum, gathering information, memorizing facts, pace	Opinion paragraph	**Manage your time wisely.** Talk about spending and managing time. Create a chart to see how students spend their time.	spr, str, scr spring, sprint street, strong screen, screw	…use words for school activities and homework. …talk about events in the past using the present perfect and *yet*, *already*, and *ever*. … talk about doing homework and make excuses. …write an opinion paragraph.
Social Science: Amazing young people co-found, compose, exceptional talent, gifted, inspiration, keep in touch, social media, symphony **Around the World: Seeds of Peace** conflict, educators, issues, neutral, participants	Biography	**Appreciate yourself.** Talk about amazing qualities and talents. Make an Amazing Me collage.	spl, squ, thr splash, split squash, squid three, throat	…use words related to achievements and personal goals. …use the present perfect and the present perfect progressive. …talk about achievements and accomplishments. …write a short biography.
Social Sciences: Ethics acceptable, based on, ethical, ethics, excuse, harmless, morally, perspective, respectful, traits, treat **Around the World: Proverbs** moss, proverb, reap, regret, saying, sound advice, sow	Story ending	**Do the right thing.** Talk about the right choice in a dilemma. Make a class handbook about doing the right thing.	nch, nth, mpt crunch, lunch month, tenth prompt, tempt	…use words related to dilemmas and consequences. …use conditional sentences. …give advice using *should*. …write a story ending.
Science and Technology: Predictions for the future futurist, microscopic, nanotechnology, revolutionize, wireless **Around the World: Power for the future** climate change, dam, electricity, geothermal, hydroelectric, megawatt, power plant, solar	Formal and informal emails	**Make smart decisions.** Talk about how the decisions you make now affect the future. Write a letter about plans for the future.	/s/, /z/, /ɪz/ eats, cooks, sleeps runs, sings, swims dances, washes, watches	…use words for personal ambitions and future predicitons. …use the future progressive with *definitely* and *probably*. …talk about the future and how certain something is. …write formal and informal emails.
Life Science: Super power or super science? adhesive, electrode, fascinating, gecko, gesture, interact, skyscraper, spell out, work on **Around the World: Superheroes** android, industry, meteorite, mischievous, native, originate	Character traits	**Take positive steps for the future.** Talk about the positive things we can do for our future world. Make a class book about positive steps for the future.	/t/, /d/, /ɪd/ looked, walked, watched called, cleaned, climbed ended, painted, wanted	…use words for super powers. …use *if* to talk about imagined situations. …talk about what I would do in imagined situations. …write a description of a superhero.
Life Science: The weirdest living things absorb, adapt, blink, break down, digest, give birth, infection, injure, nectar, nutrients, protein, rays, slippery **Around the World: Ancient civilizations** article, civilization, contribution, cultivation, influence, legacy	From story to play	**Appreciate school.** Talk about the practical uses of school subjects. Create a book of names from ancient Greece that are used today.	er, est cheaper, easier, faster, happier best, longest	…use words for school subjects and school topics. …compare things using *more/fewer/less* and the *most/the fewest/the least*. …talk about school subjects and make comparisons. …rewrite a story as a play.
Earth Science: Aurora Borealis altitude, clapping, interact, nitrogen, oxygen, phenomenon, pole, solar wind, stand out, swirling **Around the World: Mysterious findings** artifacts, clearing, diameter, rapid, sighting	Cause and effect	**Be curious.** Talk about the importance of being curious. Create a booklet about two mysteries.	un, inter, re, pre, super unhappy international recycle, reduce preused Superman	…use words for scientific mysteries. …use question tags with *be*, *can*, and *do*. …talk about mysterious phenomena. …write a cause and effect paragraph.
History: Accidental discoveries archeologist, artifact, carving, dig, goddess, pharaoh, remains, tomb, treasure **Around the World: The new seven world wonders** compile, gladiator, sea level, structure	Report	**Take pride in your town or city.** Talk about interesting places in my town or city. Create a map for a bicycle trip to famous or interesting places in your town or city.	able, ful, ly comfortable, washable beautiful, peaceful deeply, slowly	…use words for famous places and monuments. …use the passive voice and relative clauses. …talk about famous places and structures. …write a report about a country.
Language Arts: A formula for success climax, formula, plot, producer, script, structure **Around the World: Unique musical instruments** bagpipes, concertina, distinctive, squeezed, steel drums	Movie review	**Appreciate different opinions.** Share and discuss different opinions. Make an opinion map to compare, discuss, and record classmates' opinions about a topic.	sion, tion, ation decision, television fiction, option celebration, invitation	…use words for entertainment and events. …use reported speech. …talk about entertainment and people's opinions. …write a movie review.

Big English Song

From the mountaintops to the bottom of the sea,
From a big blue whale to a baby bumblebee –
If you're big, if you're small, you can have it all,
And you can be anything you want to be!

**It's bigger than you. It's bigger than me.
There's so much to do, and there's so much to see!
The world is big and beautiful, and so are we!
Think big! Dream big! Big English!**

So in every land, from the desert to the sea,
We can all join hands and be one big family.
If we love, if we care, we can go anywhere!
The world belongs to everyone; it's ours to share.

**It's bigger than you. It's bigger than me.
There's so much to do, and there's so much to see!
The world is big and beautiful, and so are we!
Think big! Dream big! Big English!**

**It's bigger than you. It's bigger than me.
There's so much to do, and there's so much to see!
The world is big and beautiful and waiting for me.
A one, two, three…
Think big! Dream big! Big English!**

Welcome to Class!

Objectives

Reading
- Can identify specific information in a short, simple text.
- Can identify key words and phrases in a short, simple text.

Listening
- Can understand the gist of a short, simple dialog.
- Can identify specific information in a short, simple dialog.

Speaking
- Can ask and answer questions about information in a short, simple text.
- Can ask and answer questions about everyday experiences relating to school.
- Can give simple advice.

Writing
- Can write simple sentences about personal experiences.
- Can write simple sentences to give advice.

Grammar
- Can ask and answer questions about past experiences using *Have you ever... ?*
- Can give advice using *should* and *shouldn't*.

Key Language

Key Vocabulary

School life
advice
assignment
English
essay
field trip
history
homework
math
schedule
test

Expressions
What's up?
Got it!
Wish me luck!
Good luck!
You'll be great!

Grammar/Structures

Have you <u>ever</u> **been** late for school? Yes, I **have**./No, I **haven't**.

You **should** always listen to the teacher.

You **shouldn't** leave your homework until the last minute.

Welcome Unit Overview **T**

Lesson 1

Lesson Flow

Warm-up › Lesson Objective › Pre-reading › Reading › Comprehension 1 › Comprehension 2 › Speaking › Think Big › Lesson Objective

Lesson Objective

I will understand a longer text and talk about being a good learner.

Key Language

advice, assignment, English, essay, field trip, history, homework, math, schedule, test

---

Welcome to Class!

1 Read and answer. Which of the good habits do you have?

HOW TO BE A TOP LEARNER FOR LIFE!
Do you want to be a good learner? We can show you how!

1 LISTEN UP!
Listening in class is important. We listen so that we know what we need to do, and to show respect to the teacher. However, we should also listen to our classmates when they talk, too. We can get new ideas from listening to others. And, when the teacher gives you advice on how to improve – what should you do? Listen, of course!

2 GET INTO GOOD HABITS!
Put your school schedule on your door or on your bedroom wall. Make a note in your diary or on the schedule when you need to hand in your homework. Don't leave your homework or assignments until the last minute. Start your homework a day earlier. This will give you time to check your work before you give it to the teacher.

3 DON'T GIVE UP!
Have you ever thought you just can't do your math or history homework? It's a horrible sensation, and one that we all feel sometimes. Don't just sit there, ask for help! You should ask someone at home to explain what to do – but not do the homework or essay for you. You should also ask a teacher for help, or go to a homework club at school. Lastly, don't say "I can't!"; say, "I can't yet!" Remember, you will understand it one day.

4 ENJOY LEARNING
Everyone loves their favorite subject. Maybe yours is art or computers? However, it's also important to enjoy the other subjects, too. Maybe you don't love studying math because you think it's difficult. If you practice hard and get a little better, you might just like it more. Or, find a part of math that you like – perhaps geometry or solving math problems. Try to find something in every subject to enjoy.

2 Read and say true or false. Find the paragraph for each statement.
1. We should only listen to the teacher in class. _____
2. Asking for help is important. _____
3. It's not important to try and enjoy all subjects. _____
4. Asking someone to help with homework is a good idea. _____
5. You should start doing homework days before it's due – not the night before. _____

a Welcome Unit

Welcome to Class!

3 Write the verb. Then write an example sentence for each.

1. _do_ my homework
   I did my homework on time last week, but then I left it at home!
2. _____ an assignment
   _____
3. _____ school schedule
   _____
4. _____ math
   _____
5. _____ (English) is difficult
   _____
6. _____ someone to explain
   _____
7. _____ your work
   _____

4 Work with a partner. Ask and answer.
1. Do you / always / do / homework / on time?
2. Do / always / look / school schedule?
3. How / do / remember / difficult words in English?
4. How long / spend / write / assignments?
5. When / should / start / homework?
6. Who / can / ask for help / homework?

> Do you always do your homework on time?

> Well, I try, but if I find it really difficult. Sometimes it isn't on time.

THINK BIG What can you do differently to be a better learner?

Welcome Unit b

Warm-up

- Divide the class into small groups. Write on the board: *Why do you think learning is important?* and tell them to discuss the question in their groups.
- When they are ready, invite each group to report back their ideas to the rest of the class.

S a/b

Lesson Objective

INVOLVE

Introduce the lesson objective. Say: *Today I will learn to understand a longer text and read and talk about being a good learner.*

- Students will read a longer text and relate it to their own lives, do a comprehension activity and match paragraphs and main ideas, write sentences to practice new vocabulary, ask and answer about being a good learner, and discuss how they can be a better learner.

Pre-reading

- Have students read aloud the title of the text in Activity 1. Ask them what they think it means to be *a top learner* and why it might be useful to be this *for life*. Encourage students to share their ideas.

Reading

1 Read and answer. Which of the good habits do you have?

- Explain to students that they need to decide which of the paragraphs describes something that they already do.
- Give students sufficient time to read the text.

MONITOR

Discuss students' answer as a class.

Comprehension 1

2 Read and say *true* or *false*. Find the paragraph for each statement.

- Read the directions aloud. Make sure students understand that the activity has two parts: first they have to decide if the statement is true or false, then they have to match the idea with a paragraph in the text. Encourage them to do the first part of the activity without re-reading the text.
- Give students sufficient time to complete the activity.

MONITOR

Check answers as a class. *(Answers: 1 false, paragraph 1; 2 true, paragraph 3; 3 false, paragraph 4; 4 true, paragraph 3; 5 true, paragraph 2)*

Comprehension 2

3 Write the verb. Then write an example sentence for each.

- Read the directions aloud. Make sure students understand that the activity has two parts: first they have to find the verb for each verb phrase, then they have to write a sentence using that verb phrase.
- Give students sufficient time to complete the activity. Encourage them to write sentences relating to their personal experience.

MONITOR

Check answers as a class. *(Answers: 2 do/write, 3 look at, 4 study/practise/learn, 5 remember, 6 ask, 7 start; students' own sentences)*

Speaking

4 Work with a partner. Ask and answer.

- Read the directions and Item 1 aloud. Have two volunteers read out the speech bubbles.
- Put students into pairs, and give them sufficient time to do the activity.

MONITOR

Invite different pairs to ask and answer each item in front of the class.

Think Big

21st Century Critical Thinking

- Read the question aloud. Ask students to share their ideas. Tell them to consider the ideas they read about in the reading text and to think about how they can apply these to their own lives. Invite students to tell their ideas to the class.
- Then ask students to think of further ideas about how they can become better learners. Ask: *Who is a good learner that you know? What tips can you learn from them?* Encourage a class discussion.

Lesson Objective

INVOLVE

Revisit the lesson objective: *Now I have learned to understand a longer text and read and talk about being a good learner.*

- Encourage awareness of what the students have learned. Have students close their books. Ask them yes/no questions about good learning habits discussed during the lesson.

Extra Practice and Application Activity

- Put students into small groups. Explain that they are going to work together to design an app to help students be better learners. Give each group a sheet of paper and tell them to write notes and draw their ideas.
- Give the groups sufficient time to do the activity. Encourage them to use their imaginations.
- When they are ready, invite each group to present their app to the rest of the class. Invite them to draw and write on the board to help explain how their app will work.

T a/b

Lesson 2

Lesson Flow

Warm-up › Lesson Objective › Pre-listening › Listening › Comprehension 1 › Comprehension 2 › Presentation 1 › Practice 1 › Presentation 2 › Practice 2 › Lesson Objective

Lesson Objective

I will talk about school, write about past experiences, and give simple advice.

Key Language

Have you <u>ever</u> **been** late for school? Yes, I **have**./No, I **haven't**.

You **should** always listen to the teacher.

You **shouldn't** leave your homework until the last minute.

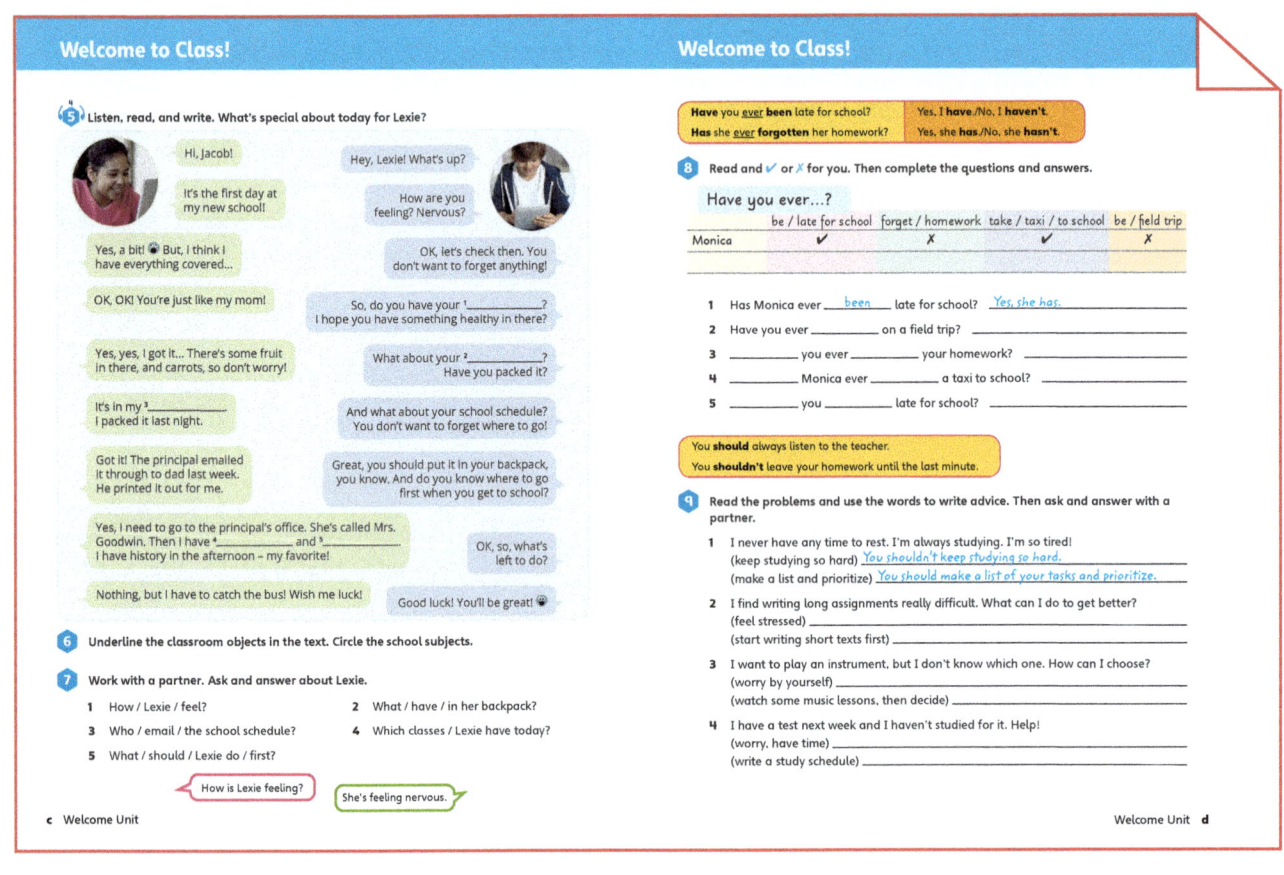

Warm-up

- Create a spidergram on the board. Write in the middle of the spidergram *How to be a good learner*. Then invite different students to come to the board to write their ideas along the legs of the spidergram.

Lesson Objective

INVOLVE

Introduce the lesson objective. Say: *Today I will learn to talk about school, write about past experiences, and give simple advice.*

- Students will listen to an online conversation, identify vocabulary items in a text, do a pairwork comprehension activity, and use the present perfect with *ever* and *should* for giving advice.

Pre-listening

- Ask students to look at the pictures of the girl and the boy and to say what they think they are doing. (Answer: They are chatting online.) Tell students that they will listen to and read a series of messages between Lexie and Jacob, on a special day for Lexie.

Listening 🎧 P.T138 4

5 Listen, read, and write. What's special about today for Lexie?

- Read the directions aloud. Play Audio Track 4 and have students listen and read along.
- Then play the audio again and have students write the missing words.

MONITOR

Check answers as a class. (Answers: *It's Lexie's first day at a new school;* 1 *lunchbox,* 2 *pencil case,* 3 *backpack,* 4 *math,* 5 *English*)

Comprehension 1

6 Underline the classroom objects in the text. Circle the school subjects.

- Read the directions aloud, and model what students have to do.
- Give students sufficient time to do the activity.

MONITOR

Check answers as a class. (Answers: *classroom objects – pencil case, backpack; school subjects – math, English, history*)

Comprehension 2

7 Work with a partner. Ask and answer about Lexie.

- Read the directions aloud. Then read Item 1 aloud, and have two volunteers read out the speech bubbles. Put students into pairs and make sure they know what they have to do.
- Give the pairs sufficient time to complete the activity.

Presentation 1

- Read the questions and answers in the first grammar box aloud, emphasizing the words highlighted in bold and underscored.
- Ask students different questions, using *Have you ever… ?* to elicit *Yes, I have.* or *No, I haven't.* (e.g. *Have you ever been early for school? Have you ever walked to school?*)

Practice 1

8 Read and ✓ or ✗ for you. Then complete the questions and answers.

- Read the directions aloud. Explain that students should first complete the table with answers for themselves, then complete the questions, and use the table to answer the questions.
- Give students sufficient time to complete the activity.

MONITOR

Check answers as a class. (Answers: 2 *been, students' own answers;* 3 *Have, forgotten, students' own answers;* 4 *Has, taken, Yes, she has.* 5 *Have, ever been, students' own answers*)

Presentation 2

- Read the sentences in the second grammar box aloud, emphasizing the words highlighted in bold.
- Give more examples using *should* and *shouldn't* (e.g. *You should ask for help. You shouldn't be late for school.*), and elicit further examples from students.

Practice 2

9 Read the problems and use the words to write advice. Then ask and answer with a partner.

- Read the directions and the examples aloud. Explain that first students write advice for each problem using *should* and *shouldn't*, and then they take turns with a partner to give and receive advice.
- Give students sufficient time to write the advice. Then put them into pairs so that they can ask and answer.

MONITOR

Invite different pairs to ask and answer each of the problems and advice in front of the class. (Possible answers: 2 *You shouldn't feel stressed. You should start writing short texts first.* 3 *You shouldn't worry by yourself. You should watch some music lessons, then (you can) decide.* 4 *You shouldn't worry, you (still) have time. You should write a study schedule (and stick to it).*)

Lesson Objective

INVOLVE

Revisit the lesson objective: *Now I have learned to talk about school, write about past experiences, and give simple advice.*

- Encourage awareness of what students have learned by inviting volunteers to ask the class *Have you ever… ?* questions. You can follow up each question with advice using *should* and *shouldn't* (e.g. *Have you ever thought you can't do your homework? Yes, I have. You should ask for help.*)

Extra Practice and Application Activity

- Give each student a sheet of paper and tell them to write four *Have you ever… ?* questions. Encourage them to use their imaginations to think of interesting past experiences to ask a partner about.
- Put students into pairs and tell them to take turns to ask and answer their *Have you ever… ?* questions. Give the pairs sufficient time to do the activity.
- When they have finished, invite different pairs to ask and answer one of their questions in front of the class.

T c/d

1 All About School

Objectives

Reading

- Can understand short school-related messages in emails, text messages, and social media posts.
- Can connect the information in a text with the information given in charts, graphs, or diagrams.
- Can identify the main ideas in straightforward, structured magazine articles on familiar topics.
- Can get the gist of short, factual school texts.

Listening

- Can understand some details in extended dialogs on familiar everyday topics.
- Can identify the main points in short talks on familiar topics, if delivered slowly and clearly.

Speaking

- Can give a simple excuse for something they have done wrong (e.g. arriving late to class).
- Can give an opinion in a structured discussion, if guided by questions.

Writing

- Can write a simple structured paragraph giving their opinion on a familiar topic, given a model.
- Can integrate numerical information into an informational text to give more precise details, given a model.

Grammar

- Can use the present perfect with *ever/yet/already*.
- Can tell when to use the past simple and when to use the present perfect.

Unit Projects

Family Connection

Encourage students to share their daily school schedules with family members, highlighting things they have and haven't studied yet in each subject. Students can also keep charts at home to share their progress in various school subjects. Remind them to check off activities once they are completed. Model: *We've already studied schools around the world and learned language for making and giving excuses, but we haven't had a test yet.*

Key Language

Key Vocabulary

School activities

do a book report

do homework

finish a project

hand in an assignment

study for a test

Expressions

barely have time to

get into

give out (candy)

under so much stress

Not exactly.

Yeah, yeah, yeah.

You're crazy.

Content Words

according to

behavior

depressed

ideal

on average

published

reach

behave

curriculum

gathering information

memorizing facts

pace

Grammar/Structures

Has she **done** her homework <u>yet</u>?

Yes, she **has**. She **has** <u>already</u> **done** it./No, she **hasn't**. She **hasn't done** it <u>yet</u>.

Have they <u>ever</u> **hosted** an exchange student?

Yes, they **have**./No, they **haven't**.

He **has** <u>already</u> **finished** the report. He **finished** it <u>yesterday</u>.

He **hasn't finished** the report <u>yet</u>. He **didn't finish** it <u>yesterday</u>.

Phonics

The sounds: *spr, str, scr*

Excuse Me! Bulletin Board

Create a bulletin-board display titled *Excuse Me!* to collect examples of especially creative or unbelievable excuses. Cut out a variety of speech bubbles for students to complete as they explore Unit 1. Begin the display by filling in one or two of the bubbles with sample excuses: *I haven't studied for the test yet because I've just moved here! I haven't read the book because it fell in the pool and is still wet! I've already done my homework, but I left it at my grandfather's house.* Highlight the words *yet* and *already* by writing them in second colors or bolder letters.

Language in Context Lesson

Lesson Flow

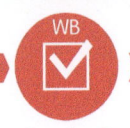

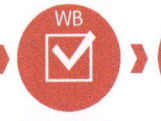

Warm-up › Lesson Objective › Presentation › Practice 1 (WB) › Practice 2 (WB) › Practice 3 (SB) › Speaking › Think BIG › Lesson Objective › Homework

Lesson Objective

I will learn to talk about school activities and excuses.

Key Language

do a book report, do homework, finish a project, hand in an assignment, study for a test; give out (candy)

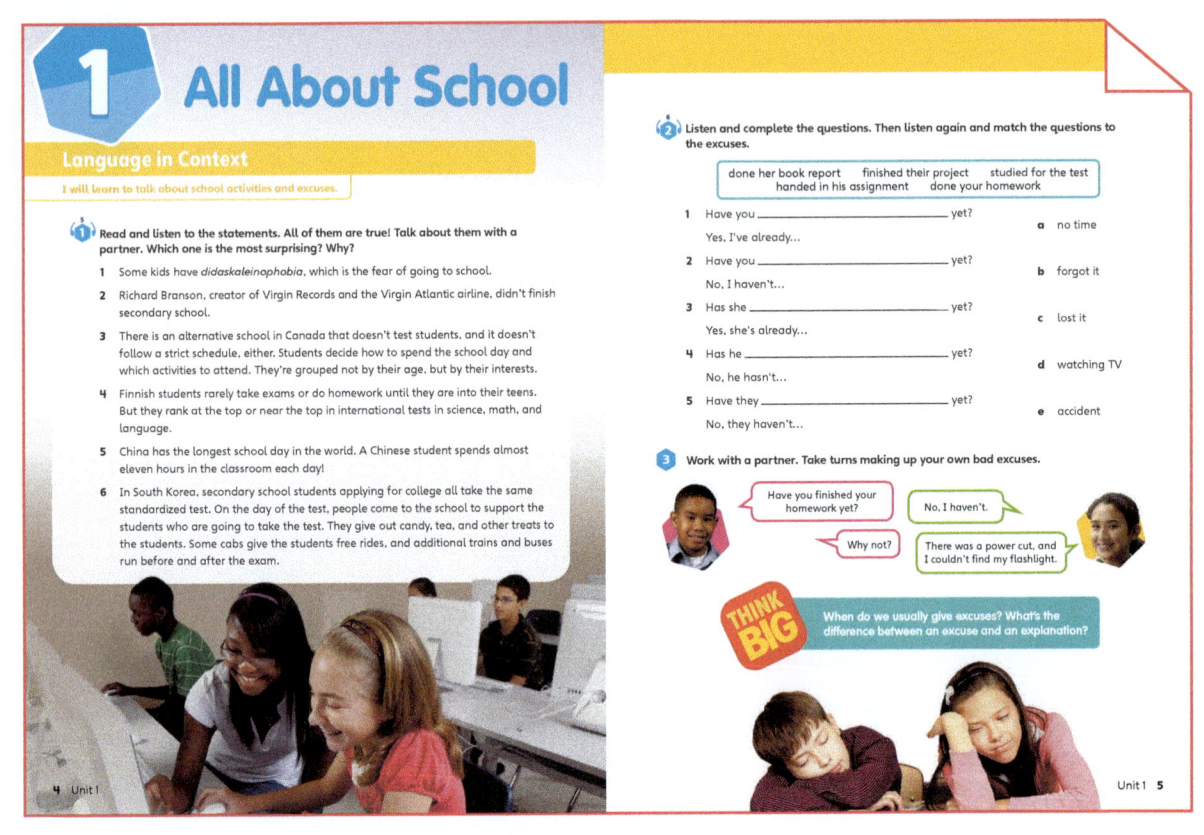

Warm-up

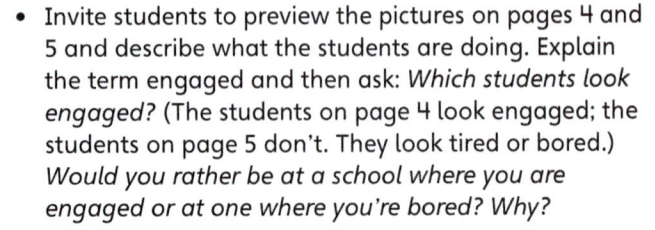

- Invite students to preview the pictures on pages 4 and 5 and describe what the students are doing. Explain the term *engaged* and then ask: *Which students look engaged?* (The students on page 4 look engaged; the students on page 5 don't. They look tired or bored.) *Would you rather be at a school where you are engaged or at one where you're bored? Why?*

Lesson Objective

INVOLVE

Explain the lesson objective. Say: *Today I will learn to talk about school activities and excuses.*

- Tell students that they will read and talk about school activities and different schools around the world.

Presentation

Materials: World map or globe

1 Read and listen to the statements. All of them are true! Talk about them with a partner. Which one is the most surprising? Why?

- Read the directions aloud. Have students read the statements independently. Then play Audio Track 5. Suggest that students rank the list from 1 to 6, with 1 being the most surprising statement, 2 the next most surprising statement, and so on.

- Have partners compare their rankings. Which school facts surprised them the most?

- Have students find these countries on a world map or globe: Canada, Finland, China, and South Korea.

S4/5 Unit 1

MONITOR

Check for understanding. Ask: *What is didaskaleinophobia?* (the fear of going to school) *Did Richard Branson finish secondary school?* (No, he didn't.) *How are Finnish schools unusual?* (They don't test students until they are teenagers.)

Practice 1 WB p. 2/ act. 1

1 What school activities do you see in the pictures? Write the numbers.

- Read the directions aloud. Have students describe what they see in the pictures. Ask volunteers to read the activity descriptions aloud.
- Have students complete the activity independently, then compare their answers with a partner.

Practice 2 WB p. 2/ act. 2

2 Read and ✓. What would you like your school to have?

- Read the directions aloud. Have students read the numbered items and look at the three columns of checkboxes. Ask a volunteer to read the school activities.
- Have students complete the activity independently.
- Have students compare their answers with a partner, then tally the checks and discuss the results.

Practice 3 P. T138

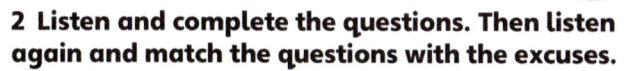

2 Listen and complete the questions. Then listen again and match the questions with the excuses.

- Read the directions and the questions aloud. Then play Audio Track 6. Then have students work in pairs to complete the activity, saying what the student should have done.

MONITOR

Have volunteers share their answers with the class. (Answers: 1 done your homework; c, 2 studied for the test; a, 3 done her book report; b, 4 handed in his assignment; e, 5 finished their project; d)

Speaking

3 Work with a partner. Take turns making up your own bad excuses.

- Read the directions aloud. Ask: *What is a bad excuse?* (Sample answers: an excuse that isn't true/an excuse that is very hard to believe)
- Have two volunteers read the speech bubbles. Ask students to work in pairs to create dialogs that include bad excuses.

Think BIG

21st Century Communication

- On the board, write: *1 I haven't finished my project because my computer broke down and I had no access to the internet. 2 I haven't done my homework because I didn't have much time.* Ask students which one is an excuse and which one is an explanation (1 explanation, 2 excuse). Then have students give you more examples of excuses and explanations.

Lesson Objective

INVOLVE

Revisit the lesson objective: *Now I have learned to talk about school activities and excuses.*

- Encourage awareness of what the students have learned by quickly eliciting some of the excuses and school activities they learned about in the lesson.

Homework P. T138 WB p. 3/ act. 3 & 4

3 ✓ the verbs you use with each phrase. Then listen and check your answers.

- Direct students to WB Activity 3 on page 3. Tell students to look at the numbered school tasks, decide which verbs are used with each phrase, then listen to the audio and check their answers.

4 Read. Match the name with the excuse. Write the letter.

- Direct students to WB Activity 4 on page 3. Tell students to read the text in the speech bubbles, then match the names with the advice.

Think BIG

- Direct students to WB Think Big on page 3. Tell students to complete the sentences with an excuse or some advice.

Extra Application and Practice Activity

- On the board, write: *The dog ate it.* Explain that this is an excuse we give when we have no real excuse to give and that it's a silly one. Ask students to make up their own silly excuses and write them on the board.

1 All About School

Language in Context

I will learn to talk about school activities and excuses.

1 Read and listen to the statements. All of them are true! Talk about them with a partner. Which one is the most surprising? Why?

1. Some kids have *didaskaleinophobia*, which is the fear of going to school.

2. Richard Branson, creator of Virgin Records and the Virgin Atlantic airline, didn't finish secondary school.

3. There is an alternative school in Canada that doesn't test students, and it doesn't follow a strict schedule, either. Students decide how to spend the school day and which activities to attend. They're grouped not by their age, but by their interests.

4. Finnish students rarely take exams or do homework until they are into their teens. But they rank at the top or near the top in international tests in science, math, and language.

5. China has the longest school day in the world. A Chinese student spends almost eleven hours in the classroom each day!

6. In South Korea, secondary school students applying for college all take the same standardized test. On the day of the test, people come to the school to support the students who are going to take the test. They give out candy, tea, and other treats to the students. Some cabs give the students free rides, and additional trains and buses run before and after the exam.

2 Listen and complete the questions. Then listen again and match the questions to the excuses.

> done her book report   finished their project   studied for the test
> handed in his assignment   done your homework

1 Have you _____ yet?
   Yes, I've already…

2 Have you _____ yet?
   No, I haven't…

3 Has she _____ yet?
   Yes, she's already…

4 Has he _____ yet?
   No, he hasn't…

5 Have they _____ yet?
   No, they haven't…

a no time
b forgot it
c lost it
d watching TV
e accident

3 Work with a partner. Take turns making up your own bad excuses.

Have you finished your homework yet?

No, I haven't.

Why not?

There was a power cut, and I couldn't find my flashlight.

THINK BIG

When do we usually give excuses? What's the difference between an excuse and an explanation?

Unit 1   5

Reading Lesson

Lesson Flow

Warm-up › Lesson Objective › Pre-reading › Reading › Comprehension 1 › Comprehension 2 › Think BIG › Lesson Objective › Homework

Lesson Objective

I will understand a text about giving advice.

Key Language

advice, detective, field trip, freedom, meeting, situation; homeschool, manage, research, study, transfer; alternative, helpful, traditional; barely have time to, get into, under so much stress

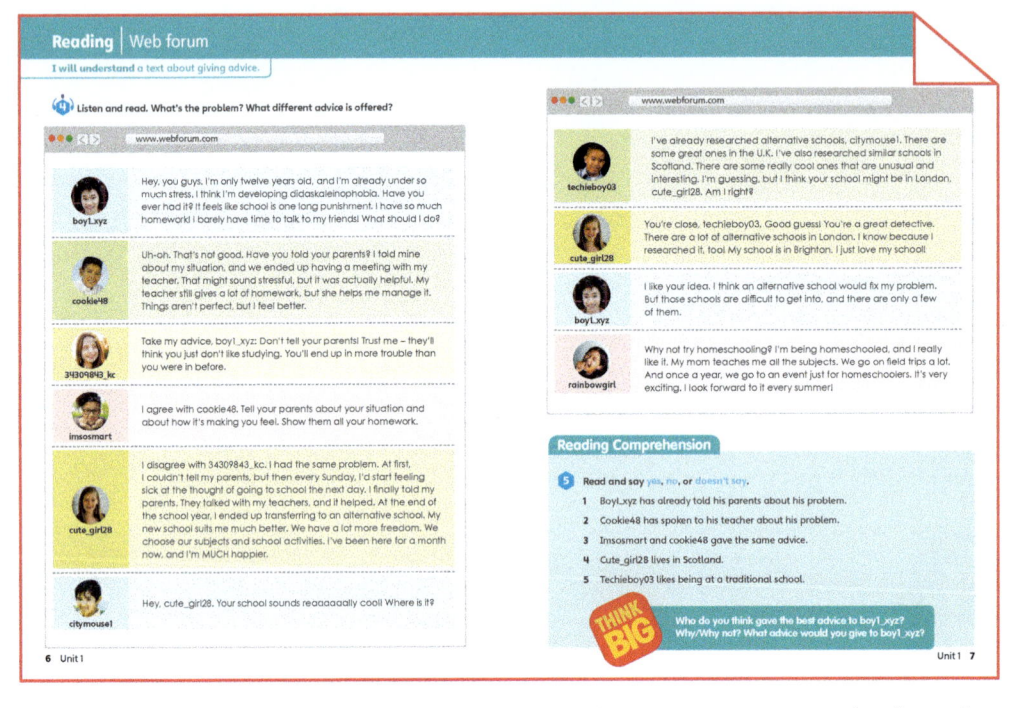

Warm-up

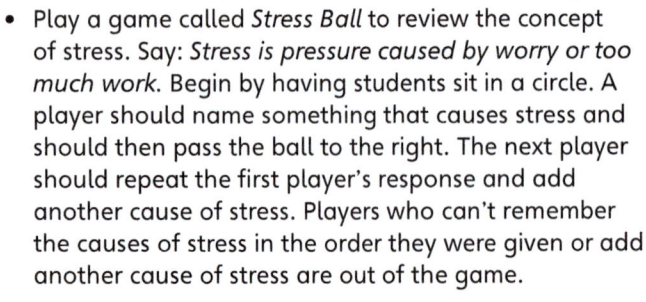

- Play a game called *Stress Ball* to review the concept of stress. Say: *Stress is pressure caused by worry or too much work.* Begin by having students sit in a circle. A player should name something that causes stress and should then pass the ball to the right. The next player should repeat the first player's response and add another cause of stress. Players who can't remember the causes of stress in the order they were given or add another cause of stress are out of the game.
- Check answers from the HW in the last lesson.

Lesson Objective

INVOLVE

Introduce the lesson objective. Say: *Today I will learn to understand a text about giving advice.*

- Students will listen to, read, talk, and answer questions about a web forum.

Pre-reading

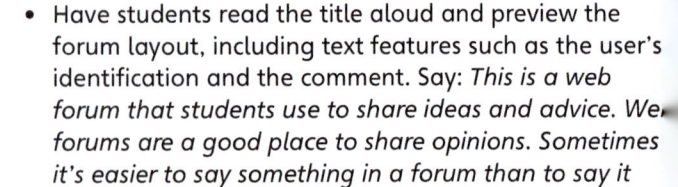

- Have students read the title aloud and preview the forum layout, including text features such as the user's identification and the comment. Say: *This is a web forum that students use to share ideas and advice. Web forums are a good place to share opinions. Sometimes it's easier to say something in a forum than to say it face to face.*
- Remind students that they read about didaskaleinophobia on page 4. Ask: *If you have this problem, what are you afraid of?* (going to school)

Reading 🎧8

4 Listen and read. What's the problem? What different advice is offered?

- Read the directions aloud. Play Audio Track 8 and have students listen and read along.

ASSIST

Replay the audio as needed. Say: *A traditional school follows teaching ideas that have been used for a long time. An alternative school is one that follows new or unusual teaching ideas.*

Comprehension 1

- Ask the question in the directions: *What different advice is offered?* (talk to the parents/teacher, search for an alternative school, try homeschooling)

MONITOR

Ask more questions to check for understanding. Ask: *How does boy1_xyz feel about school?* (He feels like it's punishment, and he's stressed.) *What happened when cookie48 told his parents about a similar situation?* (They had a meeting with his teacher, who now helps him manage his homework. He feels better.)

21st Century Media Literacy

- Point out that all of the comments on a web forum are anonymous – users don't know one another's real names. Have students discuss the advantages and disadvantages of anonymous postings. Point out that being anonymous can make it easier for someone to say what he or she really feels about something. Remind students, however, that being anonymous is not a license to comment in a bullying or hurtful way. Anonymous commenters should still be considerate of others' feelings.

Comprehension 2

5 Read and say yes, no, or doesn't say.

Read the directions aloud. Ask: *What does it mean if you choose doesn't say?* (The information is not stated in the forum.) Have students complete the activity independently.

MONITOR

Check answers as a class. Have volunteers explain why the false statements are not correct. *(Answers: 1 no – he hasn't told them yet, 2 yes, 3 yes, 4 no – cute_girl28 goes to school in Brighton, 5 doesn't say)*

CHALLENGE

Invite students to write additional items for classmates to answer with *yes/no/doesn't say*. Model: *Rainbowgirl wants to transfer to another school.* (No; she is happy being homeschooled.) *Boy1_xyz decides he'll talk with his parents about his problem.* (doesn't say)

Think BIG

21st Century Problem Solving

- Read the questions aloud with students.
- Say: *Online forums can help you solve a problem. You can post a question and get a lot of advice. Then you can decide which advice is best for you.*
- Encourage students to use the reading text for additional support as they answer in pairs.

MONITOR

As pairs work, listen for proper pronunciation, appropriate intonation, and correct use of language.

Lesson Objective

INVOLVE

Revisit the lesson objective: *Now I have learned to understand a text about giving advice.*

- Encourage awareness of what the students have learned by quickly eliciting a few things they remember about the advice given in the forum, for example, telling your parents about a stressful situation.

Homework 🎧9 WB p. 4/ act. 5 & 6

5 Listen and read. Circle T for *true* or F for *false*.

- Direct students to WB Activity 5 on page 4. Tell students to play the audio, and listen and read along. Tell students to look at Items 1–4 and circle T or F.

6 Answer the question

- Direct students to WB Activity 6 on page 4. Tell students to answer the question for themselves.

Extra Application and Practice Activity

- Invite students to write comments that they would share in response to boy1_xyz's post. Remind students that the language used in an online forum is friendly and informal and that many users don't use complete sentences. Say: *However, it's important to be as clear as possible when giving advice. Clear writing is more likely to persuade others that you're right.* Encourage students to use a computer if available and then print out a copy of their comments to share with the class.

Unit 1 **T6/7**

Reading | Web forum

I will understand a text about giving advice.

4 Listen and read. What's the problem? What different advice is offered?

---

www.webforum.com

boy1_xyz
Hey, you guys. I'm only twelve years old, and I'm already under so much stress. I think I'm developing didaskaleinophobia. Have you ever had it? It feels like school is one long punishment. I have so much homework! I barely have time to talk to my friends! What should I do?

cookie48
Uh-oh. That's not good. Have you told your parents? I told mine about my situation, and we ended up having a meeting with my teacher. That might sound stressful, but it was actually helpful. My teacher still gives a lot of homework, but she helps me manage it. Things aren't perfect, but I feel better.

34309843_kc
Take my advice, boy1_xyz: Don't tell your parents! Trust me – they'll think you just don't like studying. You'll end up in more trouble than you were in before.

imsosmart
I agree with cookie48. Tell your parents about your situation and about how it's making you feel. Show them all your homework.

cute_girl28
I disagree with 34309843_kc. I had the same problem. At first, I couldn't tell my parents, but then every Sunday, I'd start feeling sick at the thought of going to school the next day. I finally told my parents. They talked with my teachers, and it helped. At the end of the school year, I ended up transferring to an alternative school. My new school suits me much better. We have a lot more freedom. We choose our subjects and school activities. I've been here for a month now, and I'm MUCH happier.

citymouse1
Hey, cute_girl28. Your school sounds reaaaaaally cool! Where is it?

techieboy03: I've already researched alternative schools, citymouse1. There are some great ones in the U.K. I've also researched similar schools in Scotland. There are some really cool ones that are unusual and interesting. I'm guessing, but I think your school might be in London, cute_girl28. Am I right?

cute_girl28: You're close, techieboy03. Good guess! You're a great detective. There are a lot of alternative schools in London. I know because I researched it, too! My school is in Brighton. I just love my school!

boy1_xyz: I like your idea. I think an alternative school would fix my problem. But those schools are difficult to get into, and there are only a few of them.

rainbowgirl: Why not try homeschooling? I'm being homeschooled, and I really like it. My mom teaches me all the subjects. We go on field trips a lot. And once a year, we go to an event just for homeschoolers. It's very exciting. I look forward to it every summer!

Reading Comprehension

5 Read and say yes, no, or doesn't say.

1. Boy1_xyz has already told his parents about his problem.
2. Cookie48 has spoken to his teacher about his problem.
3. Imsosmart and cookie48 gave the same advice.
4. Cute_girl28 lives in Scotland.
5. Techieboy03 likes being at a traditional school.

THINK BIG
Who do you think gave the best advice to boy1_xyz? Why/Why not? What advice would you give to boy1_xyz?

Unit 1 7

Language in Action Lesson

Lesson Flow

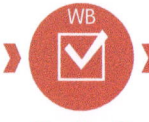

Warm-up › Lesson Objective › Pre-listening › Listening › Comprehension › Role Play › Practice 1 (SB) › Practice 2 (WB) › Lesson Objective › Homework

Lesson Objective

I will listen to a dialog about school activities and excuses.

Key Language

exchange student, license, phone call, pocket money, version; finish, get, meet, see, walk; Not exactly., Yeah, yeah, yeah., You're crazy.

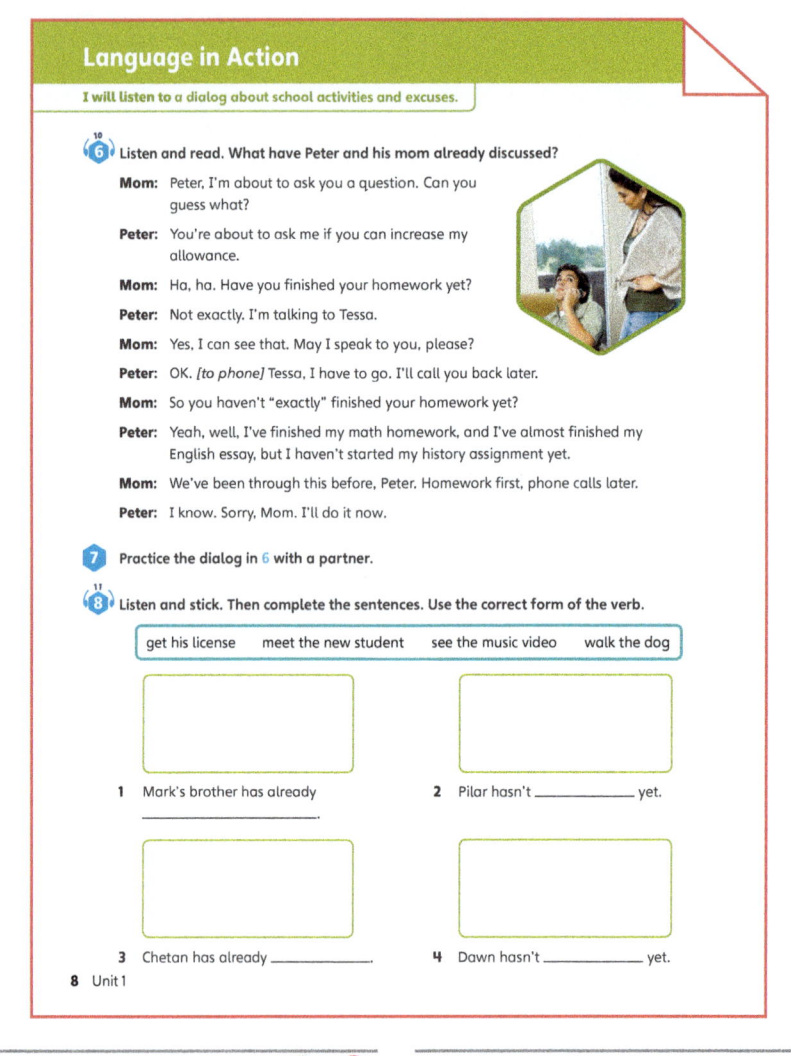

Language in Action

I will listen to a dialog about school activities and excuses.

6 Listen and read. What have Peter and his mom already discussed?

Mom: Peter, I'm about to ask you a question. Can you guess what?

Peter: You're about to ask me if you can increase my allowance.

Mom: Ha, ha. Have you finished your homework yet?

Peter: Not exactly. I'm talking to Tessa.

Mom: Yes, I can see that. May I speak to you, please?

Peter: OK. *[to phone]* Tessa, I have to go. I'll call you back later.

Mom: So you haven't "exactly" finished your homework yet?

Peter: Yeah, well, I've finished my math homework, and I've almost finished my English essay, but I haven't started my history assignment yet.

Mom: We've been through this before, Peter. Homework first, phone calls later.

Peter: I know. Sorry, Mom. I'll do it now.

7 Practice the dialog in 6 with a partner.

8 Listen and stick. Then complete the sentences. Use the correct form of the verb.

get his license   meet the new student   see the music video   walk the dog

1. Mark's brother has already _____.
2. Pilar hasn't _____ yet.
3. Chetan has already _____.
4. Dawn hasn't _____ yet.

8 Unit 1

Warm-up

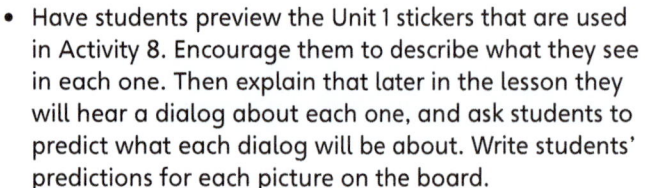

- Have students preview the Unit 1 stickers that are used in Activity 8. Encourage them to describe what they see in each one. Then explain that later in the lesson they will hear a dialog about each one, and ask students to predict what each dialog will be about. Write students' predictions for each picture on the board.
- Check answers from the HW in the last lesson.

Lesson Objective

INVOLVE

Introduce the lesson objective. Say: *Today I will listen to a dialog about school activities and excuses.*

- Students will read, listen to, and practice a dialog. Students will also listen to conversations about school life.

S8   Unit 1

Pre-listening 🔊

- Point to the picture. Ask: *What do you see?* (A boy with his mother. The boy is on the phone.) Introduce the boy and the woman as Peter and his mom. Tell students that they will hear Peter and his mom talking about finishing his homework.

Listening 🎧10 🔊

6 Listen and read. What have Peter and his mom already discussed?

- Read the directions aloud. Play Audio Track 10 and have students listen and read along.
- Invite two students to read the dialog aloud and repeat.
- Invite partners to talk about the conversation. Ask them to describe Peter's problem.

MONITOR
As students practice, listen for correct pronunciation and use of language.

ASSIST
As you notice errors, say words correctly and have students repeat.

Comprehension 💡

- Ask the question in the directions: *What have Peter and his mom already discussed?* (They've discussed the rule "Homework first, phone calls later.")

MONITOR
Ask more questions to check for understanding. Ask: *Has Peter finished his homework yet?* (He's finished his math homework, but not his English and history homework.) *Why hasn't Peter finished his homework?* (He's talking to his friend on the phone.)

Role Play 🎭 BIG world

7 Practice the dialog in 6 with a partner.

- Read the directions aloud. Invite pairs to read the dialog aloud, switch parts, and repeat.

MONITOR
As students read, listen for proper pronunciation, and appropriate intonation.

ASSIST
As you notice errors, say words or sentences correctly and have students repeat after you.

Practice 1 🎧11 P.T138 ☑

Materials: Stickers

6 Listen and stick. Then complete the sentences. Use the correct form of the verb.

- Help students find the Unit 1 stickers at the back of the Student's Book. Ask them to describe each sticker. Then read the directions and point out the sentences.
- Play Audio Track 11. Say: *You will use the words and phrases from the box and change the verb to the correct form.*

- Have students place the stickers on the page and complete the sentences independently.

MONITOR
As students work, make sure that they place the stickers in the correct order. Check answers as a class. (Answers: *1 gotten his license, 2 walked the dog, 3 met the new student, 4 seen the music video*) Ask questions to check for understanding. Ask: *Why didn't Marc ask his brother for a ride to school?* (He didn't know his brother had gotten his license already.) *How did Pilar's dad know she hadn't walked the dog yet?* (In the sticker, you can see that the dog is sitting inside, in front of the door.)

ASSIST
Review past participle forms of the verbs in the box: *get–gotten, see–seen, meet–met, walk–walked*.

Practice 2 🎧12 WB p. 5/ act. 7 ☑

7 Listen and read. Circle the correct answers.

- Read the directions aloud. Ask volunteers to read the numbered sentences aloud.
- Play Audio Track 12 and have students listen and read along. Then students complete the activity by circling the correct words.
- Have students compare answers with a partner, then check answers as a class.

Lesson Objective 📈

INVOLVE
Revisit the lesson objective: *Now I have listened to a dialog about school activities and excuses.*

- Encourage awareness of what the students have learned by quickly eliciting a few things they remember about the dialog, for example, what homework Peter hasn't finished yet.

Homework 🎧13 P.T138 WB p. 5/ act. 8 & 9 🎒

8 Look at 7. Circle the correct answers.

- Direct students to WB Activity 7 on page 5. Tell students to read the underlined expressions in the dialog again and then circle the correct meaning of each expression.

9 Circle the correct expression. Then listen and check.

- Direct students to WB Activity 9 on page 5. Tell students to read the dialogs, circle the correct expressions, and then listen to the audio to check their answers.

Extra Application and Practice Activity

- Invite students to role-play a dialog based on one of the situations in Activity 9. Encourage students to extend the dialogs to include at least one idea that they didn't hear.

Unit 1 **T8**

Language in Action

I will listen to a dialog about school activities and excuses.

6 Listen and read. What have Peter and his mom already discussed?

Mom: Peter, I'm about to ask you a question. Can you guess what?

Peter: You're about to ask me if you can increase my allowance.

Mom: Ha, ha. Have you finished your homework yet?

Peter: Not exactly. I'm talking to Tessa.

Mom: Yes, I can see that. May I speak to you, please?

Peter: OK. *[to phone]* Tessa, I have to go. I'll call you back later.

Mom: So you haven't "exactly" finished your homework yet?

Peter: Yeah, well, I've finished my math homework, and I've almost finished my English essay, but I haven't started my history assignment yet.

Mom: We've been through this before, Peter. Homework first, phone calls later.

Peter: I know. Sorry, Mom. I'll do it now.

7 Practice the dialog in 6 with a partner.

8 Listen and stick. Then complete the sentences. Use the correct form of the verb.

get his license   meet the new student   see the music video   walk the dog

1 Mark's brother has already _____.

2 Pilar hasn't _____ yet.

3 Chetan has already _____.

4 Dawn hasn't _____ yet.

8 Unit 1

Grammar

I will learn to use the present perfect with *yet*, *ever*, and *already* to talk about the past.

Has she **done** her solo <u>yet</u>?	Yes, she **has**. She **has** <u>already</u> **done** it.
	No, she **hasn't**. She **hasn't done** it <u>yet</u>.
Have they <u>ever</u> **won** an award?	Yes, they **have**.
	No, they **haven't**.

Tip: Use the present perfect to talk about an event that happened at an indefinite time in the past. The specific time is unknown or unimportant.

9 Use the words to write questions in your notebook. Then write two answers for each question.

1. you/do/your homework/yet

    Have you done your homework yet?

    Yes, I've already done it.   *No, I haven't done it yet.*

2. he/finish his test/yet
3. they/ever/join an after-school club
4. your parents/talk with the teacher/yet
5. she/give the book back/yet

He **has** <u>already</u> **finished** the project.	He **finished** it <u>yesterday</u>.
He **hasn't finished** the project <u>yet</u>.	He **didn't finish** it <u>yesterday</u>.

Tip: Use the present perfect when no specific time is given. Use the past simple when giving a specific time in the past.

10 Look at Jan's to-do list. Write the questions and answers in your notebook.

1. (talk) Has Jan…

    Has Jan talked to Jenny yet?

    Yes, she has. She talked to her at 4:00.

2. (walk the dog) Has Jan…
3. (start reading) Has Jan…
4. (write assignment) Has Jan…
5. (finish science project) Has Jan…

Things to do:
1. Call Jenny at 4:00. ✔
2. Walk the dog at 4:15. ✔
3. Start reading my book. ✘
4. Write assignment. ✔
5. Finish science project. ✘

Unit 1

Grammar Lesson

Lesson Flow

Warm-up › Lesson Objective › Presentation 1 › Practice 1 (SB) › Practice 2 (WB) › Presentation 2 › Practice 3 (SB) › Practice 4 (WB) › Lesson Objective › Homework

Lesson Objective

I will learn to use the present perfect with *yet*, *ever*, and *already* to talk about the past.

Key Language

Has she **done** her solo <u>yet</u>? Yes, she **has**. She **has** <u>already</u> **done** it./No, she **hasn't**. She **hasn't done** it <u>yet</u>.

He **has** <u>already</u> **finished** the project. He **finished** it <u>yesterday</u>.

He **hasn't finished** the project <u>yet</u>. He **didn't finish** it yesterday.

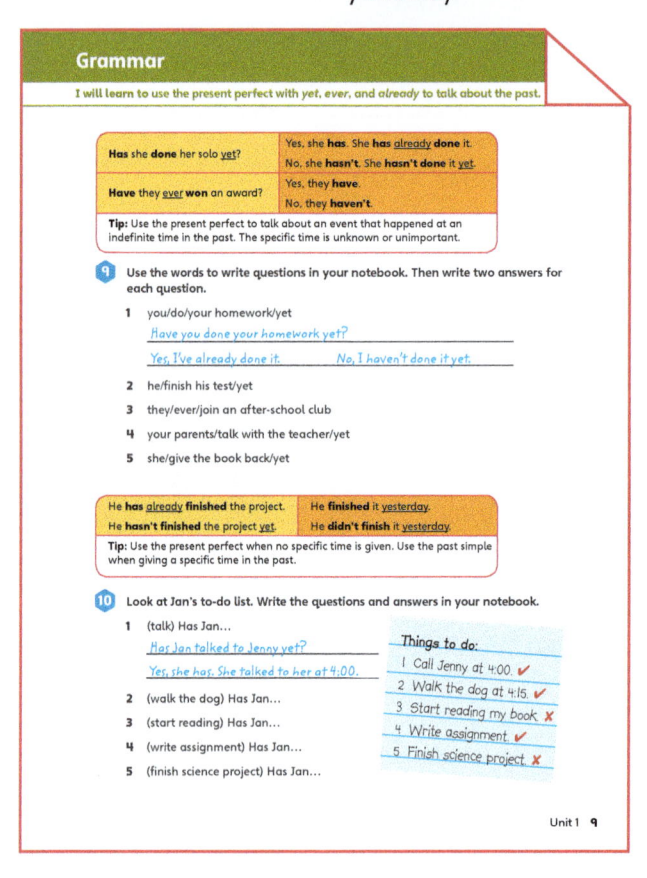

Warm-up

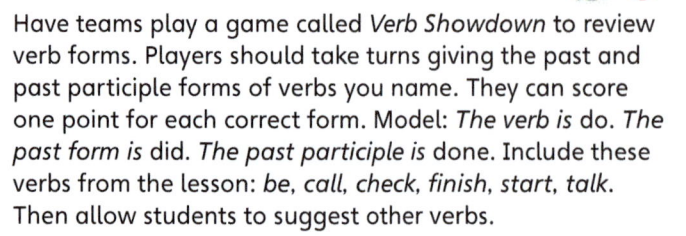

Have teams play a game called *Verb Showdown* to review verb forms. Players should take turns giving the past and past participle forms of verbs you name. They can score one point for each correct form. Model: *The verb is* do. *The past form is* did. *The past participle is* done. Include these verbs from the lesson: *be, call, check, finish, start, talk*. Then allow students to suggest other verbs.

- Check answers from the HW in the last lesson.

Lesson Objective

INVOLVE

Introduce the lesson objective. Say: *Today I will learn to use the present perfect with* yet, ever, *and* already *to talk about the past*.

- Students will use *yet*, *ever*, and *already* to talk about activities that have and have not happened.

S9 Unit 1

Presentation 1

- Have volunteers read the questions and answers in the first grammar box aloud.
- Read out the text in the Tip box. Ask students to name the verb in each sentence in the grammar box and explain how the words *yet*, *ever*, and *already* add information to the questions and answers.
- Refer students back to the Language in Action dialog and elicit or highlight the grammar structures in the dialog.

Practice 1

9 Use the words to write questions in your notebook. Then write two answers for each question.

- Read the directions aloud and read Item 1 as a class.

MONITOR

Check answers as a class. (Answers: 2 Has he finished his test yet? Yes, he's already finished it. No, he hasn't finished it yet. 3 Have they ever joined an after-school club? Yes, they have. No, they haven't. 4 Have your parents talked with the teacher yet? Yes, they have. No, they haven't. 5 Has she given the book back yet? Yes, she's already given it back. No, she hasn't given it back yet.)

Practice 2 WB p. 6/ act. 10

10 Read about Michael and Ted. Then write the answers or questions.

- Ask volunteers to read the sentences in the grammar box.
- Read the directions aloud and explain that students have to read the text and then write the question or answer for each item.
- Have students complete the activity independently, then check answers as a class.

Presentation 2

- Have volunteers read the questions and answers in the second grammar box aloud.
- Provide and then ask students to complete additional sample sentences with the correct verb in the past simple or present perfect: *She… the essay last night.* (wrote) *She… already… the essay.* (has, written) *She… not… the essay yet.* (has, written)

Practice 3

10 Look at Jan's to-do list. Write the questions and answers in your notebook.

- Read the directions aloud. Then invite volunteers to read Jan's to-do list aloud. Say: *A check means that Jan has finished the activity. An X means that she hasn't finished it yet.* Read item 1 as a class.

- Have students complete the activity independently or in pairs in their notebooks.

MONITOR

Check answers as a class. (Answers: 2 Has Jan walked the dog yet? Yes, she has. She checked it at 4:15. 3 Has Jan started reading her book yet? No, she hasn't. 4 Has Jan written her essay yet? Yes, she has. 5 Has Jan finished her science project yet? No, she hasn't.)

Practice 4 WB p. 7/ act. 11

11 Look at Sarita's to-do list. Then complete the sentences.

- Read the directions aloud. Explain that students have to complete the sentences using the present perfect.
- Have students complete the activity independently, then have students their answers with a partner.

Lesson Objective

INVOLVE

Revisit the lesson objective: *Now I have learned to use the present perfect with yet, ever, and already to talk about the past.*

- Encourage awareness of what the students have learned by quickly eliciting some sentences with the present perfect and *yet*, *ever*, and *already*.

Homework WB p. 7/ act. 12 & 13

12 Use the correct form of the verbs in parentheses.

- Direct students to WB Activity 12 on page 7. Explain that students have to complete the dialogs with the correct form of the verb.

13 Circle the correct form of the verb.

- Direct students to WB Activity 13 on page 7. Tell students to circle the correct form of the verb to complete the sentences.

Extra Application and Practice Activity

- Have students create scrambled sentences to practice the present perfect. First, ask students to write sentences using *yet*, *ever*, and *already*. Then have them write the words for each sentence on separate index cards, shuffle the cards, and then put them into a set. Have students exchange sets and try to arrange the cards to form sentences.

Content Connection Lesson

Lesson Flow

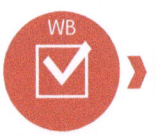

Warm-up › Lesson Objective › Pre-reading › Reading › Practice 1 (SB) › Practice 2 (WB) › Think BIG › Lesson Objective › Homework

Lesson Objective
I will learn about good sleep habits.

Key Language
according to, behavior, depressed, ideal, on average, published, reach

---

Content Connection | Life Science

I will learn about good sleep habits.

11 Listen and read. How much sleep should teens get every night?

CONTENT WORDS
according to, behavior, depressed, ideal, on average, published, reach

Ideal Sleeping for Health

Good sleep habits are important for good health. But how much sleep is ideal? Actually, it depends on a person's age. According to sleep scientists, younger people need the most sleep, and older people need less sleep. That may not surprise you, but the problem is that teens, on average, do not sleep enough.

In 2016, the American Academy of Sleep Medicine published a new report. It said that teens 13–18 years old should sleep 8–10 hours every day. Many scientists believe that if teens don't get enough sleep, they might become depressed, or have behavior or learning problems.

Many teens may not sleep enough because their body clock starts to change. When you're 10 years old, your body might tell you that you're tired around 8 or 9 p.m. But when you reach 13 or 14, your body clock moves about two hours. Your body starts to tell you that you're tired around 10 or 11 p.m. It takes time to get used to this change, and teens often feel sleepy in the morning.

Unfortunately, the beginning of the school day in the U.S.A., and in many parts of the world, does not match the need for teen sleep. If teens fall asleep at 10 or 11 p.m. and wake up around 6 a.m. for school, on average they may only get 7–8 hours of sleep. Some high schools in the U.S.A. have changed their schedule because of this. Instead of starting at 7:30 a.m., for example, they are starting around 8:30.

12 Look at the passage. Fill in the missing numbers to complete the sentences.

1. Teens should sleep _____ to _____ hours a night.
2. Teens begin to feel tired around _____ or _____ at night.
3. Some high schools in the U.S.A. are starting their days later, at around _____.

THINK BIG Do you get enough sleep every night? Why/Why not?

Warm-up

- Ask: *How much sleep do you get a night? Is sleep important? Why/Why not?* Have students discuss the questions as a class. Make a note of their ideas on the board.
- Check answers from the HW in the last lesson.

Lesson Objective

INVOLVE

Introduce the lesson objective. Say: *Today I will learn about good sleep habits.*

- Students will listen to, read, and talk about good sleep habits and their sleep habits.

Pre-reading

- Have students read the Content Words in the box. Tell students that they will learn the meaning of the words in the context of the article. Or, if you wish, have pairs of students look up the words in a dictionary before reading the text.
- Invite a volunteer to read, the title aloud and describe the picture. Have students predict what the text is about.

Reading

1 Listen and read. How much sleep should teens get every night?

- Read the directions and play Audio Track 14. Have students listen and read along in their books. Have students find the answer in the passage. (*It is said that teens 13–18 years old should sleep 8–10 hours a day.*)

MONITOR

- Check answers as a class.
- Refer the students back to the notes on the board from the Warm-up. Have them say whether their initial thoughts reflect the information in the passage. Discuss as a class.

Practice 1

2 Look at the passage. Fill in the missing numbers to complete the sentences.

- Read the directions aloud. Have students read the passage again and underline all the numbers. Have them read the gapped sentences and identify the correct numbers in the text through context.

MONITOR

- Have volunteers say the answers and point out where in the text they found the answer. (*Answers: 1. 8; 10. 2. 10; 11. 3. 8:30.*)

Practice 2 WB p. 8/ act. 14

4 Read and complete. Then listen and check.

Read the directions aloud. Have students read and complete the text with the words in the box.

Think BIG

21st Century Critical Thinking

Read the questions aloud as students follow in their books. Have students discuss the questions in small groups of three or four. Walk around and help students express their responses in English by modeling words and phrases and have them repeat.

- Invite students to share their responses with the class. Do a class survey to find out how many students get enough sleep every night. Have students suggest ways in which they can get more quality sleep.

Lesson Objective

INVOLVE

Revisit the lesson objective: *Now I have learned about good sleep habits.*

- Encourage awareness of what the students have learned by eliciting a few things they remember about the passage. Ask: *What may happen if teens don't get enough sleep?* (They may become depressed, or have behavior or learning problems.) *Why may teens not get enough sleep?* (Their bodies are changing quickly. They have busy schedules. They spend a lot of time with friends. They don't know they need more sleep.) *How do schools in the U.S. help teens?* (They begin later.)

Homework WB p. 8/ act. 15 & 16

15 Did they get enough sleep last night? Read and circle Y for *Yes* and N for *No*.

- Direct students to WB Activity 15 on page 8. Tell students to read the text and circle *Y* or *N* for each item.

16 Look at 15. Write advice for the teens who didn't get enough sleep last night.

- Direct students to WB Activity 16 on page 8. Read the directions aloud. Tell students to read the texts in Activity 15 again and write their own advice to teens who didn't get enough sleep last night.

Extra Application and Practice Activity

Materials: Index cards

- To check vocabulary, play a game. Write some of the words from the reading onto index cards. Have students take turns to pick a card and give a clue about the meaning of the word. The others should try to guess the word.

Unit 1 **T10**

Content Connection | Life Science

I will learn about good sleep habits.

11 Listen and read. How much sleep should teens get every night?

CONTENT WORDS
according to   behavior   depressed   ideal
on average   published   reach

Ideal Sleeping for Health

Good sleep habits are important for good health. But how much sleep is ideal? Actually, it depends on a person's age. According to sleep scientists, younger people need the most sleep, and older people need less sleep. That may not surprise you, but the problem is that teens, on average, do not sleep enough.

In 2016, the American Academy of Sleep Medicine published a new report. It said that teens 13–18 years old should sleep 8–10 hours every day. Many scientists believe that if teens don't get enough sleep, they might become depressed, or have behavior or learning problems.

Many teens may not sleep enough because their body clock starts to change. When you're 10 years old, your body might tell you that you're tired around 8 or 9 p.m. But when you reach 13 or 14, your body clock moves about two hours. Your body starts to tell you that you're tired around 10 or 11 p.m. It takes time to get used to this change, and teens often feel sleepy in the morning.

Unfortunately, the beginning of the school day in the U.S.A., and in many parts of the world, does not match the need for teen sleep. If teens fall asleep at 10 or 11 p.m. and wake up around 6 a.m. for school, on average they may only get 7–8 hours of sleep. Some high schools in the U.S.A. have changed their schedule because of this. Instead of starting at 7:30 a.m., for example, they are starting around 8:30.

12 Look at the passage. Fill in the missing numbers to complete the sentences.

1. Teens should sleep _____ to _____ hours a night.
2. Teens begin to feel tired around _____ or _____ at night.
3. Some high schools in the U.S.A. are starting their days later, at around _____.

THINK BIG
Do you get enough sleep every night? Why/Why not?

10   Unit 1

Culture Connection | Around the World

I will learn about a different type of school.

13 **Listen and read.** What time does Anna's school finish?

CONTENT WORDS
behave   curriculum   gathering information
memorizing facts   pace

A School Day with a Difference

"Moi, Sofia!" "Terve, Aleksi!" That's how students and teachers say hello to each other at Anna Hansson's school in Finland. Students at this school call their teachers by their first names. Anna shouts "Moi" to her friends, too, when she arrives at school at 7:45 in the morning. She's been a student there since first grade, so she knows everybody.

Anna's school is different from most schools in Europe and the United States. First, Anna and her classmates decide, along with their teacher, what their weekly activities will be. Also, students work at their own pace and don't always do the same things. Some may be doing math, and others might be doing something practical. This month, Anna has practiced cooking and making a magazine in different workshops.

Anna and her classmates don't learn by memorizing facts. Working together and gathering information is more important in this system. They ask their teacher for help whenever they need it. Students are generally very focused and active, and the teacher doesn't have to tell them to behave.

Chores have always been part of the curriculum at Anna's school. They include taking care of plants, collecting trash, recycling, and composting. Students also help in the library and in the kitchen.

School is over by two o'clock. Most parents work, so in the afternoon, there are clubs and hobby groups before students go home. Students can study Japanese, learn an instrument, and do arts and crafts. When Anna returns home in the evening, she's free to do what she likes because she hardly ever has any homework!

14 Look at the passage and complete the sentences.

1 Anna and her classmates can _____ what they will do in school every week.
2 Bad behavior isn't a problem because students are usually _____.
3 _____ like collecting trash are part of the school curriculum.
4 Anna is free to _____ after school.

THINK BIG

What are the similarities and differences between your school and Anna's school?

Culture Connection Lesson

Lesson Flow

Warm-up › Lesson Objective › Pre-reading › Reading › Practice 1 › Practice 2 › Think BIG › Video › Lesson Objective › Homework

Lesson Objective

I will learn about a different type of school.

Key Language

behave, curriculum, gathering information, memorizing facts, pace

---

Culture Connection | Around the World

I will learn about a different type of school.

13 Listen and read. What time does Anna's school finish?

CONTENT WORDS
behave   curriculum   gathering information
memorizing facts   pace

A School Day with a Difference

"Moi, Sofia!" "Terve, Aleksi!" That's how students and teachers say hello to each other at Anna Hansson's school in Finland. Students at this school call their teachers by their first names. Anna shouts "Moi" to her friends, too, when she arrives at school at 7:45 in the morning. She's been a student there since first grade, so she knows everybody.

Anna's school is different from most schools in Europe and the United States. First, Anna and her classmates decide, along with their teacher, what their weekly activities will be. Also, students work at their own pace and don't always do the same things. Some may be doing math, and others might be doing something practical. This month, Anna has practiced cooking and making a magazine in different workshops.

Anna and her classmates don't learn by memorizing facts. Working together and gathering information is more important in this system. They ask their teacher for help whenever they need it. Students are generally very focused and active, and the teacher doesn't have to tell them to behave.

Chores have always been part of the curriculum at Anna's school. They include taking care of plants, collecting trash, recycling, and composting. Students also help in the library and in the kitchen.

School is over by two o'clock. Most parents work, so in the afternoon, there are clubs and hobby groups before students go home. Students can study Japanese, learn an instrument, and do arts and crafts. When Anna returns home in the evening, she's free to do what she likes because she hardly ever has any homework!

14 Look at the passage and complete the sentences.

1 Anna and her classmates can _____ what they will do in school every week.
2 Bad behavior isn't a problem because students are usually _____.
3 _____ like collecting trash are part of the school curriculum.
4 Anna is free to _____ after school.

THINK BIG What are the similarities and differences between your school and Anna's school?

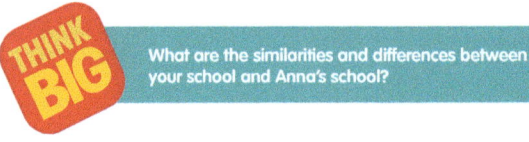

Unit 1 **11**

Warm-up

Write a two-column chart on the board with the headings *Things I Like About My School Day* and *Things I Dislike About My School Day*. Have students copy and complete the chart with three things they like about the school day and three things they dislike. Allow students to share freely in pairs.

- Check answers from the HW in the last lesson.

S11 Unit 1

Lesson Objective

INVOLVE

Introduce the lesson objective. Say: *Today I will learn about a different type of school.*

- Students will listen to, read, and talk about a school in Finland and connect the text to their personal experience.

Pre-reading

- Write the Content Words on the board: *behave, curriculum, gathering information, memorizing facts, pace*. Have students look for and circle these words in the article.
- Read the title of the article. Have students predict what the article is going to be about. Then, have students take a minute to scan the main ideas and revise their predictions.

Reading

13 Listen and read. What time does Anna's school finish?

- Read the directions aloud. Play Audio Track 16.

MONITOR

Discuss the answer as a class. (Answer: *School is over by two o'clock.*)

ASSIST

Replay the audio as needed. Use simple language and gestures to explain unfamiliar words.

Practice 1

14 Look at the passage and complete the sentences.

- Ask students to complete the activity independently.

MONITOR

Put students in pairs, and have them take turns reading the sentences aloud. Walk around the class and monitor students' pronunciation. (Answers: 1 *decide, along with their teacher*, 2 *very focused and active*, 3 *Chores*, 4 *do what she likes*.)

CHALLENGE

On strips of paper, ask students to write other fill-in-the-blank sentences based on the text. Invite volunteers to write their sentences on the board. Challenge students to close their books and complete the sentences.

Practice 2   WB p. 9/ act. 17

17 Listen and read. Then complete the chart.

- Read the directions aloud. Explain to students that they have to listen and read the text and complete the chart with the correct information.
- Have a volunteer read the title aloud.
- Play Audio Track 17 and have students listen and read along.
- Have students discuss the answers with a partner, then check answers as a class.

Think BIG

21st Century Critical Thinking

- On the board, write a four-row chart with the following headings: *Differences between Anna's School and Ours; Similarities between Anna's School and Ours; Advantages of Anna's School; Disadvantages of Anna's School.*

ASSIST

Make sure students understand the meanings of differences, similarities, advantages, and disadvantages.

- Have students complete the graphic organizer individually.
- Invite volunteers to share their ideas with the class. Ask students whether they agree or disagree.

Video   Documentary   U 01

- Refer to the Video Guide for pre-watching and post-watching activities.

Lesson Objective

INVOLVE

Revisit the lesson objective: *Now I have learned about a different type of school.*

- Encourage awareness of what the students have learned by quickly eliciting a few things they remember about the article, for example, which chores are part of the curriculum.

Homework   WB p. 9/ act. 18

18 Read 17 again and circle T for *true* or F for *false*.

- Direct students to WB Activity 18 on page 9. Tell students to read the sentences and circle T or F.

Extra Application and Practice Activity

National Adjectives: Write *Finland* and *Finnish* on the board. Say: *Finland is the name of a country. Finnish is an adjective. Finnish is the way we refer to schools in Finland.* Have students say the adjective for each of these countries: *Poland (Polish), Spain (Spanish), France (French), Japan (Japanese), India (Indian), Afghanistan (Afghan), Argentina (Argentinian), Holland (Dutch), China (Chinese), Brazil (Brazilian), Indonesia (Indonesian), Russia (Russian),* and *Greece (Greek).*

- Group students, and give each group a subject, such as history, math, or science. Have them create a dialog of students studying the subject, either in their own school or in a Finnish school. Allow students to perform their dialogs for the class.

Unit 1   **T11**

Writing Lesson

Lesson Flow

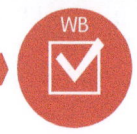

Warm-up › Lesson Objective › Practice 1 (WB) › Practice 2 (SB) › Practice 3 (SB) › Practice 4 (SB) › Speaking › Lesson Objective › Homework

Lesson Objective

I will learn to write an opinion paragraph about school issues.

Writing | Opinion paragraph

I will learn to write an opinion paragraph about school issues.

15 Read the opinion paragraph about homework.

> **Homework Does Not Make Students Learn Better**
>
> Does homework make students learn better? In my opinion, it does not. In fact, having a lot of homework makes students dislike school and become stressed. Students who are anxious and don't like school cannot learn well. Students who have hours and hours of homework cannot relax and spend quality time with their families. I believe that school schedules should allow students to get most of their schoolwork done at school. In this way, when they get home, they can be free to enjoy time with their family or just relax. In my opinion, a more relaxed student will perform better in class. Too much homework prevents this!

16 Complete the chart below with information from 15.

Title rewritten as question:	
Main opinion:	
Reason:	
Suggestion:	
Conclusion:	

17 Copy the chart above into your notebook and complete it with your ideas about one of the titles below. Then use it to write an opinion paragraph.
- Memorizing facts makes students learn better.
- School uniforms should be required.

18 In pairs, take turns sharing your opinions on school issues. Do you agree?

12 Unit 1

Warm-up

Materials: Newspapers and magazines

21st Century Media Literacy

Say: *A fact is known to be true. It can be proven. An opinion is a personal view. It's based on a person's judgment.* Allow students to scan newspapers and magazines and share examples of facts and opinions. Point out that news articles mainly contain facts, but opinions are also stated and supported in editorials and editorial features.

- Check answers from the HW in the last lesson.

Lesson Objective

INVOLVE

Introduce the lesson objective. Say: *Today I will learn to write an opinion paragraph about school issues.*

- Students will read an opinion paragraph about homework. Then they will write their own opinion paragraph about homework or another school issue. Say: *An issue is a subject for discussion. People often have different opinions about important issues.*

S12 Unit 1

Practice 1 WB p. 10/ act. 19

19 Choose one of the school issues below. Write your opinion.
- Have volunteers read the tips for writing a well-written opinion paragraph in the purple box aloud.
- Read the directions. Have volunteers choose an issue independently.

Practice 2

15 Read the opinion paragraph about homework.
- Read the directions aloud. Invite volunteers to read the paragraph aloud.

MONITOR
Check for understanding. Ask: *What's the writer's opinion about homework?* (A lot of it creates stress. It doesn't help make students better learners.) *When does the writer think students should do most of their schoolwork?* (when they're at school)

ASSIST
Use simple language to explain unfamiliar words, and point out antonyms. For example, say: *Stressed* and *relaxed* are opposites. *If you're stressed out, you feel a lot of pressure. If you're relaxed, you feel calm.*

Practice 3

16 Complete the chart below with information from 15.
- Read the directions aloud. Say: *The topic of an opinion paragraph can be stated as a question. The paragraph then gives the writer's answer.* Then have students work independently or in pairs to complete the activity in their notebooks.

MONITOR
Check answers as a class. (Possible answers: Title rewritten as question: *Does homework make students learn better?* Main opinion: *No, homework doesn't make students learn better or do better in school.* Reason: *Homework creates stress, and stress makes students dislike school and perform poorly.* Suggestion: *Students should be able to get most of their work done at school.* Conclusion: *Limiting homework will result in happier students who do better at school.*)

Practice 4

17 Copy the chart above into your notebook and complete it with your ideas about one of the titles below. Then use it to write an opinion paragraph.
- Read the directions, issues, and steps aloud. Then have students work independently to plan and write an opinion paragraph.

MONITOR
Check that students complete their outlines before they begin to draft paragraphs. Check for correct grammar and punctuation.

ASSIST
Have students use the school facts on page 4 to help them think of issues for their opinion paragraphs. Say: *You might get ideas by thinking about schools in other countries, such as China or Finland.*

Speaking

18 In pairs, take turns sharing your opinions on school issues. Do you agree?
- Ask students to work with a partner to discuss what each of them has written. Do they share their partner's opinions or not?
- Ask pairs to report to the class on any issues on which they do not agree.

Lesson Objective

INVOLVE
Revisit the lesson objective: *Now I have learned to write an opinion paragraph about school issues.*
- Encourage awareness of what the students have learned by quickly eliciting how to write a well-written opinion paragraph.

Homework WB p. 10/ act. 20 & 21

20 Write an outline for your topic in 19. Complete the chart.
- Direct students to WB Activity 20 on page 10. Tell students to write information for their paragraph in the chart.

21 Write an opinion paragraph on a separate piece of paper. Use your notes from 20.
- Direct students to WB Activity 21 on page 10. Tell students to write their opinion paragraph using the information in Activity 20.

Extra Application and Practice Activity

- Have students revise their opinion paragraphs based on class feedback. Then encourage them to submit their work to school, local, or online publications.

Unit 1 **T12**

Writing | Opinion paragraph

I will learn to write an opinion paragraph about school issues.

15 Read the opinion paragraph about homework.

> **Homework Does Not Make Students Learn Better**
>
> Does homework make students learn better? In my opinion, it does not. In fact, having a lot of homework makes students dislike school and become stressed. Students who are anxious and don't like school cannot learn well. Students who have hours and hours of homework cannot relax and spend quality time with their families. I believe that school schedules should allow students to get most of their schoolwork done at school. In this way, when they get home, they can be free to enjoy time with their family or just relax. In my opinion, a more relaxed student will perform better in class. Too much homework prevents this!

16 Complete the chart below with information from 15.

Title rewritten as question:	
Main opinion:	
Reason:	
Suggestion:	
Conclusion:	

17 Copy the chart above into your notebook and complete it with your ideas about one of the titles below. Then use it to write an opinion paragraph.

- Memorizing facts makes students learn better.
- School uniforms should be required.

18 In pairs, take turns sharing your opinions on school issues. Do you agree?

12 Unit 1

Life skills | Manage your time wisely.

I will learn to talk about how I spend and manage my time.

19 How do you spend your time? Read the list of activities and add two more. Check (✔) the ones you have to do each week and write the number of hours.

Activity	Approximate hours per week
____ take music lessons	____
____ travel to and from school	____
____ eat	____
____ sleep	____
____ study or do homework	____
____ play sports or exercise	____
____ participate in school clubs	____
____ do chores	____
____ watch TV	____
____ chat with friends online or on the phone	____
____ _____	____
____ _____	____

20 Look at 19. Do you think you manage your time wisely? Talk with a partner.

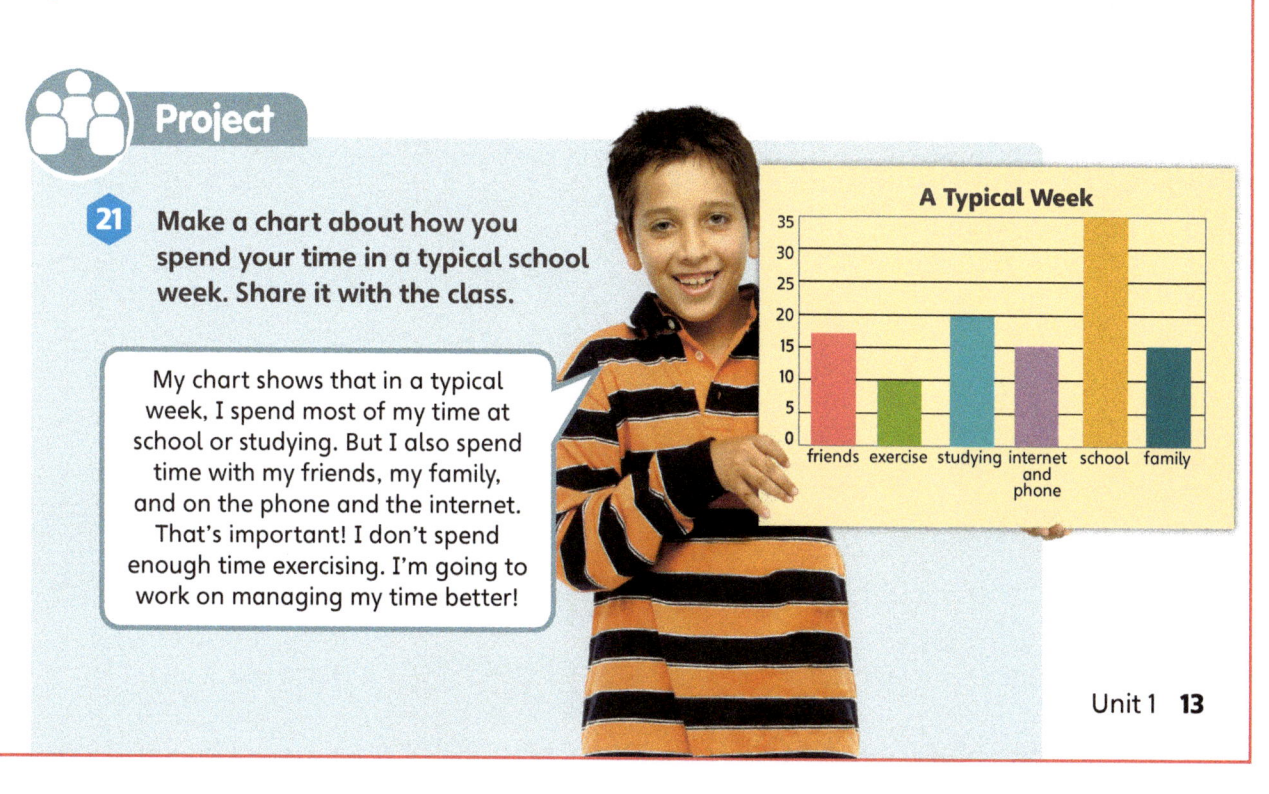

Project

21 Make a chart about how you spend your time in a typical school week. Share it with the class.

> My chart shows that in a typical week, I spend most of my time at school or studying. But I also spend time with my friends, my family, and on the phone and the internet. That's important! I don't spend enough time exercising. I'm going to work on managing my time better!

Life Skills Lesson

Lesson Flow

Warm-up › Lesson Objective › Practice (SB) › Speaking › Project › Lesson Objective

Lesson Objective

I will learn to talk about how I spend and manage my time.

Life skills | Manage your time wisely.

I will learn to talk about how I spend and manage my time.

19 How do you spend your time? Read the list of activities and add two more. Check (✓) the ones you have to do each week and write the number of hours.

Activity	Approximate hours per week
___ take music lessons	_____
___ travel to and from school	_____
___ eat	_____
___ sleep	_____
___ study or do homework	_____
___ play sports or exercise	_____
___ participate in school clubs	_____
___ do chores	_____
___ watch TV	_____
___ chat with friends online or on the phone	_____
___ _____	_____
___ _____	_____

20 Look at 19. Do you think you manage your time wisely? Talk with a partner.

Project

21 Make a chart about how you spend your time in a typical school week. Share it with the class.

> My chart shows that in a typical week, I spend most of my time at school or studying. But I also spend time with my friends, my family, and on the phone and the internet. That's important! I don't spend enough time exercising. I'm going to work on managing my time better!

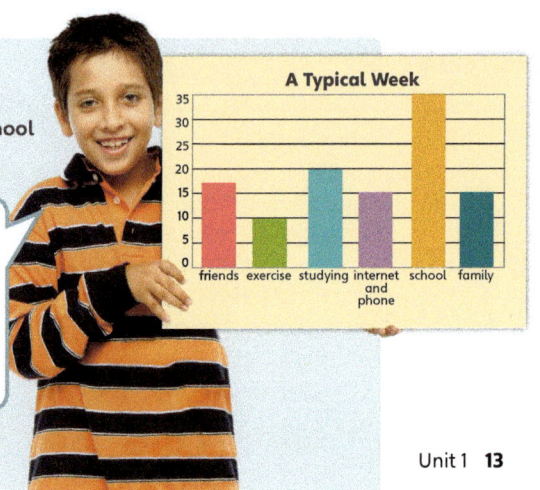

A Typical Week (chart showing: friends, exercise, studying, internet and phone, school, family)

Warm-up

- Ask students to talk in small groups about how much time they spend doing things such as talking on the phone, listening to music, cleaning their rooms, and exercising. Go around the room and take notes about how students are quantifying their time. They are probably using general approximations such as these: *I talk on the phone all night. I listen to music whenever I can. I hardly ever clean my room! I exercise as much as I can every day.* As a class, talk about words and phrases students used, and then tell students that they will get more specific and show how they generally spend their time over the course of a week.
- Check answers from the HW in the last lesson.

Lesson Objective

INVOLVE

Introduce the lesson objective. Say: *Today I will learn to talk about how I spend and manage my time.*

- Students will share ideas about how they manage their time. Then they will create graphs showing how they spend time during a typical week.

Practice

19 How do you spend your time? Read the list of activities and add two more. Check (✔) the ones you have to do each week and write the number of hours.

- Read the directions aloud. Say: *To estimate how many hours you sleep each week, first estimate how many hours you sleep in one night. Then multiply your estimate by seven.* Have students complete the activity independently, using calculators if necessary.

MONITOR

Make sure that students check each activity they do during most weeks and then provide reasonable estimates for how many hours they spend doing each activity.

ASSIST

Provide students with vocabulary to discuss other activities they may want to add. Suggest activities such as *read for fun, take care of pets, help others,* and *cook.*

21st Century Critical Thinking

- Ask: *Why is it useful to look at how you spend a typical week instead of a typical day?* (Students should point out that there are some activities they don't do every day; looking at a typical week gives a better idea of how they spend time all days of the week, including weekdays and weekends.)

Speaking

20 Look at 19. Do you think you manage your time wisely? Talk with a partner.

- Read the directions aloud. Have students work in pairs to talk about how they manage their time.

MONITOR

Ask students to report to the class about how wisely they use their time and the importance of what they do each week.

Project

21 Make a chart about how you spend your time in a typical school week. Share it with the class.

- Read the directions aloud. Review the parts of a bar chart: the title, labels, and bars. Answer any questions students have about the data shown on the sample chart. Then ask them to complete their charts independently.
- Have students share their charts with the class. Challenge students to generalize about their activities. Write this model on the board: *This year, I've spent a lot of time exercising because I'm on a sports team.*

Lesson Objective

INVOLVE

Revisit the lesson objective: *Now I have learned to talk about how I spend and manage my time.*

- Encourage awareness of what the students have learned by quickly eliciting what they remember about creating charts.

Extra Application and Practice Activity

- Display all of the charts. Help students generalize to decide which chart best reflects how most of the class spends time during a week.

ASSIST

Have students collect data from the individual charts and create a bar chart showing the class averages. Say: *To find the average amount of time we (sleep) each week, add the estimates and then divide by the number of students.*

Unit 1 **T13**

Listening and Speaking Lesson

Lesson Flow

Warm-up › Lesson Objective › Presentation › Practice 1 › Practice 2 › Speaking › Lesson Objective

Lesson Objectives

I will review the sounds *spr*, *str*, and *scr*.

I will learn to talk about school activities and excuses.

Listening and Speaking

I will review the sounds *spr*, *str*, and *scr*.
I will learn to talk about school activities and excuses.

22 Listen, read, and repeat.

1. spr   2. str   3. scr

23 Listen and blend the sounds.

1. spr-i-ng   spring   2. str-ee-t   street
3. scr-ee-n   screen   4. spr-i-n-t   sprint
5. str-o-ng   strong   6. scr-ew   screw

24 Listen and chant.

I'm fast, I'm strong,
I can sprint all day long.
In the spring, in the street,
Greeting people that I meet!

25 Look at the list of school activities and think of some really bad excuses for why you haven't done these things yet. Work in a group. Ask and answer questions.

finish your research project   do your homework   join any after-school clubs
study for the test   write your book review

Have you done your homework yet?

No, I haven't. I lost my book on my way home!

No, I haven't. I started to do it, but my dog ran off with it and ate it!

No, I haven't. I had to train his dog not to eat homework, so I ran out of time!

14 Unit 1

Warm-up

- Invite two students to the front of the classroom, and have them stand back to back so that they can't see each other. Have Student A give Student B instructions for completing a simple activity, such as packing a backpack neatly, putting on a coat, or folding a shirt. Student B should slowly follow the instructions, after first listening to all of them. To check Student B's progress, Student A should ask questions that begin with "Have you." Model: *Have you put the books on the table yet? Have you put the books in order from largest to smallest already?* Repeat with other volunteers.

Lesson Objective

INVOLVE

Introduce the lesson objective. Say: *Today I will learn to use the sounds* spr, str, *and* scr *and talk about school activities and excuses.*

- Students will identify the letters and distinguish between the sounds *spr*, *str*, and *scr* individually and as part of words. Then they will review the unit by talking about excuses.

Presentation

22 Listen, read, and repeat.

- Read the directions aloud. Play Audio Track 18 and have students listen and point to each sound as it is said. Have students repeat.

MONITOR

As students repeat, check they are pointing to the correct sound and listen for correct pronunciation.

Practice 1

23 Listen and blend the sounds.

- Read the directions aloud. Play Audio Track 19 and have students listen and point to each item as it is sounded out and blended on the audio. Have them repeat after each item.

MONITOR

As students repeat, check they are pointing to the correct word and listen for correct pronunciation and appropriate intonation.

ASSIST

Replay the audio as needed.

Practice 2

24 Listen and chant.

- Read the directions aloud. Read the chant while students follow in their books.
- Play Audio Track 20 and have students listen. Replay the audio several times and encourage them to join in.

MONITOR

As students repeat the chant, listen for proper pronunciation, appropriate intonation, and correct use of language.

Speaking

25 Look at the list of school activities and think of some really bad excuses for why you haven't done these things yet. Work in a group. Ask and answer questions.

- Ask volunteers to read the directions and the speech bubbles aloud. Have students complete the activity in small groups.

MONITOR

Listen to students' questions and answers to make sure they're using the target vocabulary and grammar correctly.

ASSIST

Provide students with the past participle of the verbs they will use to ask questions about the activities in the word box: *done, written, studied, joined, finished.* Write this sentence frame on the board: *Have you… yet?*

21st Century Leadership

Allow students to take turns leading class discussions. Remind leaders that they should make sure that the class stays focused on the topic. Leaders can also ask questions and involve volunteers to be sure everyone participates.

Lesson Objective

INVOLVE

Revisit the lesson objective: *Now I have learned to use the sounds* spr, str, *and* scr *and talked about school activities and excuses.*

- Encourage awareness of what the students have learned by quickly eliciting the words from the lesson with the sounds *spr*, *str*, and *scr*.

Extra Application and Practice Activity

- Invite students to create cartoons or comic strips that use bad excuses as punch lines. Say: *The punch line is the part of a joke that makes it funny.* Display students' work in the classroom. Have each student read his or her cartoon or comic strip to the class, explaining the punch line to the rest of the students.

Listening and Speaking

I will review the sounds *spr*, *str*, and *scr*.
I will learn to talk about school activities and excuses.

22 Listen, read, and repeat.

1. spr   2. str   3. scr

23 Listen and blend the sounds.

1. spr-i-ng   spring
2. str-ee-t   street
3. scr-ee-n   screen
4. spr-i-n-t   sprint
5. str-o-ng   strong
6. scr-ew   screw

24 Listen and chant.

> I'm fast, I'm strong,
> I can sprint all day long.
> In the spring, in the street,
> Greeting people that I meet!

25 Look at the list of school activities and think of some really bad excuses for why you haven't done these things yet. Work in a group. Ask and answer questions.

> finish your research project   do your homework   join any after-school clubs
> study for the test   write your book review

- Have you done your homework yet?
- No, I haven't. I lost my book on my way home!
- No, I haven't. I started to do it, but my dog ran off with it and ate it!
- No, I haven't. I had to train his dog not to eat homework, so I ran out of time!

14   Unit 1

Review

26 Listen to Lucas and Nina talking about their school. Take notes in the chart below.

	Lucas	Nina
book report		
assignment		
project		
homework		

27 Work in pairs and make sentences about Lucas and Nina. What have they already done? What haven't they done yet?

Nina forgot her writing assignment.

Lucas has already finished his book report.

I Can

- use words for school activities and homework.
- talk about events in the past using the present perfect and *yet*, *already*, and *ever*.
- talk about doing homework and make excuses.
- write an opinion paragraph.

Unit 1 15

Review Lesson

Lesson Flow

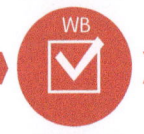

Warm-up › Lesson Objective › Practice 1 (SB) › Practice 2 (WB) › Practice 3 (WB) › Practice 4 (SB) › Self-assessment › Homework

Lesson Objective

To review the words and structures of the unit.

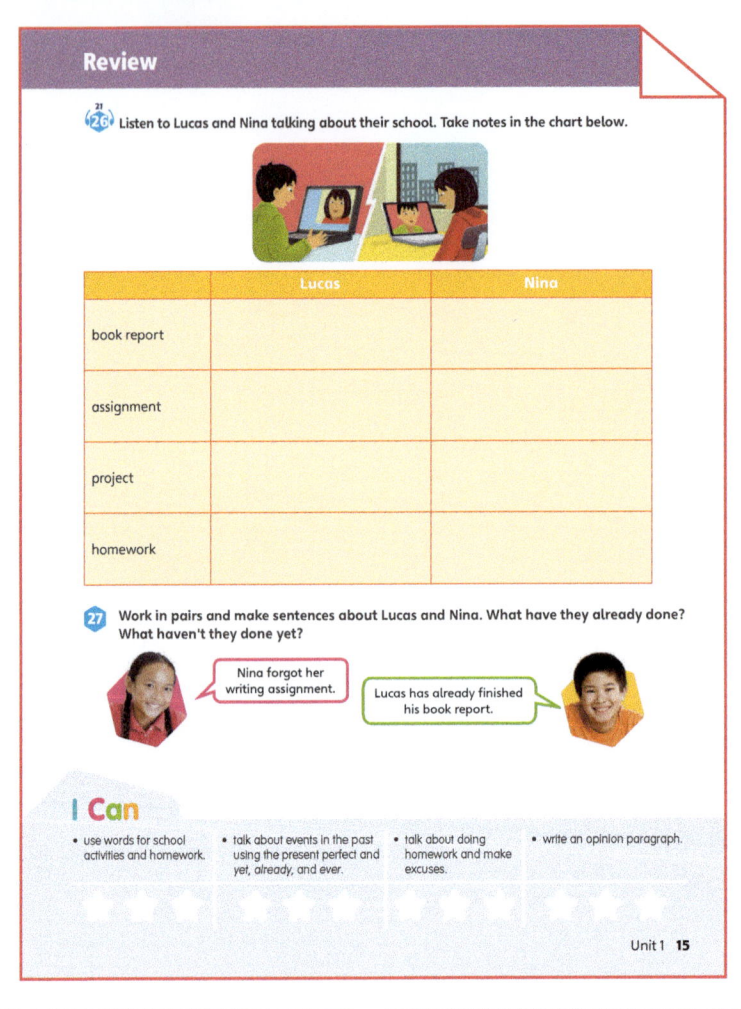

Review

26 Listen to Lucas and Nina talking about their school. Take notes in the chart below.

	Lucas	Nina
book report		
assignment		
project		
homework		

27 Work in pairs and make sentences about Lucas and Nina. What have they already done? What haven't they done yet?

- Nina forgot her writing assignment.
- Lucas has already finished his book report.

I Can

- use words for school activities and homework.
- talk about events in the past using the present perfect and yet, already, and ever.
- talk about doing homework and make excuses.
- write an opinion paragraph.

Unit 1 15

Warm-up

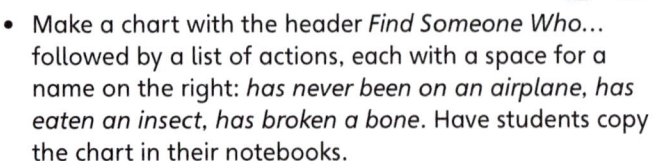

- Make a chart with the header *Find Someone Who…* followed by a list of actions, each with a space for a name on the right: *has never been on an airplane, has eaten an insect, has broken a bone*. Have students copy the chart in their notebooks.
- Tell students to walk around and ask one another if they have done the things in the chart. Tell them to write down the names of those who say yes.
- Ask different students to report back to the class, e.g. *Jorge has broken a bone.*

Lesson Objective

INVOLVE

Introduce the lesson objective: Say: *Today I will review the words and structures of the unit.*

- Students will review the vocabulary and grammar they learned in Unit 1. They will review the unit by using *yet* and *always* and the present perfect to talk about past experiences.
- Then students will complete the *I Can* section, which helps them to assess their own learning and progress.

Practice 1 🎧 P. T139 [21]

26 Listen to Lucas and Nina talking about their school. Take notes in the chart below.

- Read the directions aloud. Say: *You are going to hear a conversation between two students sharing their ideas.* Play Audio Track 21. Then have students complete the activity independently.

MONITOR

To check answers, name an activity and have students explain how they completed the chart for that activity. *(Answers: book report – Lucas, handed in yesterday; Nina, just finished; assignment – Lucas, doing it today; Nina, finished it on Wednesday; project – Lucas, started with science club; Nina, wants to join; homework – Lucas, started it last night; Nina, hasn't started yet)*

Practice 2 WB p. 11/ act. 22

22 Read about Anna's day. Use the words to write questions. Then write the answers.

- Read the directions aloud. Explain to students that they need to write complete questions and answers using the present perfect.
- Have students work independently.
- Have students compare answers with a partner, then check answers as a class.

Practice 3 WB p. 11/ act. 23

23 Complete the sentences. Use the correct form of the verbs in parentheses.

- Read the directions aloud. Explain to students that they have to use the correct forms of the verbs to complete the sentences.

Practice 4

27 Work in pairs and make sentences about Lucas and Nina. What have they already done? What haven't they done yet?

- Read the directions aloud. Read Item 1 aloud and model: *I want to write sentences about whether or not Nina and Lucas have taken the test.* Play the first three lines of Audio Track 21. Say: *Nina hasn't studied for the test yet. Lucas handed in his book report yesterday.*
- Have students complete the activity independently.

MONITOR

Check answers as a class. *(Possible answers: 2 Lucas hasn't handed in his writing assignment yet. Nina has already finished the writing assignment. She will hand it in tomorrow. 3 Nina hasn't joined any after-school clubs yet. Lucas has already joined the art club. He has already started a project with the science club. 4 Nina hasn't started the math homework yet. Lucas has already started the math homework. He started it last night.)*

Self-assessment

I Can

- This section asks students to assess their own learning and reflect on their progress. Help students appreciate their progress. Say: *The I Can statements show what you have learned in this unit.*
- Read the statements aloud. Explain that students should think about how well they know the language in the unit and should color in the stars. They should color three stars if they feel the unit was easy, two stars if they need some help, and one star if the unit was hard and they need more help. Have students work independently.

Suggestions for Remediation

Assessment Pack
- Direct students who need help with grammar and vocabulary to the Unit 1 Practice Tests in the Assessment Pack.

WB Unit 1/ p. 98
- Direct students who need help with grammar in particular to the Unit 1 Extra Grammar Practice (Workbook, page 98).
- For further vocabulary work, students can access games in the Big English Student World.

Homework WB p. 11/ act. 24

24 Look at 23. Write excuses using the ideas in the box.

- Direct students to WB Activity 24 on page 11. Explain to students that they have to look at WB Activity 23, choose one idea from the box, and write an excuse.

Extra Application and Practice Activity

- Pair students, and have them create a dialog between a famous celebrity and a magazine reporter. Explain that the reporter should ask about what the celebrity has and hasn't done.
- Invite several pairs to perform their dialogs in front of the class.

Assessment Pack

- To assess student progress at the end of the unit, have students complete the Unit 1 Unit Test in the Assessment Pack.
- To assess whether students have reached the listening and speaking targets for this unit, carry out the Unit 1 Oral Assessment in the Assessment Pack.
- Arrange one-to-one sessions with each student and use the prompts to evaluate their listening and speaking abilities.

2 Amazing Young People

Objectives

Reading

- Can follow the sequence of events in simple narrative texts by recognizing common linking words/phrases.
- Can extract specific information in short texts on familiar topics.
- Can identify supporting details in simple, structured paragraphs on familiar topics, if guided by questions.

Listening

- Can identify basic biographical information in short, simple talks about famous people from the past, if delivered slowly and clearly.
- Can understand the main information in short, simple dialogs about familiar activities, if spoken slowly and clearly.
- Can recognize familiar key words and phrases in short, basic descriptions (e.g. of objects, people, or animals), if spoken slowly and clearly.

Speaking

- Can express their opinions on familiar topics, using simple language.
- Can give an opinion in a structured discussion, if guided by questions.

Writing

- Can write a short, simple biography of a famous person with basic paragraph structure, given prompts or a model.
- Can create a poster to advertise an event or product, given a model.

Grammar

- Can use the present perfect with *for/since* to talk about the duration of states and conditions.

Unit Projects

Family Connection

Encourage students to talk with family members about amazing or impressive young people they have known or read about. Remind students to take notes about their conversations so they can share ideas with the class. Students can also share stories about amazing young people they are learning about in Unit 2. Tell students to record their family members' reactions.

Key Language

Key Vocabulary

Achievements

become a doctor
climb a mountain
invent something
meet a world leader
play an instrument
speak another language
start a company
win a tournament
write and publish a book

Expressions

developing country
drop out
have a special gift
I'm just kidding.
It feels funny.
You're joking, right?

Content Words

co-found
compose
exceptional talent
gifted
inspiration
keep in touch
social media
symphony

conflict
educators issues
neutral
participants

Grammar/Structures

How long **have** you **lived** here? I've **lived** here <u>for</u> five years./I've **lived** here <u>since</u> I was six.

How long **has** she **been singing**? She**'s been singing** <u>since</u> she was four./She**'s been singing** <u>for</u> 10 years.

Phonics

The sounds: *spl, squ, thr*

We're Young and We're Amazing Bulletin Board

Create a *We're Young and We're Amazing* bulletin-board display to celebrate accomplishments by young people, including those profiled in the unit. Begin the display by cutting out banners, awards, or ribbons from construction paper. Post several on the display, along with pictures or details about amazing young people. Place remaining cut-outs in an envelope attached to the display and encourage students to add new people to the display. Students may wish to use glitter, confetti, or other art supplies to highlight amazing accomplishments.

Language in Context Lesson

Lesson Flow

Warm-up → Lesson Objective → Presentation → Practice 1 (WB) → Practice 2 (SB) → Practice 3 (SB) → Speaking → Think BIG → Lesson Objective → Homework

Lesson Objective

I will learn to talk about achievements and reaching goals.

Key Language

book, company, contestant, doctor, game show, language, leader, millionaire, mountain, poor, reality show, tournament, world; achieve, become, climb, meet, play, publish, speak, start, take, write; amazing, award-winning; developing country

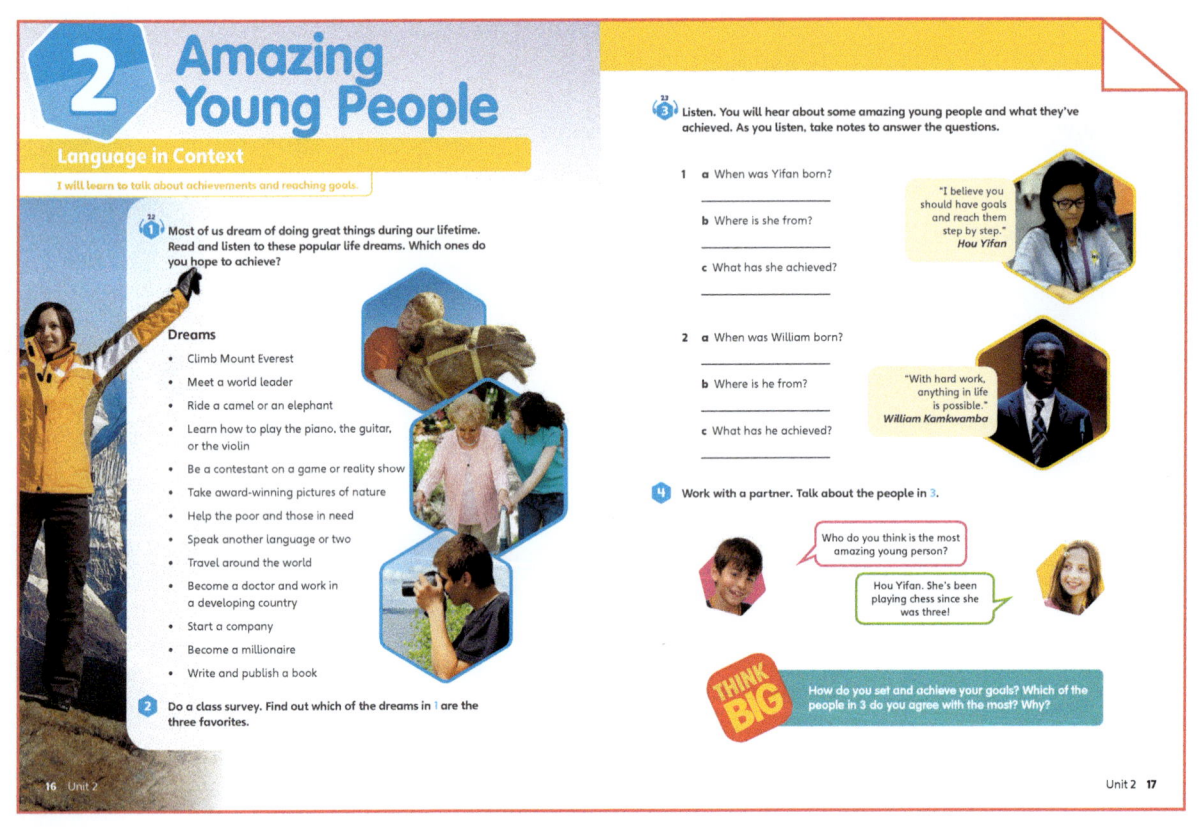

---

2 Amazing Young People

Language in Context

I will learn to talk about achievements and reaching goals.

1 Most of us dream of doing great things during our lifetime. Read and listen to these popular life dreams. Which ones do you hope to achieve?

Dreams
- Climb Mount Everest
- Meet a world leader
- Ride a camel or an elephant
- Learn how to play the piano, the guitar, or the violin
- Be a contestant on a game or reality show
- Take award-winning pictures of nature
- Help the poor and those in need
- Speak another language or two
- Travel around the world
- Become a doctor and work in a developing country
- Start a company
- Become a millionaire
- Write and publish a book

2 Do a class survey. Find out which of the dreams in 1 are the three favorites.

3 Listen. You will hear about some amazing young people and what they've achieved. As you listen, take notes to answer the questions.

1. a When was Yifan born? _____
   b Where is she from? _____
   c What has she achieved? _____

   "I believe you should have goals and reach them step by step." — Hou Yifan

2. a When was William born? _____
   b Where is he from? _____
   c What has he achieved? _____

   "With hard work, anything in life is possible." — William Kamkwamba

4 Work with a partner. Talk about the people in 3.

- Who do you think is the most amazing young person?
- Hou Yifan. She's been playing chess since she was three!

THINK BIG: How do you set and achieve your goals? Which of the people in 3 do you agree with the most? Why?

16 Unit 2 | Unit 2 17

Warm-up

- Write *dream* on the board. Say: *You have two kinds of dreams. You have dreams at night when you sleep. You also have dreams for the future. You might dream of becoming a doctor, an actor, or a politician.* Invite students to take turns completing this sentence to discuss their dreams for the future: *I dream that I will… .*
- Check answers from the HW in the last lesson.

Lesson Objective

INVOLVE

Explain the lesson objective. Say: *Today I will learn to talk about achievements and reaching goals.*

- Tell students that they will read and talk about what they want to achieve and what some young people have already achieved.

Presentation

Materials: World map or globe

1 Most of us dream of doing great things during our lifetime. Read and listen to these popular life dreams. Which ones do you hope to achieve?

- Read the directions aloud. Ask students to describe the photos. Ask volunteers to read the accomplishments from the bulleted list aloud. Play Audio Track 22.

- Have students choose which of the life dreams they would most like to achieve.

Practice 1 — WB p. 12/ act. 1

1 Match the pictures with the sentences about life dreams. Write the numbers.

- Read the directions aloud. Have students describe what they see in the pictures. Ask volunteers to read the sentences aloud.

Practice 2

Materials: Index cards

2 Do a class survey. Find out which of the dreams in 1 are the three favorites.

- Read the directions aloud. Have students make a tally of their choices.

21st Century Information Literacy

- Ask students to write their dreams on index cards. Then have them work together to sort the cards and create a graph of the three favorites from the bulleted list. Ask: *What kind of graph will show our survey data clearly?* (a bar graph/a circle graph/a pictograph) *How does a graph help you understand data or information quickly?* (Graphs let you see information visually. It can be easier to compare quantities by looking at visual information.)

Practice 3 — P. T140

3 Listen. You will hear about some amazing young people and what they've achieved. As you listen, take notes to answer the questions.

- Read the directions aloud. Have students preview the questions they'll answer. Say: *These questions will help you listen for a purpose. You'll listen to find the answers.* Play Audio Track 23. Pause after each description to allow students time to write their answers.

MONITOR

Check answers as a class. (Answers: 1 a. Yifan was born in 1994. b. She's from China. c. She's won major chess tournaments. 2 a. William was born in 1987. b. He's from Malawi. c. He has built useful machines by using materials from a junkyard.

Speaking

Work with a partner. Talk about the people in 3.

- Read the directions aloud. Have volunteers read the speech bubbles aloud. Have students work in pairs to talk about the amazing young people from the text.

Think BIG

21st Century Critical Thinking

- Ask students the questions and write their answers on the board. Then have them use the ideas from the board to ask each other the questions and answer them. Encourage them to express themselves as best they can.

Lesson Objective

INVOLVE

Revisit the lesson objective: *Now I have learned to talk about achievements and reaching goals.*

- Encourage awareness of what the students have learned by quickly eliciting some of the achievements and personal goals they learned about in the lesson.

Homework — WB pp. 12 & 13/ act. 2, 3, 4, & 5

2 Write down four of your dreams and rank them: 1 = most important, 4 = least important.

- Direct students to WB Activity 2 on page 12. Tell students to write down four of their dreams for the future and rank them in order of importance.

3 Look at 2. Which dream will be the most difficult to achieve? Draw a box around it. Which dream will be the easiest to achieve? Underline it. Which dream can you achieve right now? Write it here:

- Direct students to WB Activity 3 on page 12. Tell students to draw a box around the most difficult dream to achieve, underline the one that is easiest, and write the one that they can achieve right now.

4 Read. Then circle T for *true* or F for *false*.

- Direct students to WB Activity 4 on page 13. Tell students to read the text and then circle the sentences T or F.

5 Complete the sentences. Use the words in the box.

- Direct students to WB Activity 5 on page 13. Tell students to complete the sentences with the words in the box.

Think BIG

- Direct students to WB Think Big on page 13. Tell students to write answers to the questions.

Extra Application and Practice Activity

- Have students create awards to give to the amazing young people they've learned about. Encourage students to give their award a specific name. Model: *Most Amazing Athlete, Most Amazing Thinker, Most Amazing Helper.* Invite students to show their award to the class and then discuss which young person should receive the award.

Unit 2 T16/17

2 Amazing Young People

Language in Context

I will learn to talk about achievements and reaching goals.

1 Most of us dream of doing great things during our lifetime. Read and listen to these popular life dreams. Which ones do you hope to achieve?

Dreams

- Climb Mount Everest
- Meet a world leader
- Ride a camel or an elephant
- Learn how to play the piano, the guitar, or the violin
- Be a contestant on a game or reality show
- Take award-winning pictures of nature
- Help the poor and those in need
- Speak another language or two
- Travel around the world
- Become a doctor and work in a developing country
- Start a company
- Become a millionaire
- Write and publish a book

2 Do a class survey. Find out which of the dreams in **1** are the three favorites.

3 Listen. You will hear about some amazing young people and what they've achieved. As you listen, take notes to answer the questions.

1 a When was Yifan born?
      _____

   b Where is she from?
      _____

   c What has she achieved?
      _____

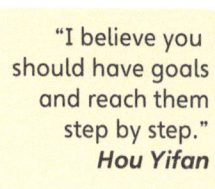

"I believe you should have goals and reach them step by step."
Hou Yifan

2 a When was William born?
      _____

   b Where is he from?
      _____

   c What has he achieved?
      _____

"With hard work, anything in life is possible."
William Kamkwamba

4 Work with a partner. Talk about the people in 3.

Who do you think is the most amazing young person?

Hou Yifan. She's been playing chess since she was three!

THINK BIG

How do you set and achieve your goals? Which of the people in 3 do you agree with the most? Why?

Reading Lesson

Lesson Flow

Warm-up › Lesson Objective › Pre-reading › Reading › Comprehension 1 › Comprehension 2 › Think BIG › Lesson Objective › Homework

Lesson Objective

I will understand a text about an amazing person's achievements.

Key Language

astronaut, biography, car, college, community, company, computer, DJ, equipment, money, technology; achieve, buy, fix, rebuild, save, start, take apart, work; local; have a special gift, It feels funny.

Reading | Biography

I will understand a text about an amazing person's achievements.

5 Listen and read. Why is Jimmy different from the kids around him?

JIMMY WOODARD: COMPUTER WHIZ KID

by Chris Winger

Where do you see yourself at seventeen? Owning a business? Owning a car? Saving for college? Chances are you'll eventually do these things, but maybe not when you're seventeen… unless you're someone like Jimmy Woodard!

Jimmy Woodard is a high school student from Manchester, Vermont, U.S.A. In many ways, Jimmy is a normal teenager who spends a lot of time online every day. But in other ways, Jimmy has always been different from the kids around him. When Jimmy was very young, his parents realized he had a special gift. While other children were playing with toys, Jimmy would take his toys apart to find out how they worked. But Jimmy's gift really became obvious when he started using computers. Jimmy was only six when he started using his parents' computer. That's not so unusual these days. However, in Jimmy's case, if he had a problem with the computer, he figured out how to fix it by himself!

When Jimmy was in fifth grade, his technology teacher gave him a computer to work on. Jimmy took the computer apart and put it back together again. Since then, Jimmy has been working with computers in his school, even helping teachers with their technology problems.

When he was fourteen, Jimmy decided to open his own technology consulting company. Since that time, he's brought in about 200 regular customers. One of them is former astronaut Gerald Carr. "It feels funny sometimes," said Jimmy with a smile. "I can't believe I'm helping an astronaut with his computer!"

Jimmy has done more than just work on computers. Since he was eleven or twelve, Jimmy has been helping and working in his community. He's managed the sound and lights for a local TV show and for theatrical performances. Jimmy has also worked as a DJ. "I've been a DJ at more than fifty dance events already," he said. "It's really fun."

Jimmy has saved a lot of money over the past three years. "I've just bought my own car," he said happily. "I've used some of my money to buy more computers or equipment for my company. But I'm trying to save the rest of it for college." As for his future, Jimmy explained, "I don't know what I want to do yet. I know I want to do something with computers. But I'm interested in a lot of different things. I'd like to live in a big city someday. I can't wait to see what happens next."

Reading Comprehension

6 Number the events in the order they happened in Jimmy's life.
- a Jimmy rebuilt a computer.
- b Jimmy bought a car.
- c Jimmy started his own company.
- d Jimmy took his toys apart to find out how they worked.
- e Jimmy started using his parents' computer.

THINK BIG What goals do you want to achieve in the future? Why?

Warm-up

21st Century Technology Literacy

- Discuss when students started using computers. Ask: *When did you learn how to use a computer? What could you do on a computer when you were six? When you were eight?* Record class answers on the board to find out who started using a computer at the youngest age. Then have students explain steps they might follow to teach a younger sister or brother about computers.

- Check answers from the HW in the last lesson.

Lesson Objective

INVOLVE

Introduce the lesson objective. Say: *Today I will learn to understand a text about an amazing person's achievements.*

- Students will listen to, read, talk, and answer questions about biography.

S18/19 Unit 2

Pre-reading

- Have students read the title aloud and preview the pictures. Say: *A whiz kid is a young person who is very, very good at something.* Have students look at the pictures and the title and guess what Jimmy Woodard has already accomplished.

Reading

5 Listen and read. Why is Jimmy different from the kids around him?

- Read the directions aloud. Play Audio Track 24 and have students listen and read along.

ASSIST

Replay the audio as needed. Pause after each paragraph and use simple language to explain unfamiliar words and phrases. Say: *Consulting means giving advice. An astronaut travels in space. A DJ plays music at parties and other events.*

Word Origins: Explain that *biography* comes from the Greek roots *bio* (life) and *graph* (writing). Help students use these to define *biography* ("writing about someone's life").

Comprehension 1

- Ask the question in the directions: *Why is Jimmy different from the kids around him?* (He's a whiz kid.)

MONITOR

Ask more questions to check for understanding. Ask: *How old is Jimmy Woodard?* (17) *What has he already done?* (He has owned a company, has bought his own car, and has saved money for college.) *What's Jimmy's special gift?* (He loves and understands computers.) *How did a technology teacher help Jimmy when he was in fifth grade?* (The teacher gave Jimmy a computer. Jimmy took it apart and put it back together.) *What kind of company did Jimmy start?* (a technology consulting company) *Who is Gerald Carr?* (He is a former astronaut and one of Jimmy's customers.)

Comprehension 2

6 Number the events in the order they happened in Jimmy's life.

- Read the directions aloud. Invite volunteers to read the events aloud.
- Have students work in pairs to find each event in the biography and number the events in the correct order. Have students write their answers in their notebooks.

MONITOR

Check answers as class.
(Answers: 1 d, 2 e, 3 a, 4 c, 5 b)

ASSIST

Replay the audio as needed and pause after each event so students can check the order of events.

Think BIG

21st Century Critical Thinking

- Remind students that asking and answering questions can help us understand and think about what we read.
- Read the question aloud. Have students work in pairs.

MONITOR

As students work, listen for proper pronunciation, appropriate intonation, and correct use of language.

ASSIST

Provide students with sentence frames to complete as they discuss Jimmy's life. Write these frames on the board: *Jimmy is different from other kids because he's already… . When he is older, Jimmy will… . Jimmy's story is amazing because… .*

Lesson Objective

INVOLVE

Revisit the lesson objective: *Now I have learned to understand a text about an amazing person's achievements.*

- Encourage awareness of what the students have learned by quickly eliciting a few things they remember about the text, for example, how old Jimmy was when he started using a computer.

Homework WB p. 14/ act. 6

6 Listen and read. Then answer the questions.

- Direct students to WB Activity 6 on page 14. Tell students to first read the questions and then play Audio Track 25 and listen and read along. Tell students to answer the questions.

Extra Application and Practice Activity

- Invite students to draw scenes from Jimmy's life. Suggest that each student choose one scene to illustrate. Tell students they can also draw events that they predict will happen when Jimmy is older.
- After students complete their pictures, encourage them to work together to hang the drawings in chronological order around the classroom. Say: *Chronological order is time order. We'll hang the scenes from first to last.*

Reading | Biography

I will understand a text about an amazing person's achievements.

🔊 **5** Listen and read. Why is Jimmy different from the kids around him?

JIMMY WOODARD: COMPUTER WHIZ KID

by Chris Winger

Where do you see yourself at seventeen? Owning a business? Owning a car? Saving for college? Chances are you'll eventually do these things, but maybe not when you're seventeen… unless you're someone like Jimmy Woodard!

Jimmy Woodard is a high school student from Manchester, Vermont, U.S.A. In many ways, Jimmy is a normal teenager who spends a lot of time online every day. But in other ways, Jimmy has always been different from the kids around him. When Jimmy was very young, his parents realized he had a special gift. While other children were playing with toys, Jimmy would take his toys apart to find out how they worked. But Jimmy's gift really became obvious when he started using computers. Jimmy was only six when he started using his parents' computer. That's not so unusual these days. However, in Jimmy's case, if he had a problem with the computer, he figured out how to fix it by himself!

When Jimmy was in fifth grade, his technology teacher gave him a computer to work on. Jimmy took the computer apart and put it back together again. Since then, Jimmy has been working with computers in

18 Unit 2

his school, even helping teachers with their technology problems.

When he was fourteen, Jimmy decided to open his own technology consulting company. Since that time, he's brought in about 200 regular customers. One of them is former astronaut Gerald Carr. "It feels funny sometimes," said Jimmy with a smile. "I can't believe I'm helping an astronaut with his computer!"

Jimmy has done more than just work on computers. Since he was eleven or twelve, Jimmy has been helping and working in his community. He's managed the sound and lights for a local TV show and for theatrical performances. Jimmy has also worked as a DJ. "I've been a DJ at more than fifty dance events already," he said. "It's really fun."

Jimmy has saved a lot of money over the past three years. "I've just bought my own car," he said happily. "I've used some of my money to buy more computers or equipment for my company. But I'm trying to save the rest of it for college." As for his future, Jimmy explained, "I don't know what I want to do yet. I know I want to do something with computers. But I'm interested in a lot of different things. I'd like to live in a big city someday. I can't wait to see what happens next."

Reading Comprehension

6 Number the events in the order they happened in Jimmy's life.

a Jimmy rebuilt a computer.

b Jimmy bought a car.

c Jimmy started his own company.

d Jimmy took his toys apart to find out how they worked.

e Jimmy started using his parents' computer.

THINK BIG What goals do you want to achieve in the future? Why?

Language in Action Lesson

Lesson Flow

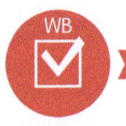

Warm-up › Lesson Objective › Pre-listening › Listening › Comprehension › Role Play › Practice 1 (SB) › Practice 2 (WB) › Lesson Objective › Homework

Lesson Objective

I will listen to a dialog about an amazing person's achievements.

Key Language

biography, builder, diagram, electricity, guy, inventor, program, research, rock band, water, windmill; build, dance, design, do, make, play, study, write; medical, running; drop out, I'm just kidding., You're joking, right?

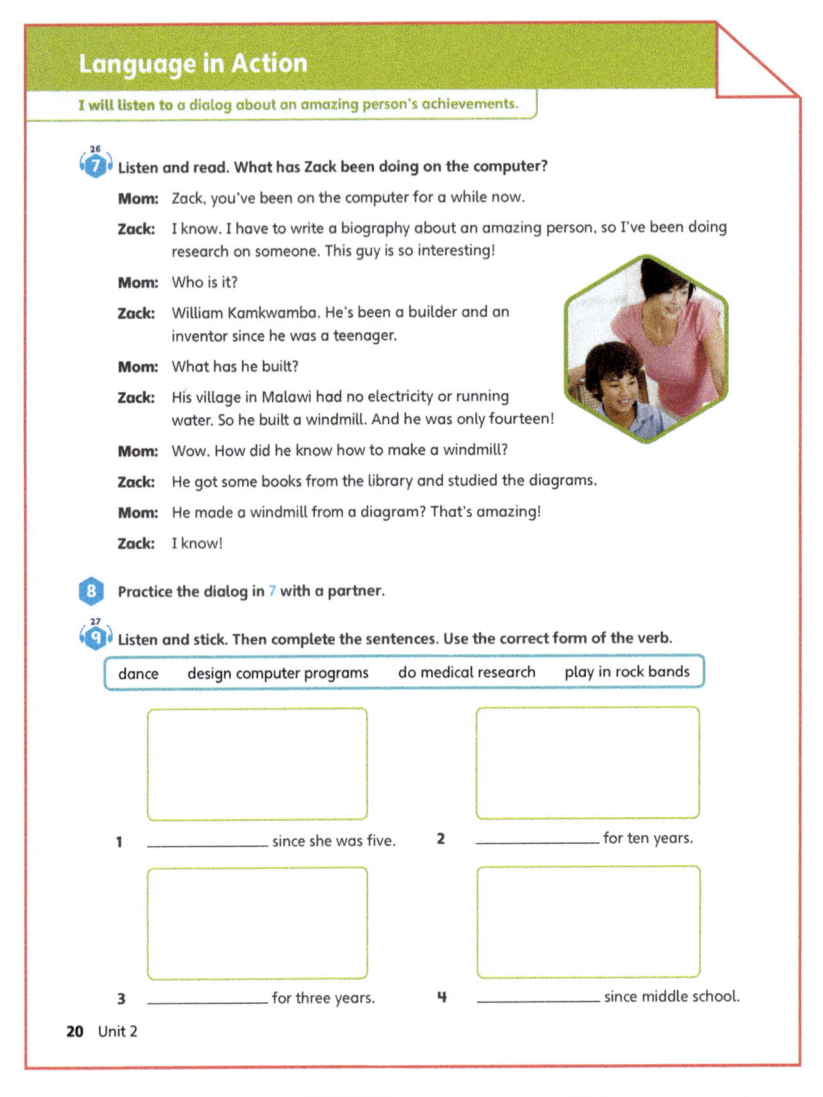

Language in Action

I will listen to a dialog about an amazing person's achievements.

7 Listen and read. What has Zack been doing on the computer?

Mom: Zack, you've been on the computer for a while now.

Zack: I know. I have to write a biography about an amazing person, so I've been doing research on someone. This guy is so interesting!

Mom: Who is it?

Zack: William Kamkwamba. He's been a builder and an inventor since he was a teenager.

Mom: What has he built?

Zack: His village in Malawi had no electricity or running water. So he built a windmill. And he was only fourteen!

Mom: Wow. How did he know how to make a windmill?

Zack: He got some books from the library and studied the diagrams.

Mom: He made a windmill from a diagram? That's amazing!

Zack: I know!

8 Practice the dialog in 7 with a partner.

9 Listen and stick. Then complete the sentences. Use the correct form of the verb.

dance   design computer programs   do medical research   play in rock bands

1 _____ since she was five.
2 _____ for ten years.
3 _____ for three years.
4 _____ since middle school.

20 Unit 2

Warm-up

Materials: Various diagrams

- Give students copies of diagrams in other languages or with the labels blacked out. Challenge them to name what the diagram shows or describes. Have students vote on which seems most accurate. Then reveal the actual purpose of the diagram.
- Tell students they are going to read about a young boy in Africa who built a windmill, using only a diagram.
- Check answers from the HW in the last lesson.

S20 Unit 2

Lesson Objective

INVOLVE
- Introduce the lesson objective. Say: *Today I will listen to a dialog about an amazing person's achievements.*
- Students will read, listen to, and practice a dialog. Students will also listen to conversations about amazing achievements.

Pre-listening

- Point to the picture. Ask: *What do you see?* (A boy with his mother or a teacher. They're looking at something, probably a computer) Introduce the boy and the woman as Zack and his mom. Tell students that they will hear Zack and his mom talking about an amazing achievement.

Listening

7 Listen and read. What has Zack been doing on the computer?
- Read the directions aloud. Play Audio Track 26 and have students listen and read along.
- Invite two students to read the dialog aloud and repeat.

Comprehension

- Ask the question in the directions: *What has Zack been doing on the computer?* (Zack has been doing research about an amazing person.)

MONITOR
Ask more questions to check for understanding. Encourage students to answer in complete sentences where appropriate. Ask: *What is Zack working on?* (He's writing a biography about an amazing person.) *Why did Zack choose to write about William Kamkwamba?* (Zack thinks William has done something amazing.) *What has William done?* (He's built a windmill, using only a diagram.)

Role Play

8 Practice the dialog in 7 with a partner.
- Read the directions aloud. Invite pairs to read the dialog aloud, switch parts, and repeat.

MONITOR
As students read, listen for proper pronunciation, and appropriate intonation.

ASSIST
As you notice errors, say words or sentences correctly and have students repeat after you.

Practice 1 P. T140

Materials: Stickers

9 Listen and stick. Then complete the sentences. Use the correct form of the verb.
- Help students find the Unit 2 stickers at the back of the Student's Book. Ask them to describe each sticker. Then read the directions and point out the sentences.
- Play Audio Track 27. Have students place the stickers on the page and complete the sentences independently.

MONITOR
As students work, make sure that they place the stickers in the correct order. Check answers as a class. *(Answers: 1 She's been dancing. 2 He's been doing medical research. 3 He's been designing computer programs. 4 They've been playing in rock bands.)*

ASSIST
Point out that present perfect progressive verbs always use *been*. Have students find an example in the dialog in Activity 8 (*…I've been doing research*). Review the present perfect progressive forms of the verbs in the box before having students listen to the audio.

Practice 2 WB p. 15/ act. 7

7 Listen and read. Circle T for *true* or F for *false*.
- Read the directions aloud. Ask volunteers to read the numbered sentences aloud.
- Play Audio Track 28. Have students complete the activity.

Lesson Objective

INVOLVE
Revisit the lesson objective: *Now I have listened to a dialog about an amazing person's achievements.*
- Encourage awareness of what the students have learned by quickly eliciting a few things they remember about the dialog, for example, what William Kamkwamba has achieved.

Homework WB p. 15/ act. 8 & 9

8 Look at 7. Read the underlined expressions. Match the expressions with their meanings. Write the letters.
- Direct students to WB Activity 8 on page 15. Tell students to read the underlined expressions in the dialog again and then match each expression with the words with the same meaning.

9 Answer the questions.
- Direct students to WB Activity 9 on page 15. Tell students to answer the questions.

Extra Application and Practice Activity

- Ask students to write sentences describing what the class has been doing in this unit. Model: *We've been reading about amazing young people. I've been learning new words. She's been teaching us about verbs.* Then have students exchange sentences and underline verbs in the present perfect progressive.

Language in Action

I will listen to a dialog about an amazing person's achievements.

7 Listen and read. What has Zack been doing on the computer?

Mom: Zack, you've been on the computer for a while now.

Zack: I know. I have to write a biography about an amazing person, so I've been doing research on someone. This guy is so interesting!

Mom: Who is it?

Zack: William Kamkwamba. He's been a builder and an inventor since he was a teenager.

Mom: What has he built?

Zack: His village in Malawi had no electricity or running water. So he built a windmill. And he was only fourteen!

Mom: Wow. How did he know how to make a windmill?

Zack: He got some books from the library and studied the diagrams.

Mom: He made a windmill from a diagram? That's amazing!

Zack: I know!

8 Practice the dialog in 7 with a partner.

9 Listen and stick. Then complete the sentences. Use the correct form of the verb.

| dance   design computer programs   do medical research   play in rock bands |

1 _____ since she was five.

2 _____ for ten years.

3 _____ for three years.

4 _____ since middle school.

20   Unit 2

Grammar

I will learn to use the present perfect and present perfect progressive.

> How long **has** she **played** the piano?
> She**'s played** the piano <u>for</u> five years.
>
> How long **have** they **known** about William Kamkwamba?
> They**'ve known** about him <u>since</u> they saw a movie about him.

10 Read the information and then complete the sentences about each amazing person. Use the present perfect and for or since.

> Hou Yifan is twenty-three and a chess player. She started playing chess when she was three.

1 She _____ chess _____ twenty years.
2 She _____ chess _____ she was three.

3 He _____ things _____ he was fourteen.
4 He _____ things _____ sixteen years.

> William Kamkwamba is thirty and an engineer. He started building things when he was fourteen.

> How long **has** your brother **been playing** tennis?
> He**'s been playing** tennis <u>since</u> he was five.
>
> How long **have** you and your sister **been bungee jumping**?
> We**'ve been bungee jumping** <u>for</u> two years.

11 Read the answers. Ask the questions. Use the present perfect progressive.

1 _____
He's been saving money for college since he was thirteen.

2 _____
We've been volunteering at the hospital for two years.

3 _____
She's been filming her documentary since August.

4 _____
I've been playing the piano since I was at nursery school.

5 _____
They've been friends for seven years.

Grammar Lesson

Lesson Flow

Warm-up › Lesson Objective › Presentation 1 › Practice 1 › Practice 2 › Presentation 2 › Practice 3 › Practice 4 › Lesson Objective › Homework

Lesson Objective

I will learn to use the present perfect and present perfect progressive.

Key Language

How long **have** you **lived** here? I**'ve lived** here <u>for</u> five years./I**'ve lived** here <u>since</u> I was six.

How long **has** she **been singing**? She**'s been singing** <u>since</u> she was four./She**'s been singing** <u>for</u> 10 years.

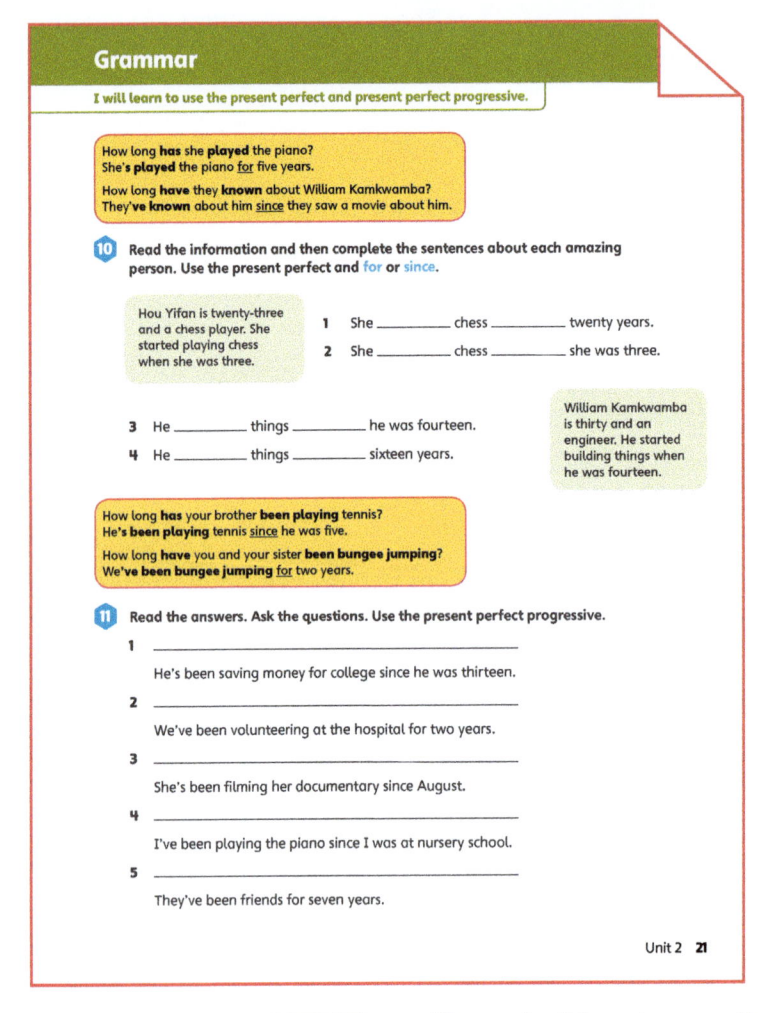

Grammar

I will learn to use the present perfect and present perfect progressive.

How long **has** she **played** the piano?
She**'s played** the piano <u>for</u> five years.
How long **have** they **known** about William Kamkwamba?
They**'ve known** about him <u>since</u> they saw a movie about him.

10 Read the information and then complete the sentences about each amazing person. Use the present perfect and for or since.

Hou Yifan is twenty-three and a chess player. She started playing chess when she was three.

1 She _____ chess _____ twenty years.
2 She _____ chess _____ she was three.

3 He _____ things _____ he was fourteen.
4 He _____ things _____ sixteen years.

William Kamkwamba is thirty and an engineer. He started building things when he was fourteen.

How long **has** your brother **been playing** tennis?
He**'s been playing** tennis <u>since</u> he was five.
How long **have** you and your sister **been bungee jumping**?
We**'ve been bungee jumping** <u>for</u> two years.

11 Read the answers. Ask the questions. Use the present perfect progressive.

1 _____
He's been saving money for college since he was thirteen.
2 _____
We've been volunteering at the hospital for two years.
3 _____
She's been filming her documentary since August.
4 _____
I've been playing the piano since I was at nursery school.
5 _____
They've been friends for seven years.

Unit 2   **21**

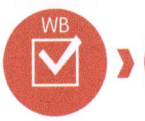

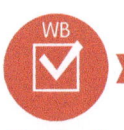

Warm-up

Materials: Different color index cards

- Review *for* and *since* by having students play *Silly Sentences*. Say: *First, write down an amount of time. You might write "2 minutes," "8 weeks," or "16 years." Next, write down a specific time in the past. You might write down "6:30 this morning," "last Sunday," or "1995."* Then write this sentence on the board: *I played one video game for…* . Have students complete the sentence with the amount of time they wrote down. Then write this sentence: *It's been raining since…* . Have students complete the sentence with the specific times they wrote down. Ask: *Which sentences make sense? Which are very silly?*

- Check answers from the HW in the last lesson.

S21 Unit 2

Lesson Objective

INVOLVE

- Introduce the lesson objective. Say: *Today I will learn to use the present perfect and present perfect progressive.*
- Students will use *for* and *since* to talk about how long people have done activities.

Presentation 1

- Have volunteers read the questions and answers in the first grammar box aloud.
- Refer students back to the Language in Action dialog and elicit or highlight the grammar structures in the dialog.

ASSIST

- Review the difference between *for* and *since*. Discuss the difference between these two sentences: *She's lived here for three years. She's lived here since she was three years old.* Say: For *comes before an amount of time*; since *comes before a specific time, age, or event in the past.*

Practice 1

10 Read the information and then complete the sentences about each amazing person. Use the present perfect and *for* or *since*.

- Read the directions and invite volunteers to read the text in the boxes about Hou Yifan and William Kamkwamba aloud. Do Item 1 as a class. Then have students complete the activity independently in their notebooks.

MONITOR

- Check answers as a class. (Answers: 1 She has played chess for sixteen years. 2 She has played chess since she was three. 3 He has built things since he was fourteen. 4 He has built things for sixteen years.)

CHALLENGE

- Have students rewrite the sentences in Activity 10, using contractions of *has*. Model: *She's played chess for sixteen years.*

Practice 2 WB p. 16/ act. 10

10 Look and match the phrases with *since* or *for*.

- Ask volunteers to read the sentences in the grammar box.
- Read the directions aloud and explain that students have to draw a line between the phrases and either *for* or *since*.
- Have students complete the activity independently, then check answers as a class.

Presentation 2

- Have volunteers read the questions and answers in the second grammar box aloud.

ASSIST

- Say: *The present perfect progressive can begin with* have *or* has. Model: *We have been studying grammar. She has been studying grammar.*

Practice 3

11 Read the answers. Ask the questions. Use the present perfect progressive.

- Read the directions and invite volunteers to read answers. Do the first item together as a class and then have students complete the activity independently.

MONITOR

- Invite volunteers to read their questions aloud. (Answers: 1 How long has he been saving money for college? 2 How long have you been volunteering at the hospital? 3 How long has she been filming her documentary? 4 How long have you been playing the piano? 5 How long have they been friends?)

Practice 4 WB p. 17/ act. 12

12 Read. Answer the questions. Use the present perfect progressive.

- Read the directions aloud. Explain that students have to write answers to the questions using the present perfect progressive.
- Have volunteers read the sentences in the grammar box and the questions aloud.
- Have students complete the activity independently.

Lesson Objective

INVOLVE

- Revisit the lesson objective: *Now I have learned to use the present perfect and present perfect progressive.*
- Encourage awareness of what the students have learned by quickly eliciting some sentences with the present perfect progressive and *since* and *for*.

Homework WB pp. 16 & 17/ act. 11 & 13

11 Complete the sentences. Use the present perfect form of the verbs in parentheses and *for* or *since*.

- Direct students to WB Activity 11 on page 16. Explain that the students have to complete the sentences with the present perfect form and *for* or *since*.

13 Answer the questions in complete sentences.

- Direct students to WB Activity 13 on page 17. Tell students to answer the questions using the present perfect progressive.

Extra Application and Practice Activity

- Have students work in pairs. Each partner should write down a present perfect progressive verb. Then they should switch verbs and use their partner's verb in a complete sentence. Model: *Has been practicing: My neighbor's been practicing the saxophone for eight years. Have been visiting: We've been visiting Florida every summer since I was six years old.*

Unit 2 T21

Content Connection Lesson

Lesson Flow

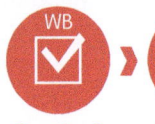

Warm-up › Lesson Objective › Pre-reading › Reading › Practice 1 (WB) › Practice 2 (SB) › Think BIG › Video › Lesson Objective › Homework

Lesson Objective

I will learn about amazing young people.

Key Language

co-found, compose, exceptional talent, gifted, inspiration, keep in touch, social media, symphony

---

Content Connection | Social Science

I will learn about amazing young people.

29 / 12 Listen and read. Then answer the questions.

CONTENT WORDS
co-found, compose, exceptional talent, gifted, inspiration, keep in touch, social media, symphony

1 Who went to Harvard?
2 Who created Apple?
3 Who played the piano?

Amazing Young People Through the Ages

Do you think kids are too young to make a difference in the world? Do you think only adults can start companies and win awards? If so, think again! Throughout history, there have always been gifted young people with exceptional talents and abilities for their age. As children or teenagers, they did amazing things that changed lives. Read on for inspiration!

Wolfgang Amadeus Mozart was one very famous gifted child. He could play the piano at the age of three and the violin at six. Amadeus composed his first symphony at the age of eight and wrote an opera at fourteen. He went on to become one of the most important music composers of all time.

Fourteen-year-old Nadia Comăneci scored a perfect 10 in gymnastics at the 1976 Olympic Games. She was the first person ever to do this! People still remember Nadia for her exceptional skills and abilities as a gymnast.

What about kids and technology? Mark Zuckerberg was only nineteen when he started Facebook with some friends of his at Harvard University. The social media platform has changed the way people around the world keep in touch with each other. Also at age nineteen, Steve Jobs was learning the skills that helped create Apple, and Bill Gates was ready to co-found a company called Microsoft!

13 Look at the passage. Correct the sentences.

1 Mozart composed his first opera at eight.
2 People remember Nadia Comăneci for her soccer skills.
3 Mark Zuckerberg created Facebook alone.

THINK BIG What do you think all of these young people had in common when they were young?

22 Unit 2

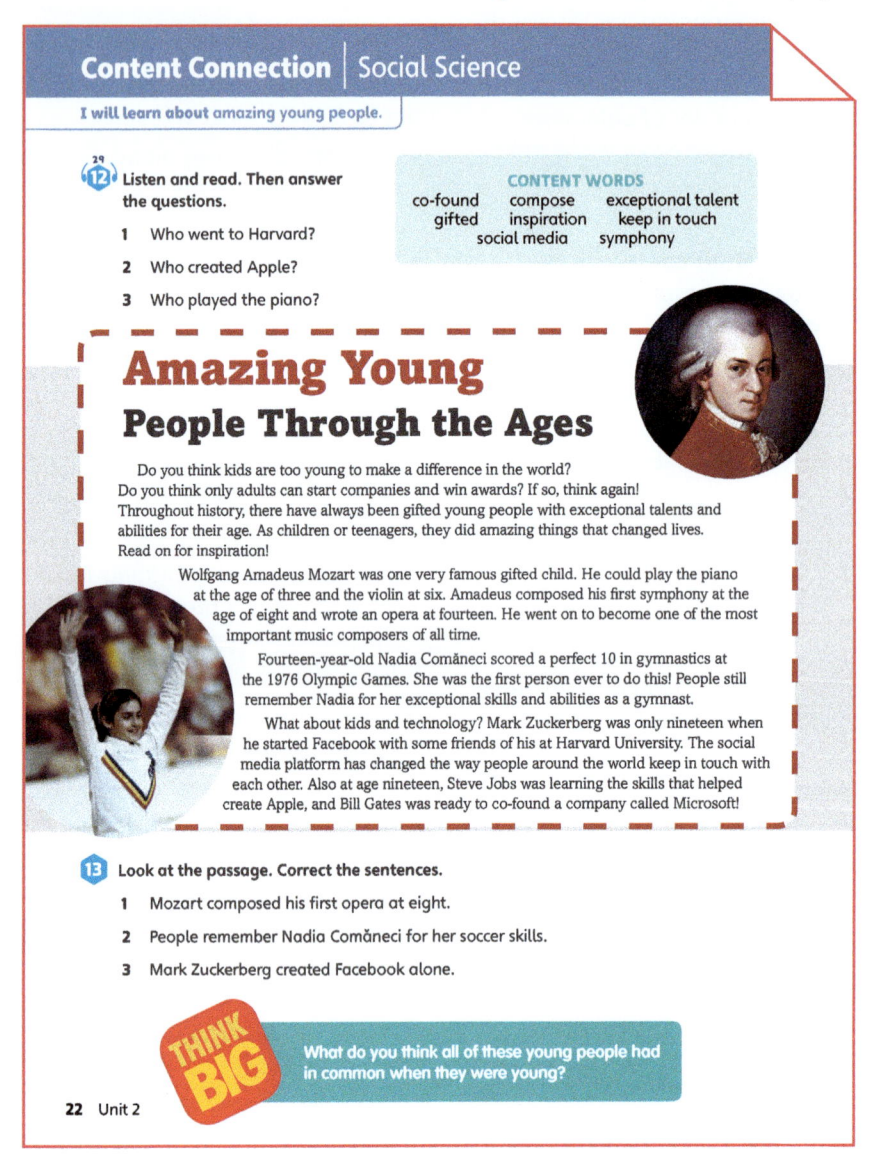

Warm-up

- Have students play *Who Am I?* Write these names on the board: *Wolfgang Amadeus Mozart, Louis Braille, Nadia Comăneci, Pelé, Steve Jobs, Mark Zuckerberg*.

Ask a student to choose one of these people and give one-word clues until his or her classmates guess the identity of the person. Model: *Brazil, soccer, player, famous.* (Pelé)

- Check answers from the HW in the last lesson.

Lesson Objective

INVOLVE

- Introduce the lesson objective. Say: *Today I will learn about amazing young people.*
- Students will listen to, read, and talk about a social science text about people who accomplished amazing things when they were young.

Pre-reading

- Write the word *gifted* on the board. Have students make predictions as to the word's meaning. Do not confirm or correct their prediction yet.
- Point to the pictures and have students describe what they see.

Reading 🎧29

12 Listen and read. Then answer the questions.

- Read the directions aloud.
- Ask volunteers to read the three questions, and have students listen for this information.
- Play Audio Track 29 and have students listen and read along.

MONITOR

Pair students, and have them share their answers, referring to phrases from the text. *(Answers: 1 Mark Zuckerberg went to Harvard. 2 Steve Jobs created Apple. 3 Mozart played the piano.)* Allow students to come up with their own conclusions but encourage the use of the Content Words.

21st Century Technology Literacy

- Have students talk about why Zuckerberg's site was so successful. Ask: *How do people use Facebook? How do you think they did these things before Facebook existed?*

Practice 1 WB p. 18/ act. 14

14 Match the words with the definitions. Write the letters.

- Read the directions aloud. Explain that the students have to match each word in the left-hand column with its definition in the right-hand column.
- Have volunteers read the words and definitions aloud.
- Have students work independently.
- Have students compare the answers with a partner, then check answers as a class.

Practice 2

13 Look at the passage. Correct the sentences.

- Read the first false sentence to the class. Have students look back at the text and identify the phrase that gives the correct information (*"Amadeus composed his first symphony at the age of eight." paragraph 2*).
- Have students continue in pairs, writing the corrected sentences in their notebooks.

MONITOR

Check answers as a class. *(1 Mozart composed his first symphony at eight. 2 People remember Nadia Comăneci for her gymnastic skills. 3 Mark Zuckerberg created Facebook with his friends.)*

Think BIG

21st Century Critical Thinking

- Read the question aloud. Have students work in small groups to talk about these amazing young people and what they had in common.

Comparing and Contrasting: Ask: *What do these young people have in common? How were they the same?* Say: *When we want to find out what people have in common we are comparing them.* Ask: *What makes each person different?* Say: *When we want to find out how people are different we are contrasting them.*

Video Documentary U 02

- Refer to the Video Guide for pre-watching and post-watching activities.

Lesson Objective

INVOLVE

- Revisit the lesson objective: *Now I have learned about amazing young people.*
- Encourage awareness of what the students have learned by quickly eliciting a few things they remember about the passage, for example, how old Amadeus Mozart was when he could play the violin.

Homework 🎧P. T140 WB p. 18/ act. 15 & 16

15 Read and complete with the words from 14. Then listen and check.

- Direct students to WB Activity 15 on page 18. Tell students to read the text and to complete it with the words from Activity 14. They should then play Audio Track 30 and check their answers.

16 Read 15 again and circle the correct word.

- Direct students to WB Activity 16 on page 18. Tell students to choose the correct word in each sentence.

Extra Application and Practice Activity

- Invite students to create puzzles by writing sentences using the Content Words and then rewriting their sentences with blanks in place of the Content Words. Have students exchange sentences with a partner and try to guess the missing words.

Unit 2 **T22**

Content Connection | Social Science

I will learn about amazing young people.

12 Listen and read. Then answer the questions.

1. Who went to Harvard?
2. Who created Apple?
3. Who played the piano?

CONTENT WORDS
co-found   compose   exceptional talent
gifted   inspiration   keep in touch
social media   symphony

Amazing Young People Through the Ages

Do you think kids are too young to make a difference in the world? Do you think only adults can start companies and win awards? If so, think again! Throughout history, there have always been gifted young people with exceptional talents and abilities for their age. As children or teenagers, they did amazing things that changed lives. Read on for inspiration!

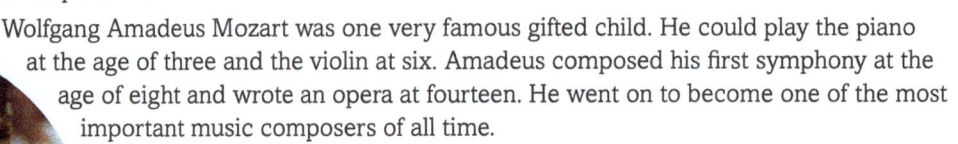

Wolfgang Amadeus Mozart was one very famous gifted child. He could play the piano at the age of three and the violin at six. Amadeus composed his first symphony at the age of eight and wrote an opera at fourteen. He went on to become one of the most important music composers of all time.

Fourteen-year-old Nadia Comăneci scored a perfect 10 in gymnastics at the 1976 Olympic Games. She was the first person ever to do this! People still remember Nadia for her exceptional skills and abilities as a gymnast.

What about kids and technology? Mark Zuckerberg was only nineteen when he started Facebook with some friends of his at Harvard University. The social media platform has changed the way people around the world keep in touch with each other. Also at age nineteen, Steve Jobs was learning the skills that helped create Apple, and Bill Gates was ready to co-found a company called Microsoft!

13 Look at the passage. Correct the sentences.

1. Mozart composed his first opera at eight.
2. People remember Nadia Comăneci for her soccer skills.
3. Mark Zuckerberg created Facebook alone.

THINK BIG

What do you think all of these young people had in common when they were young?

Culture Connection | Around the World

I will learn about a peace organization.

14 Listen and read. How many new "Seeds" are chosen each year?

CONTENT WORDS
conflict   educators   issues
neutral   participants

Seeds of Peace

Throughout history, there has hardly ever been a moment when the whole world was at peace. Every day, we hear about individuals, politicians, and world leaders trying to bring peace to countries at war. Sometimes they succeed, but often they don't. However, there's another group of people, one you probably haven't heard about, that is trying to do the same thing. They're mainly teenagers who've seen war and conflict and want to change things. These teenagers belong to an organization called Seeds of Peace.

Seeds of Peace was started in 1993 by a reporter named John Wallach. The group began with forty-six teenagers and educators. Since then, it has grown to more than 5,000 participants from twenty-seven different countries.

Each summer, 350 new "Seeds" from countries in conflict are carefully chosen by the Seeds of Peace. These teenagers attend the Seeds of Peace international summer camp, where they meet and live with teenagers whose countries are "enemy" countries. The camp is a neutral environment where young people can discuss the issues between their countries and talk about their personal experiences.

After the summer camp is over, these teenagers return to their countries. They go home not only with memories of new friendships, but also with the idea that they can be leaders who can work together for a better future for themselves and for the whole world. They've learned that the fighting around them doesn't have to go on forever.

15 Look at the passage. Circle the correct words.

1. Seeds of Peace was started by **a group of educators / a reporter**.
2. The teenagers who become Seeds **have never seen / have experienced** conflict in their countries.
3. At the camp, young people **work in groups to create / talk to people from** "enemy" countries.
4. The camp helps young people **talk about conflict / learn about conflict** in their country.

THINK BIG Why do you think Seeds of Peace campers are more hopeful about world peace after the camp?

Culture Connection Lesson

Lesson Flow

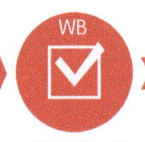

Warm-up › Lesson Objective › Pre-reading › Reading › Practice 1 › Practice 2 › Think BIG › Lesson Objective › Homework

Lesson Objective

I will learn about a peace organization.

Key Language

conflict, educators, issues, neutral, participants

Culture Connection | Around the World

I will learn about a peace organization.

14 Listen and read. How many new "Seeds" are chosen each year?

CONTENT WORDS
conflict   educators   issues
neutral   participants

Seeds of Peace

Throughout history, there has hardly ever been a moment when the whole world was at peace. Every day, we hear about individuals, politicians, and world leaders trying to bring peace to countries at war. Sometimes they succeed, but often they don't. However, there's another group of people, one you probably haven't heard about, that is trying to do the same thing. They're mainly teenagers who've seen war and conflict and want to change things. These teenagers belong to an organization called Seeds of Peace.

Seeds of Peace was started in 1993 by a reporter named John Wallach. The group began with forty-six teenagers and educators. Since then, it has grown to more than 5,000 participants from twenty-seven different countries.

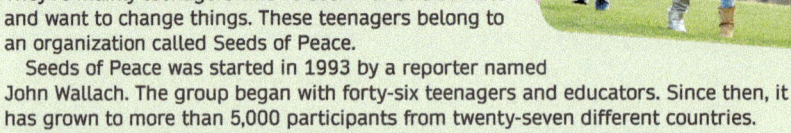

Each summer, 350 new "Seeds" from countries in conflict are carefully chosen by the Seeds of Peace. These teenagers attend the Seeds of Peace international summer camp, where they meet and live with teenagers whose countries are "enemy" countries. The camp is a neutral environment where young people can discuss the issues between their countries and talk about their personal experiences.

After the summer camp is over, these teenagers return to their countries. They go home not only with memories of new friendships, but also with the idea that they can be leaders who can work together for a better future for themselves and for the whole world. They've learned that the fighting around them doesn't have to go on forever.

15 Look at the passage. Circle the correct words.

1. Seeds of Peace was started by **a group of educators / a reporter**.
2. The teenagers who become Seeds **have never seen / have experienced** conflict in their countries.
3. At the camp, young people **work in groups to create / talk to people from** "enemy" countries.
4. The camp helps young people **talk about conflict / learn about conflict** in their country.

THINK BIG Why do you think Seeds of Peace campers are more hopeful about world peace after the camp?

Unit 2   23

S23   Unit 2

Warm-up

Materials: World map or globe

21st Century Global Awareness

- Play *That's a Border!* to review world geography. Divide the class into two teams. Players should take turns using a world map or globe to choose a country and only reveal the countries that border it. Players on the other team should try to guess the country. Give teams one point for each country they can name.
- Say: *The dividing lines between countries are called borders. Many countries share borders with no problems. They are at peace. But some countries that share a border may have problems. These problems, or conflicts, can lead to war.*

- Check answers from the HW in the last lesson.

Lesson Objective

INVOLVE

Introduce the lesson objective. Say: *Today I will learn about a peace organization*.

- Students will listen to, read, and talk about a camp that supports world peace, and connect the text to their personal experiences.

Pre-reading

- Write the words *conflict* and *war* on the board. Ask students if they can think of any things that can lead to conflict and war between countries. Write their ideas on the board as well (e.g., *religion, land, weapons, terrorism*, etc.)
- Point to the picture. Have students predict what the article is going to be about. Then, have students take a minute to scan the main ideas and review their predictions.

Reading

14 Listen and read. How many new "Seeds" are chosen each year?

- Read the directions aloud. Play Audio Track 31.

Analogies: Say: *An analogy compares two things. The students at this summer camp aren't literally "seeds," but they are like seeds because they help ideas grow.* Have students describe how Seeds of Peace members are and aren't like real seeds, to help them understand how the program name uses an extended analogy or metaphor.

MONITOR

Discuss the answer as a class. (Answer: 350 new "Seeds" are chosen each year.)

Practice 1

15 Look at the passage. Circle the correct words.

- Ask students to complete the activity independently.

MONITOR

Replay the audio as necessary. Encourage students to scan the article to find information relevant to the sentences.

To check answers, ask individual students to read out the sentence, stating the paragraph where the information appears, e.g., *Seeds of peace was started by a reporter. This is in paragraph 2.* (Answers: 2 have experienced, 3 talk to people from, 4 talk about conflict)

Practice 2 WB p. 18/ act. 17

17 Listen and read. What is the purpose of Earthdance International?

- Read the directions aloud. Explain to students that they have to listen and read the text and answer the question.
- Play Audio Track 32 and have listen and read along.
- Have students discuss the answer with a partner, then check answers as a class.

Think BIG

21st Century Empathy

- Read the question aloud, and elicit answers from different students. Use the question to begin a discussion about developing empathy. Discuss what *empathy* means – looking at a situation from someone else's point of view, "putting yourself in someone else's shoes." Ask students if they can share an example of a time when they looked at a situation from someone else's perspective.

Lesson Objective

INVOLVE

Revisit the lesson objective: *Now I have learned about a peace organization*.

- Encourage awareness of what the students have learned by quickly eliciting a few things they remember about the passage, for example, the number of countries who have sent participants to the Seeds of Peace international summer camp.

Homework WB p. 19/ act. 18

18 Complete the sentences with the words in the box.

- Direct students to WB Activity 18 on page 19. Tell students to complete the sentences with the words in the box.

Extra Application and Practice Activity

- Have students design a crossword or word search puzzles using the vocabulary items in the lesson. Ask them to exchange puzzles and solve them. Invite students to read out the words and say how they are related to the lesson.

Unit 2 T23

Writing Lesson

Lesson Flow

Warm-up › Lesson Objective › Practice 1 (WB) › Practice 2 (SB) › Practice 3 (SB) › Practice 4 (SB) › Speaking › Lesson Objective › Homework

Lesson Objective

I will learn to write a biography about an amazing person.

Writing | Biography

I will learn to write a biography about an amazing person.

16 Read the biography.

My Brother Josh

My brother, Josh, is amazing! He was born in 1998 in Melbourne, Australia. Josh went to Melmoth Primary School there and was at the top of his class.

In 2008, my family moved to Bristol, in the U.K. Josh has been very busy since we moved. He has played the drums with the school band, has been on the school soccer team, and has joined the drama club.

Josh is really busy, but he always takes time out to do things with me. That's what makes him so amazing!

17 Look at 16. Copy and complete the timeline about Josh.

Things he's been doing:
_____
_____
_____

Born in _____ (year)
_____ (place)

He went to _____ (school)

In 2008, his family _____

18 Interview an older relative or do research on an amazing person. Create a timeline about that person, then use it to write their biography.

19 Take turns sharing your biographies in pairs. What makes the people amazing?

24 Unit 2

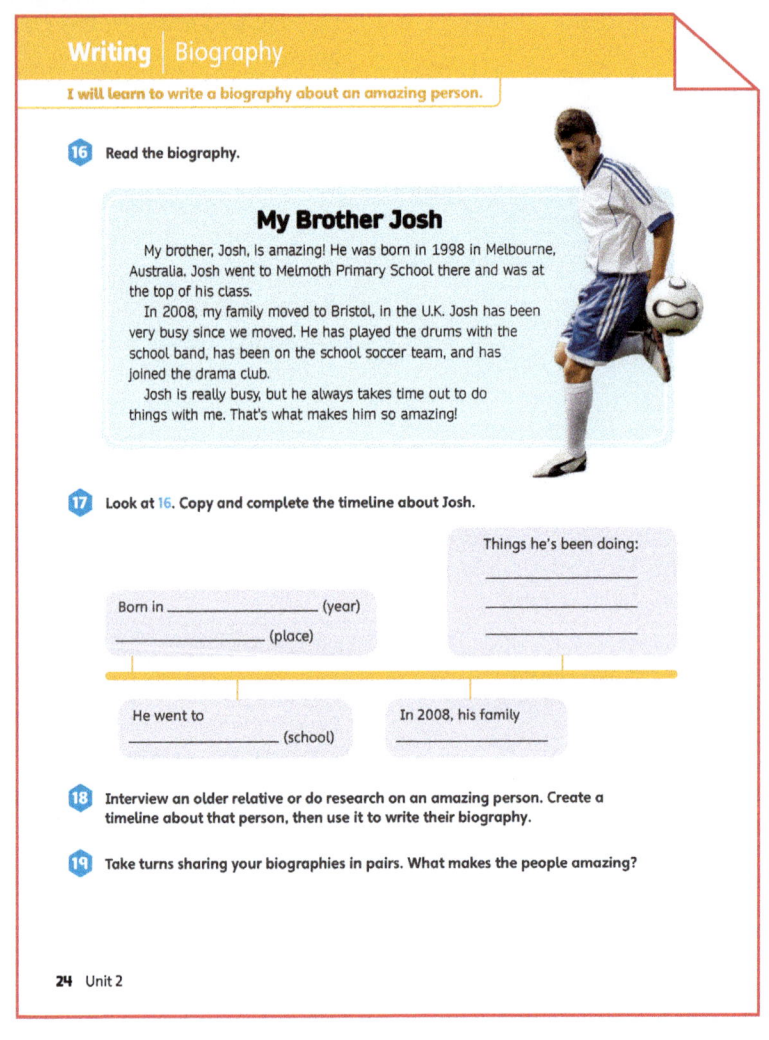

Warm-up

Materials: Index cards

- Help students review time order. Ask each student to write events in his or her own life on index cards, shuffle the cards, and challenge a partner to put the events in order. Model: *I was born on August 31. My family moved here when I was four. We visited my grandparents in Italy last summer. I started sixth grade this September.* Encourage students to ask questions when they can't decide on the order of events in their partner's life.
- Check answers from the HW in the last lesson.

Lesson Objective

INVOLVE

Introduce the lesson objective. Say: *Today I will learn to write a biography about an amazing person.*

- Students will interview relatives, create timelines, and then write biographies to share what they found out.

Practice 1 — WB p. 20/ act. 19

19 Unscramble the questions. Imagine you are interviewing Stephen Hillenburg, the creator of *SpongeBob SquarePants*.

- Have volunteers read the tips for writing a well-written biography in the purple box aloud.
- Read the directions. Have volunteers read the answers aloud.
- Have students complete the activity independently.

MONITOR

Check answers as a class. (Answers: 1 Where were you born 2 What did you study in college, 3 What are some of your most important memories, 4 What are some of your accomplishments)

Practice 2

16 Read the biography.

- Read the directions aloud. Invite volunteers to read the model biography aloud.

MONITOR

Help with pronunciation of school and place names as needed.

Practice 3

17 Look at 16. Copy and complete the timeline about Josh.

- Read the directions. Have students look at the timeline, and discuss the kind of information that is needed to complete each entry.
- Have students complete the timelines independently.

MONITOR

Check answers as a class. (Answers: 1998, Melbourne, Melmoth Primary School, moved to Bristol, has played the drums with the school band, has been on the school soccer team, has joined the drama club)

Practice 4

18 Interview an older relative or do research on an amazing person. Create a timeline about that person, then use it to write their biography.

- Read the directions and steps aloud. Have students decide who they're going to write about. Ask students to interview family members, if possible. Alternatively, they can research a famous person.
- Then have students complete the interview and writing activity independently. Remind them to create a timeline for the important events in their amazing person's life.

ASSIST

Help students create a list of interview questions to use. For example: *When and where were you born? Where did you live when you were growing up? Where did you go to school? Where have you worked so far? What are some of your greatest achievements? How old were you when you achieved these?*

Speaking

19 Take turns sharing your biographies in pairs. What makes the people amazing?

- Ask students to work with a partner to discuss what each of them has written.
- Ask pairs to report to the class on what makes the people they have written about amazing.

MONITOR

As students work, walk around the class and monitor students' pronunciation.

21st Century Communication

- Remind students to use follow-up questions when they interview people. Say: *A follow-up question is a question that helps you get more details about an answer.* Model: *I asked my grandma to name her greatest achievement. She said it was learning how to fix cars. I didn't know she could do that! I was very interested so I asked follow-up questions. How old were you when you learned that? Was it hard to learn? Why was it so useful?*

Lesson Objective

INVOLVE

Revisit the lesson objective: *Now I have learned to write a biography about an amazing person.*

- Encourage awareness of what the students have learned by quickly eliciting how to write a well-written descriptive paragraph.

Homework — WB p. 20/ act. 20

20 Write a short biography of Stephen Hillenburg. Use the information in 19. Write two more questions. Do research and find the answers. Add the information to the biography.

- Direct students to WB Activity 20 on page 20. Tell students to write a short biography of Stephen Hillenburg using the information in Activity 19. Tell them to think of two more questions and to research the answers.

Extra Application and Practice Activity

- Have students compile their biographies in a classroom book entitled *Amazing People*. Suggest that they work together to create a cover illustration that reflects all of the biographies included in the collection. Students can also include photographs, their own drawings, or other illustrations.

Writing | Biography

I will learn to write a biography about an amazing person.

16 Read the biography.

My Brother Josh

My brother, Josh, is amazing! He was born in 1998 in Melbourne, Australia. Josh went to Melmoth Primary School there and was at the top of his class.

In 2008, my family moved to Bristol, in the U.K. Josh has been very busy since we moved. He has played the drums with the school band, has been on the school soccer team, and has joined the drama club.

Josh is really busy, but he always takes time out to do things with me. That's what makes him so amazing!

17 Look at 16. Copy and complete the timeline about Josh.

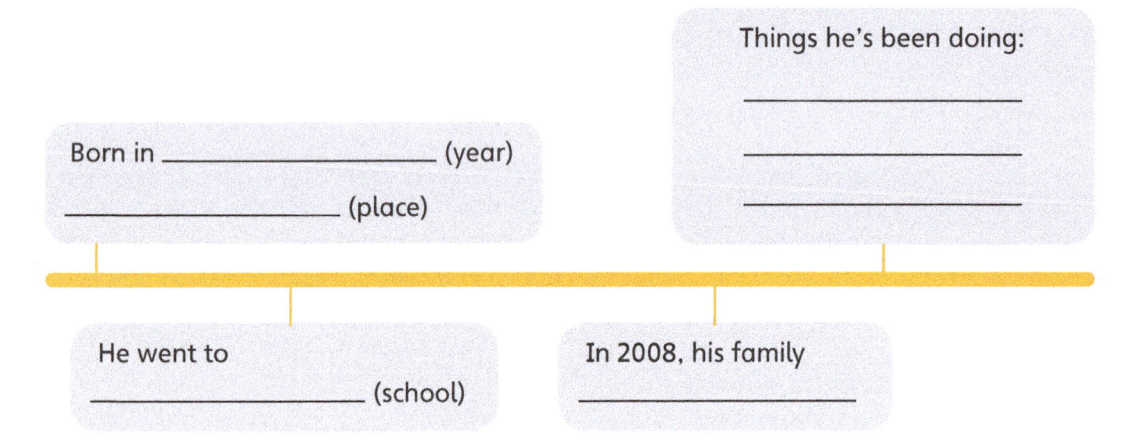

Things he's been doing:
_____
_____
_____

Born in _____ (year)
_____ (place)

He went to
_____ (school)

In 2008, his family
_____

18 Interview an older relative or do research on an amazing person. Create a timeline about that person, then use it to write their biography.

19 Take turns sharing your biographies in pairs. What makes the people amazing?

Life skills | Appreciate yourself.

I will learn to talk about my qualities and talents.

20 Just like the young people in this unit, all of us have amazing qualities and talents. Write in the chart about yourself, then work with your classmates to complete the chart.

	My good qualities	What I'm good at	My classmate thinks I'm amazing because...
Ex.	I'm friendly.	playing the drums	I'm very smart.
1			
2			
3			

21 Now study your chart. Is your classmate's opinion of you the same as/different from your opinion about yourself?

Project

22 Make an **Amazing Me** collage.

1. Include pictures or drawings of yourself doing things you enjoy.
2. Include drawings, pictures from magazines, and words and phrases that show who you are and what you like.
3. Write your name on the back and display your collage in the classroom.

23 Take turns guessing the person who made each collage. Then interview that person.

AMAZING ME!
Family
DANCE
Creativity

Life Skills Lesson

Lesson Flow

Warm-up › Lesson Objective › Practice 1 (SB) › Practice 2 (SB) › Project › Speaking › Lesson Objective

Lesson Objective

I will learn to talk about my qualities and talents.

Life skills | Appreciate yourself.

I will learn to talk about my qualities and talents.

20 Just like the young people in this unit, all of us have amazing qualities and talents. Write in the chart about yourself, then work with your classmates to complete the chart.

	My good qualities	What I'm good at	My classmate thinks I'm amazing because…
Ex.	I'm friendly.	playing the drums	I'm very smart.
1			
2			
3			

21 Now study your chart. Is your classmate's opinion of you the same as/different from your opinion about yourself?

Project

22 Make an *Amazing Me* collage.
1. Include pictures or drawings of yourself doing things you enjoy.
2. Include drawings, pictures from magazines, and words and phrases that show who you are and what you like.
3. Write your name on the back and display your collage in the classroom.

23 Take turns guessing the person who made each collage. Then interview that person.

AMAZING ME! — Family — DANCE — Creativity

Warm-up

- Say: *When we talk about amazing people, we can talk about their qualities and talents. A quality is a good point about someone. A talent is something a person does well.* Write these sentence frames on the board: *She's amazing! She's very… (a quality). She can… (a talent).* Invite students to think of different ways to complete each sentence. (Sample answers: smart/friendly/patient/caring; run fast/solve problems/invent things/fix anything)
- Check answers from the HW in the last lesson.

Lesson Objective

INVOLVE

Introduce the lesson objective. Say: *Today I will learn to talk about my qualities and talents.*

- Students will share their own qualities and talents. Then they'll create a collage that celebrates what makes them amazing.

Practice 1

20 Just like the young people in this unit, all of us have amazing qualities and talents. Write in the chart about yourself, then work with your classmates to complete the chart.

- Read the page title, directions, steps, and chart headings aloud with students. Then have a volunteer read the model row in the chart aloud.
- Have students complete the first and second columns of the chart independently. Then have students work in pairs to complete the third column.

MONITOR

Make sure students complete the first two columns of their charts before talking with their partners.

ASSIST

Provide students with vocabulary as needed. Interview students to help them think of qualities and talents to complete their charts. Ask: *Are you more patient or more energetic? How are you helpful? What do you like doing in your free time?*

Practice 2

21 Now study your chart. Is your classmate's opinion of you the same as/different from your opinion about yourself?

- Read the directions and questions aloud. Have students continue working in pairs to talk about their charts and compare their opinions.

MONITOR

Check that students are using appropriate language and gestures.

21st Century Social Skills

- Ask: *What's the difference between appreciating yourself and showing off? Why is one a good quality and the other a problem?* (Sample answers: *Appreciating yourself* means you celebrate your qualities and talents. *Showing off* means you talk with too much pride about yourself./*Showing off* can annoy people. *Appreciating yourself* makes you confident and helps you connect with others.)

Project

22 Make an Amazing Me collage.

- Read the directions and steps with students. Ask: *What does the model collage tell you about this student?* (Sample answers: She likes dancing./She values creativity./She likes cooking.) Then have students create their collages.

Managing Art Projects: Have students work on a table covered with newspapers. Encourage students to lay out the decorations for their collages before gluing them down. Remind students that cleaning up is the important last step of any art project.

MONITOR

Remind students not to write their names on the front of their collages.

Speaking

23 Take turns guessing the person who made each collage. Then interview that person.

- Display students' collages. Then have each student stand in front of a classmate's collage and guess who created it. Poll the class to see who agrees with each guess. Then have students interview each other about their collages.

Lesson Objective

INVOLVE

Revisit the lesson objective: *Now I have learned to talk about my qualities and talents.*

- Encourage awareness of what the students have learned by quickly eliciting what they remember about their partner's opinion in Activity 20.

Extra Application and Practice Activity

- Encourage students to make generalizations about the collages. Model: *A lot of us included our families. We think our families are amazing, too!*

Unit 2 **T25**

Listening and Speaking Lesson

Lesson Flow

Warm-up › Lesson Objective › Presentation › Practice 1 › Practice 2 › Speaking › Lesson Objective

Lesson Objectives

I will review the sounds *spl*, *squ*, and *thr*.

I will learn to talk about past experiences.

Listening and Speaking

I will review the sounds *spl*, *squ*, and *thr*.
I will learn to talk about past experiences.

24 Listen, read, and repeat.

1. spl   2. squ   3. thr

25 Listen and blend the sounds.

1. spl-a-sh   splash
2. squ-i-d   squid
3. thr-ee   three
4. spl-i-t   split
5. squ-a-sh   squash
6. thr-oa-t   throat

26 Listen and chant.

Take a dive in the deep blue sea.
Splish! Splash!
One squid, two whales,
And three dolphins swimming free.

27 Play the Memory game. Work in a small group and make sentences using the verbs in the box.

know   live   play   study   watch

I've known Ben since I was six years old.

Mary has known Ben since she was six years old.
I've lived in Liverpool for ten years.

Mary has known Ben since she was six years old.
Tom has lived in Liverpool for ten years.
I've been playing soccer since I was in first grade.

Mary has known Ben since... oh, no! I forgot! Let's start again.

26   Unit 2

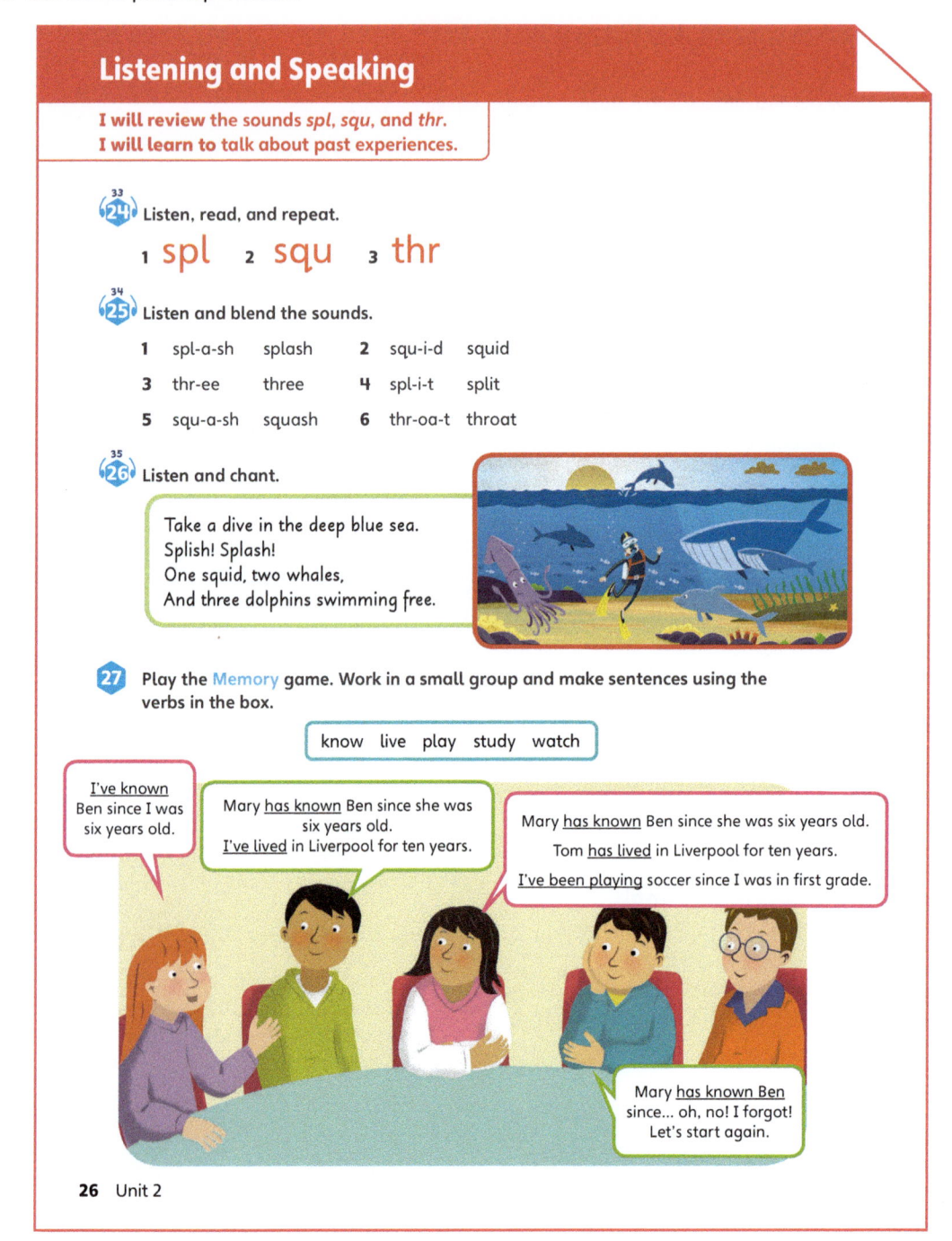

Warm-up

- Have students sit or stand in a circle and review verb forms. The first student should say a verb. The next student should say the simple past form of the verb. The third student should give present perfect form with *has*. The fourth student should start with a new verb. Model: *play/played/has played; give/gave/has given; love/loved/has loved; drink/drank/has drunk; think/thought/has thought.*

Lesson Objective

INVOLVE

Introduce the lesson objective. Say: *Today I will learn to use the sounds* spl, squ, *and* thr *and talk about past experiences.*

- Students will identify the letters and distinguish between the sounds *spl, squ,* and *thr* individually and as part of words. Then they will review the unit by talking about important life events and accomplishments in the past.

Presentation

24 Listen, read, and repeat.

- Read the directions aloud. Play Audio Track 33 and have students listen and point to each sound as it is said. Have students repeat.

MONITOR

As students repeat, check they are pointing to the correct sound and listen for correct pronunciation.

Practice 1

25 Listen and blend the sounds.

- Read the directions aloud. Play Audio Track 34 and have students listen and point to each item as it is sounded out and blended on the audio. Have them repeat after each item.

MONITOR

As students repeat, check they are pointing to the correct word and listen for correct pronunciation and appropriate intonation.

ASSIST

Replay the audio as needed.

Practice 2

26 Listen and chant.

- Read the directions aloud. Read the chant while students follow in their books.
- Play Audio Track 35 and have students listen. Replay Audio Track 35 several times and encourage them to join in.

MONITOR

As students repeat the chant, listen for proper pronunciation, appropriate intonation, and correct use of language.

Speaking

27 Play the Memory game. Work in a small group and make sentences using the verbs in the box.

- Read the directions and steps aloud. You may wish to have students remain in the class circle from the Warm-up and do the activity as a class before having students break into small groups and continuing. Have four students model the steps by reading the examples in the book aloud, but have Student 4 remember correctly and then continue the memory game with his or her own information.

MONITOR

Check that students use present perfect verbs correctly as they add to the series.

ASSIST

Provide students with the past participle form of the verbs in the box: *known, lived, played, studied, watched.*

CHALLENGE

Encourage students to include some sentences that use the present perfect progressive of verbs from the box. Model: *We've been living in our house for six years. We've been studying amazing people since September 25th. Zelda has been playing the piano since she was eight.*

21st Century Problem Solving

- Say: *This game is hard because you have to remember a long list of sentences. One way to help you remember them is to picture what the sentences describe. This is called visualizing.* Have students try one round, visualizing the list they're trying to remember. Point out that closing their eyes may help some students visualize more clearly. Ask: *Did visualizing help you remember a longer list? What other strategies can you use to help you remember things?*

Lesson Objective

INVOLVE

Revisit the lesson objective: *Now I have learned to use the sounds* spl, squ, *and* thr *and talked about past experiences.*

- Encourage awareness of what the students have learned by quickly eliciting the words from the lesson with the sounds *spl, squ,* and *thr.*

Extra Application and Practice Activity

- Invite partners to role-play interviews about past events in front of the class. Encourage them to include one or two verbs from the box at the top of the page in the present perfect or present perfect progressive. Model: *Have you ever played an instrument? Yes, I play the flute. When did you start? I've been playing the flute for six months now.* Have classmates raise their hands whenever they hear a verb in the present perfect or present perfect progressive.

Listening and Speaking

I will review the sounds *spl*, *squ*, and *thr*.
I will learn to talk about past experiences.

24 Listen, read, and repeat.

1. **spl**   2. **squ**   3. **thr**

25 Listen and blend the sounds.

1. spl-a-sh   splash
2. squ-i-d   squid
3. thr-ee   three
4. spl-i-t   split
5. squ-a-sh   squash
6. thr-oa-t   throat

26 Listen and chant.

Take a dive in the deep blue sea.
Splish! Splash!
One squid, two whales,
And three dolphins swimming free.

27 Play the Memory game. Work in a small group and make sentences using the verbs in the box.

know   live   play   study   watch

I've known Ben since I was six years old.

Mary has known Ben since she was six years old.
I've lived in Liverpool for ten years.

Mary has known Ben since she was six years old.
Tom has lived in Liverpool for ten years.
I've been playing soccer since I was in first grade.

Mary has known Ben since... oh, no! I forgot! Let's start again.

26   Unit 2

Review

28 **Complete the paragraph with for or since.**

This is Jen and Ally. Jen is from Germany, but she has lived in Ohio ¹_____ 2008. Jen has been learning English ² _____ six years. Ally has been Jen's best friend ³ _____ two years. They like in-line skating, but Jen hasn't done it ⁴ _____ she was a little girl. Ally is teaching her how to do it again. They want to invite their friends to skate with them at the town park. They've been talking about this ⁵ _____ about a month! Maybe they'll go next weekend.

29 **Complete the sentences. Use the present perfect progressive and for or since.**

win soccer tournaments   play the piano   invent things   take cooking classes

1 She _____
   she was six years old.

2 He _____
   the past eight years.

3 They _____
   fourth grade.

4 He _____
   an hour.

I Can

- use words related to achievements and personal goals.
- use the present perfect and the present perfect progressive.
- talk about achievements and accomplishments.
- write a short biography.

Review Lesson

Lesson Flow

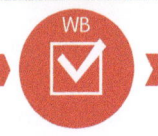

Warm-up › Lesson Objective › Practice 1 (SB) › Practice 2 (WB) › Practice 3 (WB) › Practice 4 (SB) › Self-assessment › Homework

Lesson Objective

To review the words and structures of the unit.

Review

28 Complete the paragraph with *for* or *since*.

This is Jen and Ally. Jen is from Germany, but she has lived in Ohio ¹ _____ 2008. Jen has been learning English ² _____ six years. Ally has been Jen's best friend ³ _____ two years. They like in-line skating, but Jen hasn't done it ⁴ _____ she was a little girl. Ally is teaching her how to do it again. They want to invite their friends to skate with them at the town park. They've been talking about this ⁵ _____ about a month! Maybe they'll go next weekend.

29 Complete the sentences. Use the present perfect progressive and *for* or *since*.

win soccer tournaments   play the piano   invent things   take cooking classes

1 She _____ she was six years old.
2 He _____ the past eight years.
3 They _____ fourth grade.
4 He _____ an hour.

I Can

- use words related to achievements and personal goals.
- use the present perfect and the present perfect progressive.
- talk about achievements and accomplishments.
- write a short biography.

Unit 2   27

Warm-up

Materials: Magazines and newspapers

- Divide the class into groups of three or four and give each group a few newspaper or magazine articles to scan. Draw a three-column chart on the board with the headings *Past Simple*, *Present Perfect*, and *Present Perfect Progressive*. Have students copy the chart in their notebooks and complete it with verbs they find in their articles.

MONITOR

As students are working, check that they are putting the verbs in the correct columns, and make corrections as necessary.

Lesson Objective

INVOLVE

Introduce the lesson objective. Say: *Today I will review the words and structures of the unit.*

- Students will review the vocabulary and grammar they learned in Unit 2. They will review the unit by using *for* and *since* and the present perfect progressive to talk about past experiences.
- Then students will complete the *I Can* section, which helps them to assess their own learning and reflect on their progress.

S27   Unit 2

Practice 1

28 Complete the paragraph with *for* or *since*.

- Read the directions aloud. Have students complete the paragraph independently.

MONITOR

Check answers as a class. Ask students to give the answer and then read each completed sentence aloud. *(Answers: 1 since, 2 for, 3 since, 4 since, 5 for)*

ASSIST

Review the difference between *for* and *since*. Explain that *for* comes before a length of time (two years) and *since* comes before a specific point of time (2008) in the past.

Practice 2 WB p. 21/ act. 21

21 Complete the paragraphs. Use the present perfect and *for* or *since*.

- Read the directions aloud. Explain to students that they need to complete the paragraph using the present perfect and *for* or *since*.
- Have students work independently.
- Have students compare answers with a partner. Check answers as a class.

Practice 3 WB p. 21/ act. 22

22 Look at 21. Answer the questions in complete sentences.

- Read the directions aloud. Explain to students that they have to look at the paragraph in Activity 21 again and then write answers to the questions in complete sentences.

Practice 4

29 Complete the sentences. Use the present perfect progressive and *for* or *since*.

- Read the directions and the phrases in the box aloud. Complete Item 1 as a class. Then have students complete the activity independently.
- Have partners check each other's work to see if they have used the correct form of *have* and the present perfect progressive form of the main verb.

MONITOR

Check answers as a class. *(Answers: 1 has been winning soccer tournaments since, 2 has been inventing things for, 3 have been taking cooking lessons since, 4 has been playing the piano for)*

ASSIST

Remind students that they'll use the present perfect progressive verb and *for* if they are naming a length of time, such as *six years* or *two months*. They'll use the present perfect progressive verb and *since* if they are naming a specific time in the past, such as *2003* or *last April*.

Self-assessment

I Can

- This section asks students to assess their own learning and reflect on their progress. Help students appreciate their progress. Say: *The I Can statements show what you have learned in this unit.*
- Read the statements aloud. Explain that students should think about how well they know the language in the unit and should color in the stars. They should color three stars if they feel the unit was easy, two stars if they need some help, and one star if the unit was hard and they need more help. Have students work independently.

Suggestions for Remediation

Assessment Pack
- Direct students who need help with grammar and vocabulary to the Unit 2 Practice Tests in the Assessment Pack.

WB Unit 2/ p. 99
- Direct students who need help with grammar in particular to the Unit 2 Extra Grammar Practice (Workbook, page 99).
- For further vocabulary work students can access games in the Big English Student World.

Homework WB p. 21/ act. 23

23 Answer the questions. Use the present perfect progressive and *since*.

- Direct students to WB Activity 23 on page 21. Explain to students that they have to answer the questions using the present perfect progressive and *since*.

Extra Application and Practice Activity

- Write the sentence frames on the board: *Yesterday, I… . I have… for five years. Since 2013, I have… . Last month, I… .* Pair students, and have them complete the sentences, using the simple past or present perfect.

Assessment Pack

- To assess student progress at the end of the unit, have students complete the Unit 2 Unit Test in the Assessment Pack.
- To assess whether students have reached the listening and speaking targets for this unit, carry out the Unit 2 Oral Assessment in the Assessment Pack.
- Arrange one-to-one sessions with each student and use the prompts to evaluate their listening and speaking abilities.

Unit 2   **T27**

3 Dilemmas

Objectives

Reading

- Can identify supporting details in simple, structured paragraphs on familiar topics, if guided by questions.
- Can draw simple conclusions about the information given in a factual text on a familiar topic.
- Can get the gist of short encyclopedia entries.
- Can derive the probable meaning of simple unknown words from short, familiar contexts.

Listening

- Can get the gist of authentic recorded material on topics of personal interest, if delivered in clear standard speech.
- Can identify clearly stated opinions in extended, informal conversations on matters of personal interest, if the speakers use clear standard speech.

Speaking

- Can talk about basic personal experiences, using the first conditional.
- Can give an opinion in a structured discussion, if guided by questions.
- Can explain a problem and demand what action should be taken in an appropriate way.

Writing

- Can write short, simple structured paragraphs on familiar topics, given prompts or a model.

Grammar

- Can describe possible future outcomes of a present action or situation using the first conditional.

Unit Projects

Family Connection

Have students tell their families that they're learning about difficult choices. Encourage students to talk with family members about difficult choices they've made, as well as the consequences (results) of those choices. Remind students that they should always ask family members if they want their stories shared with the class or not. Explain that learning about real choices people make is still helpful even if students can't share them.

Key Language

Key Vocabulary

Dilemmas
cheat in a test
return a wallet
tell the truth

Results and consequences
be upset with
feel good
feel guilty
get into trouble

Expressions
answer key
bothering me
calling me names
catch the bus
finders, keepers
see it in your face
wait and see
What's going on?

Content Words

acceptable
based on
ethical
ethics
excuse
harmless
morally
perspective
respectful
traits
treat

moss
proverb
reap
regret
saying
sound advice
sow

Grammar/Structures

If you **tell** your parents you forgot, they**'ll be** upset.

You **should tell** your parents **if** you have a problem.

Phonics

The sounds: nch, nth, mpt

The Right Choice Bulletin Board

Create a bulletin-board display titled *The Right Choice*. Post one or two scenarios along with possible choices. Model: *You find a brand new smartphone on the floor in a shopping mall. You can keep it. You can take it to Lost and Found.* Place a pin next to each choice and have each student hang a paper clip from the pin for his or her choice, providing a visual pictograph of students' opinions. Add new scenarios to the board throughout the unit.

Language in Context Lesson

Lesson Flow

Warm-up › Lesson Objective › Presentation › Practice 1 (WB) › Practice 2 (SB) › Practice 3 (SB) › Speaking › Think BIG › Lesson Objective › Homework

Lesson Objective

I will learn to talk about dilemmas and making the right choice.

Key Language

dilemma; be upset with, cheat, confess, feel good, feel guilty, get into trouble, loan, lose, return; dishonest, mad; answer key

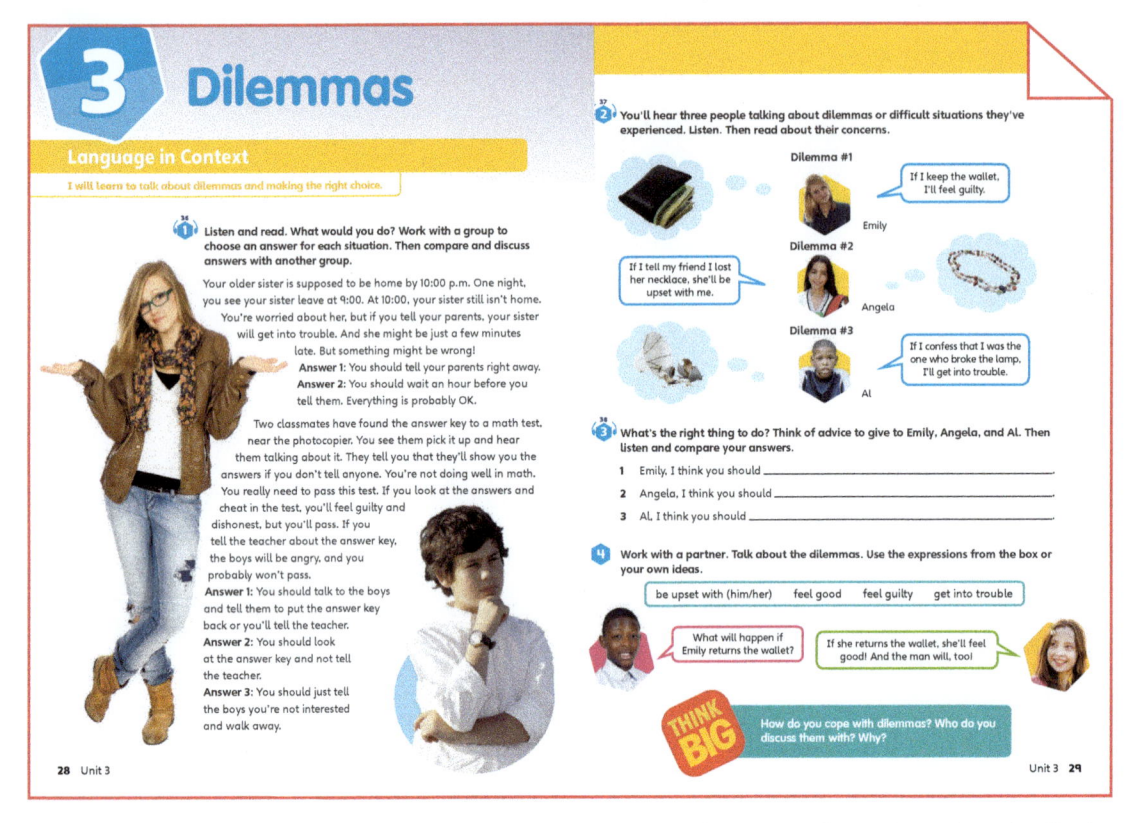

---

3 Dilemmas
Language in Context
I will learn to talk about dilemmas and making the right choice.

1 Listen and read. What would you do? Work with a group to choose an answer for each situation. Then compare and discuss answers with another group.

Your older sister is supposed to be home by 10:00 p.m. One night, you see your sister leave at 9:00. At 10:00, your sister still isn't home. You're worried about her, but if you tell your parents, your sister will get into trouble. And she might be just a few minutes late. But something might be wrong!
Answer 1: You should tell your parents right away.
Answer 2: You should wait an hour before you tell them. Everything is probably OK.

Two classmates have found the answer key to a math test, near the photocopier. You see them pick it up and hear them talking about it. They tell you that they'll show you the answers if you don't tell anyone. You're not doing well in math. You really need to pass this test. If you look at the answers and cheat in the test, you'll feel guilty and dishonest, but you'll pass. If you tell the teacher about the answer key, the boys will be angry, and you probably won't pass.
Answer 1: You should talk to the boys and tell them to put the answer key back or you'll tell the teacher.
Answer 2: You should look at the answer key and not tell the teacher.
Answer 3: You should just tell the boys you're not interested and walk away.

2 You'll hear three people talking about dilemmas or difficult situations they've experienced. Listen. Then read about their concerns.

Dilemma #1 — Emily: If I keep the wallet, I'll feel guilty.

Dilemma #2 — Angela: If I tell my friend I lost her necklace, she'll be upset with me.

Dilemma #3 — Al: If I confess that I was the one who broke the lamp, I'll get into trouble.

3 What's the right thing to do? Think of advice to give to Emily, Angela, and Al. Then listen and compare your answers.

1 Emily, I think you should _____
2 Angela, I think you should _____
3 Al, I think you should _____

4 Work with a partner. Talk about the dilemmas. Use the expressions from the box or your own ideas.

| be upset with (him/her) | feel good | feel guilty | get into trouble |

— What will happen if Emily returns the wallet?
— If she returns the wallet, she'll feel good! And the man will, too!

THINK BIG: How do you cope with dilemmas? Who do you discuss them with? Why?

Warm-up

- As a class, discuss a situation that might cause students to have to make difficult choices. For example, say: *Tim has an exam that he put off studying for until the night before. It's already late. What should he do?* Encourage students to discuss the choices and solutions in small groups.
- Check answers from the HW in the last lesson.

Lesson Objective

INVOLVE
Explain the lesson objective. Say: *Today I will learn to talk about dilemmas and making the right choice.*

- Tell students that they will read and talk about difficult choices.

Presentation

Materials: World map or globe

1 Listen and read. What would you do? Work with a group to choose an answer for each situation. Then compare and discuss answers with another group.

- Read the directions aloud. Remind students that a dilemma is a problematic situation with a difficult choice. Play Audio Track 36. Pause after each dilemma and have students discuss their answers in their groups.

MONITOR

Check that each group chooses and defends an answer for each dilemma.

21st Century Social Skills

- Ask: *How is defending an opinion different from having an argument?* (Sample answer: Two people can talk calmly and respectfully when they disagree. They don't have to become angry or shout.)

Practice 1 — WB p. 22/ act. 1

1 Look at the pictures. How do you think the people are feeling? Write the number or numbers.

- Read the directions aloud. Have students describe what they see in the pictures. Ask volunteers to read the feelings aloud.
- Have students complete the activity independently.

Practice 2 — P. T141 / 37

2 You'll hear three people talking about dilemmas or difficult situations they've experienced. Listen. Then read about their concerns.

- Read the directions aloud. Have students preview the pictures. Then play Audio Track 37. Pause after each dilemma and have volunteers read the related comment.

MONITOR

Use questions to check comprehension. Ask: *What does Emily think will happen if she keeps the wallet?* (She'll feel guilty.) *What does Angela think will happen if she tells her friend about the lost necklace?* (Her friend will be upset with her.) *What does Al think will happen if he confesses he broke the lamp?* (He'll get into trouble.)

Practice 3 — P. T141 / 38

3 What's the right thing to do? Think of advice to give to Emily, Angela, and Al. Then listen and compare your answers.

- Read the directions aloud. Say: *You'll write down your opinion and then listen to what someone else thinks. Remember that people don't always agree about what's the right thing to do.* Play Audio Track 38.

MONITOR

Have students read their advice aloud. Check that students use *should* to say what they think each person should do.

Speaking

4 Work with a partner. Talk about the dilemmas. Use the expressions from the box or your own ideas.

- Read the directions and the expressions in the box. Say: *You and a partner will discuss what will happen if these people take certain actions.* Have volunteers read the speech bubbles to model the activity.

MONITOR

Listen for correct pronunciation, appropriate intonation, and correct use of language.

Think BIG

21st Century Communication

- Read the questions aloud and encourage students to express themselves as best they can. Write answers on the board. Then ask students to write a few sentences about how they cope with dilemmas and who they discuss them with.

Lesson Objective

INVOLVE

Revisit the lesson objective: *Now I have learned to talk about dilemmas and making the right choice.*

- Encourage awareness of what the students have learned by quickly eliciting some of the dilemmas and difficult choices they learned about in the lesson.

Homework — WB pp. 22 & 23/ act. 2, 3, & 4

2 Look at 1. What do you think has happened to the people? Why do they look this way? Choose one person and ✓ all possible answers. Add three ideas of your own.

- Direct students to WB Activity 2 on page 22. Tell students to check the possible choices for one person and write three other ideas of their own.

3 Complete the dialogs. Circle the correct words.

- Direct students to WB Activity 3 on page 23. Tell students to choose the correct words.

4 Read the dilemma. What do you think? Complete the sentences. Use your own ideas.

- Direct students to WB Activity 4 on page 23. Tell students to read the dilemma and then to write sentences using their own ideas.

Think BIG

- Direct students to WB Think Big on page 23. Tell students to write answers to the questions.

Extra Application and Practice Activity

Materials: Graphic novels or comic books

- Have students retell one of the dilemmas, using illustrations and speech bubbles. Provide models from graphic novels or comic books. Students may wish to collaborate, with one student drawing part of the dilemma, the next drawing more details, and a third student drawing a possible outcome. Allow students to share their work with the class by displaying their finished artwork.

Unit 3   **T28/29**

3 Dilemmas

Language in Context

I will learn to talk about dilemmas and making the right choice.

1 Listen and read. What would you do? Work with a group to choose an answer for each situation. Then compare and discuss answers with another group.

Your older sister is supposed to be home by 10:00 p.m. One night, you see your sister leave at 9:00. At 10:00, your sister still isn't home. You're worried about her, but if you tell your parents, your sister will get into trouble. And she might be just a few minutes late. But something might be wrong!
Answer 1: You should tell your parents right away.
Answer 2: You should wait an hour before you tell them. Everything is probably OK.

Two classmates have found the answer key to a math test, near the photocopier. You see them pick it up and hear them talking about it. They tell you that they'll show you the answers if you don't tell anyone. You're not doing well in math. You really need to pass this test. If you look at the answers and cheat in the test, you'll feel guilty and dishonest, but you'll pass. If you tell the teacher about the answer key, the boys will be angry, and you probably won't pass.
Answer 1: You should talk to the boys and tell them to put the answer key back or you'll tell the teacher.
Answer 2: You should look at the answer key and not tell the teacher.
Answer 3: You should just tell the boys you're not interested and walk away.

2 You'll hear three people talking about dilemmas or difficult situations they've experienced. Listen. Then read about their concerns.

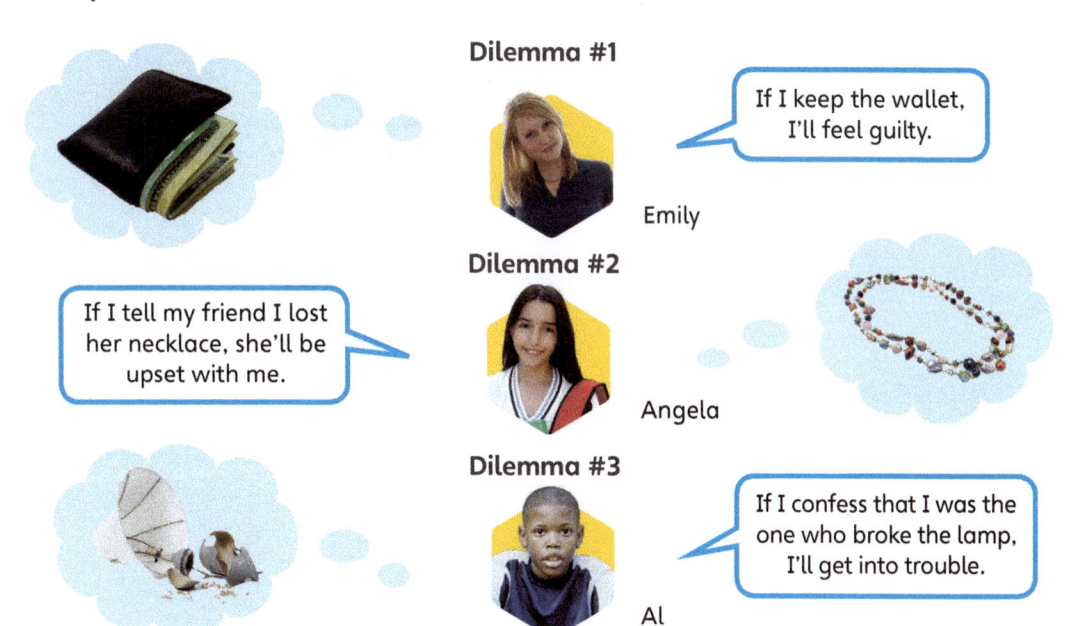

Dilemma #1

Emily: If I keep the wallet, I'll feel guilty.

Dilemma #2

Angela: If I tell my friend I lost her necklace, she'll be upset with me.

Dilemma #3

Al: If I confess that I was the one who broke the lamp, I'll get into trouble.

3 What's the right thing to do? Think of advice to give to Emily, Angela, and Al. Then listen and compare your answers.

1 Emily, I think you should _____.

2 Angela, I think you should _____.

3 Al, I think you should _____.

4 Work with a partner. Talk about the dilemmas. Use the expressions from the box or your own ideas.

> be upset with (him/her)   feel good   feel guilty   get into trouble

What will happen if Emily returns the wallet?

If she returns the wallet, she'll feel good! And the man will, too!

THINK BIG

How do you cope with dilemmas? Who do you discuss them with? Why?

Unit 3 29

Reading Lesson

Lesson Flow

Warm-up › Lesson Objective › Pre-reading › Reading › Comprehension 1 › Comprehension 2 › Think BIG › Lesson Objective › Homework

Lesson Objective

I will understand a text about a dilemma.

Key Language

problem, trouble, truth; bother, cheat, help, know, tell, trust, want; happy, upset, worried, wrong; bothering me, see it in your face, wait and see

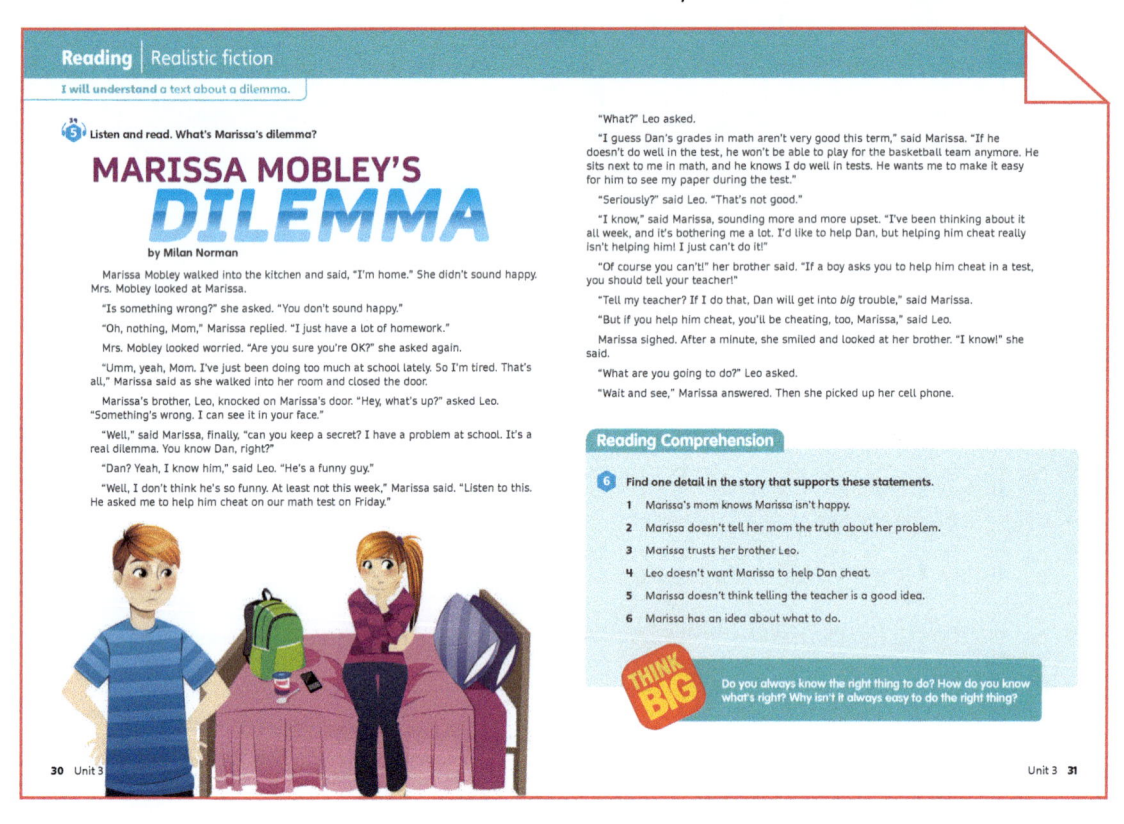

Reading | Realistic fiction

I will understand a text about a dilemma.

Listen and read. What's Marissa's dilemma?

MARISSA MOBLEY'S DILEMMA
by Milan Norman

Marissa Mobley walked into the kitchen and said, "I'm home." She didn't sound happy. Mrs. Mobley looked at Marissa.

"Is something wrong?" she asked. "You don't sound happy."

"Oh, nothing, Mom," Marissa replied. "I just have a lot of homework."

Mrs. Mobley looked worried. "Are you sure you're OK?" she asked again.

"Umm, yeah, Mom. I've just been doing too much at school lately. So I'm tired. That's all," Marissa said as she walked into her room and closed the door.

Marissa's brother, Leo, knocked on Marissa's door. "Hey, what's up?" asked Leo. "Something's wrong. I can see it in your face."

"Well," said Marissa, finally, "can you keep a secret? I have a problem at school. It's a real dilemma. You know Dan, right?"

"Dan? Yeah, I know him," said Leo. "He's a funny guy."

"Well, I don't think he's so funny. At least not this week," Marissa said. "Listen to this. He asked me to help him cheat on our math test on Friday."

"What?" Leo asked.

"I guess Dan's grades in math aren't very good this term," said Marissa. "If he doesn't do well in the test, he won't be able to play for the basketball team anymore. He sits next to me in math, and he knows I do well in tests. He wants me to make it easy for him to see my paper during the test."

"Seriously?" said Leo. "That's not good."

"I know," said Marissa, sounding more and more upset. "I've been thinking about it all week, and it's bothering me a lot. I'd like to help Dan, but helping him cheat really isn't helping him! I just can't do it!"

"Of course you can't!" her brother said. "If a boy asks you to help him cheat in a test, you should tell your teacher!"

"Tell my teacher? If I do that, Dan will get into *big* trouble," said Marissa.

"But if you help him cheat, you'll be cheating, too, Marissa," said Leo.

Marissa sighed. After a minute, she smiled and looked at her brother. "I know!" she said.

"What are you going to do?" Leo asked.

"Wait and see," Marissa answered. Then she picked up her cell phone.

Reading Comprehension

Find one detail in the story that supports these statements.

1. Marissa's mom knows Marissa isn't happy.
2. Marissa doesn't tell her mom the truth about her problem.
3. Marissa trusts her brother Leo.
4. Leo doesn't want Marissa to help Dan cheat.
5. Marissa doesn't think telling the teacher is a good idea.
6. Marissa has an idea about what to do.

THINK BIG: Do you always know the right thing to do? How do you know what's right? Why isn't it always easy to do the right thing?

Warm-up

21st Century Communication

- Say: *We learn a lot about what other people are thinking from their body language – especially their facial expressions.* Have students play *Charades*, miming simple emotions such as anger, happiness, fear, worry, sadness, and surprise. Suggest that students use body language, including facial expressions, to mime how the individuals in the dilemmas on pages 28–29 might have felt. Have the rest of the class guess. Discuss how well students guessed.

- Check answers from the HW in the last lesson.

Lesson Objective

INVOLVE

Introduce the lesson objective. Say: *Today I will learn to understand a text about a dilemma.*

- Students will listen to, read, and talk about a realistic fiction story and then answer questions about it. Say: *This unit's story leaves readers wondering what's going to happen. Later in this unit, you'll have the opportunity to decide what happens and write your own ending.*

Pre-reading

- Have students read the title aloud and preview the pictures. Ask: *What is a dilemma?* (a problematic situation in which someone must make a difficult choice)

S30 Unit 3

Reading 🎧39

5 Listen and read. What's Marissa's dilemma?

- Read the directions aloud. Play Audio Track 39 and have students listen and read along.

Comprehension 1

- Ask the question in the directions: *What is Marissa's dilemma?* (whether or not to help Dan cheat in the math test)

MONITOR

> Ask more questions to check for understanding. Ask: *How does Marissa feel when she gets home from school?* (She seems worried.) *What does Marissa tell Leo?* (Dan has asked her to help him cheat in a math test.) *Does Leo think Marissa should help Dan?* (No, he knows cheating would be wrong.) *What does he think Marissa should do?* (tell her teacher)

21st Century Social Skills

- Ask students to define *cheating in school*. (Sample answer: to use what someone else has done on an assignment or test, usually to gain an advantage) Ask: *Is cheating always wrong?* (Yes, cheating is breaking a rule that everyone knows is a dishonest thing to do.)

Comprehension 2

6 Find one detail in the story that supports these statements.

- Read the directions aloud. Have volunteers read the statements aloud. Say: *When you read a story, story details give you a lot of information. You can use these details to make inferences about the story characters and events. We'll look for clues that support each inference.*
- Complete the first item with the class. Then have students work independently.

MONITOR

> Check answers as a class. *(Sample answers: 1 Marissa's mother says, "You don't sound happy." 2 When Marissa's mother asks her if there is anything wrong, she answers, "Oh, nothing, Mom" and then again, "I've just been doing too much at school lately. So I'm tired. That's all." 3 Marissa tells her brother, "Can you keep a secret? I have a problem at school." 4 When Leo hears about Dan's idea of cheating in the math test, he says, "That's not good." 5 When Leo suggests that Marissa should talk to her teacher, she answers, "Tell my teacher? If I do that, Dan will get into big trouble." 6 Marissa sighs, not knowing what to do, but after a minute she smiles and looks at her brother and says, "I know!")*

Think BIG

21st Century Critical Thinking

- Read the questions aloud. Then have students discuss the questions about the story in pairs.
- Encourage students to write notes about what they think and hold onto them for use later in the unit.

Lesson Objective

INVOLVE

> Revisit the lesson objective: *Now I have learned to understand a text about a dilemma.*

- Encourage awareness of what the students have learned by quickly eliciting a few things they remember about the text, for example, who Marissa tells her dilemma to.

Homework 🎧40 WB p. 24/ act. 5 & 6

5 Listen and read. Circle the correct answers.

- Direct students to WB Activity 5 on page 24. Tell students to first read the numbered sentences, then play the audio and listen and read along. Tell students to circle the correct answer.

6 Answer the questions. Use your own ideas.

- Direct students to WB Activity 6 on page 24. Tell students to answer the questions with their own ideas.

Extra Application and Practice Activity

- Have students role-play one of the conversations from the story: Marissa and Dan at school, Marissa and her mother at home, or Marissa and Leo at home. Tell students they can use the words from their story or their own words. If possible, allow students to record their role plays using phones or video cameras.

Unit 3 **T31**

Reading | Realistic fiction

I will understand a text about a dilemma.

5 Listen and read. What's Marissa's dilemma?

MARISSA MOBLEY'S DILEMMA

by Milan Norman

Marissa Mobley walked into the kitchen and said, "I'm home." She didn't sound happy. Mrs. Mobley looked at Marissa.

"Is something wrong?" she asked. "You don't sound happy."

"Oh, nothing, Mom," Marissa replied. "I just have a lot of homework."

Mrs. Mobley looked worried. "Are you sure you're OK?" she asked again.

"Umm, yeah, Mom. I've just been doing too much at school lately. So I'm tired. That's all," Marissa said as she walked into her room and closed the door.

Marissa's brother, Leo, knocked on Marissa's door. "Hey, what's up?" asked Leo. "Something's wrong. I can see it in your face."

"Well," said Marissa, finally, "can you keep a secret? I have a problem at school. It's a real dilemma. You know Dan, right?"

"Dan? Yeah, I know him," said Leo. "He's a funny guy."

"Well, I don't think he's so funny. At least not this week," Marissa said. "Listen to this. He asked me to help him cheat on our math test on Friday."

30   Unit 3

"What?" Leo asked.

"I guess Dan's grades in math aren't very good this term," said Marissa. "If he doesn't do well in the test, he won't be able to play for the basketball team anymore. He sits next to me in math, and he knows I do well in tests. He wants me to make it easy for him to see my paper during the test."

"Seriously?" said Leo. "That's not good."

"I know," said Marissa, sounding more and more upset. "I've been thinking about it all week, and it's bothering me a lot. I'd like to help Dan, but helping him cheat really isn't helping him! I just can't do it!"

"Of course you can't!" her brother said. "If a boy asks you to help him cheat in a test, you should tell your teacher!"

"Tell my teacher? If I do that, Dan will get into *big* trouble," said Marissa.

"But if you help him cheat, you'll be cheating, too, Marissa," said Leo.

Marissa sighed. After a minute, she smiled and looked at her brother. "I know!" she said.

"What are you going to do?" Leo asked.

"Wait and see," Marissa answered. Then she picked up her cell phone.

Reading Comprehension

6 Find one detail in the story that supports these statements.

1. Marissa's mom knows Marissa isn't happy.
2. Marissa doesn't tell her mom the truth about her problem.
3. Marissa trusts her brother Leo.
4. Leo doesn't want Marissa to help Dan cheat.
5. Marissa doesn't think telling the teacher is a good idea.
6. Marissa has an idea about what to do.

THINK BIG Do you always know the right thing to do? How do you know what's right? Why isn't it always easy to do the right thing?

Language in Action Lesson

Lesson Flow

Warm-up › Lesson Objective › Pre-listening › Listening › Comprehension › Role Play › Practice 1 (SB) › Practice 2 (WB) › Lesson Objective › Homework

Lesson Objective

I will listen to a dialog about making the right choice.

Key Language

accident, concert, pocket money, truth; borrow, break, buy, drop, feel, go, keep, run, tell, think; broken, guilty; calling me names, finders keepers, What's going on?

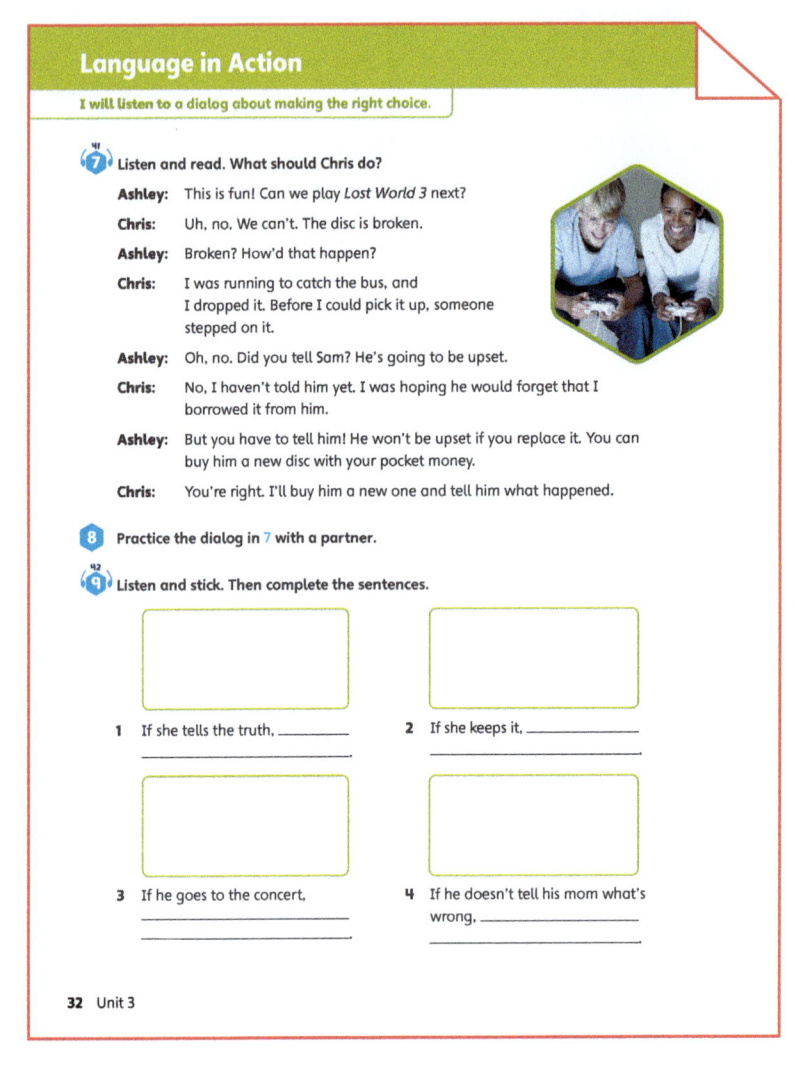

Language in Action

I will listen to a dialog about making the right choice.

7 Listen and read. What should Chris do?

Ashley: This is fun! Can we play *Lost World 3* next?
Chris: Uh, no. We can't. The disc is broken.
Ashley: Broken? How'd that happen?
Chris: I was running to catch the bus, and I dropped it. Before I could pick it up, someone stepped on it.
Ashley: Oh, no. Did you tell Sam? He's going to be upset.
Chris: No, I haven't told him yet. I was hoping he would forget that I borrowed it from him.
Ashley: But you have to tell him! He won't be upset if you replace it. You can buy him a new disc with your pocket money.
Chris: You're right. I'll buy him a new one and tell him what happened.

8 Practice the dialog in 7 with a partner.

9 Listen and stick. Then complete the sentences.

1 If she tells the truth, _____
2 If she keeps it, _____
3 If he goes to the concert, _____
4 If he doesn't tell his mom what's wrong, _____

32 Unit 3

Warm-up

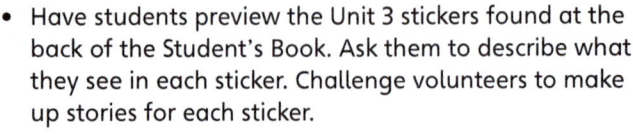

- Have students preview the Unit 3 stickers found at the back of the Student's Book. Ask them to describe what they see in each sticker. Challenge volunteers to make up stories for each sticker.
- Check answers from the HW in the last lesson.

Lesson Objective

INVOLVE

Introduce the lesson objective. Say: *Today I will listen to a dialog about making the right choice.*

- Students will read, listen to, and practice a dialog. Students will also listen to conversations about people in difficult situations.

S32 Unit 3

Pre-listening

- Point to the picture. Ask: *What do you see?* (A boy and a girl playing a video game.) Introduce the boy as Chris and the girl as Ashley. Tell students that they will hear the two friends talking about a dilemma.

Listening

7 Listen and read. What should Chris do?

- Read the directions aloud. Play Audio Track 41 and have students listen and read along.
- Invite two students to read the dialog aloud and repeat.

MONITOR

As students practice, listen for correct pronunciation and use of language.

ASSIST

As you notice errors, say words correctly and have students repeat.

Comprehension

- Ask the question in the directions: *What should Chris do?* (He should tell Sam what happened.)

MONITOR

Ask more questions to check understanding. Encourage students to answer in complete sentences. Ask: *What is* Lost World 3? (It's a video game.) *How did Chris get the game?* (He borrowed it from Sam.) *Why can't Chris and Ashley play the game?* (It's broken. Chris dropped the disc when he was running to catch the bus.) *What does Ashley think Chris should do?* (She thinks Chris should tell Sam what happened.) Ask students whether they agree with Ashley and why or why not.

CHALLENGE

Say: *What happened to the disc was an accident. What does that mean?* (Chris didn't mean to break the disc.) *What's the opposite of* accidental? (on purpose) Have students make up stories in which Chris breaks the game on purpose. (Model: *He's playing the game and gets a very bad score. He's so angry that he throws the disc at the wall.*)

Role Play

8 Practice the dialog in 7 with a partner.

- Read the directions aloud. Invite pairs to read the dialog aloud, switch parts, and repeat.

MONITOR

As students read, listen for proper pronunciation, and appropriate intonation.

ASSIST

As you notice errors, say words or sentences correctly and have students repeat after you.

Practice 1 [P. T141]

Materials: Stickers

9 Listen and stick. Then complete the sentences.

- Help students find the Unit 3 stickers at the back of the Student's Book. Read the directions aloud.
- Play Audio Track 42. Have students place the stickers on the page and complete the sentences independently. After students place each sticker, have them complete the sentences below. Complete the first item as a class and then have students complete the remaining items independently.

MONITOR

As students work, make sure that they place the stickers in the correct order. Invite volunteers to share their answers. (Sample answers: 1 *If she tells the truth, she'll feel better.* 2 *If she keeps it, she'll feel guilty every time she wears it.* 3 *If he goes to the concert, he'll worry about his brother.* 4 *If he doesn't tell his mom what's wrong, she won't be able to help him.*)

Practice 2 — WB p. 25/ act. 7

7 Listen and read. Then answer the questions.

- Read the directions aloud. Ask volunteers to read the questions aloud.
- Play Audio Track 43. Have students complete the activity.

Lesson Objective

INVOLVE

Revisit the lesson objective: *Now I have listened to a dialog about making the right choice.*

- Encourage awareness of what the students have learned by quickly eliciting a few things they remember about the dialog, for example, how the disc got broken.

Homework — WB p. 25/ act. 8 & 9

8 Look at 7. Read the underlined expressions. Match the expressions with their meanings. Write the letters.

- Direct students to WB Activity 8 on page 25. Tell students to read the underlined expressions in the dialog again and then match each expression with the words with the same meaning.

9 Answer the questions.

- Direct students to WB Activity 9 on page 25. Tell students to answer the questions.

Extra Application and Practice Activity

- Have students compare the stories they made up during the Warm-up activity with the stories on the audio. Which one was closest to the recorded version?

Language in Action

I will listen to a dialog about making the right choice.

7 Listen and read. What should Chris do?

Ashley: This is fun! Can we play *Lost World 3* next?

Chris: Uh, no. We can't. The disc is broken.

Ashley: Broken? How'd that happen?

Chris: I was running to catch the bus, and I dropped it. Before I could pick it up, someone stepped on it.

Ashley: Oh, no. Did you tell Sam? He's going to be upset.

Chris: No, I haven't told him yet. I was hoping he would forget that I borrowed it from him.

Ashley: But you have to tell him! He won't be upset if you replace it. You can buy him a new disc with your pocket money.

Chris: You're right. I'll buy him a new one and tell him what happened.

8 Practice the dialog in 7 with a partner.

9 Listen and stick. Then complete the sentences.

1 If she tells the truth, _____.

2 If she keeps it, _____.

3 If he goes to the concert, _____.

4 If he doesn't tell his mom what's wrong, _____.

32   Unit 3

Grammar

I will learn to use conditional sentences.
I will learn to use *should* to give advice.

> **If** he **pays attention** in class, he**'ll understand** the lesson.
> **If** they **don't study** for the math test, they **won't get** a good grade.
> **If** you **tell** me the truth, I**'ll help** you.
>
> **Tip:** Use a conditional sentence to express true or factual ideas in the present or future.

10 Complete the sentences. What will happen?

1 If I don't tell the truth, _____ (I, not feel good).

2 _____ (she, cheat) in the test, she will feel guilty.

3 If you help me with my book review, _____ (I, help) you with your project.

4 If he tells Mom he lost her CD, _____ (he, be) in trouble.

5 _____ (they, not return) the wallet, I'll be upset with them.

> You **should tell** your parents **if** you have a problem at school.
> **If** you don't want to get into trouble, you **shouldn't lie**.

11 Which is the best advice? Write sentences in your notebook using *should* or *shouldn't*.

1 You see someone being bullied.
   a Just walk away.   **b** Tell an adult.

2 You tear an expensive shirt in the fitting room in a store.
   a Quietly return it to the rack.   **b** Tell a sales clerk what happened.

3 Your brother's going to watch a movie that he's not allowed to see.
   a Tell your parents about it.   **b** Don't say anything to your parents.

4 Your sister's studying, and you want to listen to music.
   a Tell her to go to a friend's house.   **b** Use headphones.

5 Your friend asks you to let him copy your English homework.
   a Tell your teacher.   **b** Offer to help him do his homework.

Grammar Lesson

Lesson Flow

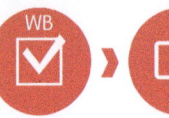

Warm-up › Lesson Objective › Presentation 1 › Practice 1 (SB) › Practice 2 (WB) › Presentation 2 › Practice 3 (SB) › Practice 4 (WB) › Lesson Objective › Homework

Lesson Objectives

I will learn to use conditional sentences.

I will learn to use *should* to give advice.

Key Language

If you tell your parents you forgot, they'll **be** upset.

You **should tell** your parents if you have a problem.

Grammar

I will learn to use conditional sentences.
I will learn to use *should* to give advice.

> If he **pays attention** in class, he'**ll understand** the lesson.
> If they **don't study** for the math test, they **won't get** a good grade.
> If you **tell** me the truth, I'**ll help** you.
> **Tip:** Use a conditional sentence to express true or factual ideas in the present or future.

10 Complete the sentences. What will happen?

1. If I don't tell the truth, _____ (I, not feel good).
2. _____ (she, cheat) in the test, she will feel guilty.
3. If you help me with my book review, _____ (I, help) you with your project.
4. If he tells Mom he lost her CD, _____ (he, be) in trouble.
5. _____ (they, not return) the wallet, I'll be upset with them.

> You **should tell** your parents **if** you have a problem at school.
> If you don't want to get into trouble, you **shouldn't lie**.

11 Which is the best advice? Write sentences in your notebook using *should* or *shouldn't*.

1. You see someone being bullied.
   a. Just walk away.   b. Tell an adult.
2. You tear an expensive shirt in the fitting room in a store.
   a. Quietly return it to the rack.   b. Tell a sales clerk what happened.
3. Your brother's going to watch a movie that he's not allowed to see.
   a. Tell your parents about it.   b. Don't say anything to your parents.
4. Your sister's studying, and you want to listen to music.
   a. Tell her to go to a friend's house.   b. Use headphones.
5. Your friend asks you to let him copy your English homework.
   a. Tell your teacher.   b. Offer to help him do his homework.

Unit 3 33

Warm-up

Materials: Index cards

- Play *Word Builder* (see *Game Bank*, page T136, for details) to review contractions. Have students write these words on index cards: *I, you, he, she, it, we, they, are, will, can, do, have.* Shuffle the cards and place them in one stack. Then write these words on cards: *not, have, will.* Use a second color card if available. Players should take turns drawing one card from each deck. If they can make a contraction, they should say the word. If not, they should say "no contraction." Return used cards to the decks. Models: *are + not = aren't; I + will = I'll; you + not = no contraction.*
- Check answers from the HW in the last lesson.

Lesson Objective

INVOLVE

Introduce the lesson objective. Say: *Today I will learn to use conditional sentences and should to give advice.*

- Students will use conditional sentences and will use *should* and *shouldn't* to give advice.

Presentation 1

- Have volunteers read the tip and sentences in the first grammar box aloud. Say: *A conditional sentence includes the word* if. *If is often the first word in the sentence.*
- Refer students back to the Language in Action dialog and elicit or highlight the grammar structures in the dialog.

Practice 1

10 Complete the sentences. What will happen?

- Read the directions and complete Item 1 as a class. Then have students complete the activity independently.

MONITOR

Check answers as a class. *(Answers: 1 I won't feel good, 2 If she cheats, 3 I'll help, 4 he'll be, 5 If they don't return)*

CHALLENGE

Point out that *if* does not necessarily appear in the beginning of a sentence. Ask: *How can you change the word order in Item 5 so this sentence does not begin with* if? (*I'll be upset with them if they don't return the wallet.*) Point out that changing the word order does not change the meaning of the sentence.

21st Century Creative Thinking

- Challenge students to think of stories behind what they read in the sentences for Activity 10. Model: *For Item 1, the story is about an older brother who asks his younger brother to lie for him. The older brother might have scratched the family car during a driving lesson. The younger brother knows what happened, but the parents don't.*

Practice 2 WB p. 26/ act. 10

10 Unscramble the phrases to complete the sentences.

- Ask volunteers to read the sentences in the grammar box.
- Read the directions aloud and explain that students have to unscramble the phrases to complete the sentences.
- Have students complete the activity independently, then check answers as a class.

Presentation 2

- Have volunteers read the sentences in the second grammar box aloud. Say: *Notice that you use* should *or* shouldn't *to give advice in a conditional sentence.*

Practice 3

11 Which is the best advice? Write sentences in your notebook using *should* **or** *shouldn't*.

- Read the directions aloud and complete Item 1 as a class. Then have students complete the activity independently.

MONITOR

For each item, poll students to see how many chose each answer. Then invite volunteers to read their sentences aloud. Check for correct use of grammar and vocabulary. *(Sample answers: 1 b; If you see someone being bullied, you should tell an adult. 2 b; If you tear an expensive shirt in the fitting room in a store, you should tell a sales clerk what happened. 3 a; If your brother's going to watch a movie that he's not allowed to see, you should tell your parents about it. 4 b; If your sister's studying, and you want to listen to music, you should use headphones. 5 b; If your friend asks you to let him copy your English homework, you should offer to help him do his homework.)*

Practice 4 WB p. 27/ act. 13

13 Complete the advice column with the correct form of the verbs in the box. Add *should* **if necessary.**

- Read the directions aloud. Explain that students have to read the advice column and then complete the sentences with the correct form of the words in the box and *should* when necessary.
- Have students complete the activity independently.

Lesson Objective

INVOLVE

Revisit the lesson objective: *Now I have learned to use conditional sentences and* should *to give advice.*

- Encourage awareness of what the students have learned by quickly eliciting some conditional sentences and sentences with *should* and *shouldn't*.

Homework WB pp. 26 & 27/ act. 11, 12, & 14

11 Match the sentences. Write the letter.

- Direct students to WB Activity 11 on page 26. Explain that the students have to match the two sentences that are connected.

12 Write sentences using the ideas in 11.

- Direct students to WB Activity 12 on page 26. Tell students to write sentences using the ideas in Activity 11.

14 Complete the sentences with advice. Use *should* **or** *shouldn't*.

- Direct students to WB Activity 14 on page 27. Tell students to complete the sentences with advice using *should* or *shouldn't*.

Extra Application and Practice Activity

- Have partners collaborate to write conditional sentences. One partner should begin a sentence with *if*, describing a situation. The other partner should complete the sentence by describing what will happen or what the person should or shouldn't do.

Unit 3 **T33**

Content Connection Lesson

Lesson Flow

Warm-up › Lesson Objective › Pre-reading › Reading › Practice 1 (WB) › Practice 2 (SB) › Think BIG › Video Lesson › Lesson Objective › Homework

Lesson Objective

I will learn about ethical behavior.

Key Language

acceptable, according to, based on, ethical, ethics, excuse, harmless, morally, perspective, respectful, traits, treat

---

Content Connection | Social Sciences

I will learn about ethical behavior.

🎧 44 / 12 Listen and read. What's ethical behavior?

CONTENT WORDS
acceptable   according to   based on
ethical   ethics   excuse
harmless   morally   perspective
respectful   traits   treat

Ethics

The saying "Treat others the way you'd want them to treat you" isn't hard to understand. It means that you should behave toward others the way you'd want them to behave toward you. It sounds simple, but it isn't always simple to do. If everyone followed this advice, the world would be a much better place.

Do you know what ethics are? Of course you do. You make choices based on ethics all the time. Ethics tell you what's right or wrong, fair or unfair, acceptable or unacceptable in a situation. Choosing to do the right thing is ethical behavior.

The word ethics comes from the Greek word ethos, which means "character". Our character is all of our traits and qualities taken together. It helps us decide what's right or wrong. What kind of character do you have? Are you respectful of your classmates? Would you cheat in a test to make sure you pass? Would you tell a "harmless" lie in order to avoid hurting someone's feelings? Would you lie to someone to get out of trouble? These are all questions of ethics.

How can you choose ethical behavior in a difficult situation? You can begin by asking yourself a few questions, but your answers must be honest. The first question is, "If I do it, will I feel bad afterward?" If we do something that's morally wrong, we'll feel guilty about it, even if we can find excuses for our actions. The second question is, "If I do it, will it hurt somebody?" If the answer is yes, then it might not be the right thing to do. You can also ask, "How would I judge someone else who did the same thing? What would my mom or dad say about it?" This helps us see things from the right perspective. And a final, but very important question is, "What's my gut feeling about it? Does it feel right?" This can give you a good idea of whether your behavior is ethical.

Behaving according to your ethics isn't always the easiest thing to do, but it's always the right thing to do.

13 Look at the passage. Read and say true or false.

1. If you want to make an ethical decision, you need to be honest with yourself.
2. If we can find a good excuse for our actions, we won't feel guilty.
3. Following our ethics is sometimes difficult, but we should always try to do it.

THINK BIG Did you ever have a problem making an ethical decision? What happened?

Warm-up

- Write on the board: *He/She did the WRONG thing*. Invite students to share situations in which story characters or people they know did *not* do the right thing. Have them say what the person did and why they think it was wrong. Model: *My neighbor borrowed my bicycle. When she returned it, the tire was flat and the bicycle had a big scratch. She left it without saying anything. She should have told me what happened.*
- Check answers from the HW in the last lesson.

Lesson Objective

INVOLVE

- Introduce the lesson objective. Say: *Today I will learn about ethical behavior.*
- Students will listen and read about ethics and learn how to make ethical decisions.

Pre-reading

- Preview the article by having students read the Content Words and discuss their meanings. Encourage students to look up any unfamiliar words in a dictionary.

Reading 🎧44

12 Listen and read. What's ethical behavior?

- Read the directions aloud. Write the question on the board: *What's ethical behavior?* Explain to students that they should be listening specifically for the answer to that question.
- Play Audio Track 44 and have students listen and read along.

MONITOR

- Have a few pairs share their ideas. (Answer: Choosing to do the right thing is ethical behavior in paragraph 2)

CHALLENGE

- Have students write a few sentences summarizing the article using the content words. In pairs or small groups, have students select a meaningful quotation from the text and write it in big letters using markers on construction paper. Ask students to come to the front, share their quotation, and explain why they chose that quotation.

Recognizing Cognates: Remind students that different languages often have similar words with similar meanings. These words are called *cognates*. For example, the Italian word for ethics is *etica*, and in Spanish it is *ética*. Explain that recognizing cognates can help students understand vocabulary.

Practice 1 🎧45 WB p. 28/ act. 15

5 Listen and read. What does "character" mean?

- Read the directions aloud. Play Audio Track 45 and have students listen and read along.
- Replay the audio and have students answer the question, then check answer as a class.

Practice 2

13 Look at the passage. Read and say *true* or *false*.

- Have students individually read the sentences and decide whether or not they are true or false.
- Place students in pairs. Have partners share their answers, explaining their reasons. (Sample answer: Item 1 is True. The third paragraph says, "You can begin by asking yourself a few questions, but your answers must be honest.")

MONITOR

- Ask different students to share their answers with the class. (Answers: 1 true, 2 false, 3 true)

Think BIG

21st Century Communication

- Read the questions aloud. Have students work in small groups to talk about their experiences making an ethical decision, then feed back to the class.

Video Documentary U 03

- Refer to the Video Guide for pre-watching and post-watching activities.

Lesson Objective

INVOLVE

- Revisit the lesson objective: *Now I have learned about ethical behavior.*
- Encourage awareness of what the students have learned by quickly eliciting a few things they remember about the passage, for example, what questions they should ask themselves when making an ethical decision.

Homework WB p. 28/ act. 16

16 Unscramble and write. Then make up a sentence with each word.

- Direct students to WB Activity 16 on page 28. Tell students to unscramble the letters and write each word. Then think of a sentence for each word.

Extra Application and Practice Activity

Materials: Magazines and newspapers

- Invite students to look through newspapers and magazines for situations that call for right or wrong decisions. Have students discuss what they would do in these situations.

Unit 3   T34

Content Connection | Social Sciences

I will learn about ethical behavior.

12 Listen and read. What's ethical behavior?

CONTENT WORDS
acceptable   according to   based on
ethical   ethics   excuse
harmless   morally   perspective
respectful   traits   treat

Ethics

The saying "Treat others the way you'd want them to treat you" isn't hard to understand. It means that you should behave toward others the way you'd want them to behave toward you. It sounds simple, but it isn't always simple to do. If everyone followed this advice, the world would be a much better place.

Do you know what ethics are? Of course you do. You make choices based on ethics all the time. Ethics tell you what's right or wrong, fair or unfair, acceptable or unacceptable in a situation. Choosing to do the right thing is ethical behavior.

The word ethics comes from the Greek word ethos, which means "character". Our character is all of our traits and qualities taken together. It helps us decide what's right or wrong. What kind of character do you have? Are you respectful of your classmates? Would you cheat in a test to make sure you pass? Would you tell a "harmless" lie in order to avoid hurting someone's feelings? Would you lie to someone to get out of trouble? These are all questions of ethics.

How can you choose ethical behavior in a difficult situation? You can begin by asking yourself a few questions, but your answers must be honest. The first question is, "If I do it, will I feel bad afterward?" If we do something that's morally wrong, we'll feel guilty about it, even if we can find excuses for our actions. The second question is, "If I do it, will it hurt somebody?" If the answer is yes, then it might not be the right thing to do. You can also ask, "How would I judge someone else who did the same thing? What would my mom or dad say about it?" This helps us see things from the right perspective. And a final, but very important question is, "What's my gut feeling about it? Does it feel right?" This can give you a good idea of whether your behavior is ethical.

Behaving according to your ethics isn't always the easiest thing to do, but it's always the right thing to do.

13 Look at the passage. Read and say true or false.

1. If you want to make an ethical decision, you need to be honest with yourself.
2. If we can find a good excuse for our actions, we won't feel guilty.
3. Following our ethics is sometimes difficult, but we should always try to do it.

THINK BIG Did you ever have a problem making an ethical decision? What happened?

Culture Connection | Around the World

I will learn about proverbs from around the world.

Proverbs from Around the World

CONTENT WORDS
moss   proverb   reap   regret
saying   sound advice   sow

Every culture has its own proverbs. Proverbs are short sayings about life that are passed on from generation to generation. They go back tens, hundreds, even thousands of years, and sum up the practical experience of the people who use them. Because proverbs give sound advice, they help us make decisions. The Chinese proverb ¹_____ is a good example. Anyone who's about to make a hasty decision, without weighing the pros and cons first, is warned of the horrible consequences of a bad choice.

Sometimes proverbs can seem to have different meanings. The English proverb ²_____ is one example. Some think that the proverb is a warning for people who keep moving and never settle down. If these people "gather no moss," then it means they haven't achieved anything. Others think that the proverb is a warning for people who never do anything. If you don't move and change with the times, you'll become like an old mossy piece of rock.

We often find that there are similar proverbs across cultures. Maybe this is because proverbs have traveled and have been translated from one language to another, or maybe it's because they're just common sense. An expression similar to ³_____ appears in many languages, and it means that you'll get what you give. One proverb in Malaysia, where crocodiles are common, is ⁴_____.

Whatever advice they give, one thing that all proverbs teach us is that although societies are changing and becoming more advanced every day, there are some basic facts about life and human nature that'll never change.

14 **Read the passage quickly and put the proverbs a–d in the correct place. Then listen and check.**

a "A rolling stone gathers no moss."

b "Don't think there are no crocodiles just because the water is calm."

c "You'll reap what you sow."

d "One step in the wrong direction can cause a thousand years of regret."

THINK BIG What's the connection between proverbs and ethics?

Culture Connection Lesson

Lesson Flow

Warm-up › Lesson Objective › Pre-reading › Reading › Practice › Think BIG › Lesson Objective › Homework

Lesson Objective

I will learn about proverbs from around the world.

Key Language

moss, proverb, reap, regret, saying, sound advice, sow

Culture Connection | Around the World

I will learn about proverbs from around the world.

Proverbs from Around the World

CONTENT WORDS
moss, proverb, reap, regret, saying, sound advice, sow

Every culture has its own proverbs. Proverbs are short sayings about life that are passed on from generation to generation. They go back tens, hundreds, even thousands of years, and sum up the practical experience of the people who use them. Because proverbs give sound advice, they help us make decisions. The Chinese proverb [1]_____ is a good example. Anyone who's about to make a hasty decision, without weighing the pros and cons first, is warned of the horrible consequences of a bad choice.

Sometimes proverbs can seem to have different meanings. The English proverb [2]_____ is one example. Some think that the proverb is a warning for people who keep moving and never settle down. If these people "gather no moss," then it means they haven't achieved anything. Others think that the proverb is a warning for people who never do anything. If you don't move and change with the times, you'll become like an old mossy piece of rock.

We often find that there are similar proverbs across cultures. Maybe this is because proverbs have traveled and have been translated from one language to another, or maybe it's because they're just common sense. An expression similar to [3]_____ appears in many languages, and it means that you'll get what you give. One proverb in Malaysia, where crocodiles are common, is [4]_____.

Whatever advice they give, one thing that all proverbs teach us is that although societies are changing and becoming more advanced every day, there are some basic facts about life and human nature that'll never change.

14 Read the passage quickly and put the proverbs a–d in the correct place. Then listen and check.

a "A rolling stone gathers no moss."
b "Don't think there are no crocodiles just because the water is calm."
c "You'll reap what you sow."
d "One step in the wrong direction can cause a thousand years of regret."

THINK BIG What's the connection between proverbs and ethics?

Warm-up

- Have students create *Word Search Puzzles* (see *Game Bank*, page T137, for details) to preview vocabulary items. Model creating a simple word search on the board. Explain that words can be hidden horizontally, vertically, or diagonally. Then have students create puzzles that include these words: *moss, proverb, reap, regret, saying, advice,* and *sow*. Have students exchange puzzles and find the hidden words.
- Check answers from the HW in the last lesson.

Lesson Objective

INVOLVE

Introduce the lesson objective. Say: *Today I will learn about proverbs from around the world.*

- Students will listen to, read, and talk about proverbs from around the world and connect them to their own experiences.

Pre-reading

- Write on the board: *proverbs*. Have students scan the first paragraph of the article and find the meaning of this word *(short sayings about life that are passed on from generation to generation)*.

Reading

14 Read the passage quickly and put the proverbs a–d in the correct place. Then listen and check.

- Read the first paragraph of the passage aloud with the class. Elicit which proverb best completes the paragraph *(d)*. Have a couple of students offer explanations as to why this is the best choice. Elicit: *In the paragraph, it talks about "the horrible consequences of a bad choice." If you make a bad choice, you will feel regret.*
- Have students read the rest of the article independently and select the most appropriate proverbs to fill in the blanks.
- Play Audio Track 46. Have students listen and read along in their books, checking their answers.

MONITOR

Check answers as a class. *(Answers: 1 d, 2 a, 3 c, 4 b)*

Practice   WB p. 29/ act. 17

17 Match the proverbs with their meanings. Write the letters.

- Read the directions aloud. Explain to students that they have to match each proverb in the left-hand column with its meaning in the right-hand column.
- Have volunteers read the proverbs aloud.
- Have students work with a partner, then check answers as a class.

Think BIG

21st Century Critical Thinking

- Ask students to think about the connection between ethical behavior and using proverbs. Write a few proverbs on the board, and ask students to suggest what kind of ethical behavior might result from people following the advice in the proverb. For example, for the proverb "Better late than never," students might give an example of a friend who made a mistake and didn't apologize at first, but then went back and told her friend she was sorry.

Lesson Objective

INVOLVE

Revisit the lesson objective: *Now I have learned about proverbs from around the world.*

- Encourage awareness of what the students have learned by quickly eliciting a few things they remember about the passage, for example, the meaning of one or two of the proverbs.

Homework   WB p. 29/ act. 18

18 Listen and read. Match the stories with the proverbs above. Write 1, 2, or 3.

- Direct students to WB Activity 18 on page 29. Tell students to match each story with a proverb in Activity 17.

Extra Application and Practice Activity

- Have students invent a new proverb. Suggest that they write a proverb related to something they are familiar with (e.g., sports, music, video games).
- Ask volunteers to share their proverbs with the class and write them on the board. Have students explain the literal meaning of their proverb as well as the advice it gives for life.
- If there is time, allow students to make posters of their own proverbs, and display them in the classroom.

21st Century Technology Literacy

- Allow students to use the internet to search for similar proverbs. Point out that there are several sites with proverbs that can be searched by keywords. Help students compare sites to decide which ones are most useful for finding proverbs to complete the activities in this lesson.

Unit 3   T35

Writing Lesson

Lesson Flow

Warm-up › Lesson Objective › Practice 1 › Practice 2 › Practice 3 › Speaking › Lesson Objective › Homework

Lesson Objectives

I will write a story ending.

Writing | Story ending

I will learn to write a story ending.

15 Look at 5. Work with a partner. Answer the questions about "Marissa Mobley's Dilemma".
1. Who are the characters in "Marissa Mobley's Dilemma"?
2. How does Marissa feel when she gets home from school?
3. Who knocks on Marissa's door?
4. What's Marissa's dilemma?
5. What advice does Marissa's brother give her?
6. At the end of the story on page 31, what do you think Marissa is going to do?

16 How do you think the story ends? Discuss these possible endings with a partner. Think of a reason that makes each one possible.

- Marissa helps Dan cheat.
  Reason: _____

- Marissa tells her teacher about Dan.
  Reason: _____

- Marissa tells Dan she can't help him.
  Reason: _____

- Marissa helps Dan study.
  Reason: _____

17 With your partner, write an ending to the story. Add details, such as how the other story characters react to Marissa's decision and how she feels about it.

18 Share your story ending with another pair. Discuss. Talk about what Marissa did and whether it was the right thing to do.

36 Unit 3

Warm-up

- Have students form a story circle to review the story "Marissa Mobley's Dilemma" on pages 30–31. Have students work together to retell the story, going around the circle. Students should each add a detail or event until they have summarized the story. Encourage students to describe events in time order, but allow them to go back and add important details that were left out.
- Check answers from the HW in the last lesson.

Lesson Objective

INVOLVE

Introduce the lesson objective. Say: *Today I will learn to write a story ending.*

- Students will write an ending for a story and then compare their endings.

Practice 1

15 Look at 5. Work with a partner. Answer questions about "Marissa Mobley's Dilemma".

- Read the directions aloud. Then have students work in pairs to answer the questions.

MONITOR

Check answers as a class. (Answers: 1 Marissa, her mother Mrs. Mobley, her brother Leo, and her classmate Dan. 2 She feels unhappy. 3 Her brother Leo. 4 Whether or not she should help her classmate Dan cheat in the math test. 5 Her brother advises her to talk to her teacher. 6 Student's own answer.)

ASSIST

Have students find phrases in the story on pages 30–31 that answer each question.

Practice 2

16 How do you think the story ends? Discuss these possible endings with a partner. Think of a reason that makes each one possible.

- Read the directions aloud. Say: *Readers are left wondering how the story ends, but there are clues that support different possible endings.* Model the first item: *Marissa might help Dan cheat because she likes him.* Have students complete the activity in pairs by using details from the story.

MONITOR

Check answers as a class. *Have volunteers share the clues they found to support each ending.* (Sample answers: 1 Marissa likes Dan. 2 Leo thinks she should tell her teacher. 3 Marissa is upset, which shows that she doesn't want to cheat. 4 Studying would help Dan without cheating.)

Practice 3

17 With your partner, write an ending to the story. Add details, such as how the other story characters react to Marissa's decision and how she feels about it.

- Read the directions aloud. Suggest that pairs reread the story on pages 30–31 before they write their ending so that they match the tone and style. Remind them to include both descriptions of what happened and dialog.

ASSIST

Have students use verbs in the past simple to say what happened in the story. Provide students with additional vocabulary to complete their stories.

Speaking

18 Share your story ending with another pair. Discuss. Talk about what Marissa did and whether it was the right thing to do.

- Read the directions aloud. Invite pairs to exchange their story endings.

MONITOR

Students can read each other's endings silently or aloud and then discuss what Marissa did in each version. Check correct use of vocabulary and grammar.

21st Century Problem Solving

- Remind students that a dilemma like Marissa's (pages 30–31) is a problem. The ending of the story should say whether Marissa solves her problem. Say: *Most problems can be solved. A good solution takes care of the situation and doesn't cause other problems.* Have students discuss whether or not each ending in Activity 16 causes a new problem for Marissa.

Lesson Objective

INVOLVE

Revisit the lesson objective: *Now I have learned to write a story ending.*

- Encourage awareness of what the students have learned by quickly eliciting how to write a well-written story ending.

Homework WB p. 30/ act. 19, 20, 21, & 22

19 Look at 5. Circle the traits that describe Gary's character in "Gary's Dilemma".

- Direct students to WB Activity 19 on page 30. Tell students to circle the traits that describe Gary from the story in WB Activity 5 on page 24.

20 Complete the sentences about Gary. Include one of the traits you circled in 19 and ideas from the story. Use the ideas in the box or your own ideas.

- Direct students to WB Activity 20 on page 30. Tell students to complete the sentences about Gary using the traits they circled in Activity 19, ideas from the story, the ideas in the box or their own ideas.

21 Think about Gary's character. What does he do the next day? Think about these questions.

- Direct students to WB Activity 21 on page 30. Tell students to think about what Gary does the next day and write short answers to the question.

22 Write an ending to *Gary's Dilemma* in your notebook. Look at 19, 20, and 21 to help you.

- Direct students to WB Activity 22 on page 30. Tell students to write the ending to Gary's Dilemma.

Extra Application and Practice Activity

- Have students vote for their favorite story ending. Ask students to explain the reasons for their votes.

Unit 3 T36

Writing | Story ending

I will learn to write a story ending.

15 Look at 5. Work with a partner. Answer the questions about "Marissa Mobley's Dilemma".

1. Who are the characters in "Marissa Mobley's Dilemma"?
2. How does Marissa feel when she gets home from school?
3. Who knocks on Marissa's door?
4. What's Marissa's dilemma?
5. What advice does Marissa's brother give her?
6. At the end of the story on page 31, what do you think Marissa is going to do?

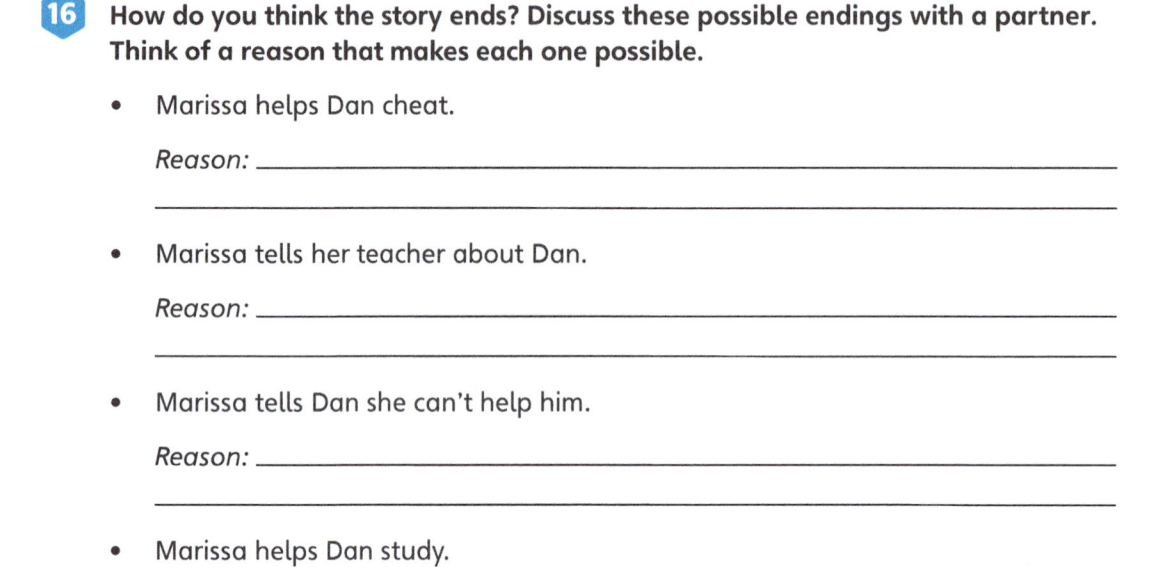

16 How do you think the story ends? Discuss these possible endings with a partner. Think of a reason that makes each one possible.

- Marissa helps Dan cheat.

  Reason: _____
  _____

- Marissa tells her teacher about Dan.

  Reason: _____
  _____

- Marissa tells Dan she can't help him.

  Reason: _____
  _____

- Marissa helps Dan study.

  Reason: _____
  _____

17 With your partner, write an ending to the story. Add details, such as how the other story characters react to Marissa's decision and how she feels about it.

18 Share your story ending with another pair. Discuss. Talk about what Marissa did and whether it was the right thing to do.

Life skills | Do the right thing.

I will learn to talk about the right choice in a dilemma.

19 Read about three situations and three possible courses of action for each one. Which one is the right thing to do? Discuss with a partner.

Situation	#1	#2	#3
You're getting into your mom's car. You see an envelope full of money on the ground.	Tell your mom about it and ask if you can keep the money.	Pick up the money quietly and don't tell your mom about it.	Tell your mom and ask her how you can return the money.
Your teacher gives you the highest mark for your book review and uses it as a model for the rest of the class. Your older sister wrote the book review for you.	Do nothing. Be happy and accept the mark and the compliment.	Tell your teacher you didn't write the review and apologize.	Tell your parents what you did, but don't tell your teacher.
Your teacher goes out of the room during a big test. Your classmate, who's the best student in the class, tries to show you her answers.	Copy your classmate's answers – after all, she offered. It'd be silly to say no.	Compare your answers with hers, but change only a few to match hers.	Tell your classmate, "No, thank you."

Project

20 Make a page to go in a class handbook about doing the right thing.

1 Choose a dilemma from the unit or use one of your own. Describe it at the top of the page.
2 Write three possible courses of action.
3 Use a picture from a magazine or draw one to show the right thing to do.
4 Present your page to the class. Read it aloud. Then say what you think the right thing to do is.
5 Bind the pages together to make a class handbook.

Dilemma: You're at a park. You see a man sitting on a bench with a tablet. He leaves the park, and you notice he's left his tablet on the bench. You've always wanted one, but you don't have enough money to buy one. What should you do?

1 Sit on the bench and cover the tablet so no one sees it.
2 Don't say anything but hold onto the tablet in case the man comes back for it. Secretly hope he doesn't!
3 Run after the man and return the tablet to him.

I think she should run after the man and return the tablet to him. If she doesn't, she'll feel terrible later.

Life Skills Lesson

Lesson Flow

Warm-up › Lesson Objective › Speaking › Project › Lesson Objective

Lesson Objective

I will learn to talk about the right choice in a dilemma.

Life skills | Do the right thing.

I will learn to talk about the right choice in a dilemma.

19 Read about three situations and three possible courses of action for each one. Which one is the right thing to do? Discuss with a partner.

Situation	#1	#2	#3
You're getting into your mom's car. You see an envelope full of money on the ground.	Tell your mom about it and ask if you can keep the money.	Pick up the money quietly and don't tell your mom about it.	Tell your mom and ask her how you can return the money.
Your teacher gives you the highest mark for your book review and uses it as a model for the rest of the class. Your older sister wrote the book review for you.	Do nothing. Be happy and accept the mark and the compliment.	Tell your teacher you didn't write the review and apologize.	Tell your parents what you did, but don't tell your teacher.
Your teacher goes out of the room during a big test. Your classmate, who's the best student in the class, tries to show you her answers.	Copy your classmate's answers – after all, she offered. It'd be silly to say no.	Compare your answers with hers, but change only a few to match hers.	Tell your classmate, "No, thank you."

Project

20 Make a page to go in a class handbook about doing the right thing.

1. Choose a dilemma from the unit or use one of your own. Describe it at the top of the page.
2. Write three possible courses of action.
3. Use a picture from a magazine or draw one to show the right thing to do.
4. Present your page to the class. Read it aloud. Then say what you think the right thing to do is.
5. Bind the pages together to make a class handbook.

Dilemma: You're at a park. You see a man sitting on a bench with a tablet. He leaves the park, and you notice he's left his tablet on the bench. You've always wanted one, but you don't have enough money to buy one. What should you do?

1. Sit on the bench and cover the tablet so no one sees it.
2. Don't say anything but hold onto the tablet in case the man comes back for it. Secretly hope he doesn't!
3. Run after the man and return the tablet to him.

> I think she should run after the man and return the tablet to him. If she doesn't, she'll feel terrible later.

Warm-up

- Have students review useful opposites. Say: *Right and wrong are opposites.* Then write these ten words on the board: *bad, decline, fair, find, foolish, guilty, happy, honest, possible, take.* Challenge students to write down opposites for each word within a one-minute time limit. Give them one point for each correct opposite. (Sample answers: *good, accept, unfair, lose, smart, innocent, sad, dishonest, impossible, give*)
- Check answers from the HW in the last lesson.

Lesson Objective

INVOLVE

Introduce the lesson objective. Say: *Today I will learn to talk about the right choice in a dilemma.*

- Students will talk about doing the right thing in different situations. Then they'll create pages for a class handbook about doing the right thing.

Speaking

19 Read about three situations and three possible courses of action for each one. Which one is the right thing to do? Discuss with a partner.

- Read the page title and directions aloud. Have volunteers read each situation aloud. Say: *A course of action involves a choice you make.*
- Have students work in pairs to discuss the situations. Suggest that they begin by reading aloud the three courses of action for each situation. Students might start by eliminating one course of action that they think is clearly wrong and then discuss which of the remaining choices is better.

MONITOR

Check that students choose and defend a specific course of action. Take a class poll to find out which courses of action were most popular. Remind students that not everyone always agrees about what is the right thing to do in a situation.

ASSIST

Try to use simple language to explain unfamiliar words. Say: *To accept means to say "yes." To decline means to say "no."*

Project

Materials: Magazines, newspapers and construction paper

20 Make a page to go in a class handbook about doing the right thing.

- Read the directions and steps aloud. Allow students to draw their illustration or to cut out a picture from a newspaper or magazine and glue it to the page.
- Have students complete the activity independently. Then have them collaborate and review one another's work before deciding on the best way to organize their handbook and a title for it.

Class Handbook: When students are ready to complete Activity 20, distribute construction paper with holes punched along one side. Allow students to use as many pages as they need for their descriptions of dilemmas, the three courses of action, and their solutions. Help them bind the pages with string or ribbon.

MONITOR

Check that students' pages depict a dilemma clearly, give three possible courses of action, and say which one is best. Students might illustrate the best thing to do on the back of their pages. In this way, others can make their own decision and compare.

ASSIST

Encourage students to review dilemmas from the unit and to scan magazines and newspapers for dilemmas, before choosing one to write about.

21st Century Collaboration

- Remind students to include dilemmas that are relevant to their own lives and their friends' and families' lives. In this way, they can ask them for ideas about how they would solve the dilemmas, too.

Lesson Objective

INVOLVE

Revisit the lesson objective: *Now I have learned to talk about the right choice in a dilemma.*

- Encourage awareness of what the students have learned by quickly eliciting what they remember about their partner's opinion in Activity 19.

Extra Application and Practice Activity

- Have students share the class handbook with another class, with friends, or with family members.

Listening and Speaking Lesson

Lesson Flow

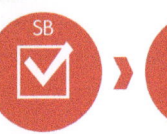

Warm-up › Lesson Objective › Presentation › Practice 1 › Practice 2 › Speaking › Lesson Objective

Lesson Objectives

I will review the sounds *nch*, *nth*, and *mpt*.

I will learn to talk about doing the right thing.

Listening and Speaking

I will review the sounds *nch*, *nth*, and *mpt*.
I will learn to talk about doing the right thing.

21 (48) Listen, read, and repeat.

1. nch   2. nth   3. mpt

22 (49) Listen and blend the sounds.

1. l-u-nch — lunch
2. t-e-nth — tenth
3. p-r-o-mpt — prompt
4. c-r-u-nch — crunch
5. m-o-nth — month
6. t-e-mpt — tempt

23 (50) Listen and chant.

I make lunch
On the tenth of the month,
An apple and chips.
Do you want any candy?
Don't tempt me!
Crunch! Crunch!

Packed lunch

24 Work in groups of three. Choose a situation from the box or create your own. Students 1 and 2 role-play the situation. Student 3 states the right thing to do.

"Oh, no! My ball's just broken the window of that house!"

"If you break something, you should tell the owner."

"You should go up to the front door and talk to the owner."

You:
- lose your friend's CD.
- see someone cheat in a test.
- spill juice on your friend's new shirt.
- see a man drop his wallet.
- break your friend's cell phone.
- are asked to lie for your brother/sister.
- break a window at home.
- forget Mother's Day.

38   Unit 3

Warm-up

- Have students play *Rhyme Time* (see *Game Bank*, page T136, for details) to review key vocabulary. Students should take turns choosing a vocabulary word and then giving a word that rhymes with it. Classmates should try to guess the vocabulary word. Say: *Remember that words in Unit 3 are about dilemmas, results, and consequences.* Model: *My clue is seat. The secret word is cheat.*

Lesson Objective

INVOLVE
Introduce the lesson objective. Say: *Today I will learn to use the sounds* nch, nth, *and* mpt, *and talk about doing the right thing.*

- Students will identify the letters and distinguish between the sounds *nch, nth,* and *mpt,* individually and as part of words. Then they will review dilemmas and consequences.

Presentation

21 Listen, read, and repeat.

- Read the directions aloud. Play Audio Track 48 and have students listen and point to each sound as it is said. Have students repeat.

MONITOR
As students repeat, check they are pointing to the correct sound and listen for correct pronunciation.

Practice 1

22 Listen and blend the sounds.

- Read the directions aloud. Play Audio Track 49 and have students listen and point to each item as it is sounded out and blended on the audio. Have them repeat after each item.

MONITOR
As students repeat, check they are pointing to the correct word and listen for correct pronunciation and appropriate intonation.

ASSIST
Replay the audio as needed.

Practice 2

23 Listen and chant.

- Read the directions aloud. Read the chant while students follow in their books.
- Play Audio Track 50 and have students listen. Replay the audio several times and encourage them to join in.

MONITOR
As students repeat the chant, listen for proper pronunciation, appropriate intonation, and correct use of language.

Speaking

24 Work in groups of three. Choose a situation from the box or create your own. Students 1 and 2 role-play the situation. Student 3 states the right thing to do.

- Read the directions aloud. Invite volunteers to role-play a conversation about one situation and to state the right thing to do.
- Have students work in groups to complete the activity.

MONITOR
Check that students form conditional statements correctly.

ASSIST
Write this sentence frame on the board: *If... , you should... .* For a situation about cheating, model: *If you see someone cheating, you should tell the teacher.*

21st Century Social Skills

- Explain that using a conditional sentence with *should* is a polite way to give advice. Have students compare two pieces of advice. Say: *(1) If you walk a dog, you should always clean up after it. (2) You're walking a dog? You have to clean up after it!* Ask: *Which advice sounds more friendly? Why?* (The first piece of advice is more friendly.) Encourage students to role-play friendly and less friendly ways to give advice in each situation from this lesson.

Lesson Objective

INVOLVE
Revisit the lesson objective: *Now I have learned to use the sounds* nch, nth, *and* mpt, *and talked about doing the right thing.*

- Encourage awareness of what the students have learned by quickly eliciting the words from the lesson with the sounds *nch, nth,* and *mpt.*

Extra Application and Practice Activity

Materials: Index cards, envelopes or paper clips

- Have students create scrambled sentences for conditional sentences from the lesson. Students should choose conditional sentences and write one word from each on an index card. They should then mix the cards up and place them in an envelope or clip them together. Have students switch card sets and try to rearrange the words to form each original sentence. Point out that card sets may form more than one accurate sentence.

Listening and Speaking

I will review the sounds *nch*, *nth*, and *mpt*.
I will learn to talk about doing the right thing.

21 Listen, read, and repeat.

1. nch   2. nth   3. mpt

22 Listen and blend the sounds.

1. l-u-nch   lunch
2. t-e-nth   tenth
3. p-r-o-mpt   prompt
4. c-r-u-nch   crunch
5. m-o-nth   month
6. t-e-mpt   tempt

23 Listen and chant.

I make lunch
On the tenth of the month,
An apple and chips.
Do you want any candy?
Don't tempt me!
Crunch! Crunch!

Packed lunch

24 Work in groups of three. Choose a situation from the box or create your own. Students 1 and 2 role-play the situation. Student 3 states the right thing to do.

Oh, no! My ball's just broken the window of that house!

If you break something, you should tell the owner.

You should go up to the front door and talk to the owner.

You:
- lose your friend's CD.
- see someone cheat in a test.
- spill juice on your friend's new shirt.
- see a man drop his wallet.
- break your friend's cell phone.
- are asked to lie for your brother/sister.
- break a window at home.
- forget Mother's Day.

38   Unit 3

Review

25 Complete the sentences with expressions from the box.

| be upset with | feel good about | feel guilty (3x) | get into trouble |

1 Claudia saw a man drop his wallet. When she picked it up, she saw that there was a lot of money in it. She was tempted to keep it, but she knew that wasn't right. She thought about what to do. By the time she decided to return the man's wallet, he was gone. Claudia _____. She _____ herself for not deciding quickly enough.

2 Anna saw two classmates looking at each other's papers during an exam. She didn't know what to do. She knew it was wrong to cheat, but she didn't want her friends to _____.
Anna _____ about not saying anything.

3 Mike was at a toy store and was holding a robot when he accidentally broke it. He didn't have the money to pay for the toy, so he put it back on the shelf and quickly left the shop. Michael _____. He didn't _____ what he did.

26 Read the problems in 25 again. Choose one. In your notebook, write what you think the person should have done.

27 Complete the sentences with the correct form of *will* and the verb in parentheses.

1 (tell) If you _____ her the truth, she _____ believe you.

2 (not return) If they _____ his wallet, he _____ get lunch.

3 (cheat) If she _____ in the test, she _____ get a good grade.

4 (promise) If I _____ to do something, I _____ do it!

I Can

- use words related to dilemmas and consequences.
- use conditional sentences.
- give advice using *should*.
- write a story ending.

Unit 3 39

Review Lesson

Lesson Flow

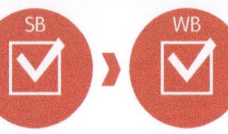

Warm-up › Lesson Objective › Practice 1 (SB) › Practice 2 (WB) › Practice 3 (SB) › Practice 4 (SB) › Self-assessment › Homework

Lesson Objective

To review the words and structures of the unit.

Review

25 Complete the sentences with expressions from the box.

> be upset with   feel good about   feel guilty (3x)   get into trouble

1. Claudia saw a man drop his wallet. When she picked it up, she saw that there was a lot of money in it. She was tempted to keep it, but she knew that wasn't right. She thought about what to do. By the time she decided to return the man's wallet, he was gone. Claudia _____. She _____ herself for not deciding quickly enough.

2. Anna saw two classmates looking at each other's papers during an exam. She didn't know what to do. She knew it was wrong to cheat, but she didn't want her friends to _____.
Anna _____ about not saying anything.

3. Mike was at a toy store and was holding a robot when he accidentally broke it. He didn't have the money to pay for the toy, so he put it back on the shelf and quickly left the shop. Michael _____. He didn't _____ what he did.

26 Read the problems in 25 again. Choose one. In your notebook, write what you think the person should have done.

27 Complete the sentences with the correct form of *will* and the verb in parentheses.

1. (tell) If you _____ her the truth, she _____ believe you.
2. (not return) If they _____ his wallet, he _____ get lunch.
3. (cheat) If she _____ in the test, she _____ get a good grade.
4. (promise) If I _____ to do something, I _____ do it!

Unit 3 **39**

Warm-up

- Draw a two-column chart on the board with the following headings: *Times You Feel Guilty* and *Times You Feel Upset*. Ask volunteers to share times when people might feel these emotions (or when they have felt these emotions themselves). Use these ideas to discuss the meanings of *guilty* and *upset*.
- Check answers from the HW in the last lesson.

Lesson Objective

INVOLVE

Introduce the lesson objective. Say: *Today I will review the words and structures of the unit.*

- Students will review the vocabulary and grammar they learned in Unit 3.
- Then students will complete the *I Can* section, which helps them to assess their own learning and reflect on their progress.

S39 Unit 3

Practice 1

25 Complete the sentences with expressions from the box.

- Read the directions aloud. Have students complete the activity independently.

MONITOR

Check answers as a class. *(Answers: 1 felt guilty, was upset with; 2 get into trouble, felt guilty; 3 felt guilty, feel good about)*

Practice 2 WB p. 31/ act. 23

23 Match the expressions with the situations. Write the letters.

- Read the directions aloud. Explain to students that they need to match each expression with the correct situation.
- Have students work independently.
- Have students compare answers with a partner, then check answers as a class.

Practice 3

26 Read the problems in 25 again. Choose one. In your notebook, write what you think the person should have done.

- Read the directions aloud. Have students complete the activity independently.

MONITOR

Have volunteers share their advice with the class. Check that they used the target vocabulary and grammar correctly. *(Sample answers: Claudia should have returned the wallet earlier. Anna should have told her teacher what she saw. Michael should have gone back to the store and admitted what he did.)*

Practice 4

27 Complete the sentences with the correct form of *will* and the verb in parentheses.

- Read the directions aloud. Have students complete the activity independently.

MONITOR

Check answers by having students read the completed sentences aloud. *(Answers: 1 tell, will; 2 don't return, won't; 3 cheats, won't; 4 promise, will)*

ASSIST

Say: *You will use* will *once in each sentence. The word in parentheses should agree with its subject.*

CHALLENGE

Remind students that conditional sentences can begin or end with an *if* clause. Have students reverse the order of each sentence. Model: *If others tease my friend, I will be kind to him.*

Self-assessment

I Can

- This section asks students to assess their own learning and reflect on their progress. Help students appreciate their progress. Say: *The* I Can *statements show what you have learned in this unit.*
- Read the statements aloud. Explain that students should think about how well they know the language in the unit and should color in the stars. They should color three stars if they feel the unit was easy, two stars if they need some help, and one star if the unit was hard and they need more help. Have students work independently.

Suggestions for Remediation

Assessment Pack

- Direct students who need help with grammar and vocabulary to the Unit 3 Practice Tests in the Assessment Pack.

WB Unit 3/ p. 110

- Direct students who need help with grammar in particular to the Unit 3 Extra Grammar Practice (Workbook, page 100).
- For further vocabulary work, students can access games in the Big English Student World.

Homework WB p. 31/ act. 24

24 Write what will happen. Use *will* and the words in parentheses.

- Direct students to WB Activity 24 on page 31. Explain to students that they have to look at each situation and write what they think will happen.

Extra Application and Practice Activity

21st Century Problem Solving

- Make a list of all of the advice students gave for each situation. Then have students vote to see which advice they think is the best.

Assessment Pack

- To assess student progress at the end of the unit, have students complete the Unit 3 Unit Test in the Assessment Pack.
- To assess whether students have reached the listening and speaking targets for this unit, carry out the Unit 3 Oral Assessment in the Assessment Pack.
- Arrange one-to-one sessions with each student and use the prompts to evaluate their listening and speaking abilities.

Checkpoint 1–3 Lesson 1

Lesson Flow

Warm-up › Lesson Objective › Self-assessment › Practice

Lesson Objective

To think about how well I can use what I have learned in Units 1–3.

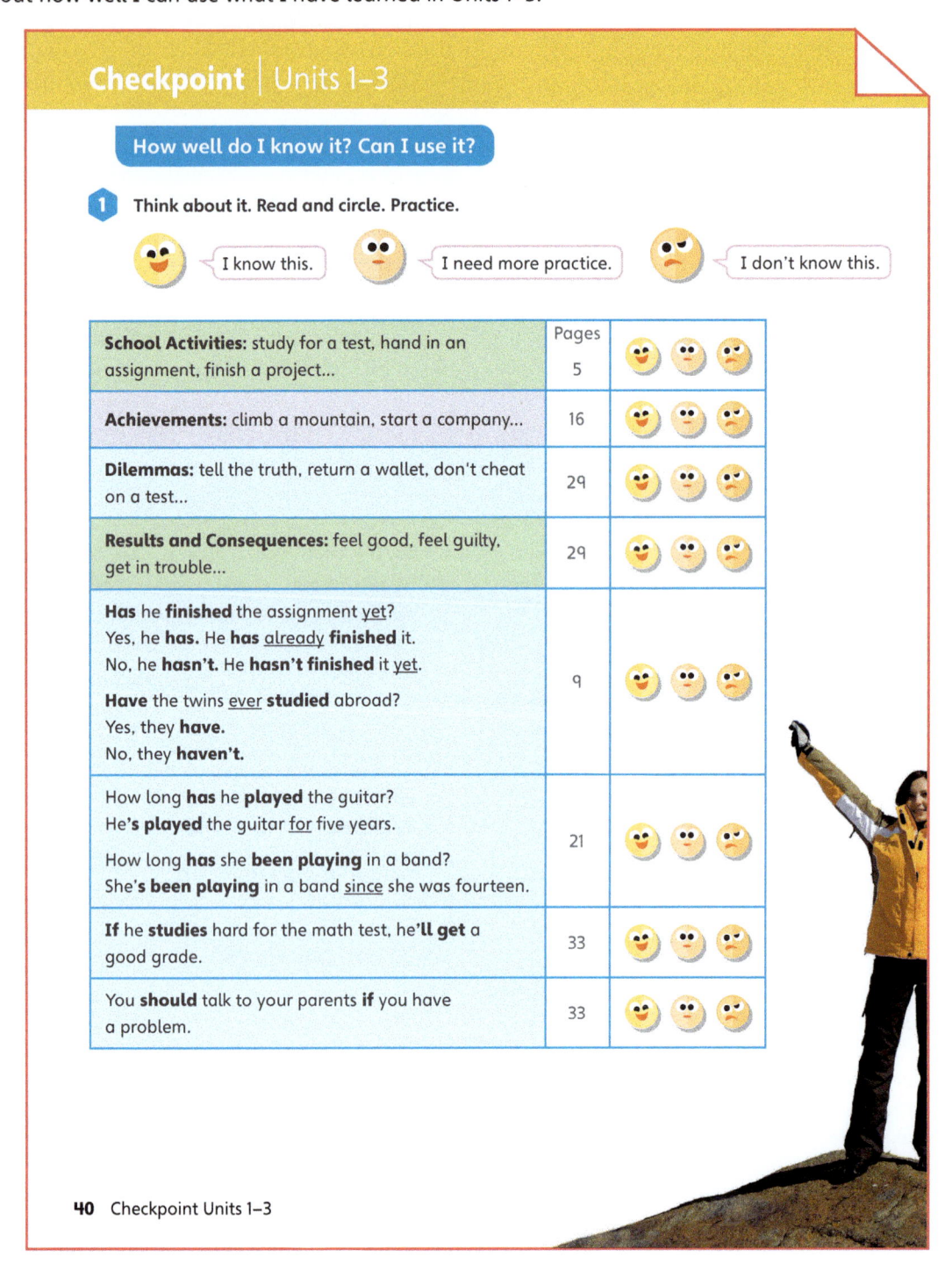

Checkpoint | Units 1–3

How well do I know it? Can I use it?

1 Think about it. Read and circle. Practice.

😊 I know this.   😐 I need more practice.   😠 I don't know this.

	Pages			
School Activities: study for a test, hand in an assignment, finish a project...	5	😊	😐	😠
Achievements: climb a mountain, start a company...	16	😊	😐	😠
Dilemmas: tell the truth, return a wallet, don't cheat on a test...	29	😊	😐	😠
Results and Consequences: feel good, feel guilty, get in trouble...	29	😊	😐	😠
Has he **finished** the assignment <u>yet</u>? Yes, he **has**. He **has** <u>already</u> **finished** it. No, he **hasn't**. He **hasn't finished** it <u>yet</u>. **Have** the twins **ever studied** abroad? Yes, they **have**. No, they **haven't**.	9	😊	😐	😠
How long **has** he **played** the guitar? He**'s played** the guitar <u>for</u> five years. How long **has** she **been playing** in a band? She**'s been playing** in a band <u>since</u> she was fourteen.	21	😊	😐	😠
If he **studies** hard for the math test, he**'ll get** a good grade.	33	😊	😐	😠
You **should** talk to your parents **if** you have a problem.	33	😊	😐	😠

40 Checkpoint Units 1–3

Warm-up

Materials: Index cards

- Have students play *Word Clues* to review key vocabulary from Units 1–3. (See *Game Bank*, page T137, for details.) Partners should write words or phrases on index cards. Players then take turns choosing a word and giving one-word clues until their partner guesses the word. Model: *test, assignment, project (school activities)*.

Lesson Objective

INVOLVE
- Introduce the lesson objective: *Today I will think about how well I can use what I have learned in Units 1–3.*
- Students will review key language in Units 1–3.

Self-assessment

1 Think about it. Read and circle. Practice.
- Read the descriptions aloud as students point to the face icons at the top of the page. Have them use markers or colored pencils to complete the checklist. They will choose a different color when they review this list at the end of the Checkpoint.

MONITOR
- Follow the suggestions below to review the key language in these units. Listen for correct use of vocabulary and grammar. Remind students that they will be asked to assess their own abilities.

ASSIST
- Encourage students to turn to the page references in the checklist when they need additional support or to refresh their memories.

21st Century Self-Direction
- Remind students that there are no right or wrong answers on the checklist. Emphasize that they should circle the face that shows how they feel about their progress with each skill. Say: *This page will help us find out what you know well and what you should continue to study.*

School Activities (page 5)
Have groups create a school timeline for a fictional student. Encourage them to include things the student does on each day of the week.

Achievements (page 16)
Ask: *What are three things you would like to do before you are twenty?* Have students write and compare their lists.

Dilemmas (page 29)
Ask: *What is a dilemma?* (a difficult situation in which you must make a hard choice) Have students give examples of dilemmas and challenge others to say what they would do in each situation.

Results and Consequences (page 29)
Have students describe possible consequences of courses of action taken to resolve dilemmas. Ask: *What will happen if you take that course of action? How will you feel if you make that choice?*

Has he finished the assignment yet? Yes, he has. / No, he hasn't. (page 9)
Have students complete these sentence frames: *Has he…? Has she…? Have they…?* Then have them write answers.

He's played for… / He's played since… (page 21)
Ask: *What is something you have done for a long time? How long have you done it?* Then have classmates report each other's answers. Model: *Jin has played soccer for five years.* Remind students they should use the progressive form when they wish to emphasize the duration of an activity. Model: *I have been waiting in line for concert tickets for two hours!*

If he studies, he'll get… / You should study… (page 33)
Challenge students to use *if* in a sentence. Say: *You can write a conditional sentence or give advice.* Model: *If you help me with English, I will help you with math. You should read the newspaper if you want to find out what is happening.*

Practice WB pp. 32 & 33 / act. 1, 2, & 3

1 Unscramble the words. Complete the phrases.
- Direct students to WB Activity 1 on page 32. Read the directions aloud. Ask the students to unscramble the word in each box, and then use the words to complete the phrases.

2 Find a song that makes you think about school days, goals, or dilemmas. Complete the chart.
- Direct students to WB Activity 2 on page 33. Read the directions aloud. Students choose a song that makes them think, and then answer the questions about it.

3 Draw pictures to illustrate your song. Then write the story of your song on a separate piece of paper.
- Direct students to WB Activity 3 on page 33. Read the directions aloud. Students draw pictures about the song. They should use their answers in WB Activity 2 for ideas. They then use the same answers to write a story about the song. It could be about how it makes them feel and why, or the story of the song itself.

Checkpoint 1–3 Lesson 2

Lesson Flow

Warm-up › Lesson Objective › Pre-listening › Listening › Practice 1 › Practice 2

Lesson Objective

To put together what I have learned in Units 1–3.

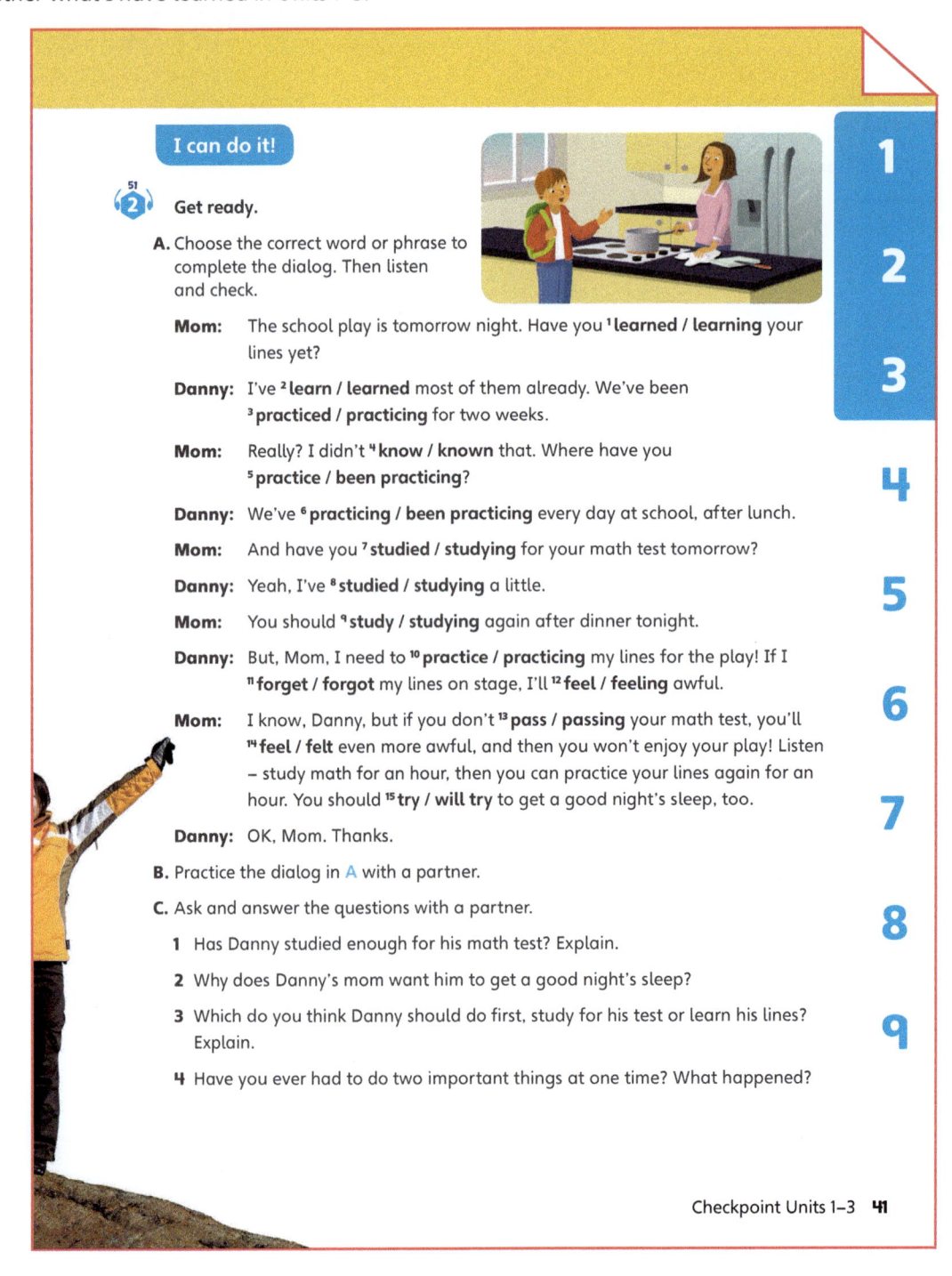

I can do it!

🔊 2 Get ready.

A. Choose the correct word or phrase to complete the dialog. Then listen and check.

Mom: The school play is tomorrow night. Have you ¹**learned / learning** your lines yet?

Danny: I've ²**learn / learned** most of them already. We've been ³**practiced / practicing** for two weeks.

Mom: Really? I didn't ⁴**know / known** that. Where have you ⁵**practice / been practicing**?

Danny: We've ⁶**practicing / been practicing** every day at school, after lunch.

Mom: And have you ⁷**studied / studying** for your math test tomorrow?

Danny: Yeah, I've ⁸**studied / studying** a little.

Mom: You should ⁹**study / studying** again after dinner tonight.

Danny: But, Mom, I need to ¹⁰**practice / practicing** my lines for the play! If I ¹¹**forget / forgot** my lines on stage, I'll ¹²**feel / feeling** awful.

Mom: I know, Danny, but if you don't ¹³**pass / passing** your math test, you'll ¹⁴**feel / felt** even more awful, and then you won't enjoy your play! Listen – study math for an hour, then you can practice your lines again for an hour. You should ¹⁵**try / will try** to get a good night's sleep, too.

Danny: OK, Mom. Thanks.

B. Practice the dialog in A with a partner.

C. Ask and answer the questions with a partner.

1. Has Danny studied enough for his math test? Explain.
2. Why does Danny's mom want him to get a good night's sleep?
3. Which do you think Danny should do first, study for his test or learn his lines? Explain.
4. Have you ever had to do two important things at one time? What happened?

Warm-up

Materials: Newspapers and magazines

- Have students review verb forms by scanning newspapers and magazines for examples of these forms: present, present perfect, present perfect progressive, past, future. Invite volunteers to read sentences aloud, leaving out the main verb in the sentence. Listeners can try to guess the verb that completes the sentence.

- You may wish to have students review forms for verbs that will be used in this activity: *feel, forget, know, learn, pass, practice, study, try*. Name a verb and have volunteers give other forms.

Lesson Objective

INVOLVE

Introduce the Lesson Objective: *Today I will put together what I have learned in Units 1–3.*

- Students will complete and practice a dialog. Then they will share ideas with a partner.

Pre-listening

- Read the directions and dialog names aloud.
- Tell students they will listen to Danny and his mother talking about a school play and his homework.

Listening

2 Get ready.

A Choose the correct word or phrase to complete the dialog. Then listen and check.

- Do the first one as a class. Have students read aloud Mom's question, completing it with the correct choice: *Have you* learned *your lines yet?*
- Have students complete the dialog independently. Remind them that reading aloud as they work can help them find the correct verb forms.

MONITOR

Play Audio Track 51 twice. First, have students focus on listening comprehension. Then have them check to see if they wrote the correct verb forms. *(Answers: 1 learned, 2 learned, 3 practicing, 4 know, 5 been practicing, 6 been practicing, 7 studied, 8 studied, 9 study, 10 practice, 11 forget, 12 feel, 13 pass, 14 feel, 15 try)*

ASSIST

Play the audio for students. You could also suggest that they circle clue words that help them decide which verb form to choose. For example, they can circle *yet*, which goes with a past participle form, or *been*, which is followed by an *-ing* form.

Practice 1

B Practice the dialog in A with a partner.

- Read the directions aloud and invite students to practice the dialog. Encourage students to change roles to review all of the unit language.

MONITOR

Listen for correct pronunciation, intonation, and use of language as students practice the dialog.

21st Century Cross-Cultural Skills

Allow students to record their dialogs using smartphones. Remind them to rehearse the dialog several times. Suggest that they create a reader's script by copying the page and using a colored pencil to circle words they should emphasize and add arrows to indicate strong up or down intonations. Remind students to speak clearly during taping, and then review their recordings to monitor their own language production.

Practice 2

C Ask and answer the questions with a partner.

- Read the directions aloud. Have student pairs ask and answer questions about Danny's situation, and compare it with their own experiences.

MONITOR

Have students share their responses with the class. Encourage volunteers to share dilemmas that they have faced similar to Danny's situation. Listen for correct use of language.

ASSIST

Have students complete these sentences to discuss Danny's dilemma: *Danny should study for his test if he wants to… . Danny should learn his lines if he wants to… .*

- Remind students that irregular verbs do not follow the rules for forming past or past participle forms. Write *forget, forgot, forgotten* on the board. Ask: *Why is this verb irregular?* (It does not add *-ed* for the past or the past participle.) Have students give the forms for other verbs that change spelling in the past and have past participles that end with *-n*: *give (gave/given), know (knew/known), get (got/gotten), grow (grew/grown), ride (rode/ridden), see (saw/seen), write (wrote/written).*

Checkpoint 1-3 Lesson 3

Lesson Flow

Warm-up › Lesson Objective › Speaking

Lesson Objective

To put together what I have learned in Units 1–3.

Checkpoint | Units 1–3

3 Get set.

STEP 1 Cut out the cards on page 133.

STEP 2 Lay out all the cards on your desk.
Now you're ready to **Go**!

4 Go!

A. Work with a partner. Look at the questions. You will use them to create two dialogs.

B. Create the first dialog. Student A reads these questions and Student B chooses five responses from the cutouts. Read the dialog aloud.

C. Switch roles and create the second dialog. The new Student A reads these questions, and the new Student B answers the questions with the remaining cutouts.

Student A
1 Have you chosen the topic of your project yet?
2 Why did you choose that topic?
3 What do you need to do for the project?
4 Have you already started the project?
5 Do you need to buy anything for the project?

Have you chosen the topic of your project yet?

Yes, I want to do a project about the solar system.

D. Now make up your own dialog using the hints below. Role-play your dialog in front of another pair.

Student A	Student B
You're the mom or dad of Student B. You want to know all about your son or daughter's project.	You're doing a project on a topic that you're really interested in. You've already started the project, but you haven't finished yet.

42 Checkpoint Units 1–3

Warm-up

3 Get set.

- Have students preview the dialog cards on page 133. Say: *You will use these cards to create two dialogs. Both dialogs will be about school projects. One project is about the solar system. The other project is about an artist.* Have students read the cards aloud and ask questions about any unfamiliar vocabulary.
- Read the directions and steps aloud. Have students cut out and display the cards.

Lesson Objective

INVOLVE

Introduce the Lesson Objective: *Today I will put together what I have learned in Units 1–3.*

- Students will organize two dialogs. Then they will act out a dialog of their own based on a new situation.

Speaking

4 Go!

A Work with a partner. Look at the questions. You will use them to create two dialogs.

- Read the directions aloud. Have partners work together to create the first dialog. Say: *The first dialog is about a solar system project. The solar system includes our sun, eight planets, and their moons.*

B Create the first dialog. Student A reads these questions and Student B chooses five responses from the cutouts. Read the dialog aloud.

- Have pairs work together to complete their dialogs.

C Switch roles and create the second dialog. The new Student A reads these questions, and the new Student B answers the questions with the remaining cutouts.

- Have two volunteers read the sample dialog in the speech bubbles.

MONITOR

Check that they formed two logical dialogs.

Sample Dialog 1

1 Have you chosen the topic of your project yet? Yes, I want to do a project about the solar system.

2 Why did you choose that topic? I've been studying about the solar system in school, and I like it.

3 What do you need to do for the project? I need to build a model of the solar system and write a report about it.

4 Have you already started the project? Yes, I've written my report, but I haven't built the model yet.

5 Do you need to buy anything for the project? I need to buy some glue so I can finish my model.

Sample Dialog 2

1 Have you chosen the topic of your project yet? Yes, I want to do a project about Pablo Picasso.

2 Why did you choose that topic? I've been studying about him in art class, and I like his paintings.

3 What do you need to do for the project? I need to write a report about him and make a big poster to show some of his art.

4 Have you already started the project? No, I haven't. I'm going to start looking at some websites about him on the Internet.

5 Do you need to buy anything for the project? Yes, I need to get some ink for our printer. I need to print out some of his paintings.

ASSIST

Help students sort the answers into two dialogs: one about the solar system project and the other about the Pablo Picasso project.

- Have pairs practice their dialog.

D Now make up your own dialog using the hints below. Role-play your dialog in front of another pair.

- Invite students to create their own dialogs. Read the directions and dialog descriptions aloud.

21st Century Collaboration

- Remind students that ideas from all members create a better dialog. Point out that students can contribute ideas for both parts.

MONITOR

Have students share their new dialogs with the class. Listen for correct grammar, vocabulary, and use of language.

ASSIST

Have students reorder the questions in C and change the answers.

Checkpoint 1–3 Lesson 4

Lesson Flow

Warm-up › Lesson Objective › Practice › Video › Self-assessment 1 › Self-assessment 2

Lesson Objective

To think about how well I can use what I have learned in Units 1–3.

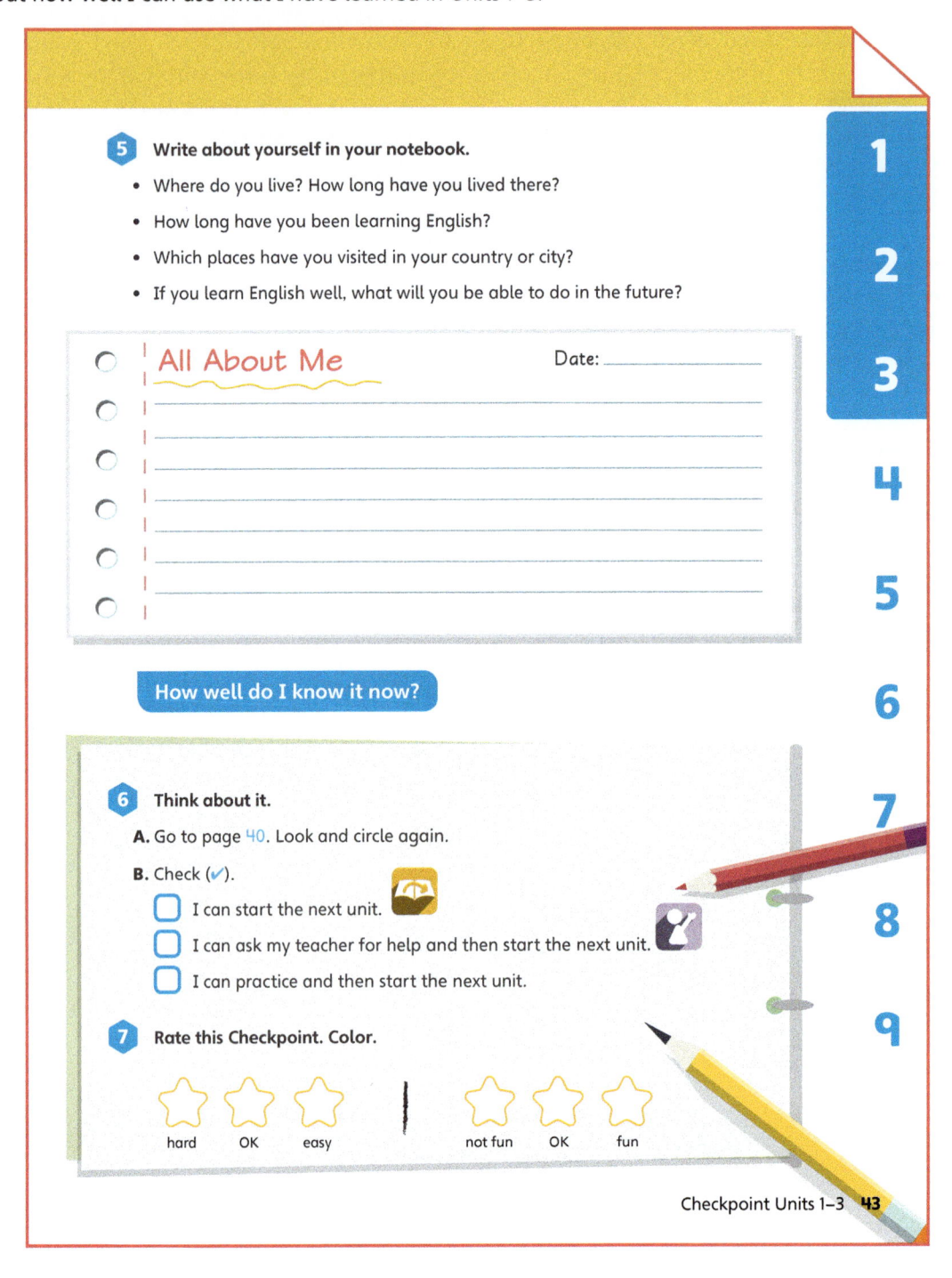

5 Write about yourself in your notebook.
- Where do you live? How long have you lived there?
- How long have you been learning English?
- Which places have you visited in your country or city?
- If you learn English well, what will you be able to do in the future?

All About Me   Date: _____

How well do I know it now?

6 Think about it.
A. Go to page 40. Look and circle again.
B. Check (✔).
- ☐ I can start the next unit.
- ☐ I can ask my teacher for help and then start the next unit.
- ☐ I can practice and then start the next unit.

7 Rate this Checkpoint. Color.

☆ ☆ ☆ | ☆ ☆ ☆
hard OK easy   not fun OK fun

Checkpoint Units 1–3   43

S43 Checkpoint Units 1–3

Warm-up

- Write this jumble on the board: *A J L N O R U*. Challenge students to find and define the scrambled word. (*JOURNAL*; sample definition: a written record of your personal experiences) Point out that the word *journal* comes from an Old French word that means "day." Ask: *How is the word* day *related to a journal?* (Many people write in a journal every day; they write about everyday experiences.) Invite students to share their experiences with writing journals.

- Point out that writing a journal can be helpful in two ways. Say: *You can learn from your own ideas by writing them down. You can also look back at an old journal and remember what you were thinking. Writing a journal is like taking a photograph of your thoughts.*

Lesson Objective

INVOLVE

- Introduce the lesson objective: *Today I will think about how well I can use what I have learned in Units 1–3.*

- Students will write about famous places and the world of entertainment. Then they will look back at Units 1–3 and think about how well they can use what they have learned.

Practice

5 Write about yourself in your notebook.

- Read the directions, questions, and journal title aloud.
- Have students begin by writing today's date. Then have them write answers to the questions. Encourage students to write at least one answer to each question. Provide students with additional journal pages as needed.

MONITOR

- Check students' work for correct use of language.
- Invite students to read aloud their *All About Me* entries and compare them with their classmates' entries.

Video Drama U 1–3

- Refer to the Video Guide for pre-watching and post-watching activities.

Self-assessment 1

6 Think about it.

A Go to page 40. Look and circle again.

- Read the directions aloud.

21st Century Self-Direction

- Have students turn to page 40 and think about each of the checklist items again. Remind students to take their time to think about each item carefully. Suggest that they read each item aloud and look back to the pages given as they review their skills.
- Make sure that students use a different colored pencil or marker as they reassess their understanding and use of each checklist item.

B Check (✓).

- Say: *Now choose the statement that describes how you feel about Units 1–3.* Students can use the "Read and circle" exercise on page 40 to help them choose a response. If they circled ten to twelve smiling faces, they can start the next unit with confidence. If they circled fewer than ten smiling faces, they should probably check one of the other choices.

Self-assessment 2

7 Rate this Checkpoint. Color.

- Read the directions aloud. Point out that students will color only one star in each section. Say: *First, you will say if the Checkpoint was easy, OK, or hard. Then you will say if it was fun, OK, or not fun.*
- Have students complete the rating individually.

Using Checkpoint Evaluations: Student evaluations of the Checkpoint (*easy/hard, fun/not fun*) can give you insight into students' reactions to classroom activities. Review their answers to help you engage and motivate them as they continue to review Units 1–3 and move on to the next units. Consider whether students require additional assistance, deeper challenges, or more inspiring activities.

4 Dreams for the Future

Objectives

Reading

- Can understand short school-related messages in emails, text messages, and social media posts.
- Can distinguish between fact and opinion in a simple text.
- Can draw simple conclusions about the information given in a factual text on a familiar topic.

Listening

- Can understand the main information in short, simple dialogs about familiar activities, if spoken slowly and clearly.
- Can identify clearly stated opinions in extended, informal conversations on matters of personal interest, if the speakers use clear standard speech.

Speaking

- Can make simple predictions about the future, given a model.

Writing

- Can write short, simple personal emails/letters describing future plans, given prompts or a model.

Grammar

- Can use the future continuous with reference to actions in progress at a specific time in the future.

Unit Projects

Family Connection

Have students tell their families that they're talking in class about their dreams for the future. Encourage students to interview family members to find out what they think they'll be doing in five, fifteen, or twenty-five years. Suggest that students take notes so that they can share their family members' future ambitions with the class.

Key Language

Key Vocabulary

Dreams
- be famous
- earn a good salary
- live in another country
- raise a family
- run my own business
- speak a foreign language
- take adventurous vacations
- work in my dream job
- work in the music industry

Expressions
- big break
- flying around
- for a start
- It's hard to imagine.
- meet the next
- on the red carpet
- work long hours
- You're such a dreamer.

Content Words

- futurist
- microscopic
- nanotechnology
- revolutionize
- wireless
- climate change
- dam
- electricity
- geothermal
- hydroelectric
- megawatt
- power plant
- solar

Grammar/Structures

Where **will** you **be living** fifty years from now?

In fifty years, I**'ll** probably **be living** in France.

I definitely **won't be living** with my parents.

Will you **be raising** a family? Yes, definitely./Probably not.

I'll probably.../I definitely **won't**...

Phonics

The sounds: s, es

Future Life Bulletin Board

Create a *Future Life* bulletin-board display to collect students' predictions about what they'll be doing at different points in the future. Divide the display into three or four sections, and label each one with a year, e.g., *In 2025...* . Encourage each student to write predictions on thin paper strips or ribbons and pin them up in the appropriate section. Model: *I'll be living in another country. I won't be living on Earth.* Tell students not to sign their predictions, and have classmates guess who contributed each prediction.

Language in Context Lesson

Lesson Flow

Warm-up → Lesson Objective → Presentation → Practice 1 (WB) → Practice 2 (SB) → Practice 3 (SB) → Speaking → Think BIG → Lesson Objective → Homework

Lesson Objective

I will talk about personal ambitions.

Key Language

business, country, dream, family, job, music industry, salary, vacation; be, bring up, earn, live in, run, take, work in; adventurous, dream, famous, foreign, several; It's hard to imagine.

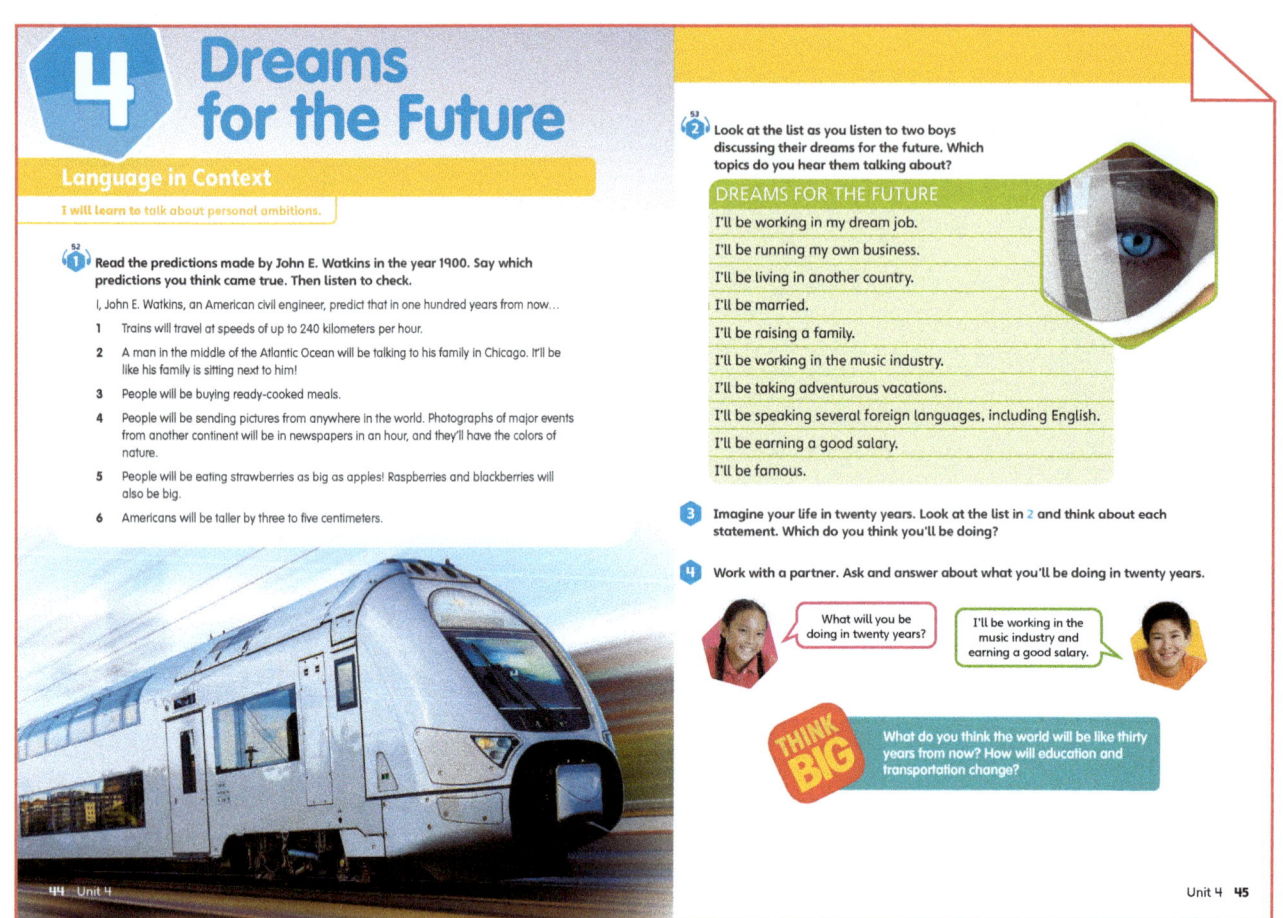

---

4 Dreams for the Future

Language in Context

I will learn to talk about personal ambitions.

1 Read the predictions made by John E. Watkins in the year 1900. Say which predictions you think came true. Then listen to check.

I, John E. Watkins, an American civil engineer, predict that in one hundred years from now…

1. Trains will travel at speeds of up to 240 kilometers per hour.
2. A man in the middle of the Atlantic Ocean will be talking to his family in Chicago. It'll be like his family is sitting next to him!
3. People will be buying ready-cooked meals.
4. People will be sending pictures from anywhere in the world. Photographs of major events from another continent will be in newspapers in an hour, and they'll have the colors of nature.
5. People will be eating strawberries as big as apples! Raspberries and blackberries will also be big.
6. Americans will be taller by three to five centimeters.

2 Look at the list as you listen to two boys discussing their dreams for the future. Which topics do you hear them talking about?

DREAMS FOR THE FUTURE
- I'll be working in my dream job.
- I'll be running my own business.
- I'll be living in another country.
- I'll be married.
- I'll be raising a family.
- I'll be working in the music industry.
- I'll be taking adventurous vacations.
- I'll be speaking several foreign languages, including English.
- I'll be earning a good salary.
- I'll be famous.

3 Imagine your life in twenty years. Look at the list in 2 and think about each statement. Which do you think you'll be doing?

4 Work with a partner. Ask and answer about what you'll be doing in twenty years.

- What will you be doing in twenty years?
- I'll be working in the music industry and earning a good salary.

THINK BIG: What do you think the world will be like thirty years from now? How will education and transportation change?

Warm-up

Materials: Calendar

- Refer students to a calendar and review how to say various years (e.g. *nineteen eighty-four* for 1984, *two thousand one* for 2001, and *twenty fifty* for 2050).
- Invite students to challenge their classmates to answer questions about the future. Model: *In what year will you turn twenty-five years old? In what year will you turn fifty? How old will you be in the year 2050?*
- Check answers from the HW in the last lesson.

Lesson Objective

INVOLVE

- Explain the lesson objective. Say: *Today I will learn to talk about personal ambitions.*
- Tell students that they will read and talk about predictions for the future.

Presentation 🎧 P.T142 52

Materials: World map or globe

1 Read the predictions made by John E. Watkins in the year 1900. Say which predictions you think came true. Then listen to check.

- Read the directions aloud. Say: *Watkins made these predictions in an article he published in a magazine called* Ladies' Home Journal. *The title of the article was "What May Happen in the Next Hundred Years."*
- Have students read the predictions and decide which ones came true.
- Play Audio Track 52. Have students check their answers.

MONITOR

Check answers as a class. *(Answers: Students should check all predictions except Item 5.)*

Practice 1 WB p. 34/ act. 1

1 Match the pictures with the predictions. Write the numbers. Then ✓ when you think the predictions may come true.

- Read the directions aloud. Ask volunteers to read the predictions for the future aloud.
- Have students complete the activity independently.

Practice 2 🎧 P.T143 53

2 Look at the list as you listen to two boys discussing their dreams for the future. Which topics do you hear them talking about?

- Read the directions aloud and have students preview the items in the chart. Say: *You will hear Sam and Jake talk about the future.* Play Audio Track 53 and have students complete the activity independently.

MONITOR

Check students' work by asking them to name items that Sam and Jake discuss. *(Answers: Students should check these predictions: I'll be working in my dream job; I'll be living in another country; I'll be working in the music industry; I'll be taking adventurous vacations; I'll be speaking several foreign languages, including English.)*

Practice 3

3 Imagine your life in twenty years. Look at the list in 2 and think about each statement. Which do you think you'll be doing?

- Read the directions aloud and have students complete the activity independently.

Speaking

4 Work with a partner. Ask and answer about what you'll be doing in twenty years.

- Read the directions aloud. Then have volunteers read the speech bubbles aloud.

MONITOR

Listen for correct use of language.

Think BIG

21st Century Critical Thinking

- Read the questions aloud and encourage students to express themselves as best they can. Write answers on the board. Then have them each write one sentence about how they think the world will be different in thirty years from now.

Lesson Objective

INVOLVE

Revisit the lesson objective: *Now I have learned to talk about personal ambitions.*

- Encourage awareness of what the students have learned by eliciting predictions from the lesson.

Homework WB pp. 34 & 35/ act. 2, 3, 4, & 5

2 Look at 1. Explain one of your predictions.

- Direct students to WB Activity 2 on page 34. Tell students to choose one of their predictions from Activity 1 and to explain why they think it will come true.

3 Match the pictures with the phrases.

- Direct students to WB Activity 3 on page 35. Tell students to match each picture with the correct phrase.

4 Complete the sentences with the phrases in 3.

- Direct students to WB Activity 4 on page 35. Tell students to complete the sentences with phrases in 3.

5 Unscramble the sentences. Are they true or false for you? Circle T for *true* or F for *false*.

- Direct students to WB Activity 5 on page 35. Tell students first to unscramble the words, then circle *T* or *F* so the sentences are true for them.

Think BIG

- Direct students to WB Think Big on page 35. Tell students to write answers to the questions.

Extra Application and Practice Activity

Materials: Slips of paper, bowl

- Have students write predictions for what they'll be doing twenty years from now on slips of paper and place them in a bowl. Students take one and say whether they will be doing it. Add their predictions to the Unit 4 bulletin board *Future Life* display.

Unit 4 **T44/45**

4 Dreams for the Future

Language in Context

I will learn to talk about personal ambitions.

1 Read the predictions made by John E. Watkins in the year 1900. Say which predictions you think came true. Then listen to check.

I, John E. Watkins, an American civil engineer, predict that in one hundred years from now…

1. Trains will travel at speeds of up to 240 kilometers per hour.
2. A man in the middle of the Atlantic Ocean will be talking to his family in Chicago. It'll be like his family is sitting next to him!
3. People will be buying ready-cooked meals.
4. People will be sending pictures from anywhere in the world. Photographs of major events from another continent will be in newspapers in an hour, and they'll have the colors of nature.
5. People will be eating strawberries as big as apples! Raspberries and blackberries will also be big.
6. Americans will be taller by three to five centimeters.

2 Look at the list as you listen to two boys discussing their dreams for the future. Which topics do you hear them talking about?

DREAMS FOR THE FUTURE

I'll be working in my dream job.

I'll be running my own business.

I'll be living in another country.

I'll be married.

I'll be raising a family.

I'll be working in the music industry.

I'll be taking adventurous vacations.

I'll be speaking several foreign languages, including English.

I'll be earning a good salary.

I'll be famous.

3 Imagine your life in twenty years. Look at the list in 2 and think about each statement. Which do you think you'll be doing?

4 Work with a partner. Ask and answer about what you'll be doing in twenty years.

What will you be doing in twenty years?

I'll be working in the music industry and earning a good salary.

THINK BIG

What do you think the world will be like thirty years from now? How will education and transportation change?

Reading Lesson

Lesson Flow

Warm-up › Lesson Objective › Pre-reading › Reading › Comprehension 1 › Comprehension 2 › Think BIG › Lesson Objective › Homework

Lesson Objective

I will understand a text about ambitions for the future.

Key Language

business, family; be, bring up, live in, run; successful, work long hours

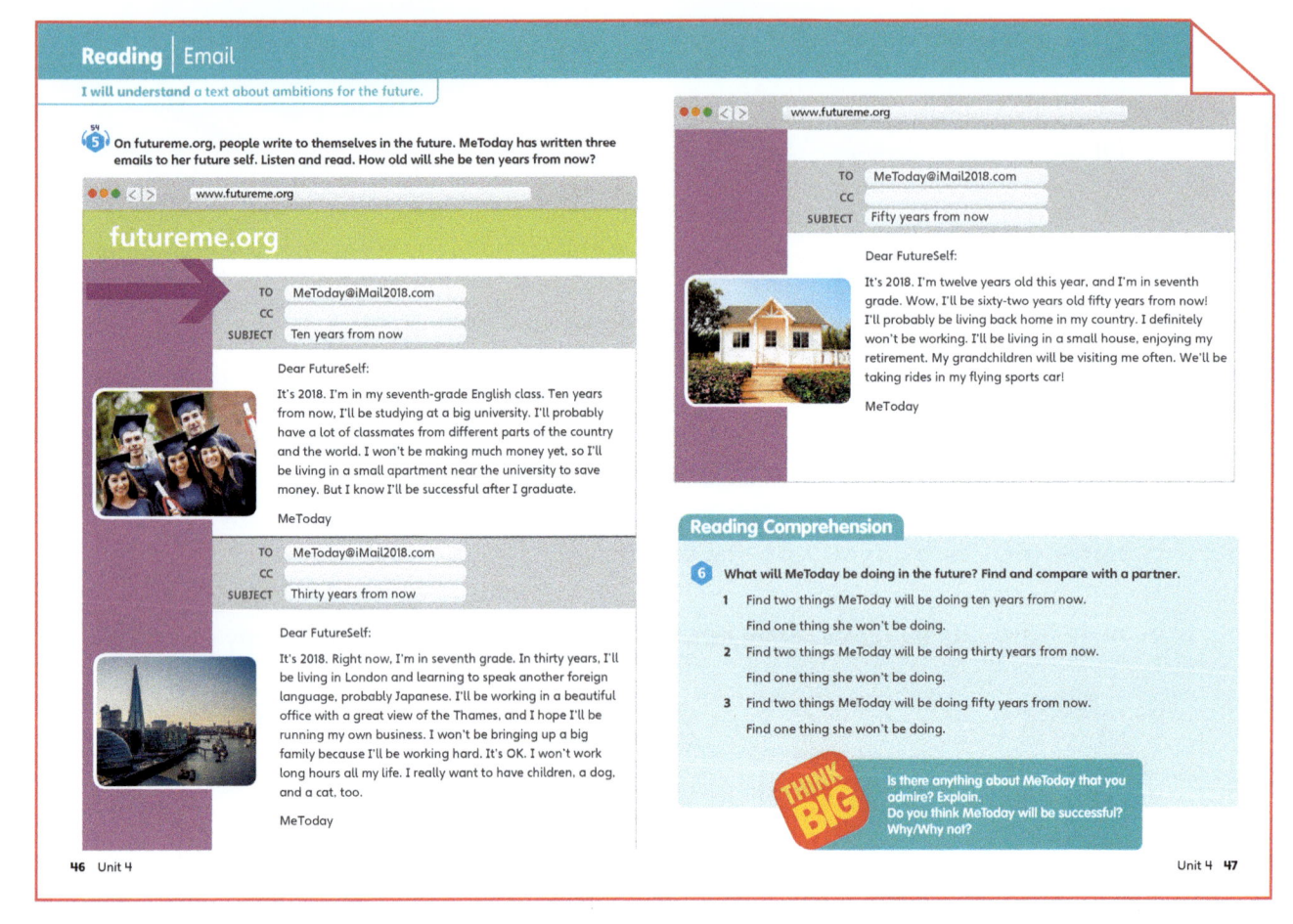

Reading | Email

I will understand a text about ambitions for the future.

5. On futureme.org, people write to themselves in the future. MeToday has written three emails to her future self. Listen and read. How old will she be ten years from now?

futureme.org

TO: MeToday@iMail2018.com
CC:
SUBJECT: Ten years from now

Dear FutureSelf:
It's 2018. I'm in my seventh-grade English class. Ten years from now, I'll be studying at a big university. I'll probably have a lot of classmates from different parts of the country and the world. I won't be making much money yet, so I'll be living in a small apartment near the university to save money. But I know I'll be successful after I graduate.

MeToday

TO: MeToday@iMail2018.com
CC:
SUBJECT: Thirty years from now

Dear FutureSelf:
It's 2018. Right now, I'm in seventh grade. In thirty years, I'll be living in London and learning to speak another foreign language, probably Japanese. I'll be working in a beautiful office with a great view of the Thames, and I hope I'll be running my own business. I won't be bringing up a big family because I'll be working hard. It's OK. I won't work long hours all my life. I really want to have children, a dog, and a cat, too.

MeToday

TO: MeToday@iMail2018.com
CC:
SUBJECT: Fifty years from now

Dear FutureSelf:
It's 2018. I'm twelve years old this year, and I'm in seventh grade. Wow, I'll be sixty-two years old fifty years from now! I'll probably be living back home in my country. I definitely won't be working. I'll be living in a small house, enjoying my retirement. My grandchildren will be visiting me often. We'll be taking rides in my flying sports car!

MeToday

Reading Comprehension

6. What will MeToday be doing in the future? Find and compare with a partner.
   1. Find two things MeToday will be doing ten years from now.
      Find one thing she won't be doing.
   2. Find two things MeToday will be doing thirty years from now.
      Find one thing she won't be doing.
   3. Find two things MeToday will be doing fifty years from now.
      Find one thing she won't be doing.

THINK BIG
Is there anything about MeToday that you admire? Explain.
Do you think MeToday will be successful? Why/Why not?

Warm-up

- Write some general categories on the board: *transportation, travel, communication, meals, holidays.* Have students work in small groups to make predictions about what each will be like in fifty years. Model: *We'll be living on Earth and traveling to the Moon fifty years from now.* Have groups share their predictions and the class vote on which predictions they agree with.
- Check answers from the HW in the last lesson.

Lesson Objective

INVOLVE

Introduce the lesson objective. Say: *Today I will learn to understand a text about ambitions for the future.*

- Students will listen to, read, and talk about emails written to be read in the future.

Pre-reading

- Have students read the subject lines aloud and preview the pictures. Ask: *What future events might these pictures predict?* (Sample answers: graduating from college, living in a big city, having a house)

Reading 🎧 54 🌍 📖

5 On futureme.org, people write to themselves in the future. MeToday has written three emails to her future self. Listen and read. How old will she be ten years from now?

- Read the directions aloud. Play Audio Track 54 and have students listen and read along.

ASSIST

> Replay the audio as needed. Pause after each message and use simple language to explain unfamiliar words and phrases.

- Ask the question in the directions: *How old will she be ten years from now?* (She'll be twenty-two years old.)

Comprehension 1 💡

MONITOR

> Ask more questions to check for understanding. Ask: *Who is MeToday writing to?* (herself in the future) *Who is FutureSelf?* (FutureSelf *is* MeToday in the future; it is the same person but ten, thirty, or fifty years later.)

Comprehension 2 🌍 💡

6 What will MeToday be doing in the future? Find and compare with a partner.

- Read the directions aloud and have students complete the activity independently. Then have students work in pairs to compare their sentences.

MONITOR

> Check as a class. (Sample answers: 1 In ten years, MeToday will be studying at a big university and living in a small apartment. MeToday won't be making much money. 2 In thirty years, MeToday will be living in London and learning to speak another foreign language. MeToday won't be bringing up a big family. 3 In fifty years, MeToday will be living in a small house. MeToday won't be working.)

Think BIG

21st Century Critical Thinking

- Read the questions aloud. Say: *When you admire someone, you like and respect them.* Then discuss the meaning of *successful* with students.

MONITOR

> As students work, listen for proper pronunciation, appropriate intonation, and correct use of language.

ASSIST

> Model: *When I think about whether or not I admire MeToday, I think about what I respect in the emails. In the first email, MeToday predicts going to college. In the second email, MeToday predicts learning Japanese. In the last email, MeToday predicts having grandchildren. I respect all of these things, so I decided that I admire MeToday.*

CHALLENGE

> Ask: *Why might writing an email or a letter to yourself in the future help you reach your goals?* (Sample answers: Thinking about the future can help you decide what's important to you. When you write these letters, you'll think about the goals you need to set to make your dreams for the future come true.)

Lesson Objective 📈

INVOLVE

> Revisit the lesson objective: *Now I have learned to understand a text about ambitions for the future.*

- Encourage awareness of what the students have learned by quickly eliciting a few things they remember about the text, for example, what does MeToday predict she'll be doing in ten years in the first email.

Homework 🎧 55 | WB p. 36/ act. 6 & 7 🎒

6 Listen and read the email. Then ✓ the predictions Christina makes about her classmates.

- Direct students to WB Activity 6 on page 36. Tell students to play the audio and listen and read along. Tell students to check the predictions Christina makes about her classmates.

7 Make a prediction about what you'll be doing in 20 years and explain why.

- Direct students to WB Activity 7 on page 36. Tell students to write one prediction about what they'll be doing in 20 years and to explain why.

Extra Application and Practice Activity

Materials: Index cards, string

> - Have students create a timeline that shows events in MeToday's life, beginning with the present and extending to at least fifty years in the future. Encourage students to include events described in MeToday's three emails as well as other possible events. Encourage students to take turns adding events until they've completed the timeline. Have students compare and contrast their timelines.

Unit 4   **T46/47**

Reading | Email

I will understand a text about ambitions for the future.

5 On futureme.org, people write to themselves in the future. MeToday has written three emails to her future self. Listen and read. How old will she be ten years from now?

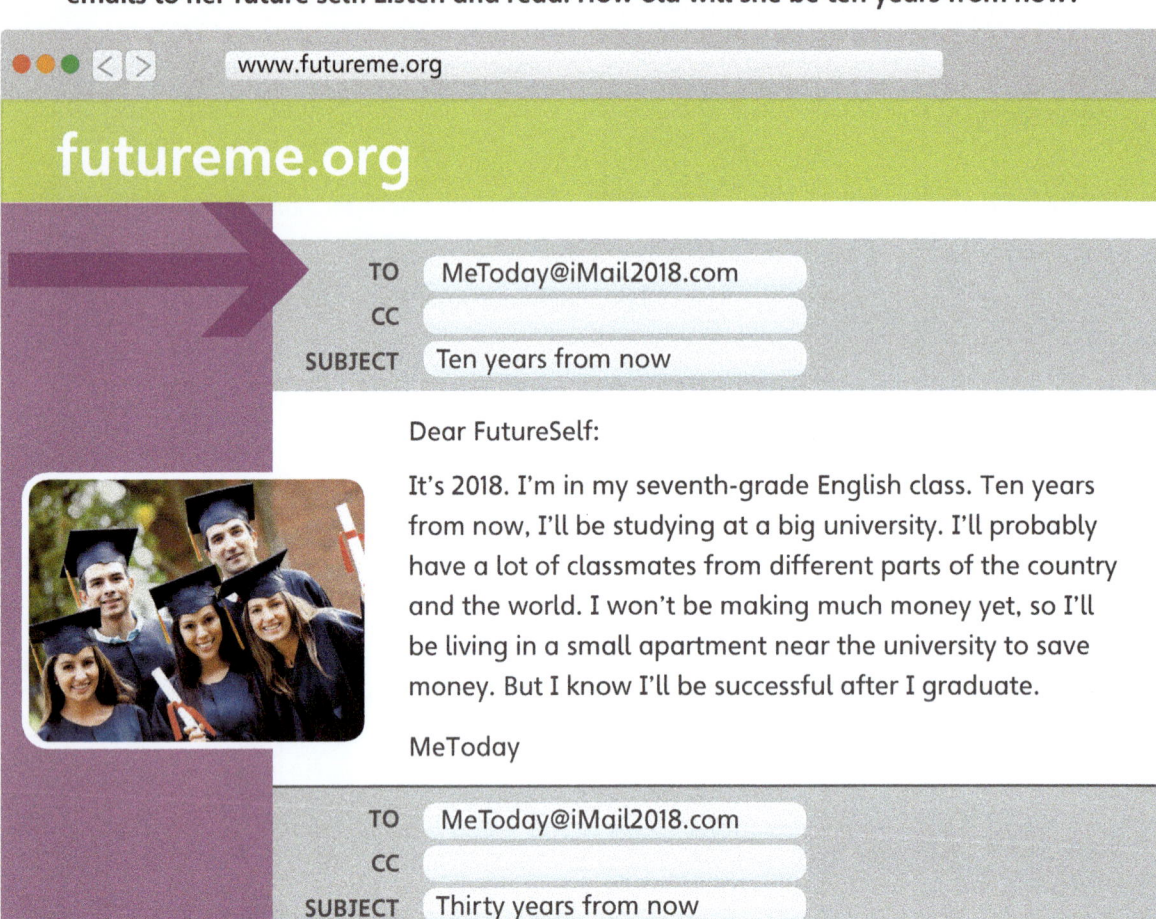

futureme.org

www.futureme.org

TO: MeToday@iMail2018.com
CC:
SUBJECT: Ten years from now

Dear FutureSelf:

It's 2018. I'm in my seventh-grade English class. Ten years from now, I'll be studying at a big university. I'll probably have a lot of classmates from different parts of the country and the world. I won't be making much money yet, so I'll be living in a small apartment near the university to save money. But I know I'll be successful after I graduate.

MeToday

TO: MeToday@iMail2018.com
CC:
SUBJECT: Thirty years from now

Dear FutureSelf:

It's 2018. Right now, I'm in seventh grade. In thirty years, I'll be living in London and learning to speak another foreign language, probably Japanese. I'll be working in a beautiful office with a great view of the Thames, and I hope I'll be running my own business. I won't be bringing up a big family because I'll be working hard. It's OK. I won't work long hours all my life. I really want to have children, a dog, and a cat, too.

MeToday

www.futureme.org

TO: MeToday@iMail2018.com
CC:
SUBJECT: Fifty years from now

Dear FutureSelf:

It's 2018. I'm twelve years old this year, and I'm in seventh grade. Wow, I'll be sixty-two years old fifty years from now! I'll probably be living back home in my country. I definitely won't be working. I'll be living in a small house, enjoying my retirement. My grandchildren will be visiting me often. We'll be taking rides in my flying sports car!

MeToday

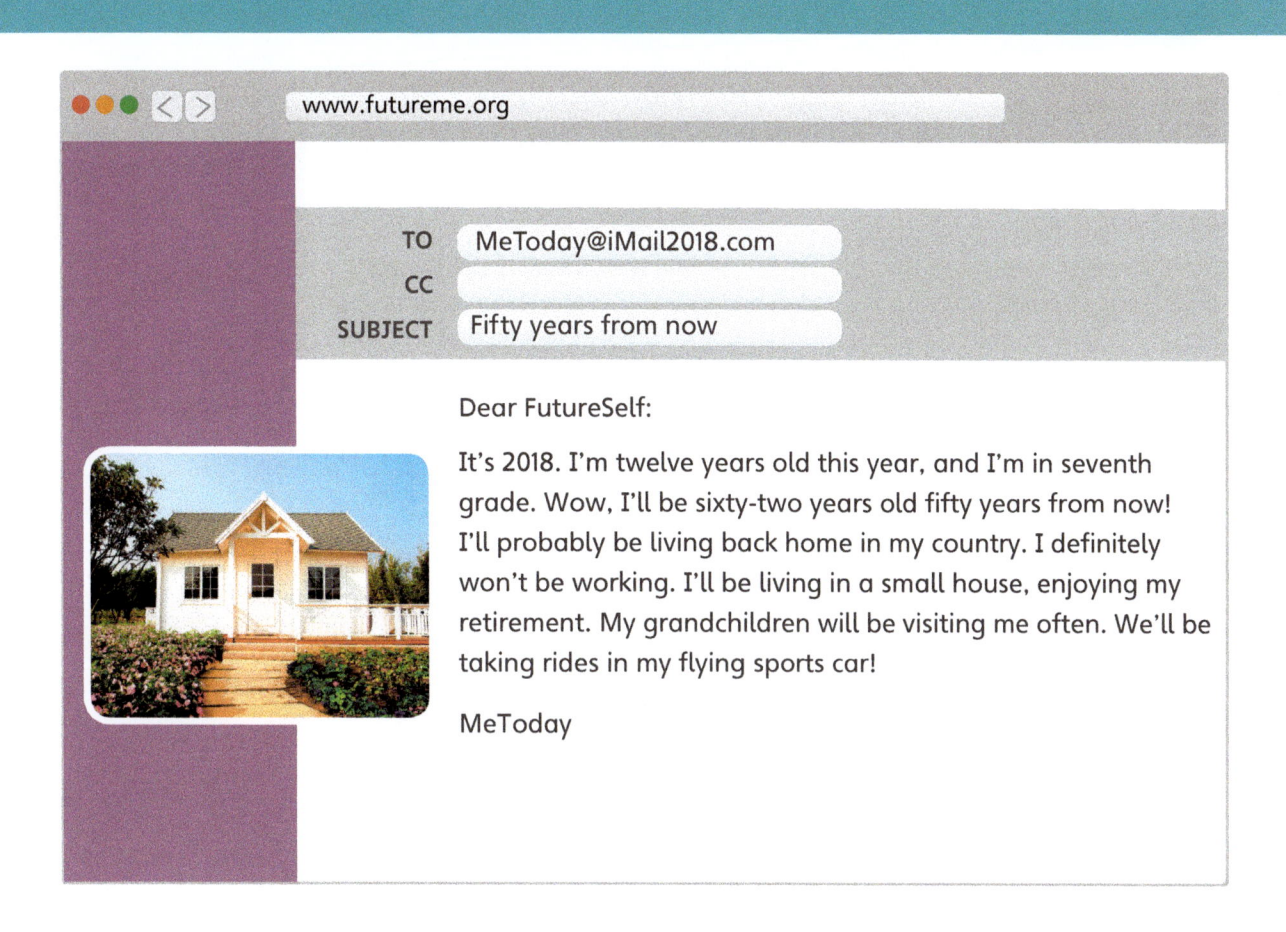

Reading Comprehension

6 What will MeToday be doing in the future? Find and compare with a partner.

1. Find two things MeToday will be doing ten years from now.
   Find one thing she won't be doing.

2. Find two things MeToday will be doing thirty years from now.
   Find one thing she won't be doing.

3. Find two things MeToday will be doing fifty years from now.
   Find one thing she won't be doing.

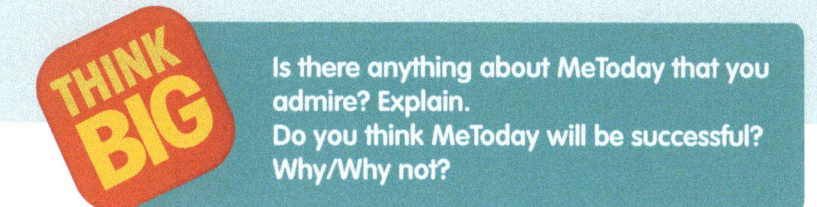

THINK BIG
Is there anything about MeToday that you admire? Explain.
Do you think MeToday will be successful? Why/Why not?

Language in Action Lesson

Lesson Flow

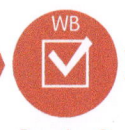

Warm-up › Lesson Objective › Pre-listening › Listening › Comprehension › Role Play › Practice 1 (SB) › Practice 2 (WB) › Lesson Objective › Homework

Lesson Objective

I will listen to a dialog about predictions for the future.

Key Language

dreamer, fuel, oil, source, space, spaceship, years; discover, fly around, live in, run out of, travel to, work on; big break, flying around, for a start, meet the next, on the red carpet, You're such a dreamer.

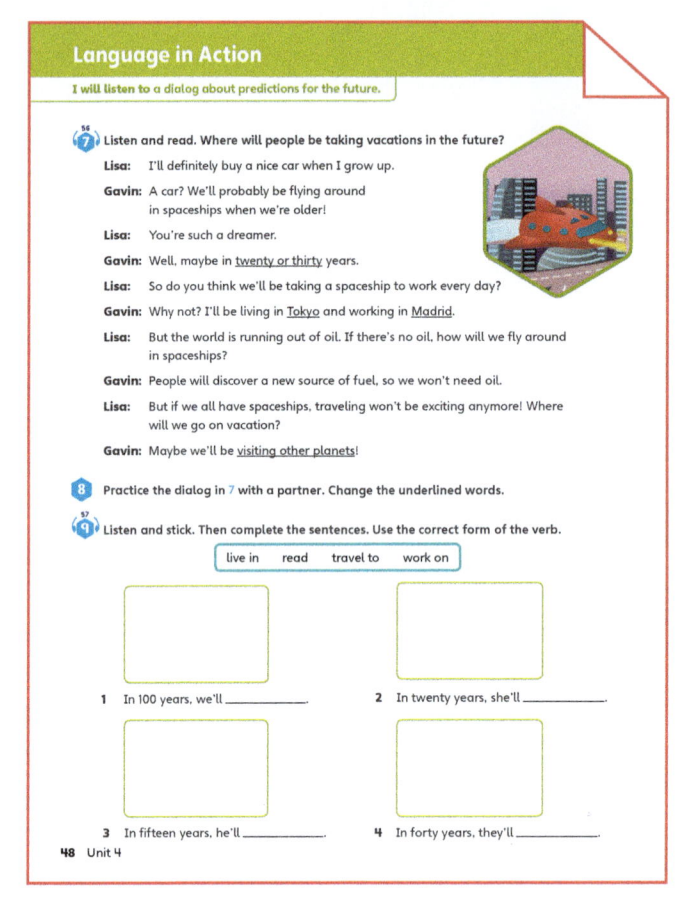

Language in Action

I will listen to a dialog about predictions for the future.

7 Listen and read. Where will people be taking vacations in the future?

Lisa: I'll definitely buy a nice car when I grow up.
Gavin: A car? We'll probably be flying around in spaceships when we're older!
Lisa: You're such a dreamer.
Gavin: Well, maybe in <u>twenty or thirty</u> years.
Lisa: So do you think we'll be taking a spaceship to work every day?
Gavin: Why not? I'll be living in <u>Tokyo</u> and working in <u>Madrid</u>.
Lisa: But the world is running out of oil. If there's no oil, how will we fly around in spaceships?
Gavin: People will discover a new source of fuel, so we won't need oil.
Lisa: But if we all have spaceships, traveling won't be exciting anymore! Where will we go on vacation?
Gavin: Maybe we'll be <u>visiting other planets</u>!

8 Practice the dialog in 7 with a partner. Change the underlined words.

9 Listen and stick. Then complete the sentences. Use the correct form of the verb.

live in   read   travel to   work on

1 In 100 years, we'll _____.
2 In twenty years, she'll _____.
3 In fifteen years, he'll _____.
4 In forty years, they'll _____.

48 Unit 4

Warm-up

- Ask: *When do you think people will be able to buy their own spaceships?* Have each student write down a year. Then have students compare their answers, identifying the earliest and latest predictions. Then invite students to work together to find a class average prediction: *Our class predicts that people will be able to buy their own spaceships in the year…* . (To find the class average, add all of the predictions together and then divide by the number of predictions.)
- Check answers from the HW in the last lesson.

Lesson Objective

INVOLVE

Introduce the lesson objective. Say: *Today I will listen to a dialog about predictions for the future.*

- Students will read, listen to, and practice a dialog. Students will also listen to conversations about predictions for the future.

Pre-listening

- Point to the picture. Ask: *What do you see?* (A flying car or spaceship in a future city.) Tell students that they will hear the two friends, Lisa and Gavin, talking about the future.

Listening

7 Listen and read. Where will people be taking vacations in the future?

- Read the directions aloud. Play Audio Track 56 and have students listen and read along.
- Invite two students to read the dialog aloud and repeat.

Comprehension

- Ask the question in the directions: *Where will people be taking vacations in the future?* (They will be visiting other planets.)

MONITOR

Ask more questions to check understanding. Encourage students to answer in complete sentences where appropriate. *Why does Gavin think cars will be old-fashioned in the future?* (Gavin thinks people will be flying around in spaceships instead.) *What problem does Lisa mention?* (The world is running out of oil.) *What solution does Gavin predict?* (He thinks people will invent a new source of fuel.)

CHALLENGE

Discuss Lisa's final comment. Say: *Lisa suggests that traveling won't be exciting if we all have spaceships. Why?* (Sample answer: With spaceships, we could move around the planet easily. Sometimes when you do something too often, it loses some of its excitement.) Ask students if they agree with Lisa's assumption.

Role Play

8 Practice the dialog in 7 with a partner. Change the underlined words.

- Read the directions aloud. Invite pairs to read the dialog aloud, switch parts, and repeat.

21st Century Technology Literacy

- Creating their own recordings of dialogs will help many students improve pronunciation and intonation. Remind students to speak loudly and clearly when practicing dialogs. Then have them listen to their recordings, note specific things they want to improve, and record again.

Practice 1

Materials: Stickers

9 Listen and stick. Then complete the sentences. Use the correct form of the verb.

- Help students find the Unit 4 stickers at the back of the Student's Book. Ask them to describe the stickers. Then read the directions and the words in the box.
- Play Audio Track 57. Have students place the stickers on the page and complete the sentences independently.

MONITOR

Check answers as a class. (Answers: 1 In 100 years, we'll be traveling to other planets. 2 In twenty years, she'll be living in Paris. 3 In fifteen years, he'll be working on a big movie. 4 In forty years, they'll be reading emails they wrote to themselves.)

Practice 2

8 Listen and read. Then circle the correct answers.

- Read the directions aloud. Ask volunteers to read the questions and answer choices aloud.
- Play Audio Track 63. Have students complete the activity.

Lesson Objective

INVOLVE

Revisit the lesson objective: *Now I have listened to a dialog about predictions for the future.*

- Encourage awareness of what the students have learned by quickly eliciting a few things they remember about the dialog, for example, how Gary thinks they will fly around in spaceships without any oil.

Homework

9 Read the dialog in 8 again. Does Brandon think he'll be successful? Why/Why not?

- Direct students to WB Activity 9 on page 37. Tell students to write answers for the questions.

Extra Application and Practice Activity

- Have students invent words people might use in the future by following the model of *email (electronic mail)*. Model: *I can combine* bad *and* adventure *to create* badventure, *which is an adventure that turns out badly. Or I can add* roam *and* homework *to create* roamwork, *which is schoolwork you do while traveling.*

Unit 4 **T48**

Language in Action

I will listen to a dialog about predictions for the future.

7 Listen and read. Where will people be taking vacations in the future?

Lisa: I'll definitely buy a nice car when I grow up.

Gavin: A car? We'll probably be flying around in spaceships when we're older!

Lisa: You're such a dreamer.

Gavin: Well, maybe in twenty or thirty years.

Lisa: So do you think we'll be taking a spaceship to work every day?

Gavin: Why not? I'll be living in Tokyo and working in Madrid.

Lisa: But the world is running out of oil. If there's no oil, how will we fly around in spaceships?

Gavin: People will discover a new source of fuel, so we won't need oil.

Lisa: But if we all have spaceships, traveling won't be exciting anymore! Where will we go on vacation?

Gavin: Maybe we'll be visiting other planets!

8 Practice the dialog in 7 with a partner. Change the underlined words.

9 Listen and stick. Then complete the sentences. Use the correct form of the verb.

live in   read   travel to   work on

1 In 100 years, we'll _____.

2 In twenty years, she'll _____.

3 In fifteen years, he'll _____.

4 In forty years, they'll _____.

48 Unit 4

Grammar

I will learn to use the future progressive to talk about personal ambitions.

What **will** you **be doing** ten years from now?	I'll <u>definitely</u> **be studying** at a big university.
Where **will** you **be living** in twenty years?	I <u>probably</u> **won't be living** in Europe.

Tip: Use the future progressive to talk about what you'll be doing in the future. For degrees of certainty (how likely something is), use either *definitely* or *probably*.

10 What will you or won't you be doing forty years from now? Make complete sentences. Use the future progressive of the verbs and *definitely* or *probably*.

1 (live in another country) _____
2 (run my own business) _____
3 (go to the moon on vacation) _____
4 (go on white-water rafting trips) _____
5 (teach chemistry at college) _____

Will you **be running** a business?	No, <u>definitely</u> not./I <u>definitely</u> **won't**…
	Yes, <u>definitely</u>./I'll <u>definitely</u>…
	<u>Probably</u> not./I <u>probably</u> **won't**…
	Yes, <u>probably</u>./I'**ll** <u>probably</u>…

11 Make Yes/No questions about the future. Use the ideas below or your own ideas. Take turns asking and answering questions with a partner.

- raise a family
- run a business
- live in a big city
- earn a good salary
- travel around the globe
- make a difference to the world
- speak a foreign language
- act in movies/on TV

Grammar Lesson

Lesson Flow

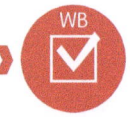

Warm-up › Lesson Objective › Presentation 1 › Practice 1 (SB) › Practice 2 (WB) › Presentation 2 › Practice 3 (SB) › Practice 4 (WB) › Lesson Objective › Homework

Lesson Objective

I will learn to use the future progressive to talk about personal ambitions.

Key Language

Where **will** you **be living** fifty years from now? In fifty years, I'**ll** probably **be living** in France. I definitely **won't be living** with my parents.

Will you **be raising** a family? Yes, definitely./Probably not. I'll probably.../I definitely **won't**...

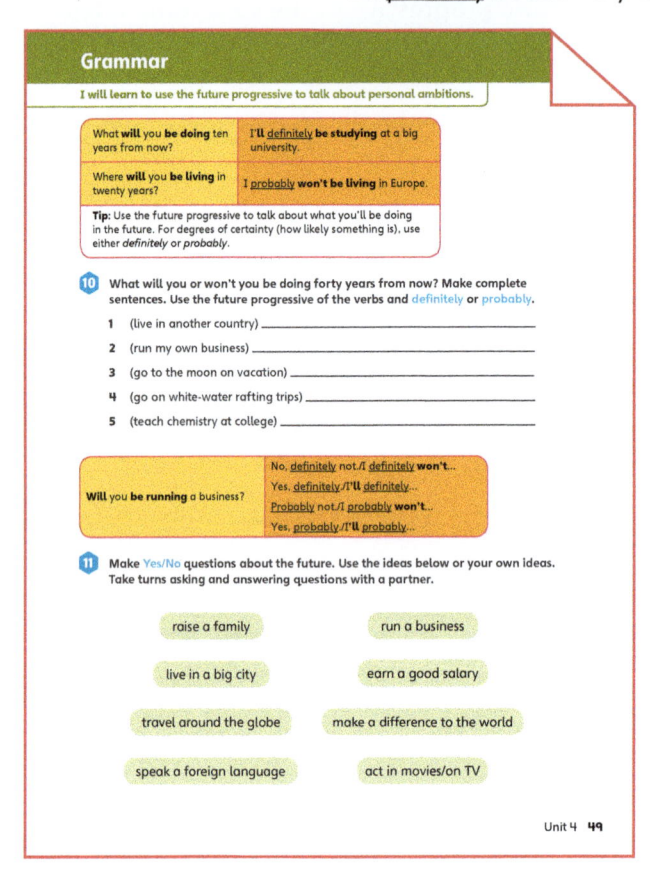

Grammar

I will learn to use the future progressive to talk about personal ambitions.

| What **will** you **be doing** ten years from now? | I'll definitely **be studying** at a big university. |
| Where **will** you **be living** in twenty years? | I probably **won't be living** in Europe. |

Tip: Use the future progressive to talk about what you'll be doing in the future. For degrees of certainty (how likely something is), use either *definitely* or *probably*.

10 What will you or won't you be doing forty years from now? Make complete sentences. Use the future progressive of the verbs and *definitely* or *probably*.

1 (live in another country) _____
2 (run my own business) _____
3 (go to the moon on vacation) _____
4 (go on white-water rafting trips) _____
5 (teach chemistry at college) _____

| **Will** you **be running** a business? | No, definitely not./I definitely **won't**... Yes, definitely./I'll definitely... Probably not./I probably **won't**... Yes, probably./I'll probably... |

11 Make Yes/No questions about the future. Use the ideas below or your own ideas. Take turns asking and answering questions with a partner.

- raise a family
- run a business
- live in a big city
- earn a good salary
- travel around the globe
- make a difference to the world
- speak a foreign language
- act in movies/on TV

Unit 4 **49**

Warm-up

Materials: Index cards

- Have students work in pairs to review -ing forms of verbs. Say: *A verb that ends in* -ing *can describe an action that's happening right now, in the past, or even in the future.* Explain that one student should name a verb and the other should name the -ing form. Model: *make/making, do/doing, live/living, stop/stopping.* Encourage students to use these lesson verbs: *bring up, go, enjoy, live in, run, study, take, work.*

- Check answers from the HW in the last lesson.

Lesson Objective

INVOLVE

Introduce the lesson objective. Say: *Today I will learn to use the future progressive to talk about personal ambitions.*

- Students will use the future progressive to talk about what will be happening in the future.

S49 Unit 4

Presentation 1

- Have volunteers read the sentences in the first grammar box aloud. Ask: *What -ing verbs are used in these sentences?* (doing, studying, living)
- Refer students back to the Language in Action dialog and elicit or highlight the grammar structures in the dialog.

ASSIST

Say: *The future progressive combines* will be *and an* -ing *verb:* will be living, will be studying. *To say what will not be happening, you can use* will not *or* won't. *You can say,* "I will not be living in Paris," *or* "I won't be living in Paris."

Practice 1

Materials: Dice

10 What will you or won't you be doing forty years from now? Make complete sentences. Use the future progressive of the verbs and *definitely* or *probably*.

- Read the directions and complete Item 1 as a class. Then have students complete the activity independently.

MONITOR

Check answers as a class. (Sample answers: 1 I'll definitely be living in another country. 2 I'll probably be running my own business. 3 I definitely won't be going to the moon on vacation. 4 I'll probably won't be going on white-water rafting trips. 5 I'll probably be teaching chemistry at college.)

Concrete Modeling: Have students use dice to model the concepts of *definitely* and *probably*. Show students a die. Ask: *What will definitely happen when I roll this die?* (Sample answers: You will roll a number between one and six./You will roll a number less than seven.) *What will probably happen when I roll this die?* (You will roll a number greater than one./You will roll a number less than six.)

Practice 2 WB p. 38/ act. 10

10 Match. Then answer the questions. Use the future progressive form of the verbs and *definitely* or *probably*.

- Ask volunteers to read the sentences in the grammar box.
- Read the directions aloud and explain that students have to match the verbs on the left-hand side of each maze with the noun phrases on the right-hand side of each maze. Then they should answer the questions about Pablo and Carine using the future progressive form and *definitely* or *probably*.
- Have students complete the activity independently.

Presentation 2

- Have volunteers read the sentences in the second grammar box aloud. Then have them complete the sentences for themselves in their notebooks.

Practice 3

11 Make *Yes/No* questions about the future. Use the ideas below or your own ideas. Take turns asking and answering your questions with a partner.

- Read the directions aloud. Have students write their questions independently in their notebooks. Be sure they exchange questions and write their partner's answers. Then ask them to answer their partner's questions.

MONITOR

Have students compare their questions. Model examples of questions: *Will you be living in this town ten years from now? Will you be working in a hospital in the future? Will you be driving a flying car in fifty years?*

ASSIST

Remind students to use *definitely* or *probably*.

Practice 4 WB p. 39/ act. 11

11 Answer the questions. Use the information in 10.

- Read the directions aloud. Explain that students have to answer the *yes/no* questions about Pablo and Carine with the information in Activity 10.
- Have students complete the activity independently.

Lesson Objective

INVOLVE

Revisit the lesson objective: *Now I have learned to use the future progressive to talk about personal ambitions.*

- Encourage awareness of what the students have learned by quickly eliciting some future progressive yes/no questions and answers with *definitely/probably*.

Homework WB p. 39/ act. 12 & 13

12 Answer the questions about your future life in college. Use *probably* or *definitely*.

- Direct students to WB Activity 12 on page 39. Tell students to answer about their future life in college.

13 Choose a friend. Write a question about your friend's future life in college. Ask your friend the question and write their answer.

- Direct students to WB Activity 13 on page 39. Tell students to write a question about a friend's future life in college. Have them ask him or her the question and to write the answer.

Extra Application and Practice Activity

- Have students write sentences that predict what they probably will and probably won't be doing next week, next month, and next year.

Unit 4 **T49**

Content Connection Lesson

Lesson Flow

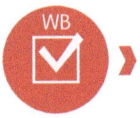

Warm-up › Lesson Objective › Pre-reading › Reading › Practice 1 (SB) › Practice 2 (WB) › Think BIG › Video Lesson › Lesson Objective › Homework

Lesson Objective

I will learn about predictions for the future.

Key Language

futurist, microscopic, nanotechnology, revolutionize, wireless

---

Content Connection | Science and Technology

I will learn about predictions for the future.

🎧 12 Listen and read. How will we be learning new skills in the future?

CONTENT WORDS
futurist   microscopic   nanotechnology
revolutionize   wireless

The Next Big Thing
Experts' Predictions for the Future

Futurists are people whose job is to look ahead and help us plan for the future. Futurists can't say what the future will definitely be like, but they use their knowledge to say what will probably happen and what we can prepare ourselves for. How will we be learning fifty years from now?

Nanotechnology

Nanotechnology is the science of incredibly small things. As a unit of measure, a nanometer is one billionth of a meter! When something is nano-sized, it's so small, it's invisible! With nanotechnology, we'll have microscopic computerized robots called nanobots. Because nanobots can be built into almost anything – even appliances – household chores will be easier. Nanobots could also be used to travel through your body and treat problems and disease without expensive and painful operations.

Brain-to-Computer Communication

How about this for an amazing prediction? One day, everyone and everything will be linked through wireless technology. Nanocomputers will be in your system, so your brain, just like a computer, will be able to receive downloads and uploads. Would you like to learn a new language or how to tango? As soon as you think the thought, your brain will download the new language or the dance steps, and you'll be learning them instantly!

All these new technologies promise to revolutionize the way we live and experience things. Maybe now the big question is "Are we ready for them?"

13 Look at the passage. Read and say yes, no, or doesn't say.
1. Futurists can't predict exactly what the future will be like.
2. Nanobots could make operations more painful.
3. With brain-to-computer communication, learning will be expensive.

THINK BIG If you could learn something by uploading it to your brain instantly, what would you like to learn? Why?

50 Unit 4

Warm-up

- Have students make predictions for the future by changing statements about the present. Model: *Today, people drive cars to work. In the future, people will fly spaceships to work. Today, a laptop weighs about a kilogram. In the future, a laptop will weigh about 100 grams.*
- Check answers from the HW in the last lesson.

Lesson Objective

INVOLVE

Introduce the lesson objective. Say: *Today I will learn about predictions for the future.*

- Students will listen to and read about scientific predictions for the future.

Pre-reading

- Preview the article by reading the subheadings in the article aloud. Have students read the Content Words and discuss their meanings. Encourage students to look up any unfamiliar words in a dictionary.

Reading 🎧 59

12 Listen and read. How will we be learning new skills in the future?

- Read the directions aloud. Write the question on the board: *How will we be learning new skills in the future?* Explain to students that they should be listening specifically for the answer to that question.
- Play Audio Track 59 and have students listen and read along.

ASSIST

Replay the audio as necessary. Have students point to the content words in the text and use context clues to describe their meaning. Model: *"Futurists are people whose job is to look ahead and help us plan for the future."* It sounds like a futurist is a person who plans for the future.

MONITOR

Pair students, and have them discuss what they learned about how people will learn new skills in the future. *(Answer: In the future, everyone and everything will be linked through wireless technology. Anything we would like to learn will be downloaded by our brain and we will be learning it instantly.)*

21st Century Health Literacy

- Have students think about and discuss how some of the ideas in the article might improve health in the future. Ask: *How might doctors be using nanobots in the future?* (Sample answer: They might be using nanobots to diagnose illnesses or perform surgery.)

Practice 1

13 Look at the passage. Read and say *yes*, *no*, or *doesn't say*.

- Read the first sentence. Ask students to scan through the text and find the paragraph that discusses this idea. Elicit that it appears in paragraph 1. Ask students whether or not the sentence is true (*yes*) or false (*no*), or if the text does not mention the idea at all (*doesn't say*)

ASSIST

Point out that the article's subheads can help readers find information in the text.

- Have students work independently to read the rest of the sentences, identify which paragraph (if any) refers to the idea, and decide whether or not the sentence is *yes*, *no*, or *doesn't say*.

MONITOR

Check as a class. (Answers: 1 yes – paragraph 1, 2 no – paragraph 2, 3 doesn't say – paragraph 3).

Practice 2 🎧 60 P. T144 WB p. 40/ act. 14

14 Read and complete with the words in the box. Then listen and check.

- Read the directions aloud. Have students read and complete the text with the word in the box.
- Play Audio Track 60 and have students check their answers.

Think BIG

21st Century Innovation

- Read the first two questions aloud. Then ask: *What are some things that are hard to learn?* Elicit different responses, e.g. *playing an instrument, complex math, how to become a doctor.* Have students explain what they would like to learn by "uploading it instantly" and why.
- Read the final question, and discuss some of the potential negative aspects of the future technologies students have read about.

Video Documentary U 04

- Refer to the Video Guide for pre-watching and post-watching activities.

Lesson Objective

INVOLVE

Revisit the lesson objective: *Now I have learned about predictions for the future.*

- Encourage awareness of what the students have learned by quickly eliciting a few things they remember about the passage, for example, about nanotechnology.

Homework WB p. 40/ act. 15

15 Read 14 again and circle the correct answers.

- Direct students to WB Activity 15 on page 40. Tell students to read the passage in Activity 13 again and circle the correct answer for each sentence.

Extra Application and Practice Activity

- Invite partners to role-play skits that show their predictions about a normal day one hundred years from now. After the class views a skit, ask students to talk about the predictions. Model: *(Susanna) and (Maria) think people will be using lots of nanobots in one hundred years.*

Unit 4   **T50**

Content Connection | Science and Technology

I will learn about predictions for the future.

12 Listen and read. How will we be learning new skills in the future?

CONTENT WORDS
futurist   microscopic   nanotechnology
revolutionize   wireless

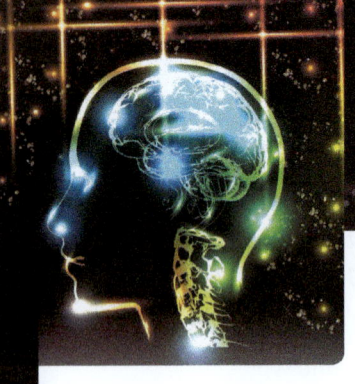

The Next Big Thing
Experts' Predictions for the Future

Futurists are people whose job is to look ahead and help us plan for the future. Futurists can't say what the future will definitely be like, but they use their knowledge to say what will probably happen and what we can prepare ourselves for. How will we be learning fifty years from now?

Nanotechnology

Nanotechnology is the science of incredibly small things. As a unit of measure, a nanometer is one billionth of a meter! When something is nano-sized, it's so small, it's invisible! With nanotechnology, we'll have microscopic computerized robots called nanobots. Because nanobots can be built into almost anything – even appliances – household chores will be easier. Nanobots could also be used to travel through your body and treat problems and disease without expensive and painful operations.

Brain-to-Computer Communication

How about this for an amazing prediction? One day, everyone and everything will be linked through wireless technology. Nanocomputers will be in your system, so your brain, just like a computer, will be able to receive downloads and uploads. Would you like to learn a new language or how to tango? As soon as you think the thought, your brain will download the new language or the dance steps, and you'll be learning them instantly!

All these new technologies promise to revolutionize the way we live and experience things. Maybe now the big question is "Are we ready for them?"

13 Look at the passage. Read and say yes, no, or doesn't say.

1. Futurists can't predict exactly what the future will be like.
2. Nanobots could make operations more painful.
3. With brain-to-computer communication, learning will be expensive.

THINK BIG

If you could learn something by uploading it to your brain instantly, what would you like to learn? Why?

Culture Connection | Around the World

I will learn about renewable energy projects around the world.

14 Listen and read. How much energy does each power plant produce?

CONTENT WORDS
climate change   dam   electricity
geothermal   hydroelectric
megawatt   power plant   solar

Power for the Future

There are more than 7 billion people on Earth right now, and according to the United Nations, there will be about 9 billion by the year 2050. International reports say that the world's demand for energy may double by that time. With climate change, it's obvious that we need better ways to answer our demands for more and more energy in the future. Luckily, in many parts of the world, large renewable energy projects are helping that effort. Here are just a few examples of what's happening now.

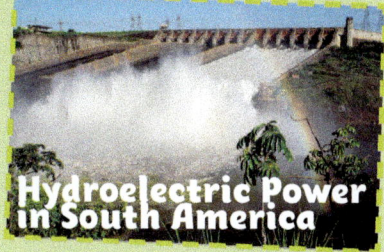

Hydroelectric Power in South America

The Itaipu Dam lies on the border of Brazil and Paraguay, and was built between 1966 and 1984. Since then, it has produced more power than any other hydroelectric dam in the world. The seven power plants at the dam can each produce 200 megawatts of energy, for a total possible production of 14,000 megawatts.

Geothermal Power in Iceland

Because of its large number of active volcanoes, Iceland is able to produce more than a quarter of its electricity and heating power from geothermal energy. Geothermal energy plants take heat energy inside the Earth and use it to create power. Two geothermal power plants in southeastern Iceland together produce over 420 megawatts of electricity.

Solar Power in Morocco

The solar power plant outside of Ouarzazate, in Morocco is one of the largest in the world. The solar panels get energy from the powerful Sahara desert sun. When the power plant is finished, it will create 580 megawatts of electricity. This is enough energy for 1.1 million people.

15 Look at the passage. Circle the correct words.

1. The United Nations says that the world's population may **double / grow to 9 billion** by 2050.

2. The Itaipu Dam **was more expensive / produces more power** than any other hydroelectric dam in the world.

3. The solar power plant in Morocco produces enough energy for **1.1 / 5.8** million people.

THINK BIG What kind of renewable energy is used in your country?

Culture Connection Lesson

Lesson Flow

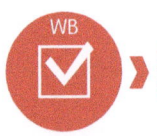

Warm-up › Lesson Objective › Pre-reading › Reading › Practice 1 (SB) › Practice 2 (WB) › Think BIG › Lesson Objective › Homework

Lesson Objective

I will learn about renewable energy projects around the world.

Key Language

climate change, dam, electricity, geothermal, hydroelectric, megawatt, power plant, solar

---

Culture Connection | Around the World

I will learn about renewable energy projects around the world.

14 Listen and read. How much energy does each power plant produce?

CONTENT WORDS
climate change, dam, electricity, geothermal, hydroelectric, megawatt, power plant, solar

Power for the Future

There are more than 7 billion people on Earth right now, and according to the United Nations, there will be about 9 billion by the year 2050. International reports say that the world's demand for energy may double by that time. With climate change, it's obvious that we need better ways to answer our demands for more and more energy in the future. Luckily, in many parts of the world, large renewable energy projects are helping that effort. Here are just a few examples of what's happening now.

Hydroelectric Power in South America

The Itaipu Dam lies on the border of Brazil and Paraguay, and was built between 1966 and 1984. Since then, it has produced more power than any other hydroelectric dam in the world. The seven power plants at the dam can each produce 200 megawatts of energy, for a total possible production of 14,000 megawatts.

Geothermal Power in Iceland

Because of its large number of active volcanoes, Iceland is able to produce more than a quarter of its electricity and heating power from geothermal energy. Geothermal energy plants take heat energy inside the Earth and use it to create power. Two geothermal power plants in southeastern Iceland together produce over 420 megawatts of electricity.

Solar Power in Morocco

The solar power plant outside of Ouarzazate, in Morocco is one of the largest in the world. The solar panels get energy from the powerful Sahara desert sun. When the power plant is finished, it will create 580 megawatts of electricity. This is enough energy for 1.1 million people.

15 Look at the passage. Circle the correct words.

1. The United Nations says that the world's population may **double / grow to 9 billion** by 2050.
2. The Itaipu Dam **was more expensive / produces more power** than any other hydroelectric dam in the world.
3. The solar power plant in Morocco produces enough energy for **1.1 / 5.8** million people.

THINK BIG What kind of renewable energy is used in your country?

Unit 4   51

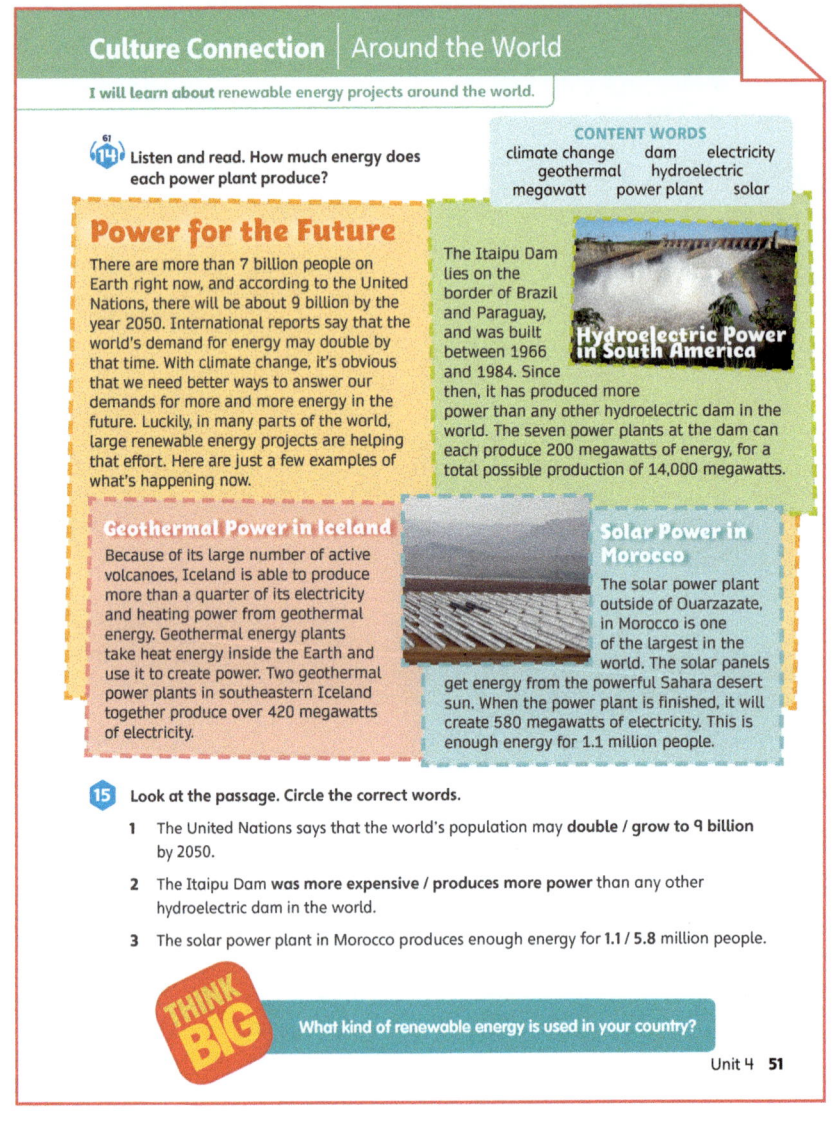

Warm-up

- On the board write the heading: *Big Problems*. Ask: *What do we mean by Big Problems?* (Answer: problems that are difficult to solve and are faced by the whole world.) Elicit examples of "Big Problems" and write them under the heading on the board.
- Tell students to think of possible solutions for one of the big problems on the board. Have students form groups of three or four and discuss their ideas.
- Have groups share their ideas with the rest of the class.
- Check answers from the HW in the last lesson.

Lesson Objective

INVOLVE

- Introduce the lesson objective. Say: *Today I will learn about renewable energy projects around the world.*
- Students will listen to, read, and talk about renewable energy projects from around the world and discuss renewable energy projects in their own country.

Pre-reading

- Have students scan the first paragraph of the passage. Ask: *What's the problem?* (demand for energy/climate change) *What's the solution?* (renewable energy)
- Have students discuss what they think renewable energy is. Elicit examples of renewable energy. *(Possible answers: wind power, water power, solar power)*. Elicit examples of energy that is not renewable *(Possible answers: oil, gas, coal, etc.)*

Reading

14 Listen and read. How much energy does each power plant produce?

- Read the second paragraph of the passage, "Geothermal Power in Iceland", aloud with the class. Elicit how much power the power plant produces.
- Have students read the rest of the passage independently and make a note of how much power each power plant produces.
- Play Audio Track 61. Have students listen and read along in their books.

MONITOR

Check answers as a class. *(Answers: Geothermal Power in Iceland = 420 megawatts of electricity, Hydroelectric Power in South America = 200 megawatts of energy, Solar Power in Morocco = 580 megawatts of electricity)*

Practice 1

15 Look at the passage. Circle the correct words.

- Read the directions aloud. Ask a volunteer to read out the first sentence. Ask the class to look at the passage again, find the appropriate paragraph for the answer. (Paragraph 1)
- Have students work independently to find the remaining answers.
- Ask students to compare their answers with a partner.

MONITOR

Check answers as a class. *(Answers: 1 grow to 9 billion, 2 produces more power, 3 1.1)*

ASSIST

To help students find the relevant information in the text ask them to underline key words in the sentences and then look for them in the text.

Practice 2   WB p. 41/ act. 16

16 Read and complete. Then listen and check.

- Read the directions aloud. Students fill in the correct word to complete each sentence. Have students complete the task independently.
- Play Audio Track 62 and have students check answers.

Think BIG

21st Century Critical Thinking

- Read the question aloud as students follow in their books. Have students discuss the question in small groups of three or four. Walk around and help students express their responses in English by modelling words and phrases and have them repeat.
- Invite students to share their responses with the class.

Lesson Objective

INVOLVE

Revisit the lesson objective: *Now I have learned about renewable energy projects around the world.*

- Encourage awareness of what the students have learned by quickly eliciting a few things they remember about the passage, for example, the kinds of renewable energy they read about.

Homework   WB p. 41/ act. 17

17 How will renewable energy help you live in the future?

- Direct students to WB Activity 17 on page 41. Read the directions aloud. Explain to students that they must think of ideas as to how renewable energy will help them live in the future and write them down. Have students read the examples to help them.

Extra Application and Practice Activity

21st Century Initiative

- Have students make a list of things they can do to help improve the environment. Model: *I want the environment to be safe to live in. I can help fight pollution now. I can join groups that are working to protect the environment. I can write to leaders and share my opinion.*

Unit 4   **T51**

Writing Lesson

Lesson Flow

Warm-up › Lesson Objective › Practice 1 (WB) › Practice 2 (SB) › Practice 3 (SB) › Practice 4 (SB) › Lesson Objective › Homework

Lesson Objective

I will learn to write formal and informal emails.

Writing | Formal and informal emails

I will learn to write formal and informal emails.

16 With a partner, read these two emails and decide which is formal and which is informal.

Email 1:
TO: teachme123@iMail.com
SUBJECT: Next week's assignment

Dear Ms. Priscott,

I'll be working on next week's assignment this weekend because I have play rehearsals all week, but I need more information about it.
I have some questions:
- What type of assignment will we be writing?
- I'm planning to write about future technology. Is this topic OK?
- What is the deadline for the assignment?

Thank you for your help.

Thomas Brown

Email 2:
TO: howcoolisit1@iMail.com
SUBJECT: This weekend

Hey Leo,

Any plans 4 tomorrow? Wanna hang out at my house? I'm staying home all day cuz I hafta babysit my little sister. Wanna do homework together?

Got the new video game, btw. It's brilliant!

Just text me b4 u come over. OK? CU soon.

Thomas

17 With another pair, discuss the differences between the formal and informal emails in 16.

18 In your notebook, write two emails, one to a teacher and one to a friend.

Formal
TO:
CC:
SUBJECT:

Dear _____,

Informal
TO:
CC:
SUBJECT:

Hey _____,

52 Unit 4

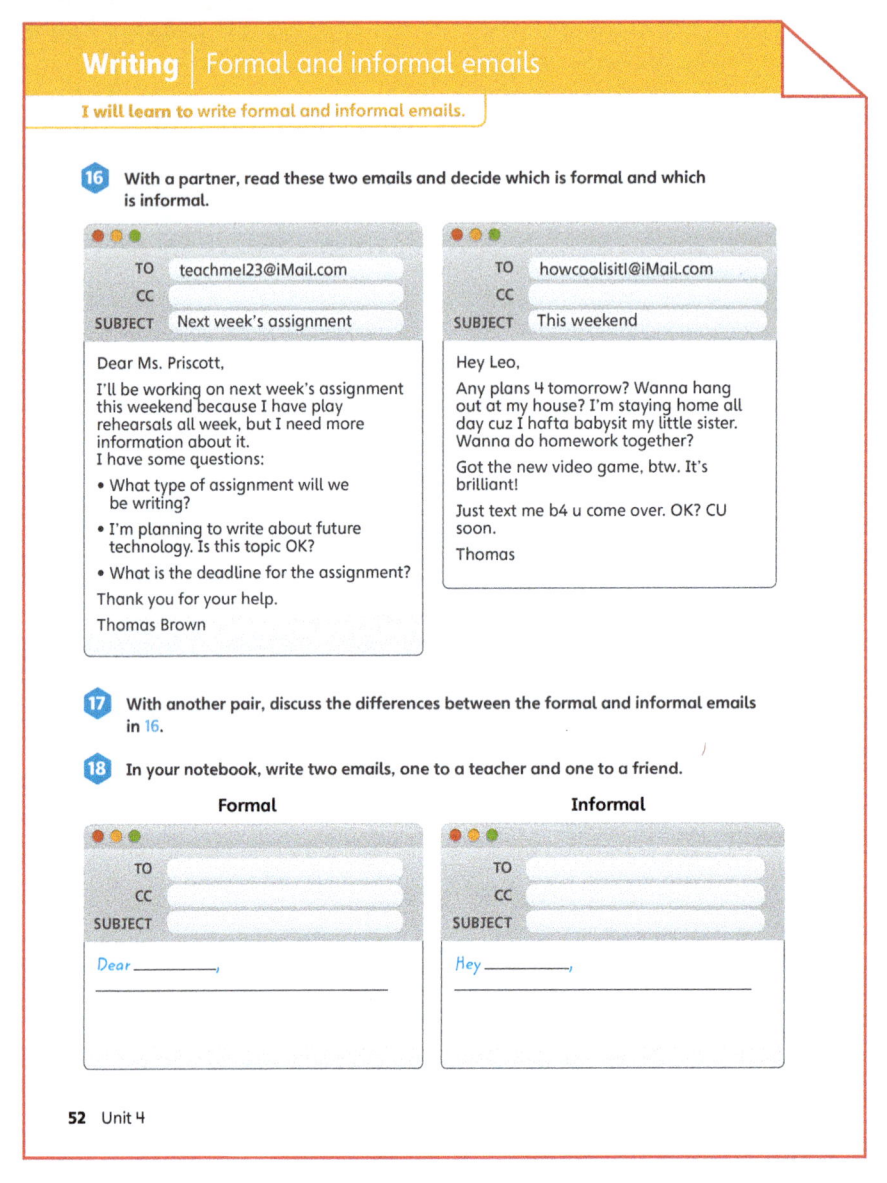

Warm-up

Materials: Magazines, newspapers, catalogs

- Review the meaning of *formal* and *informal*. Say: *Something* informal *is casual, everyday, or friendly. Something* formal *is serious and official.* Have students look through magazines, newspapers, and catalogs for examples of clothing they think is formal or informal. Allow volunteers to share their examples with the class. Ask students whether they agree or not. Then have students make generalizations about what each kind of clothing (formal and informal) looks like.
- Check answers from the HW in the last lesson.

Lesson Objective

INVOLVE

- Introduce the lesson objective. Say: *Today I will learn to write formal and informal emails.*
- Students will read and write formal and informal emails.

Practice 1 — WB p. 42/ act. 18

18 Read each sentence. Write *formal* if it belongs in a formal email or *informal* if it belongs in an informal email.

- Have volunteers read the tips for writing an email in the purple box aloud.
- Read the directions. Have volunteers read the information in the table aloud.
- Have students complete the activity independently.

Practice 2

16 With a partner, read these two emails and decide which is formal and which is informal.

- Read the directions aloud. Then have volunteers read the emails aloud.

MONITOR

Use questions to check comprehension. Ask: *Which email is formal?* (the email to Ms. Priscott) *How do you know it's formal?* (Thomas uses formal language. He writes in complete sentences and doesn't use slang.) *Why does Thomas write to Ms. Priscott?* (to get information about next week's assignment) *Why does Thomas write to Leo?* (to invite him over tomorrow) *How is the email to Leo different?* (It is informal. It uses casual language and some informal abbreviations.)

ASSIST

Help students read the informal language. Explain these words and abbreviations: *4* – for; *wanna* – want to; *cuz* – because; *btw* – by the way; *CU* – see you; *b4 u* – before you. Tell students that not all informal writing necessarily contains these kinds of abbreviations.

21st Century Social Skills

- Ask: *What might happen if Thomas sends an informal email to Ms. Priscott?* (Sample answers: She might be concerned./She might not take Thomas's request seriously./She might think he is impolite or disrespectful.) *What might happen if Thomas sends a formal email to his friend Leo?* (Sample answers: He might think something is wrong./He might think Thomas is too serious./He might tease Thomas.)

Practice 3

17 With another pair, discuss the differences between the formal and informal emails in 16.

- Ask students to work with a partner to discuss the differences between the two emails.

- Ask pairs to report to the class on some of the differences they have found.

MONITOR

As students work, walk around the class and monitor students' pronunciation.

Practice 4

18 In your notebook write two emails, one to a teacher and one to a friend.

- Read the directions aloud. Have students work independently on their emails.

MONITOR

Review the emails with the class. Have volunteers read their emails aloud and have the class point out the differences between the two.

ASSIST

Provide students with specific writing tasks, such as: *Write to a teacher to ask for information about something your class will do next month. Write to a friend to make plans for this weekend.*

Tone: Explain that we use a different tone of voice to read aloud formal and informal writing. Say: *One way to recognize tone is to read something aloud. The tone of your voice will give you a big clue about whether a piece of writing is formal or informal.* Encourage students to read the emails aloud and notice how their tone of voice reflects whether each email is formal or informal.

Lesson Objective

INVOLVE

- Revisit the lesson objective: *Now I have learned to write formal and informal emails.*
- Encourage awareness of what the students have learned by quickly eliciting the differences between a formal and informal email.

Homework — WB p. 42/ act. 19

19 Look at 18. Write a formal email to Mr. Taylor and an informal email to Tami in your notebook. In the informal email, use abbreviations from the box.

- Direct students to WB Activity 19 on page 42. Tell students to write one formal email and one informal email using the information in Activity 18.

Extra Application and Practice Activity

21st Century Technology Literacy

- Have students compile a glossary of abbreviations commonly used in informal emails. Point out that these abbreviations may also be used in online chats or text messages. (Examples include *imho* – in my humble opinion, *jk* – just kidding, *LOL* – laughing out loud, *BFF* – best friends forever.)

Unit 4 **T52**

Writing | Formal and informal emails

I will learn to write formal and informal emails.

16 With a partner, read these two emails and decide which is formal and which is informal.

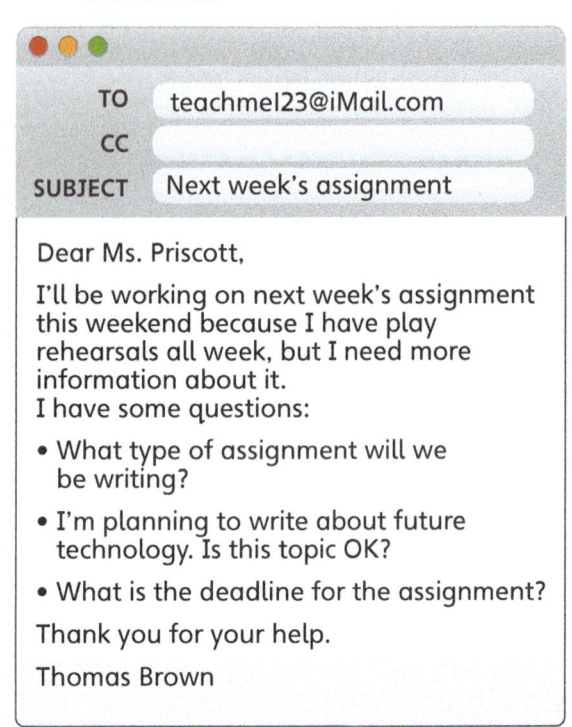

TO teachme123@iMail.com
CC
SUBJECT Next week's assignment

Dear Ms. Priscott,

I'll be working on next week's assignment this weekend because I have play rehearsals all week, but I need more information about it.
I have some questions:

- What type of assignment will we be writing?
- I'm planning to write about future technology. Is this topic OK?
- What is the deadline for the assignment?

Thank you for your help.

Thomas Brown

TO howcoolisit1@iMail.com
CC
SUBJECT This weekend

Hey Leo,

Any plans 4 tomorrow? Wanna hang out at my house? I'm staying home all day cuz I hafta babysit my little sister. Wanna do homework together?

Got the new video game, btw. It's brilliant!

Just text me b4 u come over. OK? CU soon.

Thomas

---

17 With another pair, discuss the differences between the formal and informal emails in 16.

18 In your notebook, write two emails, one to a teacher and one to a friend.

Formal

TO
CC
SUBJECT

Dear _____,
_____

Informal

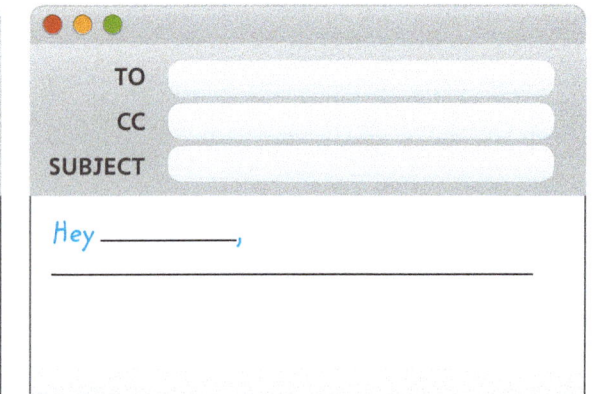

TO
CC
SUBJECT

Hey _____,
_____

52 Unit 4

Life skills | Make smart decisions.

I will learn to talk about making smart decisions.

19 Many young people don't think too much about the future. But sometimes they should. Read these statements. Think of a response to each one.

> Why do I have to learn English? I don't plan on living abroad, so I don't need it.

> My parents own a business. I don't need to finish school because I'll be running the business when I'm old enough.

> Me? Learn how to do household chores? No way! I'll have maids at home, so I won't be doing any chores in the future.

20 Discuss your responses with a partner. Did you have the same responses?

Project

21 Make a **Future Self** book. Write a letter to your future self, fifteen, thirty, even fifty years from now! Make a class book.

> Dear Future Self,
>
> Today is January 4, 2017, and I'm in seventh grade. Fifteen years from now, I'll be living on a tropical island. I'll be teaching at a school there and living near the beach. I won't be married or have children yet. I'll be...

Life Skills Lesson

Lesson Flow

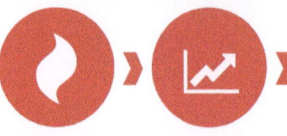

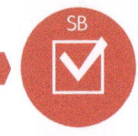

Warm-up › Lesson Objective › Practice › Speaking › Project › Lesson Objective

Lesson Objective

I will learn to talk about making smart decisions.

Life skills | Make smart decisions.

I will learn to talk about making smart decisions.

19 Many young people don't think too much about the future. But sometimes they should. Read these statements. Think of a response to each one.

> Why do I have to learn English? I don't plan on living abroad, so I don't need it.

> My parents own a business. I don't need to finish school because I'll be running the business when I'm old enough.

> Me? Learn how to do household chores? No way! I'll have maids at home, so I won't be doing any chores in the future.

20 Discuss your responses with a partner. Did you have the same responses?

Project

21 Make a *Future Self* book. Write a letter to your future self, fifteen, thirty, even fifty years from now! Make a class book.

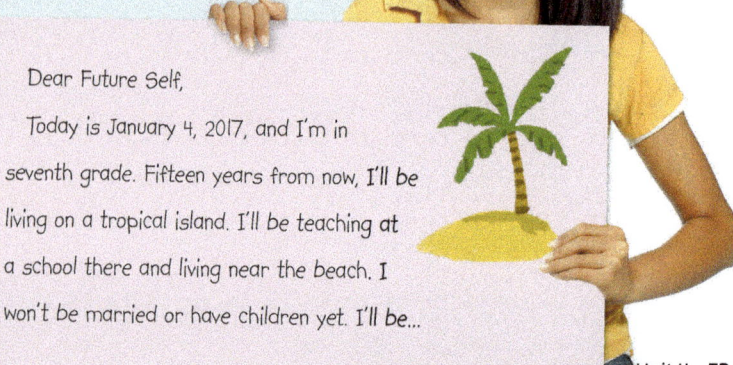

> Dear Future Self,
> Today is January 4, 2017, and I'm in seventh grade. Fifteen years from now, I'll be living on a tropical island. I'll be teaching at a school there and living near the beach. I won't be married or have children yet. I'll be...

Warm-up

- Have students review the FutureSelf emails on pages 46–47 by writing true or false statements about them. Invite students to read their statements aloud and challenge classmates to decide whether each one is true or false. Then have students change details in each false statement to make it true. Model: *FutureSelf is a website that lets you write to yourself in the future.* (True.) *MeToday is the name of a website about today's students.* (False. MeToday is the name of a student who wrote letters to be read in the future.)
- Check answers from the HW in the last lesson.

Lesson Objective

INVOLVE

Introduce the lesson objective. Say: *Today I will learn to talk about making smart decisions.*

- Students will share ideas about making decisions for the future. Then they'll write letters to themselves in the future.

Practice

19 Many young people don't think too much about the future. But sometimes they should. Read these statements. Think of a response to each one.

- Read the page title and directions aloud. Have students write responses to the statements independently. Then have partners ask each other about their responses.

MONITOR

Listen for proper pronunciation, appropriate intonation, and correct use of language.

Speaking

20 Discuss your responses with a partner. Did you have the same responses?

- Read the directions aloud. Provide a sample answer to the first item in Activity 19: *You never know what you'll decide to do in the future. You might end up living where English is the main language spoken. You should learn English. It may help you in the future!*
- Have students compare their answers with a partner, identifying similarities and differences. Ask volunteers to give reasons for their answers.

Project

21 Make a Future Self book. Write a letter to your future self, fifteen, thirty, even fifty years from now! Make a class book.

- Read the directions aloud. Then invite a volunteer to read the sample letter. Ask: *What predictions does this student make for her life fifteen years from now?* (She'll be living on a tropical island near the beach and teaching at a school. She won't be married or have children yet.)
- Have students write their letters independently. Encourage them to illustrate their letters with pictures of what they will be doing.

MONITOR

Have students share their letters and illustrations with the class. Check for correct use of language.

ASSIST

Use simple language to explain any unfamiliar words.

Class Book: Have students create a class book of Future Self letters that includes one or more letters from each student. Have students work as a class to choose an appropriate title and cover illustration. Place the book in the classroom or the school library, or share it with families during conferences.

Lesson Objective

INVOLVE

Revisit the lesson objective: *Now I have learned to talk about making smart decisions.*

- Encourage awareness of what the students have learned by quickly eliciting what they remember about their partner's responses in Activity 18.

Extra Application and Practice Activity

- Have students place individual letters in envelopes with directions to be opened on a specific date in the future. Model: *To be opened by Analia on December 14th, 2025.*

Listening and Speaking Lesson

Lesson Flow

Warm-up › Lesson Objective › Presentation › Practice 1 › Practice 2 › Speaking › Lesson Objective

Lesson Objectives

I will review the sounds *s* and *es*.

I will learn to talk about predictions.

Listening and Speaking

I will review the sounds *s* and *es*.
I will learn to talk about predictions.

22 (63) Listen, read, and repeat.

1 eat**s**   2 sing**s**   3 wash**es**

23 (64) Listen and blend the sounds.

1 c-oo-k-s   cooks   2 r-u-n-s   runs
3 w-a-tch-es watches   4 s-l-ee-p-s sleeps
5 s-w-i-m-s   swims   6 d-a-n-c-es dances

24 (65) Listen and chant.

Sol swims in the summer,
He cooks in the winter,
He dances on Fridays,
He sings in the shower,
And he sleeps for hours!

25 Do a survey. Write a question in your notebook, ask everyone in your class and record their answers. Then make a chart with your results and present it to the class.

> Will you be working in the fashion industry in thirty years?

> Yeah, I probably will be. I'm interested in designing clothes, and I love art.

Working in the Fashion Industry
(bar chart: number of students vs. definitely won't be / probably won't be / probably will be / definitely will be)

> In our class, 15 out of 30 students think they definitely won't be working in the fashion industry.

54 Unit 4

Warm-up

Materials: Timer

- Divide the class into teams, and have students play *Charades* to review unit vocabulary. They should take turns choosing a vocabulary word or phrase and miming it for their team. To increase the challenge, award 3 points for each word guessed in less than 15 seconds, 2 points for under 30 seconds, and 1 point for under a minute.

Lesson Objective

INVOLVE

Introduce the lesson objective. Say: *Today I will learn to use the sounds* s *and* es, *and talk about predictions*.

- Students will identify the letters and distinguish between the sounds *s* and *es*, individually and as part of words. Then they will review making predictions about the future.

Presentation

22 Listen, read, and repeat.

- Read the directions aloud. Play Audio Track 63 and have students listen and point to each sound as it is said. Have students repeat.

MONITOR

As students repeat, check they are pointing to the correct sound and listen for correct pronunciation.

Practice 1

23 Listen and blend the sounds.

- Read the directions aloud. Play Audio Track 64 and have students listen and point to each item as it is sounded out and blended on the audio. Have them repeat after each item.

MONITOR

As students repeat, check they are pointing to the correct word and listen for correct pronunciation and appropriate intonation.

ASSIST

Replay the audio as needed.

Practice 2

24 Listen and chant.

- Read the directions aloud. Read the chant while students follow in their books.
- Play Audio Track 65 and have students listen. Replay the audio several times and encourage them to join in.

MONITOR

As students repeat the chant, listen for proper pronunciation, appropriate intonation, and correct use of language.

Speaking

Materials: Calculators

25 Do a survey. Write a question in your notebook, ask everyone in your class and record their answers. Then make a chart with your results and present it to the class.

- Invite volunteers to read the conversation aloud. Have students work in pairs to ask and answer their own questions about what they'll be doing in thirty years.
- Read the directions aloud. Have groups choose a leader. Ask them to choose a topic for a class survey. Have each group leader poll the class about his or her group's topic.
- When the polling is completed, the leaders should return to their groups, and the groups should tally the results of the poll. Each group should create a graph with the results.
- Have volunteers from each group present the survey results to the class.

MONITOR

Check that students use target language, including degrees of certainty (*probably* and *definitely*) when asking and answering the questions. Encourage them to give reasons for their answers. Also check that students create accurate graphs.

ASSIST

Suggest that students convert the results of their surveys to percentages. Allow students to use calculators to find percentages.

21st Century Information Literacy

- Ask: *Why is it useful to change totals into percentages?* (Sample answers: Percentages are easier to understand./Percentages show parts of a whole./ Percentages give an instant idea of how popular something is.)

Lesson Objective

INVOLVE

Revisit the lesson objective: *Now I have learned to use the sounds* s *and* es, *and talked about predictions*.

- Encourage awareness of what the students have learned by quickly eliciting the words from the lesson with the sounds *s* and *es*.

Extra Application and Practice Activity

- Have students write brief articles summarizing the survey results. Remind them to use degrees of certainty (*probably* and *definitely*). Students may wish to submit finished articles to school or community newspapers or online forums.

Unit 4   T54

Listening and Speaking

I will review the sounds *s* and *es*.
I will learn to talk about predictions.

22 Listen, read, and repeat.

1 eat**s**   2 sing**s**   3 wash**es**

23 Listen and blend the sounds.

1 c-oo-k-s   cooks   2 r-u-n-s   runs
3 w-a-tch-es   watches   4 s-l-ee-p-s   sleeps
5 s-w-i-m-s   swims   6 d-a-n-c-es   dances

24 Listen and chant.

Sol swims in the summer,
He cooks in the winter,
He dances on Fridays,
He sings in the shower,
And he sleeps for hours!

25 Do a survey. Write a question in your notebook, ask everyone in your class and record their answers. Then make a chart with your results and present it to the class.

> Will you be working in the fashion industry in thirty years?

> Yeah, I probably will be. I'm interested in designing clothes, and I love art.

> In our class, 15 out of 30 students think they definitely won't be working in the fashion industry.

54   Unit 4

Review

26 Use the words from the box to complete the expressions.

> a business   a family   a foreign language   a good salary
> adventurous vacations   in a nice office

1 run _____
2 earn _____
3 take _____
4 work _____
5 raise _____
6 speak _____

27 In your notebook, write four sentences about what four of your classmates will be doing in the future. You can use the expressions in 26 and probably or definitely.

28 Ask and answer the questions in pairs. Use complete sentences.

1 What will you probably be doing tonight at 7:20?
2 Will you be traveling with friends ten years from now? Why or why not?
3 What will you definitely not be doing in the future?
4 What will you be doing forty years from now?
5 Will you be raising a family fifteen years from now?
6 Will you be traveling in space fifty years from now?

Will you be raising a family fifteen years from now?

Probably not. I'll probably be working in an another country and earning a good salary. I'll definitely be raising a family in twenty-five years.

I Can

- use words for personal ambitions and future predicitons.
- use the future progressive with *definitely* and *probably*.
- talk about the future and how certain something is.
- write formal and informal emails.

Unit 4

Review Lesson

Lesson Flow

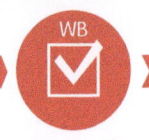

Warm-up › Lesson Objective › Practice 1 (SB) › Practice 2 (WB) › Practice 3 (SB) › Practice 4 (SB) › Self-assessment › Homework

Lesson Objective

To review the words and structures of the unit.

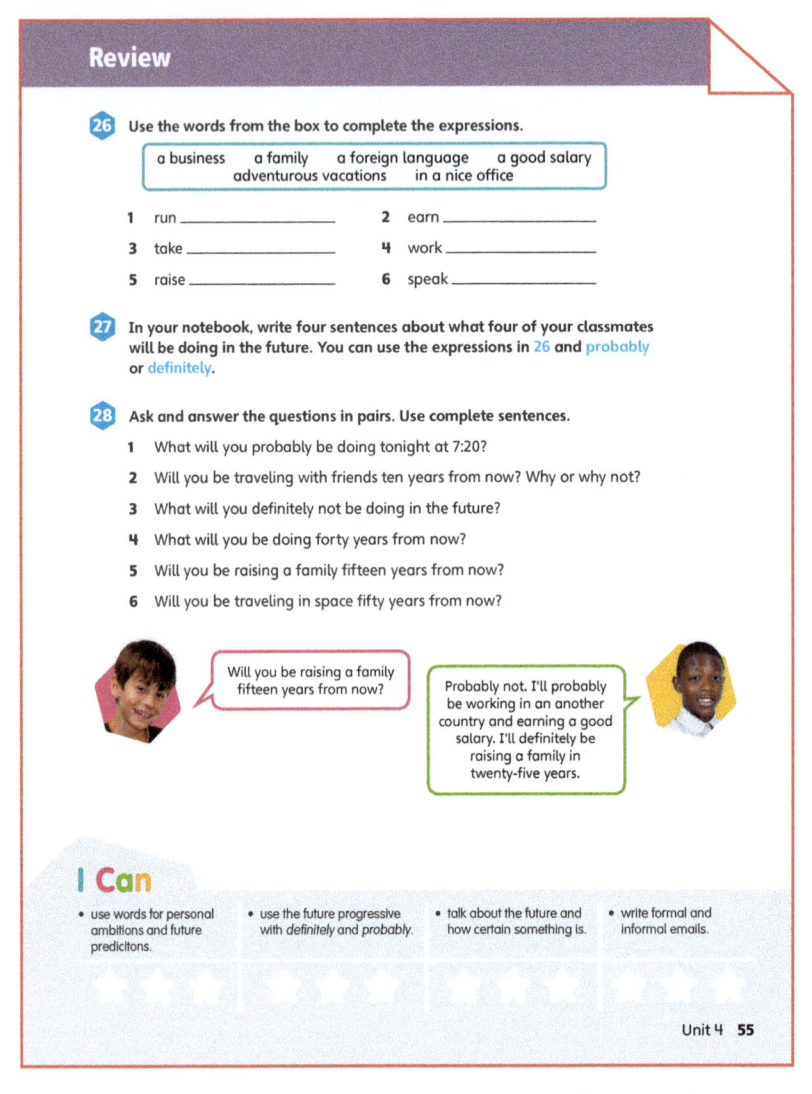

Review

26 Use the words from the box to complete the expressions.

> a business   a family   a foreign language   a good salary
> adventurous vacations   in a nice office

1 run _____
2 earn _____
3 take _____
4 work _____
5 raise _____
6 speak _____

27 In your notebook, write four sentences about what four of your classmates will be doing in the future. You can use the expressions in 26 and *probably* or *definitely*.

28 Ask and answer the questions in pairs. Use complete sentences.

1 What will you probably be doing tonight at 7:20?
2 Will you be traveling with friends ten years from now? Why or why not?
3 What will you definitely not be doing in the future?
4 What will you be doing forty years from now?
5 Will you be raising a family fifteen years from now?
6 Will you be traveling in space fifty years from now?

> Will you be raising a family fifteen years from now?

> Probably not. I'll probably be working in an another country and earning a good salary. I'll definitely be raising a family in twenty-five years.

I Can

- use words for personal ambitions and future predicitons.
- use the future progressive with *definitely* and *probably*.
- talk about the future and how certain something is.
- write formal and informal emails.

Unit 4   55

Warm-up

- Have students create word jumbles for one another to solve, using unit vocabulary. Encourage students to use the phrases in sentences.

Lesson Objective

INVOLVE

Introduce the lesson objective: Say: *Today I will review the words and structures of the unit.*

- Students will review the vocabulary and grammar they learned in Unit 4.
- Then students will complete the *I Can* section, which helps them to assess their own learning and reflect on their progress.

S55   Unit 4

Practice 1

26 Use the words from the box to complete the expressions.

- Read the directions and the words in the box aloud. Point out that some verbs will have more than one expression. Have students complete the activity independently.

MONITOR

Check answers as a class. *(Answers: 1 run a business, 2 earn a good salary, 3 take adventurous vacations, 4 work in a nice office, 5 raise a family, 6 speak a foreign language)*

Practice 2 WB p. 43/ act. 20

20 Complete the text. Use the future progressive of the verbs in parentheses.

- Read the directions aloud. Explain to students that they need to complete the sentences using the future progressive form of the verbs in parentheses.
- Have students work independently.

Practice 3

27 In your notebook, write four sentences about what four of your classmates will be doing in the future. You can use the expressions in 26 and *probably* or *definitely*.

- Read the directions aloud. Give students a minute to predict what they will be doing in the future, using one of the expressions from Activity 26 if appropriate.
- Next, have students ask four classmates what they will be doing in the future, and write down the information. Remind them to use *probably* or *definitely*.

Practice 4

28 Ask and answer the questions in pairs. Use complete sentences.

- Read the directions aloud. Have students work in pairs, taking turns asking and answering each question and then switching roles.

MONITOR

Invite different pairs to ask and answer each item in front of the class.

Self-assessment

I Can

- This section asks students to assess their own learning and reflect on their progress. Help students appreciate their progress. Say: *The I Can statements show what you have learned in this unit.*
- Read the statements aloud. Explain that students should think about how well they know the language in the unit and should color in the stars. They should color three stars if they feel the unit was easy, two stars if they need some help, and one star if the unit was hard and they need more help. Have students work independently.

Suggestions for Remediation

Assessment Pack
- Direct students who need help with grammar and vocabulary to the Unit 4 Practice Tests in the Assessment Pack.

WB Unit 4/ p. 101
- Direct students who need help with grammar in particular to the Unit 4 Extra Grammar Practice (Workbook, page 101).
- For further vocabulary work students can access games in the Big English Student World.

Homework WB p. 43/ act. 21 & 22

21 Choose a family member. Complete the sentences about his/her future using the future progressive. Use *will* or *won't* and the words from the box or your own words.

- Direct students to WB Activity 21 on page 43. Explain to students that they have to choose a family member and then write sentences about their future. Remind them to use the future progressive.

22 Answer the questions. Use *Yes, definitely, Yes, probably, No, probably not,* or *No, definitely not*.

- Direct students to WB Activity 22 on page 43. Explain to students that they have to answer the questions using *Yes, definitely, Yes, probably, No, probably not,* or *No, definitely not*.

Extra Application and Practice Activity

- Ask students to draw cartoons to illustrate one of their predictions from the unit. Have the class guess the prediction.

Assessment Pack

- To assess student progress at the end of the unit, have students complete the Unit 4 Unit Test in the Assessment Pack.
- To assess whether students have reached the listening and speaking targets for this unit, carry out the Unit 4 Oral Assessment in the Assessment Pack.
- Arrange one-to-one sessions with each student and use the prompts to evaluate their listening and speaking abilities.

5 Super Powers

Objectives

Reading

- Can follow the sequence of events in short, simple cartoon stories that use familiar key words.
- Can extract specific information (e.g. facts and numbers) from simple informational texts related to everyday life (e.g. posters, leaflets).
- Can identify key vocabulary and expressions in unfamiliar texts related to school subjects.
- Can understand the main points in simple descriptive texts on familiar topics.

Listening

- Can identify the main points in short talks on familiar topics, if delivered slowly and clearly.
- Can understand the main information in short, simple dialogs about familiar activities, if spoken slowly and clearly.

Speaking

- Can take part in a discussion on a topic of general interest, given time to prepare.
- Can suggest possible outcomes to an event or situation, given a model.

Writing

- Can complete simple forms with basic personal details.
- Can write a simple text (e.g. an invitation to a party) containing key information, given a model.
- Can write short descriptive texts on familiar topics, if provided with key words and supported by pictures.

Grammar

- Can describe hypothetical current results of a current action or situation using the second conditional.

Unit Projects

Family Connection

Have students tell their families that they are learning about superheroes and how super powers might help them solve problems. Model: *We have a lot of dishes to wash, but we also want to play basketball. If we could be in two places at once, we could do both! That would be an amazing super power.* Remind students to take notes about the super powers so they can talk about what they discussed in class.

Key Language

Key Vocabulary

Super Powers

become invisible
fly
have superhuman strength
read people's minds
run at lightning speed
travel through time

Expressions

as it should be
go back in time
Let me think.
Not only that…
quite a character
That's a hard one.
What about you?

Content Words

adhesive	android
electrode	industry
fascinating	meteorite
gecko	mischievous
gesture	native
interact	originate
skyscraper	
spell out	
work on	

Grammar/Structures

If I **were** you, I**'d choose** something else.

If you **could fly**, where **would** you **go**?

If I **could fly**, I**'d go** to the moon.

Phonics

The sounds: *ed*

Tower of Powers Bulletin Board

Create a bulletin display titled *Tower of Powers*. Write *I WISH I COULD* in large bold letters at the top of the display. Then have students add construction paper rectangles above the base to build a tower. Each rectangle should describe a super power students would like to have. Model: *be invisible, fly, remember everything I hear, jump over buildings.* Encourage students to add illustrations to show each super power in action.

Language in Context Lesson

Lesson Flow

Warm-up › Lesson Objective › Presentation › Practice 1 (WB) › Practice 2 (SB) › Practice 3 (WB) › Speaking › Think BIG › Lesson Objective › Homework

Lesson Objective

I will learn to talk about super powers.

Key Language

lightning, minds, period, lightning speed, superhuman strength, time; able, become invisible, fly, read, run, travel; What about you?, Not only that...

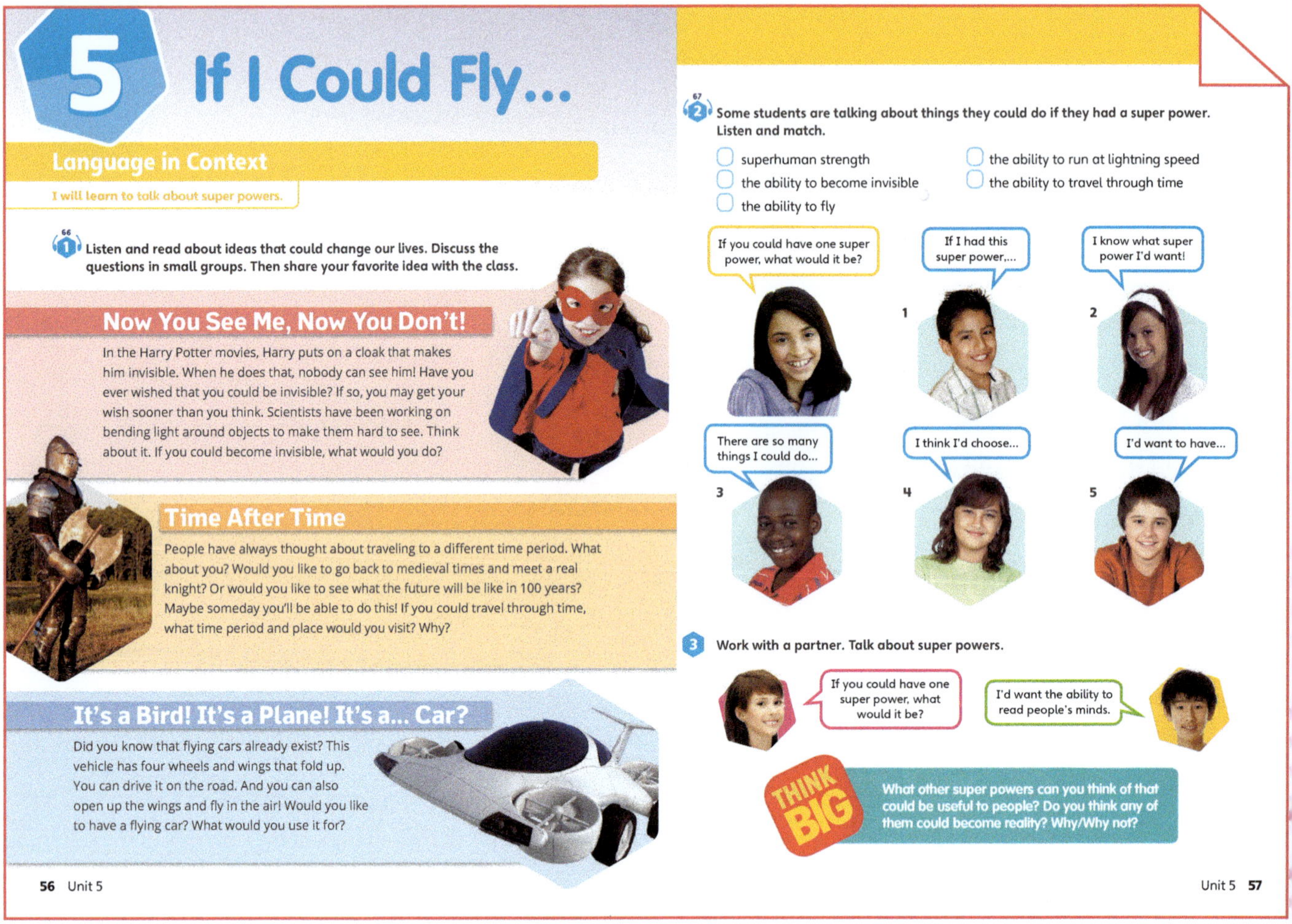

---

5 If I Could Fly...

Language in Context

I will learn to talk about super powers.

1 Listen and read about ideas that could change our lives. Discuss the questions in small groups. Then share your favorite idea with the class.

Now You See Me, Now You Don't!

In the Harry Potter movies, Harry puts on a cloak that makes him invisible. When he does that, nobody can see him! Have you ever wished that you could be invisible? If so, you may get your wish sooner than you think. Scientists have been working on bending light around objects to make them hard to see. Think about it. If you could become invisible, what would you do?

Time After Time

People have always thought about traveling to a different time period. What about you? Would you like to go back to medieval times and meet a real knight? Or would you like to see what the future will be like in 100 years? Maybe someday you'll be able to do this! If you could travel through time, what time period and place would you visit? Why?

It's a Bird! It's a Plane! It's a... Car?

Did you know that flying cars already exist? This vehicle has four wheels and wings that fold up. You can drive it on the road. And you can also open up the wings and fly in the air! Would you like to have a flying car? What would you use it for?

2 Some students are talking about things they could do if they had a super power. Listen and match.

- superhuman strength
- the ability to become invisible
- the ability to fly
- the ability to run at lightning speed
- the ability to travel through time

1. If you could have one super power, what would it be?
2. If I had this super power,...
3. I know what super power I'd want!
4. There are so many things I could do...
5. I think I'd choose...
6. I'd want to have...

3 Work with a partner. Talk about super powers.

- If you could have one super power, what would it be?
- I'd want the ability to read people's minds.

THINK BIG: What other super powers can you think of that could be useful to people? Do you think any of them could become reality? Why/Why not?

Warm-up

Materials: Comic books

- Say: *Super* can mean "very," as in "I am super happy to see you." It can also mean "more than," as in the word *superhuman*. Have students look through comic books and find pictures of heroes doing things that people cannot do. Create a two-column chart labeled *Human* and *Superhuman* to classify the actions in pictures students found. Model: *Put out fires* (Human), *Breathe fire* (Superhuman).
- Encourage volunteers to add examples of human and superhuman actions they recall seeing in movies or on television.
- Check answers from the HW in the last lesson.

Lesson Objective

INVOLVE

Explain the lesson objective. Say: *Today I will learn to talk about super powers.*

- Tell students that they will read and then talk about powers people might have in the future or would like to have.

Presentation 🎧66

1 Listen and read about ideas that could change our lives. Discuss the questions in small groups. Then share your favorite idea with the class.

- Read the directions aloud. Invite volunteers to read the boldface subheadings aloud and predict what each section will be about.
- Play Audio Track 66. Then have students work in groups to discuss the questions at the end of each paragraph.

MONITOR

Have students tell which of the ideas they would most want to come true and tell why. Check for understanding as the groups discuss.

Practice 1 | WB p. 44/ act. 1

1 Which super powers do these characters have? Match the characters with their super power. Write the number.

- Read the directions aloud. Say: *Do you know any of these characters?* Allow volunteers to describe each character and his or her super powers.
- Have students complete the activity independently.

Practice 2 🎧67

2 Some students are talking about things they could do if they had a super power. Listen and match.

- Read the directions aloud. Have students preview the pictures and the words in the box.
- Say: *You will hear some students describe super powers they would like to have.* Play Audio Track 67. Have students do the task independently.

MONITOR

Ask students to name the super power being discussed. (Answers: 1 c, 2 b, 3 a, 4 e, 5 f)

Practice 3 | WB p. 44/ act. 2

2 Look at 1 and answer the questions.

- Read the directions aloud. Ask: *What super powers were mentioned in Activity 1?* (to climb tall buildings, to run at lightning speed, to save the world from bad guys, superhuman strength, to become invisible and to travel through time and space)
- Have students complete the rest of the activity independently.

Speaking

3 Work with a partner. Talk about super powers.

- Read the directions aloud. Have two volunteers read the speech bubbles.
- Have partners talk about what they would do if they had super powers.

Think BIG

21st Century Communication

- Read the questions aloud and encourage students to express themselves as best they can. Write their answers on the board, and then place students in pairs to discuss the questions.

Lesson Objective

INVOLVE

Revisit the lesson objective: *Now I have learned to talk about super powers.*

- Encourage awareness of what the students have learned by quickly eliciting a few super powers discussed in the lesson.

Homework | WB p. 45/ act. 3, 4, & 5

3 Match the beginning of the phrases with their endings. Then label the pictures.

- Direct students to WB Activity 3 on page 45. First students match to make complete phrases. Then they write *1–4* under a–d.

4 Complete the sentences with the phrases in 3.

- Direct students to WB Activity 4 on page 45. Explain to students that they must complete each sentence with one of the phrases that they matched in 3 above.

5 Complete the sentences. If you had these super powers, what would you do?

- Direct students to WB Activity 5 on page 45. Tell students to complete the two sentences so that they are true for them.

Think BIG

- Direct students to the WB Think Big on page 45. Tell students to think about the question and write an answer.

Extra Application and Practice Activity

- Invite students to play *Charades* (see *Game Bank*, page T136, for details), using super powers they have discussed. Write the names of super powers on slips of paper, and have students take turns choosing one and miming it for the class or a team to guess.

5 If I Could Fly...

Language in Context

I will learn to talk about super powers.

🎧 **1** Listen and read about ideas that could change our lives. Discuss the questions in small groups. Then share your favorite idea with the class.

Now You See Me, Now You Don't!

In the Harry Potter movies, Harry puts on a cloak that makes him invisible. When he does that, nobody can see him! Have you ever wished that you could be invisible? If so, you may get your wish sooner than you think. Scientists have been working on bending light around objects to make them hard to see. Think about it. If you could become invisible, what would you do?

Time After Time

People have always thought about traveling to a different time period. What about you? Would you like to go back to medieval times and meet a real knight? Or would you like to see what the future will be like in 100 years? Maybe someday you'll be able to do this! If you could travel through time, what time period and place would you visit? Why?

It's a Bird! It's a Plane! It's a... Car?

Did you know that flying cars already exist? This vehicle has four wheels and wings that fold up. You can drive it on the road. And you can also open up the wings and fly in the air! Would you like to have a flying car? What would you use it for?

2 Some students are talking about things they could do if they had a super power. Listen and match.

- ☐ superhuman strength
- ☐ the ability to become invisible
- ☐ the ability to fly
- ☐ the ability to run at lightning speed
- ☐ the ability to travel through time

If you could have one super power, what would it be?

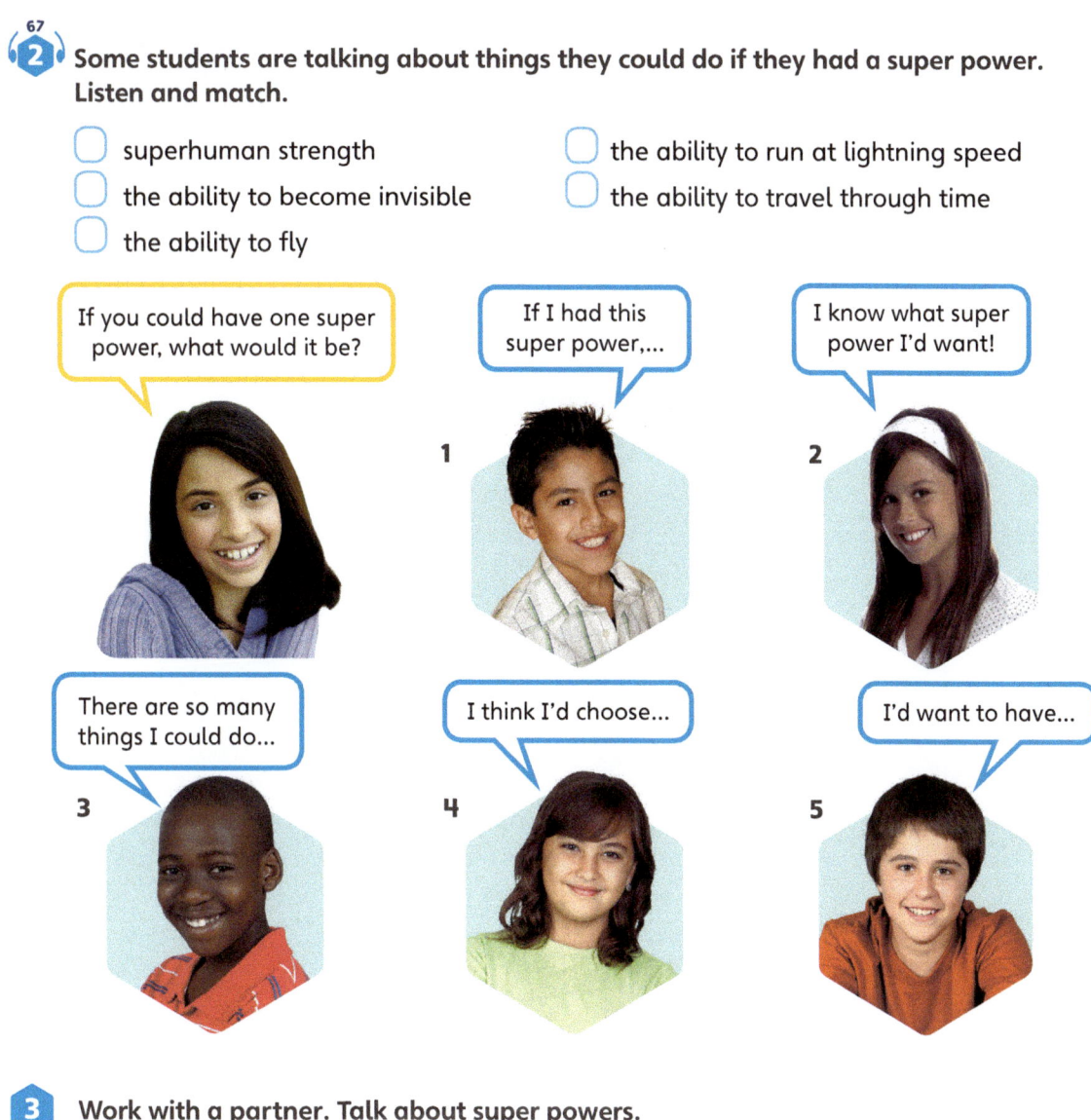

If I had this super power,…

1

I know what super power I'd want!

2

There are so many things I could do…

3

I think I'd choose…

4

I'd want to have…

5

3 Work with a partner. Talk about super powers.

If you could have one super power, what would it be?

I'd want the ability to read people's minds.

THINK BIG
What other super powers can you think of that could be useful to people? Do you think any of them could become reality? Why/Why not?

Unit 5 57

Reading Lesson

Lesson Flow

Warm-up › Lesson Objective › Pre-reading › Reading › Comprehension 1 › Comprehension 2 › Think BIG › Lesson Objective › Homework

Lesson Objective
I will understand a text about superhero.

Key Language
barbecue, birthday cake, city, dinosaur, fire, sausage, smoke, vacation, water; blow out, bring out, fly, hear, put out, scream, take, throw, tie up; calm, quiet; as it should be

---

Reading | Graphic novel

I will understand a text about a superhero.

🎧 Listen and read. What's wrong with Captain Allsafe?

CAPTAIN ALLSAFE TO THE RESCUE!
by Buster Marone

[Comic panels]
- EVERYTHING LOOKS CALM AND QUIET IN OUR CITY – JUST AS IT SHOULD BE.
- WAIT! WHAT'S THAT? I HEAR CHILDREN. THEY'RE SCREAMING!
- THIS IS A JOB FOR CAPTAIN ALLSAFE! DON'T WORRY KIDS, I'LL SAVE YOU!
- CAPTAIN ALLSAFE IS FLYING OVER THE CITY, LOOKING FOR SIGNS OF TROUBLE.
- UNTIL…
- CAPTAIN ALLSAFE SEES SOMETHING HAPPENING BELOW.
- HEY! WHAT DO YOU THINK YOU'RE DOING?
- ♪ HAPPY BIRTHDAY TO… ♪
- HEY!
- CAPTAIN ALLSAFE, IF I WERE YOU, I'D THINK ABOUT TAKING A VACATION.
- ME? GO ON VACATION?
- IF I DID THAT, THE PEOPLE OF THIS CITY WOULDN'T BE SAFE!
- WAIT! SMOKE! FIRE! THIS IS A JOB FOR CAPTAIN ALLSAFE!!!
- HEY, KIDS! THE SAUSAGES ARE…
- OH, NO! MAYBE I SHOULD TAKE A VACATION.

Reading Comprehension

5 Number the events from the story in the order they happened.
- a Captain Allsafe ties up a "dinosaur."
- b Captain Allsafe sees a "fire" and blows it out.
- c Captain Allsafe sees smoke. He throws water and puts out the "fire," pouring water onto the barbecue!
- d Captain Allsafe is flying over the city, and everything seems calm and quiet.
- e Captain Allsafe hears children screaming.
- f Captain Allsafe says that maybe he should go on vacation.
- g A woman brings out a birthday cake.

THINK BIG — Why is going on vacation important? Why is it sometimes impossible to go on vacation when you want to?

Warm-up

- Write *Captain Allsafe* on the board. Say: *We're going to read a story about this superhero. A superhero is a character who has powers that regular people don't have.* Ask: *What two words do you see in this superhero's name?* (all, safe) *What do you think this superhero wants to do?* (Sample answer: He wants to keep all people safe from danger.) *What super powers might he have?* (Sample answers: He might be able to fly or have superhuman strength.)

- Check answers from the HW in the last lesson.

Lesson Objective

INVOLVE

Introduce the lesson objective. Say: *Today I will learn to understand a text about a superhero.*

- Students will listen to, read, talk, and answer questions about a graphic novel.

S58/59 Unit 5

Pre-reading

- Say: *A graphic novel uses pictures and words to tell a story. A graphic novel is divided into* frames *or* panels.
- Have students read the title aloud and preview the first frames of the story. Invite students to compare Captain Allsafe in the story with the predictions they made about him during the Warm-up activity.

21st Century Media Literacy

- Ask: *How is a graphic novel similar to a short story? How is it different?* (Sample answers: Both a short story and a graphic novel are fictional. Both have plots, characters, settings, and conflicts. A short story uses words to describe characters and to say what happens; a graphic novel uses both words and pictures.)

Reading

4 Listen and read. What's wrong with Captain Allsafe?

- Read the directions aloud. Play Audio Track 68 and have students listen and read along.

ASSIST

Replay the audio as needed. Pause after each frame and use simple language to explain unfamiliar words and phrases.

Comprehension 1

- Ask the question in the directions: *What's wrong with Captain Allsafe?* (He needs to go on vacation.)

MONITOR

Ask more questions to check for understanding. Ask: *What does Captain Allsafe mean when he says everything is "just as it should be"?* (People in the city are safe; there are no problems or dangers.) *Why are the children screaming?* (A "dinosaur" is chasing them.) *What does Captain Allsafe do?* (He ties up the "dinosaur" so it can't chase the children.) *What fire does Captain Allsafe put out?* (the candles on a birthday cake) *What happens when the father starts cooking sausages?* (Captain Allsafe pours water on the barbecue.)

21st Century Problem Solving

- Say: *What kinds of problems does Captain Allsafe solve in this story?* (He solves problems that are really not problems. He causes problems because he jumps to conclusions.) Point out that an important part of problem solving is identifying the problem. Ask: *How could Captain Allsafe have avoided making the mistakes he did?* (He could have taken time to find out more about a situation before taking action.)

Comprehension 2

5 Number the events from the story in the order they happened.

- Read the directions aloud. Have volunteers read the events aloud. Ask: *What's happening in the first frame of the story?* (Captain Allsafe is flying over the city, and everything seems calm and quiet.) Have students work independently to order the events from first to last.

MONITOR

Check answers as a class. (Answers: 1 d, 2 e, 3 a, 4 g, 5 b, 6 c, 7 f)

Think BIG

21st Century Critical Thinking

- Read the questions aloud. Have students discuss their answers in pairs.

MONITOR

As pairs work, listen for proper pronunciation, appropriate intonation, and correct use of language.

Lesson Objective

INVOLVE

Revisit the lesson objective: *Now I have learned to understand a text about a superhero.*

- Encourage awareness of what the students have learned by eliciting an example of what Captain Allsafe does wrong in the graphic novel.

Homework   WB p. 46/ act. 6 & 7

6 Listen and read. Then circle T for *true* or F for *false*.

- Direct students to WB Activity 6 on page 46. Tell students to play Audio Track 69, listen, and then decide if each statement is true or false.

7 Answer the questions.

- Direct students to WB Activity 7 on page 46. Students answer the questions, finding the answers in 6.

Extra Application and Practice Activity

- Invite students to role-play interviews with one of the characters from the story. Remind students to ask questions that begin with *who, what, where, when, why,* and *how*. Encourage students to add details that are not in the story. Model questions and answers: Q: *What happened at your birthday party?* A: *Captain Allsafe ruined everything!* Q: *Who's Captain Allsafe?* A: *He's a superhero.* Q: *When did he arrive?* A: *When my Uncle Leo was dressed as a dinosaur. We were having a great time until Captain Allsafe tied up poor Uncle Leo!*

Unit 5   **T58/59**

Reading | Graphic novel

I will understand a text about a superhero.

4 🎧 68 Listen and read. What's wrong with Captain Allsafe?

CAPTAIN ALLSAFE TO THE RESCUE!
by Buster Marone

EVERYTHING LOOKS CALM AND QUIET IN OUR CITY – JUST AS IT SHOULD BE.

CAPTAIN ALLSAFE IS FLYING OVER THE CITY, LOOKING FOR SIGNS OF TROUBLE.

WAIT! WHAT'S THAT? I HEAR CHILDREN. THEY'RE SCREAMING!

UNTIL...

THIS IS A JOB FOR CAPTAIN ALLSAFE! DON'T WORRY KIDS, I'LL SAVE YOU!

CAPTAIN ALLSAFE SEES SOMETHING HAPPENING BELOW.

HEY! WHAT DO YOU THINK YOU'RE DOING?

♪ HAPPY BIRTHDAY TO... ♪

HEY!

CAPTAIN ALLSAFE, IF I WERE YOU, I'D THINK ABOUT TAKING A VACATION.

ME? GO ON VACATION?

IF I DID THAT, THE PEOPLE OF THIS CITY WOULDN'T BE SAFE!

58 Unit 5

Reading Comprehension

5 Number the events from the story in the order they happened.

a Captain Allsafe ties up a "dinosaur."

b Captain Allsafe sees a "fire" and blows it out.

c Captain Allsafe sees smoke. He throws water and puts out the "fire," pouring water onto the barbecue!

d Captain Allsafe is flying over the city, and everything seems calm and quiet.

e Captain Allsafe hears children screaming.

f Captain Allsafe says that maybe he should go on vacation.

g A woman brings out a birthday cake.

THINK BIG Why is going on vacation important? Why is it sometimes impossible to go on vacation when you want to?

Language in Action Lesson

Lesson Flow

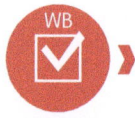

Warm-up › Lesson Objective › Pre-listening › Listening › Comprehension › Role Play › Practice 1 (SB) › Practice 2 (WB) › Lesson Objective › Homework

Lesson Objective

I will listen to a dialog about having super powers.

Key Language

mind, people, time; have, move, read, travel; go back in time, Let me think., quite a character, That's a hard one.

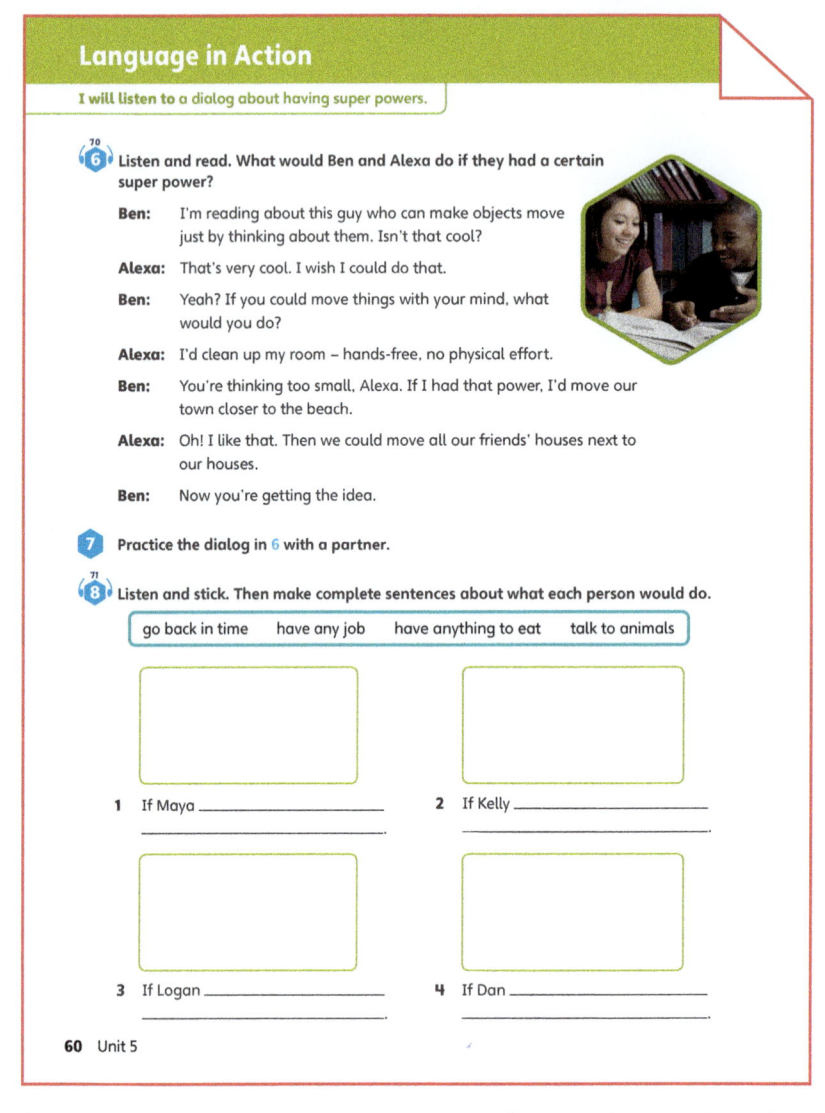

Language in Action

I will listen to a dialog about having super powers.

6 Listen and read. What would Ben and Alexa do if they had a certain super power?

Ben: I'm reading about this guy who can make objects move just by thinking about them. Isn't that cool?

Alexa: That's very cool. I wish I could do that.

Ben: Yeah? If you could move things with your mind, what would you do?

Alexa: I'd clean up my room – hands-free, no physical effort.

Ben: You're thinking too small, Alexa. If I had that power, I'd move our town closer to the beach.

Alexa: Oh! I like that. Then we could move all our friends' houses next to our houses.

Ben: Now you're getting the idea.

7 Practice the dialog in 6 with a partner.

8 Listen and stick. Then make complete sentences about what each person would do.

| go back in time | have any job | have anything to eat | talk to animals |

1 If Maya _____
2 If Kelly _____
3 If Logan _____
4 If Dan _____

60 Unit 5

Warm-up

- Have students preview the Unit 5 stickers that are used in Activity 8. Have them work in pairs to create sentences to describe each picture. One partner should begin the sentence with one word; then partners should take turns adding one word at a time until they have complete sentences. Model: *This picture shows a math test with a good grade.* Have pairs compare their descriptions with other pairs' descriptions.

CHALLENGE

Have students choose one of the pictures and give one-word clues for a partner to guess which picture is being described.

- Check answers from the HW in the last lesson.

S60 Unit 5

Lesson Objective

INVOLVE

- Introduce the lesson objective. Say: *Today I will listen to a dialog about having super powers.*
- Students will read, listen to, and practice a dialog. Students will also listen to conversations about what people would do if they had super powers.

Pre-listening

- Point to the students in the picture. Tell students that they are going to listen to two friends, Ben and Alexa, talking about super powers. Point to the names *Ben* and *Alexa* in the text.

Listening

6 Listen and read. What would Ben and Alexa do if they had a certain super power?

- Read the directions aloud. Play Audio Track 70 and have students listen and read along.
- Invite two students to read the dialog aloud and repeat.

MONITOR

As students practice, listen for correct pronunciation and use of language.

ASSIST

As you notice errors, say words correctly and have students repeat.

Comprehension

- Ask the question in the directions: *What would Ben and Alexa do if they had a certain super power?* (Alexa would clean her room. Ben would move their house closer to the beach.)

MONITOR

Ask more questions to check for understanding. Encourage students to answer in complete sentences where appropriate. Ask: *What does Alexa wish she could do?* (She wishes she could move things with her mind.) *What would she do if she had that power?* (Her first idea is that she would use it to clean up her room.) *What would Ben do?* (He would move their town closer to the beach.) *What idea does Alexa add to Ben's?* (They could move all their friends' houses next to theirs.)

Role Play

7 Practice the dialog in 6 with a partner.

- Read the directions aloud. Invite pairs to read the dialog aloud, switch parts, and repeat.

MONITOR

As students work, listen for proper pronunciation and appropriate intonation.

ASSIST

As you notice errors, say words or sentences correctly and have students repeat after you.

Practice 1

Materials: Stickers

8 Listen and stick. Then make complete sentences about what each person would do.

- Help students find the Unit 5 stickers at the back of the Student's Book. Read the directions and the phrases in the box aloud. Have students look at each picture and describe it. Then have volunteers read the sentences.
- Play Audio Track 71. They then place each sticker by the correct number. Write the first sentence as a class and then have students complete the activity independently.

MONITOR

Check answers as a class. (Answers: 1 If Maya could go back in time, she'd spend more time studying. 2 If Kelly could have any job, she'd be a doctor. 3 If Logan could have anything to eat, he'd have ice cream. 4 If Dan could talk to animals, he'd know what Kiku was saying.)

Practice 2

8 Listen and read. Then circle the correct answers.

- Read the directions aloud. Play Audio Track 72 twice. The second time, have students circle the words they do not understand. Explain their meaning.
- Have students complete the activity.

Lesson Objective

INVOLVE

Revisit the lesson objective: *Now I have listened to a dialog about having super powers.*

- Encourage awareness of what the students have learned by quickly eliciting what they remember from the dialog about what Ben and Alexa would do.

Homework

9 Look at 8. Read the underlined expressions. Match the expressions with their meanings. Write the letters.

- Direct students to WB Activity 9 on page 47. Tell students to match the expressions with their meanings.

10 Complete the sentence. Use a phrase from 9.

- Direct students to WB Activity 10 on page 47. Tell students to choose the correct phrase from 9.

Extra Application and Practice Activity

- Have students write sentences about what they'd do if they had one of the super powers described in this lesson. Then invite partners to interview each other about their super powers and plans.

Unit 5 **T60**

Language in Action

I will listen to a dialog about having super powers.

6 Listen and read. What would Ben and Alexa do if they had a certain super power?

Ben: I'm reading about this guy who can make objects move just by thinking about them. Isn't that cool?

Alexa: That's very cool. I wish I could do that.

Ben: Yeah? If you could move things with your mind, what would you do?

Alexa: I'd clean up my room – hands-free, no physical effort.

Ben: You're thinking too small, Alexa. If I had that power, I'd move our town closer to the beach.

Alexa: Oh! I like that. Then we could move all our friends' houses next to our houses.

Ben: Now you're getting the idea.

7 Practice the dialog in 6 with a partner.

8 Listen and stick. Then make complete sentences about what each person would do.

| go back in time | have any job | have anything to eat | talk to animals |

1 If Maya _____ _____.

2 If Kelly _____ _____.

3 If Logan _____ _____.

4 If Dan _____ _____.

60   Unit 5

Grammar

I will learn to use *if* to talk about imagined situations.

if clause	result clause
If I **were** you,	**I'd choose** something else.
If he **made** his bed every day,	his mom **would be** happy.
If she **could have** one super power,	she**'d become** invisible.

Tip: Use *if* to talk about situations that are not true or contrary to fact. For example: *If I were you = I'm not you.*

9 Circle the correct verbs to complete the sentences.

1 If I **could breathe / would breathe** underwater, I **will explore / would explore** the bottom of the ocean.

2 If he **can / could fly**, he **would fly / will fly** every day.

3 If you **ate / will eat** healthier food, you **are going to be / would be** stronger.

4 If we **can read / could read** people's minds, we **knew / would know** when they were lying.

If you **didn't have to go** to school, what **would** you **do** every day?	If I **didn't have to go** to school, I **would stay** home and **listen** to music all day.
If you **could go** anywhere, where **would** you **go**?	If I **could go** anywhere, I**'d go** to Paris.

10 Choose phrases from the box to complete the questions. Then answer the questions for you. Make complete sentences.

> who would you like to meet?   whose mind would you read?
> what time would you visit?   where would you go now?

1 If you could run at lightening speed, _____

Answer: _____

2 If you could meet a TV or movie star, _____

Answer: _____

3 If you could travel through time, _____

Answer: _____

4 If you could read people's minds, _____

Answer: _____

Grammar Lesson

Lesson Flow

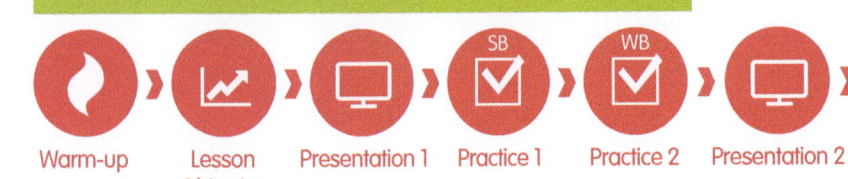

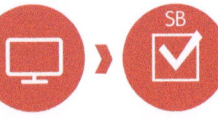

Warm-up › Lesson Objective › Presentation 1 › Practice 1 › Practice 2 › Presentation 2 › Practice 3 › Practice 4 › Lesson Objective › Homework

Lesson Objective

I will learn to use *if* to talk about imagined situations.

Key Language

If I **were** you, I'**d choose** something else.

If you **could fly**, where **would** you **go**? If I **could fly**, I'**d go** to the moon.

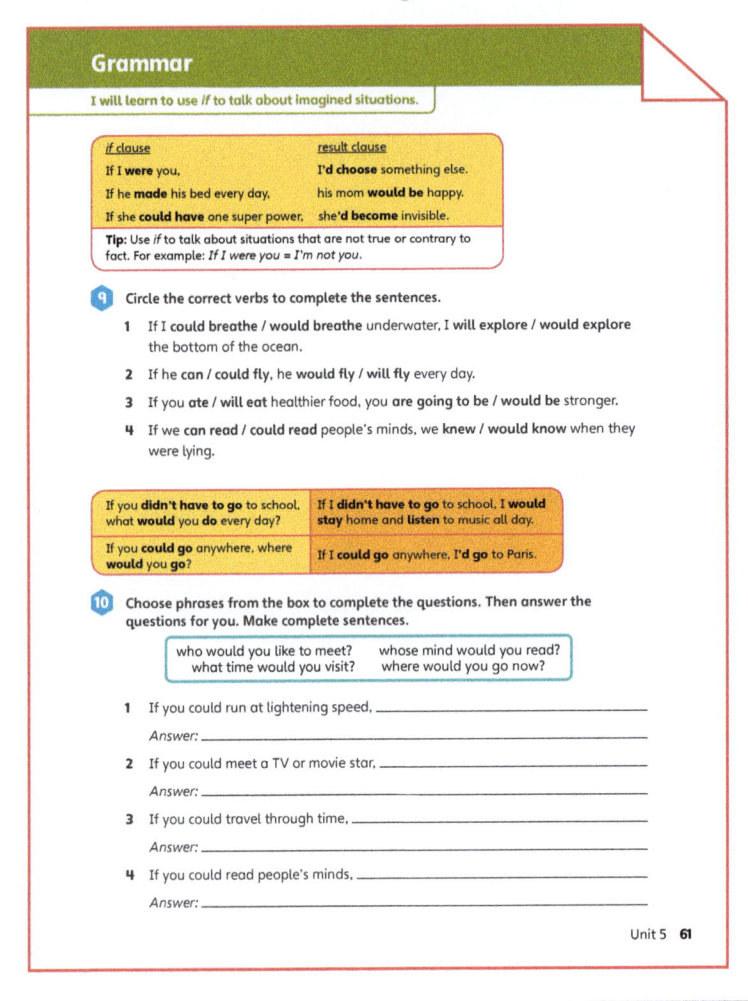

Grammar

I will learn to use *if* to talk about imagined situations.

if clause	result clause
If I **were** you,	I'**d choose** something else.
If he **made** his bed every day,	his mom **would be** happy.
If she **could have** one super power,	she'**d become** invisible.

Tip: Use *if* to talk about situations that are not true or contrary to fact. For example: *If I were you = I'm not you.*

9 Circle the correct verbs to complete the sentences.

1. If I **could breathe / would breathe** underwater, I **will explore / would explore** the bottom of the ocean.
2. If he **can / could fly**, he **would fly / will fly** every day.
3. If you **ate / will eat** healthier food, you **are going to be / would be** stronger.
4. If we **can read / could read** people's minds, we **knew / would know** when they were lying.

If you **didn't have to go** to school, what **would** you **do** every day?	If I **didn't have to go** to school, I **would stay** home and **listen** to music all day.
If you **could go** anywhere, where **would** you **go**?	If I **could go** anywhere, I'**d go** to Paris.

10 Choose phrases from the box to complete the questions. Then answer the questions for you. Make complete sentences.

> who would you like to meet?   whose mind would you read?
> what time would you visit?   where would you go now?

1. If you could run at lightening speed, _____
   Answer: _____
2. If you could meet a TV or movie star, _____
   Answer: _____
3. If you could travel through time, _____
   Answer: _____
4. If you could read people's minds, _____
   Answer: _____

Unit 5 **61**

Warm-up

- To get students ready for using sentences with *if* clauses, have them start thinking about things they would like to have or do (but don't have or can't do now) and people they would like to be when they're older. Provide some examples: *have a dog/teach him tricks; be a movie star/be recognized everywhere I go*. Have students prepare their ideas in small groups.
- Check answers from the HW in the last lesson.

Lesson Objective

INVOLVE

Introduce the lesson objective. Say: *Today I will learn to use* if *to talk about imagined situations.*

- Students will use *if* clauses and result clauses in sentences to talk about what would happen if something were true.

Presentation 1

- Have volunteers read the sentences in the first grammar box aloud.
- Review contractions that include *would* (*I'd, you'd, he'd, she'd, we'd, they'd*). Point out that these contractions combine a subject pronoun and the verb *would*.
- Refer students back to the Language in Action dialog and elicit or highlight the grammar structures in the dialog.

Practice 1

9 Circle the correct verbs to complete the sentences.

- Read the directions aloud and complete Item 1 as a class. Then have students complete the activity independently.

MONITOR

Check answers as a class. (*Answers: 1 could breathe, would explore; 2 could, would fly; 3 ate, would be; 4 could read, would know*)

CHALLENGE

Point out that a result clause can come before an *if* clause. Model: *I would explore the bottom of the sea if I could breathe underwater.* Have students change the order of the clauses in Items 2–4.

Practice 2 WB p. 49/ act. 11

11 Complete the sentences with the words given.

- Read the directions aloud. Complete Item 1 as a class, trying different options till students choose the correct answer.
- Have students complete the activity in pairs.

Presentation 2

- Have volunteers read the questions and answers in the second grammar box aloud.

CHALLENGE

Ask one or two volunteers to supply their own answers to the questions as well, using the same format.

Practice 3

10 Choose phrases from the box to complete the questions. Then answer the questions for you. Make complete sentences.

- Read the directions aloud and complete Item 1 as a class. Then have students complete the activity independently in their notebooks.

MONITOR

Invite volunteers to share their answers with the class. Check for correct use of *if* and result clauses. (*Answers: 1 where else would you go now? Student's own answer. 2 who would you like to meet? Student's own answer. 3 what time would you visit? Student's own answer. 4 whose mind would you read? Student's own answer.*)

Practice 4 WB p. 49/ act. 14

14 Unscramble the questions.

- Read the directions aloud. Explain that the students have to unscramble the words to make phrases that complete each sentence.
- Have a volunteer read the top line of words aloud. Then Complete Item 1 as a class, trying different options till students choose the correct answer.
- Have students work independently to complete the activity, then compare answers with a partner.

Lesson Objective

INVOLVE

Revisit the lesson objective: *Now I have learned to use* if *to talk about imagined situations.*

- Encourage awareness of what the students have learned by quickly eliciting responses to phrases that start with *if*. For example: *If school ends early today,… .*

Homework WB pp. 48 & 49/ act. 12, 13, 15, & 16

12 Read. Complete the sentences with the words in parentheses and *could* and *would*.

- Direct students to WB Activity 12 on page 48. Tell students to use *could* or *would* in each space, and then choose the correct form of the verb in brackets.

13 Complete the sentences about yourself.

- Direct students to WB Activity 13 on page 48. Have students write about themselves.

15 Match the questions in 14 with the answers below. Write the numbers. Then circle T for *true* or F for *false*.

- Direct students to WB Activity 15 on page 49. Tell students to choose one of the questions 1–5 from 14 to match with the answers in 15. They write the question number in the space before the answer number. Students then circle T or F to show whether the answer would be true for themselves or not.

16 Ask the questions in 14 to a friend or family member. Write his or her answers.

- Direct students to WB Activity 16 on page 49. Students write their friend or family member's answers to the questions.

Extra Application and Practice Activity

Materials: Slips of paper

- Have students write two or three sentences using this frame: *If I could…, I'd… .* Then have them write each clause on a separate slip of paper and mix up the slips. Suggest that students use what they listed on their charts for the Warm-up activity. Challenge classmates to assemble the sentences.

Unit 5 **T61**

Content Connection Lesson

Lesson Flow

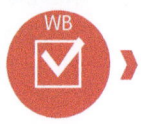

Warm-up › Lesson Objective › Pre-reading › Reading › Practice › Think BIG › Video › Lesson Objective › Homework

Lesson Objectives

I will learn about inventing super powers.

Key Language

adhesive, electrode, fascinating, gecko, gesture, interact, skyscraper, spell out, work on

---

Content Connection | Life Science

I will learn about inventing super powers.

CONTENT WORDS
adhesive electrode fascinating
gecko gesture interact skyscraper
spell out work on

Super Power or Super Science?

People have always found super powers fascinating. We love watching movies about superheroes. They can do all the things that humans can't do. Or can we? Every year, engineers create new technologies that people couldn't even imagine in the past. Here are three surprising things that scientists are already working on.

Have you ever seen a gecko climb up a wall and wondered why it doesn't fall off? Geckos have very sticky feet, which stop them from slipping off the wall. If a human could climb like a gecko, it would seem like a super power. Scientists are experimenting with plastic to make an adhesive (a kind of glue) that will let humans climb up walls, and they're close to succeeding! [1]_____

How would you like to be able to Tweet without using a keyboard? Believe it or not, there's a scientist who's trying to make this possible! His idea uses a cap with electrodes. While wearing the cap, he concentrates on one letter at a time, spelling out his message on a computer screen! He's able to tweet eight letters a minute. But in the future, who knows? [2]_____

Mark Rolston, a computer designer, thinks that computers as we know them – a monitor, a keyboard, and speakers – limit us. He believes that we need to start thinking that the computer is the room we're in and we interact with it using voice or gestures. Imagine, or example, being able to watch the news on the kitchen table, make a video call on your refrigerator, and read a recipe on the wall above your oven by activating the computer using voice or gestures. [3]_____

Read and put sentences a–c in the correct place. Then listen and check your answers.

a   This would really be a digital world!
b   Maybe we'll see skyscraper climbing as an Olympic sport one day!
c   It would certainly make texting in class easier!

THINK BIG Which of the super powers you read about would be the most useful to you? Why?

62 Unit 5

Warm-up

- Ask: *What can some animals do that people can't?* Write students' answers on the board. (Sample answers: fly, live underwater, change their skin color, live in very cold conditions) Say: *Something you can do is an ability. Animals have some abilities that people don't have. Science can help us develop new abilities.*

- Check answers from the HW in the last lesson.

Lesson Objective

INVOLVE

Introduce the lesson objective. Say: *Today I will learn about inventing super powers.*

- Students will read and talk about scientific advances.

Pre-reading

- Have students read the Content Words aloud. Ask volunteers to share meanings of these words.
- Read the heading aloud. Ask student to predict what the text will be about.
- Point to the three different-colored blocks of text. Suggest to students that each block will deal with a different example.

Reading

11 Read and put sentences a–c in the correct place. Then listen and check your answers.

- Use "reciprocal teaching" to help students understand the text through close reading. Write these four strategies on the board for students to use: *summarizing – putting ideas in your own words, clarifying – figuring out something that is confusing, asking questions – sharing something you wonder about, predicting – making an educated guess as to what will happen next.*
- Have a volunteer read the title aloud. Next, read the first paragraph aloud. Ask different students to summarize a key idea, clarify something that was confusing, ask a question, and make a prediction based on the last sentence about what surprising things scientists are working on.
- Divide the class into groups of three or four and have them continue with the reading process, stopping after each paragraph and taking turns using the reading strategies.
- Have students put sentences a, b, and c in the correct place in the text.

21st Century Technology Literacy

- Explain that an electrode conducts electricity. The scientist who tweets by thinking, places electrodes in a cap on his head. The electrodes detect electrical energy in the brain, which allows him to send messages without using his hands. Ask: *What other tasks might you do with this technology?*

MONITOR

As students are working, walk around the class and monitor their use of the strategies.

- Play Audio Track 73, and have students listen and check their answers.

MONITOR

Check answers as a class. *(Answers: 1 b, 2 c, 3 a)*

ASSIST

Reading aloud can help students practice intonation. After students have listened to the audio, encourage them to take turns reading the article aloud in small groups. Model different intonation for the questions and answers. If possible, allow students to record their readings and compare their recordings with the audio.

Practice

17 Listen and read. Match the titles A-E with the paragraphs 1-5.

- Read the directions aloud. Before playing the audio, ask a volunteer to read aloud the titles.
- Play Audio Track 74 and have students listen and follow in their books.
- Have students complete the activity independently. Replay the audio if necessary.

Think BIG

21st Century Critical Thinking

- Divide the class into small groups. Read the question aloud, and have students take turns answering it in their groups.

ASSIST

Write the word *useful* on the board. Make sure students understand its meaning.

- Ask individuals from each group to share answers from their group with the class.

Video

- Refer to the Video Guide for pre-watching and post-watching activities.

Lesson Objective

INVOLVE

Revisit the lesson objective: *Now I have learned about inventing super powers.*

- Encourage awareness of what the students have learned by eliciting from them the main point of the text. Ask: *What is the difference between a super power and science?*

Homework

18 Read 17 again and circle T for *true* or F for *false*.

- Direct students to WB Activity 18 on page 50. Tell students to scan the text to find the information for each item, then circle if they are true or false.

Extra Application and Practice Activity

Materials: Art supplies

- Have students create a "scientific superhero" comic strip based on one of the scientific advances described in the text. Tell them to create a superhero and have him or her use the scientific super power to help save the day.

Content Connection | Life Science

I will learn about inventing super powers.

CONTENT WORDS
adhesive   electrode   fascinating
gecko   gesture   interact   skyscraper
spell out   work on

Super Power or Super Science?

People have always found super powers fascinating. We love watching movies about superheroes. They can do all the things that humans can't do. Or can we? Every year, engineers create new technologies that people couldn't even imagine in the past. Here are three surprising things that scientists are already working on.

Have you ever seen a gecko climb up a wall and wondered why it doesn't fall off? Geckos have very sticky feet, which stop them from slipping off the wall. If a human could climb like a gecko, it would seem like a super power. Scientists are experimenting with plastic to make an adhesive (a kind of glue) that will let humans climb up walls, and they're close to succeeding! [1]_____

How would you like to be able to Tweet without using a keyboard? Believe it or not, there's a scientist who's trying to make this possible! His idea uses a cap with electrodes. While wearing the cap, he concentrates on one letter at a time, spelling out his message on a computer screen! He's able to tweet eight letters a minute. But in the future, who knows? [2]_____

Mark Rolston, a computer designer, thinks that computers as we know them – a monitor, a keyboard, and speakers – limit us. He believes that we need to start thinking that the computer is the room we're in and we interact with it using voice or gestures. Imagine, or example, being able to watch the news on the kitchen table, make a video call on your refrigerator, and read a recipe on the wall above your oven by activating the computer using voice or gestures. [3]_____

11 Read and put sentences a–c in the correct place. Then listen and check your answers.

a   This would really be a digital world!
b   Maybe we'll see skyscraper climbing as an Olympic sport one day!
c   It would certainly make texting in class easier!

THINK BIG
Which of the super powers you read about would be the most useful to you? Why?

Culture Connection | Around the World

I will learn about superheroes around the world.

12 Listen and read. Which superhero is also called Aldo?

CONTENT WORDS
android   industry
meteorite   mischievous
native   originate

Superheroes from Different Cultures

Although many superheroes originated in the U.S.A., there are many other countries with their own superheroes. Japan, which has the largest comic book industry in the world (called manga), has many heroes. Mexican writers started creating their own native heroes in the 1990s, and in India, comic books have been around for the last fifty years. Here are some popular examples.

Cat Girl Nuku Nuku – Japan
In everyday life, this hero is called Atsuko "Nuku Nuku" Natsume. She's an android with a cat's brain, but she goes to school every day with her "brother," Ryunosuke. Nuku Nuku is a highly advanced android with the reflexes and senses of a cat. She also has superhuman strength.

Meteorix – Mexico
He goes to school, where he's known as Aldo. He has superhuman strength and can throw bolts of blue lightning. He gained his super powers when he swallowed a piece of meteorite that fell to Earth. His mission is to protect Mexico City from dangerous criminals.

Bantul the Great – India
Bantul just does odd jobs. If he didn't have his super powers, he might not get into trouble, but he often does. He takes care of two mischievous schoolboys. He has a really big appetite, and sometimes he eats a whole whale for breakfast! Bantul is incredibly strong. He could stop a train if he stood in front of it. He can move things just by blowing air out of his mouth, and bullets can't hurt him.

13 Look at the passage. Circle the correct words.

1. Meteorix **can fly / has superhuman strength**.
2. **The U.S.A. / Japan** produces the most comic books in the world.
3. India has had a comic book industry **since the 1990s / for the last 50 years**.

THINK BIG Why do you think people like to read stories about superheroes?

Culture Connection Lesson

Lesson Flow

Warm-up › Lesson Objective › Pre-reading › Reading › Practice 1 (SB) › Practice 2 (WB) › Think BIG › Lesson Objective › Homework

Lesson Objective

I will learn about superheroes around the world.

Key Language

android, industry, meteorite, mischievous, native, originate

Culture Connection | Around the World

I will learn about superheroes around the world.

12 🎧75 Listen and read. Which superhero is also called Aldo?

CONTENT WORDS
android   industry
meteorite   mischievous
native   originate

Superheroes from Different Cultures

Although many superheroes originated in the U.S.A., there are many other countries with their own superheroes. Japan, which has the largest comic book industry in the world (called manga), has many heroes. Mexican writers started creating their own native heroes in the 1990s, and in India, comic books have been around for the last fifty years. Here are some popular examples.

Cat Girl Nuku Nuku – Japan 
In everyday life, this hero is called Atsuko "Nuku Nuku" Natsume. She's an android with a cat's brain, but she goes to school every day with her "brother," Ryunosuke. Nuku Nuku is a highly advanced android with the reflexes and senses of a cat. She also has superhuman strength.

Meteorix – Mexico 
He goes to school, where he's known as Aldo. He has superhuman strength and can throw bolts of blue lightning. He gained his super powers when he swallowed a piece of meteorite that fell to Earth. His mission is to protect Mexico City from dangerous criminals.

Bantul the Great – India 
Bantul just does odd jobs. If he didn't have his super powers, he might not get into trouble, but he often does. He takes care of two mischievous schoolboys. He has a really big appetite, and sometimes he eats a whole whale for breakfast! Bantul is incredibly strong. He could stop a train if he stood in front of it. He can move things just by blowing air out of his mouth, and bullets can't hurt him.

13 Look at the passage. Circle the correct words.

1. Meteorix **can fly / has superhuman strength**.
2. **The U.S.A. / Japan** produces the most comic books in the world.
3. India has had a comic book industry **since the 1990s / for the last 50 years**.

THINK BIG Why do you think people like to read stories about superheroes?

Warm-up

Materials: Index cards

- Ask: *Who in our class has the super power of mind reading?* Have students play a mind-reading game to find out. Write these vocabulary items on the board: *android, armor, bolt of lightning, meteorite, reflexes.* Have students create vocabulary cards for the words and take turns choosing and thinking about one card. Partners should try to guess which card their partner chose. Find out which student(s) had the most correct guesses out of five or ten attempts.
- Check answers from the HW in the last lesson.

Lesson Objective

INVOLVE

Introduce the lesson objective. Say: *Today I will learn about superheroes around the world.*

- Students will read and talk about superheroes from different cultures, including their own.

Pre-reading

- Write the Content Words on the board. Go over their meanings with the class.
- Ask: *What do you know about superheroes?*

Reading

12 Listen and read. Which superhero is also called Aldo?

MONITOR

Discuss the answer as a class. *(Answer: Meteorix)*

ASSIST

Replay the audio as needed. Use simple language and gestures to explain unfamiliar words.

Practice 1

13 Look at the passage. Circle the correct words.

- Have students work independently to read the article again and find the answers.

MONITOR

Ask several students to read out the completed sentences. *(Answers: 1 has superhuman strength, 2 Japan, 3 for the last 50 years)*

CHALLENGE

Write the following sentence starters on the board: *I think it is interesting that… . I was surprised to learn… is similar to… because… .*

- Have small groups discuss the article using these sentence starters. Invite volunteers to share their thoughts with the class.
- Have students find the Content Words in the text.

Practice 2 — WB p. 51/ act. 19

19 Listen and read. Write the names of the superheroes.

- Read the directions aloud. Before playing the audio, ask a volunteer to read aloud the three definitions.
- Play Audio Track 76 and have students listen and follow in their books.
- Have students complete the activity independently. Replay the audio if necessary.

MONITOR

Check answers as a class. *(Answers: 1 Darna, 2 Meteorix, 3 Cat Girl Nuku Nuku)*

Think BIG

Materials: Poster paper, art supplies

21st Century Critical Thinking

- Read the question aloud. Have students work individually to brainstorm at least five different reasons that people like to read stories about superheroes. (e.g. *superheroes fight evil, they have special powers, they have cool equipment*)
- Make a poster titled "Why Superheroes Are Popular," and add the reasons to the chart. Allow students to illustrate the poster if they wish, and display the poster in the classroom.

Lesson Objective

INVOLVE

Revisit the lesson objective: *Now I have learned about superheroes around the world.*

- Encourage awareness of what the students have learned by quickly eliciting a few things they remember about the passage, using the question in the Pre-reading activity.

Homework — WB p. 51/ act. 20

20 Unscramble and write words from 19. Then complete the sentences.

- Direct students to WB Activity 20 on page 51. Have students first unscramble and write the words from this lesson. Then they use each word to complete the sentences that follows.

Extra Application and Practice Activity

- Have students work in pairs or small groups to role-play a scene with one of the superheroes described in the article. Suggest that they show how the superhero changes from an everyday person into a superhero and then uses his or her powers to help someone. If possible, allow students to record their scenes using phones or video cameras.

Unit 5 T63

Writing Lesson

Lesson Flow

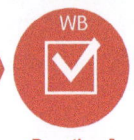

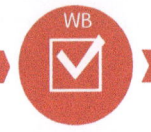

Warm-up › Lesson Objective › Practice 1 (WB) › Practice 2 (WB) › Practice 3 (SB) › Practice 4 (SB) › Speaking › Lesson Objective › Homework

Lesson Objective

I will learn to write a description of a superhero.

Writing | Character traits

I will learn to write a description of a superhero.

14 Create and describe a superhero character of your own. Use the questions to help you. Take notes and discuss with a partner.

- What are your character's superhero and everyday names?
- What is his or her everyday occupation?
- What is his or her country of origin?
- In what time period does your character live?
- What does he or she look like?
- Does he or she have a family? If so, describe each member.
- What are your character's super powers?
- What is your character's mission?

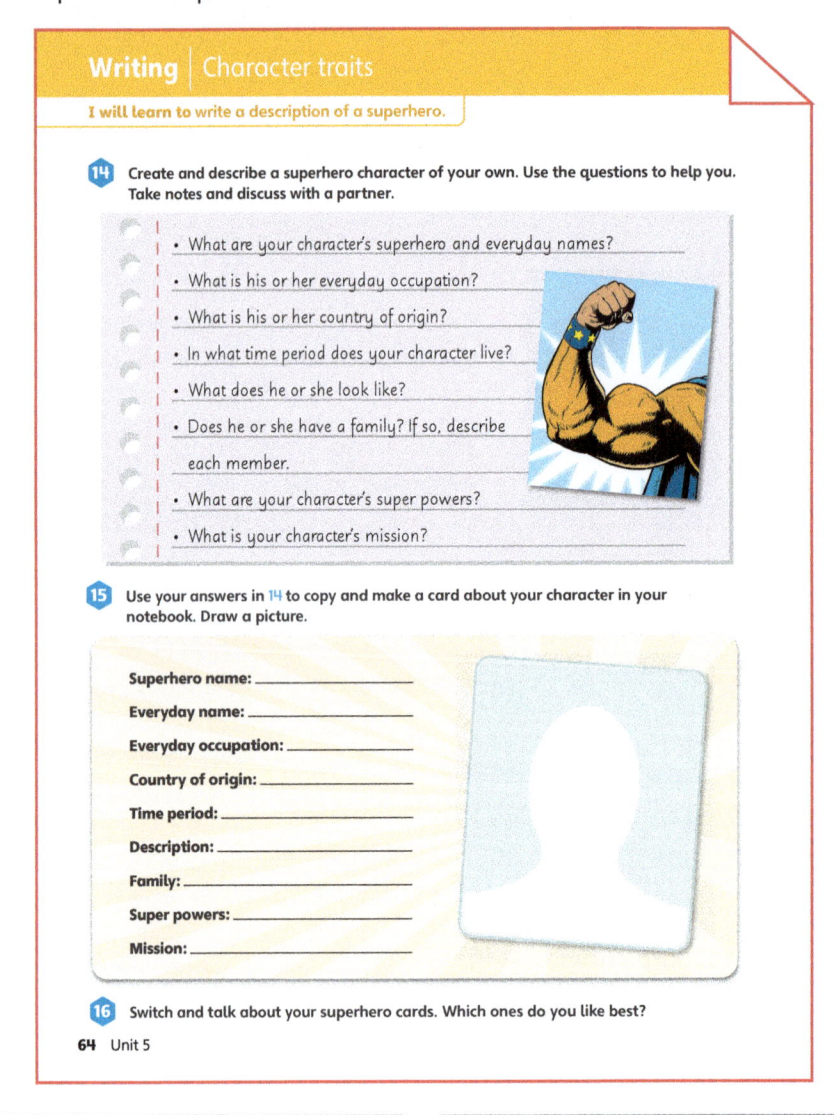

15 Use your answers in 14 to copy and make a card about your character in your notebook. Draw a picture.

Superhero name: _____
Everyday name: _____
Everyday occupation: _____
Country of origin: _____
Time period: _____
Description: _____
Family: _____
Super powers: _____
Mission: _____

16 Switch and talk about your superhero cards. Which ones do you like best?

64 Unit 5

Warm-up

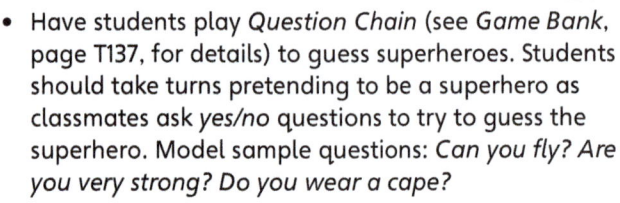

- Have students play *Question Chain* (see *Game Bank*, page T137, for details) to guess superheroes. Students should take turns pretending to be a superhero as classmates ask *yes/no* questions to try to guess the superhero. Model sample questions: *Can you fly? Are you very strong? Do you wear a cape?*
- Check answers from the HW in the last lesson.

Lesson Objective

INVOLVE

Introduce the lesson objective. Say: *Today I will learn to write a description of a superhero.*

- Students will create and then write about superheroes and their character traits.

S64 Unit 5

Practice 1 WB p. 52/ act. 21

21 Read the sentences and match them with the information in the box. What information is missing? Write the numbers.

- Read the directions aloud. Have volunteers read the information in the box aloud. Discuss the meaning of each of these.
- Do the first item with students. Read: *Her everyday name is Diana, but her superhero name is Wonder Woman. This is her name so we write* 1 *in the space.*
- Have students complete the remaining items with a partner. Check answers as a class.

Practice 2 WB p. 52/ act. 22

22 Read the missing information from 21 below. Number it according to the information in the writing box.

- Read the directions aloud. Have students read each item and then decide what information it gives about the character. Use the list in the box at the top of the page.
- Have students work independently. Check answers as a class.

Practice 3

14 Create and describe a superhero character of your own. Use the questions to help you. Take notes and discuss with a partner.

- Read the directions and questions aloud. Then have students work in pairs, taking turns asking and answering questions. Tell students to take notes.

21st Century Environmental Awareness

- Encourage students to think of ways superheroes could help improve the environment. Say: *Make a list of problems that a superhero might help with*, such as pollution, endangered animals, or lack of water. Have students choose abilities for the superheroes that will help them solve one of these environmental problems.

MONITOR
Have volunteers share their answers.

ASSIST
Provide new vocabulary as needed. Use simple language and gestures to define unfamiliar terms in the questions. To help students come up with super powers, remind them about the amazing things that animals can do and people can't (page 62). Suggest that they create superheroes with abilities animals have.

Practice 4

15 Use your answers in 14 to copy and make a card about your character in your notebook. Draw a picture.

- Read the directions aloud. Ask students to use the model card on the page as a guide. Then have them work independently to complete their cards.

MONITOR
Check that students have completed their card.

ASSIST
Provide students with vocabulary as needed to describe their characters. You could also have students create cards for existing superheroes. Provide them with comic books or other source materials for information.

Speaking

16 Switch and talk about your superhero cards. Which ones do you like best?

- Read the directions aloud. Have students work in small groups to switch and talk about their cards. Encourage them to show enthusiasm for their classmates' work.

MONITOR
Gently correct any errors as students discuss their cards.

Lesson Objective

INVOLVE
Revisit the lesson objective: *Now I have learned to write a description of a superhero.*

- Encourage awareness of what the students have learned by asking for examples of what you need to describe when describing or creating a character.

Homework WB p. 52/ act. 23

23 Write a description of Wonder Woman. Use the information in 21 and 22.

- Direct students to WB Activity 23 on page 52. Tell students to write a description of Wonder Woman using the information in the previous activities on this page.

Extra Application and Practice Activity

- Have students create superhero challenges. Have two students describe their superheroes. Another two students should describe a situation, such as putting out a forest fire, stopping corruption, etc. Have one or more students act as judges to decide which superhero would be best suited for the situation. Model a situation and the best choice: *Imagine there is a giant storm and trees are falling down. If Tim's and Martina's superheroes were there, which one would be the most helpful? If Martina's superhero were there, he could run like lightning and make sure that each tree falls safely.*

Unit 5 **T64**

Writing | Character traits

I will learn to write a description of a superhero.

14 Create and describe a superhero character of your own. Use the questions to help you. Take notes and discuss with a partner.

- What are your character's superhero and everyday names?
- What is his or her everyday occupation?
- What is his or her country of origin?
- In what time period does your character live?
- What does he or she look like?
- Does he or she have a family? If so, describe each member.
- What are your character's super powers?
- What is your character's mission?

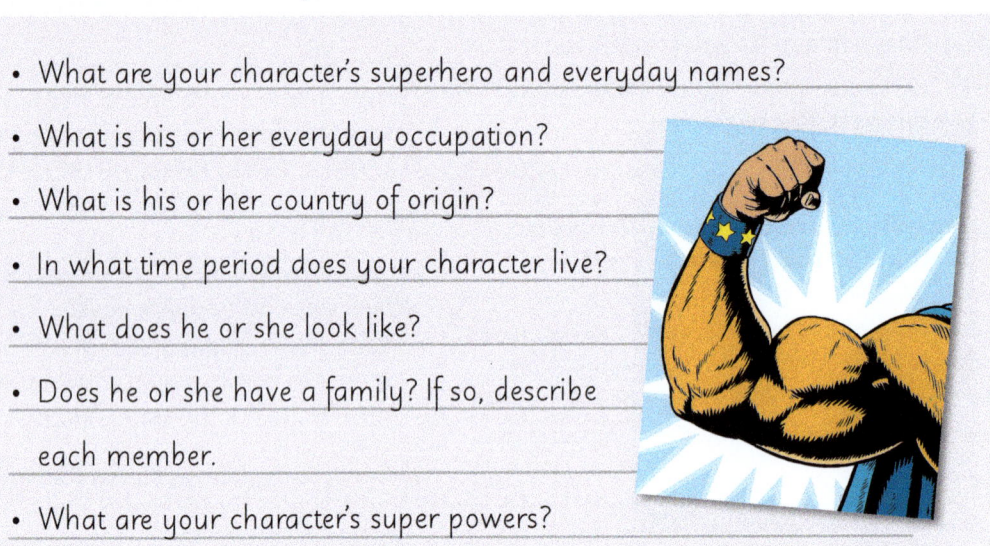

15 Use your answers in 14 to copy and make a card about your character in your notebook. Draw a picture.

Superhero name: _____

Everyday name: _____

Everyday occupation: _____

Country of origin: _____

Time period: _____

Description: _____

Family: _____

Super powers: _____

Mission: _____

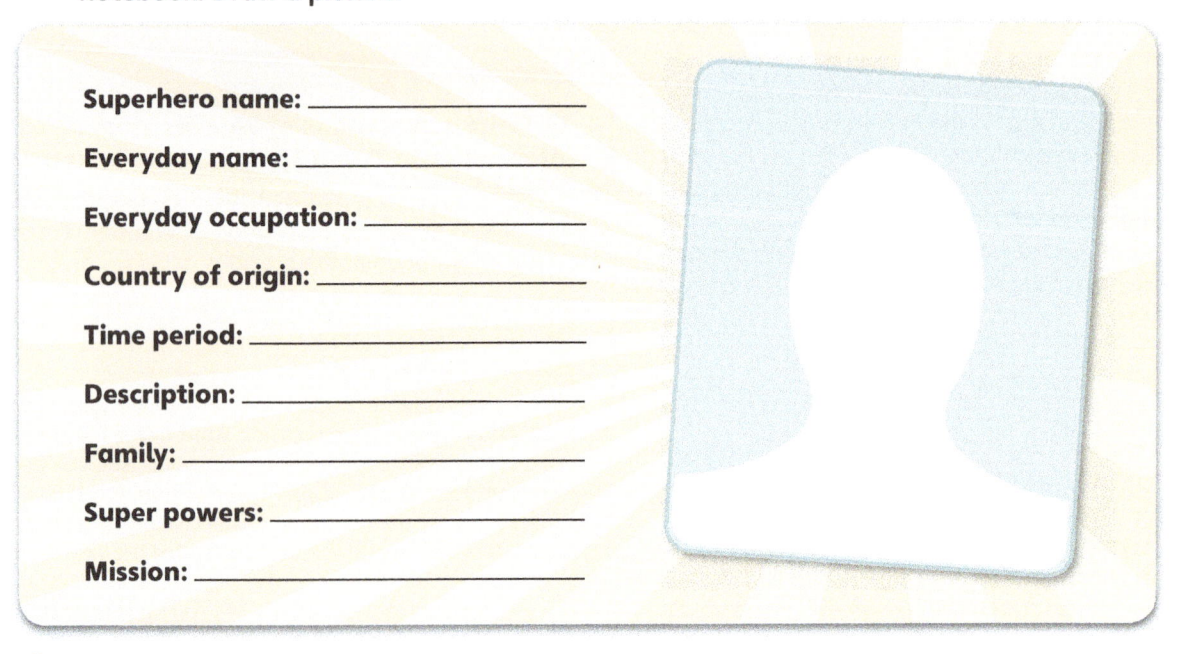

16 Switch and talk about your superhero cards. Which ones do you like best?

64 Unit 5

Life skills | Take positive steps for the future.

I will learn to talk about the positive things we can do for our future world.

17 In real life, no one has super powers. But there have been some super achievements. Discuss them with a partner and decide which three are the greatest.

We have…

1. visited the moon.
2. invented alphabets and writing.
3. invented airplanes.
4. mapped the stars.
5. invented the Internet.
6. learned how to use electricity.
7. created systems that bring clean water into homes.
8. found ways to prevent and cure many diseases.

18 Make a list of three positive steps you could take to help the future of our world. Discuss them with a partner and choose the best one.

> If I could do three things to help improve the world, I would…

> If I could do one thing, I'd help clean up our oceans and seas!

Project

19 Create a page for a class book about positive steps for the future. Share your page with the class.

1. Create a page for your best positive step for the future from 18.
2. Draw pictures or use pictures from magazines to illustrate it.
3. Show your page and talk about why the step is important.

Life Skills Lesson

Lesson Flow

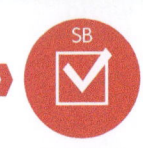

Warm-up › Lesson Objective › Practice › Speaking › Project › Lesson Objective

Lesson Objective

I will learn to talk about the positive things we can do for our future world.

Life skills | Take positive steps for the future.

I will learn to talk about the positive things we can do for our future world.

17 In real life, no one has super powers. But there have been some super achievements. Discuss them with a partner and decide which three are the greatest.

We have…

1. visited the moon.
2. invented alphabets and writing.
3. invented airplanes.
4. mapped the stars.
5. invented the Internet.
6. learned how to use electricity.
7. created systems that bring clean water into homes.
8. found ways to prevent and cure many diseases.

18 Make a list of three positive steps you could take to help the future of our world. Discuss them with a partner and choose the best one.

If I could do three things to help improve the world, I would…

If I could do one thing, I'd help clean up our oceans and seas!

Project

19 Create a page for a class book about positive steps for the future. Share your page with the class.

1. Create a page for your best positive step for the future from 18.
2. Draw pictures or use pictures from magazines to illustrate it.
3. Show your page and talk about why the step is important.

Unit 5 65

Warm-up

- Write the word *Problems* on the board. Help students create a word web to list problems on Earth today that people can do something about, such as pollution, not enough fuel, too many trees being cut down, and what people can do to help. Place students in small groups to discuss the webs, talking about both the problems and the solutions.
- Check answers from the HW in the last lesson.

Lesson Objective

INVOLVE

Introduce the lesson objective. Say: *Today I will learn to talk about the positive things we can do for our future world.*

- Students will talk about taking positive steps for the future of our world. Then they'll create a page for a class book with their best ideas for positive steps.

Practice

17 In real life, no one has super powers. But there have been some super achievements. Discuss them with a partner and decide which three are the greatest.

- Read the directions aloud. Place students in pairs. Have partners discuss the list and decide which three achievements they believe are the greatest.

MONITOR

Check that pairs identify three achievements. Then poll the class to see which ones the class thinks are the greatest.

ASSIST

Provide students with definitions as needed. Say: *To prevent means to stop.* Encourage students to give reasons for their choices. Model: *I think that Number 7 is one of the greatest achievements. We use water every day to stay clean, to cook, and to drink. I can't imagine life without clean water at home and at school.*

Speaking

18 Make a list of three positive steps you could take to help the future of our world. Discuss them with a partner and choose the best one.

- Read the directions aloud. Have students work independently to write three positive steps. Then have them work in pairs to decide which of their steps is best.

MONITOR

Make sure students use *if* clauses correctly to talk about what they would do.

ASSIST

Provide students with examples of positive steps they might take. Model: *If I could do three things to help improve the world, I'd help protect animals that are in danger, I'd plant trees to help make the air cleaner, and I'd work to make computers cheaper so everyone in the world could share ideas.*

Project

Materials: Poster paper, art supplies

21st Century Collaboration

19 Create a page for a class book about positive steps for the future. Share your page with the class.

- Read the directions and steps aloud. Point out the example page.
- Have students complete their pages independently. Then have them collaborate and review one another's work before deciding on the best way to organize their class book and a title for it.

MONITOR

Check that students' pages clearly describe a positive step for the future. Invite students to share and talk about their pages.

Lesson Objective

INVOLVE

Revisit the lesson objective: *Now I have learned to talk about the positive things we can do for our future world.*

- Encourage awareness of what the students have learned by quickly eliciting some ways people have and can make a positive difference in the world.

Extra Application and Practice Activity

- Have students collect their pages and create a class book. Encourage them to choose an appropriate title and cover illustration. Make the book available to other classes or share it with parents during school conferences.

Listening and Speaking Lesson

Lesson Flow

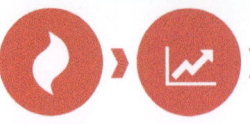

Warm-up › Lesson Objective › Presentation › Practice 1 (SB) › Practice 2 (SB) › Speaking › Lesson Objective

Lesson Objectives

I will review the sound *ed*.

I will learn to talk about imagined situations.

Listening and Speaking

I will review the sound *ed*.
I will learn to talk about imagined situations.

20 (77) Listen, read, and repeat.

1. walk**ed**　2. clean**ed**　3. paint**ed**

21 (78) Listen and blend the sounds.

1. w-a-tch-ed　watched　　2. cl-i-mb-ed　climbed
3. w-a-n-t-ed　wanted　　4. l-oo-k-ed　looked
5. c-a-ll-ed　called　　6. e-n-d-ed　ended

22 (79) Listen and chant.

> We walked in the jungle,
> And we climbed trees
> That ended in the sky!
> We looked at birds,
> And we wanted to fly!

23 In pairs take turns to interview each other using the words in the box.

> act in a movie with any actor　　become invisible
> have any kind of pet　　live anywhere　　move things with your mind
> sing with any musician or band　　travel anywhere in the world

If you could travel anywhere in the world, where would you go?

I'd go to Argentina. I'd love to see the penguins!

66　Unit 5

S66　Unit 5

Warm-up

- Remind students that many words are easy to confuse because they're very similar, such as *could* and *would*. Encourage students to keep lists of words that are easily confused. For each word, students can write a definition and sample sentence. Ask students to share any strategies they use to help them distinguish between these words.

Lesson Objective

INVOLVE

- Introduce the lesson objective. Say: *Today I will learn to use the sound ed, and talk about imagined situations.*
- Students will identify the letters and distinguish between the sounds /t/, /d/, and /id/ individually and as part of words. Then they'll review talking about what they'd do in different hypothetical situations.

Presentation

20 Listen, read, and repeat.

- Read the directions aloud. Play Audio Track 77 and have students listen and point to each sound as it is said. Have students repeat.

MONITOR

As students repeat, check they are pointing to the correct sound and listen for correct pronunciation.

Practice 1

21 Listen and blend the sounds.

- Read the directions aloud. Play Audio Track 78 and have students listen and point to each item as it is sounded out and blended on the audio. Have them repeat after each item.

MONITOR

As students repeat, check they are pointing to the correct word, and listen for correct pronunciation and appropriate intonation.

ASSIST

Replay the audio as needed.

Practice 2

22 Listen and chant.

- Read the directions aloud. Read the chant while students follow in their books.
- Play Audio Track 79 and have students listen. Replay the audio several times and encourage them to join in.

MONITOR

As students repeat the chant, listen for proper pronunciation, appropriate intonation, and correct use of language.

Speaking

Materials: World map or globe

23 In pairs, take turns to interview each other using the words in the box.

- Read the directions and steps aloud. Have two volunteers read the speech bubbles aloud. Read the phrases in the box aloud.
- Have students interview their partners.

MONITOR

Check that students know how to form each question properly before interviewing classmates. Encourage students to use complete sentences as they ask and answer questions.

ASSIST

Provide students with vocabulary as needed. Make sure students understand each situation they're asked about.

- Provide a world map or globe to help students complete the sentences about travel and places to live.

CHALLENGE

Encourage students to add one more situation to the first column of the chart. Model: *If I could be in two places at once… ; If I could run at lightning speed… ; If I could meet any character from a film… .*

Lesson Objective

INVOLVE

Revisit the lesson objective: *Now I have learned to use the sound ed, and talked about imagined situations.*

- Encourage awareness of what the students have learned by quickly eliciting the activities from the lesson with the sounds /t/, /d/, and /id/.

Extra Application and Practice Activity

21st Century Media Literacy

- Draw on the board a quick sketch of a person thinking. Use a cloud-shaped speech bubble. Say: *In comics, a speech bubble in the shape of a cloud, called a thought bubble, shows what a character is thinking.* Have students draw cartoons with a character and a thought bubble. Model: *If Paul could have any job, he'd be a famous basketball player.* A cartoon would show Paul and a thought bubble with an illustration of a famous basketball player. Invite students to share their cartoons with the class and then display them in the classroom.

Unit 5 **T66**

Listening and Speaking

I will review the sound *ed*.
I will learn to talk about imagined situations.

20 Listen, read, and repeat.

1 walked   2 cleaned   3 painted

21 Listen and blend the sounds.

1 w-a-tch-ed watched   2 cl-i-mb-ed climbed
3 w-a-n-t-ed wanted   4 l-oo-k-ed looked
5 c-a-ll-ed called   6 e-n-d-ed ended

22 Listen and chant.

We walked in the jungle,
And we climbed trees
That ended in the sky!
We looked at birds,
And we wanted to fly!

23 In pairs take turns to interview each other using the words in the box.

act in a movie with any actor   become invisible
have any kind of pet   live anywhere   move things with your mind
sing with any musician or band   travel anywhere in the world

If you could travel anywhere in the world, where would you go?

I'd go to Argentina. I'd love to see the penguins!

Review

24 Complete the sentences with the correct phrases from the box.

> become invisible   fly   had superhuman strength   read my mind
> run at lightning speed   travel through time

1 If you could _____, you'd know what I'm thinking now.
2 I wish I could _____ right now. I don't want anyone to see me.
3 In the movie, the hero _____, so he lifted the car off the railroad tracks.
4 In the story, the character could go back and forth between the past and the present. He could _____.
5 He's a gold medalist in track and field. He can practically _____!
6 If we could _____, we wouldn't need to spend money on airplanes.

25 Complete the sentences using the words or phrases in parentheses and your own information. Use **could** and **would (not)**. Then share your ideas with a partner.

1 (fly)
   If I _____, I _____.

2 (become invisible)
   If I _____, I _____.

3 (have superhuman strength)
   If I _____, I _____.

4 (run at lightning speed)
   If I _____, I _____.

5 (travel through time)
   If I _____, I _____.

I Can

- use words for super powers.
- use *if* to talk about imagined situations.
- talk about what I would do in imagined situations.
- write a description of a superhero.

Unit 5 **67**

Review Lesson

Lesson Flow

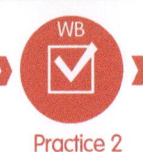

Warm-up › Lesson Objective › Practice 1 (SB) › Practice 2 (WB) › Practice 3 (WB) › Practice 4 (SB) › Self-assessment › Homework

Lesson Objective

To review the words and structures of the unit.

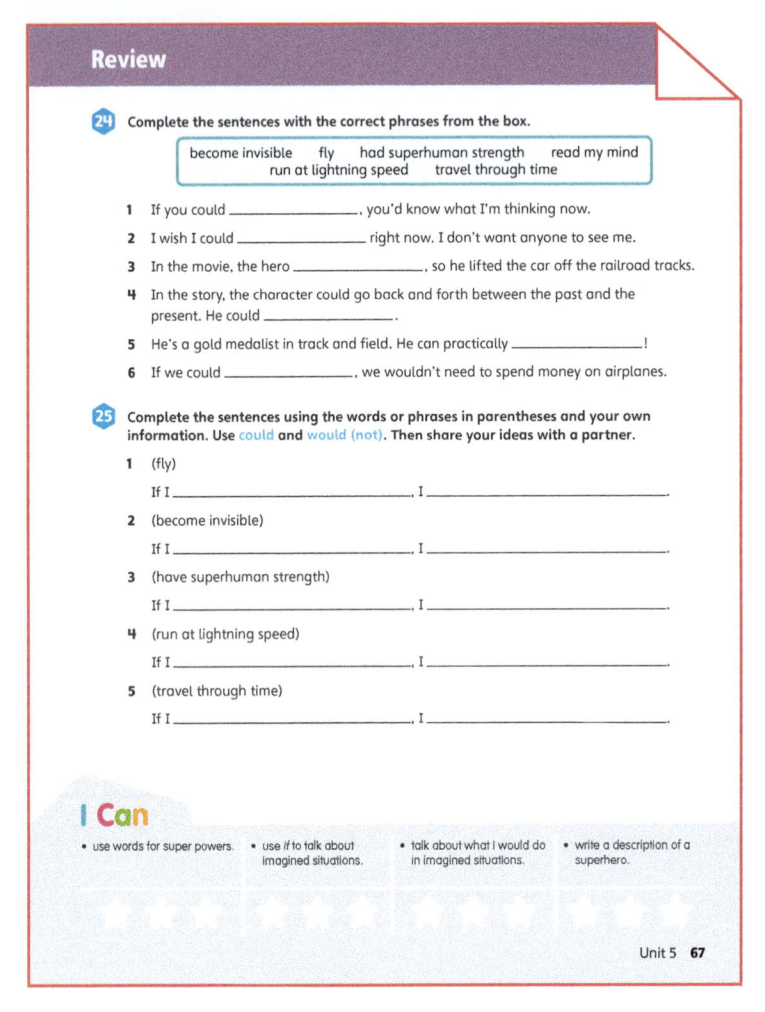

Review

24 Complete the sentences with the correct phrases from the box.

> become invisible   fly   had superhuman strength   read my mind
> run at lightning speed   travel through time

1. If you could _____, you'd know what I'm thinking now.
2. I wish I could _____ right now. I don't want anyone to see me.
3. In the movie, the hero _____, so he lifted the car off the railroad tracks.
4. In the story, the character could go back and forth between the past and the present. He could _____.
5. He's a gold medalist in track and field. He can practically _____!
6. If we could _____, we wouldn't need to spend money on airplanes.

25 Complete the sentences using the words or phrases in parentheses and your own information. Use *could* and *would (not)*. Then share your ideas with a partner.

1. (fly)
   If I _____, I _____.
2. (become invisible)
   If I _____, I _____.
3. (have superhuman strength)
   If I _____, I _____.
4. (run at lightning speed)
   If I _____, I _____.
5. (travel through time)
   If I _____, I _____.

I Can

- use words for super powers.
- use *if* to talk about imagined situations.
- talk about what I would do in imagined situations.
- write a description of a superhero.

Unit 5   67

Warm-up

- Have students create word puzzles by writing sentences, leaving blanks for unit vocabulary words. Challenge classmates to guess the words that belong in the blanks. Model: *If I could… people's minds, I would always know what my mom is really… .*

Lesson Objective

INVOLVE

Introduce the lesson objective: Say: *Today I will review the words and structures of the unit.*

- Students will review the vocabulary and grammar they have learned in Unit 5 by doing activities, including completing sentences.
- Then students will complete the *I Can* section, which helps them to assess their own learning and think about their progress.

S67   Unit 5

Practice 1

24 Complete the sentences with the correct phrases from the box.

- Read the directions aloud. Have students complete the activity independently.

MONITOR
> Check answers as a class. (Answers: 1 read my mind, 2 be come invisible, 3 had superhuman strength, 4 travel through time, 5 run at lightning speed, 6 fly)

Practice 2   WB p. 53/ act. 24

24 Read and match. Write the letters.

- Read the directions aloud. Read the first phrase aloud. As a class work through a–d to consider which is correct.
- Have the students work independently, then check answers as a class.

Practice 3   WB p. 53/ act. 25

25 Complete the sentences with your own ideas.

- Read the directions aloud. Read Item 1 aloud and model a possible answer: *If you would talk to me...*
- Have the students work independently to write their own answers.
- Discuss their answers as a class.

Practice 4

25 Complete the sentences using the words or phrases in parentheses and your own information. Use *could* and *would (not)*. Then share your ideas with a partner.

- Read the directions aloud. Complete Item 1 as a class.
- Have students complete the sentences independently in their notebooks.
- Have students share their ideas in pairs.

Self-assessment

I Can

- This section asks students to assess their own learning and think about their progress. Help students appreciate their progress. Say: *The I Can statements show what you have learned in this unit.*
- Read the statements aloud. Explain that students should think about how well they know the language in the unit and should color in the stars. They should color three stars if they feel the unit was easy, two stars if they need some help, and one star if the unit was hard and they need more help. Have students work independently.

Suggestions for Remediation

Assessment Pack
- Direct students who need help with grammar and vocabulary to the Unit 5 Practice Tests in the Assessment Pack.

WB Unit 5/ p. 102
- Direct students who need help with grammar in particular to the Unit 5 Extra Grammar Practice (Workbook, page 102).
- For further vocabulary work, students can access games in the Big English Student World.

Homework   WB p. 53/ act. 26 & 27

26 Read. Circle the correct answers.
- Direct students to WB Activity 26 on page 53. Have students circle the correct answers. Do Item 1 as a class.

27 Answer the questions with your own ideas.
- Direct students to WB Activity 27 on page 53. Students write their own answers.

Extra Application and Practice Activity

- Have students work in small groups and list superhuman powers from the unit. Then have them use the powers to complete the sentence frame: *If I could..., I'd....* Have students write the frames again but, this time, just list the second part of the sentence. Tell groups to swap with another group, which should then fill in the first part of the sentence. Have the two groups compare what they wrote. Are the super powers they listed the same?
- When ending a unit, have students help out by taking down the bulletin-board display to prepare for the next unit. As they do this, encourage them to share what they have learned by using or creating each part of the display. Allow students to take home and share with their families what they made for the displays.

Assessment Pack

- To assess student progress at the end of the unit, have students complete the Unit 5 Unit Test in the Assessment Pack.
- To assess whether students have reached the listening and speaking targets for this unit, carry out the Unit 5 Oral Assessment in the Assessment Pack.
- Arrange one-to-one sessions with each student and use the prompts to evaluate their listening and speaking abilities.

6 The Coolest School Subjects

Objectives

Reading

- Can follow extended stories and texts written in simple, familiar language, if supported by pictures.
- Can understand simple details in short animal fact files containing some unfamiliar language, if supported by pictures.

Listening

- Can understand the main information in short, simple dialogs about familiar activities, if spoken slowly and clearly.
- Can understand most of the concrete details in informal conversations on familiar, everyday topics, if the speakers talk slowly and clearly.
- Can understand the main points in extended, factual talks on topics of general interest, if delivered in clear standard speech.

Speaking

- Can give an opinion in a structured discussion, if guided by questions.

Writing

- Can begin and end a simple story using an appropriate fixed expression.
- Can briefly narrate a familiar historical event, given prompts or a model.

Grammar

- Can compare facts (e.g. about people, animals, or objects) using *more/fewer/less than* and *the most/fewest/least*.

Unit Projects

Family Connection

Have students tell their families that they're learning about the coolest school subjects. Tell them to share superlatives from the unit such as *coolest, biggest, earliest, smallest, slowest,* and *strangest.* Encourage students and their families to find superlatives in newspapers, movies, and websites. Tell students to interview family members to find out which school subjects they think are the coolest and then to share them with the class.

Key Language

Key Vocabulary

Areas of Study
art
English
literature
math
music
P.E.
science (biology)
social studies

Things We Learn About in School
artists
democracy
exercise
grammar
legends
mammals
murals
myths
playwrights
prime numbers

Expressions
A promise is a promise.
as it turned out
in someone's favor
Let me see.
Seriously?
sounds familiar
sounds like fun
Speaking of…
study group

Content Words

absorb
adapt
blink
break down
digest
give birth
infection
injure
nutrients
protein
rays
slippery

article
civilization
contribution
cultivation
influence
legacy

Grammar/Structures

My teacher gives **more** homework **than** your teacher. There are **fewer** playwrights in the U.S.A **than** in the U.K. I do **less** exercise **than** my sister.

My brother has **the most** homework of anyone I know. Jenny has **the fewest** cards. She has **the least** space.

Phonics

The sounds: er, est

Superlative Subjects Bulletin Board

Create a bulletin-board display titled *Superlative Subjects*. Attach seven paper rectangles in different colors and label them *Art, English, Literature, Math, P.E., Science,* and *Social Science*. Throughout the unit, invite students to add specific topics to each subject category, including both the topic and a superlative. Model: *Art – The oldest paintings are in caves. Math – The biggest number is infinity.* Students can add pictures or cartoons to illustrate the sentences.

Unit 6 Overview **T**

Language in Context Lesson

Lesson Flow

Warm-up › Lesson Objective › Presentation › Practice 1 (WB) › Practice 2 (SB) › Practice 3 (SB) › Speaking › Think BIG › Lesson Objective › Homework

Lesson Objective

I will learn to talk about topics we learn about in school.

Key Language

art, artist, democracy, English, grammar, literature, mammal, math, mural, P.E., playwright, prime number, science (biology), social studies

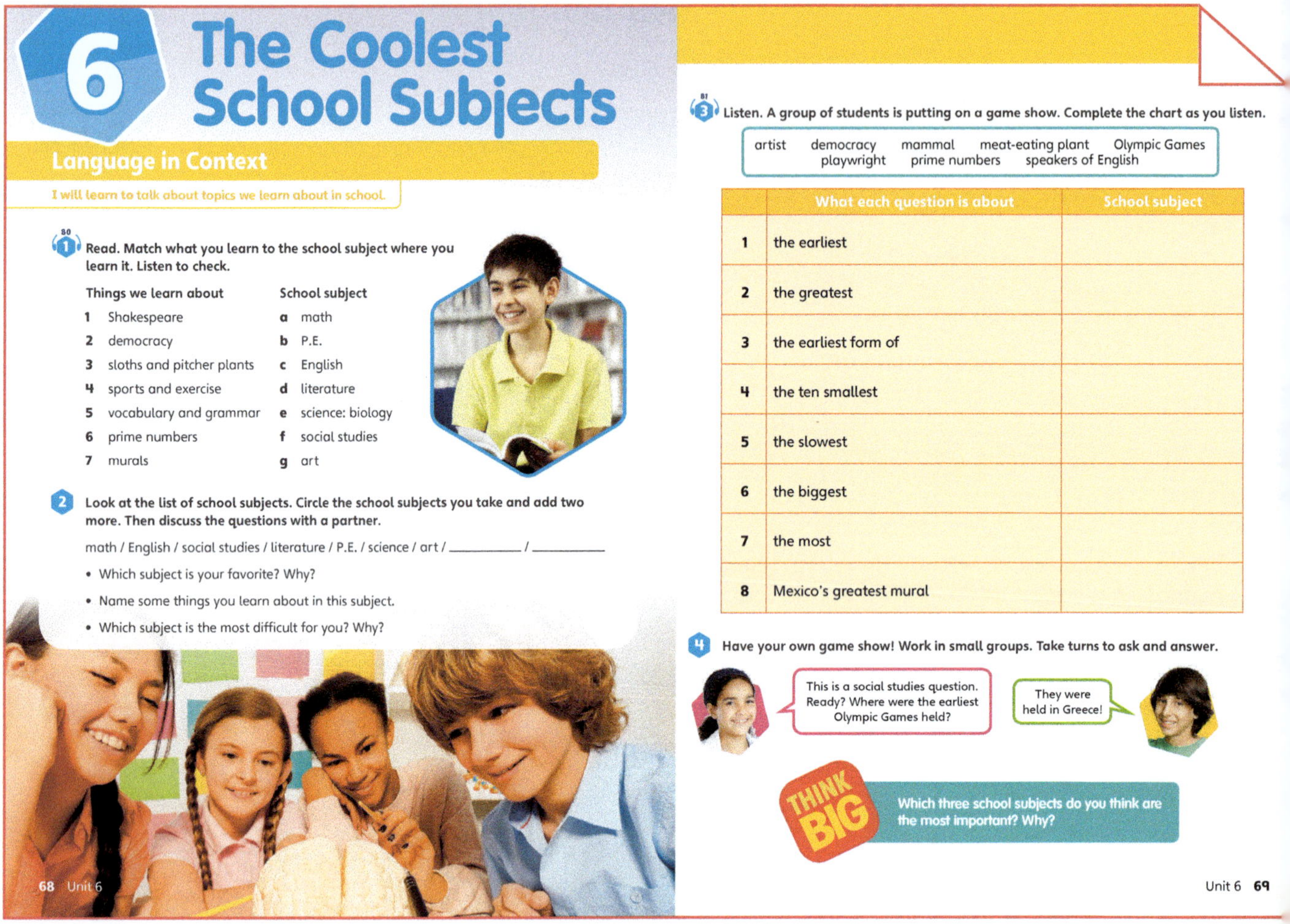

---

6 The Coolest School Subjects

Language in Context

I will learn to talk about topics we learn about in school.

1 Read. Match what you learn to the school subject where you learn it. Listen to check.

Things we learn about
1. Shakespeare
2. democracy
3. sloths and pitcher plants
4. sports and exercise
5. vocabulary and grammar
6. prime numbers
7. murals

School subject
a. math
b. P.E.
c. English
d. literature
e. science: biology
f. social studies
g. art

2 Look at the list of school subjects. Circle the school subjects you take and add two more. Then discuss the questions with a partner.

math / English / social studies / literature / P.E. / science / art / _____ / _____

- Which subject is your favorite? Why?
- Name some things you learn about in this subject.
- Which subject is the most difficult for you? Why?

3 Listen. A group of students is putting on a game show. Complete the chart as you listen.

artist   democracy   mammal   meat-eating plant   Olympic Games
playwright   prime numbers   speakers of English

	What each question is about	School subject
1	the earliest	
2	the greatest	
3	the earliest form of	
4	the ten smallest	
5	the slowest	
6	the biggest	
7	the most	
8	Mexico's greatest mural	

4 Have your own game show! Work in small groups. Take turns to ask and answer.

This is a social studies question. Ready? Where were the earliest Olympic Games held?

They were held in Greece!

THINK BIG Which three school subjects do you think are the most important? Why?

Warm-up

- Have students play *Question Chain* (see *Game Bank*, page T137, for details) to describe school subjects with superlatives. Write these adjectives on the board: *coolest*, *hardest*, *most interesting*, *best*, *worst*. One student should think of a school subject that can be described using one of these adjectives. Classmates should then take turns asking yes/no questions in order to guess the subject.
- Model: *Is it your hardest subject?* (no) *Is it your best subject?* (yes) *Is it music?* (yes)
- Check answers from the HW in the last lesson.

Lesson Objective

INVOLVE

- Explain the lesson objective. Say: *Today I will learn to talk about topics we learn about in school.*
- Tell students that they will read and talk about what they learn in different school subjects.

S68/69 Unit 6

Presentation 🎧 P.T145 / 80

1 Read. Match what you learn to the school subject where you learn it. Listen to check.

- Point to the column labeled *Things we learn about*. Say: *You may not know all of the topics, but you can guess.*
- Have students read the headings of the two columns aloud. Then have volunteers read the items in each column aloud. Ask students to complete the activity.
- Read the directions aloud. Play Audio Track 80 and have students listen and check their answers.

MONITOR

Check answers as a class. (*Answers: 1 d, 2 f, 3 e, 4 b, 5 c, 6 a, 7 g*)

Practice 1 WB p. 54/ act. 1

1 Match the pictures with the school subjects. Write the numbers.

- Read the directions aloud. Say: *Do you recognize anything in these pictures?* Allow volunteers to say what each picture is, and describe it.
- Look at the first picture with the students. Say: *This is an ancient Greek building*, so it must relate to world history.
- Have students complete the activity.

Practice 2

2 Look at the list of school subjects. Circle the school subjects you take and add two more. Then discuss the questions with a partner.

- Read the directions, questions, and subjects aloud. Have students complete the first part of the activity independently before discussing with a partner.

Practice 3 🎧 P.T145 / 81

3 Listen. A group of students is putting on a game show. Complete the chart as you listen.

- Read the directions and the phrases in the box aloud. Play Audio Track 81 and have students listen and complete the activity independently in their notebooks.

MONITOR

Have volunteers share and compare their answers with the class. (*Answers: 1 Olympic Games, social studies; 2 playwright, literature; 3 democracy, social studies; 4 prime numbers, math; 5 mammal, biology; 6 meat-eating plant, biology; 7 speakers of English, social studies; 8 artist, art*)

Speaking

4 Have your own game show! Work in small groups. Take turns to ask and answer.

- Read the directions and steps aloud. Say: *The host* runs *the game show. The* contestants *are the players.* Have two volunteers read the speech bubbles aloud. Then have students perform their game show in groups.

MONITOR

Listen for proper pronunciation, appropriate intonation, and correct use of language.

Think BIG

21st Century Communication

- Read the directions aloud, and have students discuss the questions in pairs. Encourage students to support their views with details.

Lesson Objective

INVOLVE

Revisit the lesson objective: *Now I have learned to talk about topics we learn about in school.*

- Encourage awareness of what students have learned by quickly eliciting a few school subjects discussed in the lesson.
- Tell students they will learn more about some of the topics introduced in this lesson, such as sloths and pitcher plants, later in this unit.

Homework WB pp. 54 & 55/ act. 2, 3, & 4

2 If you could choose three subjects to add to your school schedule, what would they be? ✓ or add your own ideas.

- Direct students to WB Activity 2 on page 54. Students choose their own answers.

3 Unscramble the words. Use the words to complete the sentences.

- Direct students to WB Activity 3 on page 55. Students should first write the word in the space, then use it to complete the sentence that follows.

4 Match the sentences with the subjects. Write the letters.

- Direct students to WB Activity 4 on page 55. Tell students to read the sentences and match them with the subjects.

Think Big

- Direct students to WB Think Big on page 55. Tell students to write their own views.

Extra Application and Practice Activity

- Have students write additional questions that can be used in the class game show. Encourage them to include questions that relate to the seven school subjects named in Activities 1 and 2 in the SB.
- Allow students to create recordings or videos of their game shows. Encourage them to use sound effects, music, set design, and costumes to create the feeling of a game show.

6 The Coolest School Subjects

Language in Context

I will learn to talk about topics we learn about in school.

1 Read. Match what you learn to the school subject where you learn it. Listen to check.

Things we learn about
1. Shakespeare
2. democracy
3. sloths and pitcher plants
4. sports and exercise
5. vocabulary and grammar
6. prime numbers
7. murals

School subject
a. math
b. P.E.
c. English
d. literature
e. science: biology
f. social studies
g. art

2 Look at the list of school subjects. Circle the school subjects you take and add two more. Then discuss the questions with a partner.

math / English / social studies / literature / P.E. / science / art / _____ / _____

- Which subject is your favorite? Why?
- Name some things you learn about in this subject.
- Which subject is the most difficult for you? Why?

68 Unit 6

3 Listen. A group of students is putting on a game show. Complete the chart as you listen.

| artist | democracy | mammal | meat-eating plant | Olympic Games | playwright | prime numbers | speakers of English |

	What each question is about	School subject
1	the earliest	
2	the greatest	
3	the earliest form of	
4	the ten smallest	
5	the slowest	
6	the biggest	
7	the most	
8	Mexico's greatest mural	

4 Have your own game show! Work in small groups. Take turns to ask and answer.

This is a social studies question. Ready? Where were the earliest Olympic Games held?

They were held in Greece!

THINK BIG Which three school subjects do you think are the most important? Why?

Unit 6 69

Reading Lesson

Lesson Flow

Warm-up › Lesson Objective › Pre-reading › Reading › Comprehension 1 › Comprehension 2 › Comprehension 3 › Think BIG › Lesson Objective › Homework

Lesson Objective

I will understand a text about a Greek myth.

Key Language

(in their) favor, gift, goddess, myth, problem; judge, offer; A promise is a promise., as it turned out, in someone's favor

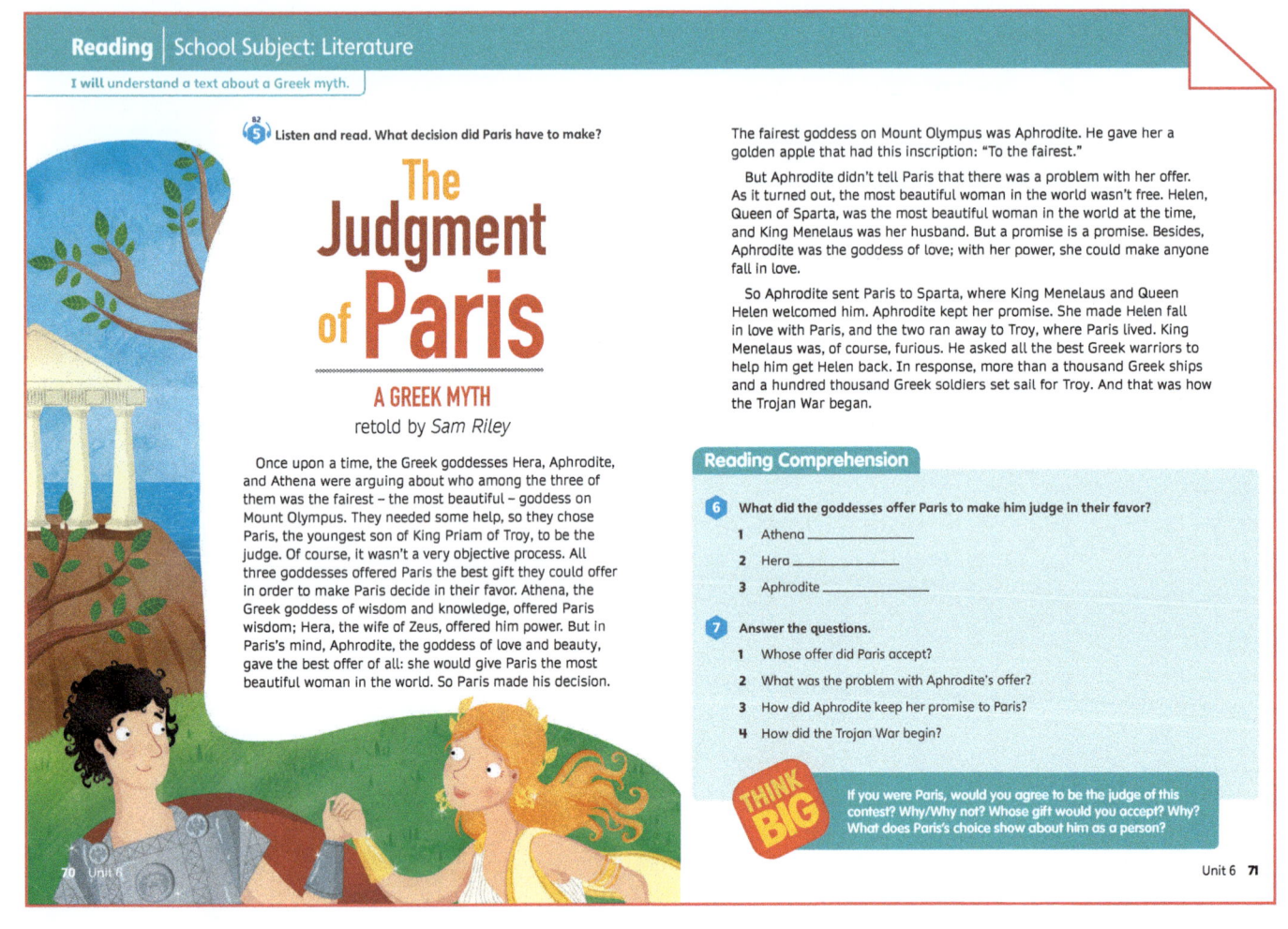

Reading | School Subject: Literature

I will understand a text about a Greek myth.

Listen and read. What decision did Paris have to make?

The Judgment of Paris
A GREEK MYTH
retold by *Sam Riley*

Once upon a time, the Greek goddesses Hera, Aphrodite, and Athena were arguing about who among the three of them was the fairest – the most beautiful – goddess on Mount Olympus. They needed some help, so they chose Paris, the youngest son of King Priam of Troy, to be the judge. Of course, it wasn't a very objective process. All three goddesses offered Paris the best gift they could offer in order to make Paris decide in their favor. Athena, the Greek goddess of wisdom and knowledge, offered Paris wisdom; Hera, the wife of Zeus, offered him power. But in Paris's mind, Aphrodite, the goddess of love and beauty, gave the best offer of all: she would give Paris the most beautiful woman in the world. So Paris made his decision.

The fairest goddess on Mount Olympus was Aphrodite. He gave her a golden apple that had this inscription: "To the fairest."

But Aphrodite didn't tell Paris that there was a problem with her offer. As it turned out, the most beautiful woman in the world wasn't free. Helen, Queen of Sparta, was the most beautiful woman in the world at the time, and King Menelaus was her husband. But a promise is a promise. Besides, Aphrodite was the goddess of love; with her power, she could make anyone fall in love.

So Aphrodite sent Paris to Sparta, where King Menelaus and Queen Helen welcomed him. Aphrodite kept her promise. She made Helen fall in love with Paris, and the two ran away to Troy, where Paris lived. King Menelaus was, of course, furious. He asked all the best Greek warriors to help him get Helen back. In response, more than a thousand Greek ships and a hundred thousand Greek soldiers set sail for Troy. And that was how the Trojan War began.

Reading Comprehension

6 What did the goddesses offer Paris to make him judge in their favor?
1 Athena _____
2 Hera _____
3 Aphrodite _____

7 Answer the questions.
1 Whose offer did Paris accept?
2 What was the problem with Aphrodite's offer?
3 How did Aphrodite keep her promise to Paris?
4 How did the Trojan War begin?

THINK BIG If you were Paris, would you agree to be the judge of this contest? Why/Why not? Whose gift would you accept? Why? What does Paris's choice show about him as a person?

Warm-up

Materials: Magazines

- Say: *A judgment is a decision.* Have the class practice making judgments by holding a *Cutest Contest*. Give each student or team a magazine and challenge them to find the cutest picture.
- Say: *Your picture might show a person, a baby, an animal, or any other cute image.* If students are using the internet, allow them to print out cute photos to share with the class. Then have students describe and display their cute pictures and have the class vote to find the winner. Say: *In our class's judgment, this is the cutest photo!*
- Check answers from the HW in the last lesson.

Lesson Objective

INVOLVE

- Introduce the lesson objective. Say: *Today I will understand a text about a Greek myth.*
- Students will listen to, read, talk, and answer questions about the retelling of a Greek myth.

Pre-reading

- Say: *A myth is a traditional story. Myths are often about heroes, gods, or supernatural beings. Many myths tell how something began.*
- Have a volunteer read the title aloud. Encourage students to predict what the myth will be about. Tell them to use the title and the illustration to help them. Explain that the word *Paris* in the title refers to a young man, rather than the city.
- Tell students that the city of Paris wasn't named for the Paris of Greek mythology. The name of the French city came from the Celtic Gaelic name of some of the earliest people to live there, the *Parisii*.

Reading

5 Listen and read. What decision did Paris have to make?

- Read the directions aloud. Play Audio Track 82 and have students listen and read along.

Comprehension 1

- Ask the question in the directions: *What decision did Paris have to make?* (Answer: He had to decide who was the fairest and most beautiful: Hera, Aphrodite, or Athena.)

MONITOR

Ask more questions to check for understanding. Ask: *Why were Hera, Aphrodite, and Athena arguing?* (They were arguing about who was the fairest or most beautiful.) *What did Paris decide? Why?* (He decided that Aphrodite was the fairest because she promised him the most beautiful woman in the world.) *Who was the most beautiful woman in the world?* (Helen, the Queen of Sparta) *What war began because of Paris's judgment? Why?* (The Trojan War began. Helen was already married to King Menelaus of Greece. Aphrodite made Helen fall in love with Paris and he took her away to Troy. The Greeks fought to get her back, beginning the Trojan War.)

21st Century Critical Thinking

- Point out that the writer says that the process of deciding who was the fairest wasn't very objective. Say: *An* objective *decision is one that is not influenced by emotions or bias.* Ask: *Why wasn't the process objective?* (Paris didn't decide who was the fairest based on their beauty, but rather based on what he could get from them.)

Comprehension 2

6 What did the goddesses offer Paris to make him judge in their favor?

- Read the directions aloud. Have students work independently to complete the activity in their notebooks.

MONITOR

Check answers as a class. (Answers: 1 wisdom. 2 power. 3 the most beautiful woman in the world.)

Comprehension 3

7 Answer the questions.

- Read the directions and questions aloud. Have students work independently to write their answers in their notebooks.

MONITOR

Invite volunteers to read their answers for the rest of the class to check their own work. (Answer: 1 He accepted Aphrodite's offer. 2 The most beautiful woman in the world was married to another man. 3 She made Helen fall in love with Paris. 4 King Menelaus and more than a thousand Greek ships set sail for Troy.)

Think BIG

21st Century Critical Thinking

- Read the directions aloud. Have students discuss their ideas with a partner.

MONITOR

As students share ideas, check for problems with comprehension and accurate use of vocabulary, syntax, and grammar.

Lesson Objective

INVOLVE

- Revisit the lesson objective: *Now I have understood a text about a Greek myth.*
- Encourage awareness of what students have learned by eliciting something students remember from *The Judgment of Paris*.

Homework — WB p.56/ act. 5

5 Listen and read. Then answer the questions.

- Direct students to WB Activity 5 on page 56. Tell students to play Audio Track 83, listen, and answer the questions about this Greek myth.

Extra Application and Practice Activity

- Have students decide what actors they would cast in a movie version of the myth. Ask: *What actor would be the best choice for each character? Why?* Have students share their ideas with the class.

Unit 6 **T70/71**

Reading | School Subject: Literature

I will understand a text about a Greek myth.

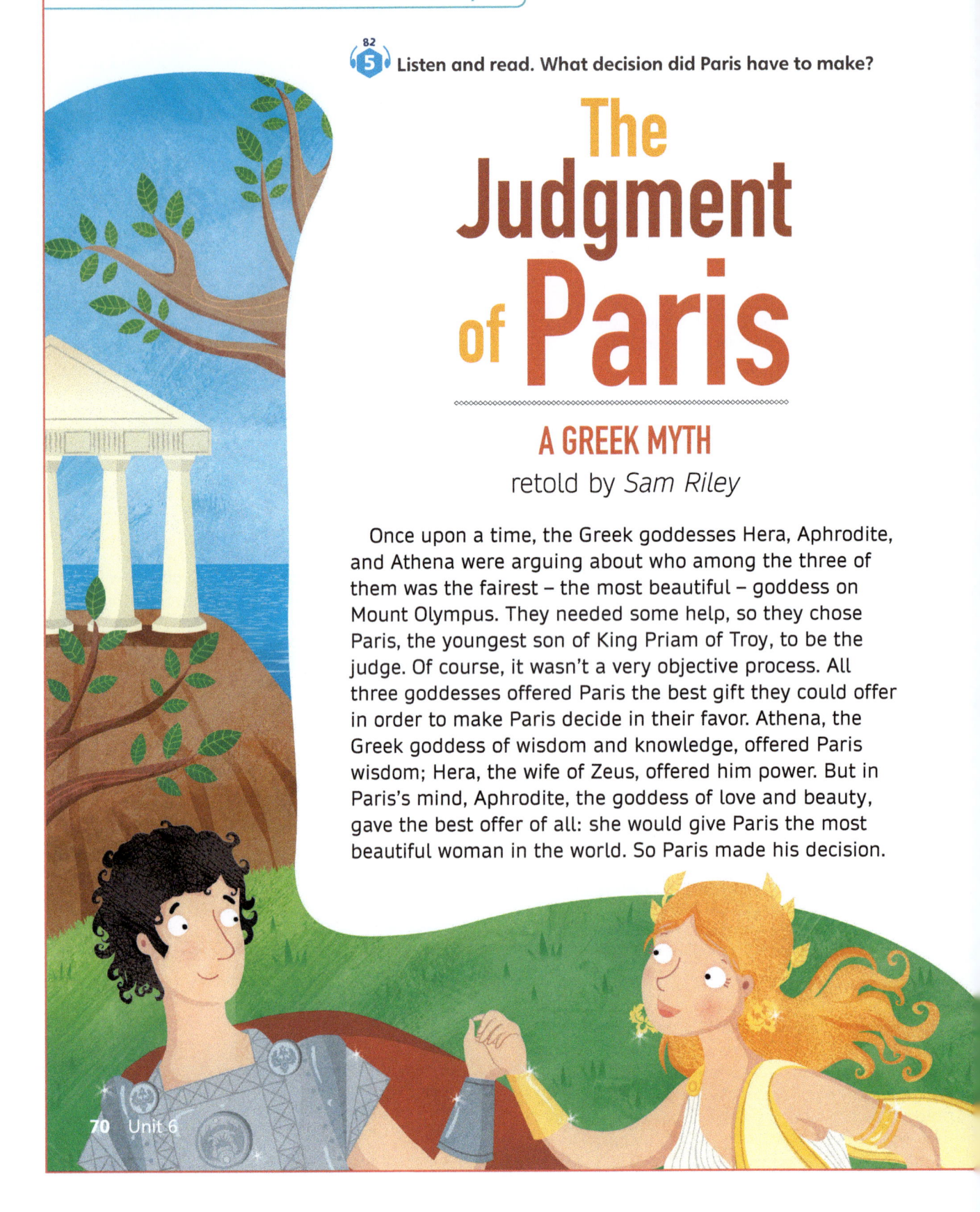

5 Listen and read. What decision did Paris have to make?

The Judgment of Paris

A GREEK MYTH

retold by *Sam Riley*

Once upon a time, the Greek goddesses Hera, Aphrodite, and Athena were arguing about who among the three of them was the fairest – the most beautiful – goddess on Mount Olympus. They needed some help, so they chose Paris, the youngest son of King Priam of Troy, to be the judge. Of course, it wasn't a very objective process. All three goddesses offered Paris the best gift they could offer in order to make Paris decide in their favor. Athena, the Greek goddess of wisdom and knowledge, offered Paris wisdom; Hera, the wife of Zeus, offered him power. But in Paris's mind, Aphrodite, the goddess of love and beauty, gave the best offer of all: she would give Paris the most beautiful woman in the world. So Paris made his decision.

The fairest goddess on Mount Olympus was Aphrodite. He gave her a golden apple that had this inscription: "To the fairest."

But Aphrodite didn't tell Paris that there was a problem with her offer. As it turned out, the most beautiful woman in the world wasn't free. Helen, Queen of Sparta, was the most beautiful woman in the world at the time, and King Menelaus was her husband. But a promise is a promise. Besides, Aphrodite was the goddess of love; with her power, she could make anyone fall in love.

So Aphrodite sent Paris to Sparta, where King Menelaus and Queen Helen welcomed him. Aphrodite kept her promise. She made Helen fall in love with Paris, and the two ran away to Troy, where Paris lived. King Menelaus was, of course, furious. He asked all the best Greek warriors to help him get Helen back. In response, more than a thousand Greek ships and a hundred thousand Greek soldiers set sail for Troy. And that was how the Trojan War began.

Reading Comprehension

6 What did the goddesses offer Paris to make him judge in their favor?

1 Athena _____

2 Hera _____

3 Aphrodite _____

7 Answer the questions.

1 Whose offer did Paris accept?

2 What was the problem with Aphrodite's offer?

3 How did Aphrodite keep her promise to Paris?

4 How did the Trojan War begin?

THINK BIG If you were Paris, would you agree to be the judge of this contest? Why/Why not? Whose gift would you accept? Why? What does Paris's choice show about him as a person?

Language in Action Lesson

Lesson Flow

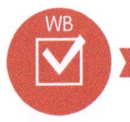

Warm-up › Lesson Objective › Pre-listening › Listening › Comprehension › Role Play › Practice 1 (SB) › Practice 2 (WB) › Lesson Objective › Homework

Lesson Objective

I will listen to a dialog about a literature assignment.

Key Language

legend, myth, play; base on, escape, open; amazing, depressing, difficult, endangered, familiar, favorite; Let me see., Seriously?, sounds familiar, sounds like fun, Speaking of... , study group

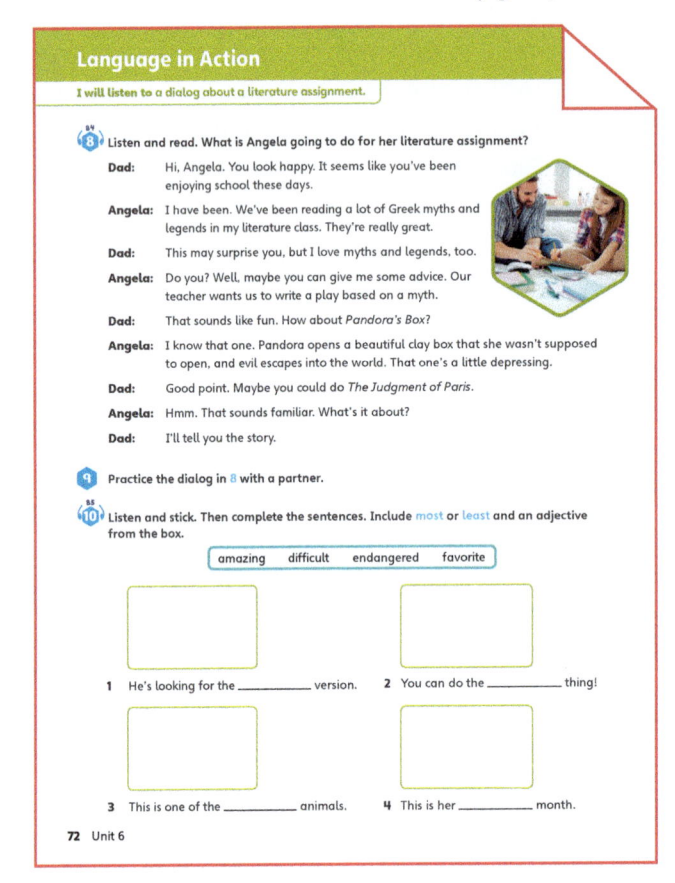

Language in Action

I will listen to a dialog about a literature assignment.

8 Listen and read. What is Angela going to do for her literature assignment?

Dad: Hi, Angela. You look happy. It seems like you've been enjoying school these days.

Angela: I have been. We've been reading a lot of Greek myths and legends in my literature class. They're really great.

Dad: This may surprise you, but I love myths and legends, too.

Angela: Do you? Well, maybe you can give me some advice. Our teacher wants us to write a play based on a myth.

Dad: That sounds like fun. How about *Pandora's Box*?

Angela: I know that one. Pandora opens a beautiful clay box that she wasn't supposed to open, and evil escapes into the world. That one's a little depressing.

Dad: Good point. Maybe you could do *The Judgment of Paris*.

Angela: Hmm. That sounds familiar. What's it about?

Dad: I'll tell you the story.

9 Practice the dialog in 8 with a partner.

10 Listen and stick. Then complete the sentences. Include *most* or *least* and an adjective from the box.

| amazing | difficult | endangered | favorite |

1 He's looking for the _____ version.
2 You can do the _____ thing!
3 This is one of the _____ animals.
4 This is her _____ month.

72 Unit 6

Warm-up

21st Century Cross-Cultural Awareness

- Invite students to brainstorm characters from myths. Write the list on the board. Students can begin by naming characters from "The Judgment of Paris" on pages 70–71 (Paris, Athena, Hera, Aphrodite, Helen) Use the list as topics for playing *Charades*.
- Provide students with other familiar names from world mythology to use, such as Anansi the Spider (African), Thor (Norse), and Pegasus (Greek).

- Check answers from the HW in the last lesson.

Lesson Objective

INVOLVE

Introduce the lesson objective. Say: *Today I will listen to a dialog about a literature assignment.*

- Students will read, listen to, and practice a dialog. Students will make comparisons as they listen and talk about what some students are doing in their school subjects.

Pre-listening 🔊

- Point to Dad and Angela in the picture. Point out their names in the text and remind students that this is a script for a dialog. Tell students that they are going to listen to Angela and her dad talking about her literature assignment.

Script Format: Use the dialog in Activity 6 to model one way that a play is different from a myth or legend in story form. Say: *In addition to dialog like in this activity, a play includes stage directions in parentheses that set the scene or tell actors how to act. A play is meant to be performed for an audience.*

Listening 🎧 84 🔊

8 Listen and read. What is Angela going to do for her literature assignment?

- Read the directions aloud. Play Audio Track 84 and have students listen and read along.
- Invite a pair to read the dialog aloud and repeat.

MONITOR
As students practice, listen for correct pronunciation and use of language.

ASSIST
As you notice errors, say words correctly and have students repeat.

Comprehension 💡

- Ask the question in the directions: *What is Angela going to do for her literature assignment?* (She's going to write a play based on a myth.)

MONITOR
Ask more questions to check for understanding. Encourage students to answer in complete sentences where appropriate. Ask: *What myths does Angela's father suggest?* (He suggests "Pandora's Box" and "The Judgment of Paris.")

CHALLENGE
Invite students to share the story of "Pandora's Box," or model as follows: *There's nothing bad in the world. Zeus gives Pandora a box and tells her never to look inside. Her curiosity is too great and she opens the box. Terrible things fly out, such as sadness, greed, old age, death, hatred, and violence. Pandora shuts the box, but these terrible things are now in the world. The only thing that remains in the box is something good: hope.*

Role Play 🎭

9 Practice the dialog in 8 with a partner.

- Read the directions aloud. Have students pair to read the dialog aloud, switch parts, and repeat.

MONITOR
As students work, listen for correct pronunciation and use of language.

ASSIST
As you notice errors, say words or sentences correctly and have students repeat.

Practice 1 🎧 85 P.T146 ✓

Materials: Stickers

10 Listen and stick. Then complete the sentences. Include *most* or *least* and an adjective from the box.

- Help students find the Unit 6 stickers at the back of the Student's Book. Ask them to describe each sticker. Read the directions and sentences aloud.
- Play Audio Track 85. Have students listen, place the stickers on the page, and complete the sentences, using *most* or *least* and adjectives from the box.

MONITOR
As students work, make sure that they place the stickers in the correct order. Then check answers as a class. (Answers: 1 least difficult, 2 most amazing, 3 most endangered, 4 least favorite)

Practice 2 🎧 86 WB p. 57/ act. 6 ✓

6 Listen and read. Then circle the correct answers.

- Read the directions aloud. Play Audio Track 86 twice. The second time, have students circle the correct letter.

Lesson Objective 📈

INVOLVE
Revisit the lesson objective: *Now I have listened to a dialog about a literature assignment.*

- Encourage awareness of what students have learned by eliciting what they remember from the dialog between Angela and her father.

Homework 🎧 87 P.T146 WB p. 57/ act. 7 & 8 🖨

7 Look at 6. Read the underlined expressions. Match the expressions with the sentences. Write the letters.

- Direct students to WB Activity 7 on page 57. Students match 1–4 with a–d.

8 Complete the dialog with the expressions in 7. Then listen and check your answers.

- Direct students to WB Activity 8 on page 57. Students complete the activity, then listen to the audio to check.

Extra Application and Practice Activity

- Ask students to tell you more adjectives they know that they can use to describe a myth, animal, person, and story. (*boring, dangerous, intelligent, exciting,* etc.) Write their answers on the board. Have students make their own sentences with the adjectives.

Unit 6 **T72**

Language in Action

I will listen to a dialog about a literature assignment.

8 Listen and read. What is Angela going to do for her literature assignment?

Dad: Hi, Angela. You look happy. It seems like you've been enjoying school these days.

Angela: I have been. We've been reading a lot of Greek myths and legends in my literature class. They're really great.

Dad: This may surprise you, but I love myths and legends, too.

Angela: Do you? Well, maybe you can give me some advice. Our teacher wants us to write a play based on a myth.

Dad: That sounds like fun. How about *Pandora's Box*?

Angela: I know that one. Pandora opens a beautiful clay box that she wasn't supposed to open, and evil escapes into the world. That one's a little depressing.

Dad: Good point. Maybe you could do *The Judgment of Paris*.

Angela: Hmm. That sounds familiar. What's it about?

Dad: I'll tell you the story.

9 Practice the dialog in **8** with a partner.

10 Listen and stick. Then complete the sentences. Include **most** or **least** and an adjective from the box.

| amazing   difficult   endangered   favorite |

1 He's looking for the _____ version.

2 You can do the _____ thing!

3 This is one of the _____ animals.

4 This is her _____ month.

72   Unit 6

Grammar

I will learn to use *more/fewer/less than* and *the most/fewest/least* to talk about facts.

China has **more** speakers of English **than** the U.S.A.

I take **fewer** school subjects **than** my brother.

Teachers in Finland give **less** homework **than** teachers in the U.K. do.

Tip: Use *fewer* with countable things. Use *less* with amounts that aren't countable.

---

11 Complete these facts about plants and animals. Use more, fewer, or less.

1. Sloths spend _____ time doing any form of activity than most animals. Most of their time is spent sleeping or just hanging out – upside down!

2. There are _____ dogs and cats than fish as pets in the U.K. There are approximately 40 million fish in tanks and ponds and 17 million pet dogs and cats in the U.K.

3. The panda spends _____ time sleeping than eating. Pandas eat bamboo for 14 to 16 hours a day!

4. Trees use carbon dioxide to make food. The _____ trees there are, the _____ carbon dioxide in the atmosphere.

The Amazon rain forest has **the most** species of plants and animals on Earth.

Germany and Switzerland have **the fewest** pet dogs per capita.

Which country has **the least** amount of air pollution?

---

12 Complete the text with the fewest, the least, or the most.

Antarctica is full of extremes. It is ¹_____ remote region on Earth. There are no permanent residents. This makes Antarctica ²_____ populated continent on the planet. In spite of the snowy conditions, Antarctica is actually considered a desert. It has ³_____ amount of rainfall of any place in the world. Not surprisingly, Antarctica has ⁴_____ flowering plants of any other continent. The McMurdo Dry Valleys, one of ⁵_____ extreme desert regions in the world, is the largest ice-free region in Antarctica.

Grammar Lesson

Lesson Flow

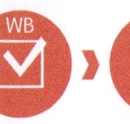

Warm-up › Lesson Objective › Presentation 1 › Practice 1 (SB) › Practice 2 (WB) › Presentation 2 › Practice 3 (SB) › Practice 4 (WB) › Lesson Objective › Homework

Lesson Objective

I will learn to use *more/fewer/less than* and *the most/fewest/least* to talk about facts.

Key Language

My teacher gives **more** homework **than** your teacher.
There are **fewer** playwrights in the U.S.A. **than** in the U.K.
I do **less** exercise **than** my sister.

My brother has **the most** homework of anyone I know.
Jenny has **the fewest** cards. She has **the least** space.

Grammar

I will learn to use *more/fewer/less than* and *the most/fewest/least* to talk about facts.

China has **more** speakers of English **than** the U.S.A.
I take **fewer** school subjects **than** my brother.
Teachers in Finland give **less** homework **than** teachers in the U.K. do.

Tip: Use *fewer* with countable things. Use *less* with amounts that aren't countable.

11 Complete these facts about plants and animals. Use *more*, *fewer*, or *less*.

1. Sloths spend _____ time doing any form of activity than most animals. Most of their time is spent sleeping or just hanging out – upside down!
2. There are _____ dogs and cats than fish as pets in the U.K. There are approximately 40 million fish in tanks and ponds and 17 million pet dogs and cats in the U.K.
3. The panda spends _____ time sleeping than eating. Pandas eat bamboo for 14 to 16 hours a day!
4. Trees use carbon dioxide to make food. The _____ trees there are, the _____ carbon dioxide in the atmosphere.

The Amazon rain forest has **the most** species of plants and animals on Earth.
Germany and Switzerland have **the fewest** pet dogs per capita.
Which country has **the least** amount of air pollution?

12 Complete the text with *the fewest*, *the least*, or *the most*.

Antarctica is full of extremes. It is ¹_____ remote region on Earth. There are no permanent residents. This makes Antarctica ²_____ populated continent on the planet. In spite of the snowy conditions, Antarctica is actually considered a desert. It has ³_____ amount of rainfall of any place in the world. Not surprisingly, Antarctica has ⁴_____ flowering plants of any other continent. The McMurdo Dry Valleys, one of ⁵_____ extreme desert regions in the world, is the largest ice-free region in Antarctica.

Unit 6 73

Warm-up

- Have students play *Question Chain* (see *Game Bank*, page T137, for details) to use superlative adjectives to talk about what they've learned about in different school subjects. Write these phrases on the board: *biggest animal, strangest plant, greatest mural, longest piece of music, hardest language (to learn)*, etc. Have one student think of a school topic that can be described using one of these phrases. Ask the other students to take turns asking yes/no questions to guess the secret topic. Model: *Is it English?* (no) *Is it a Chinese language?* (yes) *Is it Mandarin?* (yes).
- Check answers from the HW in the last lesson.

Lesson Objective

INVOLVE

Introduce the lesson objective. Say: *Today I will learn to use more/fewer/less than and the most/fewest/least to talk about facts.*

- Students will compare amounts using *more/most*, *fewer/fewest*, and *less/least*.

S73 Unit 6

Presentation 1

- Have volunteers read the sentences and tip in the first grammar box aloud. Say: *We use* more, fewer, *and* less *plus a noun, and often* than, *to compare two amounts.* Ask: *What two things are compared in each sentence?* (the number of English speakers in China and the U.S.A., the number of school subjects my brother and I have, the amount of homework given in Finland and the U.K.).

CHALLENGE

Have students suggest alternative *more than, fewer than,* and *less than* sentences, using the same format.

Practice 1

1 Complete these facts about plants and animals. Use *more*, *fewer*, or *less*.

- Read the directions aloud and complete the first item as a class. Then have students complete the activity independently.

MONITOR

Check answers as a class. *(Answers: 1 less; 2 fewer; 3 less; 4 more, less)*

ASSIST

Use simple language to explain unfamiliar vocabulary. Say: *Hanging out* is spending time without doing anything. *Approximately* means "about." *Carbon dioxide* is a gas. *The atmosphere* is the air around Earth.

CHALLENGE

Have students make their own sentences with *more*, *fewer*, and *less* to present to the class.

21st Century Environmental Literacy

- Ask: *Why is it a problem if there's more carbon dioxide in the atmosphere?* (Sample answer: If there's more carbon dioxide in the atmosphere, Earth might get hotter, which can cause glaciers to melt and health problems for people and animals to increase.)

Practice 2 — WB p. 58/ act. 9

9 Circle the correct words to complete these facts about countries.

- Read the directions aloud.
- Have a volunteer read Item 1. As a class, discuss the possible answers and have students circle the answer (*less*).
- Have students complete the activity.

Presentation 2

- Have volunteers read the sentences in the second grammar box aloud.

ASSIST

Use simple language to explain unfamiliar vocabulary.

Practice 3

Materials: World map or globe

12 Complete the text with *the fewest*, *the least*, or *the most*.

- Read the directions aloud and complete the first item as a class. Then have students complete the activity independently in their notebooks.

MONITOR

Check answers as a class. *(Answers: 1 the most, 2 the least, 3 the least, 4 the fewest, 5 the most)*

CHALLENGE

Have students make their own sentences with *the fewest*, *the least*, and *the most*.

21st Century Global Awareness

- Have students find Antarctica on a world map or globe and share what they know about this continent. Ask: *Why is Antarctica important even though very few people live there?* (Sample answers: The continent contains freshwater glaciers./Much of Earth's ice is found here.)

Practice 4 — WB p. 58/ act. 11

11 Draw lines to connect the sentence parts.

- Read the directions aloud. Have students make six sentences by connecting one part of each sentence from each column.
- Have students complete the activity independently.

Lesson Objective

INVOLVE

Revisit the lesson objective: *Now I have learned to use* more/fewer/less than *and* the most/fewest/least *to talk about facts.*

- Encourage awareness of what students have learned by quickly eliciting from students some statements with *more than* and *the most*, and *fewer* and *fewest*.

Homework — WB p. 59/ act. 10 & 12

10 Answer the questions. Write complete sentences.

- Direct students to WB Activity 10 on page 59. Have students answer the questions using full sentences.

12 Read the answers and write the questions.

- Direct students to WB Activity 12 on page 59. Students write questions from the answers.

Extra Application and Practice Activity

- Have students write questions and answers based on the facts in the lesson. Model: *Does a panda spend more time sleeping or eating?* (eating)

Unit 6 **T73**

Content Connection Lesson

Lesson Flow

Warm-up › Lesson Objective › Pre-reading › Reading › Practice 1 (SB) › Practice 2 (WB) › Think BIG › Lesson Objective › Homework

Lesson Objective

I will learn about some rare animal abilities.

Key Language

absorb, adapt, blink, break down, digest, give birth, infection, injure, nectar, nutrients, protein, rays, slippery

---

Content Connection | Life Science

I will learn about some rare animal abilities.

13 Listen and read. Which rare abilities are described?

CONTENT WORDS
absorb, adapt, blink, break down, digest, give birth, infection, injure, nectar, nutrients, protein, rays, slippery

The Weirdest Living Things

Over time, animals on our planet have developed so that they can survive in the best way possible. Some animals have rare abilities that make them particularly interesting.

Sloths are the slowest creatures on Earth. Everything they do is slow. They eat slowly, blink slowly, and move slowly. They're so slow that they need a month to move one kilometer! They're also the sleepiest animals alive; they sleep up to twenty hours a day! They eat fruit and leaves, and because they're so slow and sleepy, they burn energy very slowly. Sloths live in trees in the rain forests of South and Central America. Because they're always in trees, they've learned to eat, sleep, and even give birth upside down.

The **pitcher plant** of Southeast Asia's rain forests is the largest meat-eating plant in the world. It's so big that it can even digest rats. But how? First, the plant attracts insects and small animals with a sweet-smelling sticky nectar. Second, the cup-shaped plant is an excellent trap. It has slippery sides, so once the insects and other animals are inside, there's no escape! However, the pitcher plant doesn't "eat" food the way animals do. First, it needs to use chemicals to break down the protein and other nutrients in the meat, and then it absorbs them.

The grass- and plant-eating **hippopotamus** might be one of the deadliest creatures in Africa, but it has very sensitive skin, so living in the African heat is difficult. A hippo needs to spend most of its time in lakes or rivers. The water helps the hippo stay cool, but it doesn't protect it from the sun's rays. Luckily, the hippo has adapted so that it can produce its own sunscreen! Two acids in the hippo's skin combine to make a special gel that absorbs all the sun's harmful rays. It also stops skin infections when the hippo gets injured in fights.

14 Look at the passage. Answer the questions.

1. Why do sloths burn energy slowly?
2. Why can't insects that get into a pitcher plant climb out?
3. What is hippo sunscreen made of?

THINK BIG Which other animals have rare abilities? What rare abilities do humans have?

74 Unit 6

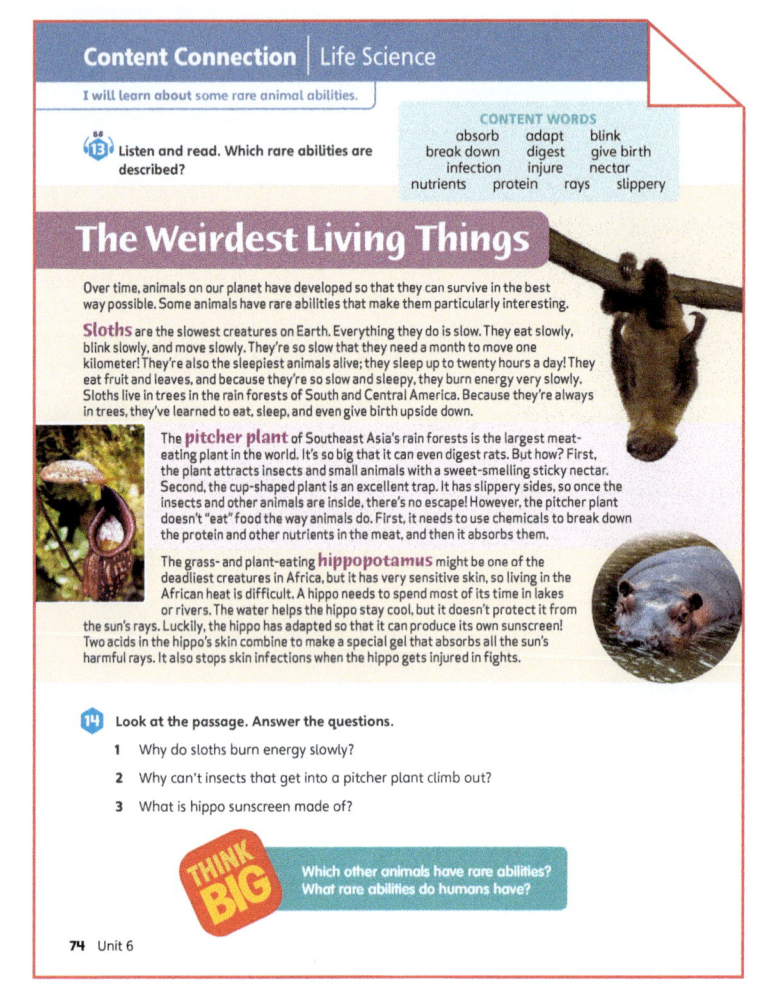

Warm-up

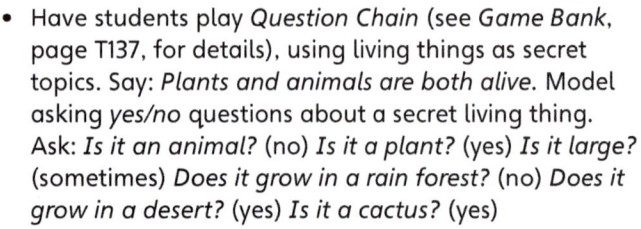

- Have students play Question Chain (see Game Bank, page T137, for details), using living things as secret topics. Say: *Plants and animals are both alive.* Model asking yes/no questions about a secret living thing. Ask: *Is it an animal?* (no) *Is it a plant?* (yes) *Is it large?* (sometimes) *Does it grow in a rain forest?* (no) *Does it grow in a desert?* (yes) *Is it a cactus?* (yes)
- Check answers from the HW in the last lesson.

Lesson Objective

INVOLVE

Introduce the lesson objective. Say: *Today I will learn about some rare animal abilities.*

- Students will read and talk about some unusual abilities of living things.

Pre-reading

- Have students read the Content Words aloud. Ask volunteers to share their understanding of these words.

CHALLENGE

Ask students to write sentences using at least five of the Content Words.

- Write on the board: *Animals with Special Abilities*. Ask students to brainstorm some special things that particular animals can do, e.g. *Bears can hibernate*.
- Next, write *chameleon* on the board. Ask students to describe the animal. Then ask: *What is the chameleon's special ability?* (It can change color.) *How is the special ability used?* (They hide from danger.)

21st Century Communication

- Say: *We use superlatives to give exact factual information. But we can also use them to exaggerate.* Explain that the superlative facts in this article are true, but the title might be considered an exaggeration. Ask: *What are some other plants and animals that might be called "the weirdest living things"?*
- Read the title aloud. Ask student to predict what the text will be about.
- Point to the three different-colored blocks of text. Suggest to students that each block will deal with a different animal. Read the purple-bolded words: *sloths*, *pitcher plant*, and *hippopotamus*.

Reading 🎧88 📖

13 Listen and read. Which rare abilities are described?

- Have a volunteer read the first paragraph aloud. Ask different students to summarize the key idea. Clarify anything that was confusing to the students.
- Divide the class into groups of three or four and have them continue with the reading process, stopping after each paragraph to summarize the clear idea and explain anything students are having difficulty with.
- Now play Audio Track 88 and have students listen and read along.

21st Century Visual Literacy

- Ask how the pictures in these lessons help them. Elicit that the pictures often help students complete items on the page, such as the one that shows that sloths spend most of their time hanging!
- Place students in pairs, and have partners discuss which special abilities are described in the article. Invite volunteer pairs to share their ideas.

MONITOR

Ask questions to gauge students' comprehension, e.g. *Which living things sleep up to 20 hours a day?* (sloths) *Which living things produce their own sunscreen?* (hippos) *Which living things can digest insects and small animals?* (pitcher plants)

Practice 1 ☑

14 Look at the passage. Answer the questions.

- Read the directions aloud. Have students answer the questions in pairs, noting where they found the information in the text.

Practice 2 🎧89 📄P.T147 WB p. 60/ act. 13 🌍 ☑

13 Read and complete. Then listen and check.

- Read the directions aloud. Have students read and complete the text with the word in the box.
- Play Audio Track 89 and have students check their answers, then check them as a class.

MONITOR

Check answers as a class. (Answers: 1 pitcher plant, 2 nutrients, 3 water, 4 slippery, 5 nectar, 6 absorbs, 7 insects)

Think BIG 💭

21st Century Environmental Awareness

- Read the questions with the students.
- Have students work individually to look in the text for information about rare abilities some animals have.

MONITOR

Invite different volunteers to share their answers, including where they found the information in the text.

Lesson Objective 📈

INVOLVE

Revisit the lesson objective: *Now I have learned about some rare animal abilities.*

- Encourage awareness of what students have learned by eliciting from them examples of some rare animal abilities.

Homework WB p. 60/ act. 14 🎒

14 Read 13 again and answer the questions.

- Direct students to WB Activity 14 on page 60. Tell students to read the text in Activity 13 again and answer the questions in full sentences.

Extra Application and Practice Activity

- Use animal facts from the lesson to play a trivia game with students. Divide the class into two teams. Alternate asking a student from each team a question about one of the animals. (e.g. *Which animal has its own sunscreen?*) If the student names the correct animal, his or her team scores a point.

Unit 6   **T74**

Content Connection | Life Science

I will learn about some rare animal abilities.

CONTENT WORDS
absorb   adapt   blink
break down   digest   give birth
infection   injure   nectar
nutrients   protein   rays   slippery

13 Listen and read. Which rare abilities are described?

The Weirdest Living Things

Over time, animals on our planet have developed so that they can survive in the best way possible. Some animals have rare abilities that make them particularly interesting.

Sloths are the slowest creatures on Earth. Everything they do is slow. They eat slowly, blink slowly, and move slowly. They're so slow that they need a month to move one kilometer! They're also the sleepiest animals alive; they sleep up to twenty hours a day! They eat fruit and leaves, and because they're so slow and sleepy, they burn energy very slowly. Sloths live in trees in the rain forests of South and Central America. Because they're always in trees, they've learned to eat, sleep, and even give birth upside down.

The **pitcher plant** of Southeast Asia's rain forests is the largest meat-eating plant in the world. It's so big that it can even digest rats. But how? First, the plant attracts insects and small animals with a sweet-smelling sticky nectar. Second, the cup-shaped plant is an excellent trap. It has slippery sides, so once the insects and other animals are inside, there's no escape! However, the pitcher plant doesn't "eat" food the way animals do. First, it needs to use chemicals to break down the protein and other nutrients in the meat, and then it absorbs them.

The grass- and plant-eating **hippopotamus** might be one of the deadliest creatures in Africa, but it has very sensitive skin, so living in the African heat is difficult. A hippo needs to spend most of its time in lakes or rivers. The water helps the hippo stay cool, but it doesn't protect it from the sun's rays. Luckily, the hippo has adapted so that it can produce its own sunscreen! Two acids in the hippo's skin combine to make a special gel that absorbs all the sun's harmful rays. It also stops skin infections when the hippo gets injured in fights.

14 Look at the passage. Answer the questions.

1. Why do sloths burn energy slowly?
2. Why can't insects that get into a pitcher plant climb out?
3. What is hippo sunscreen made of?

THINK BIG
Which other animals have rare abilities?
What rare abilities do humans have?

74   Unit 6

Culture Connection | Around the World

I will learn about ancient civilizations.

15 Listen and read. Who should we thank for chocolate?

CONTENT WORDS
article   civilization
contribution   cultivation
influence   legacy

Ancient Civilizations and Their Legacies

What do we take for granted in the world today – language, writing, theater, politics? Even the subjects we learn about in school? In this article, we look at two civilizations that have had an important influence on the modern world.

The Greeks have had a great influence on modern culture. From 800 to 146 BC, the ancient Greeks shaped the worlds of art, literature, and philosophy. Homer wrote his great works of literature in the 7th century BC, and Western philosophy was born with Socrates, Plato, and Aristotle. The fascinating events and the myths and legends of ancient Greece have been a rich source of inspiration for movies, plays, and many famous works of art.

The ancient Greeks also gave the world a sporting legacy: the Olympic Games. The first games took place in the Greek city of Olympia in 776 BC. Today, as in ancient Greece, the modern Olympic Games still take place every four years.

Perhaps the Greeks' greatest contribution to modern culture, however, was in politics. The ancient Greeks introduced the concept of democracy. The word comes from the Greek word demokratia – demos meaning "people" and kratos meaning "rule." Nations and elections around the world today are still based on the principles developed by the Greeks.

Ancient Greece, of course, is only one of the world's great civilizations. Ancient American peoples also left us important legacies in math, astronomy, agriculture, and medicine. For example, around the 7th century BC, the Maya developed a 365-day calendar system by observing Earth's revolution around the sun. They also began to use the concept of zero (0) in math, independently of other cultures.

What about farming? If you enjoy chocolate, you can thank the people of the Aztec empire, which was at its peak between the 14th and 16th centuries. The Aztecs were known for advancing the cultivation of cacao, a key ingredient in chocolate. The Inca civilization, which was powerful in Peru when the Aztecs were powerful in Mexico, introduced terraced farming, which is a special way of organizing land for growing crops. This type of farming is still practiced today. Many of the herbal remedies that we use to treat illnesses were also discovered by the Inca people.

16 Look at the passage. Say Greeks, Maya, or Inca.

1 They knew a lot about plant medicine.
2 They developed an advanced political system.
3 They developed a way of farming that's still used today.
4 They used astronomy to measure time.

THINK BIG

What else do you know about these ancient civilizations? Which other civilizations could you add to the time line?

Culture Connection Lesson

Lesson Flow

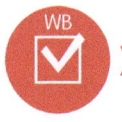

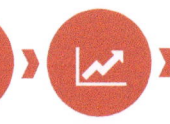

Warm-up › Lesson Objective › Pre-reading › Reading › Practice 1 (SB) › Practice 2 (WB) › Think BIG › Video › Lesson Objective › Homework

Lesson Objective

I will learn about ancient civilizations.

Key Language

article, civilization, contribution, cultivation, influence, legacy

---

Culture Connection | Around the World

I will learn about **ancient civilizations**.

15 Listen and read. Who should we thank for chocolate?

CONTENT WORDS
article civilization
contribution cultivation
influence legacy

Ancient Civilizations and Their Legacies

What do we take for granted in the world today – language, writing, theater, politics? Even the subjects we learn about in school? In this article, we look at two civilizations that have had an important influence on the modern world.

The Greeks have had a great influence on modern culture. From 800 to 146 BC, the ancient Greeks shaped the worlds of art, literature, and philosophy. Homer wrote his great works of literature in the 7th century BC, and Western philosophy was born with Socrates, Plato, and Aristotle. The fascinating events and the myths and legends of ancient Greece have been a rich source of inspiration for movies, plays, and many famous works of art.

The ancient Greeks also gave the world a sporting legacy: the Olympic Games. The first games took place in the Greek city of Olympia in 776 BC. Today, as in ancient Greece, the modern Olympic Games still take place every four years.

Perhaps the Greeks' greatest contribution to modern culture, however, was in politics. The ancient Greeks introduced the concept of democracy. The word comes from the Greek word demokratia – demos meaning "people" and kratos meaning "rule." Nations and elections around the world today are still based on the principles developed by the Greeks.

Ancient Greece, of course, is only one of the world's great civilizations. Ancient American peoples also left us important legacies in math, astronomy, agriculture, and medicine. For example, around the 7th century BC, the Maya developed a 365-day calendar system by observing Earth's revolution around the sun. They also began to use the concept of zero (0) in math, independently of other cultures.

What about farming? If you enjoy chocolate, you can thank the people of the Aztec empire, which was at its peak between the 14th and 16th centuries. The Aztecs were known for advancing the cultivation of cacao, a key ingredient in chocolate. The Inca civilization, which was powerful in Peru when the Aztecs were powerful in Mexico, introduced terraced farming, which is a special way of organizing land for growing crops. This type of farming is still practiced today. Many of the herbal remedies that we use to treat illnesses were also discovered by the Inca people.

16 Look at the passage. Say *Greeks*, *Maya*, or *Inca*.

1. They knew a lot about plant medicine.
2. They developed an advanced political system.
3. They developed a way of farming that's still used today.
4. They used astronomy to measure time.

THINK BIG
What else do you know about these ancient civilizations? Which other civilizations could you add to the time line?

Unit 6 75

Warm-up

- Write *ancient* on the board. Say: *Ancient history refers to events that happened a long, long time ago.* Write the following list on the board in scrambled order: *Mayans, ancient Egyptians, Incas, ancient Greeks, Aztecs.*

- Encourage groups of students to try to arrange this list from the earliest to the most recent. Draw a timeline. The answer is as follows: *1 ancient Egyptians, 2 ancient Greeks, 3 Mayans, 4 Aztecs, 5 Incas.* Tell students they will learn something about these civilizations in this lesson.

- Check answers from the HW in the last lesson.

Lesson Objective

INVOLVE

- Introduce the lesson objective. Say: *Today I will learn about ancient civilizations.*
- Students will read about the legacies of ancient civilizations.

Pre-reading

- Write the words *cultivation, influence, inspiration, legacy, revolution,* and *terraced farming* on the board. Have students underline each one in the text and use context clues to determine its meaning.
- Invite a volunteer to read the title aloud. Say: *A legacy is a gift from the past that is passed from one generation to the next.*

Reading

15 Listen and read. Who should we thank for chocolate?

- Play Audio Track 90 and have students listen and read.

MONITOR

- Discuss the answer as a class. *(Answer: The Aztecs)*

ASSIST

- Replay the audio as required. If students have difficulty with the dates, explain the difference in numbering for years and centuries. For example, say: *The 16th century took place during the 1500s.*

Practice 1

16 Look at the passage. Say *Greeks, Maya,* or *Inca*.

- Read the directions aloud. Have students work independently to read the sentences and choose whether they refer to the Greeks, Maya, or Incas.
- Play Audio Track 91 again for students to check their answers.

MONITOR

- Check answers as a class. *(Answers: 1 Incas, 2 Greeks, 3 Incas, 4 Maya)*

Practice 2 WB p. 61/ act. 15

15 Listen and read. Which ancient civilization should you thank for things you have today? Write *The Aztecs, The Incas,* or *The Greeks*.

- Read the directions aloud, then play Audio Track 91 twice. The second time, have students circle the words they do not understand. Explain their meaning.
- Have students label the descriptions with the correct civilization. Prompt students to use SB Activity 15 on page 75 to help them.

MONITOR

- Check answers in pairs.

Think BIG

21st Century Global Awareness

- Point out that our word *theater* comes from the Greek word *theatron* and we can thank the Aztecs for the word *tomato*. The Aztecs also founded Mexico City. Maya legacies include chewing gum and complementary agriculture, in which beans, corn, and squash are grown together. Point out that similar growing strategies are used on many farms today. We have some stone-building techniques and road systems from the Incas.
- Ask students if they can think of any other things we have from ancient civilizations. The Great Wall of China and mathematical theories such as Pythagoras's rule are examples.
- Finally, ask students to think why it is important to study civilizations other than our own. Have students come up with comparisons between the modern world and the civilizations they have read about and discussed. Share their ideas with the class.

Video Documentary U 06

- Refer to the Video Guide for pre-watching and post-watching activities.

Lesson Objective

INVOLVE

- Revisit the lesson objective: *Now I have learned about ancient civilizations.*
- Encourage awareness of what students have learned by quickly eliciting a few things that we have or know today because of ancient civilizations.

Homework WB p. 61/ act. 16

16 Look at 15. Circle T for *true* or F for *false*.

- Direct students to WB Activity 16 on page 61. Tell students to read the statements and then decide if each is true or false.

Extra Application and Practice Activity

Materials: Index cards

- Invite students to create "Ancient Legacy" cards on index cards. Each card should have an illustration on one side and a description of the legacy on the back. Students can use the cards to ask and answer questions.

Unit 6 **T75**

Writing Lesson

Lesson Flow

Warm-up › Lesson Objective › Practice 1 › Practice 2 › Speaking › Lesson Objective › Homework

Lesson Objective

I will learn to rewrite a story as a play.

Writing | From story to play

I will learn to rewrite a story as a play.

17 Read the fairy tale. Note down anything a character thinks, wonders, wishes, or says.

The Ugly Duckling

A mother duck sat on her nest. One of her eggs was much larger than the others. She wondered why the egg was so big. Soon the egg hatched. Out came a very big and odd-looking duckling.

"PEEP!" said the big duckling and blinked.

"Go away!" the duckling's brother snapped. He told the duckling that he was the ugliest duckling he'd ever seen.

The poor duckling didn't know what to do, so he ran away. Fall came and went, and soon winter chilled the air. The duckling shivered, cold and alone.

Finally, spring came, and the duckling stretched his neck down to the water to drink. He saw a beautiful bird reflected in the water. He wished he could look like the bird in the reflection. "Then people wouldn't call me an ugly duckling," he said.

A little girl throwing bread to him heard what the duckling said. "But that *is* you!" she cried. "You're not an ugly duckling – you're a swan!"

18 Rewrite the story as a play. Then read it aloud to a partner.

Narrator:	Mother Duck looks at her eggs.
Mother Duck: *[to herself]*	_____
Narrator:	The egg hatches. Out comes the Ugly Duckling.
Ugly Duckling:	_____
Ugly Duckling's brother:	_____
Narrator:	The Ugly Duckling runs away. Fall and winter come and go. Spring arrives. The Ugly Duckling looks down at the water and sees something.
Ugly Duckling: *[to himself]*	_____
Little Girl:	_____

19 Work with a partner. Find a fairy tale. In your notebook, rewrite it as a play. Read your play aloud to the class.

76 Unit 6

Warm-up

- Say: *A fairy tale is a story for young people. Many fairy tales have characters that are magical or have unreal powers, such as talking animals.* Have students brainstorm a list of fairy tales and characters.

- Have students play *Picture Charades*, using characters and tales from their list as topics. Players should take turns choosing a tale or character and drawing a picture until classmates guess the topic.

- Check answers from the HW in the last lesson.

S76 Unit 6

Lesson Objective

INVOLVE

Introduce the lesson objective. Say: *Today I will learn to rewrite a story as a play.*

- Students will read a fairy tale and rewrite fairy tales as plays.

Practice 1

17 Read the fairy tale. Note down anything a character thinks, wonders, wishes, or says.

- Read the the directions aloud. Then have volunteers read the fairy tale aloud. Encourage them to use appropriate emotion and intonation as they read.
- Then have students complete the activity independently in their notebooks.

MONITOR

Have students read the sentences they noted down aloud. (Sample answers: She wondered why the egg was so big./"PEEP!"/"Go away!"/He told the duckling that he was the ugliest duckling he'd ever seen./He wished he could look like the bird in the reflection./"Then people wouldn't call me an ugly duckling"./"But that is you!"/"You're not an ugly duckling – you're a swan!")

ASSIST

Remind students that a character's exact words are written inside quotation marks.

Practice 2

18 Rewrite the story as a play. Then read it aloud to a partner.

- Read the directions aloud. Have students work independently to complete the activity and then read their play to a partner.

MONITOR

Check answers by inviting volunteers to read their play aloud. (Sample play:

Mother Duck [to herself]:	That's strange. Why is this egg so big?
Ugly Duckling:	PEEP!
Ugly Duckling's brother:	Go away! You're the ugliest duckling I've ever seen!
Ugly Duckling [to himself]:	I wish I could look like the bird in the reflection.
Little Girl:	But that is you!)

ASSIST

Help students compare the model sentences with the original ones in the tale. Help students rewrite what the duckling's brother did. ("He told the duckling that he was the ugliest duckling he'd ever seen" changes to "You're the ugliest duckling I've ever seen!")

Speaking

19 Work with a partner. Find a fairy tale. In your notebook, rewrite it as a play. Read your play aloud to the class.

- Read the directions aloud. Remind students that a play includes character names, what they say (dialog), and what they do (stage directions). Have students complete the activity in pairs in their notebooks.

MONITOR

As pairs share their plays, check that they've written dialog that shows what the characters say or think, and stage directions that show what they do.

ASSIST

Provide students with fairy tales they can consider adapting, such as "Snow White," "Little Red Riding Hood," "Rapunzel," or "Hansel and Gretel."

Lesson Objective

INVOLVE

Revisit the lesson objective: *Now I have learned to rewrite a story as a play.*

- Encourage awareness of what students have learned by asking students the difference between a story and a play. See the box at the top of page 62 of the WB.

Homework WB p. 62/ act. 17 & 18

17 Read the story of Daedalus and Icarus in 5 again. Answer the questions.

- Direct students to WB Activity 17 on page 62. Tell students to answer the questions using the story in WB Activity 5 on page 56.

18 Choose one of the events in 17. Rewrite the event as a play in your notebook.

- Direct students to WB Activity 18 on page 62. Tell students to write a play using one of the events they wrote about in Activity 17, ideas from the story in Activity 5 and the box at the top of the page.

Extra Application and Practice Activity

- Have students perform their plays for the class, using simple costumes, props, and settings. Students might prefer to perform the plays using finger, hand, paper bag, or shadow puppets. If possible, allow students to record their plays.

21st Century Collaboration

- Point out that students can improvise as they create and perform their plays. Suggest that they begin by deciding on a tone, such as serious or funny. If possible, record improvisations and then have students choose the best lines for their written versions.

Writing | From story to play

I will learn to rewrite a story as a play.

17 Read the fairy tale. Note down anything a character thinks, wonders, wishes, or says.

The Ugly Duckling

A mother duck sat on her nest. One of her eggs was much larger than the others. She wondered why the egg was so big. Soon the egg hatched. Out came a very big and odd-looking duckling.

"PEEP!" said the big duckling and blinked.

"Go away!" the duckling's brother snapped. He told the duckling that he was the ugliest duckling he'd ever seen.

The poor duckling didn't know what to do, so he ran away. Fall came and went, and soon winter chilled the air. The duckling shivered, cold and alone.

Finally, spring came, and the duckling stretched his neck down to the water to drink. He saw a beautiful bird reflected in the water. He wished he could look like the bird in the reflection. "Then people wouldn't call me an ugly duckling," he said.

A little girl throwing bread to him heard what the duckling said. "But that *is* you!" she cried. "You're not an ugly duckling – you're a swan!"

18 Rewrite the story as a play. Then read it aloud to a partner.

Narrator:	Mother Duck looks at her eggs.
Mother Duck: *[to herself]*	_____
Narrator:	The egg hatches. Out comes the Ugly Duckling.
Ugly Duckling:	_____
Ugly Duckling's brother:	_____
Narrator:	The Ugly Duckling runs away. Fall and winter come and go. Spring arrives. The Ugly Duckling looks down at the water and sees something.
Ugly Duckling: *[to himself]*	_____
Little Girl:	_____

19 Work with a partner. Find a fairy tale. In your notebook, rewrite it as a play. Read your play aloud to the class.

Life skills | Appreciate school.

I will learn to talk about the practical uses of school subjects.

20 The subjects you learn in school have practical and important uses in everyday life. Can you think of a practical use for each of your subjects? Complete the chart. Then share your ideas with a partner.

School subject	Topic learned	Everyday use
Literature	Myths and legends	help us recognize our faults; teach us valuable lessons about life and people
Math		
Social studies		
Science		
Art and music		
Health and P.E.		
English		

Project

21 Work with a group. Make a book of names from ancient Greece that we use today.

1. Write the Greek name and say what it stood for.
2. Draw a picture.
3. Share your page. Explain why it's a good name to use today.

Amazon

The Amazons were female Greek warriors. They were brave and strong. There's a company with this name that sells products online. The name makes people think that the company is strong.

Unit 6 77

Life Skills Lesson

Lesson Flow

Warm-up › Lesson Objective › Speaking › Project › Lesson Objective

Lesson Objective

I will learn to talk about the practical uses of school subjects.

Life skills | Appreciate school.

I will learn to talk about the practical uses of school subjects.

20 The subjects you learn in school have practical and important uses in everyday life. Can you think of a practical use for each of your subjects? Complete the chart. Then share your ideas with a partner.

School subject	Topic learned	Everyday use
Literature	Myths and legends	help us recognize our faults; teach us valuable lessons about life and people
Math		
Social studies		
Science		
Art and music		
Health and P.E.		
English		

Project

21 Work with a group. Make a book of names from ancient Greece that we use today.

1. Write the Greek name and say what it stood for.
2. Draw a picture.
3. Share your page. Explain why it's a good name to use today.

Amazon

The Amazons were female Greek warriors. They were brave and strong. There's a company with this name that sells products online. The name makes people think that the company is strong.

Warm-up

- Write this word scramble on the board: *A A C E E I P P R T*. Challenge students to rearrange the letters to find the word (*appreciate*) and define it. (Sample definition: *to care about something or value something highly*) Then have students complete this sentence: *I really appreciate…* . Invite students to read and compare their sentences.
- Check answers from the HW in the last lesson.

Lesson Objective

INVOLVE

Introduce the lesson objective. Say: *Today I will learn to talk about the practical uses of school subjects.*

- Students will think about why it's important to appreciate school and write about how they can use what they learn there every day. Then they'll create books to show how words from ancient Greece are used today.

Speaking

20 The subjects you learn in school have practical and important uses in everyday life. Can you think of a practical use for each of your subjects? Complete the chart. Then share your ideas with a partner.

- Read the page title and directions aloud.
- Have students look at the chart, and complete the first item as a class. Model: *Why is literature useful in everyday life? Well, we read myths and legends. Even though we aren't heroes, these stories help us recognize our faults. They teach us valuable lessons about life and people.* Then have students work independently or in pairs to complete the chart.

MONITOR

Check that students list everyday uses for school subjects and topics.

ASSIST

Remind students that math includes algebra and geometry; social science includes history and geography; science includes biology, technology, and astronomy; and English includes vocabulary and grammar. Students can refer to the unit activities to list topics. Provide students with vocabulary to describe everyday uses for school subjects.

Project

Materials: Poster paper, art supplies

21st Century Research

21 Work with a group. Make a book of names from ancient Greece that we use today.

- Read the directions and steps aloud. Have volunteers read the model book page aloud. Ask: *What name from ancient Greece does this page explain?* (Amazon) Have groups work together to find and choose an ancient Greek name. Guide students to use the internet to research the names.
- Encourage students to create two illustrations for each book page: one that shows what the Greek name stood for in ancient times and another that shows how it's used today.

MONITOR

Check that students use complete sentences in their books.

ASSIST

Provide these additional Greek words and names for students to choose from: *Atlas, Aurora, Delphi, Elysium, Eos, Helios, Hyperion, Medusa, Midas, Odyssey, Olympus, Orion, Poseidon, Spartan.*

Class Album: Suggest that students arrange pages in the class album alphabetically by the Greek names. Encourage the class to choose an appropriate title and cover illustration for the album. Place the finished book in the classroom or school library so it can be shared with other students or classroom visitors.

Lesson Objective

INVOLVE

Revisit the lesson objective: *Now I have learned to talk about the practical uses of school subjects.*

- Encourage awareness of what students have learned by quickly eliciting examples of what students learn from different school subjects.

Extra Application and Practice Activity

- Have students read a page from the book aloud but leave out the Greek name. Encourage classmates to guess it.

Listening and Speaking Lesson

Lesson Flow

Warm-up › Lesson Objective › Presentation › Practice 1 (SB) › Practice 2 (SB) › Practice 3 (SB) › Speaking › Lesson Objective

Lesson Objectives

I will review the sounds *er* and *est*.

I will learn to talk about who has the most or the least of something.

Listening and Speaking

I will review the sounds *er* and *est*.
I will learn to talk about who has the most or the least of something.

22 Listen, read, and repeat.

1. **er**   2. **est**

23 Listen and blend the sounds.

1. f-a-s-t-er   faster
2. ea-s-i-er   easier
3. b-e-s-t   best
4. ch-ea-p-er   cheaper
5. h-a-pp-i-er   happier
6. l-o-n-g-e-s-t   longest

24 Listen and chant.

Running is faster than walking,
Walking is cheaper than driving,
Driving is easier than flying,
Flying is harder than cycling,
Cycling is the best!

25 Make a sentence using the words in each row of the chart.

Student	Adjective	Activity
1 Hannah	most	has books in her backpack
2 Robert	fewest	has coins in his pockets
3 Cheryl	most	has songs on her MP3 player
4 Dan	most	has after-school activities every week
5 Paula	fewest	plays video games every day
6 Mark	least amount of	watches TV every day
7 Francis	most	watches movies every month
8 Laura	least amount of	has free time every week

26 Work with a partner. Ask and answer questions about the sentences you made in **25**.

Who has the most books in her backpack?

Hannah does.

78 Unit 6

Warm-up

Materials: Dice, timer

- Have students play a dice game to review *most*, *fewest*, and *least*. Players should roll two dice and write down the number. Then they should start a timer and keep rolling until they roll the same number. Have them write down the number of rolls and the amount of time it took and then talk with the group to compare results. Model: *Jan took the most number of rolls to match her number. Ian took the fewest number of rolls. Lexy took the most time. Alana took the least time.*

Lesson Objective

INVOLVE

Introduce the lesson objective. Say: *Today I will learn to use the sounds* er *and* est, *and talk about who has the most or least of something.*

- Students will identify the letters and distinguish between the sounds *er* and *est*, individually, and as part of words. They'll also use *most*, *fewest*, and *least* to ask and answer questions.

Presentation

22 Listen, read, and repeat.

- Read the directions aloud. Play Audio Track 92 and have students listen and point to each sound as it is said. Have students repeat.

MONITOR

As students repeat, check they are pointing to the correct sound and listen for correct pronunciation.

Practice 1

23 Listen and blend the sounds.

- Read the directions aloud. Play Audio Track 93 and have students listen and point to each item as it is sounded out and blended on the audio. Have them repeat after each item.

MONITOR

As students repeat, check they are pointing to the correct word, and listen for correct pronunciation and appropriate intonation.

ASSIST

Replay the audio as needed.

Practice 2

24 Listen and chant.

- Read the directions aloud. Read the chant while students follow in their books.
- Play Audio Track 94 and have students listen. Replay the audio several times and encourage them to join in.

MONITOR

As students repeat the chant, listen for proper pronunciation, appropriate intonation, and correct use of language.

Practice 3

25 Make a sentence using the words in each row of the chart.

- Read the directions aloud. Complete the first item as a class. Then have students complete the activity independently.

MONITOR

Pair students, and have partners take turns comparing amounts. *(Answers: 1 Hannah has the most books in her backpack. 2 Robert has the fewest coins in his pockets. 3 Cheryl has the most songs on her MP3 player. 4 Dan has the most after-school activities every week. 5 Paula plays the fewest video games every day. 6 Mark watches the least amount of TV every day. 7 Francis watches the most movies every month. 8 Laura has the least amount of free time every week.)*

ASSIST

Remind students that these superlatives are adjectives and come before a noun.

Speaking

26 Work with a partner. Ask and answer questions about the sentences you made in 25.

- Read the directions and steps aloud. Have two volunteers read the speech bubbles aloud.
- Have students ask and answer questions about their sentences in pairs.

MONITOR

Listen for proper pronunciation, appropriate intonation, and correct use of language.

Lesson Objective

INVOLVE

Revisit the lesson objective: *Now I have learned to use the sounds* er *and* est, *and talked about who has the most or least of something.*

- Encourage awareness of what students have learned by quickly eliciting from them words from the lesson with *er* and *est* at the end.

Extra Application and Practice Activity

- Invite students to read their sentences from Activity 24 aloud, leaving out the superlatives. Have classmates guess which superlative was used to complete the sentence.

21st Century Leadership

- Ask: *How would you help a student who's just beginning to study Unit 6?* Encourage students to give specific advice about studying comparative and superlative adjectives or talking about school subjects. Have students write down their advice so it can be shared with students in future classes.

Listening and Speaking

I will review the sounds *er* and *est*.
I will learn to talk about who has the most or the least of something.

22 Listen, read, and repeat.

1. er   2. est

23 Listen and blend the sounds.

1. f-a-s-t-er   faster
2. ea-s-i-er   easier
3. b-e-s-t   best
4. ch-ea-p-er   cheaper
5. h-a-pp-i-er   happier
6. l-o-n-g-e-s-t   longest

24 Listen and chant.

> Running is faster than walking,
> Walking is cheaper than driving,
> Driving is easier than flying,
> Flying is harder than cycling,
> Cycling is the best!

25 Make a sentence using the words in each row of the chart.

Student	Adjective	Activity
1 Hannah	most	has books in her backpack
2 Robert	fewest	has coins in his pockets
3 Cheryl	most	has songs on her MP3 player
4 Dan	most	has after-school activities every week
5 Paula	fewest	plays video games every day
6 Mark	least amount of	watches TV every day
7 Francis	most	watches movies every month
8 Laura	least amount of	has free time every week

26 Work with a partner. Ask and answer questions about the sentences you made in **25**.

Who has the most books in her backpack?

Hannah does.

78   Unit 6

Review

27 Circle the correct words. Then, with a partner, research the answer to each question.

1. Which country has **most / more** pet dogs: Germany or the U.S.A.?
2. Which animal spends **least / less** time eating: a cat or a panda?
3. What is the **larger / largest** mammal on the planet: the elephant or the blue whale?
4. Which country gives the **least / fewest** homework: China, the U.S.A., or Finland?
5. Which animal is the **slower / slowest**: a snail, a sloth, or a turtle?
6. Which place is the **fewest / least** populated place on Earth: the Galapagos Islands, Easter Islands, or Antarctica?
7. Which is a **biggest / bigger** planet: Mars or Earth?
8. Which planet has the **fewest / least** moons: Venus, Earth, or Mars?

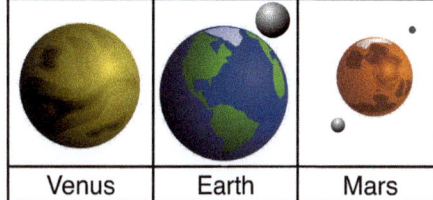

Venus	Earth	Mars

28 Complete the sentences with a word or phrase from the box.
Then write the school subject.

| mural   democracy   myths   vocabulary   artist |
| playwright   prime number   mammal |

1. Leonardo da Vinci was a famous _____. _____
2. Shakespeare was a famous English _____. _____
3. We're going to paint a _____ on the wall. _____
4. A sloth is a _____. _____
5. I'm learning _____ for the quiz tomorrow. _____
6. A _____ can be divided only by 1 and itself. _____
7. He loves to read about Greek _____. _____
8. A government whose leaders are elected by the people is called a _____. _____

I Can

- use words for school subjects and school topics.
- compare things using *more/fewer/less* and *the most/the fewest/the least*.
- talk about school subjects and make comparisons.
- rewrite a story as a play.

Unit 6

Review Lesson

Lesson Flow

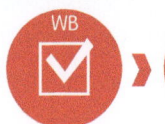

Warm-up › Lesson Objective › Practice 1 (SB) › Practice 2 (WB) › Practice 3 (WB) › Practice 4 (SB) › Self-assessment › Homework

Lesson Objective

To review the words and structures of the unit.

Review

27 Circle the correct words. Then, with a partner, research the answer to each question.

1. Which country has **most / more** pet dogs: Germany or the U.S.A.?
2. Which animal spends **least / less** time eating: a cat or a panda?
3. What is the **larger / largest** mammal on the planet: the elephant or the blue whale?
4. Which country gives the **least / fewest** homework: China, the U.S.A., or Finland?
5. Which animal is the **slower / slowest**: a snail, a sloth, or a turtle?
6. Which place is the **fewest / least** populated place on Earth: the Galapagos Islands, Easter Islands, or Antarctica?
7. Which is a **biggest / bigger** planet: Mars or Earth?
8. Which planet has the **fewest / least** moons: Venus, Earth, or Mars?

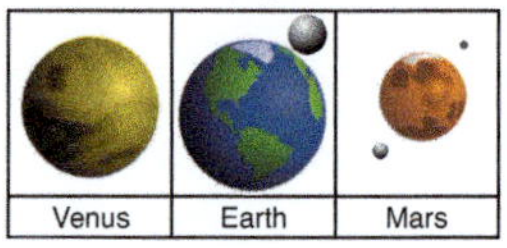

(Images labeled: Venus, Earth, Mars)

28 Complete the sentences with a word or phrase from the box. Then write the school subject.

> mural   democracy   myths   vocabulary   artist
> playwright   prime number   mammal

1. Leonardo da Vinci was a famous _____. _____
2. Shakespeare was a famous English _____. _____
3. We're going to paint a _____ on the wall. _____
4. A sloth is a _____. _____
5. I'm learning _____ for the quiz tomorrow. _____
6. A _____ can be divided only by 1 and itself. _____
7. He loves to read about Greek _____. _____
8. A government whose leaders are elected by the people is called a _____. _____

I Can

- use words for school subjects and school topics.
- compare things using *more/fewer/less* and *the most/the fewest/the least*.
- talk about school subjects and make comparisons.
- rewrite a story as a play.

Unit 6   79

Warm-up

Materials: Index cards, paper clips

- Have students create scrambled sentences to review unit vocabulary. Ask them to first write a sentence that uses a unit vocabulary word. Then they should write the sentence again on index cards, writing one word on each card. Have them mix up the cards, clip them together, and challenge a classmate to arrange the cards to make a sentence that makes sense.

Lesson Objective

INVOLVE

Introduce the lesson objective: Say: *Today I will review the words and structures of the unit.*

- Students will review the vocabulary and grammar they have learned in Unit 6 by doing activities, including matching and completing sentences.
- Then students will complete the *I Can* section, which helps them to assess their own learning and think about their progress.

Practice 1

27 Circle the correct words. Then, with a partner, research the answer to each question.

- Read the directions aloud. Have students complete the activity in pairs. Allow them to use library or internet resources to answer the questions.

MONITOR

Ask students to say what sources they used to find each answer. Check answers as a class. *(Sample answers: 1 more, the U.S.A.; 2 less, a cat; 3 the largest, the blue whale; 4 least, Finland; 5 the slowest, sloth; 6 least, Antarctica; 7 bigger, Earth; 8 fewest, Venus)*

21st Century Technology Literacy

- Remind students to be careful when finding answers on the internet. Say: *Not all information on the internet is true. Check that a website is reliable before you use it as a source.* Tell students that sites whose URLs that end in .gov (government) or .org (organizations) are usually reliable. Point out that .edu (education) sites are often reliable, but may include student posted pages, which may not have been carefully checked.

Practice 2 WB p. 63/ act. 19

19 Read and match. Write the letters.

- Read the directions aloud. Read the first sentence part aloud. As a class work through a–d to consider which is correct.
- Have the students work independently to complete the activity, then check the answers as a class.

Practice 3 WB p. 63/ act. 20

20 Read and complete the sentences.

- Read the directions aloud. Have students read the sentences carefully, then complete them using *more* or *fewer*.
- Do Item 1 as a class, then have students complete the activity independently.

Practice 4

28 Complete the sentences with a word or phrase from the box. Then write the school subject.

- Read the directions and the words and phrases in the box aloud. Have students complete the activity independently.

MONITOR

Check answers as a class. *(Answers: 1 artist, art; 2 playwright, literature; 3 mural, art; 4 mammal, science: biology; 5 vocabulary, English; 6 prime number, math; 7 myths, literature; 8 democracy social science)*

Ask students to name clues from each sentence that helped them complete it.

Self-assessment

I Can

- This section asks students to assess their own learning and think about their progress. Help students appreciate their progress. Say: *The I Can statements show what you have learned in this unit.*
- Read the statements aloud. Explain that students should think about how well they know the language in the unit and should color in the stars. They should color three stars if they feel the unit was easy, two stars if they need some help and one star if the unit was hard and they need more help. Have students work independently.

Suggestions for Remediation

Assessment Pack
- Direct students who need help with grammar and vocabulary to the Unit 6 Practice Tests in the Assessment Pack.

WB Unit 6/ p. 103
- Direct students who need help with grammar in particular to the Unit 6 Extra Grammar Practice (Workbook, page 103).
- For further vocabulary work, students can access games in the Big English Student World.

Homework WB p. 63/ act. 21

21 Complete the sentences. Use *the least*, *the fewest*, or *the most* and the underlined words.

- Direct students to WB Activity 21 on page 63. Students write their own answers.

Extra Application and Practice Activity

- Have students write *true/false* statements based on the facts in the lesson and then challenge classmates to identify them as *true* or *false*.

Assessment Pack

- To assess student progress at the end of the unit, have students complete the Unit 6 Unit Test in the Assessment Pack.
- To assess whether students have reached the listening and speaking targets for this unit, carry out the Unit 6 Oral Assessment in the Assessment Pack.
- Arrange one-to-one sessions with each student and use the prompts to evaluate their listening and speaking abilities.

Unit 6 T79

Checkpoint 4–6 Lesson 1

Lesson Flow

Warm-up › Lesson Objective › Self-assessment › Practice

Lesson Objective

To think about how well I can use what I have learned in Units 4–6.

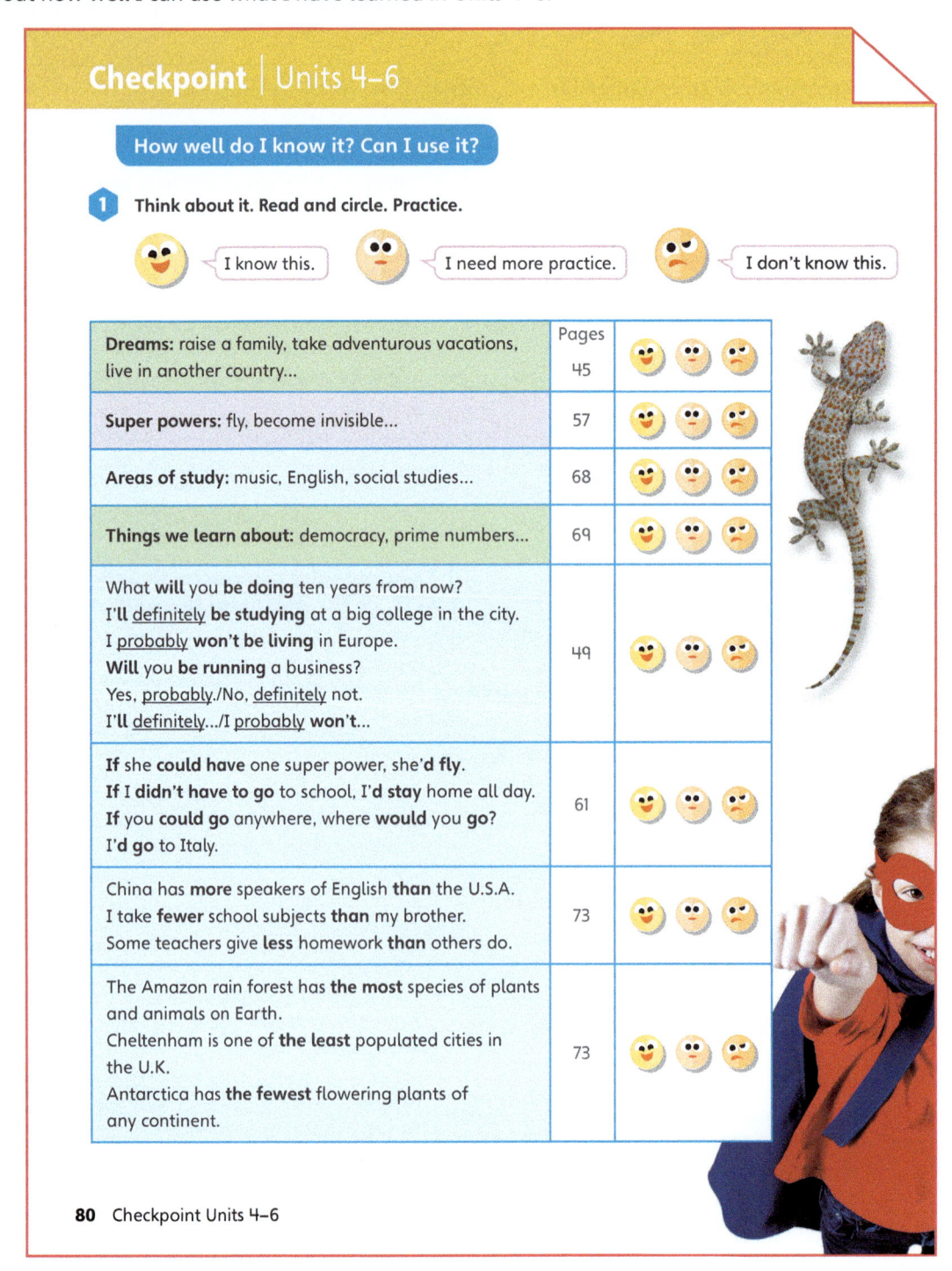

Checkpoint | Units 4–6

How well do I know it? Can I use it?

1 Think about it. Read and circle. Practice.

😃 I know this.   😐 I need more practice.   😠 I don't know this.

	Pages			
Dreams: raise a family, take adventurous vacations, live in another country…	45	😃	😐	😠
Super powers: fly, become invisible…	57	😃	😐	😠
Areas of study: music, English, social studies…	68	😃	😐	😠
Things we learn about: democracy, prime numbers…	69	😃	😐	😠
What **will** you **be doing** ten years from now? I'll <u>definitely</u> **be studying** at a big college in the city. I <u>probably</u> **won't be living** in Europe. **Will** you **be running** a business? Yes, <u>probably</u>./No, <u>definitely</u> not. I'll <u>definitely</u>…/I <u>probably</u> **won't**…	49	😃	😐	😠
If she **could have** one super power, she'**d fly**. If I **didn't have to go** to school, I'**d stay** home all day. If you **could go** anywhere, where **would** you **go**? I'**d go** to Italy.	61	😃	😐	😠
China has **more** speakers of English **than** the U.S.A. I take **fewer** school subjects **than** my brother. Some teachers give **less** homework **than** others do.	73	😃	😐	😠
The Amazon rain forest has **the most** species of plants and animals on Earth. Cheltenham is one of **the least** populated cities in the U.K. Antarctica has **the fewest** flowering plants of any continent.	73	😃	😐	😠

80   Checkpoint Units 4–6

Warm-up

- On the board, write: *What dreams do students in this class have?* Remind students that dreams are things people want to have, do, or be someday. Have students draw a picture of their dream and take turns displaying their picture for their classmates to guess the dream. Then discuss the other meaning of *dreams*: things we imagine when we sleep. Ask students to share any of these kinds of dreams they can remember.

Lesson Objective

INVOLVE

Introduce the lesson objective: *Today I will think about how well I can use what I have learned in Units 4–6.*

- Students will review key language in Units 4–6.

Self-assessment

Materials: Slips of paper, envelope, sticky notes, magazines, dice

1 Think about it. Read and circle. Practice.

- Read the descriptions aloud as students point to the face icons at the top of the page. Have them use markers or colored pencils to complete the checklist. They will choose a different color when they review this list at the end of the Checkpoint.

MONITOR

Follow the suggestions below to review the key language in these units. Listen for correct use of vocabulary and grammar. Remind students that they will be asked to assess their own abilities.

ASSIST

Encourage students to turn to the page references in the checklist when they need additional support or to refresh their memories.

> **21st Century Self-Direction**
>
> - Remind students that they completed Checkpoints to review the skills they learned in Units 1–3. Have students review those Checkpoints to recall how they used a checklist to monitor their own progress. As students complete the checklist for Units 4–6, emphasize that there are no right or wrong answers. Students should circle face icons that show how they feel about each skill.

Dreams (page 45)

Have students write predictions on slips of paper and place them in an envelope. Model: *You will be raising a family. You will be living in Madrid.* Students take turns naming a time in the future and then choosing a prediction to complete the sentence. Model: *In eight years, I will be...*

Super powers (page 57)

Have students use sticky notes to label the super powers of people shown in magazine photos. Model: *He can read minds.*

Areas of study (page 68)

Ask students to rank areas of study from their favorite to their least favorite. Invite students to compare their lists and rankings.

Things we learn about (page 69)

Ask students to write definitions for things we learn about and share them with classmates, who try to guess the school subject where it's learned.

I'll be studying/I won't be living (page 49)

Have students roll two dice and use the number rolled to ask a partner a question about the future. Encourage partners to repeat numbers in their answers. Model: A: *What will you be doing in eight years?* B: *In eight years, I'll be traveling in Asia.*

If she could have... , she would... . (page 61)

Invite partners to write new sticky notes for people in pictures in Unit 5, telling about their secret wishes. Model: *If she could go anywhere, she would go to India. If he could have one super power, he'd fly.*

more than/fewer than/less than (page 73)

Ask students to compare the numbers and amounts of things in the classroom. Model: *Sam has more markers than Edith. Edith has less homework than Sam.*

the most/the fewest/the least (page 73)

Have students ask and answer questions that include the most, the fewest, or the least. Allow students to use the internet. Model: *What continent has the most glaciers?* (Antarctica) *What country has the least amount of rainfall?* (Egypt)

Practice WB pp. 64 & 65/ act. 1, 2, 3, & 4

1 Write about yourself. Look at Units 4, 5, and 6 to help you.

- Direct students to WB Activity 1 on page 64. Read the directions aloud. Ask the students to look at the pictures and write unit vocabulary about them in the boxes.

2 Make a list of your superheroes – real or imaginary.

- Direct students to WB Activity 2 on page 65. Read the directions aloud. Students list superheroes.

3 Look at 2. Choose one superhero and make some notes about your choice.

- Direct students to WB Activity 3 on page 65. Read the directions aloud. Students choose one superhero from their list in WB Activity 2, and write about him or her.

4 Look at 2 and 3. Write a song about your superhero. Use some of these sentences in your song. Add your own sentences.

- Direct students to WB Activity 4 on page 65. Read the directions aloud. Students use words and sentences from WB activities 2 and 3, as well as the lines in this activity, to write a song about their chosen superhero.

Checkpoint 4–6 Lesson 2

Lesson Flow

Warm-up › Lesson Objective › Pre-listening › Listening › Practice 1 › Practice 2

Lesson Objective

To put together what I have learned in Units 4–6.

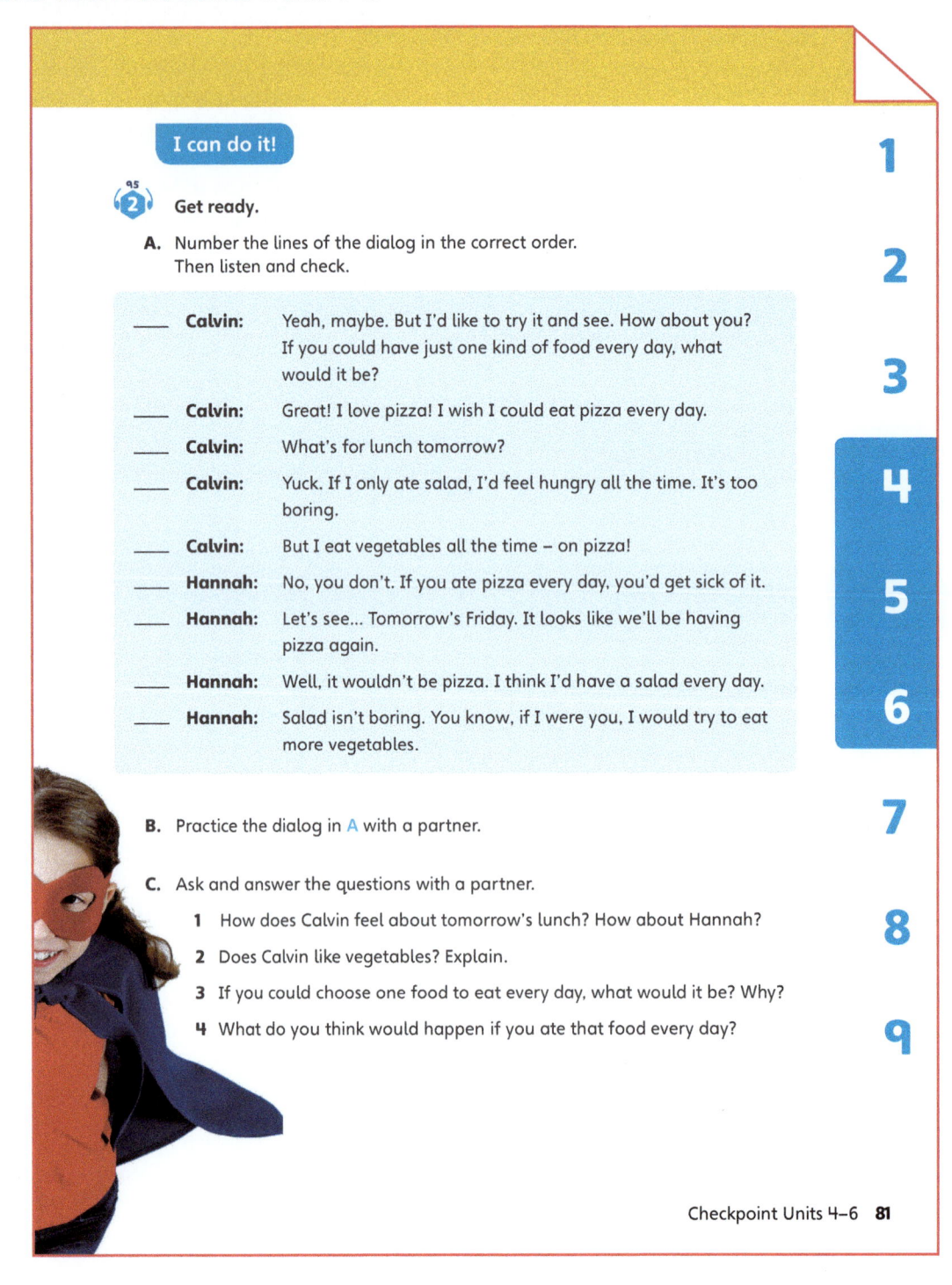

I can do it!

🎧 2 Get ready.

A. Number the lines of the dialog in the correct order.
   Then listen and check.

___ Calvin: Yeah, maybe. But I'd like to try it and see. How about you? If you could have just one kind of food every day, what would it be?

___ Calvin: Great! I love pizza! I wish I could eat pizza every day.

___ Calvin: What's for lunch tomorrow?

___ Calvin: Yuck. If I only ate salad, I'd feel hungry all the time. It's too boring.

___ Calvin: But I eat vegetables all the time – on pizza!

___ Hannah: No, you don't. If you ate pizza every day, you'd get sick of it.

___ Hannah: Let's see… Tomorrow's Friday. It looks like we'll be having pizza again.

___ Hannah: Well, it wouldn't be pizza. I think I'd have a salad every day.

___ Hannah: Salad isn't boring. You know, if I were you, I would try to eat more vegetables.

B. Practice the dialog in A with a partner.

C. Ask and answer the questions with a partner.
   1. How does Calvin feel about tomorrow's lunch? How about Hannah?
   2. Does Calvin like vegetables? Explain.
   3. If you could choose one food to eat every day, what would it be? Why?
   4. What do you think would happen if you ate that food every day?

Checkpoint Units 4–6 **81**

S81 Checkpoint Units 4–6

Warm-up

- Ask each student to write down three favorite foods. Ask: *Would you like to eat your favorite food every day? Why or why not?* (Sample answers: I would love to have noodles every day./If I could, I would have a different sauce every time./No, I'd get bored if I ate mangoes every day.)
- Then have students compare their responses to identify the foods mentioned most frequently and take a class poll to determine which food is most popular.

Lesson Objective

INVOLVE

Introduce the Lesson Objective: *Today I will put together what I have learned in Units 4–6.*

- Students will complete and practice a dialog. Then they will share ideas with a partner.

Pre-listening

- Read the directions and dialog names aloud.
- Tell students they will listen to Calvin and Hannah talk about what they like to eat. Explain that the lines in the activity are jumbled up.

Listening

2 Get ready.

A Number the lines of the dialog in the correct order. Then listen and check.

21st Century Critical Thinking

- Ask: *How can you tell that Calvin's first line does not begin the dialog?* (The first line starts with the answer to a question: "Yeah, maybe." The dialog must be out of order because a question must come before this line.)

- Have volunteers read the dialog sentences aloud. Then have students suggest which sentence begins the dialog. (*Calvin: What's for lunch tomorrow?*) Ask students to continue numbering the lines of dialog independently.

MONITOR

Play Audio Track 95 and have students check that they numbered the lines correctly. (Answers: 5, 3, 1, 7, 9, 4, 2, 6, 8) Use questions to check comprehension. Ask: *What is for lunch tomorrow?* (pizza) *Which student likes pizza the most?* (Calvin) *What food does Hannah like more than pizza?* (salad) *How does Calvin feel about salad?* (He thinks it is boring.)

ASSIST

Play the audio for students before they number the sentences. You could also suggest that students copy the eight lines of dialog onto separate cards. Have them use different colors for Calvin and Hannah. Then have them put the cards in order so the dialog makes sense.

Practice 1

B Practice the dialog in A with a partner.

- Read the directions aloud and invite students to practice the dialog. Encourage students to change roles to review all of the unit language.

MONITOR

Listen for correct pronunciation, intonation, and use of language as students practice the dialog.

- Allow students to use smartphones to record their dialogs. Encourage them to review their lines to check their own language production.

Practice 2

C Ask and answer the questions with a partner.

- Read the directions aloud. Have student pairs ask and answer questions about the dialog.

MONITOR

Have students share their responses with the class. Listen for correct use of language.

ASSIST

Provide students with sentence frames they can complete to answer items: *If I could choose one food to eat every day, I would choose… . If I ate this food every day, I think I would… .*

- Remind students that punctuation can help them decide how to say a line of dialog. Have students circle the end punctuation in the dialog. Point out that a sentence that ends with a question mark often ends with rising intonation. A sentence that ends with an exclamation point should be spoken in an excited and energetic way.

21st Century Cross-Cultural Skills

Ask: *If you could eat only food from one country every day, which one would it be? Why?* Have students share their answers with the class and describe the different kinds of food they would eat. You may wish to suggest countries, such as China, France, Japan, Mexico, and Thailand.

Checkpoint Units 4–6   **T81**

Checkpoint 4–6 Lesson 3

Lesson Flow

Warm-up › Lesson Objective › Speaking

Lesson Objective

To put together what I have learned in Units 4–6.

Checkpoint | Units 4–6

3 Get set.

STEP 1 Cut out the Mystery Classmate card on page 135.

STEP 2 Ask one classmate questions about himself/herself to fill in the card. Be sure to write neatly.

STEP 3 Mix up all the cards in a bag. Then each student takes one of the cards from the bag. Make sure it's not your own card.
Now you're ready to Go!

4 Go!

A. Work in a group. Take turns reading aloud the information (except for the name) on your card. Each group member copies the chart into a notebook and completes it by writing who he or she thinks the other group members are reading about.

Card number	Who read it?	Who do you think it's about?
Example	Andy	Anna
1		
2		
3		
4		

B. Talk about your guesses. Give reasons for your choices.

> I think Andy's card is about Anna. She loves playing soccer, and she'll be working in a hospital someday.

> I'm not sure. I don't think Anna likes chocolate.

C. Each student says whose card he/she read in Step A. Check your guesses. Which person in your group solved the most mysteries?

82 Checkpoint Units 4–6

Warm-up

3 Get set.

- Have students preview the Mystery Classmate cards on page 135. Say: *You will use this card to interview a classmate.* Have students read the card aloud and ask questions about any unfamiliar vocabulary.
- Read the directions and the steps aloud. Then have partners complete the steps.

Lesson Objective

INVOLVE

Introduce the Lesson Objective: *Today I will put together what I have learned in Units 4–6.*

- Students will interview classmates and then try to guess classmates' identities based on clues from the Mystery Classmate cards.

Speaking

4 Go!

A Work in a group. Take turns reading aloud the information (except for the name) on your card. Each group member copies the chart into a notebook and completes it by writing who, he or she thinks the other group members are reading about.

- Read the directions aloud. Model choosing one card and reading the clues aloud without revealing the name of the student. Then have groups work together to read the information on their cards aloud. Have individual students write their guesses on their charts. Remind them to write down the name of the person who read each card.
- Suggest that students use sticky notes to cover up the names of the students at the top of each card. This will help students from accidentally reading the names aloud and will also allow students to guess the mystery classmate's identity.

MONITOR

Check that students complete the cards with logical answers.

ASSIST

Have students cross out a pronoun in each sentence (so that the pronoun left is correct). This will make the mystery classmate easier to guess because listeners will know if the student is a boy or a girl. You could also provide students with possible choices to complete sentences: *He/She plays more... than...* : *soccer, basketball, baseball, tennis, video games, board games, piano; He/She reads fewer... than...* : *newspapers, magazines, books, comic books, short stories, biographies, novels, mysteries.*

CHALLENGE

Have students write additional clues, using language structures from Units 4–6. Model: *If he/she could be a superhero, he/she would be... . Next year, he/she will definitely be... . In thirty years, he/she will probably... .*

B Talk about your guesses. Give reasons for your choices.

- Read the directions aloud. Have two students read the model dialog in the speech bubbles.
- Have students discuss their guesses within their groups. Encourage them to give reasons for their choices.

MONITOR

Listen for correct grammar, vocabulary, and use of language as students discuss the results for each title.

C Each student says whose card he/she read in Step A. Check your guesses. Which person in your group solved the most mysteries?

- Read the directions. Have each student in a group stand and announce whose card he or she read. Then have students tally their correct responses. Announce which student (or students) guessed the most mystery classmates correctly. Ask these students to talk about why they were so successful at guessing the identities of their classmates.

21st Century Social Skills

- Point out that appreciating other people and remembering their interests are important social skills. Tell students who guessed many names correctly that they did a good job with these social skills. Encourage them to share tips with others to explain how they did so well.

Checkpoint 4–6 Lesson 4

Lesson Flow

Warm-up › Lesson Objective › Practice (SB) › Video › Self-assessment 1 › Self-assessment 2

Lesson Objective

To think again about how well I can use what I have learned in Units 4–6.

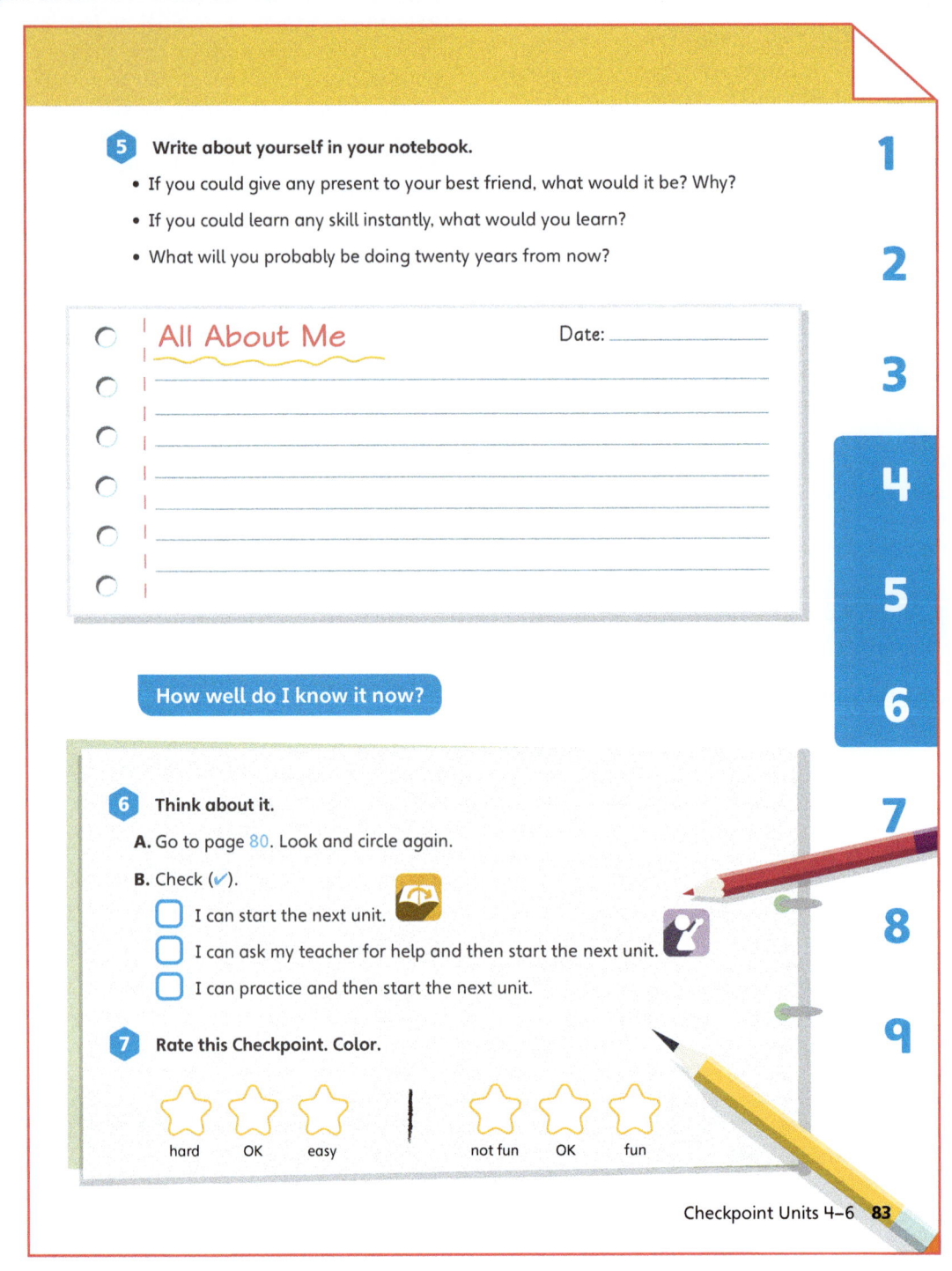

---

5 Write about yourself in your notebook.
- If you could give any present to your best friend, what would it be? Why?
- If you could learn any skill instantly, what would you learn?
- What will you probably be doing twenty years from now?

All About Me   Date: _____

How well do I know it now?

6 Think about it.
A. Go to page 80. Look and circle again.
B. Check (✓).
- ☐ I can start the next unit.
- ☐ I can ask my teacher for help and then start the next unit.
- ☐ I can practice and then start the next unit.

7 Rate this Checkpoint. Color.

☆ ☆ ☆ | ☆ ☆ ☆
hard OK easy   not fun OK fun

Checkpoint Units 4–6   83

S83   Checkpoint Units 4–6

Warm-up

- Show students a gift box or bag, or draw one on the board. Say: *This is a gift for a 12-year-old boy (girl). What gift could be in this box?* Have students brainstorm ideas and then write their suggestions on the board. Point out that they might decide to use some of these ideas when they write their *All About Me* journals.

Lesson Objective

INVOLVE

Introduce the lesson objective: *Today I will think about how well I can use what I have learned in Units 4–6.*

- Students will write about themselves, and what they would like to do. Then they will look back at Units 4–6 and think about how well they can use what they have learned.

Practice

5 Write about yourself in your notebook.

- Read the directions, questions, and journal title aloud.
- Have students begin by writing today's date. Then have them write answers to the questions. Encourage students to use complete sentences. Provide students with additional journal pages as needed.

MONITOR

Check students' work for correct use of language.

- Invite students to read aloud their *All About Me* entries and compare them with their classmates' entries.
- Explain that students can calculate how old they will be in twenty years to help them think about what they might be doing at that time.

Video Drama U 4-6

- Refer to the Video Guide for pre-watching and post-watching activities.

Self-assessment 1

6 Think about it.
A Go to page 80. Look and circle gain.

21st Century Self-Direction

- Have students turn to the "Read and circle" exercise on page 80 and think about each of the checklist items again. Remind students to take their time to think about each category carefully. Suggest that they look at the reference pages listed as they review their skills.
- Ask students to use a different colored marker or pencil as they reassess their understanding and use of each checklist item.
- Students may want to circle the same face icon when they revisit the exercise. Encourage them to draw the second circle outside the first so that both colors are visible, rather than covering up the first circle with the second color.

B Check (✓).

- Say: *Now choose the statement that describes how you feel about Units 4–6.* Students can use the "Read and circle" exercise on page 80 to help them choose a response. If they circled ten to twelve smiling faces, they can start the next unit with confidence. If they circled fewer than ten smiling faces, they should probably check one of the other choices.

Self-assessment 2

7 Rate this Checkpoint. Color.

- Read the directions aloud. Point out that students will color only one star in each section. Say: *First, you will say if the Checkpoint was easy, OK, or hard. Then you will say if it was fun, OK, or not fun.*
- Have students complete the rating individually.

Using Checkpoint Evaluations: Student evaluations of the Checkpoint (easy/hard, fun/not fun) can give you insight into students' reactions to classroom activities. Review their answers to help you engage and motivate them as they continue to review Units 4-6 and move on to the next units. Consider whether students require additional assistance, deeper challenges, or more inspiring activities.

7 Mysteries!

Objectives

Reading

- Can draw simple conclusions about the information given in a factual text on a familiar topic.
- Can extract specific information in short texts on familiar topics.

Listening

- Can understand the details of extended conversations on familiar topics, if delivered in clear standard speech.

Speaking

- Can give an opinion in a structured discussion, if guided by questions.

Writing

- Can describe the steps in a simple technical process, clearly signaling the sequence of actions.
- Can give a reason for an action in an informational text, given a model.
- Can complete a table or form with specific information extracted from a short, simple, written text on a familiar topic.

Grammar

- Can correctly use affirmative/negative and negative/affirmative question tags.

Unit Projects

Family Connection

Have students tell their families that they're learning about mysterious phenomena. Encourage students and their families to look for news articles and watch TV shows about mysterious or unexplained events. Suggest that families keep a Mystery Diary in which they take notes about the mysteries that make them the most curious. Allow students to share notes and ideas from their Mystery Diaries with the class.

Key Language

Key Vocabulary

Mysteries
Atlantis
Aurora Borealis (Northern Lights)
Bermuda Triangle
crop circles
Great Pyramids
Kryptos
Nazca Lines
sailing stones

Mystery-Related Words
explanation
phenomenon
proof
scientific
theory
unsolved

Expressions
buy this whole story
cool stuff
hang on a minute
hooked on
it makes you wonder
no sign of it
That's ridiculous.
much to everyone's surprise

Content Words

altitude
clapping
interaction
nitrogen
oxygen
phenomenon
pole
solar wind
stand out
swirling

artifacts
clearing
diameter
rapid
sighting

Grammar/Structures

The geoglyphs **are** in Peru, **aren't** they?

Astronauts **aren't** going to Pluto, **are** they?

Experts **can** explain the Aurora Borealis, **can't** they?

Scientists **can't** explain crop circles, **can** they?

It **didn't** make sense, **did** it?

Phonics

The sounds: *un, inter, re, pre, super*

What's the Big Mystery? Bulletin Board

Create a *What's the Big Mystery?* bulletin-board display to share photographs, drawings, or descriptions of mysterious phenomena. Cut out a large question mark as the focal point for the display. Then surround the question mark with illustrations of the mysteries and index cards about them. Students can begin with the mysteries on the Unit Opener. Encourage them to add more information about these mysteries to the display.

Language in Context Lesson

Lesson Flow

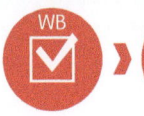

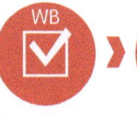

Warm-up ▸ Lesson Objective ▸ Presentation ▸ Practice 1 (WB) ▸ Practice 2 (SB) ▸ Practice 3 (WB) ▸ Speaking ▸ Think BIG ▸ Lesson Objective ▸ Homework

Lesson Objective

I will learn to talk about mysterious places and things.

Key Language

Atlantis, Aurora Borealis (Northern Lights), Bermuda Triangle, crop circles, explanation, Kryptos, Nazca Lines, phenomenon, proof, theory; wonder; scientific, unsolved; it makes you wonder, no sign of it

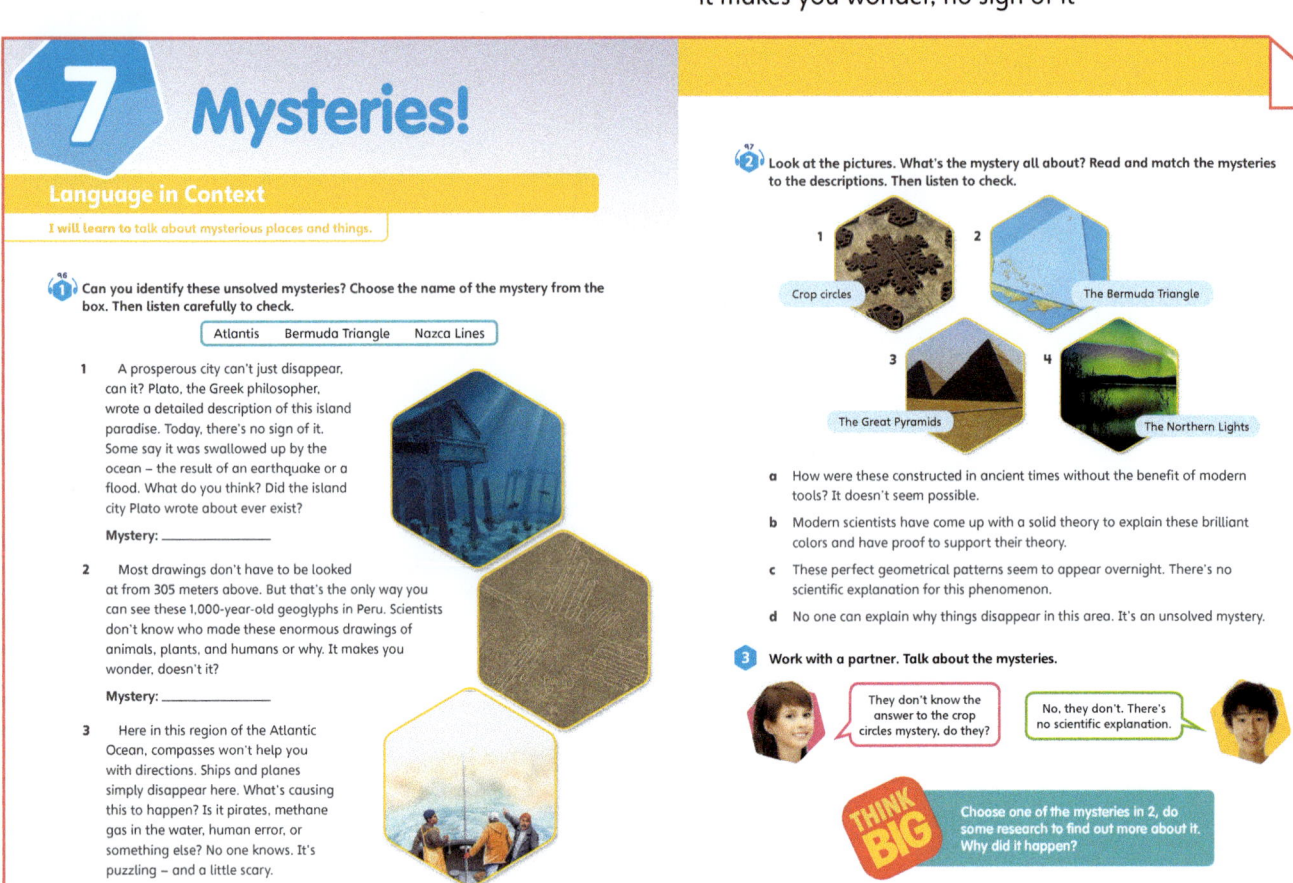

---

7 Mysteries!

Language in Context

I will learn to talk about mysterious places and things.

1 Can you identify these unsolved mysteries? Choose the name of the mystery from the box. Then listen carefully to check.

[Atlantis   Bermuda Triangle   Nazca Lines]

1. A prosperous city can't just disappear, can it? Plato, the Greek philosopher, wrote a detailed description of this island paradise. Today, there's no sign of it. Some say it was swallowed up by the ocean – the result of an earthquake or a flood. What do you think? Did the island city Plato wrote about ever exist?

   Mystery: _____

2. Most drawings don't have to be looked at from 305 meters above. But that's the only way you can see these 1,000-year-old geoglyphs in Peru. Scientists don't know who made these enormous drawings of animals, plants, and humans or why. It makes you wonder, doesn't it?

   Mystery: _____

3. Here in this region of the Atlantic Ocean, compasses won't help you with directions. Ships and planes simply disappear here. What's causing this to happen? Is it pirates, methane gas in the water, human error, or something else? No one knows. It's puzzling – and a little scary.

   Mystery: _____

2 Look at the pictures. What's the mystery all about? Read and match the mysteries to the descriptions. Then listen to check.

1. Crop circles
2. The Bermuda Triangle
3. The Great Pyramids
4. The Northern Lights

a. How were these constructed in ancient times without the benefit of modern tools? It doesn't seem possible.

b. Modern scientists have come up with a solid theory to explain these brilliant colors and have proof to support their theory.

c. These perfect geometrical patterns seem to appear overnight. There's no scientific explanation for this phenomenon.

d. No one can explain why things disappear in this area. It's an unsolved mystery.

3 Work with a partner. Talk about the mysteries.

> They don't know the answer to the crop circles mystery, do they?

> No, they don't. There's no scientific explanation.

THINK BIG Choose one of the mysteries in 2, do some research to find out more about it. Why did it happen?

Warm-up

- Ask students if they have read or watched any interesting mysteries. Discuss how detectives go about solving mysteries (e.g. collecting clues, making deductions or inferences, and drawing conclusions).
- Tell students that scientists and archeologists follow a similar process: researching, looking at evidence, and drawing conclusions to solve mysteries in nature or from history around the world.
- Check answers from the HW in the last lesson.

Lesson Objective

INVOLVE
- Explain the lesson objective. Say: *Today I will learn to talk about mysterious places and things.*
- Tell students that they will listen and read about unsolved mysteries.

Presentation

1 Can you identify these unsolved mysteries? Choose the name of the mystery from the box. Then listen carefully to check.
- Read the directions and the words in the box aloud. Ask volunteers to share their understanding of the words. Then have students read and answer independently.
- Play Audio Track 96 and have students listen and check their answers.

MONITOR
- Check answers as a class. *(Answers: 1 Atlantis, 2 Nazca Lines, 3 Bermuda Triangle)*

Practice 1 WB p. 66/ act. 1

1 Match the pictures with the explanations of these unsolved mysteries. Do you think these explanations are possible? Circle *Possible* or *Not Possible*.
- Read the directions aloud.
- Look at Picture 1. Have volunteers read the 4 items. Ask: *Which does this picture relate to?* Have students write *1* in the space before the third item.
- Have students complete the activity independently.

Practice 2

2 Look at the pictures. What's the mystery all about? Read and match the mysteries to the descriptions. Then listen to check.
- Read the directions aloud. Invite volunteers to read the descriptions of the mysteries aloud.
- Have students complete the activity, then play Audio Track 97 and have students listen and check their answers.

MONITOR
- Check answers as a class. *(Answers: 1 c, 2 d, 3 a, 4 b)*

Practice 3 WB p. 67/ act. 2

Complete the dialogs. Then listen and check your answers.
- Read the directions aloud. Have a volunteer read the first line.
- Have students read the words in the box. Point out that they need to read the next sentence to know the answer. Complete Item 1 as a class *(Northern Lights)*.
- Play Audio Track 98 and have students check their answers.

Speaking

3 Work with a partner. Talk about mysteries.
- Read the directions aloud. Then have volunteers read the speech bubbles aloud. Draw students' attention to the question tag, "do they?", at the end of the first speech bubble. Explain that people use question tags when they want someone to agree with them.
- Have students work in pairs asking and answering about unsolved mysteries, using question tags.

MONITOR
Listen for proper pronunciation, appropriate intonation, and correct use of language.

ASSIST
Say: *A question tag turns a sentence into a question. Questions that end with tags don't begin with question words, such as* who, what, where, when, *or* why.

Think BIG

21st Century Information Literacy
- Read the questions aloud. Have students complete the activity in groups or in pairs. Encourage students to use the internet for their research. Have students present their findings to the class.

Lesson Objective

INVOLVE
- Revisit the lesson objective: *Now I have learned to talk about mysterious places and things.*
- Encourage awareness of what students have learned by quickly eliciting a few mysterious places and things discussed in the lesson.

Homework WB p. 67/ act. 3

3 Read the sentences about the places in 2. Circle T for *true* or F for *false*. Correct the false sentences.
- Direct students to WB Activity 3 on page 67. Students circle true or false, and then write corrected sentences.

Think BIG
- Direct students to WB Think Big on page 67. Students write their own views.

Extra Application and Practice Activity

21st Century Information Literacy
- Divide the class into small groups, and have each group research one of the two mysteries not included in the text: *Kryptos* and *crop circles*. Ask students to search online. Discuss students' findings as a class. Ask questions such as: *What parts of the mystery have been solved? What parts are still unsolved?*

7 Mysteries!

Language in Context

I will learn to talk about mysterious places and things.

1 Can you identify these unsolved mysteries? Choose the name of the mystery from the box. Then listen carefully to check.

> Atlantis   Bermuda Triangle   Nazca Lines

1. A prosperous city can't just disappear, can it? Plato, the Greek philosopher, wrote a detailed description of this island paradise. Today, there's no sign of it. Some say it was swallowed up by the ocean – the result of an earthquake or a flood. What do you think? Did the island city Plato wrote about ever exist?

    Mystery: _____

2. Most drawings don't have to be looked at from 305 meters above. But that's the only way you can see these 1,000-year-old geoglyphs in Peru. Scientists don't know who made these enormous drawings of animals, plants, and humans or why. It makes you wonder, doesn't it?

    Mystery: _____

3. Here in this region of the Atlantic Ocean, compasses won't help you with directions. Ships and planes simply disappear here. What's causing this to happen? Is it pirates, methane gas in the water, human error, or something else? No one knows. It's puzzling – and a little scary.

    Mystery: _____

2 Look at the pictures. What's the mystery all about? Read and match the mysteries to the descriptions. Then listen to check.

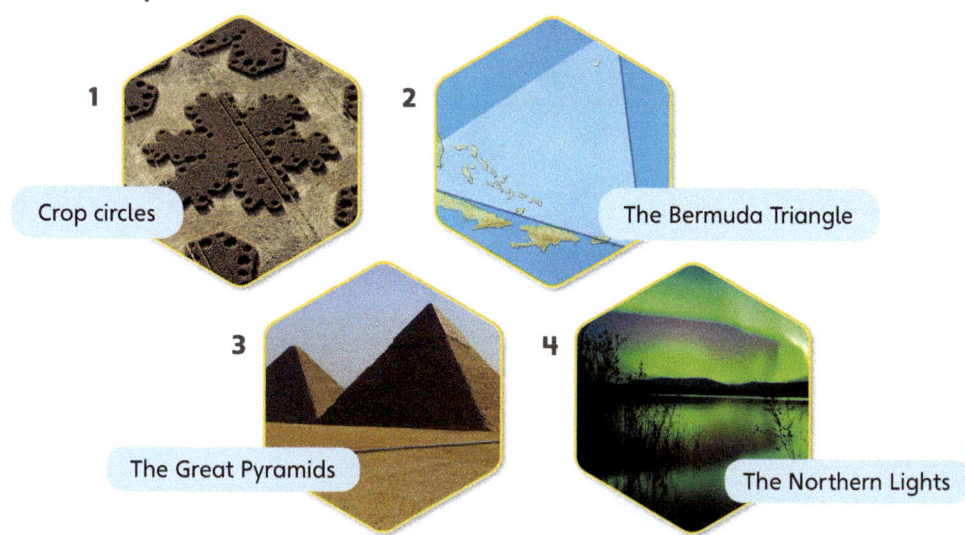

1 Crop circles
2 The Bermuda Triangle
3 The Great Pyramids
4 The Northern Lights

a   How were these constructed in ancient times without the benefit of modern tools? It doesn't seem possible.

b   Modern scientists have come up with a solid theory to explain these brilliant colors and have proof to support their theory.

c   These perfect geometrical patterns seem to appear overnight. There's no scientific explanation for this phenomenon.

d   No one can explain why things disappear in this area. It's an unsolved mystery.

3 Work with a partner. Talk about the mysteries.

They don't know the answer to the crop circles mystery, do they?

No, they don't. There's no scientific explanation.

THINK BIG Choose one of the mysteries in 2, do some research to find out more about it. Why did it happen?

Reading Lesson

Lesson Flow

Warm-up › Lesson Objective › Pre-reading › Reading › Comprehension 1 › Comprehension 2 › Think BIG › Lesson Objective › Homework

Lesson Objective

I will understand a text about a mysterious place.

Key Language

explanation, phenomenon, rock, theory, wind; doubt, move; heavy; buy this whole story, much to everyone's surprise, Told you...

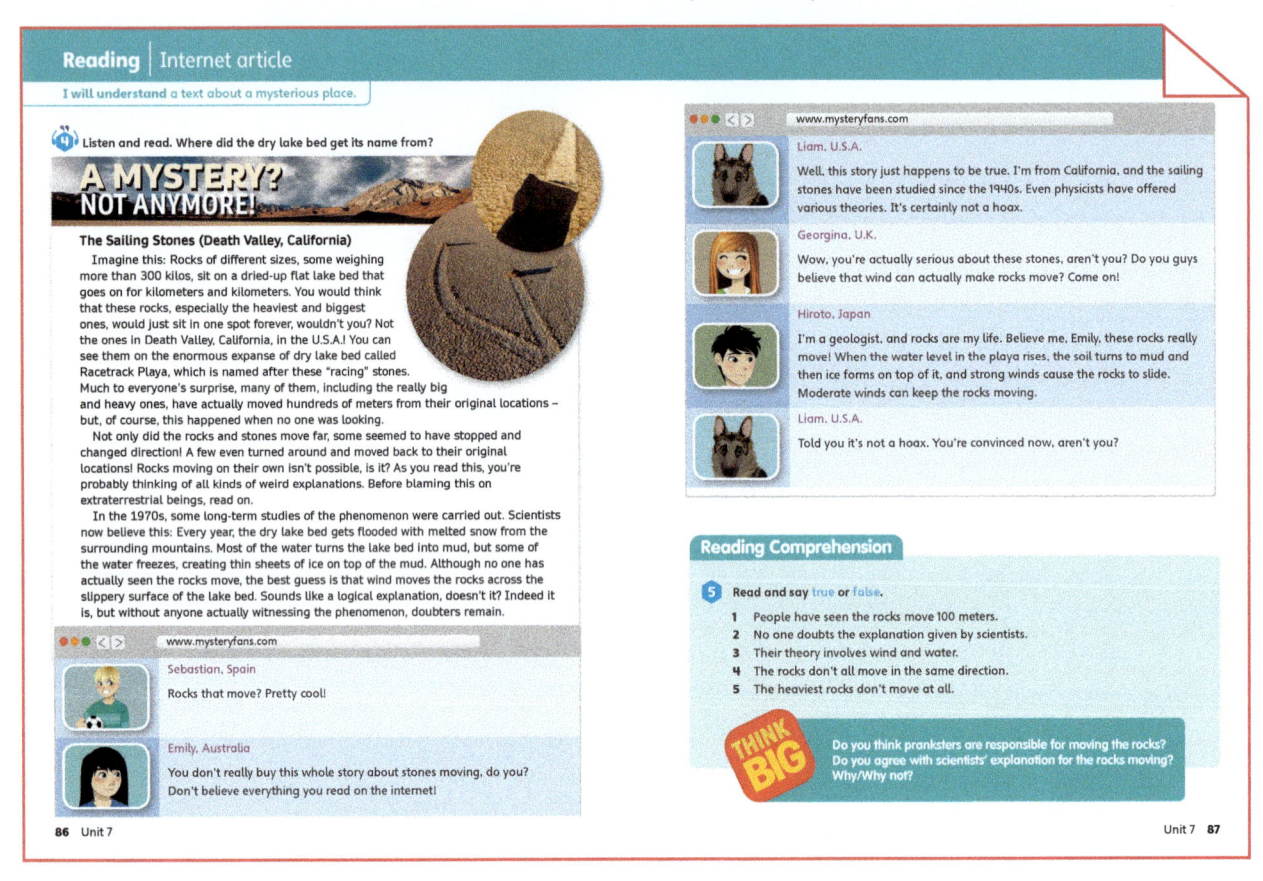

Reading | Internet article

I will understand a text about a mysterious place.

Listen and read. Where did the dry lake bed get its name from?

A MYSTERY? NOT ANYMORE!

The Sailing Stones (Death Valley, California)

Imagine this: Rocks of different sizes, some weighing more than 300 kilos, sit on a dried-up flat lake bed that goes on for kilometers and kilometers. You would think that these rocks, especially the heaviest and biggest ones, would just sit in one spot forever, wouldn't you? Not the ones in Death Valley, California, in the U.S.A.! You can see them on the enormous expanse of dry lake bed called Racetrack Playa, which is named after these "racing" stones. Much to everyone's surprise, many of them, including the really big and heavy ones, have actually moved hundreds of meters from their original locations – but, of course, this happened when no one was looking.

Not only did the rocks and stones move far, some seemed to have stopped and changed direction! A few even turned around and moved back to their original locations! Rocks moving on their own isn't possible, is it? As you read this, you're probably thinking of all kinds of weird explanations. Before blaming this on extraterrestrial beings, read on.

In the 1970s, some long-term studies of the phenomenon were carried out. Scientists now believe this: Every year, the dry lake bed gets flooded with melted snow from the surrounding mountains. Most of the water turns the lake bed into mud, but some of the water freezes, creating thin sheets of ice on top of the mud. Although no one has actually seen the rocks move, the best guess is that wind moves the rocks across the slippery surface of the lake bed. Sounds like a logical explanation, doesn't it? Indeed it is, but without anyone actually witnessing the phenomenon, doubters remain.

www.mysteryfans.com

Sebastian, Spain
Rocks that move? Pretty cool!

Emily, Australia
You don't really buy this whole story about stones moving, do you? Don't believe everything you read on the internet!

---

www.mysteryfans.com

Liam, U.S.A.
Well, this story just happens to be true. I'm from California, and the sailing stones have been studied since the 1940s. Even physicists have offered various theories. It's certainly not a hoax.

Georgina, U.K.
Wow, you're actually serious about these stones, aren't you? Do you guys believe that wind can actually make rocks move? Come on!

Hiroto, Japan
I'm a geologist, and rocks are my life. Believe me, Emily, these rocks really move! When the water level in the playa rises, the soil turns to mud and then ice forms on top of it, and strong winds cause the rocks to slide. Moderate winds can keep the rocks moving.

Liam, U.S.A.
Told you it's not a hoax. You're convinced now, aren't you?

Reading Comprehension

5 Read and say true or false.
1. People have seen the rocks move 100 meters.
2. No one doubts the explanation given by scientists.
3. Their theory involves wind and water.
4. The rocks don't all move in the same direction.
5. The heaviest rocks don't move at all.

THINK BIG
Do you think pranksters are responsible for moving the rocks?
Do you agree with scientists' explanation for the rocks moving?
Why/Why not?

Warm-up

21st Century Media Literacy

- Point out that many internet sites allow readers to post comments. Ask: *Why do you think people like to post comments?* (Sample answers: They may have strong reactions to an article and want to share them./They might have questions./They might know more information about the topic and want to share it.) *Have you ever posted a comment on an internet site? If so, what made you want to share your ideas?*

- Check answers from the HW in the last lesson.

Lesson Objective

INVOLVE

Introduce the lesson objective. Say: *Today I will learn to understand a text about a mysterious place.*

- Students will read and talk about an internet article and comments about it.

Pre-reading

- Have students read the title aloud and preview the pictures. Say: *Sailing is usually used to describe boats. A sailboat moves with wind and a large piece of cloth, called a sail. Why is the term* sailing stones *a little mysterious?* (Sample answer: Stones are heavy and don't usually move easily.)

Reading

4 Listen and read. Where did the dry lake bed get its name from?

- Read the directions aloud. Play Audio Track 99 and have students listen and read along.
- Ask the question in the directions: *Where did the dry lake bed get its name from?* (It is named after the "racing" stones, which move hundreds of meters.)

Comprehension 1

MONITOR

Ask more questions to check for understanding. Ask: *Where are the sailing stones found?* (in Death Valley, California) *What's mysterious about these giant stones?* (They move hundreds of meters on flat land.) *What explanation do some scientists give?* (They say the rocks move because of water and wind. Water from the surrounding mountains turns the area into slippery mud. Then strong wind moves the rocks.) *Does everyone agree with this theory?* (No. Some people doubt it.)

21st Century Communication

- Say: *Sometimes we can understand facts and ideas by making comparisons. Do you know how big a 300-kilo rock is? What object can you compare that size to?* (Sample answers: a heavy bathtub/a motorcycle) *Write a sentence that compares the sailing stones to the object.* (Sample answer: The sailing stones can weigh more than a motorcycle!)

Comprehension 2

5 Read and say *true* or *false*.

- Read the directions aloud. Have students complete the activity independently.

MONITOR

Check answers as a class. (Answers: 1 false, 2 false, 3 true, 4 true, 5 false)

CHALLENGE

Invite students to change one or more words in each false statement to make it true. (Sample answers: 1 No one has seen the rocks move. 2 Some doubt the explanation given by scientists. 3 Even the heaviest rocks move.)

Think BIG

Materials: Paperweights or smooth stones

21st Century Critical Thinking

- Read the questions aloud. Provide students with classroom objects to use in modeling the movements of the sailing stones. For example, students might use books, erasers, or paperweights to represent the stones. They can use crumpled paper to represent desert sand when it is dry and flat plastic, such as a plastic file folder, to represent the land when it is slippery. Model how much more easily objects move on the slippery surface. Say: *When something is slippery, there is less friction. Friction is the rubbing of one thing against another. When there is a lot of friction, objects don't move easily.*

MONITOR

Check for problems with comprehension and errors in vocabulary, syntax, and grammar as students discuss the theories.

Lesson Objective

INVOLVE

Revisit the lesson objective: *Now I have learned to understand a text about a mysterious place.*

- Encourage awareness of what students have learned by eliciting something students remember from the article.

Homework   WB p. 68/ act. 4

4 Listen and read. Then answer the questions.

- Direct students to WB Activity 4 on page 68. Tell students to play Audio Track 100, listen, and answer the questions. Students must write in full sentences.

Extra Application and Practice Activity

21st Century Technology Literacy

- Tell students that in August 2014, scientists finally solved the mystery of the sailing stones. They observed the movement of the stones by fitting them with motion-activated GPS units. They discovered that thin sheets of floating ice form under the rocks. Winds move the ice, pushing rocks in front of them through the soft mud.
- Invite students to write their own comments about the article based on the new information. Remind students to follow the format used in the postings to the internet article for their own comments. Say: *Begin by writing your first name and where you live. Then write your comment. You can respond to the article or any of the comments.*

Unit 7   **S86/87**

Reading | Internet article

I will understand a text about a mysterious place.

4) Listen and read. Where did the dry lake bed get its name from?

A MYSTERY? NOT ANYMORE!

The Sailing Stones (Death Valley, California)

Imagine this: Rocks of different sizes, some weighing more than 300 kilos, sit on a dried-up flat lake bed that goes on for kilometers and kilometers. You would think that these rocks, especially the heaviest and biggest ones, would just sit in one spot forever, wouldn't you? Not the ones in Death Valley, California, in the U.S.A.! You can see them on the enormous expanse of dry lake bed called Racetrack Playa, which is named after these "racing" stones. Much to everyone's surprise, many of them, including the really big and heavy ones, have actually moved hundreds of meters from their original locations – but, of course, this happened when no one was looking.

Not only did the rocks and stones move far, some seemed to have stopped and changed direction! A few even turned around and moved back to their original locations! Rocks moving on their own isn't possible, is it? As you read this, you're probably thinking of all kinds of weird explanations. Before blaming this on extraterrestrial beings, read on.

In the 1970s, some long-term studies of the phenomenon were carried out. Scientists now believe this: Every year, the dry lake bed gets flooded with melted snow from the surrounding mountains. Most of the water turns the lake bed into mud, but some of the water freezes, creating thin sheets of ice on top of the mud. Although no one has actually seen the rocks move, the best guess is that wind moves the rocks across the slippery surface of the lake bed. Sounds like a logical explanation, doesn't it? Indeed it is, but without anyone actually witnessing the phenomenon, doubters remain.

www.mysteryfans.com

Sebastian, Spain

Rocks that move? Pretty cool!

Emily, Australia

You don't really buy this whole story about stones moving, do you? Don't believe everything you read on the internet!

www.mysteryfans.com

Liam, U.S.A.

Well, this story just happens to be true. I'm from California, and the sailing stones have been studied since the 1940s. Even physicists have offered various theories. It's certainly not a hoax.

Georgina, U.K.

Wow, you're actually serious about these stones, aren't you? Do you guys believe that wind can actually make rocks move? Come on!

Hiroto, Japan

I'm a geologist, and rocks are my life. Believe me, Emily, these rocks really move! When the water level in the playa rises, the soil turns to mud and then ice forms on top of it, and strong winds cause the rocks to slide. Moderate winds can keep the rocks moving.

Liam, U.S.A.

Told you it's not a hoax. You're convinced now, aren't you?

Reading Comprehension

5 Read and say true or false.

1 People have seen the rocks move 100 meters.
2 No one doubts the explanation given by scientists.
3 Their theory involves wind and water.
4 The rocks don't all move in the same direction.
5 The heaviest rocks don't move at all.

THINK BIG

Do you think pranksters are responsible for moving the rocks? Do you agree with scientists' explanation for the rocks moving? Why/Why not?

Language in Action Lesson

Lesson Flow

Warm-up › Lesson Objective › Pre-listening › Listening › Comprehension › Role Play › Practice 1 (SB) › Practice 2 (WB) › Lesson Objective › Homework

Lesson Objective

I will listen to a dialog about solving a mystery.

Key Language

Atlantis, Aurora Borealis (Northern Lights), clue, code breaker, Kryptos, machine, message, mystery; break, crack (a code), decode, give away, work out; beautiful, encrypted, secret; cool stuff, hang on a minute, hooked on, That's ridiculous., Totally., work out (the code)

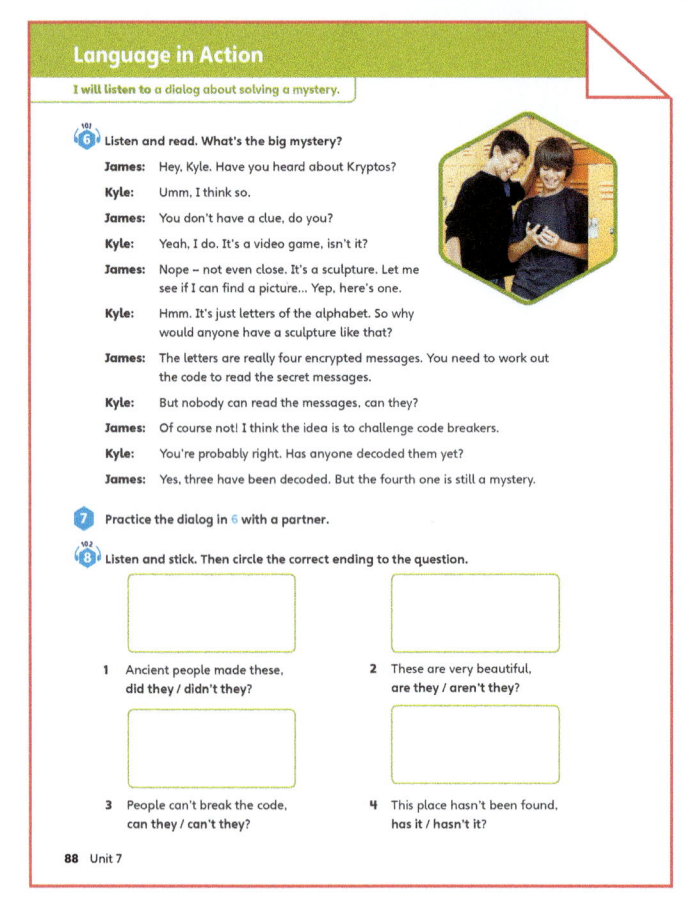

Language in Action

I will listen to a dialog about solving a mystery.

6 Listen and read. What's the big mystery?

- **James:** Hey, Kyle. Have you heard about Kryptos?
- **Kyle:** Umm, I think so.
- **James:** You don't have a clue, do you?
- **Kyle:** Yeah, I do. It's a video game, isn't it?
- **James:** Nope – not even close. It's a sculpture. Let me see if I can find a picture… Yep, here's one.
- **Kyle:** Hmm. It's just letters of the alphabet. So why would anyone have a sculpture like that?
- **James:** The letters are really four encrypted messages. You need to work out the code to read the secret messages.
- **Kyle:** But nobody can read the messages, can they?
- **James:** Of course not! I think the idea is to challenge code breakers.
- **Kyle:** You're probably right. Has anyone decoded them yet?
- **James:** Yes, three have been decoded. But the fourth one is still a mystery.

7 Practice the dialog in 6 with a partner.

8 Listen and stick. Then circle the correct ending to the question.

1. Ancient people made these, did they / didn't they?
2. These are very beautiful, are they / aren't they?
3. People can't break the code, can they / can't they?
4. This place hasn't been found, has it / hasn't it?

88 Unit 7

Warm-up

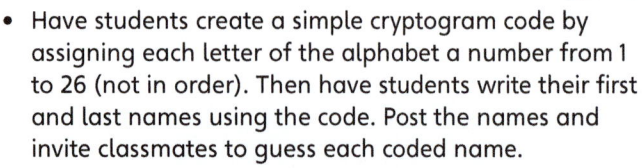

- Have students create a simple cryptogram code by assigning each letter of the alphabet a number from 1 to 26 (not in order). Then have students write their first and last names using the code. Post the names and invite classmates to guess each coded name.
- Say: *This simple code is a substitution code in which each letter is replaced with a number. Many codes are much more complicated – and harder to solve.*
- Check answers from the HW in the last lesson.

Lesson Objective

INVOLVE

Introduce the lesson objective. Say: *Today I will listen to a dialog about solving a mystery.*

- Students will read, listen to, and practice a dialog. Students will also listen to conversations about unsolved mysteries and use question tags.

Pre-listening

- Tell students that they are going to listen to James and Kyle and find out what the big mystery is.
- Point to James and Kyle in the picture and the text.

Listening

6 Listen and read. What's the big mystery?

- Read the directions aloud. Play Audio Track 101 and have students listen and read along.
- Invite two boys to read the dialog aloud and repeat.

Comprehension

- Ask the question in the directions: *What's the big mystery?* (The fourth encrypted message.)

MONITOR

Ask more questions to check for understanding. Encourage students to answer in complete sentences, where appropriate. Ask: *What's Kryptos?* (a sculpture) *How do code breakers read the secret messages?* (They have to work out the code.)

21st Century Global Awareness

- Say: *Kryptos is a sculpture at the CIA headquarters in Virginia in the United States. The CIA is the Central Intelligence Agency.* Ask: *Why do you think governments might use codes?* (Sample answer: They want to keep certain information secret.)

Role Play

7 Practice the dialog in 6 with a partner.

- Read the directions aloud. Have students pair to read the dialog aloud, switch parts, and repeat.

MONITOR

As students practice, listen for proper pronunciation and use of language.

ASSIST

Model a falling intonation for a question tag when you expect someone to agree with your answer and a rising intonation when you aren't sure.

Practice 1

Materials: Stickers

8 Listen and stick. Then circle the correct ending to the question.

- Help students find the Unit 7 stickers at the back of the Student's Book.
- Read the directions aloud. Have students look at the pictures and describe what they see. Then have volunteers read the statements aloud.
- Play Audio Track 102. Have students complete the activity independently.

MONITOR

Check answers as a class. (Answers: 1 d, didn't they; 2 c, aren't they; 3 b, can they; 4 a, has it)

ASSIST

Remind students to listen for the main idea when they match the pictures. Say: *You may hear some words you don't know. Don't get nervous. Keep listening. You don't need to understand every word to understand the main idea. The first time you listen, try to find the right picture. You'll have a chance to listen again for details.*

Practice 2 WB p. 69/ act. 5

5 Listen and read. Then circle T for *true* or F for *false*.

- Read the directions aloud.
- Play Audio Track 103 twice. The second time, have students circle the words they do not understand. Explain their meaning.
- Read Item 1 as a class. Prompt students to find the answer in the text.
- Students complete the activity, circling *T* or *F*.

Lesson Objective

INVOLVE

Revisit the lesson objective: *Now I have listened to a dialog about solving a mystery.*

- Encourage awareness of what students have learned by eliciting what they remember from the dialog between James and Kyle.

Homework WB p. 69/ act. 6 & 7

6 Look at 5. Read the underlined expressions. Match the expressions with their meanings. Write the letters.

- Direct students to WB Activity 6 on page 69. Students match 1–4 with a sentence that explains the meaning.

7 Complete with the expressions in 6. Then listen and check.

- Direct students to WB Activity 7 on page 69. Students complete the activity using the four expressions in the previous activity, then listen to Audio Track 104 to check their answers.

Extra Application and Practice Activity

Materials: Poster paper, art supplies

- Have students choose a mystery discussed so far in the unit and create a poster to advertise it. Encourage students to include a drawing suggestive of the mystery and persuasive language about why people should want to find out more about it. Suggest that they include a question tag, too. Model: *You'll be amazed when you see the sailing stones. You'll find yourself wondering how these giant rocks can actually move. It makes you want to come to Death Valley, California, to see them, doesn't it?*

Unit 7   T88

Language in Action

I will listen to a dialog about solving a mystery.

6 Listen and read. What's the big mystery?

James: Hey, Kyle. Have you heard about Kryptos?

Kyle: Umm, I think so.

James: You don't have a clue, do you?

Kyle: Yeah, I do. It's a video game, isn't it?

James: Nope – not even close. It's a sculpture. Let me see if I can find a picture... Yep, here's one.

Kyle: Hmm. It's just letters of the alphabet. So why would anyone have a sculpture like that?

James: The letters are really four encrypted messages. You need to work out the code to read the secret messages.

Kyle: But nobody can read the messages, can they?

James: Of course not! I think the idea is to challenge code breakers.

Kyle: You're probably right. Has anyone decoded them yet?

James: Yes, three have been decoded. But the fourth one is still a mystery.

7 Practice the dialog in **6** with a partner.

8 Listen and stick. Then circle the correct ending to the question.

1. Ancient people made these, **did they / didn't they?**

2. These are very beautiful, **are they / aren't they?**

3. People can't break the code, **can they / can't they?**

4. This place hasn't been found, **has it / hasn't it?**

88 Unit 7

Grammar

I will learn to use question tags with *be*, *can*, and *do* to confirm information.

AFFIRMATIVE STATEMENTS	NEGATIVE TAGS	NEGATIVE STATEMENTS	POSITIVE TAGS
The geoglyphs **are** in Peru,	**aren't** they?	Atlantis **isn't** real,	**is** it?
Experts **can** explain them,	**can't** they?	Scientists **can't** find it,	**can** they?
We **love** mysteries,	**don't** we?	It **doesn't** make sense,	**does** it?

9 Circle the correct question tags.

1. The Northern Lights are a natural phenomenon, **are they / aren't they**?

2. Scientists can't explain the Northern Lights, **can they / can't they**?

3. The Nazca Lines aren't made by aliens, **are they / aren't they**?

4. People in ancient times made the Nazca lines, **did they / didn't they**?

5. The sailing stones can be seen only in the U.S.A., **can they / can't they**?

6. The sailing stones don't really move, **do they / don't they?**

10 Prepare to interview an archeologist about Atlantis. Make question tags.

1. A: In your article, you claimed that Atlantis existed, _____
   B: Yes, I did...

2. A: You don't know the exact location of the city, _____
   B: No, I don't...

3. A: Your article claims that you have found artifacts, _____
   B: Yes, it does...

4. A: Most scientists disagree with your research, _____
   B: Yes, they do, but...

11 Write responses for the archeologist in the interview in 10. Then role-play the interview with a partner.

Grammar Lesson

Lesson Flow

Warm-up › Lesson Objective › Presentation › Practice 1 (SB) › Practice 2 (WB) › Practice 3 (WB) › Practice 4 (SB) › Practice 5 (SB) › Lesson Objective › Homework

Lesson Objective

I will learn to use question tags with *be*, *can*, and *do* to confirm information.

Key Language

The geoglyphs **are** in Peru, **aren't** they?

Astronauts **aren't** going to Pluto, **are** they?

Experts **can** explain the Aurora Borealis, **can't** they?

Scientists **can't** explain crop circles, **can** they?

We **love** mysteries, **don't** we?

It **didn't** make sense, **did** it?

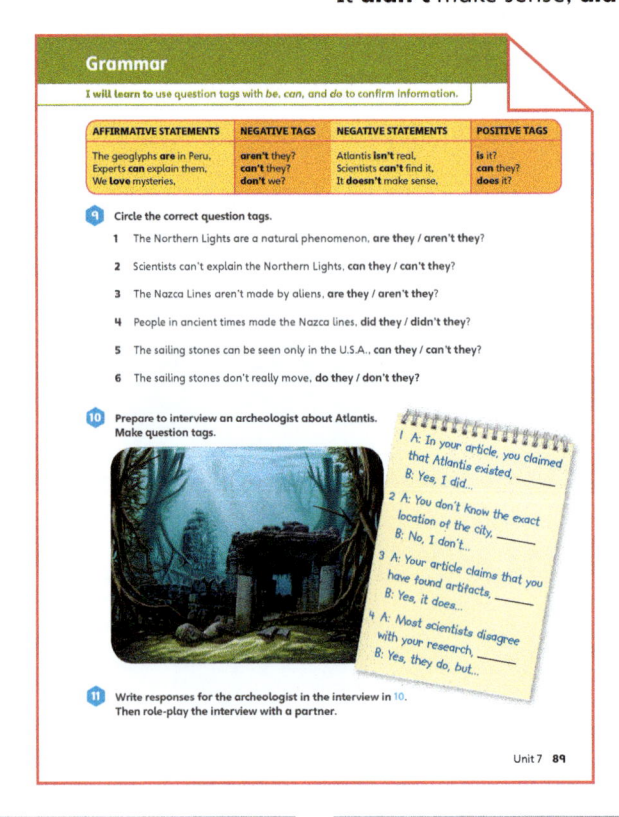

Warm-up

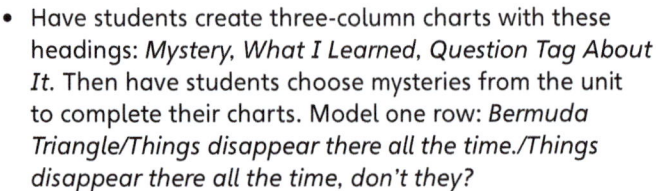

- Have students create three-column charts with these headings: *Mystery, What I Learned, Question Tag About It*. Then have students choose mysteries from the unit to complete their charts. Model one row: *Bermuda Triangle/Things disappear there all the time./Things disappear there all the time, don't they?*
- Have students complete the charts in pairs.
- Check answers from the HW in the last lesson.

Lesson Objective

INVOLVE

Introduce the lesson objective. Say: *Today I will learn to use question tags with* be, can, *and* do *to confirm information.*

- Students will learn how to use question tags to confirm information. Say: *Sometimes when you're talking, you believe someone will agree with you. You can ask a question tag to find out if you're right.*

Presentation

- Have volunteers read the grammar chart labels and question tags aloud. Ask: *What kind of question tag do you use after an affirmative statement?* (a negative tag) *What kind of question tag do you use after a negative statement?* (a positive tag)
- Refer students back to the Language in Action dialog and elicit or highlight the grammar structures in the dialog.

CHALLENGE

Have students suggest alternative *more than*, *fewer than*, and *less than* sentences, using the same format.

21st Century Communication

- Say: *You can use question tags to confirm or check information. In an interview, question tags help you make sure information is correct. These questions are sometimes considered leading questions because you lead someone to give the answer or the information you want.* Have students give examples of situations in which they might use question tags at school, at home, or with friends.

Practice 1

1 Circle the correct question tags.

- Read the directions aloud and complete Item 1 as a class. Then have students complete the activity independently.

MONITOR

Check answers as a class. (Answers: 1 aren't they, 2 can they, 3 are they, 4 didn't they, 5 can't they, 6 do they)

Practice 2 — WB p. 70/ act. 8

8 Complete the sentences with question tags.

- Read the directions aloud, and the question tags.
- Read the first item as a class and allow students to try the different question tags at the end of the sentence. Choose the correct one (*isn't it*) and students write the answer.
- Have students complete the activity independently.

Practice 3 — WB p. 70/ act. 9

9 Complete the sentences with question tags.

- Read the directions aloud.
- Complete Item 1 as a class. Then have students work independently to complete the activity.

Practice 4

10 Prepare to interview an archeologist about Atlantis. Make question tags.

- Read the directions aloud. Complete Item 1 as a class. Then have students complete the activity independently in their notebooks.

MONITOR

Check answers as a class. (Answers: 1 didn't you? 2 do you? 3 doesn't it? 4 don't they?)

- As students read the answers aloud, have them use falling intonation. Say: *This interviewer seems to believe he or she already knows the answers, and just wants confirmation. So we should use falling intonation.*

Practice 5

11 Write responses for the archeologist in the interview in 10. Then role-play the interview with a partner.

- Read the directions aloud. Say: *You can make up information for the archeologist, based on the activity and what you know.* Complete the archeologist's first response as a class. Then have students complete the activity independently in their notebooks.

Lesson Objective

INVOLVE

Revisit the lesson objective: *Now I have learned to use question tags with* be, can, *and* do *to confirm information.*

- Encourage awareness of what students have learned by quickly eliciting from students examples of question tags.

Homework — WB p. 71/ act. 10 & 11

10 Unscramble the sentences with question tags.

- Direct students to WB Activity 10 on page 71. Students unscramble the sentences and write question tags.

11 Zack is writing a play about Atlantis. Complete the dialog with the question tags in the box.

- Direct students to WB Activity 11 on page 71. Students write a question tag at the end of each sentence to complete the dialog.

Extra Application and Practice Activity

Materials: Newspapers

- Invite students to add question tags to statements from newspapers. Model: *The mayor won the election by a huge number of votes, didn't she?* Then have pairs use their questions to discuss their news.

Unit 7 **T89**

Content Connection Lesson

Lesson Flow

Warm-up › Lesson Objective › Pre-reading › Reading › Practice 1 › Practice 2 › Think BIG › Lesson Objective › Homework

Lesson Objective

I will learn about the Northern Lights.

Key Language

altitude, clapping, interaction, nitrogen, oxygen, phenomenon, pole, solar wind, stand out, swirling

---

Content Connection | Earth Science

I will learn about the Northern Lights.

12 Listen and read. What is another name for the Aurora Borealis?

CONTENT WORDS
altitude clapping
interaction nitrogen
oxygen phenomenon
pole solar wind
stand out swirling

The Aurora Borealis

Albert Einstein, whose work we still study today, once said this about nature: "What I see in nature is a magnificent structure that we can comprehend only very imperfectly and that must fill a thinking person with a feeling of humility." We could surely say this while looking at the Aurora Borealis!

The Aurora Borealis, also called the Northern Lights, is a magnificent display of swirling colored lights that's visible in northern countries. Each year, people travel closer to the North Pole to see it and enjoy its beauty.

What causes this strange phenomenon? For a long time, no one could answer this question. People thought it was just a mysterious natural event or even the spirits of animals they had hunted. Recently, however, science has provided an explanation. The different colors of an aurora are the result of solar winds interacting with different gases at different altitudes. Oxygen produces yellow-green and red colors, and nitrogen produces violet and blue colors.

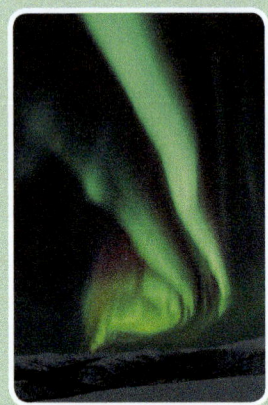

The Northern Lights are easiest to see in the Arctic from the fall to the early spring. This is the time of year when the nights are long and dark and the colors really stand out. However, during strong solar storms, you can sometimes see the Aurora Borealis as far south as Texas. At the South Pole, a similar phenomenon occurs at the same time as the one in the north. This is called the Aurora Australis, or the Southern Lights.

Scientists have discovered a lot about the Aurora Borealis, but some things are still a mystery. For example, people have said that a clapping sound comes at the same time as the light display. Whatever the explanation, the aurora's magical and mysterious beauty has inspired and continues to inspire painters, poets, and songwriters.

13 Look at the passage. Read and say true or false.

1. Albert Einstein discovered the Aurora Borealis.
2. The colors of the Northern Lights are created when gases react with solar winds.
3. The Aurora Borealis can be seen at the South Pole.

THINK BIG Does nature make you feel humble? Which things in nature do you think are really beautiful?

Warm-up

- Pair students, and ask partners to take turns asking and answering with question tags about a mystery from the unit. Model: *It's a little scary, isn't it?* (Yes, it is.) *Ships disappear here, don't they?* (Yes, they do.) *It's the Bermuda Triangle, isn't it?* (Yes it is.)
- Check answers from the HW in the last lesson.

Lesson Objective

INVOLVE

- Introduce the lesson objective. Say: *Today I will learn about the Northern Lights.*
- Students will read, understand, and discuss a science text about the Aurora Borealis.

Pre-reading

- Ask the class what they know about the Aurora Borealis.
- Go over the Content Words with students. Elicit or supply definitions for each word.
- Have students work in pairs to predict how the Content Words are related to the Aurora Borealis, e.g. *I think the Aurora Borealis is made of nitrogen.*
- Read the title and point out the picture. Ask: *What do you think this article is about?* Allow students to share their ideas.

Reading

12 Listen and read. What is another name for the Aurora Borealis?

- Play Audio Track 105. Have students listen and read along in their books.

MONITOR

Discuss the answer as a class. (Answer: Northern Lights)

ASSIST

Replay the audio as needed. Use simple language and gestures to explain unfamiliar words.

21st Century Cross-Cultural Awareness

- Share information about cultural and historical interpretations of the lights. Say: *In Roman mythology, Aurora was a goddess who brought the dawn each day. In Inuit (Alaska) myths, these lights represent the spirits of the hunted animals. The Menominee (Wisconsin) believe the lights are the spirits of great hunters and fishers. In the Middle Ages, many people believed that they were signs of war or famine. The Maori (New Zealand) say they're reflections of campfires and torches.*

Practice 1

13 Look at the passage. Read and say *true* or *false*.

- Read the directions, and have students complete the activity independently.

MONITOR

- Have students compare their answers in pairs. As students are working, walk around the class and listen for their justifications. (Answers: 1 false, 2 true, 3 false)
- Ask different students to correct the sentences that are false. Write their sentences on the board. (1 Albert Einstein didn't discover the Aurora Borealis. 3 The Aurora Australis is at the South Pole, and the Aurora Borealis is at the North Pole.)

Practice 2

12 Read and complete the text with the words in the box. Then listen and check.

- Read the directions aloud, and have students complete the activity independently.
- Play Audio Track 106. Have students listen and check their answers independently.

MONITOR

Check answers as a class. (Answers: 1 swirling, 2 phenomenon, 3 solar wind, 4 Oxygen, 5 nitrogen)

Think BIG

21st Century Values and Environmental Awareness

- Reread the quote from Albert Einstein at the beginning of the article. Explain that *humility* is related to the word *humble*. Discuss the quote as a way to elicit what *humble* means.
- Invite a volunteer to read the first question, and discuss it as a class.
- Pair students, and have partners brainstorm things in nature that seem particularly beautiful to them. Invite volunteer pairs to share their ideas, and write them on the board.

Lesson Objective

INVOLVE

Revisit the lesson objective: *Now I have learned about the Northern Lights.*

- Encourage awareness of what students have learned by eliciting from them another name for the Northern Lights, and some information about it.

Homework

13 Read 12 again and choose the correct answers.

- Direct students to WB Activity 13 on page 72. Tell students to complete the sentences by choosing *a* or *b*.

Extra Application and Practice Activity

- Have students create an infographic based on the reading that explains what the Aurora Borealis is and what causes it. Make sure they label and explain the images in their infographic. Tell students they should use at least four of the Content Words.

Unit 7 **T90**

Content Connection | Earth Science

I will learn about the Northern Lights.

12 Listen and read. What is another name for the Aurora Borealis?

CONTENT WORDS
altitude, clapping, interaction, nitrogen, oxygen, phenomenon, pole, solar wind, stand out, swirling

The Aurora Borealis

Albert Einstein, whose work we still study today, once said this about nature: "What I see in nature is a magnificent structure that we can comprehend only very imperfectly and that must fill a thinking person with a feeling of humility." We could surely say this while looking at the Aurora Borealis!

The Aurora Borealis, also called the Northern Lights, is a magnificent display of swirling colored lights that's visible in northern countries. Each year, people travel closer to the North Pole to see it and enjoy its beauty.

What causes this strange phenomenon? For a long time, no one could answer this question. People thought it was just a mysterious natural event or even the spirits of animals they had hunted. Recently, however, science has provided an explanation. The different colors of an aurora are the result of solar winds interacting with different gases at different altitudes. Oxygen produces yellow-green and red colors, and nitrogen produces violet and blue colors.

The Northern Lights are easiest to see in the Arctic from the fall to the early spring. This is the time of year when the nights are long and dark and the colors really stand out. However, during strong solar storms, you can sometimes see the Aurora Borealis as far south as Texas. At the South Pole, a similar phenomenon occurs at the same time as the one in the north. This is called the Aurora Australis, or the Southern Lights.

Scientists have discovered a lot about the Aurora Borealis, but some things are still a mystery. For example, people have said that a clapping sound comes at the same time as the light display. Whatever the explanation, the aurora's magical and mysterious beauty has inspired and continues to inspire painters, poets, and songwriters.

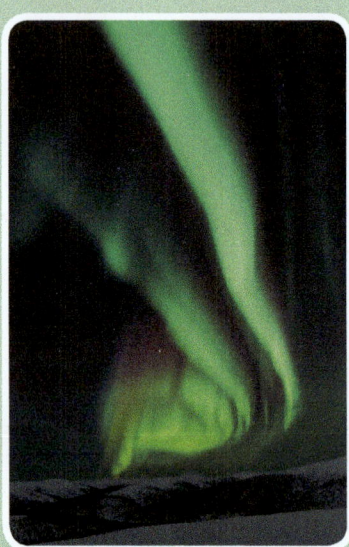

13 Look at the passage. Read and say *true* or *false*.

1 Albert Einstein discovered the Aurora Borealis.
2 The colors of the Northern Lights are created when gases react with solar winds.
3 The Aurora Borealis can be seen at the South Pole.

THINK BIG
Does nature make you feel humble? Which things in nature do you think are really beautiful?

Culture Connection | Around the World

I will learn about mysterious stories around the world.

CONTENT WORDS
artifacts   clearing   diameter   rapid   sighting

🔊 107
14 Listen and read. Where does the Sasquatch come from?

Mysterious Findings

There are stories of strange discoveries, unexplained artifacts, and mysterious sightings from all over the world. Studying them is popular with curious people and scientists who want to find explanations. Here are two interesting examples from Costa Rica and Tibet.

Stone Spheres

Take a look at this photograph. These stones don't look natural, do they? In 1930, while clearing an area of the Costa Rican jungle workers came upon a number of these balls, which are estimated to date back to 600 BC. Since then, several hundred have been discovered, and they're all perfectly constructed! They vary in size from the size of tennis balls to spheres that are eight feet in diameter and weigh sixteen tons.

Studies have shown that the balls are made of granodiorite, a rock that is easy to break when its temperature changes rapidly from hot to cold. However, even with today's technology, getting the stones this perfect would be extremely difficult. The mystery remains: Who made the stones and why? And how did they give them such a perfect shape?

The Yeti

You've heard of the yeti, haven't you? So have I. But like most people, I wonder if it's real or just a legend. People believe that the yeti, also called the abominable snowman, resembles a gorilla. Many believe that the yeti lives in the Himalayan regions of Tibet and Nepal, which is where the legend began. But people also talk about a yeti-like creature in Canada and Alaska, where it's called Sasquatch.

Over the years, scientists and explorers have tried to find evidence for the story of the yeti. So far, only footprints have been found. There's no proof that a yeti or any other creature made them, and photographs are never clear. Many scientists think that they were probably made by bears. So why do people continue to believe the yeti exists? Maybe because there's no proof that it doesn't exist, and people like mysteries!

15 Look at the passage. Match to complete the sentences.

1. The stone spheres were discovered by…
2. Granodiorite is…
3. The legend of the yeti comes from…
4. The yeti is also called…

a. the people of the Himalayas.
b. workers in the jungle.
c. the abominable snowman.
d. a kind of rock.

THINK BIG

What explanations are there in the article for the mysteries? Can you think of any more?

Culture Connection Lesson

Lesson Flow

Warm-up › Lesson Objective › Pre-reading › Reading › Practice 1 (SB) › Practice 2 (WB) › Think BIG › Video › Lesson Objective › Homework

Lesson Objective

I will learn about mysterious stories around the world.

Key Language

artifacts, clearing, diameter, rapid, sighting

Culture Connection | Around the World

I will learn about mysterious stories around the world.

CONTENT WORDS
artifacts, clearing, diameter, rapid, sighting

🎧 107 Listen and read. Where does the Sasquatch come from?

Mysterious Findings

There are stories of strange discoveries, unexplained artifacts, and mysterious sightings from all over the world. Studying them is popular with curious people and scientists who want to find explanations. Here are two interesting examples from Costa Rica and Tibet.

Stone Spheres

Take a look at this photograph. These stones don't look natural, do they? In 1930, while clearing an area of the Costa Rican jungle workers came upon a number of these balls, which are estimated to date back to 600 BC. Since then, several hundred have been discovered, and they're all perfectly constructed! They vary in size from the size of tennis balls to spheres that are eight feet in diameter and weigh sixteen tons.

Studies have shown that the balls are made of granodiorite, a rock that is easy to break when its temperature changes rapidly from hot to cold. However, even with today's technology, getting the stones this perfect would be extremely difficult. The mystery remains: Who made the stones and why? And how did they give them such a perfect shape?

The Yeti

You've heard of the yeti, haven't you? So have I. But like most people, I wonder if it's real or just a legend. People believe that the yeti, also called the abominable snowman, resembles a gorilla. Many believe that the yeti lives in the Himalayan regions of Tibet and Nepal, which is where the legend began. But people also talk about a yeti-like creature in Canada and Alaska, where it's called Sasquatch.

Over the years, scientists and explorers have tried to find evidence for the story of the yeti. So far, only footprints have been found. There's no proof that a yeti or any other creature made them, and photographs are never clear. Many scientists think that they were probably made by bears. So why do people continue to believe the yeti exists? Maybe because there's no proof that it doesn't exist, and people like mysteries!

15 Look at the passage. Match to complete the sentences.

1. The stone spheres were discovered by...
2. Granodiorite is...
3. The legend of the yeti comes from...
4. The yeti is also called...

a. the people of the Himalayas.
b. workers in the jungle.
c. the abominable snowman.
d. a kind of rock.

THINK BIG What explanations are there in the article for the mysteries? Can you think of any more?

Unit 7 91

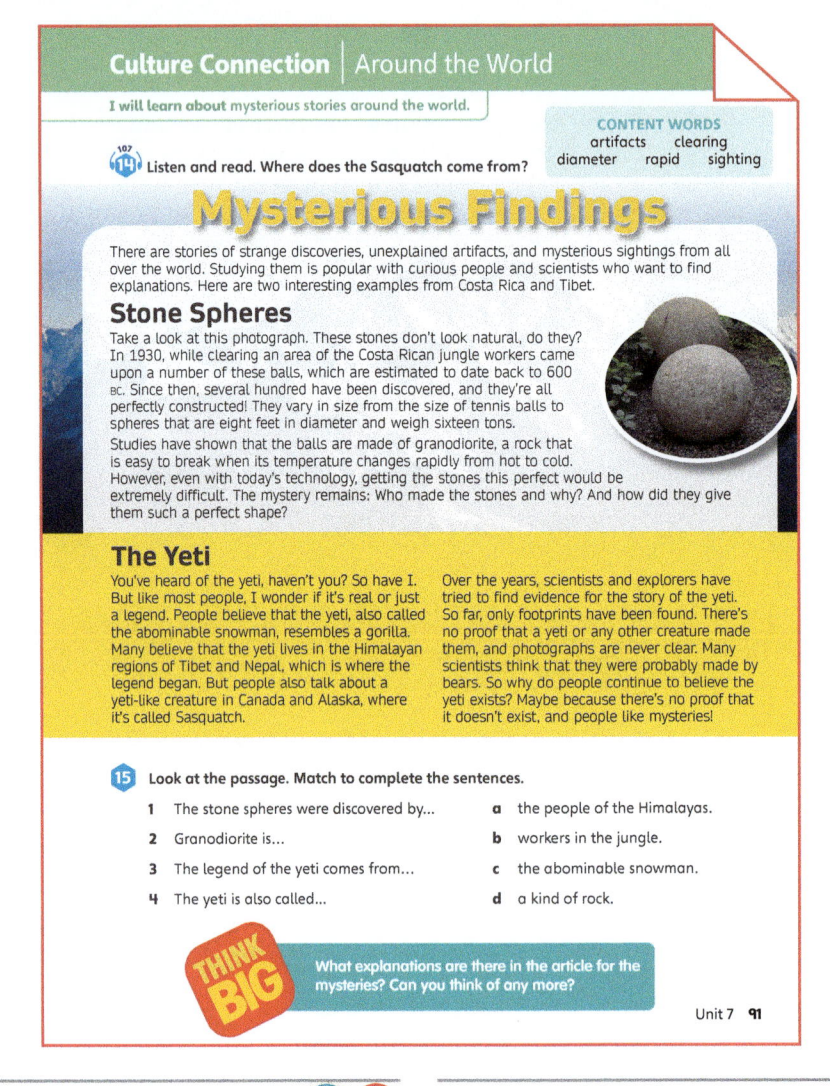

Warm-up

- Write on slips of paper: *Peru*; *the Atlantic Ocean*; *England*; *Egypt*; *the Northern Hemisphere*; *Death Valley, California*; *Virginia*; *Costa Rica*. Have students work in small groups and take turns drawing a slip and using a question tag to guess the mystery there. Model: *Egypt. The mystery is about the Great Pyramids, isn't it?*
- Check answers from the HW in the last lesson.

Lesson Objective

INVOLVE

Introduce the lesson objective. Say: *Today I will learn about mysterious stories around the world.*

- Students will read a text about mysterious findings in different cultures. Tell students *findings* means "discoveries."

S91 Unit 7

Pre-reading

- Write the words *artifacts, diameter, rapid, sighting,* and *clearing* on the board. Have students underline each one in the text and use context clues to determine its meaning.
- Invite a volunteer to read the title aloud. Point to the two blocks of different-colored texts and read the subheadings. Have students predict what the text is about.

Reading

4 Listen and read. Where does the Sasquatch come from?

- Play Audio Track 107 and have students listen and read along.

MONITOR

Discuss the answer as a class. *(Answer: Many believe that the yeti lives in the Himalayan regions of Tibet and Nepal. The Sasquatch is a yeti-like creature in Canada and Alaska.)*

ASSIST

Replay the audio as needed. Use simple language and gestures to explain unfamiliar words.

Practice 1

5 Look at the passage. Match to complete the sentences.

- Read the directions aloud. Have students read through the first and second parts of the four sentences, and make predictions as to the correct answers. Do not confirm or correct their predictions yet.

MONITOR

Check answers as a class. Ask students how accurate their predictions were. *(Answers: 1 b, 2 d, 3 a, 4 c)*

- Write the following questions on the board: *What do you remember about the stone spheres? What do you remember about the yeti?*
- Have students close their books and answer the questions with a partner.

MONITOR

As a class, discuss how well students remembered the main points of the article.

CHALLENGE

Have students create an additional multiple-choice question based on the text. Invite different students to share their multiple-choice questions, and elicit the answers from the class.

Practice 2 — WB p. 73/ act. 15

15 Listen and read. The circle T for *true* or F for *false*.

- Read the directions aloud.
- Play Audio Track 108 twice. The second time, have students circle words they do not understand. Explain their meaning.

Think BIG

21st Century Critical Thinking

- Elicit from students some different people who can make discoveries (e.g. *explorers, archeologists, scientists*).
- Have a volunteer read the first question. Discuss as a class.
- Place students in small groups and have them discuss the second question. A group member reports back to the class the students' further explanations for the mysteries.

Video — Documentary U 07

- Refer to the Video Guide for pre-watching and post-watching activities.

Lesson Objective

INVOLVE

Revisit the lesson objective: *Now I have learned about mysterious stories around the world.*

- Encourage awareness of what students have learned by quickly eliciting a few facts from the article.

Homework — WB p. 73/ act. 16

16 Read and circle the correct answers.

- Direct students to WB Activity 15 on page 73. Tell students to read the sentence and circle the correct choice.

Extra Application and Practice Activity

21st Century Collaboration

- In their same groups, have students work together to write a paragraph about one of the mysteries, as well as their thoughts on the mystery and its possible explanations. Encourage them to include the thoughts or opinions of all members in the group.

ASSIST

Provide the following sentence frames: *One interesting mystery is… . An explanation from the article is… . Another possible explanation is… . In our opinion,… .*

Unit 7 T91

Writing Lesson

Lesson Flow

Warm-up › Lesson Objective › Practice 1 (WB) › Practice 2 (SB) › Practice 3 (SB) › Practice 4 (SB) › Speaking › Lesson Objective › Homework

Lesson Objective

I will learn to write a paragraph about the cause and effect of something.

Writing | Cause and effect

I will learn to write a paragraph about the cause and effect of something.

16 Read this explanation for why the sailing stones move.

> **What Causes the Sailing Stones to Move?**
>
> The Racetrack Playa in Death Valley gets seven to ten centimeters of rain a year, but the rainfall comes in bursts. During the storms, the ground floods, and the fine soil turns into mud and ice.
>
> The winds, which can reach 145 kilometers per hour, can actually overcome the force of friction and cause the stones to move. Once the stones are already moving, much less powerful winds can keep them in motion.

17 Complete the chart below with information from 16.

Cause:		Effect:
_____ comes in bursts.	→	The ground _____ and the fine _____ turns into mud and ice.

Cause:		Effect:
Powerful _____ blow.	→	The wind pushes on the _____ and they slide in the mud and ice.

18 Choose a topic and make a chart like the one in 17. Use your chart to write a paragraph about your topic.

19 Share your paragraph with the class.

92 Unit 7

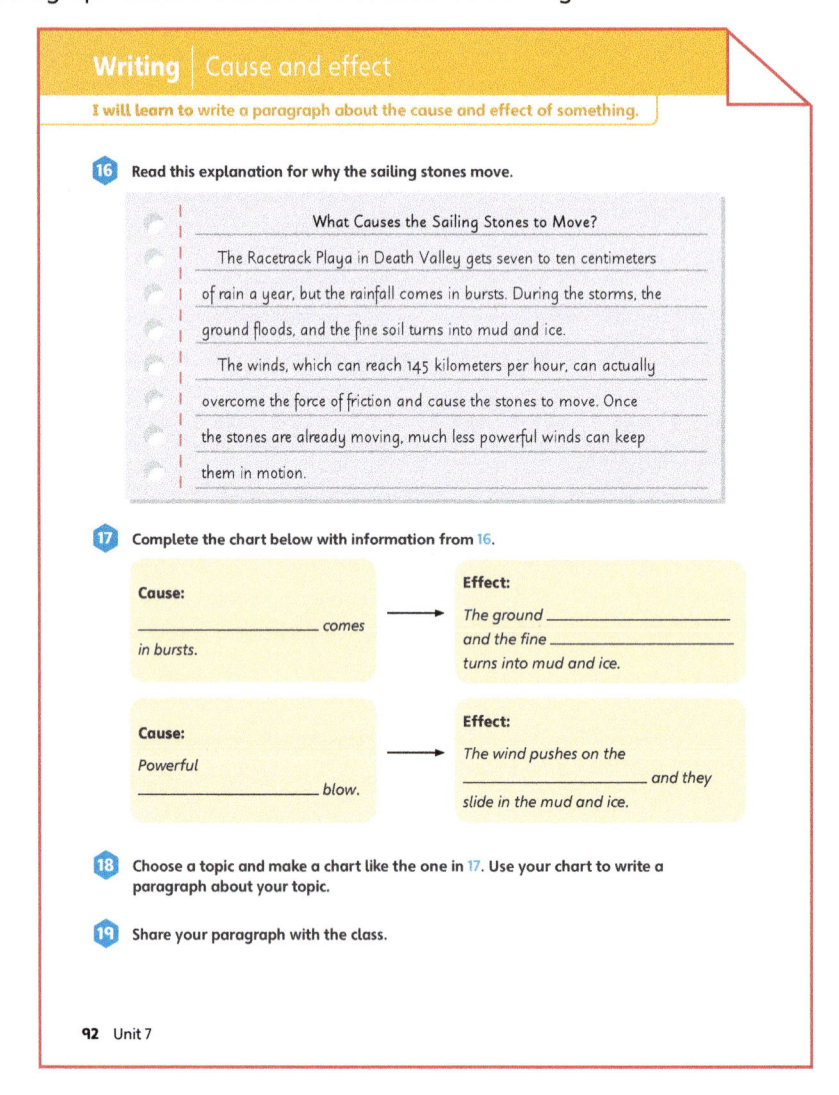

Warm-up

Materials: Marbles, sandpaper, plastic, smooth paper

21st Century Self-Directed Learning

- Give students marbles and paper of various textures, including sandpaper. Have them design experiments to show how the texture of the paper affects the movement of the marbles. (Students should conclude that marbles move the fastest and most easily on smooth surfaces, such as plastic or very smooth paper; they move less easily and may stop moving on rough surfaces, such as sandpaper.)

- Check answers from the HW in the last lesson.

Lesson Objective

INVOLVE

Introduce the lesson objective. Say: *Today I will learn to write a paragraph about the cause and effect of something.*

- Students will read and write cause-and-effect paragraphs.

Practice 1   WB p. 74/ act. 16

16 Read the paragraph. Underline the causes. Circle the effects.

- Have a volunteer read the information in the purple box aloud. Tell students that they are going to read a paragraph and separate the cause from the effect.
- Read the directions aloud. Have students complete the activity. Check the answers as a class.

Practice 2

16 Read this explanation for why the sailing stones move.

- Read the directions aloud. Then have volunteers read the paragraph aloud. Encourage them to connect their experiment with marbles in the Warm-up with the phenomenon of the sailing stones. *(Possible answer: The stones move more easily when the land is smooth with mud and ice.)*

MONITOR

Use questions to check comprehension. Ask: *What happens when it rains at Racetrack Playa?* (The ground floods and the dirt turns into mud and ice.)

ASSIST

Suggest that students use C for each cause and E for each effect. Model: *I'll use C next to "rain" because it causes a change in the ground. I'll use E next to "the fine dirt turns into mud" because that's an effect.*

Practice 3

17 Complete the chart below with information from 16.

- Say: *The cause is the reason something happens. The effect is what happens as a result. To find a cause, ask, "Why?" To find an effect, ask, "What happens as a result?"*
- Read the directions aloud. Say: *A cause-and-effect diagram can help you understand what happens and why. You can use it to write a cause-and-effect paragraph.* Have students complete the activity individually.

MONITOR

Check answers as a class. *(Answers: Cause: **Rain** comes in bursts. Effect: The ground **floods** and the fine **soil** turns into mud and ice. Cause: Powerful **winds** blow. Effect: The wind pushes on the **rocks** and they slide in the mud and ice.)*

Practice 4

18 Choose a topic and make a chart like the one in 17. Use your chart to write a paragraph about your topic.

- Read the directions aloud. Have students work in small groups to discuss possible topics. Allow students time to research and plan. Suggest that they use science books or other resources.

MONITOR

Check that students complete their cause-and-effect charts before writing their paragraphs and then use the information in their paragraphs.

Speaking

19 Share your paragraph with the class.

- Read the directions aloud and invite volunteers to read their cause-and-effect paragraphs aloud.

MONITOR

As pairs share their paragraphs with the class, check that they've included information about cause and effect correctly. Encourage other students to offer helpful feedback.

Lesson Objective

INVOLVE

Revisit the lesson objective: *Now I have learned to write a paragraph about the cause and effect of something.*

- Encourage awareness of what students have learned by asking students to describe the difference between a cause, and an effect.

Homework   WB p. 74/ act. 17

17 Write a cause-and-effect paragraph about something that's happened to you or something you've read about in your science lessons. Use the chart below to organize your ideas.

- Direct students to WB Activity 17 on page 74. Students plan and write a cause-and-effect paragraph.
- Point out the box on the top of the page. This information will guide students.

Extra Application and Practice Activity

- Invite students to draw illustrations to accompany their cause-and-effect paragraphs. Have students show the illustrations before sharing their writing, and have classmates guess their topic.

Unit 7   **T92**

Writing | Cause and effect

I will learn to write a paragraph about the cause and effect of something.

16 Read this explanation for why the sailing stones move.

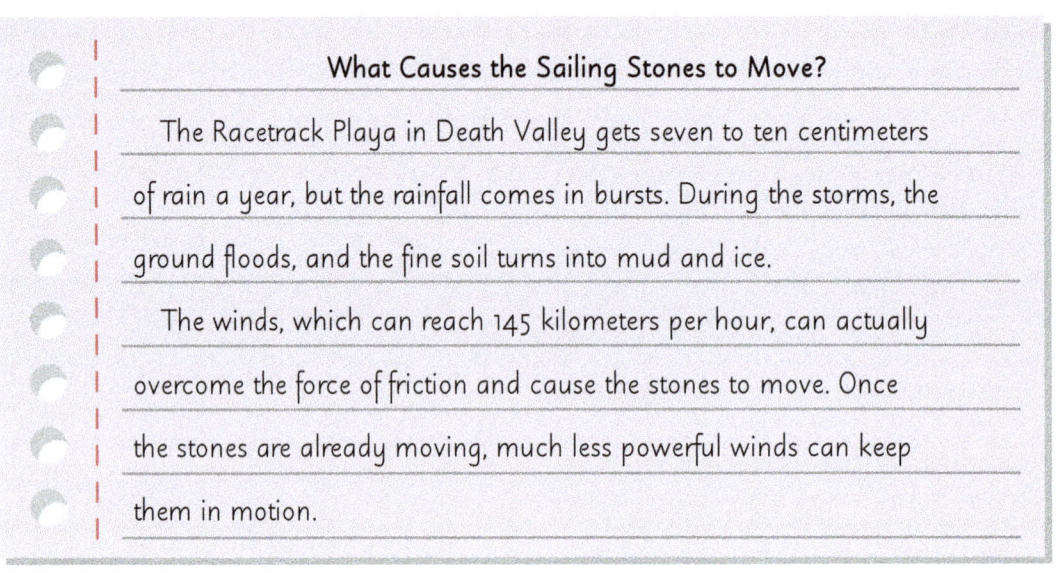

What Causes the Sailing Stones to Move?

The Racetrack Playa in Death Valley gets seven to ten centimeters of rain a year, but the rainfall comes in bursts. During the storms, the ground floods, and the fine soil turns into mud and ice.

The winds, which can reach 145 kilometers per hour, can actually overcome the force of friction and cause the stones to move. Once the stones are already moving, much less powerful winds can keep them in motion.

17 Complete the chart below with information from **16**.

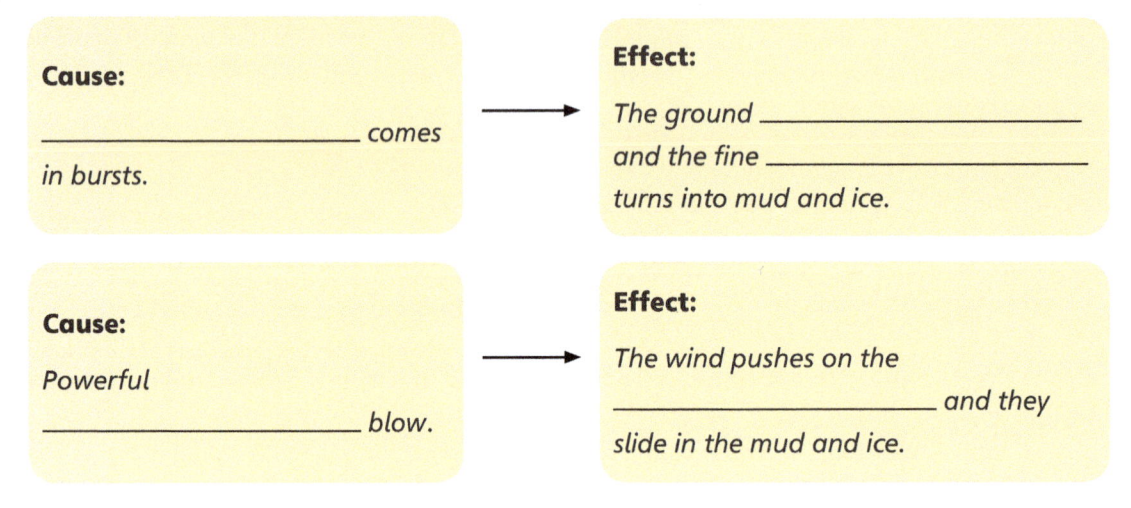

Cause:
_____ comes in bursts.

→ **Effect:**
The ground _____ and the fine _____ turns into mud and ice.

Cause:
Powerful _____ blow.

→ **Effect:**
The wind pushes on the _____ and they slide in the mud and ice.

18 Choose a topic and make a chart like the one in **17**. Use your chart to write a paragraph about your topic.

19 Share your paragraph with the class.

Life skills | Be curious.

I will learn to talk about the importance of being curious.

20 Is curiosity important? Say which statements you agree with. Then discuss your opinions with a partner.

1. Curiosity makes us ask questions, and questions help us learn.
2. Curiosity makes us unhappy and dissatisfied.
3. Curiosity encourages us to be creative.
4. Curiosity leads to inventions and discoveries.
5. Curiosity makes us look indecisive, like we don't know something.

21 Keep a curiosity diary every day for a week. Use the ideas below to give examples of your curiosity.

Ask questions. / Be observant. / Find answers. / Study one new topic every day. / Try something new. / Read a lot!

> Monday, March 17
>
> I was observant. I looked at a frog under a magnifying glass.

> At Ringing Rocks Park in Pennsylvania, U.S.A., when you hit the rocks with a hammer, they sound like bells. No one knows why it happens.

Project

22 Did the things you read in this unit make you curious? Learn more about mysterious phenomena.

A Make a booklet with a partner. Research information about two mysteries. Use these headers:
- General Information
- Research Done
- Theories Found
- My Conclusion

B When you've finished, share your booklet with another pair.

Mystery #1:
Ringing Rocks Park,
Pennsylvania, U.S.A.

General Information
The rocks sound like bells when you hit them.

Research Done
http://www.travelandleisure.com/travel-guide/bucks-county/activities/ringing-rocks-park

Theories Found
There are no explanations for this phenomenon.

My Conclusion
I think they must be made of something unusual.

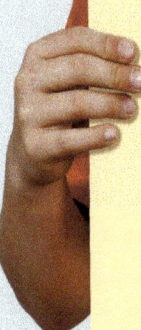

Unit 7   93

Life Skills Lesson

Lesson Flow

Warm-up › Lesson Objective › Speaking › Practice › Project › Lesson Objective

Lesson Objective

I will learn to talk about the importance of being curious.

Life skills | Be curious.

I will learn to talk about the importance of being curious.

20 Is curiosity important? Say which statements you agree with. Then discuss your opinions with a partner.

1. Curiosity makes us ask questions, and questions help us learn.
2. Curiosity makes us unhappy and dissatisfied.
3. Curiosity encourages us to be creative.
4. Curiosity leads to inventions and discoveries.
5. Curiosity makes us look indecisive, like we don't know something.

21 Keep a curiosity diary every day for a week. Use the ideas below to give examples of your curiosity.

Ask questions. / Be observant. / Find answers. / Study one new topic every day. / Try something new. / Read a lot!

> Monday, March 17
> I was observant. I looked at a frog under a magnifying glass.

> At Ringing Rocks Park in Pennsylvania, U.S.A., when you hit the rocks with a hammer, they sound like bells. No one knows why it happens.

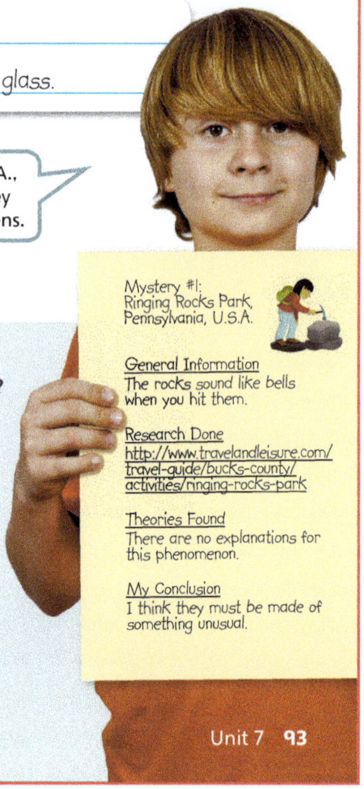

Project

22 Did the things you read in this unit make you curious? Learn more about mysterious phenomena.

A Make a booklet with a partner. Research information about two mysteries. Use these headers:
- General Information
- Research Done
- Theories Found
- My Conclusion

B When you've finished, share your booklet with another pair.

Mystery #1:
Ringing Rocks Park,
Pennsylvania, U.S.A.

General Information
The rocks sound like bells when you hit them.

Research Done
http://www.travelandleisure.com/travel-guide/bucks-county/activities/ringing-rocks-park

Theories Found
There are no explanations for this phenomenon.

My Conclusion
I think they must be made of something unusual.

Unit 7   93

Warm-up

21st Century Cross-Cultural Skills

- Share this saying with students: "Curiosity killed the cat, but satisfaction brought him back." Ask: *What does the first part of this saying mean?* (Sample answer: Being curious can get you in trouble.) *What does the second part mean?* (Sample answer: Being curious can also be rewarding.) Point out that in many cultures, cats are said to have more than one life because they get out of life-threatening situations. The number of lives varies. (Some say that in English culture, cats have nine lives; and that in Spanish culture, they have seven.)
- Check answers from the HW in the last lesson.

Lesson Objective

INVOLVE

Introduce the lesson objective. Say: *Today I will learn to talk about the importance of being curious.*

- Students will discuss being curious and then make a booklet about mysterious phenomena.

Speaking

20 Is curiosity important? Say which statements you agree with. Then discuss your opinions with a partner.

- Read the directions aloud. Have students complete the activity independently and then compare their answers with a partner.

MONITOR

Make sure that students choose at least three statements. Be sure that students discuss each statement and why they agree or disagree. Listen for proper pronunciation, appropriate intonation, and correct use of language.

ASSIST

Encourage students to use question tags in their discussions. Model: *Curiosity makes us ask questions, doesn't it? Curiosity doesn't make us unhappy, does it?*

Practice

21 Keep a curiosity diary every day for a week. Use the ideas below to give examples of your curiosity.

- Read the directions and example aloud.
- Have students complete their diaries independently. Then have them work in pairs to compare their experiences. Model: *I decided to learn about one new thing. I saw an article about Zimbabwe. I didn't know very much about that country, so I spent half an hour reading about it on the internet.*

MONITOR

Listen for proper pronunciation, appropriate intonation, and correct use of language.

ASSIST

Say: *Try to write in your curiosity diary every day. You don't have to write complete sentences. Note down topics that you'd like to know more about.*

Project

Materials: Poster paper, art supplies

22 Did the things you read in this unit make you curious? Learn more about mysterious phenomena.

21st Century Collaboration

- Read the directions aloud. Tell students that collaborating can help them test their ideas to make sure they're logical and clear. Have students create booklets. Suggest that students work in pairs to describe and illustrate two mysteries. Then have students share their booklets with another pair.

21st Century Leadership

- Have students take turns being the leader during pair activities. Switching the leadership role can help prevent one student from dominating. Suggest that leaders set specific goals for each meeting and end each session by discussing whether or not those goals were met.

MONITOR

Check that partners complete each category for two mysterious phenomena. Be sure that they find general information for each topic, list research done and theories found, and write a conclusion.

ASSIST

If needed, help students find resources for each topic.

Lesson Objective

INVOLVE

Revisit the lesson objective: *Now I have learned to talk about the importance of being curious.*

- Encourage awareness of what students have learned by asking for a few reasons why it is important to be curious.

Extra Application and Practice Activity

Materials: World map or globe

- As a class, make a world map of mysterious phenomena, using pins to mark the locations of the ones that students described in their booklets.

Unit 7 T93

Listening and Speaking Lesson

Lesson Flow

Warm-up › Lesson Objective › Presentation › Practice 1 (SB) › Practice 2 (SB) › Practice 3 (SB) › Speaking › Lesson Objective

Lesson Objectives

I will review the sounds *un*, *inter*, *re*, *pre*, and *super*.

I will learn to talk about famous mysteries.

Listening and Speaking

I will review the sounds *un*, *inter*, *re*, *pre*, and *super*.
I will learn to talk about famous mysteries.

23 Listen, read, and repeat.

1. un 2. inter 3. re 4. pre 5. super

24 Listen and blend the sounds.

1. un-h-a-pp-y   unhappy
2. inter-n-a-t-io-n-a-l   international
3. re-c-y-c-le   recycle
4. pre-u-s-ed   preused
5. Super-m-a-n   Superman
6. re-d-u-ce   reduce

25 Listen and chant.

> Celebrate International Earth Day!
> Recycle your Superman T-shirt
> And your pre-washed bottles.
> Reduce unhealthy food,
> Try healthy food! It's good!

26 Work in a small group. Do a survey. Which mystery is your favorite? Make a chart to show what your classmates' favorite mystery is.

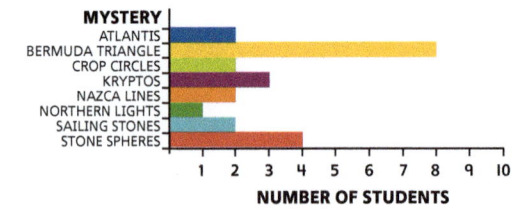

MYSTERY
- ATLANTIS
- BERMUDA TRIANGLE
- CROP CIRCLES
- KRYPTOS
- NAZCA LINES
- NORTHERN LIGHTS
- SAILING STONES
- STONE SPHERES

NUMBER OF STUDENTS (1–10)

27 Ask and answer questions about the results. Use question tags when you can.

- The Bermuda Triangle is our favorite mystery, isn't it?
- Yeah. I wonder why.
- I think it's because it's still unsolved.
- Maybe, but I think it's because it's creepy.

Warm-up

- Have partners take turns thinking of one of the mysteries from this unit, giving its first letter, and challenging others to guess the mystery. Model: A: *I'm thinking of a mystery that begins with* y. B: *It's the yeti, isn't it?* A: *You guessed it!*

Lesson Objective

INVOLVE

Introduce the lesson objective. Say: *Today I will learn to use the sounds* un, inter, re, pre, *and* super, *and talk about famous mysteries.*

- Students will identify the letters and distinguish between the sounds *un*, *inter*, *re*, *pre*, and *super* individually and as part of words. Then they'll review the unit by talking about mysterious phenomena and using question tags.

Presentation

23 Listen, read, and repeat.

- Read the directions aloud. Play Audio Track 109 and have students listen and point to each sound as it is said. Have students repeat.

MONITOR

As students repeat, check they are pointing to the correct sound and listen for correct pronunciation.

Practice 1

24 Listen and blend the sounds.

- Read the directions aloud. Play Audio Track 110 and have students listen and point to each item as it is sounded out and blended on the audio. Have them repeat after each item.

MONITOR

As students repeat, check they are pointing to the correct word, and listen for correct pronunciation and appropriate intonation.

ASSIST

Replay the audio as needed.

Practice 2

25 Listen and chant.

- Read the directions aloud. Read the chant while students follow in their books.
- Play Audio Track 111 and have students listen. Replay the audio several times and encourage them to join in.

MONITOR

As students repeat the chant, listen for proper pronunciation, appropriate intonation, and correct use of language.

Practice 3

26 Work in a small group. Do a survey. Which mystery is your favorite? Make a chart to show what your classmates' favorite mystery is.

- Read the directions aloud. On the board write the mysteries presented in the chart, and have students copy them in their notebooks. Have students work in small groups to complete the survey.

MONITOR

Have each student write his or her name by their topic of choice on the chart on the board.

21st Century Information Literacy

- Have students work in pairs to create charts with the class results. They can use the chart in this activity as a model. Point out that the chart students are making is in the form of a bar graph. Ask: *How does a bar graph show information?* (Each bar represents an amount.) *How do the labels help you interpret the graph?* (The labels name each mystery and show the number of students that voted for it.)

Speaking

27 Ask and answer questions about the results. Use question tags when you can.

- Read the directions aloud. Have volunteers read the speech bubbles aloud. Model other question tags that can be used to talk about the data: *The sailing stones aren't very popular with our class, are they? Atlantis is popular, isn't it?*

ASSIST

Provide students with statements about their charts that can be turned into question tags. Model: *Six of us voted for the Bermuda Triangle.* (didn't we?) *We don't need to include a bar for crop circles.* (do we?)

Lesson Objective

INVOLVE

Revisit the lesson objective: *Now I have learned to use the sounds* un, inter, re, pre, *and* super, *and talked about famous mysteries.*

- Encourage awareness of what students have learned by quickly eliciting from them words from the lesson that have the sounds *un*, *inter*, *re*, *pre*, and *super*.

Extra Application and Practice Activity

21st Century Leadership

- Have students use computer software to create their charts. Students may also wish to create a chart for a different question, such as *Which mystery do you think would make the best subject for a movie?*

Unit 7 **T94**

Listening and Speaking

I will review the sounds *un*, *inter*, *re*, *pre*, and *super*.
I will learn to talk about famous mysteries.

23 Listen, read, and repeat.

1. un   2. inter   3. re   4. pre   5. super

24 Listen and blend the sounds.

1. un-h-a-pp-y   unhappy
2. inter-n-a-t-io-n-a-l   international
3. re-c-y-c-le   recycle
4. pre-u-s-ed   preused
5. Super-m-a-n   Superman
6. re-d-u-ce   reduce

25 Listen and chant.

> Celebrate International Earth Day!
> Recycle your Superman T-shirt
> And your pre-washed bottles.
> Reduce unhealthy food,
> Try healthy food! It's good!

26 Work in a small group. Do a survey. Which mystery is your favorite? Make a chart to show what your classmates' favorite mystery is.

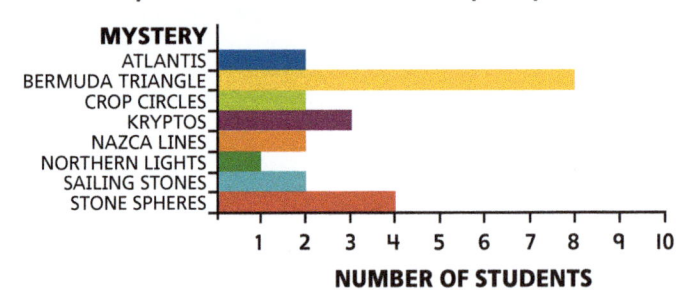

MYSTERY
- ATLANTIS: 2
- BERMUDA TRIANGLE: 8
- CROP CIRCLES: 2
- KRYPTOS: 3
- NAZCA LINES: 2
- NORTHERN LIGHTS: 1
- SAILING STONES: 2
- STONE SPHERES: 4

NUMBER OF STUDENTS

27 Ask and answer questions about the results. Use question tags when you can.

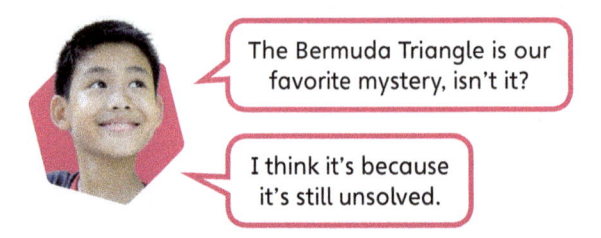

- The Bermuda Triangle is our favorite mystery, isn't it?
- Yeah. I wonder why.
- I think it's because it's still unsolved.
- Maybe, but I think it's because it's creepy.

Review

28 Complete the sentences using question tags. Then give answers to show you agree or disagree.

1 All unsolved mysteries are worth investigating, _____?
   _____

2 Most unsolved mysteries are hoaxes, _____?
   _____

3 Some mysteries can't be solved even with scientific research, _____?
   _____

4 Having a curious mind is important, _____?
   _____

5 Curiosity makes new discoveries and inventions possible, _____?
   _____

6 Einstein had a curious mind, _____?
   _____

29 Complete the sentences with words from the box.

| phenomenon | proof | scientific | theory | unsolved |

1 So far, there's no _____ explanation for how the stones became so perfectly round.

2 One _____ that explains the mystery of Atlantis is that it disappeared during a large earthquake.

3 Actually, there's no reliable _____ that the city of Atlantis existed.

4 The Aurora Borealis is a natural _____ that has been explained.

5 The mystery of the stone spheres is still _____.

I Can

- use words for scientific mysteries.
- use question tags with *be, can,* and *do.*
- talk about mysterious phenomena.
- write a cause and effect paragraph.

Unit 7 **95**

Review Lesson

Lesson Flow

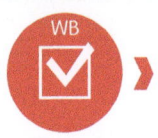

Warm-up › Lesson Objective › Practice 1 (SB) › Practice 2 (WB) › Practice 3 (WB) › Practice 4 (SB) › Self-assessment › Homework

Lesson Objective

To review the words and structures of the unit.

Review

28 Complete the sentences using question tags. Then give answers to show you agree or disagree.

1. All unsolved mysteries are worth investigating, _____?
   _____
2. Most unsolved mysteries are hoaxes, _____?
   _____
3. Some mysteries can't be solved even with scientific research, _____?
   _____
4. Having a curious mind is important, _____?
   _____
5. Curiosity makes new discoveries and inventions possible, _____?
   _____
6. Einstein had a curious mind, _____?
   _____

29 Complete the sentences with words from the box.

| phenomenon | proof | scientific | theory | unsolved |

1. So far, there's no _____ explanation for how the stones became so perfectly round.
2. One _____ that explains the mystery of Atlantis is that it disappeared during a large earthquake.
3. Actually, there's no reliable _____ that the city of Atlantis existed.
4. The Aurora Borealis is a natural _____ that has been explained.
5. The mystery of the stone spheres is still _____.

I Can

- use words for scientific mysteries.
- use question tags with be, can, and do.
- talk about mysterious phenomena.
- write a cause and effect paragraph.

Unit 7 95

Warm-up

Materials: Index cards

- Have students play *Word Clues* (see *Game Bank*, page T137, for details) to review key vocabulary from Unit 7. Give students index cards and invite them to create game cards by writing one unit word or phrase on each card. Players should take turns looking at a word and giving one-word clues for partners. Model: *My clues are* sculpture, code, unsolved *and* letters. (Kryptos)
- Teams may wish to play *Word Clues* as a competition.

Lesson Objective

INVOLVE

Introduce the lesson objective: Say: *Today I will review the words and structures of the unit.*

- Students will review the vocabulary and grammar they have learned in Unit 7 by doing activities, including completing sentences.
- Then students will complete the *I Can* section, which helps them to assess their own learning and think about their progress.

Practice 1

28 Complete the sentences using question tags. Then give answers to show you agree or disagree.

- Read Item 1 aloud and elicit the appropriate question tag from the class. *(aren't they?)*
- Have a volunteer consider sample response. Ask another student to give a different sample response. (e.g. *No, I think it's good that there are things we don't understand.*)
- Pair students and have them continue the process, taking turns adding question tags to the sentences, and stating whether they agree or disagree.

MONITOR

For each question, have at least one pair share their mini-dialog with the class. *(Answers: 1 aren't they? 2 aren't they? 3 can they? 4 isn't it? 5 doesn't it? 6 didn't he?)*

Practice 2   WB p. 75/ act. 18

18 Read and choose the correct answers.

- Read the directions aloud. Read the first item aloud. As a class, work through *a* and *b* to consider which is correct.
- Have the students work independently to complete the activity.

Practice 3   WB p. 75/ act. 19

18 Correct the question tags.

- Read the directions aloud. Read the first item aloud and ask a volunteer to correct the question tag.
- Have students work independently to complete the activity.

Practice 4

29 Complete the sentences with words from the box.

- Read the directions aloud. Have volunteers read the words in the box aloud. Have students complete the activity independently.

MONITOR

Check answers as a class. *(1 scientific, 2 theory, 3 proof, 4 phenomenon, 5 unsolved)*

Self-assessment

Can

- This section asks students to assess their own learning and think about their progress. Help students appreciate their progress. Say: *The* I Can *statements show what you have learned in this unit.*
- Read the statements aloud. Explain that students should think about how well they know the language in the unit and should color in the stars. They should color three stars if they feel the unit was easy, two stars if they need some help, and one star if the unit was hard and they need more help. Have students work independently.

Suggestions for Remediation

Assessment Pack
- Direct students who need help with grammar and vocabulary to the Unit 7 Practice Tests in the Assessment Pack.

WB Unit 7/ p. 104
- Direct students who need help with grammar in particular to the Unit 7 Extra Grammar Practice (Workbook, page 104).

- For further vocabulary work, students can access games in the Big English Student World.

Homework   WB p. 75/ act. 20

20 Complete the dialogs. Use question tags. Use information you have learned about mysteries.

- Direct students to WB Activity 20 on page 75. Students use information from the unit, and question tags, to complete the sentences in the dialog.

Extra Application and Practice Activity

- Place students in small groups. Invite them to role-play a skit in which they interview someone who's investigating an unsolved mystery. Encourage students to use question tags and vocabulary words in the skit. When groups share their skit with the class, have classmates raise their hands when they hear a question tag.

Assessment Pack

- To assess student progress at the end of the unit, have students complete the Unit 7 Unit Test in the Assessment Pack.
- To assess whether students have reached the listening and speaking targets for this unit, carry out the Unit 7 Oral Assessment in the Assessment Pack.
- Arrange one-to-one sessions with each student and use the prompts to evaluate their listening and speaking abilities.

Unit 7   **T95**

8 Why Is It Famous?

Objectives

Reading

- Can draw simple conclusions about the information given in a factual text on a familiar topic.
- Can understand short, simple texts giving information about important places in a town, with the support of a map.
- Can extract specific information in short texts on familiar topics.

Listening

- Can identify key information (e.g. day, date, location) in short announcements about events, if spoken slowly and clearly.
- Can identify the main points in short talks on familiar topics, if delivered slowly and clearly.

Speaking

- Can answer simple questions after giving a presentation on a school topic.
- Can give the location of common stores or amenities in a town, using simple language, with reference to a map.

Writing

- Can write short, simple structured paragraphs on familiar topics, given prompts or a model.
- Can write simple texts with appropriate paragraph breaks, given prompts or a model.

Grammar

- Can use the past simple passive.
- Can use *who*, *that*, and *which* in relative clauses.

Unit Projects

Family Connection

Have students tell their families that they're learning about famous places and monuments around the world. Encourage students to interview family members about the most interesting places they've already visited and the places they would still most like to see. Encourage students to keep a list at home of places they read about or see in movies or on TV. Allow students to share with classmates the lists they made at home.

Key Language

Key Vocabulary

Famous Places and Structures

Big Ben	pyramid	
cathedral	Pyramid of Kukulcán	
City of Petra	St. Basil's Cathedral	
Christ the Redeemer statue	statue	
Easter Island	Statue of Liberty	
Forbidden City	Stonehenge	
Great Sphinx of Giza	Sydney Opera House	
Great Wall of China	Taj Mahal	
Machu Picchu	temple	
mausoleum	Temple of Borobudur	
monument	tower	
palace		

Expressions

- be held
- bucket list
- DNA testing
- prepare a presentation
- reclaim the land
- thanks to (someone/something)
- That makes sense.
- tourist attractions
- tribute
- work of art

Content Words

archeologist	compile
artifact	gladiator
carving	sea level
dig	structure
goddess	
pharaoh	
remains	
tomb	
treasure	

Grammar/Structures

Stonehenge **was constructed** more than 4,000 years ago.

Louis XIV was a French king **who ruled** for 72 years.

The Statue of Liberty is a landmark **that has become** a symbol of welcome.

Phonics

The sounds: *able, ful, ly*

A World of Wonders Bulletin Board

Create a bulletin-board display titled *A World of Wonders* with a world map at the center. Place pictures and illustrations of famous places and monuments around the map. As students learn about them, help the class add captions with the passive voice and relative clauses to give details. Connect each place to its location with string and a tack. Begin by displaying pictures of places from the Unit Opener. Encourage students to add more famous places as they explore Unit 8.

Language in Context Lesson

Lesson Flow

Warm-up ▸ Lesson Objective ▸ Presentation ▸ Practice 1 ▸ Practice 2 ▸ Practice 3 ▸ Practice 4 ▸ Speaking ▸ Think BIG ▸ Lesson Objective ▸ Homework

Lesson Objective

I will learn to talk about famous places.

Key Language

Forbidden City, Machu Picchu, City of Petra, St. Basil's Cathedral, Stonehenge, Sydney Opera House; built, completed, considered, constructed, dedicated, designed, located, renamed

Warm-up

- Ask: *What's the most famous place in the world?* Ask students to write down the name of a place everyone in the world has heard of. Then have students read their answers aloud and say why they think the place they named is so famous. Invite students to take a class poll to identify the top five or six answers. Help students create a pie graph showing the results.
- Check answers from the HW in the last lesson.

Lesson Objective

INVOLVE

Explain the lesson objective. Say: *Today I will learn to talk about famous places.*

- Tell students that they will read and talk about famous places and learn why they're well known.

Presentation

1 Work with a partner. Match. Then listen and check.

- Read the directions aloud. Do the first item as a class and then have students complete the activity independently in their notebooks.
- Play Audio Track 112 and have students listen and check their answers.

MONITOR

Check answers as a class. (Answers: 1 St. Basil's Cathedral in Russia, 2 the City of Petra in Jordan, 3 the Forbidden City in China, 4 Machu Picchu in Peru, 5 the Sydney Opera House in Australia, 6 Stonehenge in the U.K.)

Practice 1

2 Share your results with the class. Who identified the most places correctly?

- Read the directions aloud. Say: To identify means "to name." Have each student report their findings.

Practice 2

3 Discuss in small groups what you know about these places. Why are they famous?

- Read the directions aloud. Have students complete the activity in small groups.

Practice 3

4 Look at the pictures and read the information about each. Then listen and complete.

- Read the directions aloud. Ask volunteers to describe the pictures. Then play Audio Track 113 and have students listen.

Practice 4

5 Look at 4. Listen and match the descriptions to the places. Note down any new information you learn.

- Read the directions aloud. Play Audio Track 114. Pause after the first one and check that students have noted down the letter b for the image of Big Ben.
- Have students listen to the rest of the descriptions, writing the letters in their notebooks and taking notes.

MONITOR

Pair students, and have partners check each other's answers. (Answers: 1 b, 2 f, 3 a, 4 c, 5 d, 6 e)

Speaking

6 Work with a partner. Talk about the famous places and things. Give as much information as you can.

- Read the directions aloud. Then have volunteers read the speech bubbles aloud. Have students work in pairs to discuss the other famous places and things.

Think BIG

21st Century Information Literacy

- Read the questions aloud and explain to students that they can use the internet for research. Tell students that they can also use pictures or drawings to show their preferred landmark. Have students present their work to the class.

Lesson Objective

INVOLVE

Revisit the lesson objective: *Now I have learned to talk about famous places.*

- Encourage awareness of what students have learned by eliciting the names of a few famous places discussed in the lesson.

Homework   WB pp. 76 & 77/ act. 1, 2, 3, & 4

1 Match the pictures of famous places with the sentences. Why do you think these places are famous? Circle A for architecture, B for natural beauty, or C for mystery. You can circle more than one.

- Direct students to WB Activity 1 on page 76. Students match the pictures with the descriptions and circle A, B, or C. They can circle more than one.

2 Think about your country. What places are famous? Write the names.

- Direct students to WB Activity 2 on page 76. Students choose one to three places for each category.

3 Listen and label the pictures with the words from the box.

- Direct students to WB Activity 3 on page 77. Students listen to the audio and label each picture correctly.

4 Look at 3 and answer the questions.

- Direct students to WB Activity 4 on page 77. Students write their own answers.

Think BIG

- Direct students to WB Think Big on page 77. Students write their own views.

Extra Application and Practice Activity

Materials: Index cards

- Pair students, and have them write the countries and famous places on index cards, one name per card. Have pairs play *Concentration* with the cards.

8 Why Is It Famous?

Language in Context

I will learn to talk about famous places.

1 Work with a partner. Match. Then listen and check.

1.
2.
3.
4.
5.
6.

☐ City of Petra, Jordan
☐ St. Basil's Cathedral, Russia
☐ Forbidden City, China
☐ Stonehenge, the U.K.
☐ Machu Picchu, Peru
☐ Sydney Opera House, Australia

2 Share your results with the class. Who identified the most places correctly?

3 Discuss in small groups what you know about these places. Why are they famous?

4 Look at the pictures and read the information about each. Then listen and complete.

1 **Big Ben (the Elizabeth Tower)**
Location: London, U.K.
When it was completed: _____

2 **Taj Mahal**
Location: Agra, _____
When it was built: 1632–1654

3 **Great Sphinx of Giza**
Location: Giza, _____
When it was built: probably 2558–2532 BC

4 **Temple of Borobudur**
Location: Central Java, Indonesia
When it was built: in the _____ and _____ centuries

5 **Statue of Liberty**
Location: New York City Harbor, U.S.A.
When it was dedicated: _____

6 **Pyramid of Kukulcán (El Castillo) at Chichén Itzá**
Location: Yucatan Peninsula, Mexico
When it was built: AD _____

5 Look at 4. Listen and match the descriptions to the places. Note down any new information you learn.

6 Work with a partner. Talk about the famous places and things. Give as much information as you can.

Is Big Ben a clock, a tower, or a bell?

It's a bell. It hangs inside the Elizabeth Tower in London.

THINK BIG
What do you know about famous landmarks in your country?
Is it important to know about famous landmarks?

Unit 8   **97**

Reading Lesson

Lesson Flow

Warm-up › Lesson Objective › Pre-reading › Reading › Comprehension 1 › Comprehension 2 › Think BIG › Lesson Objective › Homework

Lesson Objective

I will understand a text about a famous place.

Key Language

bone, Easter Island, location, mystery, population, statue; discover, restore; expressionless, faraway, original, volcanic; DNA testing, thanks to (someone/something)

Reading | Nonfiction article

I will understand a text about a famous place.

7 Listen and read. What is another name for Easter Island?

Moai on Easter Island

The Mysteries of Easter Island

For hundreds of years, Easter Island has been a place shrouded in mystery. Have the mysteries of this faraway island finally been solved?

Full of mysteries, Easter Island is a small island that sits in the Pacific Ocean, about 3,500 kilometers to the west of Chile, South America. It's a volcanic island that may once have had a population of 7,000–17,000 people. Today, only 4,000 people live on the island.

Easter Island, known as Rapa Nui to the original settlers, was discovered by Dutch explorers on Easter Day in 1722. Most people know Easter Island today because of the giant statues there, called moai.

For a long time, no one was sure about where the people of Rapa Nui were from. Thanks to DNA testing of old bones, we now know that the original people of Rapa Nui were from Polynesia.

For many years, the statues were also the subject of mystery. The faces of the statues looked expressionless. Many scientists thought the statues represented dead ancestors. In 1979, scientist Sergio Rapu Haoa discovered that long ago the statues had eyes that were made of coral. Since his discovery, many of the eyes of the moai have been restored. With eyes, the statues' faces look very different. They look like proud, strong leaders who watch over Rapa Nui.

> For many years, the statues were also the subject of mystery.

Probably the biggest mystery about the statues today is still this: How were these statues – most of which are more than 4 meters tall and weigh more than 12 tons – moved from the quarry where they were carved out of volcanic rock to various locations around the island?

Some scientists believe the Rapa Nui people used trees to move the statues. They think the tree trunks were used as rollers, or sleds, to pull the statues across the island. Other scientists, however, believe the statues were "walked" across the island. They think ropes were used to rock the statues from side to side, moving them forward a little each time they were rocked. And some people even believe that the statues were moved by aliens with sophisticated technology who helped the Rapa Nui people put the statues in new locations.

Scientists have discovered a lot about this ancient culture over just the last fifty years. Maybe someday they'll solve all of its mysteries.

Moai with eyes restored

Reading Comprehension

8 Read and say true or false. Compare your answers with a partner.

1. The population of Easter Island today is about 7,000.
2. Easter Island is famous because it was discovered on Easter Day.
3. DNA of old bones was used to find out where the people of Rapa Nui were from.
4. In 1979, a scientist discovered that the moai once had eyes that were made of coral.
5. One unsolved mystery is how the statues were moved to different locations on the island.

THINK BIG — How do you think the moai were moved to their locations around the island? Explain. What other places do you know of that hold mysteries like this?

Warm-up

Materials: World map or globe, pins or colored tape

- Provide students with a large world map or globe. Then have them use pins or colored tape to find the famous structures they've read about so far in the unit. Help them find the area of the Pacific Ocean where Easter Island is located and identify it. Tell students they will find out what makes Easter Island famous. Have students take turns pointing to a place they have identified on the map or globe and asking what famous structure can be found there.
- Check answers from the HW in the last lesson.

S98/99 Unit 8

Lesson Objective

INVOLVE

- Introduce the lesson objective. Say: *Today I will learn to understand a text about a famous place.*
- Students will read and discuss a nonfiction article about Easter Island.

Pre-reading

- Have students read the title of the article aloud and ask them to preview the pictures. Have volunteers read the subtitle, pull quote ("For hundreds of years, Easter Island has been a place shrouded in mystery."), and captions aloud.
- Ask students to predict what the passage is about.

Reading 🎧 116

7 Listen and read. What is another name for Easter Island?

- Read the directions aloud. Play Audio Track 116 and have students listen and read along.

ASSIST

Pause after each paragraph and use simple language to explain unfamiliar words, including *shrouded*, *volcanic*, *settlers*, *Polynesia*, *represented*, *ancestors*, *coral*, *carved*, *sophisticated*, *quarry*, and *ancient*.

Comprehension 1

- Ask the question in the directions: *What is another name for Easter Island?* (Its other name is Rapa Nui.)

MONITOR

Ask more questions to check for understanding. Ask: *Where is Easter Island located?* (in the Pacific Ocean, west of Chile) *How many people live there today?* (about 4,000) *Where did the original settlers of the island come from?* (Polynesia) *How do we know?* (Old bones show the origin of the first settlers.) *What are moai?* (giant stone statues on Easter Island) *What are some theories about how the Rapa Nui people moved the statues?* (They used trees to roll or pull the statues; they used ropes to rock and move them; they were helped by aliens.)

- Ask students to compare the eyes in the two moai photos. Discuss how the restored eyes change the appearance of the statues.

CHALLENGE

Ask: *Why do you think the people of Rapa Nui created the moai?* (Sample answers: The statues probably had religious or cultural importance./They might have been created as guardians to protect the island./They might have been created to reflect the culture's values./They might have been memorials to important ancestors or leaders.)

Comprehension 2

8 Read and say *true* or *false*. Compare your answers with a partner.

- Read the directions aloud. Have students work independently to complete the activity before comparing and discussing their answers.

MONITOR

Check answers as a class. (Answers: 1 false, 2 false, 3 true, 4 true, 5 true)

ASSIST

Replay the audio as needed. Suggest that students note down key words in each statement and then find matching words in the article.

Think BIG

21st Century Global Awareness

- Read the questions aloud. Have students discuss their ideas with a partner.

MONITOR

As students talk, check for problems with comprehension and errors with vocabulary, syntax, and use of language. Take a class poll to determine which theory about the moai is most popular among classmates.

Lesson Objective

INVOLVE

- Revisit the lesson objective: *Now I have learned to understand a text about a famous place.*
- Encourage awareness of what students have learned by eliciting something students remember from the article.

Homework 🎧 117 | WB p. 78/ act. 5

5 Listen and read. Then answer the questions.

- Direct students to WB Activity 5 on page 78. Tell students to play the audio, listen, and answer the questions about this famous place in China. Students must write in full sentences.

Extra Application and Practice Activity

Materials: Index cards

- Have students create word puzzles by writing sentences about Easter Island and then rewriting them on index cards, leaving out a word. Have students exchange puzzles and guess the missing words. Model: *The eyes of the moai were originally colored with… .* (coral) *Some people think that… from outer space helped to move the statues on Easter Island.* (aliens)

Unit 8 T98/99

Reading | Nonfiction article

I will understand a text about a famous place.

🎧 7 Listen and read. What is another name for Easter Island?

Moai on Easter Island

The Mysteries of Easter Island

For hundreds of years, Easter Island has been a place shrouded in mystery. Have the mysteries of this faraway island finally been solved?

Full of mysteries, Easter Island is a small island that sits in the Pacific Ocean, about 3,500 kilometers to the west of Chile, South America. It's a volcanic island that may once have had a population of 7,000–17,000 people. Today, only 4,000 people live on the island.

Easter Island, known as Rapa Nui to the original settlers, was discovered by Dutch explorers on Easter Day in 1722. Most people know Easter Island today because of the giant statues there, called moai.

For a long time, no one was sure about where the people of Rapa Nui were from. Thanks to DNA testing of old bones, we now know that the original people of Rapa Nui were from Polynesia.

For many years, the statues were also the subject of mystery.

For many years, the statues were also the subject of mystery. The faces of the statues looked expressionless. Many scientists thought the statues represented dead ancestors. In 1979, scientist Sergio Rapu Haoa discovered that long ago the statues had eyes that were made of coral. Since his discovery, many of the eyes of the moai have been restored. With eyes, the statues' faces look very different. They look like proud, strong leaders who watch over Rapa Nui.

98 Unit 8

Probably the biggest mystery about the statues today is still this: How were these statues – most of which are more than 4 meters tall and weigh more than 12 tons – moved from the quarry where they were carved out of volcanic rock to various locations around the island?

Some scientists believe the Rapa Nui people used trees to move the statues. They think the tree trunks were used as rollers, or sleds, to pull the statues across the island. Other scientists, however, believe the statues were "walked" across the island. They think ropes were used to rock the statues from side to side, moving them forward a little each time they were rocked. And some people even believe that the statues were moved by aliens with sophisticated technology who helped the Rapa Nui people put the statues in new locations.

Moai with eyes restored

Scientists have discovered a lot about this ancient culture over just the last fifty years. Maybe someday they'll solve all of its mysteries.

Reading Comprehension

8 Read and say true or false. Compare your answers with a partner.

1 The population of Easter Island today is about 7,000.
2 Easter Island is famous because it was discovered on Easter Day.
3 DNA of old bones was used to find out where the people of Rapa Nui were from.
4 In 1979, a scientist discovered that the moai once had eyes that were made of coral.
5 One unsolved mystery is how the statues were moved to different locations on the island.

THINK BIG

How do you think the moai were moved to their locations around the island? Explain.
What other places do you know of that hold mysteries like this?

Language in Action Lesson

Lesson Flow

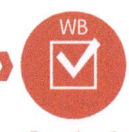

Warm-up › Lesson Objective › Pre-listening › Listening › Comprehension › Role Play › Practice 1 (SB) › Practice 2 (WB) › Lesson Objective › Homework

Lesson Objective

I will listen to a dialog about visiting famous places.

Key Language

honor, island, pyramids, (trading) ship; appreciate, build, construct, design, take pictures; bucket list, prepare a presentation, reclaim the land, thanks to (someone/something), That makes sense., tourist attraction, tribute, work of art

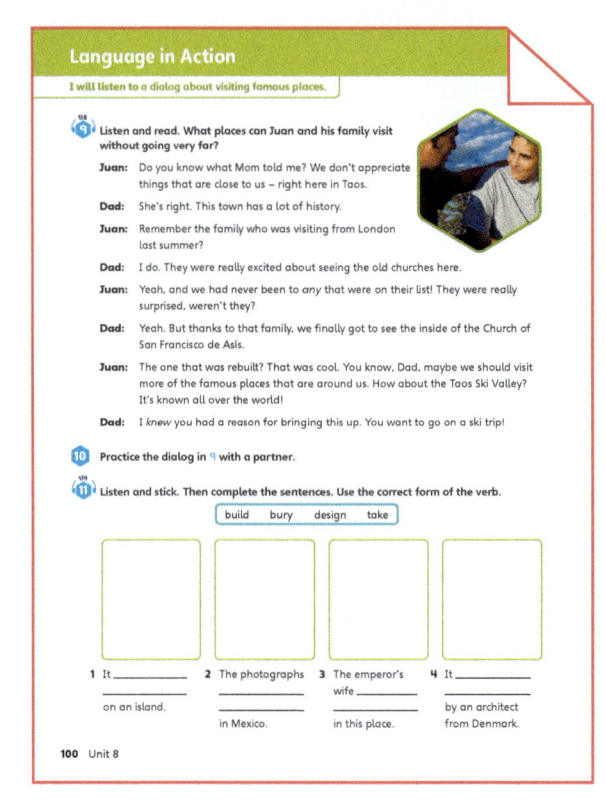

Language in Action

I will listen to a dialog about visiting famous places.

9 Listen and read. What places can Juan and his family visit without going very far?

Juan: Do you know what Mom told me? We don't appreciate things that are close to us – right here in Taos.

Dad: She's right. This town has a lot of history.

Juan: Remember the family who was visiting from London last summer?

Dad: I do. They were really excited about seeing the old churches here.

Juan: Yeah, and we had never been to *any* that were on their list! They were really surprised, weren't they?

Dad: Yeah. But thanks to that family, we finally got to see the inside of the Church of San Francisco de Asís.

Juan: The one that was rebuilt? That was cool. You know, Dad, maybe we should visit more of the famous places that are around us. How about the Taos Ski Valley? It's known all over the world!

Dad: I *knew* you had a reason for bringing this up. You want to go on a ski trip!

10 Practice the dialog in 9 with a partner.

11 Listen and stick. Then complete the sentences. Use the correct form of the verb.

build   bury   design   take

1 It _____ on an island.
2 The photographs _____ in Mexico.
3 The emperor's wife _____ in this place.
4 It _____ by an architect from Denmark.

100 Unit 8

Warm-up

- Play *Hangman* with the class, using one or more of these places as the secret phrase: *Taos, New Mexico; Sydney Opera House; Taj Mahal; pyramid*. Write a line for each letter, leaving a space between words and including punctuation. Have students guess the letters. Reveal the letters when students guess correctly.
- Check answers from the HW in the last lesson.

Lesson Objective

INVOLVE

Introduce the lesson objective. Say: *Today I will listen to a dialog about visiting famous places.*

- Students will read, listen to, and practice a dialog. Students will also listen to conversations about famous places.

Pre-listening

- Tell students that they are going to listen to Juan and his dad talking about famous places to visit.
- Point to Juan and his dad in the picture. Point out their names in the text.

S100 Unit 8

Listening 🎧 118 🔊

9 Listen and read. What places can Juan and his family visit without going very far?

- Read the directions aloud. Play Audio Track 118 and have students listen and read along.
- Invite a pair to read the dialog aloud and repeat.

MONITOR
As students practice, listen for correct pronunciation and use of language.

Comprehension 💡

- Ask the question in the directions: *What places can Juan and his family visit without going very far?* (old churches, Taos Ski Valley)

MONITOR
Ask more questions to check for understanding. Encourage students to answer in complete sentences, where appropriate. Ask: *Does Juan's mother think Taos has interesting things to see?* (Yes; she told Juan that they don't appreciate things that are close to them.) *What did Juan and his family do because of the family from London?* (They visited a famous church.)

CHALLENGE
Invite students to use internet resources to find out more about Taos and share their findings with the class.

21st Century Environmental Literacy

- Have students discuss both positive and negative effects of tourist attractions like those discussed. (*Positive effects include increased jobs and money in an area; negative effects include congestion and pollution.*) Have students discuss strategies for limiting the negative effects of tourism. (*Solutions include limiting the number of visitors allowed at certain times and passing strict laws about pollution.*)

Role Play 🌍 🎭

10 Practice the dialog in 9 with a partner.

- Read the directions aloud. Have students pair to read the dialog aloud, switch parts, and repeat.

MONITOR
As students practice, listen for correct pronunciation and correct use of language.

Practice 1 🎧 119 P. T150 ✓

Materials: Stickers

1 Listen and stick. Then complete the sentences. Use the correct form of the verb.

- Help students find the Unit 8 stickers at the back of the Student's Book. Ask them to describe each sticker. Read the directions aloud.

- Play Audio Track 119. Have students listen, place each sticker next to the appropriate number, and complete the sentences using a form of a verb from the box.

MONITOR
As students work, make sure they place the stickers correctly. Check answers as a class. (*Answers: 1 was built, 2 were taken, 3 was buried, 4 was designed*)

ASSIST
Replay the audio. Pause after each conversation and use simple language to explain unfamiliar words. For example, say: *To construct* means to build. *Marble* is a hard stone that can be polished.

Practice 2 🎧 120 WB p. 79/ act. 6 ✓

6 Listen and read. Then answer the question.

- Read the directions aloud.
- Play Audio Track 120 twice. The second time, have students circle the words they do not understand. Explain their meaning.
- Read the question as a class. Prompt students to find the answer in the text and write their answer.

Lesson Objective 📈

INVOLVE
Revisit the lesson objective: *Now I have listened to a dialog about visiting famous places.*

- Encourage awareness of what students have learned by eliciting the names of places Juan has visited or would like to visit.

Homework 🎧 121 P. T151 WB p. 79/ act. 7 & 8 🖨

7 Look at 6. Read the underlined expressions. Match the expressions with their meanings. Write the letters.

- Direct students to WB Activity 7 on page 79. Students match 1–4 with a phrase a–d that explains the meaning.

8 Complete with three of the expressions in 7. Then listen and check.

- Direct students to WB Activity 8 on page 79. Students complete the activity using three expressions from the previous activity, then listen to the audio to check their answers.

Extra Application and Practice Activity

- Explain that the phrase *bucket list* comes from the saying *to kick the bucket*, which means "to die." Tell students that a bucket list includes things you would like to do or see before you die. Have students write a bucket list that includes at least five items, two of which are places they would like to visit. Have them explain why they would like to go to each.

Unit 8 **T100**

Language in Action

I will listen to a dialog about visiting famous places.

9 Listen and read. What places can Juan and his family visit without going very far?

Juan: Do you know what Mom told me? We don't appreciate things that are close to us – right here in Taos.

Dad: She's right. This town has a lot of history.

Juan: Remember the family who was visiting from London last summer?

Dad: I do. They were really excited about seeing the old churches here.

Juan: Yeah, and we had never been to *any* that were on their list! They were really surprised, weren't they?

Dad: Yeah. But thanks to that family, we finally got to see the inside of the Church of San Francisco de Asís.

Juan: The one that was rebuilt? That was cool. You know, Dad, maybe we should visit more of the famous places that are around us. How about the Taos Ski Valley? It's known all over the world!

Dad: I *knew* you had a reason for bringing this up. You want to go on a ski trip!

10 Practice the dialog in 9 with a partner.

11 Listen and stick. Then complete the sentences. Use the correct form of the verb.

build   bury   design   take

1 It _____ _____ on an island.

2 The photographs _____ _____ in Mexico.

3 The emperor's wife _____ _____ in this place.

4 It _____ _____ by an architect from Denmark.

100 Unit 8

Grammar

I will learn to use the passive voice.
I will learn to use relative clauses with *who* and *that* to make descriptions.

Active	Passive
Archeologists discovered Machu Picchu in 1911.	Machu Picchu **was discovered** in 1911 (by archeologists).

12 Say whether each sentence is active or passive.

1. The Great Wall of China is visited by millions of tourists each year.
2. Augustus Pugin designed London's Elizabeth Tower.
3. Two hundred thousand workers constructed the Forbidden City.
4. The City of Petra was made a new wonder of the world by millions of voters.
5. The Sydney Opera House was opened to the public in 1973.

Leonardo da Vinci is the famous artist and inventor **who painted** the *Mona Lisa*. The Eiffel Tower is a landmark **that has become** the symbol of Paris, France.

Tip: A relative clause describes a noun. The relative pronouns *who* and *that* are used to describe people; *that* is used to describe things.

13 Rewrite the two sentences as one sentence in your notebook.

1. The Statue of Liberty is a landmark. It has become a symbol of welcome.
2. Van Gogh was a famous Dutch painter. He painted *Starry Night*.
3. The Great Sphinx of Giza is a famous landmark. It has become famous for its broken nose.
4. The Taj Mahal is a beautiful mausoleum. It was built in memory of Mumtaz Mahal.
5. Buckingham Palace is a landmark. It has become the most famous palace in the U.K.
6. Borobudur is a temple. It is located in Java, Indonesia.
7. The Christ the Redeemer statue is a landmark. It was built by Heitor da Silva Costa.
8. Postnik Yakovlev is a Russian architect. He helped to design St. Basil's Cathedral in Moscow.

Grammar Lesson

Lesson Flow

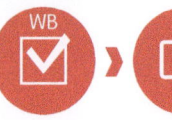

Warm-up › Lesson Objective › Presentation 1 › Practice 1 (SB) › Practice 2 (WB) › Presentation 2 › Practice 3 (SB) › Practice 4 (WB) › Lesson Objective › Homework

Lesson Objectives

I will learn to use the passive voice.

I will learn to use relative clauses with *who* and *that* to make descriptions.

Key Language

Stonehenge **was constructed** more than 4,000 years ago.

Louis XIV was a French king **who ruled** for 72 years.

The Statue of Liberty is a landmark **that has become** a symbol of welcome.

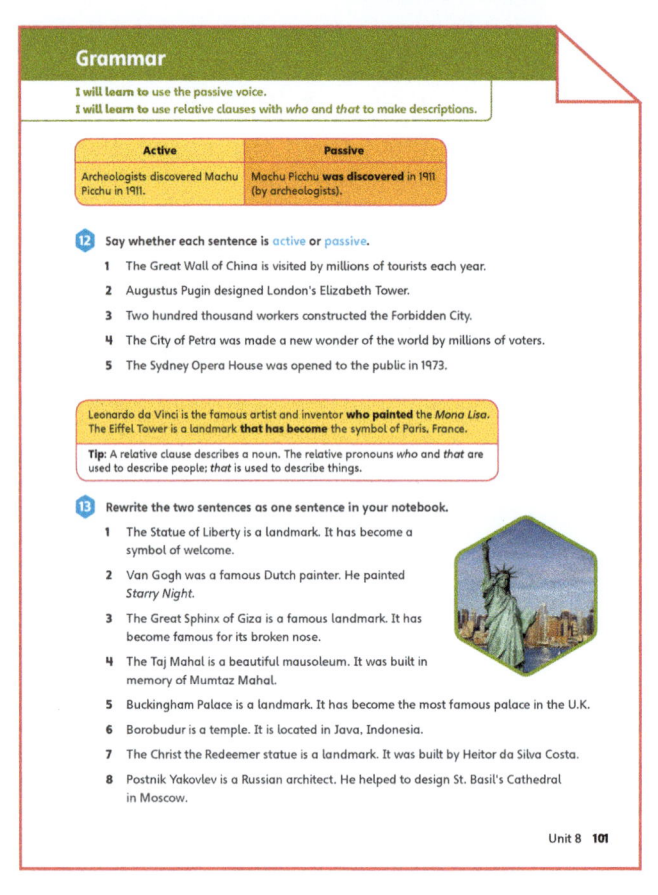

Grammar

I will learn to use the passive voice.
I will learn to use relative clauses with *who* and *that* to make descriptions.

Active	Passive
Archeologists discovered Machu Picchu in 1911.	Machu Picchu **was discovered** in 1911 (by archeologists).

12 Say whether each sentence is *active* or *passive*.
1. The Great Wall of China is visited by millions of tourists each year.
2. Augustus Pugin designed London's Elizabeth Tower.
3. Two hundred thousand workers constructed the Forbidden City.
4. The City of Petra was made a new wonder of the world by millions of voters.
5. The Sydney Opera House was opened to the public in 1973.

Leonardo da Vinci is the famous artist and inventor **who painted** the *Mona Lisa*.
The Eiffel Tower is a landmark **that has become** the symbol of Paris, France.

Tip: A relative clause describes a noun. The relative pronouns *who* and *that* are used to describe people; *that* is used to describe things.

13 Rewrite the two sentences as one sentence in your notebook.
1. The Statue of Liberty is a landmark. It has become a symbol of welcome.
2. Van Gogh was a famous Dutch painter. He painted *Starry Night*.
3. The Great Sphinx of Giza is a famous landmark. It has become famous for its broken nose.
4. The Taj Mahal is a beautiful mausoleum. It was built in memory of Mumtaz Mahal.
5. Buckingham Palace is a landmark. It has become the most famous palace in the U.K.
6. Borobudur is a temple. It is located in Java, Indonesia.
7. The Christ the Redeemer statue is a landmark. It was built by Heitor da Silva Costa.
8. Postnik Yakovlev is a Russian architect. He helped to design St. Basil's Cathedral in Moscow.

Unit 8 101

Warm-up

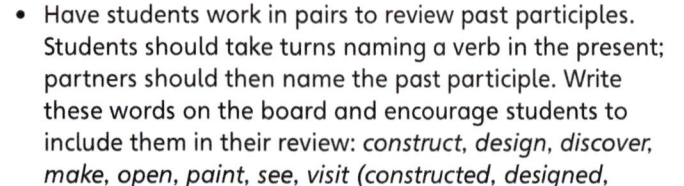

- Have students work in pairs to review past participles. Students should take turns naming a verb in the present; partners should then name the past participle. Write these words on the board and encourage students to include them in their review: *construct, design, discover, make, open, paint, see, visit* (constructed, designed, discovered, made, opened, painted, seen, visited).
- Check answers from the HW in the last lesson.

Lesson Objective

INVOLVE

Introduce the lesson objective. Say: *Today I will learn to use the passive voice, and relative clauses with* who *and* that *to make descriptions.*

- Students will use the passive voice and relative clauses in sentences.

Presentation 1

- Have volunteers read the sentences in the first grammar box aloud. Say: *In the active voice, the subject of a sentence performs the action. In the passive voice, the subject of the sentence receives the action.* Draw students' attention to the sample active-voice sentence. Ask: *What's the subject?* (archeologists) *What did they do?* (discovered Machu Picchu) *What's the subject of the passive-voice sentence?* (Machu Picchu) *Did Machu Picchu do anything?* (No; it was discovered.)

CHALLENGE

- Have volunteers write a sentence in the active voice on the board, and another rewrite it in the passive voice.

Practice 1

12 Say whether each sentence is active or passive.

- Read the directions aloud and complete Item 1 as a class. Then have students complete the activity independently.

MONITOR

- Check answers as a class. *(Answers: 1 passive, 2 active, 3 active, 4 passive, 5 passive)*

ASSIST

- Have students underline the subject and circle the verb in each sentence. Say: *The passive voice uses a form of* be *and a participle.*

CHALLENGE

- Have students rewrite each sentence, changing active-voice sentences to passive and passive-voice sentences to active.

Practice 2 WB p. 80/ act. 9

9 Complete the sentences. Use *is* or *are* and the correct form of the verb in parentheses.

- Read the directions aloud. Complete Item 1 as a class. Say: *How can we use the word* know *in the passive form?* (are known)

Presentation 2

- Have volunteers read the sentences and tip in the second grammar box aloud. Say: *A relative clause isn't a complete sentence.* Have students read the relative clauses in the examples aloud. *(who painted the Mona Lisa; that has become the symbol of Paris, France)*

Practice 3

13 Rewrite the two sentences as one sentence in your notebook.

- Read the directions aloud, then write the first item on the board, and read it as a class.
- Have students complete the activity independently.

MONITOR

- Check answers as a class. *(Answers: 1 The Statue of Liberty is a landmark that has become a symbol of welcome. 2 Van Gogh was a famous Dutch painter who painted Starry Night. 3 The Great Sphinx of Giza is a landmark that has become famous for its broken nose. 4 The Taj Mahal is a beautiful mausoleum that was built in memory of Mumtaz Mahal. 5 Buckingham Palace is a landmark that has become the most famous palace in the U.K. 6 Borobudur is a temple that is located in Java, Indonesia. 7 The Christ the Redeemer statue is a landmark that was built by Heitor da Silva Costa. 8 Postnik Yakovlev is a Russian architect who helped to design St. Basil's Cathedral in Moscow.)*

Practice 4 WB p. 81/ act. 12

12 Complete the sentences with *who* or *that*.

- Read the directions aloud. Ask: *Are the tortoises people, or things?* (Answer: things, so we write *that*.)

Lesson Objective

INVOLVE

- Revisit the lesson objective: *Now I have learned to use the passive voice, and relative clauses with* who *and* that *to make descriptions.*
- Encourage awareness of what students have learned by giving an active voice sentence from the unit, such as: *Archeologists discovered Machu Picchu in 1911.* Ask students to change it to the passive voice.

Homework WB pp. 80 & 81/ act. 10, 11, 13, & 14

10 Write *A* for active or *P* for passive next to each sentence.

- Direct students to WB Activity 10 on page 80. Students write an *A* or *P* in the space before each sentence.

11 Write sentences with the passive form of the verb.

- Direct students to WB Activity 11 on page 80. Students write sentence in the passive form.

13 Read and match. Write the letters.

- Direct students to WB Activity 13 on page 81. Students match 1–4 with information related to a–d.

14 Look at 13. Rewrite the matching sentences as one sentence.

- Direct students to WB Activity 14 on page 81. Students rewrite two matched sentences in 13 as one sentence.

Extra Application and Practice Activity

21st Century Creativity

- Place students in small groups and have them make a grammar poster for the passive voice and relative clauses. Encourage them to make sentences that can be used as examples and to use different colors to show verb form changes and pronouns.

Unit 8 **T101**

Content Connection Lesson

Lesson Flow

Warm-up › Lesson Objective › Pre-reading › Reading › Practice 1 (WB) › Practice 2 (SB) › Think BIG › Lesson Objective › Homework

Lesson Objective

I will learn about accidental discoveries of amazing places.

Key Language

archeologist, artifact, carving, dig, goddess, pharaoh, remains, tomb, treasure

---

Content Connection | History

I will learn about accidental discoveries of amazing places.

CONTENT WORDS
archeologist, artifact, carving, dig, goddess, pharaoh, remains, tomb, treasure

14 Listen and read. Which archeologist discovered the tomb of King Tutankhamen?

Accidental Discoveries

Finding things from the past is exciting, and archeologists spend years studying ancient texts and history books in order to discover ancient places. Tombs, palaces, important treasures, sometimes whole cities are hidden underground, under layers of earth and rock. Sometimes they're found with careful research and digging, but sometimes they're discovered by accident!

In 1978, a new subway system for Mexico City was being constructed near the national cathedral. As the workers were digging, they discovered a huge carved stone! Workers had archeologists brought in. They immediately confirmed that the stone was a giant carving of the Aztec moon goddess.

These were the remains of an Aztec temple from the ancient city of Tenochtitlan. Soon a pyramid was uncovered, which scientists dated to AD 1325! Built on top of the original pyramid were another six pyramids. In total, more than 7,000 different artifacts were also found at the site. Before this surprise discovery, archeologists believed that Spanish people had destroyed the temple to build the cathedral. Today, if you visit the Zócalo, which is in the heart of Mexico City, you can see the artifacts in the Templo Mayor Museum nearby.

The discovery of King Tutankhamen's tomb in the Valley of the Kings in Egypt might be the most famous accidental discovery of its kind. The Valley of the Kings is home to more than sixty tombs in which ancient pharaohs and kings are buried. In 1922, most archeologists had given up looking for tombs there because they were convinced that everything had been discovered. But one archeologist, Howard Carter, continued looking.

He wasn't disappointed. Working with some friends, he discovered the entrance to the tomb of King Tutankhamen. It's the most well-preserved ancient tomb that has ever been found. The tomb survived 3,000 years, even though robbers and floods destroyed many of the other tombs from that region. The artifacts from the tomb that once belonged to King Tutankhamen can now be seen in the Cairo Museum in Egypt.

15 Look at the passage. Read and say *Mexico* or *Egypt*.
1. Archeologists believed this discovery had been destroyed.
2. Many other discoveries were destroyed by thieves and water.
3. Archeologists had given up looking for this discovery.
4. This discovery was made in the busy city center.

THINK BIG Would you like to work as an archeologist? Why/Why not?

102 Unit 8

Warm-up

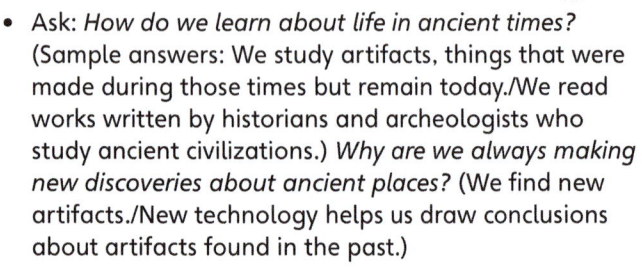

- Ask: *How do we learn about life in ancient times?* (Sample answers: We study artifacts, things that were made during those times but remain today./We read works written by historians and archeologists who study ancient civilizations.) *Why are we always making new discoveries about ancient places?* (We find new artifacts./New technology helps us draw conclusions about artifacts found in the past.)
- Check answers from the HW in the last lesson.

Lesson Objective

INVOLVE

Introduce the lesson objective. Say: *Today I will learn about accidental discoveries of amazing places.*

- Students will read a history text about two famous archeological discoveries: ancient pyramids in Mexico and the tomb of King Tutankhamen in Egypt.

Pre-reading

- Write the word *archeology* on the board. Explain to students that *archeo* is a Greek root that means "ancient history," and that the suffix *–ology* means "the study of." So the word *archeology* means "the study of ancient history."
- Read the Content Words with students and elicit or supply general meanings. Have students write the words and definitions in their notebooks.
- Read the title of the article and point to the picture. Ask: *What do you think this article is about?* Allow students to share their ideas.
- Draw their attention to the two different-colored blocks of texts and suggest that there might be two examples of accidental discoveries.

Reading

14 Listen and read. Which archeologist discovered the tomb of King Tutankhamen?

- Play Audio Track 122 and have students follow along in their books, listening for the Content Words.

ASSIST
- Play the track again as needed to allow students to find all the Content Words.
- Read the first paragraph aloud with the class. After you finish, help students use context clues from the text to add detail to their definitions of the Content Words, e.g. *An archeologist is someone who studies texts and books to discover ancient places.*
- Have students continue the process in pairs for the remainder of the article.

MONITOR
- Invite volunteers to share what they learned about the Content Words. Then, ask the class which archeologist discovered the tomb of King Tutankhamen (*Howard Carter*).

CHALLENGE
- Have students write fill-in-the-blank sentences based on the Content Words, e.g. *A(n)... discovered the Mayan ruins.* (archeologist) Ask students to trade sentences with a partner and fill in the missing words.

Practice 1   WB p. 82/ act. 15

15 Read and circle the correct answers.

- Read the directions aloud. Explain to students that they have to read the text and circle the correct answers.
- Have volunteers read the title aloud and describe the picture.

Practice 2

15 Look at the passage. Read and say *Mexico* or *Egypt*.

- Place students in pairs. Have partners take turns reading the items and saying whether they refer to Mexico or Egypt.

MONITOR
- Invite volunteers to share their answers with the class. (Answers: 1 Mexico, 2 Egypt, 3 Egypt, 4 Mexico).

21st Century Critical Thinking

- Ask: *How did sites like these become lost?* (Sample answers: They were buried over time./Writing about the locations did not survive./Historians knew about the ancient structures, but most assumed they had been destroyed and were lost forever.)

Think BIG

21st Century Creativity and Imagination

- Allow students to imagine what it would be like to be an archeologist. Encourage them to openly share their thoughts.

Lesson Objective

INVOLVE
- Revisit the lesson objective: *Now I have learned about accidental discoveries of amazing places.*
- Encourage awareness of what students have learned by eliciting from them some information about one of the accidental discoveries in the article.

Homework   WB p. 82/ act. 16

16 Listen and read. Then circle *T* for true or *F* for false.

- Direct students to WB Activity 16 on page 82. Students complete the activity, circling *T* or *F*.

Extra Application and Practice Activity

- Have students find out more about the Templo Mayor Museum in Mexico City and the Cairo Museum in Egypt. People can see the artifacts from these finds in these two museums.
- Have students work individually to write a few sentences saying which of the two museums they would most like to visit and why. Have them find or draw a picture of an artifact in the museum to use as a visual aid.
- Then ask them to present the picture and their information to the class. Discuss which students had similar opinions.

Unit 8   T102

Content Connection | History

I will learn about accidental discoveries of amazing places.

14 Listen and read. Which archeologist discovered the tomb of King Tutankhamen?

CONTENT WORDS
archeologist   artifact
carving   dig   goddess
pharaoh   remains
tomb   treasure

Accidental Discoveries

Finding things from the past is exciting, and archeologists spend years studying ancient texts and history books in order to discover ancient places. Tombs, palaces, important treasures, sometimes whole cities are hidden underground, under layers of earth and rock. Sometimes they're found with careful research and digging, but sometimes they're discovered by accident!

In 1978, a new subway system for Mexico City was being constructed near the national cathedral. As the workers were digging, they discovered a huge carved stone! Workers had archeologists brought in. They immediately confirmed that the stone was a giant carving of the Aztec moon goddess.

These were the remains of an Aztec temple from the ancient city of Tenochtitlan. Soon a pyramid was uncovered, which scientists dated to AD 1325! Built on top of the original pyramid were another six pyramids. In total, more than 7,000 different artifacts were also found at the site. Before this surprise discovery, archeologists believed that Spanish people had destroyed the temple to build the cathedral. Today, if you visit the Zócalo, which is in the heart of Mexico City, you can see the artifacts in the Templo Mayor Museum nearby.

The discovery of King Tutankhamen's tomb in the Valley of the Kings in Egypt might be the most famous accidental discovery of its kind. The Valley of the Kings is home to more than sixty tombs in which ancient pharaohs and kings are buried. In 1922, most archeologists had given up looking for tombs there because they were convinced that everything had been discovered. But one archeologist, Howard Carter, continued looking.

He wasn't disappointed. Working with some friends, he discovered the entrance to the tomb of King Tutankhamen. It's the most well-preserved ancient tomb that has ever been found. The tomb survived 3,000 years, even though robbers and floods destroyed many of the other tombs from that region. The artifacts from the tomb that once belonged to King Tutankhamen can now be seen in the Cairo Museum in Egypt.

15 Look at the passage. Read and say Mexico or Egypt.

1. Archeologists believed this discovery had been destroyed.
2. Many other discoveries were destroyed by thieves and water.
3. Archeologists had given up looking for this discovery.
4. This discovery was made in the busy city center.

THINK BIG
Would you like to work as an archeologist? Why/Why not?

102 Unit 8

Culture Connection | Around the World

I will learn about the new seven wonders of the world.

CONTENT WORDS
compile   gladiator   sea level
structure

🎧 **16** Listen and read. Where is the Temple of the Sun?

The New Seven World Wonders

What exactly are the seven wonders of the world? Who created the list and when?

The list was first compiled by the historian Herodotus in the 5th century BC. His list was created using sights that were popular with Greek sightseers. Seven were chosen because the Greeks believed seven was a perfect number.

Over the years there have been a number of different lists, but in 2001, a Swiss company decided to have a new list made with seven wonders of the modern world.

These are the places that received the final vote:

1 Petra: The structures of this city in Jordan, in western Asia, were carved into rock and sandstone.

2 Taj Mahal: When Mumtaz Mahal, the wife of Emperor Shah Jahan, died, the Indian emperor had this temple built, between 1632 and 1654.

3 Great Wall of China: Built from the 5th century BC to the 16th century. This wall was built more than 2,000 years ago to keep enemies out.

4 Kukulcán Pyramid at Chichén Itzá: Chichén Itzá is an archeological site on the Yucatan Peninsula. Kukulcán, a thirty-meter-high pyramid and temple, is its most famous landmark.

5 Machu Picchu: This ancient Incan city is 2,430 meters above sea level and consists of 150 buildings. Its most famous structure, the Temple of the Sun, is made of solid rock.

6 Statue of Christ the Redeemer: Built between 1922 and 1931. Standing 38 meters tall at the top of a mountain is a statue of Christ with his arms outstretched. The statue looks out over the city of Rio de Janeiro, Brazil.

7 Roman Colosseum: During the time of the Roman Empire, the Colosseum was used for battles between gladiators and for other forms of entertainment.

17 Look at the passage. Answer the questions.

1. Who created the first list of wonders?
2. Why were there seven?
3. When was the modern list created?
4. What was Petra made of?
5. Why was the Great Wall of China built?
6. Who was Mumtaz Mahal?
7. What is Kukulcán?
8. Which wonder was built after 1900?

THINK BIG Which are more important, natural world wonders or man-made world wonders? Why?

Culture Connection Lesson

Lesson Flow

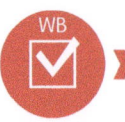

Warm-up › Lesson Objective › Pre-reading › Reading › Practice 1 › Practice 2 › Think BIG › Video › Lesson Objective › Homework

Lesson Objective

I will learn about the new seven wonders of the world.

Key Language

compile, gladiator, sea level, structure

Culture Connection | Around the World

I will learn about the new seven wonders of the world.

CONTENT WORDS
compile, gladiator, sea level, structure

16 Listen and read. Where is the Temple of the Sun?

The New Seven World Wonders

What exactly are the seven wonders of the world? Who created the list and when?

The list was first compiled by the historian Herodotus in the 5th century BC. His list was created using sights that were popular with Greek sightseers. Seven were chosen because the Greeks believed seven was a perfect number.

Over the years there have been a number of different lists, but in 2001, a Swiss company decided to have a new list made with seven wonders of the modern world.

These are the places that received the final vote:

1 Petra: The structures of this city in Jordan, in western Asia, were carved into rock and sandstone.

2 Taj Mahal: When Mumtaz Mahal, the wife of Emperor Shah Jahan, died, the Indian emperor had this temple built, between 1632 and 1654.

3 Great Wall of China: Built from the 5th century BC to the 16th century. This wall was built more than 2,000 years ago to keep enemies out.

4 Kukulcán Pyramid at Chichén Itzá: Chichén Itzá is an archeological site on the Yucatan Peninsula. Kukulcán, a thirty-meter-high pyramid and temple, is its most famous landmark.

5 Machu Picchu: This ancient Incan city is 2,430 meters above sea level and consists of 150 buildings. Its most famous structure, the Temple of the Sun, is made of solid rock.

6 Statue of Christ the Redeemer: Built between 1922 and 1931. Standing 38 meters tall at the top of a mountain is a statue of Christ with his arms outstretched. The statue looks out over the city of Rio de Janeiro, Brazil.

7 Roman Colosseum: During the time of the Roman Empire, the Colosseum was used for battles between gladiators and for other forms of entertainment.

17 Look at the passage. Answer the questions.

1. Who created the first list of wonders?
2. Why were there seven?
3. When was the modern list created?
4. What was Petra made of?
5. Why was the Great Wall of China built?
6. Who was Mumtaz Mahal?
7. What is Kukulcán?
8. Which wonder was built after 1900?

THINK BIG Which are more important, natural world wonders or man-made world wonders? Why?

Unit 8 103

Warm-up

- Write on the board: *The Most Amazing Place in the World*. Have students brainstorm some amazing places they know. Tell students that something truly amazing can be called a wonder. Ask students if they have ever heard of the phrase "seven wonders of the ancient world." Tell them that people have chosen new "wonders" for our modern world.

- Check answers from the HW in the last lesson.

Lesson Objective

INVOLVE

- Introduce the lesson objective. Say: *Today I will learn about the new seven wonders of the world.*
- Students will read and talk about the seven wonders of the world.

Pre-reading

- Write the words *empire, gladiator, landmark,* and *sea level* on the board. Have students underline each one in the article and use context clues to determine its meaning.
- Invite a volunteer to read the title and subtitle aloud. Point to the numbers 1 to 7. Have students predict what the text is about.

Reading 🎧124

16 Listen and read. Where is the Temple of the Sun?

- Play Audio Track 124 and have students listen and read.

MONITOR

- Discuss the answer as a class. *(Answer: Machu Picchu)*

ASSIST

- Replay the audio as needed. Use simple language and gestures to explain unfamiliar words.
- Draw a timeline of wonders on the board, and complete it as a class, based on dates students find in the text. (Note that some wonders were constructed over a long period of time, and the timeline should reflect this fact.) Have students copy the timeline into their notebooks.

Practice 1

17 Look at the passage. Answer the questions.

- Read the directions aloud. Pair students, and have partners take turns asking and answering the questions.

MONITOR

- Check answers as a class. *(Answers: 1 Herodotus, 2 The Greeks considered seven a perfect number. 3 2001, 4 rock and sandstone, 5 to keep enemies out, 6 the wife of emperor Shah Jahan, 7 a pyramid and a temple, 8 the statue of Christ the Redeemer)*

CHALLENGE

- Have students write vocabulary words from the reading, e.g. *pyramid, sandstone,* on strips of paper. Have students close their books, exchange strips of paper, and determine which wonder the word is related to.

Practice 2 🎧125 📋 WB p. 83/ act. 17

17 Read and complete using the words in the box. Then listen and check.

- Read the directions aloud. Students fill in the correct word to complete each sentence. Play Audio Track 125 and have students check answers.

Think BIG

21st Century Critical Thinking

- Read the questions aloud. First, ask students to discuss the difference between man-made and natural wonders. Elicit examples of each.
- In small groups, have students discuss whether they think man-made or natural wonders are more important. Invite volunteers to share their ideas and their reasoning.
- As a class, brainstorm ideas as to what we can do to help protect and take care of the wonders in our world.

Video Documentary U 08

- Refer to the Video Guide for pre-watching and post-watching activities.

Lesson Objective

INVOLVE

- Revisit the lesson objective: *Now I have learned about the new seven wonders of the world, and connected a text to personal experience.*
- Encourage awareness of what students have learned by eliciting the names of a few of the new seven wonders of the world.

Homework WB p. 83/ act. 18

18 Read 17 again and anser the questions.

- Direct students to WB Activity 18 on page 93. Students answer in complete sentences.

Extra Application and Practice Activity

- Point to the question at the end of the article, and read it aloud: *Which other place would get your vote as the eighth wonder?* Have students work individually or in pairs to decide on a possible eighth wonder of the world. Ask them to write a brief explanation.

ASSIST

- As students are working, walk around and provide language and vocabulary as needed.
- Have different students present their ideas. Then have the class vote on a new eighth wonder.

Unit 8 **T103**

Writing Lesson

Lesson Flow

Warm-up › Lesson Objective › Practice 1 (WB) › Practice 2 (SB) › Practice 3 (SB) › Practice 4 (SB) › Speaking › Lesson Objective › Homework

Lesson Objective

I will learn to write a report about a country.

Writing | Report

I will learn to write a report about a country.

18 Read the report. Then copy the idea web and use the information to complete it.

> Australia is one of the seven continents, but it's also a country. It's known as the smallest continent in the world. Do you know why it's called "the land down under"? It's because Australia is located below the equator.
> More than 22 million people live in Australia. Aborigines are the original inhabitants of Australia, but people from many different countries have come to Australia to live. Today, most people in Australia speak English.
> The capital of Australia is Canberra. Other big and important cities in Australia are Sydney, Melbourne, Brisbane, and Perth.

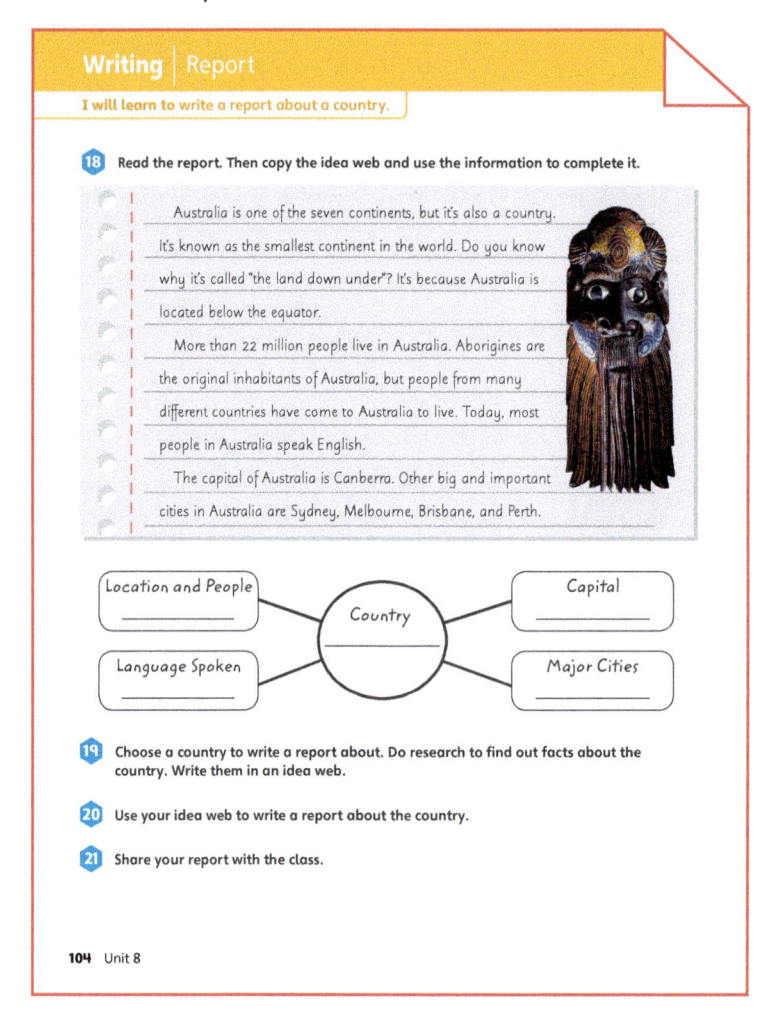

Idea web: Country — Location and People, Capital, Language Spoken, Major Cities

19 Choose a country to write a report about. Do research to find out facts about the country. Write them in an idea web.

20 Use your idea web to write a report about the country.

21 Share your report with the class.

104 Unit 8

Warm-up

Materials: World map or globe

- Do this activity to help students generate ideas for countries they'd like to use for their reports. Have students work in small groups and look back over the unit and choose the famous place they'd most like to see or visit. Have them find the place on a world map or globe. Then have them choose a country near it or the one where it's located. Have them use what they know about the country and do a little research on it. Then have groups come together and take turns providing clues for other groups to guess the country. Tell them to use more general clues at first and then more specific ones to make the activity more challenging.

- Check answers from the HW in the last lesson.

Lesson Objective

INVOLVE

Introduce the lesson objective. Say: *Today I will learn to write a report about a country.*

- Students will read and write a report about a country.

S104 Unit 8

Practice 1 — WB p. 84/ act. 19

19 Look at the facts. Write the number of each fact in the correct category.

- Have volunteers read the tips for writing a well-written report in the purple box aloud.
- Read the directions aloud. Have volunteers read the facts numbered 1–8. Tell students they are going to write the numbers of each in the correct category.
- Read the three categories aloud. As a class, discuss which facts go into which categories.
- Have students complete the activity, then check the answers as a class.

Practice 2

18 Read the report. Then copy the idea web and use the information to complete it.

- Read the directions aloud. Then have volunteers read the report aloud. Remind students that a paragraph is a group of sentences about one idea. Ask: *What's the topic of each paragraph in this report?* (First paragraph: General facts and location; Second paragraph: Population, people and languages; Third paragraph: Major cities)
- Have students complete the activity independently in their notebooks.

MONITOR

Invite volunteers to provide details to include in each part of the idea web. (Answers: Location and People – below the equator, 22 million people, Aborigines and people from many different countries; Language Spoken – English; Capital – Canberra; Major Cities – Sydney, Melbourne, Brisbane, Perth)

Practice 3

19 Choose a country to write a report about. Do research to find out facts about the country. Write them in an idea web.

- Read the directions aloud. Review research strategies with students. Say: *Look for information about the country in an encyclopedia or on the internet.*
- Have students work independently to complete the activity. Allow them to use classroom or internet resources to find information and complete idea webs.

MONITOR

Check that students consult reliable sources and complete each part of their idea webs.

ASSIST

Suggest that students write about countries mentioned in this unit, such as Chile, China, Egypt, India, Jordan, Peru, or Russia.

Practice 4

20 Use your idea web to write a report about the country.

- Read the directions aloud. Remind students that each paragraph in their reports should have a main idea.

MONITOR

Check to make sure that students complete their idea webs before writing their reports.

ASSIST

Encourage students to use the sample idea web and report to help them organize their reports.

Speaking

21 Share your report with the class.

- Read the directions aloud and invite volunteers to read their reports aloud. Tell students to read their reports, leaving out the country name so others can guess it.

MONITOR

As pairs share their reports with the class, check that they've included information about their country correctly. Encourage other students to offer helpful feedback.

Lesson Objective

INVOLVE

Revisit the lesson objective: *Now I have learned to write a report about a country.*

- Encourage awareness of what students have learned by asking students to give some examples of what should be included in a report about a country.

Homework — WB p. 84/ act. 20 & 21

20 The paragraph below should only include general facts and information about the location of India. Circle the two sentences that do NOT belong in the paragraph.

- Direct students to WB Activity 20 on page 84. Students circle the two sentences that do not give the most important information.

21 Write a report about India in your notebook. Use the information in 19 and 20.

- Direct students to WB Activity 21 on page 84. Students will use information from the previous two activities, and their own research, to write the report.
- Point out the box on the top of the page. This information will guide students.

Extra Application and Practice Activity

- Post students' reports on a bulletin board. Have the class use the reports to vote on the countries they would most like to visit.

Unit 8 T104

Writing | Report

I will learn to write a report about a country.

18 Read the report. Then copy the idea web and use the information to complete it.

Australia is one of the seven continents, but it's also a country. It's known as the smallest continent in the world. Do you know why it's called "the land down under"? It's because Australia is located below the equator.

More than 22 million people live in Australia. Aborigines are the original inhabitants of Australia, but people from many different countries have come to Australia to live. Today, most people in Australia speak English.

The capital of Australia is Canberra. Other big and important cities in Australia are Sydney, Melbourne, Brisbane, and Perth.

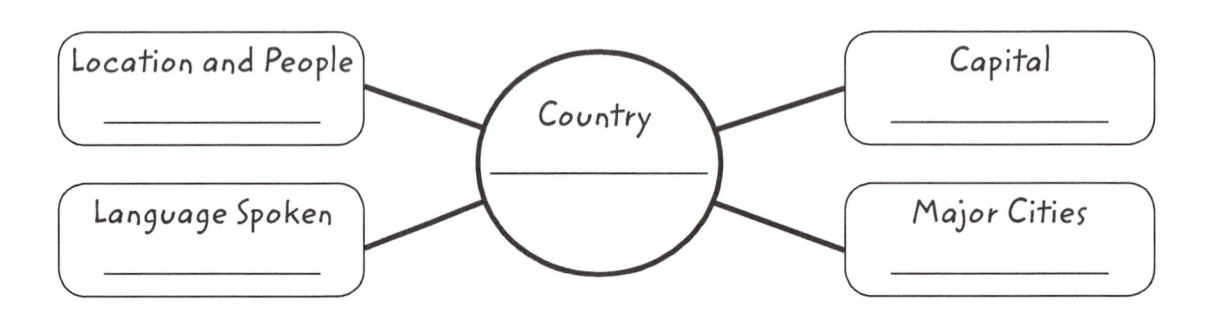

- Location and People _____
- Capital _____
- Language Spoken _____
- Major Cities _____
- Country _____

19 Choose a country to write a report about. Do research to find out facts about the country. Write them in an idea web.

20 Use your idea web to write a report about the country.

21 Share your report with the class.

Life skills | Take pride in your town or city.

I will learn to talk about the interesting places in my town or city.

22 Look at this list of features. Does your town or city (or a nearby town or city) have any of these? Copy the list and write the names and locations. Add any additional attractions to your list. Then share your ideas with a partner.

- a statue of a famous person or historical event
- an art museum
- a history, anthropology, or science museum
- a concert hall or event center
- a stadium or athletic field
- old houses or other historical structures
- religious places that are historically or culturally important
- a beautiful park or garden
- a famous restaurant
- a college or university

The Clock Tower in Chetbury was built in 1870. It used to be a town hall and a fire station. Today, it's a historic building with stores in it.

Project

23 Work in a small group. Prepare a map for a bicycle trip to six famous or interesting places in your town/city, state, or country.

1. See 22 for ideas.
2. Make a map.
3. Give a presentation of your map. Talk about each place:
   - the location
   - a short description of the place
   - when the place was built
   - why it was built

Unit 8 105

Life Skills Lesson

Lesson Flow

Warm-up › Lesson Objective › Speaking › Project › Lesson Objective

Lesson Objective

I will learn to talk about the interesting places in my town or city.

Life skills | Take pride in your town or city.

I will learn to talk about the interesting places in my town or city.

22 Look at this list of features. Does your town or city (or a nearby town or city) have any of these? Copy the list and write the names and locations. Add any additional attractions to your list. Then share your ideas with a partner.

- a statue of a famous person or historical event
- an art museum
- a history, anthropology, or science museum
- a concert hall or event center
- a stadium or athletic field
- old houses or other historical structures
- religious places that are historically or culturally important
- a beautiful park or garden
- a famous restaurant
- a college or university

> The Clock Tower in Chetbury was built in 1870. It used to be a town hall and a fire station. Today, it's a historic building with stores in it.

Project

23 Work in a small group. Prepare a map for a bicycle trip to six famous or interesting places in your town/city, state, or country.

1. See 22 for ideas.
2. Make a map.
3. Give a presentation of your map. Talk about each place:
   - the location
   - a short description of the place
   - when the place was built
   - why it was built

Unit 8 105

S105 Unit 8

Warm-up

- Have students play *What Am I?* Players should take turns thinking of a specific place, such as a building, statue, or other local attraction. Say: *Try to choose a place near here.* Encourage students to use previous pages in this unit to help them think of places. Classmates should then ask yes/no questions to find out what famous place the player "is." (The player should answer as if he or she "were" the place.) Have students keep track of how many questions it takes for classmates to guess the place. Model questions students can ask: *Are you found in our community? Do most people speak Spanish where you are? Are you made of stone? Were you built more than 100 years ago? Were you built to honor someone?*
- Check answers from the HW in the last lesson.

Lesson Objective

INVOLVE

Introduce the lesson objective. Say: *Today I will learn to talk about the interesting places in my town or city.*

- Students will think about interesting attractions near where they live. Then they will create a map for a bicycle trip to six of those places.

Speaking

22 Look at this list of features. Does your town or city (or a nearby town or city) have any of these? Copy the list and write the names and locations. Add any additional attractions to your list. Then share your ideas with a partner.

- Read the page title and discuss what it means to "take pride" in something. Then read the directions aloud. Invite volunteers to read the list of features.
- Have students name examples of each feature or local attraction. Then have them work in pairs to think of additional attractions.
- Have students work independently to complete their lists. Encourage them to include their favorite local places.

MONITOR

Check that students name specific local attractions. Provide vocabulary and spelling tips as needed.

ASSIST

Provide students with ideas for additional attractions, such as amusement parks, new buildings, public meeting places, places of natural beauty, or unusual geographic features.

Project

Materials: Poster paper, art supplies

23 Work in a small group. Prepare a map for a bicycle trip to six famous or interesting places in your town/city, state, or country.

- Read the directions, steps, and speech bubble aloud. Have students use a local map to plan their bicycle trip.
- Have groups work together to plan and describe their bicycle trips. Make sure each student in a group has a role.

21st Century Health Literacy

- Discuss the advantages of using bicycles to explore local attractions. Help students recognize that bicycles offer healthy physical activity and don't create air pollution like cars and buses can. Then discuss with them tips for safe bicycle trips. (Tips include wearing helmets, taking along water bottles, and building up strength and stamina by cycling regularly.)
- Invite groups to share their maps with the class.

21st Century Collaboration

- Encourage all group members to participate when sharing group work with the class. For this project, suggest that one student show the map and then others take turns describing the local attractions on it.

MONITOR

As students share their routes, listen for correct vocabulary, syntax, and use of target language.

Lesson Objective

INVOLVE

Revisit the lesson objective: *Now I have learned to talk about interesting places in my town or city.*

- Encourage awareness of what students have learned by asking them to name a few interesting places on their map.

Extra Application and Practice Activity

- Have students use a local map and scale to find out the distance and time needed for their planned bicycle trip. Then have groups compare their results to find out who planned the shortest and longest trips.

Listening and Speaking Lesson

Lesson Flow

Warm-up › Lesson Objective › Presentation › Practice 1 (SB) › Practice 2 (SB) › Speaking › Lesson Objective

Lesson Objectives

I will review the sounds *able*, *ful*, and *ly*.

I will learn to describe famous places.

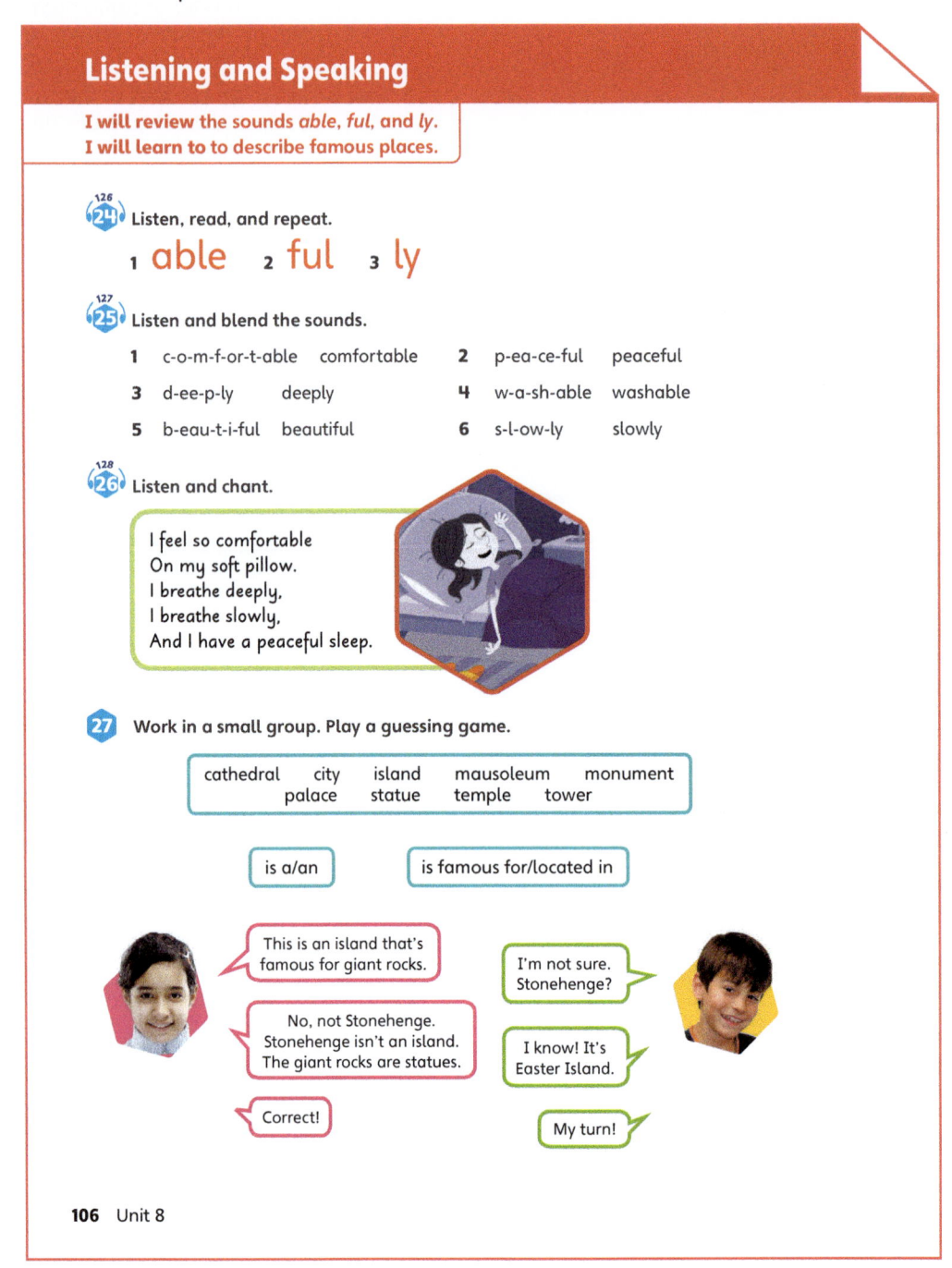

Listening and Speaking

I will review the sounds *able*, *ful*, and *ly*.
I will learn to to describe famous places.

24 / 126 Listen, read, and repeat.

1. **able**   2. **ful**   3. **ly**

25 / 127 Listen and blend the sounds.

1. c-o-m-f-or-t-able   comfortable
2. p-ea-ce-ful   peaceful
3. d-ee-p-ly   deeply
4. w-a-sh-able   washable
5. b-eau-t-i-ful   beautiful
6. s-l-ow-ly   slowly

26 / 128 Listen and chant.

> I feel so comfortable
> On my soft pillow.
> I breathe deeply,
> I breathe slowly,
> And I have a peaceful sleep.

27 Work in a small group. Play a guessing game.

| cathedral | city | island | mausoleum | monument |
| palace | statue | temple | tower |

[___ is a/an ___]   [___ is famous for/located in ___]

- This is an island that's famous for giant rocks.
- I'm not sure. Stonehenge?
- No, not Stonehenge. Stonehenge isn't an island. The giant rocks are statues.
- I know! It's Easter Island.
- Correct!
- My turn!

106   Unit 8

Warm-up

- Write the alphabet on the board and challenge students to think of the name of a place or structure that begins with each letter. Encourage students to name places they've learned about in this unit, such as those shown on the classroom bulletin-board displays. You may wish to suggest the following places for uncommon letters: Vancouver (Canada), Xi'an (China), and Zanzibar (Tanzania).

Lesson Objective

INVOLVE

Introduce the lesson objective. Say: *Today I will learn to use the sounds* able, ful, *and* ly, *and describe famous places.*

- Students will identify the letters and distinguish between the sounds *able*, *ful*, and *ly* individually and as part of words. Then they'll review the unit by talking about famous places and structures and using the passive voice and relative clauses.

Presentation

24 Listen, read, and repeat.

- Read the directions aloud. Play Audio Track 126 and have students listen and point to each sound as it is said. Have students repeat.

MONITOR

As students repeat, check they are pointing to the correct sound and listen for correct pronunciation.

Practice 1

25 Listen and blend the sounds.

- Read the directions aloud. Play Audio Track 127 and have students listen and point to each item as it is sounded out and blended on the audio. Have them repeat after each item.

MONITOR

As students repeat, check they are pointing to the correct word, and listen for correct pronunciation and appropriate intonation.

ASSIST

Replay the audio as needed.

Practice 2

26 Listen and chant.

- Read the directions aloud. Read the chant while students follow in their books.
- Play Audio Track 128 and have students listen. Replay the audio several times and encourage them to join in.

MONITOR

As students repeat the chant, listen for proper pronunciation, appropriate intonation, and correct use of language.

Speaking

27 Work in a small group. Play a guessing game.

- Read the directions aloud. Have volunteers read the words in the box aloud. Have students create lists in their notebooks of famous places or structures and their locations.
- Have volunteers read the speech bubbles aloud. Have students play the guessing game in groups.

MONITOR

Check that students have made lists using accurate information and correct language.

ASSIST

Model giving clues: *I wrote down "St. Basil's Cathedral is a cathedral that's famous for its colorful domes." To give a clue, I'll say, "This is famous for its colorful domes."*

21st Century Social Skills

- Remind students to speak clearly when giving clues and guessing. Point out that playing the guessing game will be more enjoyable when clues are challenging but not impossible. If places or things are too difficult to guess, encourage students to give additional clues.

Lesson Objective

INVOLVE

Revisit the lesson objective: *Now I have learned to use the sounds* able, ful, *and* ly, *and described famous places.*

- Encourage awareness of what students have learned by quickly eliciting from them words from the lesson that have the sounds *able*, *ful*, and *ly*.

Extra Application and Practice Activity

- As students play the game in groups or as a class, encourage them to listen for examples of passive voice or relative clauses. Ask students to share examples they heard. Model: *This structure was designed by a Dutch architect.* (passive voice) *This is a statue that was built in the 20th century.* (relative clause, passive voice)

Unit 8 **T106**

Listening and Speaking

I will review the sounds *able*, *ful*, and *ly*.
I will learn to to describe famous places.

24 Listen, read, and repeat.

1. **able**   2. **ful**   3. **ly**

25 Listen and blend the sounds.

1. c-o-m-f-or-t-able   comfortable
2. p-ea-ce-ful   peaceful
3. d-ee-p-ly   deeply
4. w-a-sh-able   washable
5. b-eau-t-i-ful   beautiful
6. s-l-ow-ly   slowly

26 Listen and chant.

I feel so comfortable
On my soft pillow.
I breathe deeply,
I breathe slowly,
And I have a peaceful sleep.

27 Work in a small group. Play a guessing game.

cathedral   city   island   mausoleum   monument
palace   statue   temple   tower

is a/an   is famous for/located in

This is an island that's famous for giant rocks.

I'm not sure. Stonehenge?

No, not Stonehenge. Stonehenge isn't an island. The giant rocks are statues.

I know! It's Easter Island.

Correct!

My turn!

106   Unit 8

Review

28 Complete each sentence with a word from the box.

> mausoleum   monument   pyramids   Statue   temple   tower

1. The _____ are burial places for ancient Egyptian pharaohs.
2. Borobudur in Indonesia is a famous Buddhist _____ dedicated to Buddha.
3. The _____ of Liberty was given to the United States by the people of France.
4. The Taj Mahal is actually a _____ where Mumtaz Mahal is buried.
5. Big Ben is a bell that is located in London's most famous clock _____.
6. Stonehenge is a famous _____ whose original purpose remains a mystery.

29 Combine the sentences. Use *who* or *that*.

1. Machu Picchu is an ancient city. It is 2,430 meters above sea level in the Andes Mountains.
   _____

2. The moai are giant rock statues. They were found on Easter Island.
   _____

3. Christ the Redeemer is a famous statue. It stands over the city of Rio de Janeiro.
   _____

4. Jørn Utzon was a Danish architect. He designed the Sydney Opera House.
   _____

5. The Great Sphinx is a monument. It has remained a mystery to this day.
   _____

I Can

- use words for famous places and monuments.
- use the passive voice and relative clauses.
- talk about famous places and structures.
- write a report about a country.

Review Lesson

Lesson Flow

Warm-up › Lesson Objective › Practice 1 (SB) › Practice 2 (WB) › Practice 3 (WB) › Practice 4 (SB) › Self-assessment › Homework

Lesson Objective

To review the words and structures of the unit.

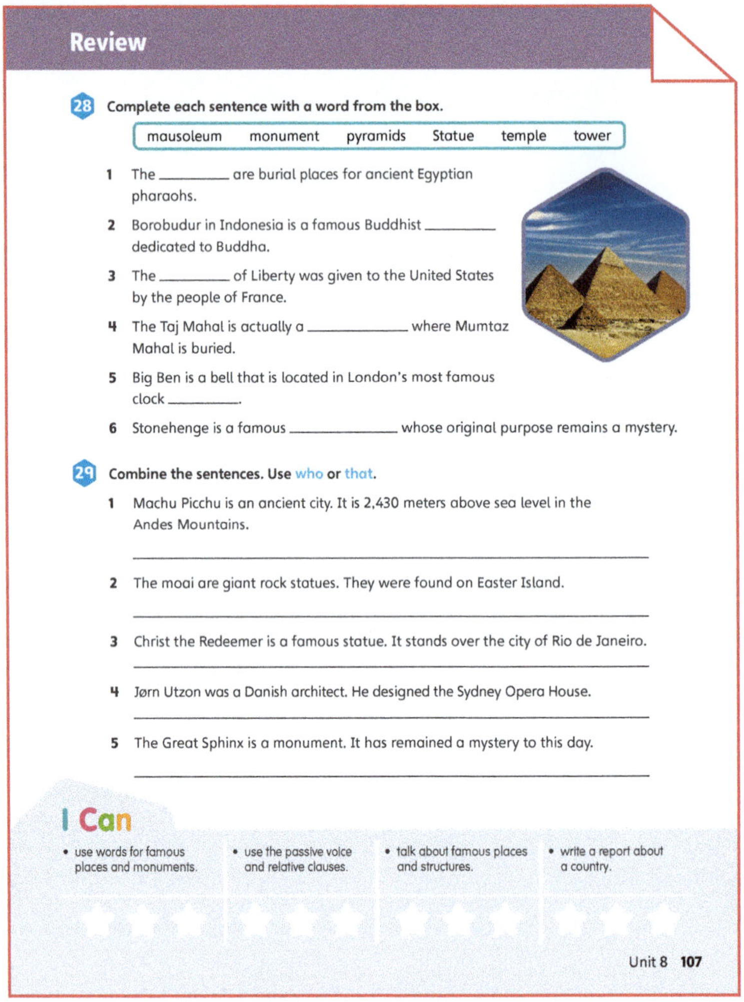

Review

28 Complete each sentence with a word from the box.

| mausoleum | monument | pyramids | Statue | temple | tower |

1. The _____ are burial places for ancient Egyptian pharaohs.
2. Borobudur in Indonesia is a famous Buddhist _____ dedicated to Buddha.
3. The _____ of Liberty was given to the United States by the people of France.
4. The Taj Mahal is actually a _____ where Mumtaz Mahal is buried.
5. Big Ben is a bell that is located in London's most famous clock _____.
6. Stonehenge is a famous _____ whose original purpose remains a mystery.

29 Combine the sentences. Use *who* or *that*.

1. Machu Picchu is an ancient city. It is 2,430 meters above sea level in the Andes Mountains.
2. The moai are giant rock statues. They were found on Easter Island.
3. Christ the Redeemer is a famous statue. It stands over the city of Rio de Janeiro.
4. Jørn Utzon was a Danish architect. He designed the Sydney Opera House.
5. The Great Sphinx is a monument. It has remained a mystery to this day.

I Can
- use words for famous places and monuments.
- use the passive voice and relative clauses.
- talk about famous places and structures.
- write a report about a country.

Warm-up

Materials: Index cards

- Have students create word cards to review key unit vocabulary. Students can write words on one side of an index card and definitions on the other and take turns reading either the word or the definition to a partner, challenging the partner to provide the information on the other side of the card.

Lesson Objective

INVOLVE

Introduce the lesson objective: Say: *Today I will review the words and structures of the unit.*

- Students will review the vocabulary and grammar they have learned in Unit 8 by doing activities, including completing and combining sentences.
- Then students will complete the *I Can* section, which helps them to assess their own learning and think about their progress.

Practice 1

28 Complete each sentence with a word from the box.

- Read the directions and the words in the box aloud. Then have students complete the items independently.

MONITOR

Check answers as a class. *(Answers: 1 pyramids, 2 temple, 3 Statue, 4 mausoleum, 5 tower, 6 monument)*

ASSIST

Remind students to read all the sentences before they begin the activity and then complete the items they're sure about first. Students can also refer to unit activities as needed.

Practice 2 · WB p. 85/ act. 22

22 Circle the correct answers.

- Read the directions aloud. Read the first item aloud. As a class, work through 1-4 to circle the correct answer.
- Have the students work independently to complete the activity.

Practice 3 · WB p. 85/ act. 23

23 Complete the statements with the correct passive form of the verbs in the box.

- Read the directions aloud. Read the first item aloud and ask a volunteer to choose the correct form of the verb.
- Have students work independently to complete the activity.

Practice 4

29 Combine the sentences. Use *who* or *that*.

- Read the directions aloud. Remind students that they can sometimes combine sentences using relative clauses. Say: *When two sentences have the same subject, you can use a relative clause instead of repeating the subject or using a pronoun for it.* Complete the first item as a class and then have students complete the activity independently.

MONITOR

Check answers as a class. *(Answers: 1 Machu Picchu is an ancient city that is 2,430 meters above sea level in the Andes Mountains. 2 The moai are giant rock statues that are found on Easter Island. 3 Christ the Redeemer is a famous statue that stands over the city of Rio de Janeiro. 4 Jørn Utzon was a Danish architect who designed the Sydney Opera House. 5 The Great Sphinx is a monument that has remained a mystery to this day.)*

Self-assessment

I Can

- This section asks students to assess their own learning and think about their progress. Help students appreciate their progress. Say: *The I Can statements show what you have learned in this unit.*

- Read the statements aloud. Explain that students should think about how well they know the language in the unit and should color in the stars. They should color three stars if they feel the unit was easy, two stars if they need some help, and one star if the unit was hard and they need more help. Have students work independently.

Suggestions for Remediation

Assessment Pack
- Direct students who need help with grammar and vocabulary to the Unit 8 Practice Tests in the Assessment Pack.

WB Unit 8/ p. 105
- Direct students who need help with grammar in particular to the Unit 8 Extra Grammar Practice (Workbook, page 105).
- For further vocabulary work, students can access games in the Big English Student World.

Homework · WB p. 85/ act. 24

24 Combine the sentences. Use *that* or *who* and the sentences in the box.

- Direct students to WB Activity 24 on page 85. Students combine sentences, each time using one item and one line from the box.

Extra Application and Practice Activity

- Have pairs of students role-play being tour guides and visitors to any of the unit's famous places or structures. Before they do, have partners list details about each place or structure, using the passive voice and relative clauses. Have partners practice their parts. Then have pairs present to the class.

Assessment Pack

- To assess student progress at the end of the unit, have students complete the Unit 8 Unit Test in the Assessment Pack.
- To assess whether students have reached the listening and speaking targets for this unit, carry out the Unit 8 Oral Assessment in the Assessment Pack.
- Arrange one-to-one sessions with each student and use the prompts to evaluate their listening and speaking abilities.

9 That's Entertainment

Objectives

Reading
- Can understand likes and preferences in short, simple personal texts (e.g. diary entries or emails).
- Can connect the information in a text with the information given in charts, graphs, or diagrams.

Listening
- Can understand most of the concrete details in informal conversations on familiar everyday topics, if the speakers talk slowly and clearly.
- Can understand the main information in short, simple dialogs about familiar activities, if spoken slowly and clearly.

Speaking
- Can give an opinion in a structured discussion, if guided by questions.

Writing
- Can describe the plot of a movie or book very briefly, using simple language.

Grammar
- Can make the necessary tense changes in reported speech.

Unit Projects

Family Connection

Have students tell their families that they're learning how to talk about the world of entertainment and people's opinions about it. Have families keep an entertainment journal of the different types of entertainment they enjoy together, including movies, TV shows, music, and video games. Have family members provide ratings and reviews. Students can then use reported speech to share their family members' opinions of each with the class.

Key Language

Key Vocabulary

Entertainment
book signing
comic book exhibit
concert
festival
movie premiere

Expressions
Deal!
He was so right!
I didn't know what to expect.
in advance
(new book) is out
set records
special effects
the world of entertainment
What for?

Content Words

climax
formula
plot
producer
script
structure

bagpipes
distinctive
concertina
squeezed
steel drums

Grammar/Structures

Sara said, "The sequel **isn't** as good as the first movie."

She said (that) the sequel **wasn't** as good as the first movie.

Paul said, "**I'm going** to the concert."

He said (that) he **was going** to the concert.

Phonics

The sounds: *sion*, *tion*, *ation*

What's the Buzz? Bulletin Board

Create a bulletin-board display titled *What's the Buzz?* Cut out pictures related to the world of entertainment, such as movie posters, CD or video-game covers, and celebrities. For each picture, have students add one or two opinions from reviews or other sources, using reported speech. Model: *The critic for* Time Magazine *said that this was the best movie of the year. But some online reviewers said that it was a big disappointment.* Tell students that "the buzz" is used to describe current opinions or gossip about a topic from the world of entertainment.

Language in Context Lesson

Lesson Flow

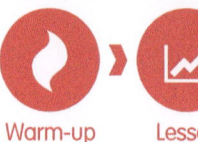

Warm-up › Lesson Objective › Presentation › Practice 1 (WB) › Practice 2 (SB) › Practice 3 (WB) › Speaking › Think BIG › Lesson Objective › Homework

Lesson Objective

I will learn to talk about entertainment and events.

Key Language

book signing, comic book exhibit, concert, festival, movie premiere, new release; cool, favorite; set records, the world of entertainment

---

9 That's Entertainment!

Language in Context

I will learn to talk about entertainment and events.

1 Read about some performers, movies, and books from the world of entertainment. Guess the name of each one. Then listen carefully to check.

1 The first three movies in this series made almost 2 billion dollars at the box office and more than 450 million dollars in DVD sales. The fourth movie in this series was sold out in the theaters before it was even released. _____

2 This young singer-songwriter has won many awards, including Artist of the Year and Best New Artist. This musician has more than 25 million followers on Twitter and has sold more than 15 million albums. _____

3 This book series has sold 450 million copies, making it the best-selling book series in history. It has now been translated into sixty-seven languages. The last four books in this series have set records as the fastest-selling books ever. _____

4 This singer's second album alone has earned her seven Grammy Awards, two Brit Awards, three American Music Awards, and at least fourteen other awards. This person has sold more than 26 million albums and has written and sung an original song for *Skyfall*, the twenty-third James Bond film. _____

5 This actor was recently named the highest-paid teenage actor in Hollywood. He has appeared in many TV shows and movies, but is best known for his role as Jacob Black. _____

2 Listen. Complete Becky's plans for the year using the words from the box. Then match the events to the pictures below.

book signing   comic book exhibit   concert   festival   movie premiere

January _____   March _____   May _____
February _____   April _____

3 Work with a partner. Talk about Becky's activities for next year and what she said she was going to do each month.

What did Becky say she was doing in January?

She said she was going to an Adele concert.

THINK BIG What do you consider good entertainment? Why?

Warm-up

- On the board, create a word web with *artist* in the center circle. Say: *The word* artist *can mean someone who creates art, like a painter or sculptor. These people make visual art – which is art you can see. But an artist can also mean anyone in the performing arts, which include singing, playing music, and acting.* Add ovals labeled *actors, singers, musicians* and *visual artists*. Have students brainstorm names of artists to complete the word web.

- Check answers from the HW in the last lesson.

Lesson Objective

INVOLVE

Explain the lesson objective. Say: *Today I will learn to talk about entertainment and events.*

- Tell students that they will read and talk about the world of entertainment, and then report about events and activities that one young person said she was going to attend or do.

Presentation

1 Read about some performers, movies, and books from the world of entertainment. Guess the name of each one. Then listen carefully to check.

- Read the directions aloud. Model Item 1: *The description says "the first three movies in this series." That means I need to guess and name a movie series. I'll need to think of a group of movies that have the same characters.* Have students write their guesses in their notebooks.
- Play Audio Track 129 and have students listen and check their answers.
- Replay the audio as needed. Use simple language and the pictures to explain unfamiliar words. Say: *To release a movie* means "to begin showing it to audiences." *A record* is a best accomplishment. If someone *sets records*, he or she does something better than it has been done before.

MONITOR

Check answers as a class. (Answers: 1 the Twilight movie series, 2 Justin Bieber, 3 the Harry Potter series, 4 Adele, 5 Taylor Lautner)

Practice 1 WB p. 86/ act. 1

1 Read the statements and ✔ the ones that describe you.

- Read the directions aloud. Place students in pairs to discuss their answers with each other.
- Students complete the activity independently.

MONITOR

Listen for correct pronunciation, intonation, and use of language as students discuss their own views on entertainment.

Practice 2

2 Listen. Complete Becky's plans for the year using the words from the box. Then match the events to the pictures below.

- Read the directions aloud. Have students preview the words in the box, the calendar, and the pictures.
- Play Audio Track 130. Have students complete the activity independently.

MONITOR

Check answers as a class. (Answers in Becky's planner: January – concert, 4; February – book signing, 1; March – comic book exhibit, 2; April – movie premiere, 5; May – festival, 3.)

Practice 3 WB p. 86/ act. 2

2 Read and circle the answers that are true for you.

- Read the directions aloud. Read the first item aloud. Have students put up their hands to indicate sometimes, often, or never. Model circling an answer: *I go to the movie theater often so I circle O.*
- Students complete the activity independently.

Speaking

3 Work with a partner. Talk about Becky's activities for next year and what she said she was going to do each month.

- Read the directions and the speech bubbles aloud.
- Have students talk about Becky's activities in pairs. Remind them to talk about each of the five months described in Activity 2.

MONITOR

Listen for correct pronunciation, appropriate intonation, and correct use of language.

Think BIG

21st Century Critical Thinking

- Read the questions aloud and write students' responses on the board. Then place students in pairs and have them write a few sentences on what makes good entertainment. Have pairs present their sentences to the class.

Lesson Objective

INVOLVE

Revisit the lesson objective: *Now I have learned to talk about entertainment and events.*

- Encourage awareness of what students have learned by eliciting the names of a few entertainment events discussed in the lesson.

Homework WB p. 87/ act. 3

3 Complete the sentences with the words in the box.

- Direct students to WB Activity 3 on page 87. Students fill in the correct word to complete each sentence.

Think BIG

- Direct students to WB Think Big on page 87. Students write their own ideas.

Extra Application and Practice Activity

21st Century Critical Thinking

- Have students use online or print resources to find out about upcoming events in their area. Suggest that they consult "What To Do" lists in magazines, in newspapers, or on internet sites. Encourage students to select two or three events they plan to go to and share them with the class. Then have others report on classmates' plans.

Unit 9 T108/109

9 That's Entertainment!

Language in Context

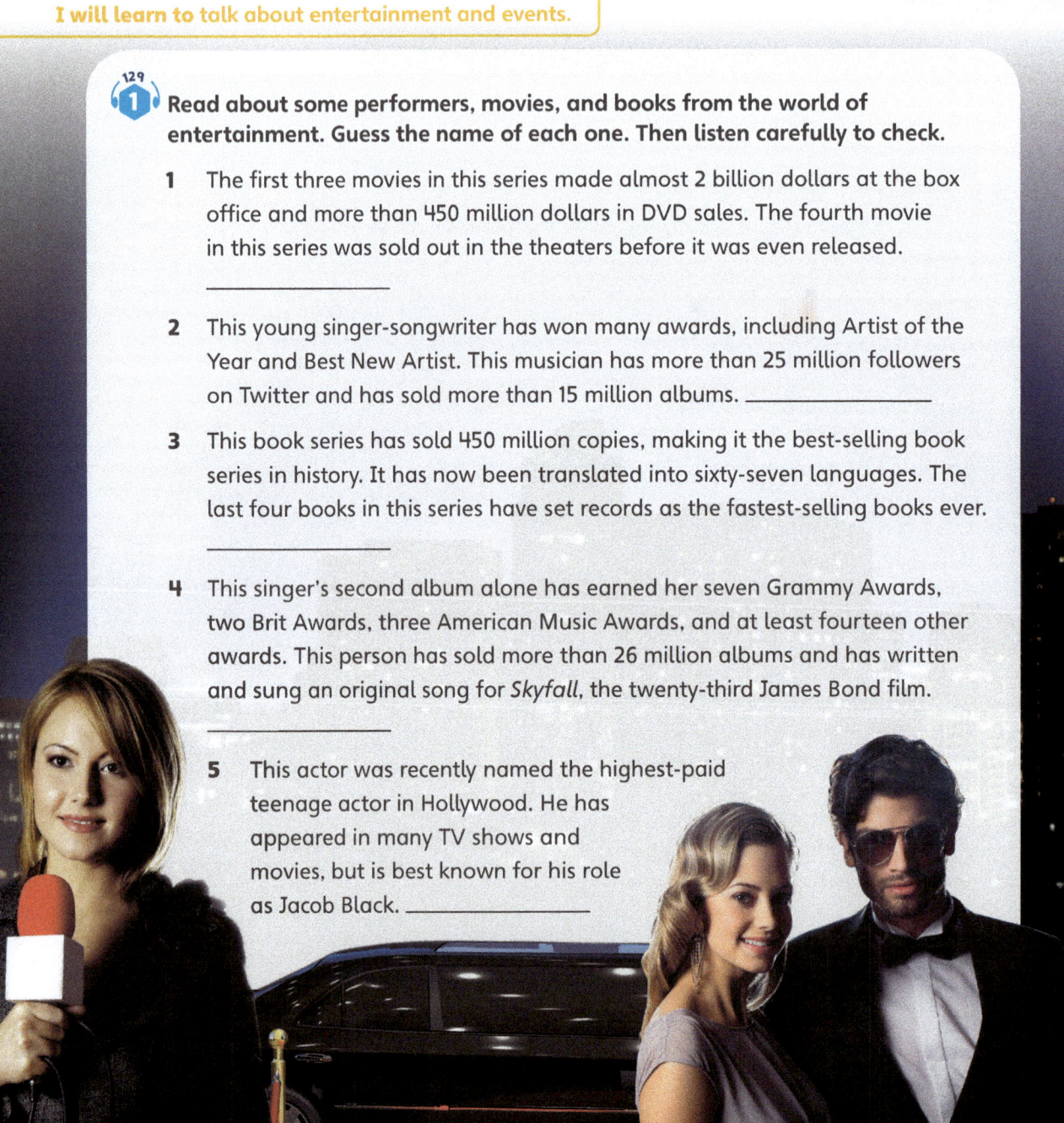

I will learn to talk about entertainment and events.

1 Read about some performers, movies, and books from the world of entertainment. Guess the name of each one. Then listen carefully to check.

1. The first three movies in this series made almost 2 billion dollars at the box office and more than 450 million dollars in DVD sales. The fourth movie in this series was sold out in the theaters before it was even released.

   _____

2. This young singer-songwriter has won many awards, including Artist of the Year and Best New Artist. This musician has more than 25 million followers on Twitter and has sold more than 15 million albums. _____

3. This book series has sold 450 million copies, making it the best-selling book series in history. It has now been translated into sixty-seven languages. The last four books in this series have set records as the fastest-selling books ever.

   _____

4. This singer's second album alone has earned her seven Grammy Awards, two Brit Awards, three American Music Awards, and at least fourteen other awards. This person has sold more than 26 million albums and has written and sung an original song for *Skyfall*, the twenty-third James Bond film.

   _____

5. This actor was recently named the highest-paid teenage actor in Hollywood. He has appeared in many TV shows and movies, but is best known for his role as Jacob Black. _____

2 Listen. Complete Becky's plans for the year using the words from the box. Then match the events to the pictures below.

| book signing | comic book exhibit | concert | festival | movie premiere |

January _____   March _____   May _____
February _____   April _____

1 
2 
3 
4 
5

3 Work with a partner. Talk about Becky's activities for next year and what she said she was going to do each month.

What did Becky say she was doing in January?

She said she was going to an Adele concert.

THINK BIG

What do you consider good entertainment? Why?

Unit 9 **109**

Reading Lesson

Lesson Flow

Warm-up › Lesson Objective › Pre-reading › Reading › Comprehension 1 › Comprehension 2 › Think BIG › Lesson Objective › Homework

Lesson Objective

I will understand a text about a new album.

Key Language

album, award, concert, festival, month, week; nominate, perform; creative, next; He was so right!, I didn't know what to expect.

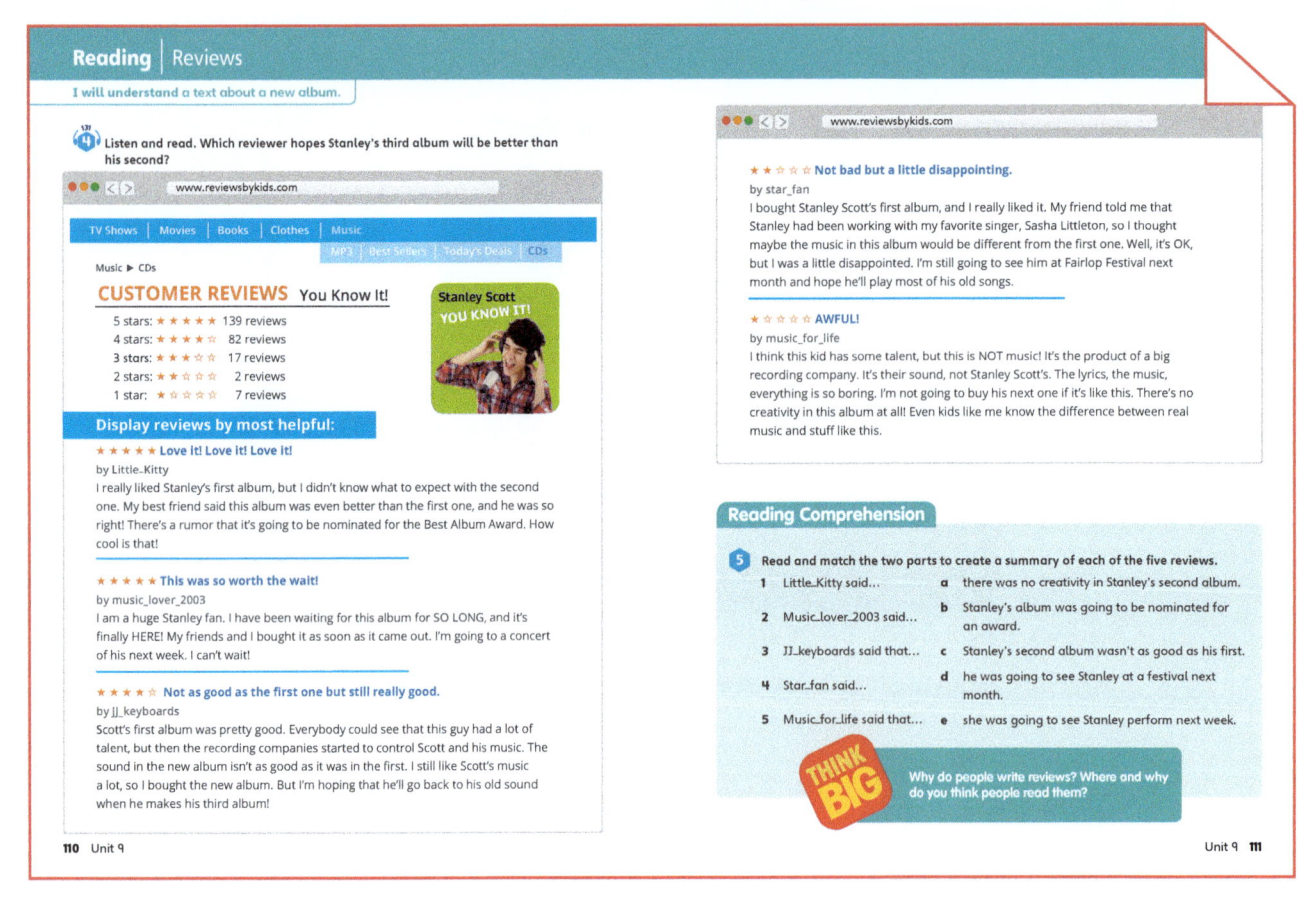

Reading | Reviews

I will understand a text about a new album.

Listen and read. Which reviewer hopes Stanley's third album will be better than his second?

www.reviewsbykids.com

TV Shows | Movies | Books | Clothes | Music
MP3 | Best Sellers | Today's Deals | CDs
Music ▸ CDs

CUSTOMER REVIEWS — You Know It!

Stanley Scott — YOU KNOW IT!

5 stars: ★★★★★ 139 reviews
4 stars: ★★★★☆ 82 reviews
3 stars: ★★★☆☆ 17 reviews
2 stars: ★★☆☆☆ 2 reviews
1 star: ★☆☆☆☆ 7 reviews

Display reviews by most helpful:

★★★★★ **Love It! Love It! Love It!**
by Little_Kitty
I really liked Stanley's first album, but I didn't know what to expect with the second one. My best friend said this album was even better than the first one, and he was so right! There's a rumor that it's going to be nominated for the Best Album Award. How cool is that!

★★★★★ **This was so worth the wait!**
by music_lover_2003
I am a huge Stanley fan. I have been waiting for this album for SO LONG, and it's finally HERE! My friends and I bought it as soon as it came out. I'm going to a concert of his next week. I can't wait!

★★★★☆ **Not as good as the first one but still really good.**
by JJ_keyboards
Scott's first album was pretty good. Everybody could see that this guy had a lot of talent, but then the recording companies started to control Scott and his music. The sound in the new album isn't as good as it was in the first. I still like Scott's music a lot, so I bought the new album. But I'm hoping that he'll go back to his old sound when he makes his third album!

★★☆☆☆ **Not bad but a little disappointing.**
by star_fan
I bought Stanley Scott's first album, and I really liked it. My friend told me that Stanley had been working with my favorite singer, Sasha Littleton, so I thought maybe the music in this album would be different from the first one. Well, it's OK, but I was a little disappointed. I'm still going to see him at Fairlop Festival next month and hope he'll play most of his old songs.

★☆☆☆☆ **AWFUL!**
by music_for_life
I think this kid has some talent, but this is NOT music! It's the product of a big recording company. It's their sound, not Stanley Scott's. The lyrics, the music, everything is so boring. I'm not going to buy his next one if it's like this. There's no creativity in this album at all! Even kids like me know the difference between real music and stuff like this.

Reading Comprehension

5. Read and match the two parts to create a summary of each of the five reviews.

1. Little_Kitty said…
2. Music_lover_2003 said…
3. JJ_keyboards said that…
4. Star_fan said…
5. Music_for_life said that…

a. there was no creativity in Stanley's second album.
b. Stanley's album was going to be nominated for an award.
c. Stanley's second album wasn't as good as his first.
d. he was going to see Stanley at a festival next month.
e. she was going to see Stanley perform next week.

THINK BIG — Why do people write reviews? Where and why do you think people read them?

Warm-up

- Pose this brain teaser: *A new movie got six reviews online. The average for all six reviews was 3 out of 5 stars. What might the ratings for each of the six reviews be?* (Sample answers: six 3-star reviews/three 4-star reviews and three 2-star reviews/three 5-star reviews and three 1-star reviews)

21st Century Critical Thinking

- Point out that looking at review averages does not always reflect the individual opinions well. Say: *Two movies got an average score of 3 stars. One movie got twenty 3-star reviews. Another movie got ten 5-star reviews and ten 1-star reviews. Which one would you rather see? Why?* (Sample answers: I'd rather see the movie that got all 3-star reviews. Most people think the movie is at least OK./I'd rather see the movie that got good and bad reviews. It's probably more interesting, even if I don't like it.)
- Check answers from the HW in the last lesson.

Lesson Objective

INVOLVE

Introduce the lesson objective. Say: *Today I will learn to understand a text about a new album.*

- Students will read and talk about online reviews of a new album.

Pre-reading

- Say: *These reviews give opinions about Stanley Scott's second album. The record is called* You Know It! *Each review has a title, a rating, the reviewer's user name, and an opinion.* Have volunteers preview the article by reading the title, the titles of the individual reviews, and the reviewers' user names aloud.

Reading

4 Listen and read. Which reviewer hopes Stanley's third album will be better than his second?

- Read the directions aloud. Play Audio Track 131 and have students listen and read along.

ASSIST

Replay the audio as needed. Pause after each review and use simple language to explain unfamiliar words and phrases. Say: *An* album *is a collection of songs. To* nominate *means "to propose someone or something for an honor or award."*

Comprehension 1

- Ask the question in the directions: *Which reviewer hopes Stanley's third album will be better than his second?* (JJ_keyboards)

MONITOR

Ask more questions to check for understanding. Ask: *Who said that this album was even better than Stanley's first album?* (Little_Kitty's best friend) *What did star_fan's friend say?* (The friend said that Stanley had been working with star_fan's favorite singer, Sasha Littleton.) *Why didn't music_for_life like the album?* (The reviewer thinks the music and lyrics are boring and not creative. The album sounds like the product of a big recording company.)

21st Century Technology Literacy

- Say: *Most people who post reviews online aren't professional reviewers. They aren't paid for their reviews. Online reviews often use informal language.* Challenge students to find a professional review and compare the style and tone of the review with these customer reviews. Remind students that reading aloud can help them identify the tone of the writing.

Comprehension 2

5 Read and match the two parts to create a summary of each of the five reviews.

- Read the directions aloud. Model the first item: *I want to match Little_Kitty with an item. First, I'll go back and read the review again. Then I'll read the choices to see which one matches what Little_Kitty said. Choice (b) says, "Stanley's album was nominated for an award." That's the right match! Little_Kitty mentions this in her review.*
- Have students work independently to complete the activity.

MONITOR

Check answers as a class. (Answers: 1 b, 2 e, 3 c, 4 d, 5 a)

Think BIG

21st Century Media Literacy

- Have students work in pairs to talk about the reviews.
- Encourage students to use their own experiences for additional support as they share ideas about analyzing media reviews.

MONITOR

As pairs work, listen for correct pronunciation, appropriate intonation, and correct use of language.

Lesson Objective

INVOLVE

Revisit the lesson objective: *Now I have learned to understand a text about a new album.*

- Encourage awareness of what students have learned by eliciting from them some opinions in the reviews.

Homework WB p. 88/ act. 4 & 5

4 Read and listen. Then circle the correct names.

- Direct students to WB Activity 4 on page 88. Tell students to play the audio, listen to the reviews, and circle the name of the reviewer who made each statement.

5 Answer the questions.

- Direct students to WB Activity 5 on page 88. Students must write their answers in full sentences.

Extra Application and Practice Activity

- Have students use print or digital resources to find reviews of recent music, movies, or TV shows. Encourage them to take notes about each review and share details with the class.

Unit 9   **T110/111**

Reading | Reviews

I will understand a text about a new album.

🎧 **4** Listen and read. Which reviewer hopes Stanley's third album will be better than his second?

www.reviewsbykids.com

| TV Shows | Movies | Books | Clothes | Music |

MP3 | Best Sellers | Today's Deals | CDs

Music ▶ CDs

CUSTOMER REVIEWS You Know It!

5 stars: ★★★★★ 139 reviews
4 stars: ★★★★☆ 82 reviews
3 stars: ★★★☆☆ 17 reviews
2 stars: ★★☆☆☆ 2 reviews
1 star: ★☆☆☆☆ 7 reviews

Stanley Scott — YOU KNOW IT!

Display reviews by most helpful:

★★★★★ **Love it! Love it! Love it!**
by Little_Kitty

I really liked Stanley's first album, but I didn't know what to expect with the second one. My best friend said this album was even better than the first one, and he was so right! There's a rumor that it's going to be nominated for the Best Album Award. How cool is that!

★★★★★ **This was so worth the wait!**
by music_lover_2003

I am a huge Stanley fan. I have been waiting for this album for SO LONG, and it's finally HERE! My friends and I bought it as soon as it came out. I'm going to a concert of his next week. I can't wait!

★★★★☆ **Not as good as the first one but still really good.**
by JJ_keyboards

Scott's first album was pretty good. Everybody could see that this guy had a lot of talent, but then the recording companies started to control Scott and his music. The sound in the new album isn't as good as it was in the first. I still like Scott's music a lot, so I bought the new album. But I'm hoping that he'll go back to his old sound when he makes his third album!

www.reviewsbykids.com

★★☆☆☆ **Not bad but a little disappointing.**
by star_fan
I bought Stanley Scott's first album, and I really liked it. My friend told me that Stanley had been working with my favorite singer, Sasha Littleton, so I thought maybe the music in this album would be different from the first one. Well, it's OK, but I was a little disappointed. I'm still going to see him at Fairlop Festival next month and hope he'll play most of his old songs.

★☆☆☆☆ **AWFUL!**
by music_for_life
I think this kid has some talent, but this is NOT music! It's the product of a big recording company. It's their sound, not Stanley Scott's. The lyrics, the music, everything is so boring. I'm not going to buy his next one if it's like this. There's no creativity in this album at all! Even kids like me know the difference between real music and stuff like this.

Reading Comprehension

5 Read and match the two parts to create a summary of each of the five reviews.

1. Little_Kitty said…
2. Music_lover_2003 said…
3. JJ_keyboards said that…
4. Star_fan said…
5. Music_for_life said that…

a. there was no creativity in Stanley's second album.
b. Stanley's album was going to be nominated for an award.
c. Stanley's second album wasn't as good as his first.
d. he was going to see Stanley at a festival next month.
e. she was going to see Stanley perform next week.

THINK BIG Why do people write reviews? Where and why do you think people read them?

Language in Action Lesson

Lesson Flow

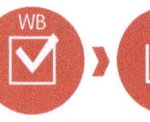

Warm-up → Lesson Objective → Pre-listening → Listening → Comprehension → Role Play → Practice 1 (SB) → Practice 2 (WB) → Lesson Objective → Homework

Lesson Objective

I will listen to a dialog about going to an event.

Key Language

album, book signing, comic book exhibit, movie premiere, new release, reviewer, video game; challenging, exciting, fantastic, good, impressive, stunning; Deal!, in advance, (new book) is out, saved up, What for?

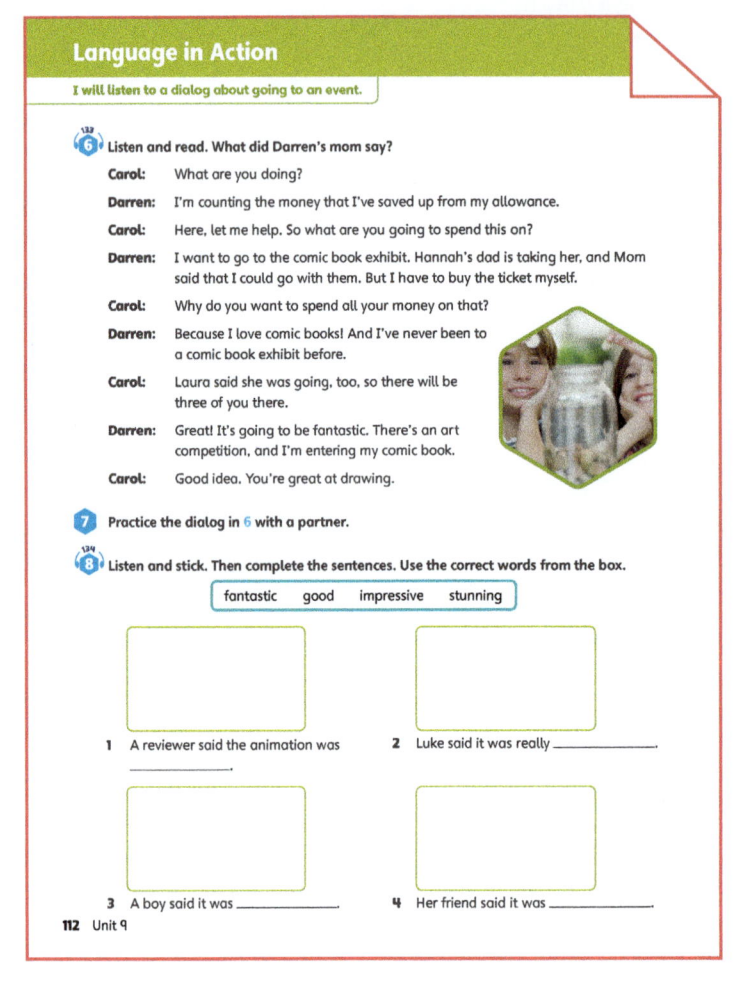

Language in Action

I will listen to a dialog about going to an event.

6 Listen and read. What did Darren's mom say?

Carol: What are you doing?

Darren: I'm counting the money that I've saved up from my allowance.

Carol: Here, let me help. So what are you going to spend this on?

Darren: I want to go to the comic book exhibit. Hannah's dad is taking her, and Mom said that I could go with them. But I have to buy the ticket myself.

Carol: Why do you want to spend all your money on that?

Darren: Because I love comic books! And I've never been to a comic book exhibit before.

Carol: Laura said she was going, too, so there will be three of you there.

Darren: Great! It's going to be fantastic. There's an art competition, and I'm entering my comic book.

Carol: Good idea. You're great at drawing.

7 Practice the dialog in 6 with a partner.

8 Listen and stick. Then complete the sentences. Use the correct words from the box.

fantastic   good   impressive   stunning

1. A reviewer said the animation was _____
2. Luke said it was really _____
3. A boy said it was _____
4. Her friend said it was _____

112 Unit 9

Warm-up

- Write *comic book exhibit* on the board. Say: *Exhibit* means "to show." Ask: *What do you think happens at a comic book exhibit?* (Sample answers: People who make comic books show new and old comics./People come to buy comic books./People dress up as their favorite comic-book characters./Workshops teach drawing or writing comics./People watch movies based on comic books.)

- Check answers from the HW in the last lesson.

Lesson Objective

INVOLVE

Introduce the lesson objective. Say: *Today I will listen to a dialog about going to an event.*

- Students will read, listen to, and practice a dialog. Students will also listen to conversations about the world of entertainment.

S112 Unit 9

Pre-listening 🔊

- Tell students that they are going to listen to Darren and Carol talking about a comic book exhibit.
- Point to the names *Darren* and *Carol* in the dialog. Point to the picture. Ask: *Why are they putting coins into a jar?* (Answer: Sometime people save money by collecting money in a jar.) Say: *Listen to what Darren is saving up for.*

Listening 🎧 133 🔊

6 Listen and read. What did Darren's mom say?

- Read the directions aloud. Play Audio Track 133 and have students listen and read along.
- Invite a pair to read the dialog aloud and repeat.

MONITOR
As students practice, listen for correct pronunciation and use of language.

Comprehension 💡

- Ask the question in the directions: *What did Darren's mom say?* (She said he could go, but he had to buy the ticket himself.)

MONITOR
Ask more questions to check for understanding. Encourage students to answer in complete sentences where appropriate. Ask: *What does Darren want to do?* (He wants to go to the comic book exhibit.) *What's one thing Darren wants to do at the comic book exhibit?* (He wants to enter his comic book in an art competition.) *What does Carol say about his idea?* (She says it's a good one and that he's great at drawing.)

Role Play 🎭

7 Practice the dialog in 6 with a partner.

- Read the directions aloud. Have students pair to read the dialog aloud, switch parts, and repeat.

MONITOR
As students practice, listen for correct pronunciation and correct use of language.

ASSIST
As you notice errors, say words or sentences correctly and have students repeat.

Practice 1 🎧 134 P.T152 ☑

Materials: Stickers

8 Listen and stick. Then complete the sentences. Use the correct words from the box.

- Help students find the Unit 9 stickers at the back of the Student's Book. Ask them to describe each sticker. Read the directions aloud.
- Play Audio Track 134. Have students place the stickers on the page and complete each sentence with a word or phrase from the box.

MONITOR
As students work, make sure they place the stickers in the correct order. Check answers as a class. (*Answers: 1 stunning, 2 good, 3 impressive, 4 fantastic*)

ASSIST
Replay the audio and have students raise their hands when they hear the people mention what someone else said. Pause the audio and help students identify: *this reviewer said, Luke said, a boy said, her friend said.* Then continue to play the audio and help students with the reported speech.

Practice 2 🎧 135 WB p. 89/ act. 6 ☑

6 Listen and read. Then answer the questions.

- Read the directions aloud, then play Audio Track 135 twice. The second time, have students circle the words they do not understand. Explain their meaning.
- Read the first question as a class. Prompt students to find the answer in the text and write their answer.
- Students complete the activity independently.

Lesson Objective 📈

INVOLVE
Revisit the lesson objective: *Now I have listened to a dialog about going to an event.*

- Encourage awareness of what students have learned by asking students what Darren wants to do at the comic exhibit.

Homework 🎧 136 P.T153 WB p. 89/ act. 7 & 8 🎒

7 Look at 6. Circle the correct answers.

- Direct students to WB Activity 7 on page 89. Students circle a or b. They find their answers in the dialog.

8 Complete with two of the expressions in 6. Then listen and check.

- Direct students to WB Activity 8 on page 89. Students complete the activity using the underlined expressions in the dialog in 6, and then listen to the audio to check.

Extra Application and Practice Activity

Materials: Magazines

- Provide students with magazines, or help them find online and print pictures of a favorite actor, movie, video game, etc. Then have partners ask each other questions about their pictures. Tell them to take notes about what their partner said. Then have partners use reported speech to relate what they learned, such as: *Rosa said that her favorite band is The Five Cupcakes. She said the band is the best rock band ever.*

Unit 9 **T112**

Language in Action

I will listen to a dialog about going to an event.

6 Listen and read. What did Darren's mom say?

Carol: What are you doing?

Darren: I'm counting the money that I've saved up from my allowance.

Carol: Here, let me help. So what are you going to spend this on?

Darren: I want to go to the comic book exhibit. Hannah's dad is taking her, and Mom said that I could go with them. But I have to buy the ticket myself.

Carol: Why do you want to spend all your money on that?

Darren: Because I love comic books! And I've never been to a comic book exhibit before.

Carol: Laura said she was going, too, so there will be three of you there.

Darren: Great! It's going to be fantastic. There's an art competition, and I'm entering my comic book.

Carol: Good idea. You're great at drawing.

7 Practice the dialog in **6** with a partner.

8 Listen and stick. Then complete the sentences. Use the correct words from the box.

fantastic   good   impressive   stunning

1 A reviewer said the animation was _____.

2 Luke said it was really _____.

3 A boy said it was _____.

4 Her friend said it was _____.

112   Unit 9

Grammar

I will learn to use reported speech to report what someone said.

Direct speech	Reported speech
Claire said, "The album **isn't** as good as the last one."	Claire/She said (that) the album **wasn't** as good as the last one.
Josh said, "**I'm going** to the premiere."	Josh/He said (that) he **was going** to the premiere.

Tip: Change the verb in the reported statement from the simple present to the simple past, or from the present progressive to the past progressive.

9 Read what each person is saying. Rewrite their words in your notebook as reported speech.

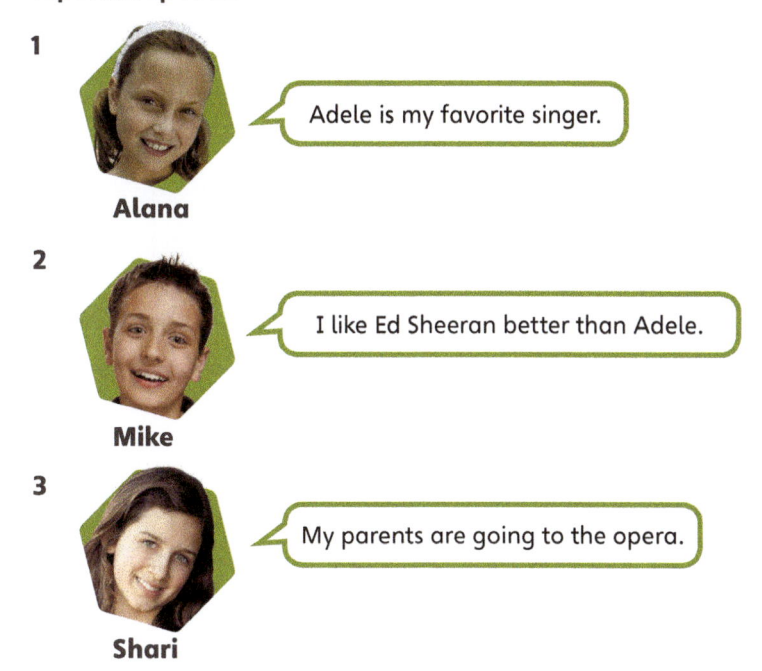

1. Alana: Adele is my favorite singer.

2. Mike: I like Ed Sheeran better than Adele.

3. Shari: My parents are going to the opera.

10 Change the direct speech to reported speech in your notebook.

1. My mom said, "His concerts are expensive."
2. Julia said, "The new comic book is getting bad reviews."
3. Rosie said, "I'm going to go to the book signing."
4. Alex said, "There are only a few tickets left."
5. James said, "I'm reading a great book right now."
6. Harry said, "The concert starts at 8:00."
7. Emma said, "Dad's coming to pick me up after the festival."
8. George said, "Her new album is much better than her last one."

Grammar Lesson

Lesson Flow

Warm-up › Lesson Objective › Presentation 1 › Practice 1 (SB) › Practice 2 (WB) › Practice 3 (WB) › Practice 4 (SB) › Lesson Objective › Homework

Lesson Objective

I will learn to use reported speech to report what someone said.

Key Language

Sara said, "The sequel **isn't** as good as the first movie." She said (that) the sequel **wasn't** as good as the first movie.

Paul said, "**I'm going** to the concert." He said (that) he **was going** to the concert.

Grammar

I will learn to use reported speech to report what someone said.

Direct speech	Reported speech
Claire said, "The album **isn't** as good as the last one."	Claire/She said (that) the album **wasn't** as good as the last one.
Josh said, "**I'm going** to the premiere."	Josh/He said (that) he **was going** to the premiere.

Tip: Change the verb in the reported statement from the simple present to the simple past, or from the present progressive to the past progressive.

9 Read what each person is saying. Rewrite their words in your notebook as reported speech.

1. Alana: Adele is my favorite singer.
2. Mike: I like Ed Sheeran better than Adele.
3. Shari: My parents are going to the opera.

10 Change the direct speech to reported speech in your notebook.

1. My mom said, "His concerts are expensive."
2. Julia said, "The new comic book is getting bad reviews."
3. Rosie said, "I'm going to go to the book signing."
4. Alex said, "There are only a few tickets left."
5. James said, "I'm reading a great book right now."
6. Harry said, "The concert starts at 8:00."
7. Emma said, "Dad's coming to pick me up after the festival."
8. George said, "Her new album is much better than her last one."

Unit 9 113

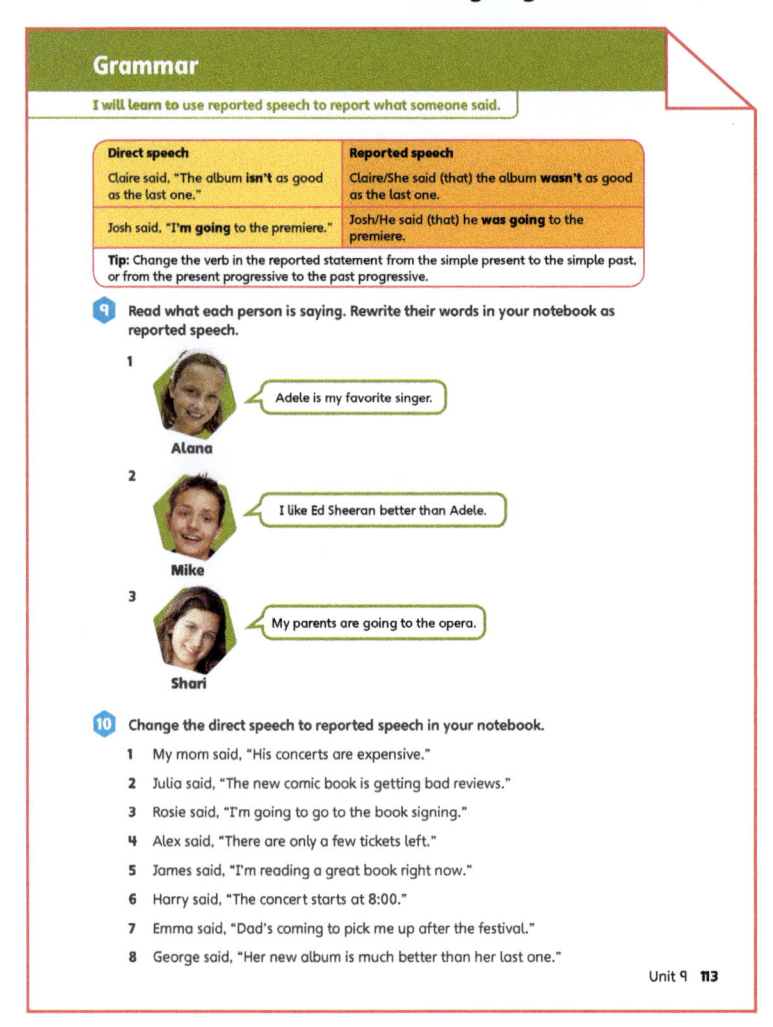

Warm-up

- Have partners play a game to review present simple and past simple verbs (feel/felt; fight/fought; find/found; fly/flew; give/gave). Give each pair some coins. Write *Heads = present simple* and *Tails = past simple* on the board. Players should take turns tossing coins and writing verbs (for example, two past verbs for two "tails" and three present verbs for three "heads"). Challenge partners to try to complete their list within a time limit (30 seconds or 1 minute). Partners score one point for each correct verb.
- Check answers from the HW in the last lesson.

S113 Unit 9

Lesson Objective

INVOLVE

Introduce the lesson objective. Say: *Today I will learn to use reported speech to report what someone said.*

- Students will use reported speech to talk about what other people say.

Presentation 1

- Have volunteers read the examples in the grammar box aloud. Ask: *What's direct speech?* (Direct speech gives a person's exact words.) *What punctuation is used in direct speech?* (Quotation marks are placed around the speaker's exact words.) *What's reported speech?* (You report what someone says, but you don't use the person's exact words.) *Do you use quotation marks in reported speech?* (no)
- Write these changes on the board: *I he/she; me him/her, my his/her.* Model: *Lisa said, "My sister is going to give me back the book." Lisa said that her sister was going to give her back the book.*
- Refer students back to the Language in Action dialog and elicit or highlight the grammar structures in the dialog.

Practice 1

9 Read what each person is saying. Rewrite their words in your notebook as reported speech.

- Read the directions aloud and complete the first item as a class. Then have students complete the activity independently.

MONITOR

Check answers as a class. (Answers: 1 Alana said (that) Adele was her favorite singer. 2 Michael said (that) he liked Ed Sheeran better than Adele. 3 Shari said (that) her parents were going to the opera.)

ASSIST

Provide students with the first part of the reported-speech sentences: *Alana said that, Michael said that, Shari said that.* Explain that the word *that* is optional in reported speech. Have students read the examples aloud, with and without *that*. Say: *Both versions are correct.*

- Point out that pronouns often change in reported speech. Draw students' attention to the second sentence in the grammar box. Ask: *What did Josh say?* (I'm going to the premiere.) *What pronoun changes when you report what he said?* (I changes to he)

Practice 2 WB p. 90/ act. 9

9 Read the dialogs and answer the questions. Use reported speech.

- Read the directions aloud. Have two volunteers read the first dialog aloud.
- Read the first item and discuss the answer. Have students write the answer: *He said he was going to a live show at Dragon's Den to see Ed Sheeran.*
- Have students work in pairs to read the dialogs and complete the activity.

Practice 3 WB p. 91/ act. 10

10 Read the dialog and complete the sentences. Use reported speech.

- Read the directions aloud. Have two volunteers read the speech bubbles. Complete Item 1 as a class.
- Have students complete the activity independently.

Practice 4

10 Change the direct speech to reported speech in your notebook.

- Read the directions aloud and complete the first item with the class. Then have students complete the activity independently

MONITOR

Check answers as a class. (Answers: 1 My mom said his concerts were expensive. 2 Julia said (that) the new comic book was getting bad reviews. 3 Rosie said (that) she was going to go to the book signing. 4 Alex said (that) there were only a few tickets left. 5 James said (that) he was reading a great book at that moment. 6 Harry said (that) the concert started at 8:00. 7 Emma said that her dad was coming to pick her up after the festival. 8 George said that her new album was much better than her last one.)

ASSIST

Discuss other changes that need to be made in the sentences for reported speech, e.g. changing *right now* to *at that moment* in Item 5 and changing *Dad* to *her dad* in Item 7.

Lesson Objective

INVOLVE

Revisit the lesson objective: *Now I have learned to use reported speech to report what someone said.*

- Encourage awareness of what students have learned by giving a direct speech sentence, and asking students to change it to reported speech.

Homework WB p. 91/ act. 11

11 Read the dialog and answer the questions. Use reported speech.

- Direct students to WB Activity 11 on page 91. Students read the dialog to answer the questions.

Extra Application and Practice Activity

- Have students rewrite dialogs from books and stories as reported speech.

Unit 9 **T113**

Content Connection Lesson

Lesson Flow

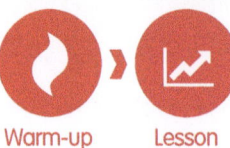

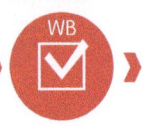

Warm-up › Lesson Objective › Pre-reading › Reading › Practice 1 (WB) › Practice 2 (SB) › Think BIG › Lesson Objective › Homework

Lesson Objective

I will learn about writing movie scripts.

Key Language

climax, formula, plot, producer, script, structure

Content Connection | Language Arts

I will learn about writing movie scripts.

11 Listen and read. What is the name of Blake Snyder's book about script writing?

CONTENT WORDS
climax   formula   plot   producer
script   structure

A Formula for Success

What makes a good story? Many writers say that there is a structure, or formula, for story writing. Of course, the plot of every story is different, but many stories follow this basic formula:
1. **Story opening:** Introduce the characters and the setting.
2. **Rising action:** Something happens to the characters that causes a problem.
3. **Climax:** The characters try to fix their problem. Either they win, or they lose.
4. **Falling action:** The characters see the result of their actions.
5. **Story ending:** The end of the story, where the problems are fixed, or not fixed.

If you look at novels and plays throughout history, it is easy to match the structure to the stories, from Shakespeare's Macbeth to J.K. Rowling's Harry Potter.

So, how is writing for movies different from writing books?

Many movie scripts follow the same structure as novels and plays, but in movies, timing is very important. Since most movies are around 100 minutes long, some writers have created a formula to show the times that each of these steps should occur.

Of course, not all script writers agree with this formula, and the times are not exact. But if you look at a lot of the big films that have come out of Hollywood in the last 20 years, there are many that seem to follow this pattern.

In fact, in 2005, a script writer named Blake Snyder wrote a book called *Save the Cat!* In this book, Snyder explains an even more detailed formula for script writing. If you want to sell your script to a movie producer, you might want to check it out.

Story opening	Rising action	Climax	Falling action	Story ending
10 min.	40 min.	35 min.	10 min.	5 min.

12 Look at the passage. Match to complete the sentences.

1   Many novels and plays share…   a   use the same formula.
2   Many Hollywood movies in the   b   at the end of the story
    last 20 years…   structure.
3   The falling action takes place…   c   the same story structure as
                                              movie scripts.

THINK BIG Can you think of a famous movie that follows this formula? Explain.

114 Unit 9

Warm-up

21st Century Media Literacy

- Have students play *Charades*, using movie titles and characters from movies as topics to mime. Players should take turns thinking of a movie topic and miming it for classmates to guess. You may wish to begin by having students brainstorm a list of favorite or memorable movies and characters.

- Check answers from the HW in the last lesson.

Lesson Objective

INVOLVE

- Introduce the lesson objective. Say: *Today I will learn about writing movie scripts.*
- Students will read a text about writing movie scripts.

Pre-reading

Materials: Word map or globe

- Read the Content Words with students and elicit or supply general meanings. Have students write the words and definitions in their notebooks.
- Read the title of the article and point to the diagram below. Ask: *What do you think this article is about? What do you think the diagram shows?* Allow students to share their ideas
- Draw their attention to the numbered items in the text, and suggest that these relate to the sections of the diagram.

Reading

11 Listen and read. What is the name of Blake Snyder's book about script writing?

- Play Audio Track 137 and have students follow along in their books, listening for the Content Words.

ASSIST

- Play the track again as needed to allow students to find all the Content Words.
- Read the first paragraph aloud with the class. After you finish, help students use context clues from the text to add detail to their definitions of the Content Words, e.g. *Many stories follow a basic formula.*
- Have students continue the process in pairs for the remainder of the article.

MONITOR

- Invite volunteers to share what they learned about the Content Words. Then, ask the class what the name of Blake Snyder's book about script writing is. *(Save the Cat!)*

Practice 1 | WB p. 92/ act. 12

12 Circle the correct answers.

- Read the directions aloud, and do Item 1 as a class.
- Have students complete the activity independently.

Practice 2

12 Look at the passage. Match to complete the sentences.

- Read the directions aloud. Have students work in pairs to complete the activity.

ASSIST

Tell students to identify the key words in the sentences, then scan the passage to find them.

MONITOR

Check answers as a class. *(Answers: 1 c, 2 a, 3 b)*

Think BIG

21st Century Media Literacy

- Read the question aloud, and put students into small groups.
- In their groups, students discuss the structure of famous movies, and try to find one that follows the basic formula for success.
- Encourage groups to create a rough diagram like the one in their Student's Book for their chosen movie, to demonstrate how closely it follows the formula.
- Have groups report back to the class on their chosen movie.

Lesson Objective

INVOLVE

Revisit the lesson objective: *Now I have learned about writing movie scripts.*

- Encourage awareness of what students have learned by eliciting from them some information from the article about movie scripts.

Homework | WB p. 92/ act. 13

13 Read and complete the text with the words in the box. Then listen and check.

- Direct students to WB Activity 13 on page 92. Tell students that they should read the text carefully and complete it, using the words in the box. They should then listen to Audio Track 138 and check their answers.

Extra Application and Practice Activity

- In their groups, have students work together to develop a story line for a new movie, based on the basic formula for success as detailed in the text in Activity 11.
- Encourage groups to prepare a presentation to share with the class, including a diagram like the one in the Student's Book, short descriptions of the main characters, and a summary of the storyline.
- Groups present their movies to the class. Have a class vote to decide which is the class favorite.

Unit 9   **T114**

Content Connection | Language Arts

I will learn about writing movie scripts.

11 Listen and read. What is the name of Blake Snyder's book about script writing?

CONTENT WORDS
climax   formula   plot   producer
script   structure

A Formula for Success

What makes a good story? Many writers say that there is a structure, or formula, for story writing. Of course, the plot of every story is different, but many stories follow this basic formula:

1. **Story opening:** Introduce the characters and the setting.
2. **Rising action:** Something happens to the characters that causes a problem.
3. **Climax:** The characters try to fix their problem. Either they win, or they lose.
4. **Falling action:** The characters see the result of their actions.
5. **Story ending:** The end of the story, where the problems are fixed, or not fixed.

If you look at novels and plays throughout history, it is easy to match the structure to the stories, from Shakespeare's Macbeth to J.K. Rowling's Harry Potter.

So, how is writing for movies different from writing books?

Many movie scripts follow the same structure as novels and plays, but in movies, timing is very important. Since most movies are around 100 minutes long, some writers have created a formula to show the times that each of these steps should occur.

Of course, not all script writers agree with this formula, and the times are not exact. But if you look at a lot of the big films that have come out of Hollywood in the last 20 years, there are many that seem to follow this pattern.

In fact, in 2005, a script writer named Blake Snyder wrote a book called *Save the Cat!* In this book, Snyder explains an even more detailed formula for script writing. If you want to sell your script to a movie producer, you might want to check it out.

Story opening	Rising action	Climax	Falling action	Story ending
10 min.	40 min.	35 min.	10 min.	5 min.

12 Look at the passage. Match to complete the sentences.

1. Many novels and plays share…
2. Many Hollywood movies in the last 20 years…
3. The falling action takes place…

a. use the same formula.
b. at the end of the story structure.
c. the same story structure as movie scripts.

THINK BIG
Can you think of a famous movie that follows this formula? Explain.

114 Unit 9

Culture Connection | Around the World

I will learn about musical instruments around the world.

13 Listen and read. Which musical instrument was invented in Trinidad and Tobago?

CONTENT WORDS
bagpipes   distinctive
concertina   squeezed   steel drums

Unique Musical Instruments

Music is as old as mankind. It's a form of communication, and just like language, many instruments are unique to a specific culture or area. This article takes a look at just a few of the instruments that we associate with different countries and their history.

Bagpipes are a very old instrument, although we don't know exactly how old because bagpipes aren't built to last a long time. Bagpipes are a bag (which was traditionally made of sheep's stomach) and pipes. Most people think of Scotland when they think of the bagpipes, but bagpipes are also used traditionally in other parts of Europe.

Steel drums were first used in the 1700s. These drums were originally created out of oil drums to celebrate Carnival in Trinidad and Tobago, but their popularity is growing around the world. The steel is bent to create a distinctive sound and a number of different notes. Many musicians play six to eight drums at a time.

The **bandoneon** is a type of concertina. Although it was invented in Germany in 1846 to play church music, it has become the symbol of the Argentine tango. Astor Piazzolla, the famous Argentine composer and musician, made the instrument world-famous in the 20th century with his tango compositions. The instrument itself is extremely complex and difficult to play, as each button plays a different note depending on whether the instrument is being squeezed in or pulled out.

These are just some of the unusual instruments that are part of different cultures. Which instruments is your country famous for?

14 Look at the passage. Read and say true or false.

1. Musicians can play six to eight drums at the same time.
2. The bagpipes are a modern musical instrument.
3. The steel drums are played during a famous period of celebration.
4. The bandoneon requires great skill.

THINK BIG

Is there a traditional kind of music in your country, such as folk music? What is it? Which instruments do the musicians use?

Culture Connection Lesson

Lesson Flow

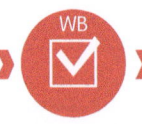

Warm-up › Lesson Objective › Pre-reading › Reading › Practice 1 (SB) › Practice 2 (WB) › Think BIG › Video › Lesson Objective › Homework

Lesson Objective

I will learn about musical instruments around the world.

Key Language

bagpipes, distinctive, concertina, squeezed, steel drums

Culture Connection | Around the World

I will learn about musical instruments around the world.

13 Listen and read. Which musical instrument was invented in Trinidad and Tobago?

CONTENT WORDS
bagpipes   distinctive
concertina   squeezed   steel drums

Unique Musical Instruments

Music is as old as mankind. It's a form of communication, and just like language, many instruments are unique to a specific culture or area. This article takes a look at just a few of the instruments that we associate with different countries and their history.

Bagpipes are a very old instrument, although we don't know exactly how old because bagpipes aren't built to last a long time. Bagpipes are a bag (which was traditionally made of sheep's stomach) and pipes. Most people think of Scotland when they think of the bagpipes, but bagpipes are also used traditionally in other parts of Europe.

Steel drums were first used in the 1700s. These drums were originally created out of oil drums to celebrate Carnival in Trinidad and Tobago, but their popularity is growing around the world. The steel is bent to create a distinctive sound and a number of different notes. Many musicians play six to eight drums at a time.

The **bandoneon** is a type of concertina. Although it was invented in Germany in 1846 to play church music, it has become the symbol of the Argentine tango. Astor Piazzolla, the famous Argentine composer and musician, made the instrument world-famous in the 20th century with his tango compositions. The instrument itself is extremely complex and difficult to play, as each button plays a different note depending on whether the instrument is being squeezed in or pulled out.

These are just some of the unusual instruments that are part of different cultures. Which instruments is your country famous for?

14 Look at the passage. Read and say true or false.
1. Musicians can play six to eight drums at the same time.
2. The bagpipes are a modern musical instrument.
3. The steel drums are played during a famous period of celebration.
4. The bandoneon requires great skill.

THINK BIG Is there a traditional kind of music in your country, such as folk music? What is it? Which instruments do the musicians use?

Unit 9   115

Warm-up

- Play recordings of a variety of types of music (classical, popular, folk) and have students name instruments they recognize or know as they hear each one.
- Check answers from the HW in the last lesson.

Lesson Objective

INVOLVE

Introduce the lesson objective. Say: *Today I will learn about musical instruments around the world.*

- Students will read and talk about unique musical instruments as well as their own experience with music.

S115   Unit 9

Pre-reading

Materials: World map or globe

- Invite a volunteer to read the title aloud. Have students predict what the text is about.
- Draw their attention to the five differently-colored blocks of text. Say: *The first block is the introduction, then the article deals with three different musical instruments.*
- Have students look at the pictures of the instruments (bagpipes, steel drums, and bandoneon). Write the names of the instruments on the board.
- Write the names of these countries on the board: *Germany*, *Scotland*, and *Trinidad and Tobago*. Find each country on a world map or globe.
- Invite volunteers to suggest in which country each of these instruments was developed, or is most used. Draw lines to link each instrument to the country that most students agree on.

Reading

13 Listen and read. Which musical instrument was invented in Trinidad and Tobago?

- Read the directions and play Audio Track 139. Have students listen and read along in their books.

MONITOR

Discuss the answer as a class. (Answer: Steel drums)

ASSIST

Replay the audio as needed. Use simple language and gestures to explain unfamiliar words.

Practice 1

14 Look at the passage. Read and say *true* or *false*.

- Place students in pairs, and have partners read the sentences and determine whether they are true or false, referring to specific parts of the article to support their answers.

ASSIST

Help students remember details from the article by having them work in small groups to create a word web for one of the instruments in the article. Groups should write the name of the instrument in the center, surrounded by related key words and phrases and a sketch of the instrument.

MONITOR

Ask different students to explain their answers to the class, e.g. *The first sentence is true. In the fourth paragraph, it says, "Many musicians play six to eight drums at a time."* Have students correct any false sentences. (Answers: 1 true, 2 false, 3 false, 4 true)

- Draw students attention to the list of instruments and countries. Were their predictions correct? (*Answers: bagpipes – Scotland, steel drums – Trinidad and Tobago, bandoneon – Germany, but also common in Argentina*)

Practice 2

14 Listen and complete the text with the words in the box. Then listen and check.

- Read the directions aloud. Students fill in the correct word to complete each sentence.
- Play Audio Track 140 for students to check their answers.

Think BIG

21st Century Cross-Cultural Skills

- Read the questions aloud. Have students work in pairs to ask and answer the questions.

MONITOR

As students discuss musical instruments, listen for correct pronunciation and use of language, and appropriate intonation.

Video

- Refer to the Video Guide for pre-watching and post-watching activities.

Lesson Objective

INVOLVE

Revisit the lesson objective: *Now I have learned about musical instruments around the world.*

- Encourage awareness of what students have learned by eliciting the names of a few of the musical instruments mentioned in the article.

Homework

15 Read 14 again and choose the correct answers.

- Direct students to WB Activity 15 on page 93. Students read the sentences and choose *a* or *b*.

Extra Application and Practice Activity

- Encourage students to use internet sources to find recordings of the instruments described in the article and share them with the class. Students can also interview music teachers or family members about unique musical instruments and use reported speech to share what they learned in class.

Auditory and Kinesthetic Learners: Such learners will benefit from creating their own musical instruments. Point out that percussion instruments can be created by using glasses filled with water or empty containers, such as plastic tubs or metal cans. Have students give their instruments names and then show and describe them to the class.

Unit 9 **T115**

Writing Lesson

Lesson Flow

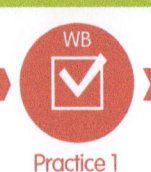

Warm-up › Lesson Objective › Practice 1 (WB) › Practice 2 (SB) › Practice 3 (SB) › Speaking › Lesson Objective › Homework

Lesson Objective

I will learn to write a movie review.

Key Language

special effects

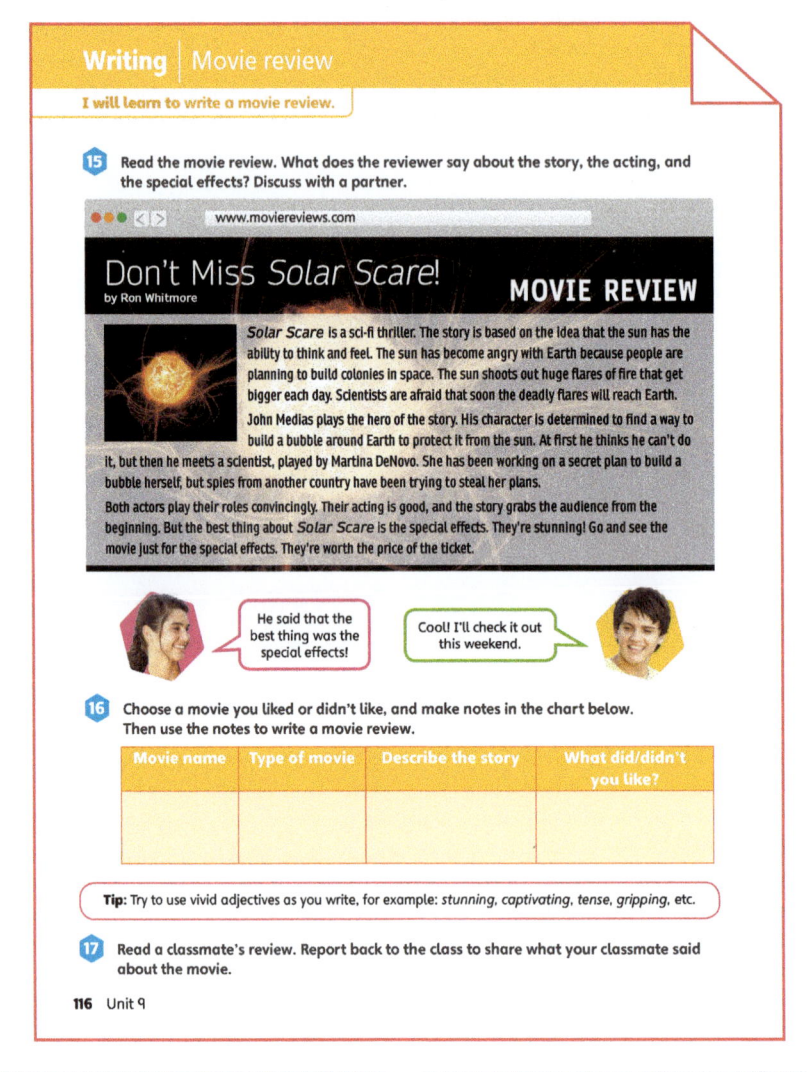

Writing | Movie review
I will learn to write a movie review.

15 Read the movie review. What does the reviewer say about the story, the acting, and the special effects? Discuss with a partner.

Don't Miss *Solar Scare*!
by Ron Whitmore

MOVIE REVIEW

Solar Scare is a sci-fi thriller. The story is based on the idea that the sun has the ability to think and feel. The sun has become angry with Earth because people are planning to build colonies in space. The sun shoots out huge flares of fire that get bigger each day. Scientists are afraid that soon the deadly flares will reach Earth.

John Medias plays the hero of the story. His character is determined to find a way to build a bubble around Earth to protect it from the sun. At first he thinks he can't do it, but then he meets a scientist, played by Martina DeNovo. She has been working on a secret plan to build a bubble herself, but spies from another country have been trying to steal her plans.

Both actors play their roles convincingly. Their acting is good, and the story grabs the audience from the beginning. But the best thing about *Solar Scare* is the special effects. They're stunning! Go and see the movie just for the special effects. They're worth the price of the ticket.

> He said that the best thing was the special effects!

> Cool! I'll check it out this weekend.

16 Choose a movie you liked or didn't like, and make notes in the chart below. Then use the notes to write a movie review.

Movie name	Type of movie	Describe the story	What did/didn't you like?

Tip: Try to use vivid adjectives as you write, for example: *stunning, captivating, tense, gripping,* etc.

17 Read a classmate's review. Report back to the class to share what your classmate said about the movie.

116 Unit 9

Warm-up

Materials: Movie reviews

- Help students find brief movie reviews on the internet or in newspapers or magazines. Then have them take turns reading the reviews aloud for the class – leaving out the title of the movie. Challenge classmates to guess the names of the movies.
- Check answers from the HW in the last lesson.

Lesson Objective

INVOLVE

Introduce the lesson objective. Say: *Today I will learn to write a movie review.*

- Say: *A good movie review lets readers know what the movie is about, but doesn't give any key details (spoilers) away. The review incorporates the reviewer's opinions and helps readers decide if they should see the movie.*
- Students will read and write a movie review.

Practice 1   WB p. 94/ act. 16

16 Put the paragraphs in order. Write 1, 2, or 3.

- Have volunteers read the tips for writing a well-written movie review in the purple box aloud.
- Read the directions aloud. Have three volunteers read one of the paragraphs each.
- Discuss with the class the order the paragraphs should be in. Have students number the paragraphs in pairs. Then check answers as a class.

Practice 2

15 Read the movie review. What does the reviewer say about the story, the acting, and the special effects? Discuss with a partner.

- Read the directions aloud. Then have volunteers read the review and the speech bubbles aloud. Invite students to talk about the review in pairs.

MONITOR

Use questions to check comprehension. Ask: *What is Solar Scare about?* (the sun getting angry with Earth and shooting flares at it) *What actors does the review mention?* (John Medias and Martina DeNovo) *What do their characters have in common?* (They're trying to find a way to protect Earth from the sun.) Be sure students can answer: *What does the reviewer have to say about the acting?* (quite good)/*the story?* (It grabs the audience from the beginning.)/*the special effects?* (the best thing about the movie/stunning)

21st Century Media Literacy

- Have students list their five favorite movies. Ask: *How many of your favorite movies have used special effects? How can you use this information to help you choose movies to see?* (Answers will vary.) Encourage students to discuss the question with a partner and share their ideas with the class.

Practice 3

16 Choose a movie you liked or didn't like, and make notes in the chart below. Then use the notes to write a movie review.

- Read the directions aloud. Have a volunteer read the steps, and the tip in the box.
- Have students work independently to complete the activity.

21st Century Communication

- Remind students that, when they write, the language they use should be appropriate for their audience. Say: *You might use informal words if you're reviewing a movie for friends. If you're posting a review on a website or publishing it in a school paper, your language should be more formal.* Model: *An informal review might say, "You have to see this movie. It's crazy!" A formal review might say, "Anyone who loves science fiction will enjoy this movie."*

MONITOR

Check that students complete the first four steps before writing their reviews. Make sure students give their opinions, rather than simply summarizing the movie.

ASSIST

Have students use the model review to help them. Provide sentence frames from it for students to complete about their movie, such as:*… is a… . The story is based on… . … plays the role of… .*

Speaking

17 Read a classmate's review. Report back to the class to share what your classmate said about the movie.

- Read the directions aloud. Invite volunteers to read their partners' reviews and then report the review to the class. Model: *Nandi said that the movie was terrible. She said the acting wasn't believable, the story was dull, and the special effects were sloppy.*

MONITOR

Listen for correct pronunciation, appropriate intonation, and correct use of language.

Lesson Objective

INVOLVE

Revisit the lesson objective: *Now I have learned to write a movie review.*

- Encourage awareness of what students have learned by asking students to quickly share some tips on how to write a movie review.

Homework   WB p. 94/ act. 17 & 18

17 Look at 16. Complete the chart about *Bubble Sky*.

- Direct students to WB Activity 17 on page 94. Students divide the information in the review in 16 into the categories in the chart.

18 Write a review of a movie playing near you this weekend. Make a chart to help you.

- Direct students to WB Activity 18 on page 94. Students choose a movie to watch at a theatre or on video. Students draw a chart like that in 16 and fill out the information. They then use the chart to write their own review.

Extra Application and Practice Activity

- Have students use reported speech to share highlights of movie reviews from the internet, newspapers, and magazines.

Unit 9   T116

Writing | Movie review

I will learn to write a movie review.

15 Read the movie review. What does the reviewer say about the story, the acting, and the special effects? Discuss with a partner.

---

www.moviereviews.com

Don't Miss *Solar Scare!*
by Ron Whitmore

MOVIE REVIEW

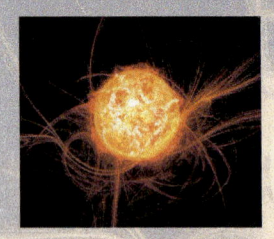

Solar Scare is a sci-fi thriller. The story is based on the idea that the sun has the ability to think and feel. The sun has become angry with Earth because people are planning to build colonies in space. The sun shoots out huge flares of fire that get bigger each day. Scientists are afraid that soon the deadly flares will reach Earth.

John Medias plays the hero of the story. His character is determined to find a way to build a bubble around Earth to protect it from the sun. At first he thinks he can't do it, but then he meets a scientist, played by Martina DeNovo. She has been working on a secret plan to build a bubble herself, but spies from another country have been trying to steal her plans.

Both actors play their roles convincingly. Their acting is good, and the story grabs the audience from the beginning. But the best thing about *Solar Scare* is the special effects. They're stunning! Go and see the movie just for the special effects. They're worth the price of the ticket.

> He said that the best thing was the special effects!

> Cool! I'll check it out this weekend.

16 Choose a movie you liked or didn't like, and make notes in the chart below. Then use the notes to write a movie review.

Movie name	Type of movie	Describe the story	What did/didn't you like?

Tip: Try to use vivid adjectives as you write, for example: *stunning, captivating, tense, gripping,* etc.

17 Read a classmate's review. Report back to the class to share what your classmate said about the movie.

Life skills | Appreciate different opinions.

I will learn to share and discuss different opinions.

18 Read the four different opinions. Match each opinion to an item from the box.

> **a** an exhibit   **b** a concert   **c** a video game   **d** a movie premiere

1 It was the best live musical performance I've ever seen. _____

2 The event, which was held in a dark hall, was badly organized and too busy for me! _____

3 It was the most exciting game I've ever played. I can't wait until they launch the sequel. _____

4 I didn't see any famous actors because it was so crowded. The movie was good though! _____

19 In small groups share your opinions about a movie, book, comic book, or album.

Project

20 Make an **Opinion Map**. Work in a small group.

1 Choose a movie, book, comic book, or album that everyone in your group knows.
2 Share your opinions about it.
3 Record what each person thinks about it on an Opinion Map.
4 Present your Opinion Map to the class:

We reviewed Lady Gaga's new album. Ali said it wasn't as good as her last one, etc.

Ali: It's not as good as her last one.

Kyle: It's great to listen to while I'm doing my homework!

Lady Gaga's New Album

Lisa: The music is too loud! It drowns out her voice.

Sam: The best! It's better than any of her other albums.

Tip: Show interest when people share their opinions. Here are some expressions:
*I think so, too.   Why do you say that?
That's interesting.   Really? I don't agree.*

Unit 9   117

Life Skills Lesson

Lesson Flow

Warm-up › Lesson Objective › Practice (SB) › Speaking › Project › Lesson Objective

Lesson Objective

I will learn to share and discuss different opinions.

Life skills | Appreciate different opinions.

I will learn to share and discuss different opinions.

18 Read the four different opinions. Match each opinion to an item from the box.

> **a** an exhibit **b** a concert **c** a video game **d** a movie premiere

1 It was the best live musical performance I've ever seen. ____

2 The event, which was held in a dark hall, was badly organized and too busy for me! ____

3 It was the most exciting game I've ever played. I can't wait until they launch the sequel. ____

4 I didn't see any famous actors because it was so crowded. The movie was good though! ____

19 In small groups share your opinions about a movie, book, comic book, or album.

Project

20 Make an **Opinion Map**. Work in a small group.

1 Choose a movie, book, comic book, or album that everyone in your group knows.
2 Share your opinions about it.
3 Record what each person thinks about it on an Opinion Map.
4 Present your Opinion Map to the class:

   We reviewed Lady Gaga's new album. Ali said it wasn't as good as her last one, etc.

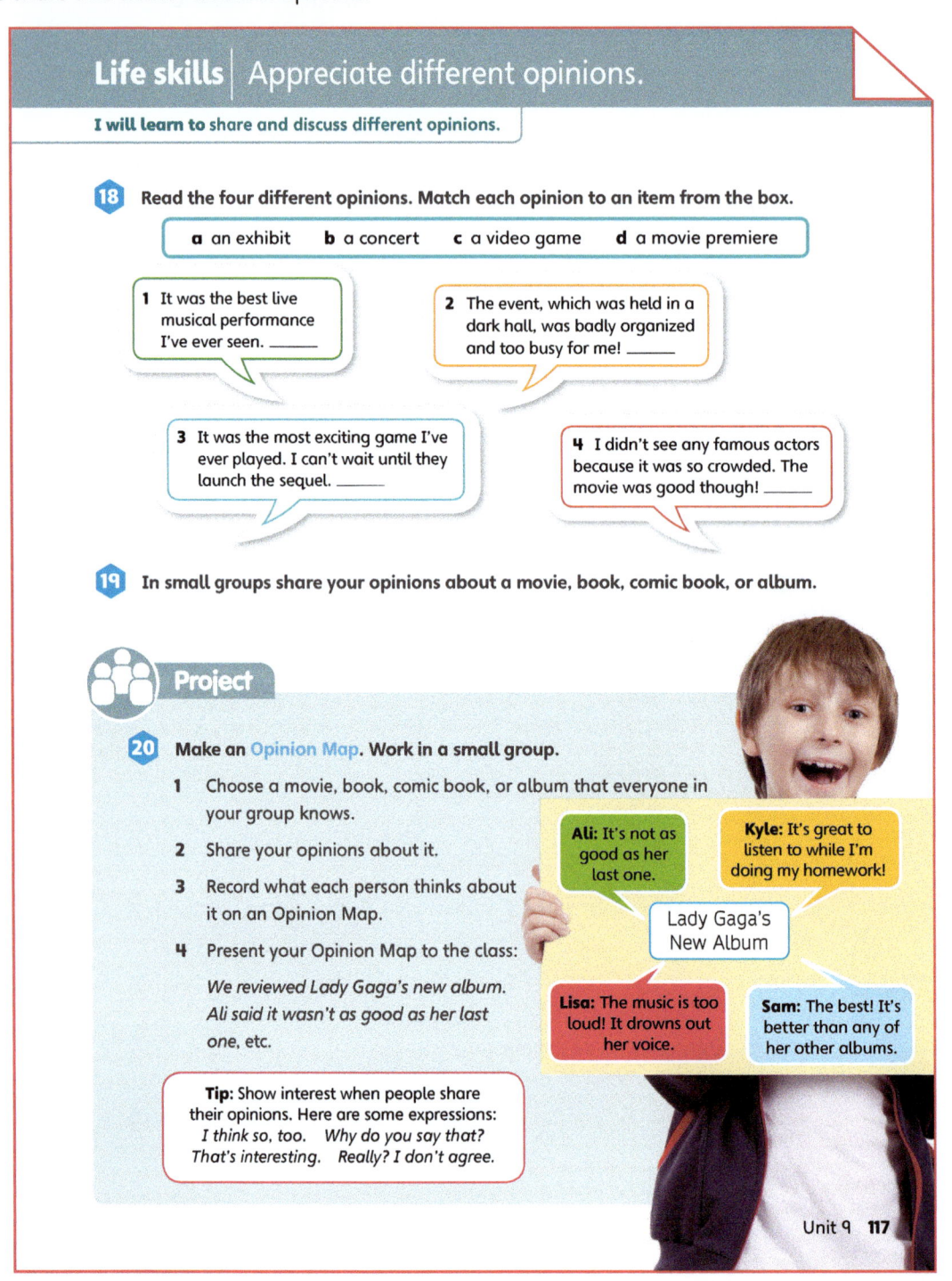

Tip: Show interest when people share their opinions. Here are some expressions:
*I think so, too.   Why do you say that?
That's interesting.   Really? I don't agree.*

Lady Gaga's New Album

- **Ali:** It's not as good as her last one.
- **Kyle:** It's great to listen to while I'm doing my homework!
- **Lisa:** The music is too loud! It drowns out her voice.
- **Sam:** The best! It's better than any of her other albums.

Unit 9 117

S117 Unit 9

Warm-up

Materials: Magazines, newspapers

21st Century

- Have students scan magazines and newspapers for movie, music, or other entertainment reviews that include strong opinions. Suggest that students look for reviews that give very high or very low ratings. Then invite volunteers to read a review aloud very slowly. Have classmates try to say whether the review is negative or positive after hearing as few words as possible.
- Check answers from the HW in the last lesson.

Lesson Objective

INVOLVE

Introduce the lesson objective. Say: *Today I will learn to share and discuss different opinions.*

- Students will read and appreciate different opinions. They'll create an Opinion Map to show their group members' opinions about a creative work.

Practice

18 Read the four different opinions. Match each opinion to an item from the box.

- Read the directions aloud. Invite volunteers to say what they know about the words in the box. (Sample answers: a An exhibit has tables and booths where people show things, such as art or comics. They might also sell them. b A concert is music played by live musicians. c A video game is a game you play on a computer, your TV, or another electronic device. d A movie premiere is the first time a movie is shown.)
- Have students work independently to complete the activity.

MONITOR

Check answers as a class. (Answers: 1 b, 2 a, 3 c, 4 d)

ASSIST

Tell students to use clues from the comments to eliminate choices. Model: *I know a video game isn't a live performance. An exhibit isn't a musical performance. So the first comment must be about a concert.*

Speaking

19 In small groups share your opinions about a movie, book, comic book, or album.

- Read the directions aloud, and have students share their opinions.

MONITOR

As they work, check for correct pronunciation, appropriate intonation, and correct use of language.

Project

Materials: Poster paper, art supplies

20 Make an *Opinion Map*. Work in a small group.

- Read the directions and steps aloud. Have volunteers read the speech bubbles aloud. Then have students work in groups to find an entertainment topic that everyone in the group knows about. Provide suggestions, if needed. Then have students cut out speech bubbles and write each person's opinion to create their Opinion Map. Finally, have volunteers use reported speech to share their group members' opinions with the class.

Variety: Point out that students can use words other than "say" to talk about what someone says about a topic. Model: *Monica said that the movie was wonderful. Alex thought it was pretty good until the end. Naomi commented that the settings were beautiful. Mike insisted that it was better than the director's last movie. Viv agreed but added that it was still a terrible movie.*

21st Century Social Skills

- Say: *Hearing other people's opinions can help you understand their point of view. It might even change your mind about one of your own opinions.* Remind students to use phrases from the **Tip** box as they share their opinions.

Lesson Objective

INVOLVE

Revisit the lesson objective: *Now I have learned to share and discuss different opinions.*

- Encourage awareness of what students have learned by asking for a few reasons why it is good to listen to people's different opinions.

Extra Application and Practice Activity

- Have students create Opinion Maps that show critics' responses to a new movie, book, music, or other entertainment topic. Encourage students to use reported speech to summarize each reviewer's opinion.

Unit 9 **T117**

Listening and Speaking Lesson

Lesson Flow

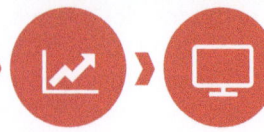

Warm-up › Lesson Objective › Presentation › Practice 1 › Practice 2 › Practice 3 › Speaking › Lesson Objective

Lesson Objectives

I will review the sounds *sion*, *tion*, and *ation*.

I will learn to talk about my favorite entertainment.

Listening and Speaking

I will review the sounds *sion*, *tion*, and *ation*.
I will learn to talk about my favorite entertainment.

21 Listen, read, and repeat.

1. sion 2. tion 3. ation

22 Listen and blend the sounds.

1. t-e-l-e-v-i-sion — television
2. f-i-c-tion — fiction
3. c-e-l-e-b-r-ation — celebration
4. d-e-c-i-sion — decision
5. o-p-tion — option
6. i-n-v-i-t-ation — invitation

23 Listen and chant.

I have an invitation
To a birthday celebration.
We'll watch science fiction
Movies on television.
Now that's a good decision!

24 Work with a partner. Copy and complete this chart for you. Then write your partner's answers.

Who's/What's your favorite...?	Me	My partner
animated movie		
action movie		
comedy movie		
comic book		
video game		
actor		
singer		
song		
album		

25 With your partner, talk about three of the items on the list. Why are those your favorites?

Krypton Kid is my favorite animated movie. The animation is fantastic. The ending is amazing!

118 Unit 9

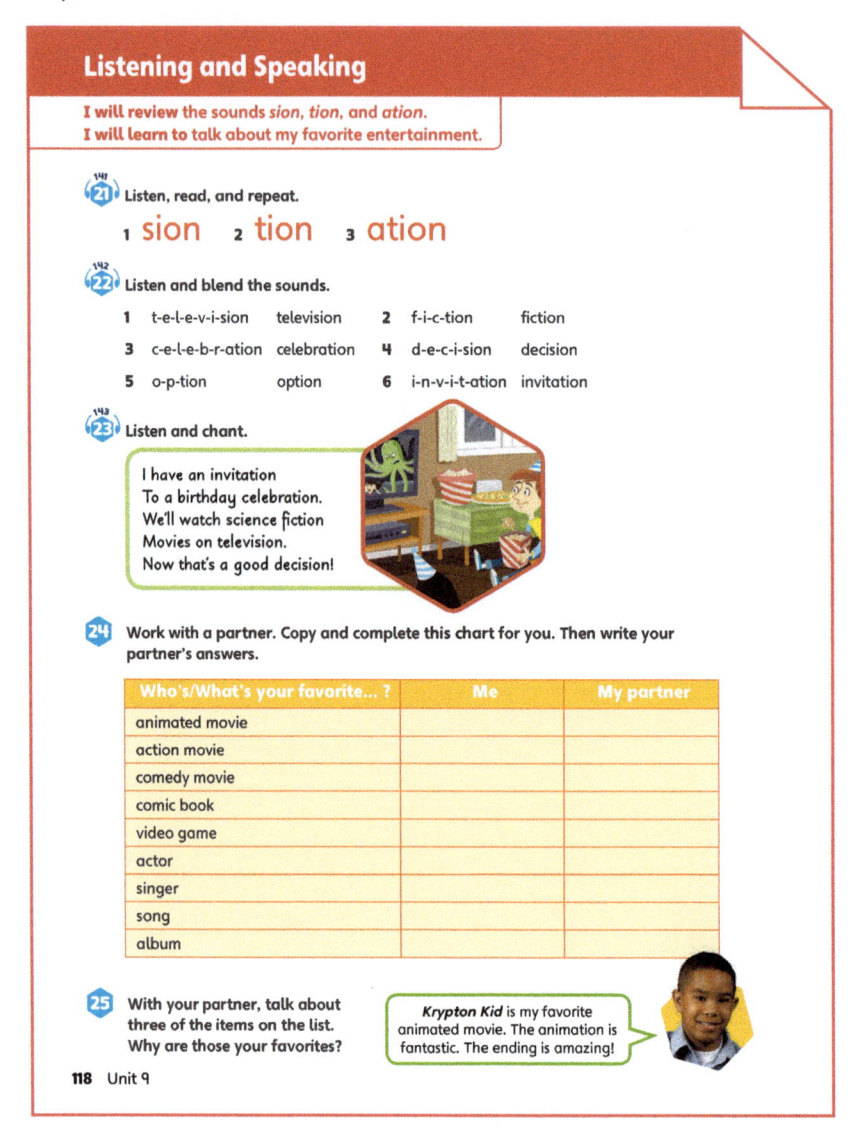

Warm-up

- Have students play *Telephone* (see *Game Bank*, page T137, for details). Have them sit in a circle. Say the name of a popular movie. Have the first student whisper a comment about it (that a reviewer might make) to the student on his or her right.

- Students should continue the chain, whispering what they heard. The last student should say the comment aloud. Then the first student should say his or her original comment. Discuss how it has changed.

21st Century Social Skills

- After playing *Telephone*, have students write down examples of comments that changed the most. Point out that this game shows how what we actually say can be changed when others repeat it. Ask students to draw conclusions about gossip. *(Sample responses: You need to think carefully before you believe what you hear about what someone else said./There's always a chance that the person reporting has made a mistake./It's always best to confirm what you heard about something someone else said before you assume it's true.)*

Lesson Objective

INVOLVE

Introduce the lesson objective. Say: *Today I will learn to use the sounds* sion, tion, *and* ation, *and talk about my favorite entertainment*.

- Students will identify the letters and distinguish between the sounds *sion*, *tion*, and *ation* individually and as part of words. Then they'll review the unit by talking about entertainment topics and opinions about them and by using reported speech.

Presentation

21 Listen, read, and repeat.

- Read the directions aloud. Play Audio Track 141 and have students listen and point to each sound as it is said. Have students repeat.

MONITOR

As students repeat, check they are pointing to the correct sound and listen for correct pronunciation.

Practice 1

22 Listen and blend the sounds.

- Read the directions aloud. Play Audio Track 142 and have students listen and point to each item as it is sounded out and blended on the audio. Have them repeat after each item.

MONITOR

As students repeat, check they are pointing to the correct word, and listen for correct pronunciation and appropriate intonation.

ASSIST

Replay the audio as needed.

Practice 2

23 Listen and chant.

- Read the directions aloud. Read the chant while students follow in their books.

- Play Audio Track 143 and have students listen. Replay the audio several times and encourage them to join in.

MONITOR

As students repeat the chant, listen for correct pronunciation, appropriate intonation, and correct use of language.

Practice 3

24 Work with a partner. Copy and complete this chart for you. Then write your partner's answers.

- Pair students, and read the directions aloud. Direct students' attention to the chart. Explain any unfamiliar entertainment forms from the first column. Say: *An* animated *movie has cartoon characters. An* action *movie has a lot of action, such as adventures or car chases*. Have students complete the second column with their choices and the third column with their partner's.

Speaking

25 With your partner, talk about three of the items on the list. Why are those your favorites?

- Read the directions aloud. Say: *Now you'll find out more about your partner's opinions*. Remind students to support their opinions with details. Tell students to use the comments in the speech bubble about *Krypton Kid* as a model. Ask: *What two details did he use?* (the animation and the ending)

ASSIST

Model questions that students can ask their partners: *What does your favorite singer's music sound like? How many times have you seen your favorite movie? Is it just as interesting the second time?*

Lesson Objective

INVOLVE

Revisit the lesson objective: *Now I have learned to use the sounds* sion, tion, *and* ation, *and talked about my favorite entertainment*.

- Encourage awareness of what students have learned by quickly eliciting from them words from the lesson that have the sounds *sion*, *tion*, and *ation*.

Extra Application and Practice Activity

- Have students create a "Hall of Fame" for the venues and people that are most popular among classmates. Encourage students to post reviews and pictures

Listening and Speaking

I will review the sounds *sion*, *tion*, and *ation*.
I will learn to talk about my favorite entertainment.

21 Listen, read, and repeat.

1. **sion**   2. **tion**   3. **ation**

22 Listen and blend the sounds.

1. t-e-l-e-v-i-sion   television
2. f-i-c-tion   fiction
3. c-e-l-e-b-r-ation   celebration
4. d-e-c-i-sion   decision
5. o-p-tion   option
6. i-n-v-i-t-ation   invitation

23 Listen and chant.

I have an invitation
To a birthday celebration.
We'll watch science fiction
Movies on television.
Now that's a good decision!

24 Work with a partner. Copy and complete this chart for you. Then write your partner's answers.

Who's/What's your favorite... ?	Me	My partner
animated movie		
action movie		
comedy movie		
comic book		
video game		
actor		
singer		
song		
album		

25 With your partner, talk about three of the items on the list. Why are those your favorites?

Krypton Kid is my favorite animated movie. The animation is fantastic. The ending is amazing!

118   Unit 9

Review

26 Complete each sentence with a word from the box.

> book signing　　comic book exhibit　　concert　　festival　　premiere　　review

1. I wanted to go to the Ne-Yo _____ last night, but it was sold out. I read Gayle Smart's _____ of it, and she said it was amazing.
2. Did you hear? The Stamford Summer Brit-pop Music _____ has been announced for June of next year. I can't wait!
3. Do you love comic books? Have you ever been to a _____? If you enjoy reading comic books, this event will blow your mind.
4. Did you hear? *Flipped* is now a movie! The _____ is next week. And the author will be at a _____ event at Bookspace on the same day.

27 Read the dialog. Then take turns with a partner to ask the questions and answer using reported speech.

Brian: What are you doing this weekend?
Carla: I'm going to a hip-hop festival. It starts tomorrow.
Brian: Cool. You're pretty good at dancing, aren't you?
Carla: I love dancing! I'm going to be in a competition next week.
Brian: Wow! So, who's going to be at the festival?
Carla: Jay Z, Kelly Rowland, Diddy, and a bunch more.
Brian: It sounds amazing.
Carla: Yeah. Want to come?
Brian: Sorry, I can't. I'm baby-sitting all day tomorrow.

1. What did Carla say she was doing this weekend?
2. What did Carla say she was going to do next week?
3. What did Brian say about the festival when he heard who was going to be there?
4. What did Brian say he was doing instead of going to the festival?

I Can

- use words for entertainment and events.
- use reported speech.
- talk about entertainment and people's opinions.
- write a movie review.

Review Lesson

Lesson Flow

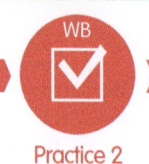

Warm-up › Lesson Objective › Practice 1 (SB) › Practice 2 (WB) › Practice 3 (WB) › Practice 4 (SB) › Self-assessment › Homework

Lesson Objective

To review the words and structures of the unit.

Review

26 Complete each sentence with a word from the box.

| book signing | comic book exhibit | concert | festival | premiere | review |

1. I wanted to go to the Ne-Yo _____ last night, but it was sold out. I read Gayle Smart's _____ of it, and she said it was amazing.
2. Did you hear? The Stamford Summer Brit-pop Music _____ has been announced for June of next year. I can't wait!
3. Do you love comic books? Have you ever been to a _____? If you enjoy reading comic books, this event will blow your mind.
4. Did you hear? *Flipped* is now a movie! The _____ is next week. And the author will be at a _____ event at Bookspace on the same day.

27 Read the dialog. Then take turns with a partner to ask the questions and answer using reported speech.

Brian: What are you doing this weekend?
Carla: I'm going to a hip-hop festival. It starts tomorrow.
Brian: Cool. You're pretty good at dancing, aren't you?
Carla: I love dancing! I'm going to be in a competition next week.
Brian: Wow! So, who's going to be at the festival?
Carla: Jay Z, Kelly Rowland, Diddy, and a bunch more.
Brian: It sounds amazing.
Carla: Yeah. Want to come?
Brian: Sorry, I can't. I'm baby-sitting all day tomorrow.

1. What did Carla say she was doing this weekend?
2. What did Carla say she was going to do next week?
3. What did Brian say about the festival when he heard who was going to be there?
4. What did Brian say he was doing instead of going to the festival?

Unit 9 119

Warm-up

Materials: Index cards

- Have students write vocabulary words from the unit on index cards. Then have students take turns drawing one card and making up a sentence about the word without actually using it. Model: *This is an event you go to when you want to watch a new movie.* (*movie premiere*) Ask classmates to guess the unit word or phrase.

Lesson Objective

INVOLVE

Introduce the lesson objective: Say: *Today I will review the words and structures of the unit.*

- Students will review the vocabulary and grammar they have learned in Unit 9 by doing activities, including completing sentences and writing in reported speech.
- Then students will complete the *I Can* section, which helps them to assess their own learning and think about their progress.

Practice 1

26 Complete each sentence with a word from the box.

- Read the directions aloud. Invite volunteers to provide definitions for each of the words or phrases in the box and then have students complete the activity independently.

MONITOR

Check answers as a class. *(Answers: 1 concert, review; 2 festival; 3 comic book exhibit; 4 premiere, book signing)*

ASSIST

Remind students that each word or phrase from the box will be used only once. Encourage them to read their completed sentences aloud to check that they make sense.

Practice 2 WB p. 95/ act. 19

19 Circle the correct events.

- Read the directions aloud. Read the first item aloud. As a class, choose between movie premiere and book signing.
- Have the students work independently to complete the activity. Then check answers as a class, writing words and definitions that students find challenging on the board.

Practice 3 WB p. 95/ act. 20

20 Change the direct speech to reported speech.

- Read the directions aloud. Have a volunteer read Item 1 aloud. As a class, change the sentence into reported speech.
- Have the students work independently to complete the activity. Then check the answers as a class.

Practice 4

27 Read the dialog. Then take turns with a partner to ask the questions and answer using reported speech.

- Read the directions aloud. First have students read the dialog independently. Then give the parts of Brian and Carol to two volunteers. Have them read their parts aloud, using appropriate gestures and intonation.
- Do the first item as a class. Then have students complete the activity independently.

MONITOR

Check answers by having students read their answers aloud. *(Answers: 1 Carla said she was going to a hip-hop festival. 2 Carla said she was going to be in a dancing competition. 3 Brian said that it sounded amazing. 4 Brian said he would be baby-sitting.)*

Self-assessment

I Can

- This section asks students to assess their own learning and think about their progress. Help students appreciate their progress. Say: *The I Can statements show what you have learned in this unit.*
- Read the statements aloud. Explain that students should think about how well they know the language in the unit and should color in the stars. They should color three stars if they feel the unit was easy, two stars if they need some help and one star if the unit was hard and they need more help. Have students work independently.

Suggestions for Remediation

Assessment Pack

- Direct students who need help with grammar and vocabulary to the Unit 9 Practice Tests in the Assessment Pack.

WB Unit 9/ p. 106

- Direct students who need help with grammar in particular to the Unit 9 Extra Grammar Practice (Workbook, page 106).
- For further vocabulary work, students can access games in the Big English Student World.

Homework WB p. 95/ act. 21

21 Change the reported speech to direct speech.

- Direct students to WB Activity 21 on page 95. Students rewrite the sentences in direct speech.

Extra Application and Practice Activity

- Have students copy the dialog in Activity 27, replacing the entertainment-related details with their own ideas. Then have students exchange dialogs with a classmate and report each other's speech to the class.

Assessment Pack

- To assess student progress at the end of the unit, have students complete the Unit 9 Unit Test in the Assessment Pack.
- To assess whether students have reached the listening and speaking targets for this unit, carry out the Unit 9 Oral Assessment in the Assessment Pack.
- Arrange one-to-one sessions with each student and use the prompts to evaluate their listening and speaking abilities.

Checkpoint 7-9 Lesson 1

Lesson Flow

Warm-up › Lesson Objective › Self-assessment › Practice

Lesson Objective

To think about how well I can use what I have learned in Units 7-9.

Checkpoint | Units 7-9

How well do I know it? Can I use it?

1. Think about it. Read and circle. Practice.

😊 I know this.   😐 I need more practice.   🙁 I don't know this.

	Pages			
Mysteries: Atlantis, Bermuda Triangle, crop circles…	85	😊	😐	🙁
Mystery-related words: phenomenon, proof…	85	😊	😐	🙁
Structures: palace, statue, tower…	97	😊	😐	🙁
Famous places: Statue of Liberty, Taj Mahal…	97	😊	😐	🙁
Entertainment: concert, movie premiere, book signing…	109	😊	😐	🙁
The sailing stones **are** in California, **aren't** they? The Aurora Borealis **isn't** a real mystery, **is** it? The agent **can** break this code, **can't** he? We **can't see** crop circles from the ground, **can** we? She **has** a curious mind, **doesn't** she? They **don't** have all the answers, **do** they?	89	😊	😐	🙁
The Taj Mahal **is visited** by millions of tourists each year. Machu Picchu **was discovered** in 1911 (by archeologists).	101	😊	😐	🙁
Leonardo da Vinci was an inventor and the famous artist **who painted** the Mona Lisa. The Eiffel Tower is a landmark **that has become** the symbol of Paris, France.	101	😊	😐	🙁
Claire said, "The album **isn't** as good as the last one." She said the album **wasn't** as good as the last one. Dana said, "Paul**'s going** to a concert." She said that Paul **was going** to a concert.	113	😊	😐	🙁

Warm-up

- Have students play *Spell Off* to review vocabulary from Units 7–9. Players take turns choosing a vocabulary word or phrase and spelling it, pausing after each letter. The first classmate to guess the word or phrase gets a point. The student with the most points at the end is the winner.

Lesson Objective

INVOLVE

- Introduce the lesson objective: *Today I will think about how well I can use what I have learned in Units 7–9.*
- Students will review key language in Units 7–9.

Self-assessment

Materials: Plastic building blocks or clay, magazines and books

1 Think about it. Read and circle. Practice.

- Read the descriptions aloud as students point to the face icons at the top of the page. Have them use markers or colored pencils to complete the checklist. They will choose a different color when they review this list at the end of the Checkpoint.

MONITOR

Follow the suggestions below to review the key language in these units. Listen for correct use of vocabulary and grammar. Remind students that they will be asked to assess their own abilities.

ASSIST

Encourage students to turn to the page references in the checklist when they need additional support or to refresh their memories.

21st Century Self-Direction

- Remind students that they completed Checkpoints to review the skills they learned in Units 1–3 and Units 4–6. Have students review those Checkpoints to recall how they used a checklist to monitor their own progress. As students complete the checklist for Units 7–9, emphasize that there are no right or wrong answers. Students should circle face icons that show how they feel about each skill.

Mysteries (page 85)

Have students complete a word web for *mysteries* that are still mysterious, such as the Bermuda Triangle, crop circles, and Nazca Lines.

Mystery-related words (page 85)

Have students take turns beginning to spell mystery-related words from Unit 7. The student who guesses a word first scores a point.

Structures (page 97)

Have students use plastic building blocks or clay to make one-minute replicas of structures and challenge classmates to guess each structure.

Famous places (page 97)

One student chooses a famous place and keeps it secret. Another student puts a pointer on a world map. The first student says if the second student is getting "colder" or "warmer" as the pointer gets farther or closer to the place. Students try to guess the famous place before the location is revealed.

Entertainment (page 109)

Have students create calendars with five entertainment events they would like to attend. Invite partners to share information about their events.

Question tags (page 89)

Have students find statements in books and magazines and make question tags about them. Model: *Bern is the capital of Switzerland, isn't it?*

Passive voice (page 101)

Ask students to complete these sentence frames: *was built in… is located in…* . Students then compare their answers and write additional examples of the passive voice.

Relative clauses (page 101)

Invite students to scan books and magazines for sentences with *who* or *that*. Have students share and name the noun *who* or *that* refers to in the clause.

Reported speech (page 113)

Have partners interview each other about forms of entertainment. Then have them report their partner's opinions to the class. Model: *Pam said that the show was exciting. Mika said the song was unforgettable.*

Practice WB pp. 96 & 97/ act. 1, 2, & 3

1 Look at the pictures. Complete the items. Add your own items on the extra lines.

- Direct students to WB Activity 1 on page 96. Read the directions aloud. Ask the students to look at the pictures and name the items pictured (1–3). For 4, they add their own item.

2 Find a famous place or event that interests you. Complete the chart.

- Direct students to WB Activity 2 on page 97. Read the directions aloud. Students choose a place and complete the chart with information about it.

3 Do research. Find more information about the place or event in 2. Write a report about it.

- Direct students to WB Activity 3 on page 97. Read the directions aloud. Students use the information in the chart, and research further if required, to write a report.

Checkpoint 7-9 Lesson 2

Lesson Flow

Warm-up › Lesson Objective › Pre-listening › Listening › Practice 1 (SB) › Practice 2 (SB)

Lesson Objective

To put together what I have learned in Units 7-9.

I can do it!

144 / 2 Get ready.

A. Choose the correct word or phrase to complete the dialog.
Then listen and check.

Tina: Hey, do you want to watch *Mystery Tour*?

Kevin: I don't know. What's it about?

Tina: It's a new show about scientists ¹ **who / who's** travel around the world and study mysterious places, like the Bermuda Triangle.

Kevin: Oh, I've heard about that show! My friend at school said it ² **was / were** really good.

Tina: Oops, wait a minute, Kevin. It's not on until 9:00. Your mom said your bedtime was at 8:30, ³ **did / didn't** she?

Kevin: That's on weeknights. On Saturdays I'm allowed to stay up until 9:30.

Tina: Oh, lucky you. You can watch it, then.

Kevin: So *Mystery Tour* is scary, isn't it?

Tina: Umm, not really. I think it's ⁴ **make / made** for people ⁵ **who / which** like science. But you're a science guy, ⁶ **are / aren't** you?

Kevin: Sort of. But I like scary shows better, like *Dark Corners*.

Tina: *Dark Corners*! That's a creepy show!

Kevin: What's wrong with creepy? Anyway, it's not on anymore.
It ⁷ **is canceled / was canceled** last month.

Tina: Probably because it was too creepy.

B. Practice the dialog in **A** with a partner.

C. Ask and answer the questions with a partner.

1 What is the TV show *Mystery Tour* about?
2 What has Kevin heard about the show?
3 Will Kevin be able to watch the show with Tina? Why/Why not?
4 Does the show sound interesting to you? Why/Why not?

Checkpoint Units 7-9 121

S121 Checkpoint Units 7-9

Warm-up

- Have students list names of new television programs. Ask: *How do you find out about new TV shows?* (Sample answers: I hear about them from friends./I see ads on TV, in magazines, online, and in public places./I read reviews in magazines and newspapers./I find them while changing channels.) *If you could choose new TV shows, what kinds would you choose?* (Answers will vary.)

Lesson Objective

INVOLVE

Introduce the Lesson Objective: *Today I will put together what I have learned in Units 7–9.*

- Students will complete and practice a dialog. Then they will talk about a TV show and share their opinions about it.

Pre-listening

- Read the directions and dialog names aloud.
- Tell students they will listen to Tina and Kevin talk about TV shows about mysterious places and events.

Listening

2 Get ready.

A Choose the correct word or phrase to complete the dialog. Then listen and check.

- Have students read the dialog independently, and circle the correct word to complete it.
- Play Audio Track 144 twice. First, have students focus on listening comprehension. Then have them check to see if they circled the correct words.

MONITOR

Check answers as a class. (Answers: 1 who, 2 was, 3 didn't, 4 made, 5 who, 6 aren't, 7 was canceled)

21st Century Media Awareness

- Invite students to use television program guides or classroom, library, or internet resources to find out about television programs that are like *Mystery Tour*. Encourage students to find out about each show's format and host, and episodes already aired. If possible, have students find and share summaries of the episodes with the class.

Practice 1

B Practice the dialog in A with a partner.

- Read the directions aloud and invite students to practice the dialog. Encourage students to change roles to review all of the unit language.

MONITOR

Listen for correct pronunciation, intonation, and use of language as students practice the dialog.

CHALLENGE

Invite students to create another dialog between Kevin and Tina after the two have watched *Mystery Tour* together. Allow partners to share their new dialogs with the class.

Practice 2

C Ask and answer the questions with a partner.

- Read the directions aloud. Have student pairs ask and answer questions about the TV show.

MONITOR

Have students share their responses with the class. (Answers: 1 *Mystery Tour* is a show about scientists who travel the world and study mysterious places. 2 A friend of Kevin's said the show was really good. 3 Kevin will be able to watch the show with Tina because he can stay up later on Saturdays. 4 Answers will vary.)

Take a class poll to find out how many students would like to watch *MysteryTour*. Listen for correct use of language as students compare ideas.

ASSIST

Provide models to help students answer questions. Model: *I think* Mystery Tour *sounds interesting because I like shows that are set all around the world.* Or: *I don't think the show sounds interesting because I already know a lot about mysteries.*

- Remind students that contractions are very common in informal speech. Say: *When you talk with friends, using contractions makes your language sound friendly and conversational.* Have students practice the dialog with and without contractions to recognize the difference in tone. Guide them to use this word order for the tags *didn't she* and *aren't you*: *did she not* and *are you not*. Remind students that contractions are not usually used in formal writing.

Checkpoint Units 7–9 **T121**

Checkpoint 7-9 Lesson 3

Lesson Flow

Warm-up › Lesson Objective › Speaking

Lesson Objective

To put together what I have learned in Units 7-9.

Checkpoint | Units 7-9

3 Get set.

STEP 1 Cut out the cards on page 137.

STEP 2 Assign a group leader. The group leader gets a set of yellow cards, the group gets a set of green cards, and each group member gets a set of orange cards.
Now you're ready to **Go**!

4 Go!

A. Work in a group of five.
- The group leader takes the yellow card. Each other member takes one of the green cards. As the leader reads each yellow card, the student with the green card that correctly completes the description reads it.
- For each title, group members turn over orange cards and describe what "your best friend" says about the title.

> My best friend said *International Mystery Solvers* was interesting.

> Really? My best friend said it was a little boring.

B. Count the positive and negative reviews for each title and decide which ones your group is going to check out. Report to the class.

> *International Mystery Solvers* got three positive reviews in our group. Let's check it out!

122 Checkpoint Units 7-9

Warm-up

3 Get set.

- Have students preview the description cards on page 137. Have students read the cards aloud and restate them in their own words. Use simple language, gestures, or illustrations to define unfamiliar terms, such as *explorers, civilization, danger zone, creature, sci-fi,* and *hard-to-solve mysteries.*

- Read the directions and steps aloud. Have students cut out and prepare the cards on page 137. Have students read Step 2 carefully so they know how many cards are needed for their group (one set of yellow cards for the group leader, one set of green cards for the group to share, and one set of orange cards for each student in the group).

CHALLENGE

Invite students to create additional review cards. Point out that each card should begin with what "Your best friend says" and have a strong negative or positive opinion. Model: *Your best friend says, "It's the best one ever!" Your best friend says, "It's beyond terrible!"*

Lesson Objective

INVOLVE

Introduce the Lesson Objective: *Today I will put together what I have learned in Units 7–9.*

- Students will ask and answer questions about forms of entertainment.

Speaking

4 Go!

A Work in a group of five.

- Read the directions aloud. Say: *First, you will match descriptions of a game, a comic book, a movie, and a book. Then you will take a card to find what your best friend said about it.* Invite volunteers to read the conversation in the speech bubbles aloud to model the activity. Then have students complete the activity with their group.

MONITOR

Check that students match cards correctly. (Answers: **International Mystery Solvers** – *It's a new video game about explorers who go from country to country searching for answers to the world's most hard-to-solve mysteries.*

Chasing Bigfoot – *It's a new comic book about a team of explorers who are looking for a giant, mysterious creature that lives in the forests of North America.*

Return to Atlantis – *It's a new movie about a group of scientists who are trying to solve the mystery of a lost island civilization.*

Inside the Bermuda Triangle – *It's a new sci-fi book about some scientists who travel by boat and plane into a danger zone in search of answers.*)

ASSIST

Help students classify each opinion card as positive or negative. Say: *A positive review says it's good; a negative review says it's bad.* (positive adjectives: *amazing, interesting;* negative adjectives: *boring, awful*).

B Count the positive and negative reviews for each title and decide which ones your group is going to check out. Report to the class.

- Read the directions aloud. Say: *When you "check something out," you find out more about it. If you check out a movie, you watch it. If you check out a game, you play it.* Have a volunteer read the speech bubble aloud. Have students continue to work together to discuss the results and decide which titles they want to check out.

MONITOR

Listen for correct grammar, vocabulary, and use of language as students discuss the results for each title.

21st Century Leadership

Remind students that a strong group leader helps focus an activity so that group members can get it done. Point out that a good leader makes sure that every team member contributes. Allow students to take turns being group leaders in order to develop everyone's leadership skills.

Checkpoint 7-9 Lesson 4

Lesson Flow

Warm-up › Lesson Objective › Practice › Video › Self-assessment 1 › Self-assessment 2

Lesson Objective

To think again about how well I can use what I have learned in Units 7–9.

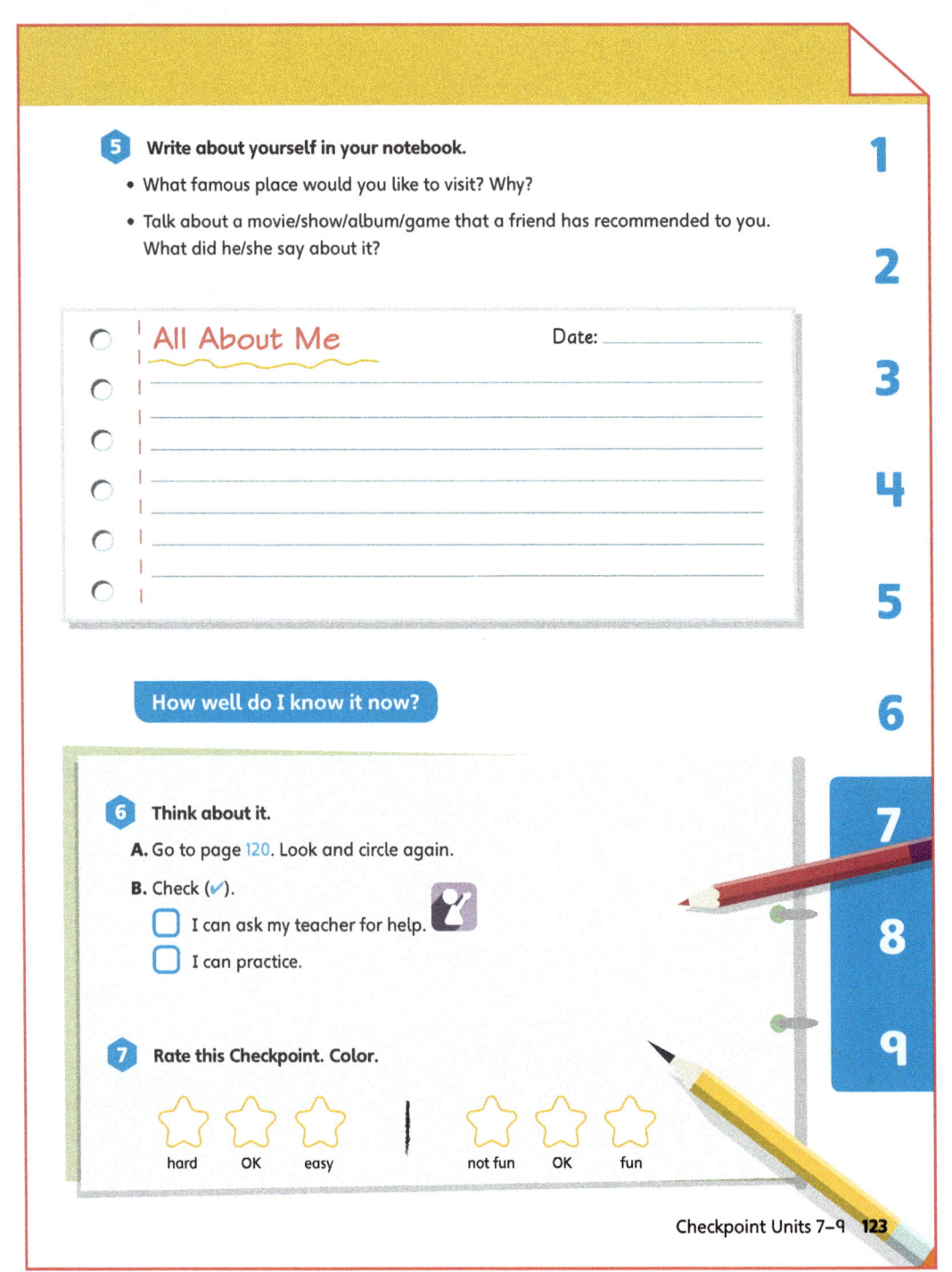

5 Write about yourself in your notebook.
- What famous place would you like to visit? Why?
- Talk about a movie/show/album/game that a friend has recommended to you. What did he/she say about it?

All About Me Date: _____

How well do I know it now?

6 Think about it.
A. Go to page 120. Look and circle again.
B. Check (✓).
- ☐ I can ask my teacher for help.
- ☐ I can practice.

7 Rate this Checkpoint. Color.

hard OK easy | not fun OK fun

Checkpoint Units 7–9

Warm-up

- Invite each student to make a recommendation from the world of entertainment. Ask: *What movie, show, album, or game would you like to recommend to the class? Why?* Invite students to come to the board and write the name of the title they recommend and tell why they think that others will enjoy it. Remind students to include their names so that classmates can remember who made each recommendation.

Lesson Objective

INVOLVE
Introduce the lesson objective: *Today I will think about how well I can use what I have learned in Units 7–9.*

- Students will write about famous places and the world of entertainment. Then they will look back at Units 7–9 and think about how well they can use what they have learned.

Practice

5 Write about yourself in your notebook.

- Read the directions, questions, and journal title aloud.
- Have students begin by writing today's date. Then have them write answers to the questions. Encourage students to use complete sentences. Provide students with additional journal pages as needed.

MONITOR
Check students' work for correct use of language.

ASSIST
Have students use a world map or globe, Unit 8, or the Internet to help them think of famous places they would like to visit. If they wish, students can write about their classmates' ideas from the Warm-up activity to answer the second question.

- Invite students to read aloud their *All About Me* entries and compare them with their classmates' entries.

Video Drama U 7–9

- Refer to the Video Guide for pre-watching and post-watching activities.

Self-assessment 1

6 Think about it.

A Go to page 120. Look and circle again.

- Read the directions aloud.

21st Century Self-Direction

- Have students turn to the "Read and circle" exercise on page 120 and think about each of the categories again. Remind students to take their time to think about each category carefully. Suggest that they look at the reference pages listed as they review their skills.
- Ask students to use a different colored pencil or marker as they reassess their understanding and use of each checklist item.
- Students may want to circle the same face icon when they revisit the exercise. Encourage them to draw the second circle outside the first so that both colors are visible, rather than covering up the first circle with the second color.

B Check (✓).

- Say: *Now choose the statement that describes how you feel about Units 7–9.* Students can use the "Read and circle" exercise on page 120 to help them choose a response. If they circled ten to twelve smiling faces, they can practice their English with confidence. If they circled fewer than ten smiling faces, they should probably check *I can ask my teacher for help.*

Self-assessment 2

7 Rate this Checkpoint. Color.

- Read the directions aloud. Point out that students will color only one star in each section. Say: *First, you will say if the Checkpoint was easy, OK, or hard. Then you will say if it was fun, OK, or not fun.*
- Have students complete the rating individually.

Cutouts for Checkpoints

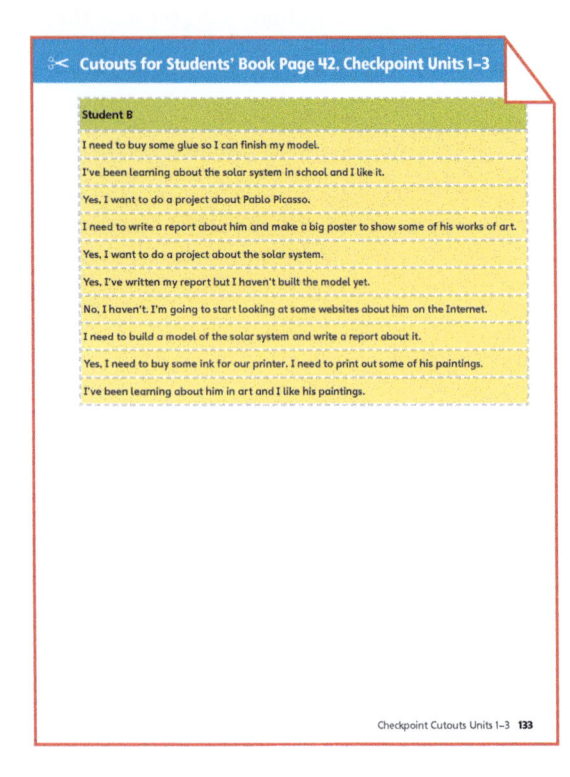

Cutouts for Students' Book Page 42, Checkpoint Units 1–3

Student B

I need to buy some glue so I can finish my model.

I've been learning about the solar system in school and I like it.

Yes, I want to do a project about Pablo Picasso.

I need to write a report about him and make a big poster to show some of his works of art.

Yes, I want to do a project about the solar system.

Yes, I've written my report but I haven't built the model yet.

No, I haven't. I'm going to start looking at some websites about him on the Internet.

I need to build a model of the solar system and write a report about it.

Yes, I need to buy some ink for our printer. I need to print out some of his paintings.

I've been learning about him in art and I like his paintings.

Checkpoint Cutouts Units 1–3 133

Cutouts for Students' Book Page 82, Checkpoint Units 4–6

Mystery Classmate: _____
(Remember: Don't read the name aloud!)

???

If this person could eat any food every day, it would be _____.

He/She plays more _____ than _____.

He/She reads fewer _____ than _____.

He/She definitely spends _____ time in front of the computer than some people I know.

If he/she didn't have to go to school every day, he/she would _____ and _____ from morning till night.

My classmate thinks he/she will probably be living in _____ in twenty years. And he'll/she'll probably be working as a(n) _____.

Who is he/she?

Checkpoint Cutouts Units 4–6 135

Cutouts for Students' Book Page 122, Checkpoint Units 7–9

Description cards

One set for the group leader | One set for each group

International Mystery Solvers It's a new video game about explorers…	…who are trying to solve the mystery of a lost island civilization.
Chasing Bigfoot It's a new comic book about a team of explorers…	…who travel by boat and plane into a danger zone in search of answers.
Return to Atlantis It's a new movie about a group of scientists…	…who are looking for a giant, mysterious creature that lives in the forests of North America.
Inside the Bermuda Triangle It's a new sci-fi book about some scientists…	…who go from country to country searching for answers to the world's most hard-to-solve mysteries.

Review cards

One set for each group member

Your best friend says, "It's amazing!"	Your best friend says, "It's interesting."
Your best friend says, "It's quite boring."	Your best friend says, "It's awful."

Checkpoint Cutouts Units 7–9 137

Stickers

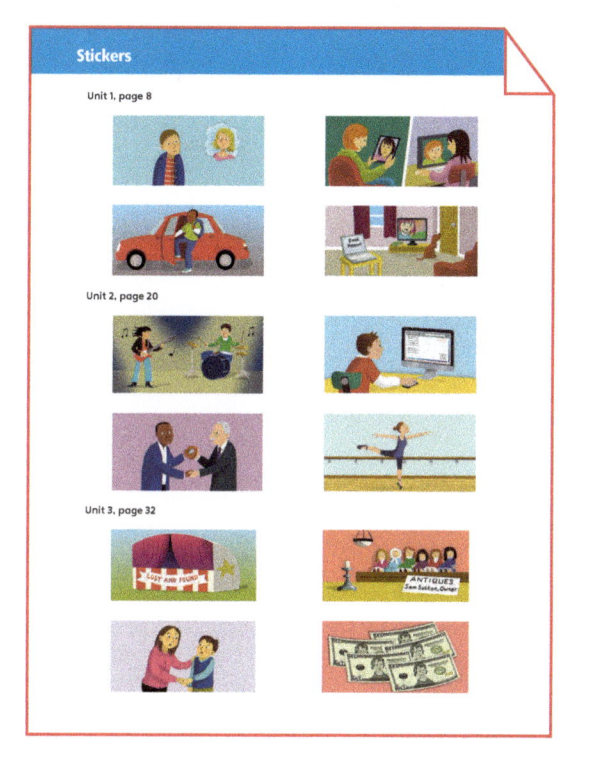

Stickers
Unit 1, page 8

Unit 2, page 20

Unit 3, page 32

Stickers
Unit 4, page 48

Unit 5, page 60

Unit 6, page 72

Stickers
Unit 7, page 88

Unit 8, page 100

Unit 9, page 112

T125

Cambridge Young Learners English: Flyers Practice Paper

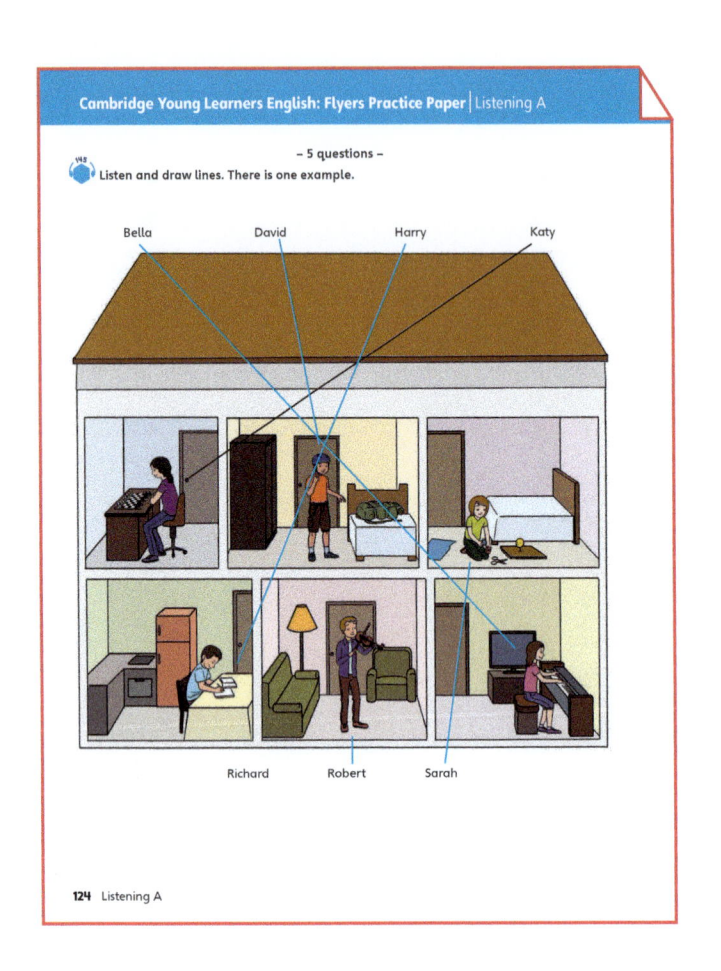

Listening A

In this part, students listen and draw lines to match names with children in a picture.

Do the test

1 Ask students to turn to page 124. Read the children's names above and below the picture, indicating to students that they repeat after you.
2 Tell students that the picture shows six children doing different activities at home. Explain that the six children are all brothers and sisters.
3 To warm up, ask students what kinds of things they like to do at home.
4 Play the first part of the recording. Go through the example.
5 Play the rest of the recording while students match the names with the children shown in the picture.
6 Let students listen to the recording again. Check the answers.

Audio Script

Narrator: **Listening A. Listen and draw lines. There is one example.**
Woman 1: Hello, Emma. Gosh, I haven't seen you for such a long time!
Woman 2: I know, Vicky. I can't believe it's been twenty years since we were at school. It's so wonderful to see you.
Woman 1: You, too! One of our classmates told me you have a lot of children now.
Woman 2: Yes, I have six! Can you believe it?
Woman 1: What are they like?
Woman 2: Well, my eldest daughter, Katy, plays chess a lot. She's been playing it since she was little. She's really very good at it.
Narrator: **Can you see the line? This is an example. Now you listen and draw lines.**
Woman 2: My daughter Bella is into music. She's been playing the piano since she was three years old.
Woman 1: Oh, really?
Woman 2: Yes, and my son Robert likes music a lot, too. He's been playing the violin for five years now.
Woman 1: That's wonderful. Do any of your other children like the arts?
Woman 2: Well, my son Harry wants to be a writer when he grows up. He loves writing stories. But sometimes he spends too much time writing, and not enough time doing his homework!
Woman 1: Ah, some children are like that.
Woman 2: Yes. My youngest daughter Sarah loves science. She's been working on a new science project for the last week or so.
Woman 1: Wonderful. So that's Katy, Bella, Robert, and…
Woman 2: … and Harry and Sarah.
Woman 1: Do you have any other children?
Woman 2: Yes – one more. My son David. He's the active one of the group.
Woman 1: What does he like doing?
Woman 2: He likes mountain climbing. He goes all the time with my husband. In fact, he's getting ready to go mountain climbing today.
Woman 1: That sounds like fun. And good exercise, too! It sounds like all your children are very talented. That's really wonderful, Emma.
Woman 2: Thanks, Vicky. I'm very proud of them.
Narrator: **Now listen again.**

Cambridge Young Learners English: Flyers Practice Paper | Listening B

– 5 questions –

Listen and write. There is one example.

Interview with a Star

	Career:	_soccer player_
1	How many years:	_12_ years
2	When playing in Olympics:	in _6_ months
3	Olympic goal:	_gold_ medal
4	Plans in ten years:	_playing soccer_
5	Message for young people:	_Never give up._

Listening B 125

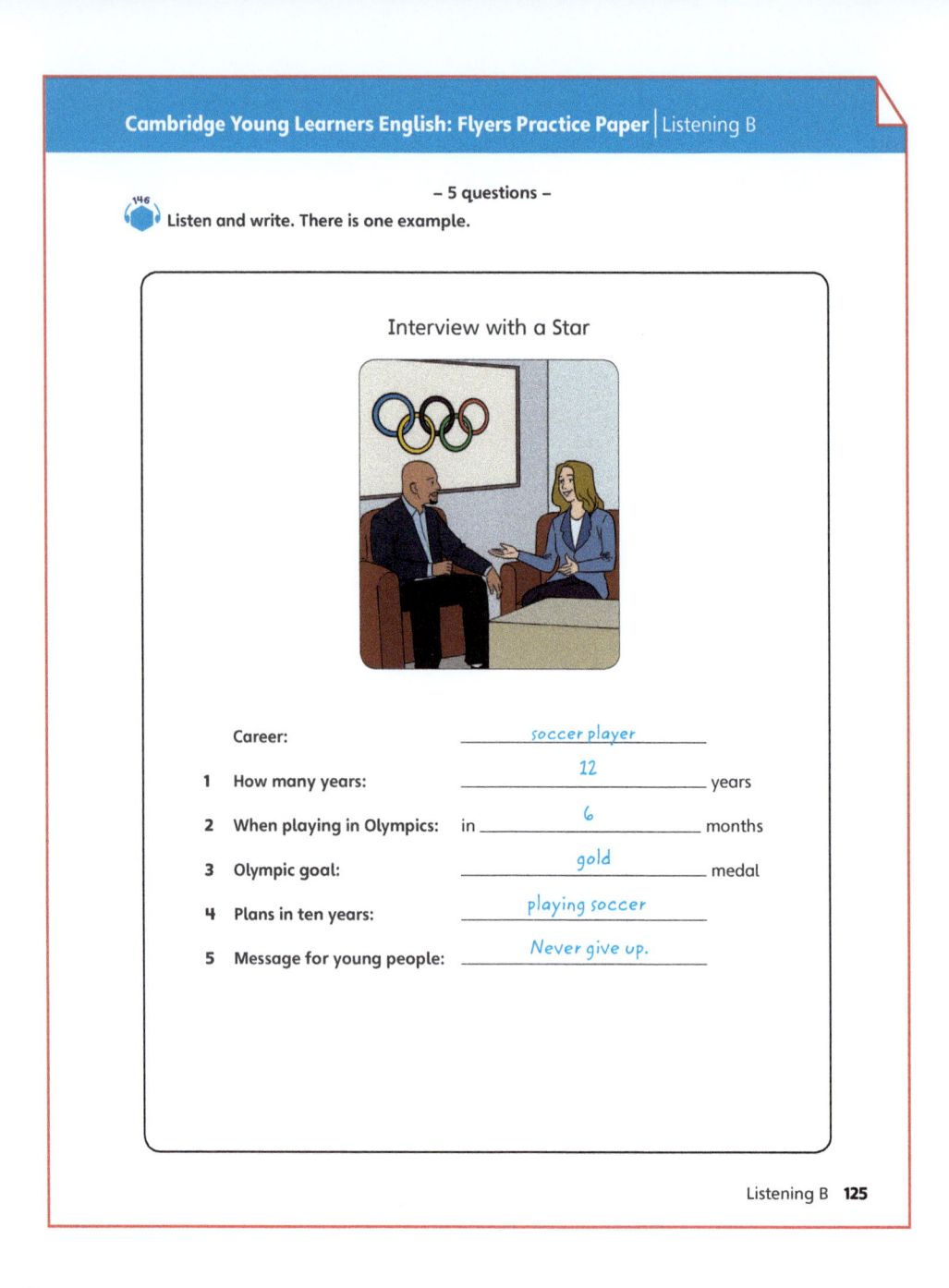

Listening B

In this part, students listen to a dialog and take notes.

Do the test

1. Ask students to turn to page 125. Explain that they will hear an interview between a talk show host and a famous soccer player. The talk show host will ask the soccer player questions about his career and future plans.
2. To warm up, invite students to practice turning each of the prompts into a question (*For how many years have you been a soccer player? When did you start playing? What's your goal for the Olympics?* etc.)
3. Play the first part of the recording. Go through the example.
4. Play the rest of the recording. Have students take notes, writing information on each line of the notepad while they listen.
5. Let students listen to the recording again. Help them check their answers.

Audio Script

Narrator: **Listening B. Listen and write. There is one example.**
Woman: Hello and welcome to our show.
Man: It's great to be here.
Woman: I'd like to ask you a few questions about your career as a soccer player.
Man: My career as a soccer player. Certainly.
Woman: OK. Let's get started.
Narrator: **Can you see the answer? Now you listen and write.**
Woman: My first question is about your early days. How long have you been playing soccer?
Man: I started playing when I was twelve.
Woman: And you're twenty-four now. So you've been playing soccer for… twelve years?
Man: That's right.
Woman: And I hear that your team has some exciting news about the Olympics.
Man: Yes, it's true. We're going to take part in the next Olympics, which is six months from now.
Woman: In six months. That's not long! How do you feel?
Man: Excited. Proud. Scared.
Woman: What a mix of feelings. What's your goal for the Olympics?
Man: We're going for the gold!
Woman: The gold medal?
Man: That's right. If we practice really hard, we'll win it. I'm sure of it.
Woman: What about the future? Where do you see yourself ten years from now?
Man: Ten years? Well, I hope I'll be still playing soccer.
Woman: You don't think you'll want to retire before then?
Man: Retire? I don't think so. I love this sport. I'll definitely still be playing.
Woman: Finally, what message do you have for young people today?
Man: Hm… Never give up.
Woman: That's a great message, to never give up. I think I need to hear that, too! Thank you for coming today.
Man: Thank you for having me. I enjoyed talking to you.
Narrator: **Now listen again.**

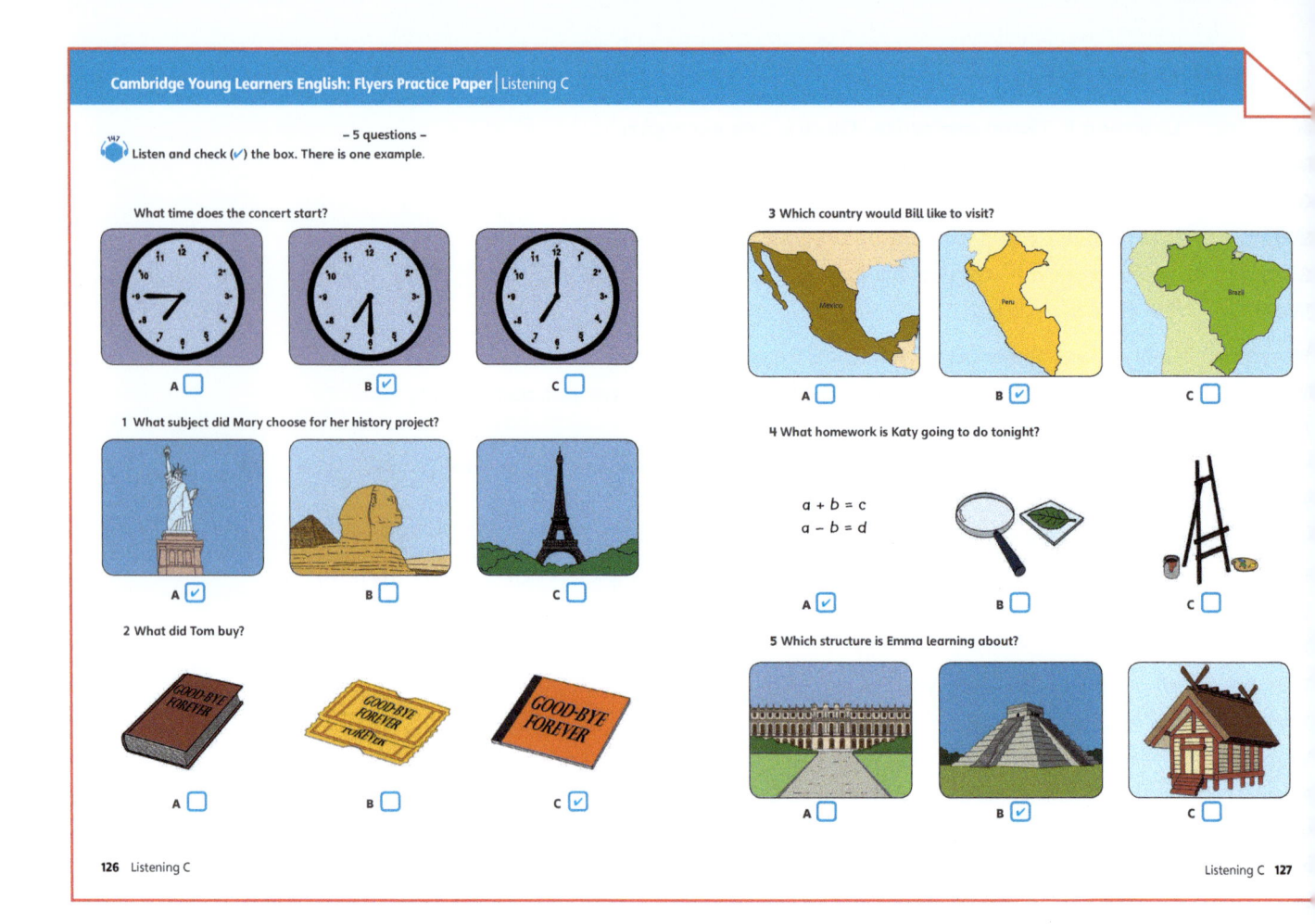

Cambridge Young Learners English: Flyers Practice Paper | Listening C

– 5 questions –

Listen and check (✓) the box. There is one example.

What time does the concert start?

A ☐   B ✓   C ☐

1 What subject did Mary choose for her history project?

A ✓   B ☐   C ☐

2 What did Tom buy?

A ☐   B ☐   C ✓

3 Which country would Bill like to visit?

A ☐   B ✓   C ☐

4 What homework is Katy going to do tonight?

$a + b = c$
$a - b = d$

A ✓   B ☐   C ☐

5 Which structure is Emma learning about?

A ☐   B ✓   C ☐

Listening C

In this part, students listen to questions and check the correct picture.

Do the test

1 Ask students to turn to pages 126–127. Look at the five questions together and prompt students to name the different objects, activities, and places shown.
2 Play the recording and pause it after the example. Go through the example with the class, making sure they understand what they need to do.
3 Play the rest of the recording. As the students listen to the questions, they look at each set of pictures and check the correct box, A, B, or C.
4 Let students listen to the recording again. Check the answers.

Audio Script

Narrator: Listening C. Listen and check the box. There is one example.
Boy: Hi, Mary.
Girl: Hi, Tom. I'm excited to see the concert tonight.
Boy: So am I. We'd better go now. What time does it start?
Girl: Um... it starts at 7:45, doesn't it?
Boy: I don't think so. I think it starts at seven thirty.
Girl: Oh, you're right. Seven thirty. And it's seven now. We have to hurry or we'll be late.

Narrator: Can you see the check? Now you listen and check the box. One. What subject did Mary choose for her history project?
Boy: What is your history project on, Mary? Did you choose anything from Europe?
Girl: No, I didn't. I thought about choosing the Great Sphinx, but decided not to.
Boy: I think the Egyptians were amazing.
Girl: You're right, they were. But I recently watched a program about the Statue of Liberty and thought, Wow! Did you know the Statue of Liberty was designed by the same man that designed the Eiffel Tower?
Boy: Yes. It was a gift from France to the United States, wasn't it?
Girl: Exactly. It has such an interesting history, so that's why I chose it.

Narrator: Two. What did Tom buy?
Boy 1: Hi Tom. What's that?
Boy 2: It's a new CD. I just bought it for my collection.
Boy 1: Oh really?
Boy 2: Yeah. It's the soundtrack to that movie called "Good-bye Forever."
Boy 1: Oh, I saw that movie and read the book. They were both great.

Narrator: Three. Which country would Bill like to visit?
Boy 1: Are you ready to start the homework?
Girl 2: Yeah. So, the first question is, would you like to visit Mexico, Brazil, or Peru?
Boy 1: I want to visit all of them. I have family in Mexico so maybe I would start there first.
Girl 2: Wait. That's not the question. Which country would you like to visit?
Boy 1: Do you mean I have to choose *one*?
Girl 2: Yes, you do.
Boy 1: Oh. Well, in that case, I think I'd have to choose Peru because I've always wanted to see Machu Picchu.

Narrator: Four. What homework is Katy going to do tonight?
Boy: How's your art assignment going, Katy?
Girl: I'm done. I painted a view of London. Have you started your research for the science project yet?
Boy: No, I haven't.
Girl: I haven't started mine either. I'm going to review for my math test tonight. Then tomorrow, I'll work on the science project.

Narrator: Five. Which structure is Emma learning about?
Girl: I'm studying history at the moment. Have you ever heard of the Temple of Kukulcán?
Boy: No, I haven't.
Girl: It's a famous pyramid in Mexico. It's also known as El Castillo.
Boy: What does "El Castillo" mean? Does it mean "palace"?
Girl: "El Castillo" is Spanish. It means "castle."
Boy: If it's a pyramid, why is it called "El Castillo"?
Girl: Because El Castillo is large and important, just like a castle.

Narrator: Now listen again.

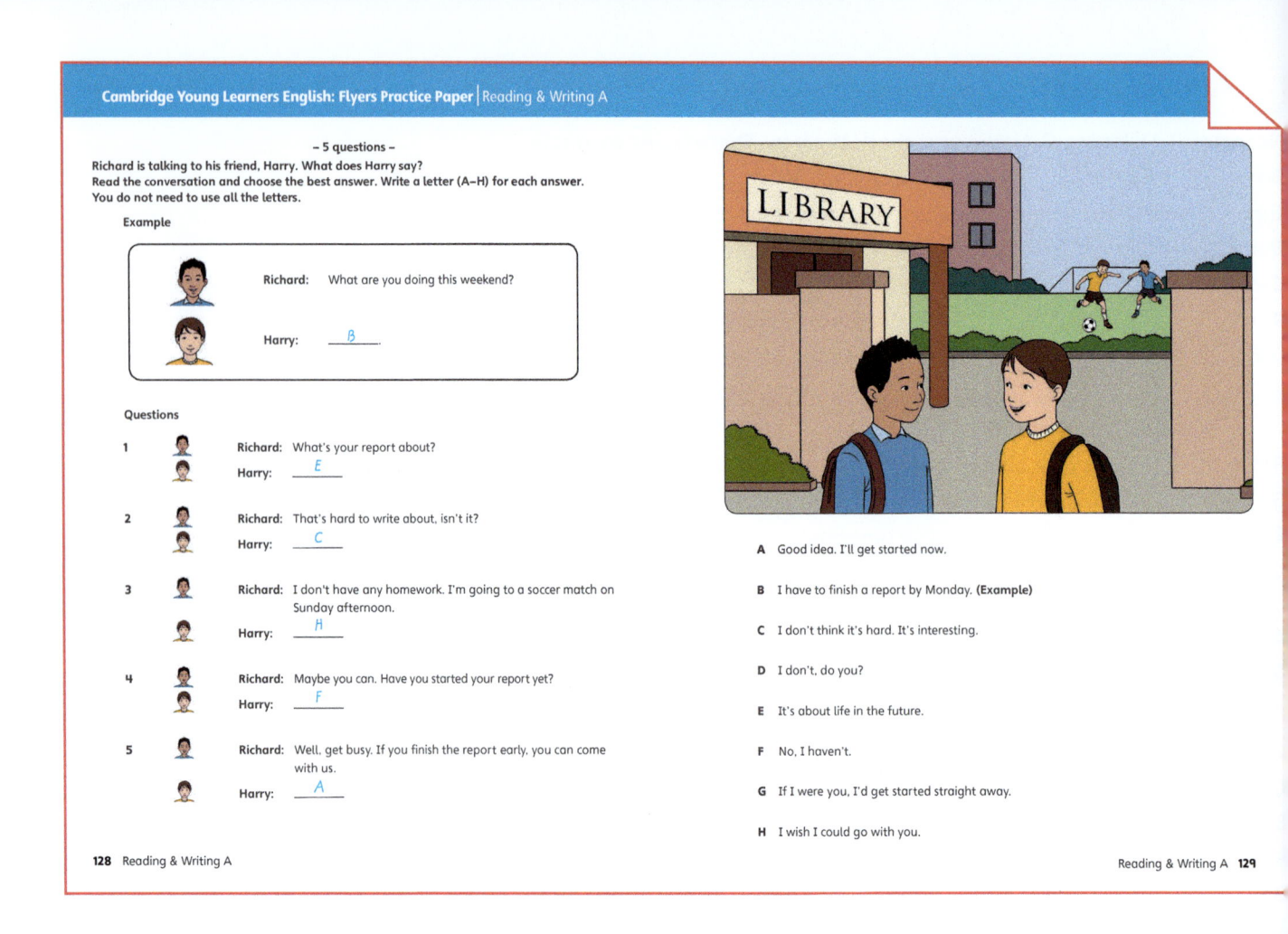

Cambridge Young Learners English: Flyers Practice Paper | Reading & Writing A

– 5 questions –

Richard is talking to his friend, Harry. What does Harry say?
Read the conversation and choose the best answer. Write a letter (A–H) for each answer.
You do not need to use all the letters.

Example

Richard: What are you doing this weekend?
Harry: __B__

Questions

1 Richard: What's your report about?
   Harry: __E__

2 Richard: That's hard to write about, isn't it?
   Harry: __C__

3 Richard: I don't have any homework. I'm going to a soccer match on Sunday afternoon.
   Harry: __H__

4 Richard: Maybe you can. Have you started your report yet?
   Harry: __F__

5 Richard: Well, get busy. If you finish the report early, you can come with us.
   Harry: __A__

A Good idea. I'll get started now.
B I have to finish a report by Monday. **(Example)**
C I don't think it's hard. It's interesting.
D I don't, do you?
E It's about life in the future.
F No, I haven't.
G If I were you, I'd get started straight away.
H I wish I could go with you.

Reading & Writing A

In this part, students read a dialog with missing text and choose from a list of sentences to fill in the blanks.

Do the test

1 Ask students to turn to pages 128–129. Look at the dialog together and point out that it only shows Richard's part of the conversation. Prompt students to think about things Harry might say in response to each of Richard's lines.
2 Ask students to read the lines on page 129.
3 Ask students to choose the appropriate line of dialog from the list on page 129 and to write the correct letter in the space provided. Remind students that there are two extra lines of dialog that are not needed. Encourage them to read through the dialog, quietly to themselves, to check that it makes sense.
4 Check answers.

Cambridge Young Learners English: Flyers Practice Paper | Reading & Writing B

– 7 questions –

Look at the picture and read the story. Write some words to complete the sentences about the story. You can use 1, 2, 3, or 4 words.

A Discovery in the Backyard

My name's Robert and I have an amazing story to tell. Most people don't believe me when I tell them about it but it's completely true.

One day, my friend Sarah brought a small potted tree to my house. My mom said it was OK for us to plant the tree in the backyard. While I was digging, I found something hard and round.

"What is it?" Sarah asked.

"I'm not sure," I said, "but I think it's a coin."

We brushed it off and looked at it more closely. It wasn't perfectly round and it wasn't very shiny but it was definitely a coin or a token of some kind. On one side was a picture of a man's face. He had a big nose and looked very serious. The word "Roma" was printed on the other side.

Sarah thought it might be a bus token from Italy. We decided to take it to the museum. An expert looked at the coin. She said it was from ancient Rome. "You've discovered an important piece of history," she said.

"This is very mysterious," I said. "I wonder how it got into my backyard?"

Like I said, most people don't believe me when I tell this story. If you don't believe me, you can go to the museum and see the coin for yourself.

Examples

The person telling this story is called ___**Robert**___.

Most people ___**don't believe**___ him when he tells this story.

Questions

1 One day, Sarah brought a small ___**potted tree**___ to Robert's house.

2 Robert's mom said it was OK to ___**plant the tree**___ in the backyard.

3 Robert found something that was ___**hard**___ and round while he was digging.

4 On one side of the coin, there was a picture of ___**a man's face**___.

5 On the other side of the coin, the word "Roma" ___**was printed**___.

6 Robert went to ___**the museum**___ and spoke to an expert.

7 The expert said the discovery was an important ___**piece of history**___.

Reading & Writing B

In this part, students complete sentences about a story using one, two, or three words.

Do the test

1 Ask students to turn to pages 130–131. Look at the picture together and prompt students to think about the topic of the story.

2 Ask students to read the story on page 130 and then read the sentences on page 131. Then ask students to underline the parts of the story that give them the information they need to complete the sentences.

3 Look at the example with the class and make sure they understand that they need to fill in the blanks using one, two, or three words. Tell students that the words they will need to use are in the story.

4 Ask students to fill in each gap with the correct word.

5 Help students check their answers.

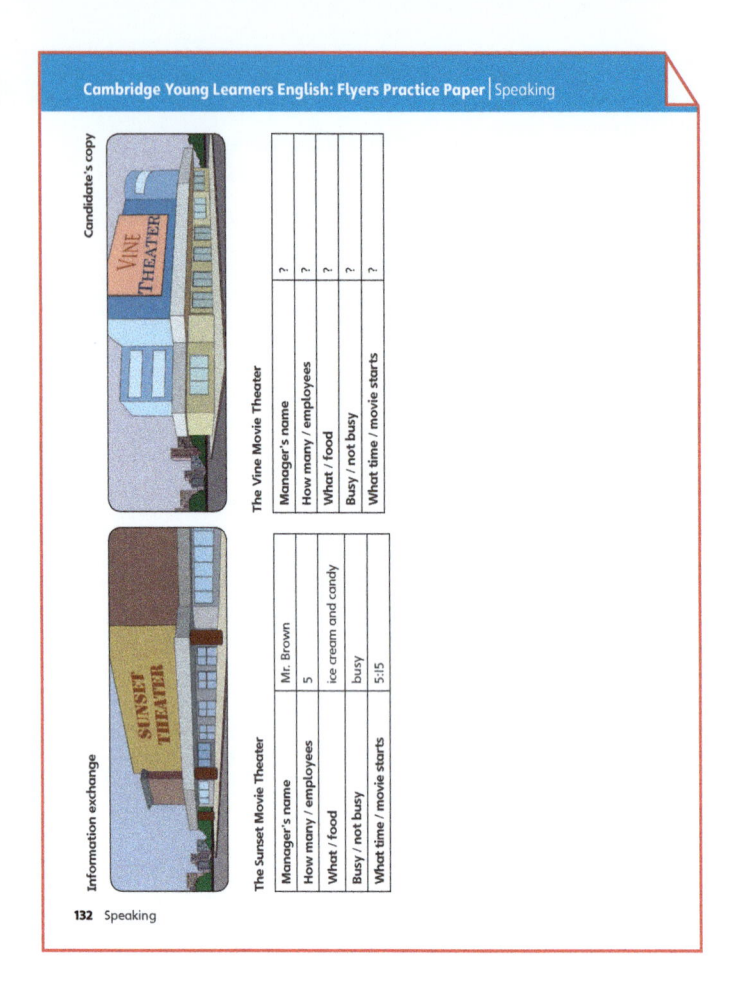

Speaking

In this part, students ask and answer questions using cues.

Do the test

1 Ask students to turn to page 132. Give them time to look at the pictures and the tables.

2 Look at the Examiner's copy (see page T135). Ask the student questions about the information they have; e.g. *I don't know anything about The Vine Movie Theater. What's the manager's name?* (Mr. Brown)

3 Now encourage the student to ask you similar questions; e.g. *How many employees are at the Sunset Movie Theater?*

What to say (Examiner)

Who is the manager at the Sunset Movie Theater?
(The manager's name is Mr. Brown.)
How many employees are there at this theater?
(There are five employees.)
What kind of food do they sell?
(They sell ice cream and candy.)
Is it a busy theater?
(Yes, it is. It's busy.)
What time does the first movie start?
(The first movie starts at 5:15.)

What to say (Candidate)

Who is the manager at the Vine Movie Theater?
(The manager's name is Mrs. Smith.)
How many employees are there at this theater?
(There are three employees.)
What kind of food do they sell?
(They sell pizza.)
Is it a busy theater?
(No, it isn't. It's not busy.)
What time does the first movie start?
(The first movie starts at 3:30.)

Cambridge Young Learners English: Flyers Practice Paper | Speaking

Information exchange

Examiner's copy

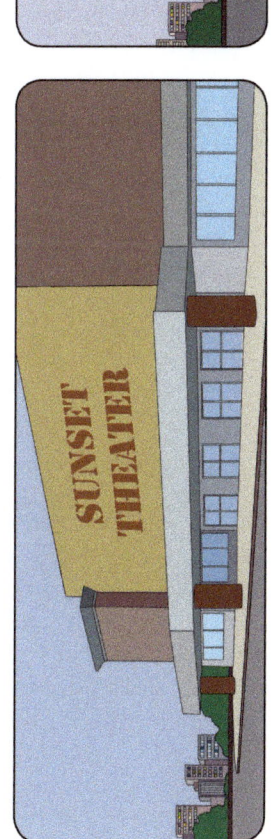

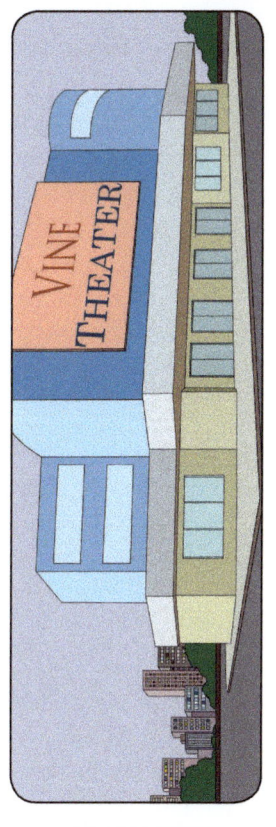

The Sunset Movie Theater

Manager's name	?
How many / employees	?
What / food	?
Busy / not busy	?
What time / movie starts	?

The Vine Movie Theater

Manager's name	Mrs. Smith
How many / employees	3
What / food	pizza
Busy / not busy	not busy
What time / movie starts	3:30

Game Bank

Games are a great way for children to practice, correct, confirm, and reinforce their vocabulary, usage, and numerical skills. Help everyone in class enjoy game time by creating an environment where the competitive aspect is challenging and motivating while remaining stress-free. Model supportive, friendly reactions when children make mistakes or don't know certain vocabulary words or just need more time than others to express the answer, such as *Nice try!* and *You're getting much quicker!*

Flashcard Games

Charades and Picture Charades
Divide the class into two teams. A child from Team A picks a Flashcard from the pile, chooses one of the activities on the card, and draws a picture of the activity on the board (*Picture Charades*) or acts out the activity (*Charades*) for his/her teammates to guess. If the team guesses correctly (they can make several tries, or you can set a time limit) they win a point. Then Team B takes a turn. Students may also choose pictures from parts of the Student Book and act out or draw out these objects or activities in a similar way.

Concentration
Have students use a set of Flashcards and phrase cards and sit with a partner. Pairs put both sets of cards together, mix them up, and place them face down on a table or in front of them. Students take turns turning over two cards and naming them. If the cards match, they keep the pair. If not, they place them face down again and try to remember where they are. The student with the most cards at the end of the game wins.

Yes or No
With the whole class, review a related set of Flashcards. Encourage everyone to say the words aloud with you. Then mix up the cards (without looking) so they are in a different order. Pick a card without looking at it and hold it over your head with the picture facing the class. You try to guess which card you are holding by saying words from the lexical set. If you guess right, students shout *Yes!* If you guess wrong, they shout *No!* and you keep guessing words from the same set.

Vocabulary and Word Games

Rhyme Time
Use this game to review key vocabulary. Students take turns choosing a secret vocabulary word and then naming a word that rhymes with it. Classmates try to guess the vocabulary word. Have students use a reading passage such as one of the Connections pages to look for words to practice. Tell them that they should look for a word in the passage, and think of a word they know that rhymes with this word. Model an example by saying: *My clue is seat. The secret word is cheat.* You may wish to divide the class into teams and have them compete by presenting their words to other teams to guess.

Spell Off
Bring three students to the front of the classroom. One student chooses a secret word and spells it aloud, pausing after each letter. (Before starting, you may want to have the student write the word and show it to you in secret, so you can monitor the spelling.) As the first student spells, the other two students compete to guess the word. If a student guesses the wrong word, he or she must sit down. Another student comes to the front, and the spelling continues. If a student guesses the word correctly before the first student has finished spelling it, the student guessing must spell the word aloud. If correct, that student can choose the next secret word.

Word Builder
Use this game to practice combinations of words such as contractions. Have students write these words on index cards: *I, you, he, she, it, we, they, are, will, can, do, have*. Shuffle the cards and place them in one stack. Then write these words on card: *not, have, will*. Use a second color card if available. Players take turns drawing one card from each deck. If they can make a contraction, they say the word and score one point. Return used cards to the decks. Models: *are + not = aren't; I + will = I'll; you + not = no contraction*. You may wish to use a simliar technique to help students build phrases (Phrase Builder). For example, write words that form parts of key collocations on cards, with one word on each card (*eat + breakfast, do + homework*, etc.). Have students match the collocations.

Mad Lib
Ask students to name some comparative adjectives and write them on the board. Then write this sentence on the board: *A mouse is ___ than an elephant.* Have volunteers read the sentence substituting each comparative adjective in the blank space. You may also want to use this technique to review other types of adjectives, verb forms, and so on. The idea is to get lists of words that, when inserted into the sentence, make some silly combinations.

Odd One Out
Working in pairs or small groups, students create groups of four words: three words are related thematically (you may want to set the categories, such as *hobbies* or *parts of the body*) and a fourth word is not. Model some examples of these types of groups on the board if needed. Other pairs or teams compete to be first to find the word that doesn't belong.

Question Chain
Divide students into groups. Have each group sit in a circle. Select one of the groups to model the game. Start the game by asking the first student a question that reviews a particular group of vocabulary words – for example, *What's your favorite [school subject]?* The first student answers: *I like [studying science].* The first student then turns and asks the question to the next student. Continue around the group until all students have answered the question. You may want to write a list of questions on the board so that students can continue rounds of questions without interrupting the game.

Telephone
Use this game to practice fluency of functional language, key vocabulary, or grammar structures. Have students sit in a circle or in a long, straight line. Whisper a sentence into the ear of Student 1. Student 1 then whispers it to Student 2, and so on down the line. At the end of the line, have the last student say the sentence. Is it the same as the original sentence? If not, try to find out how and where it changed along the way. This game is best played with fairly long, complex sentences or with a lot of players, as the sentences tend to end up more easily confused as they are passed down the line.

Word Clues
Use this game to review key vocabulary. Give students index cards and invite them to create game cards by writing one key word or phrase from a particular section of the Student's Book on each card. Players take turns looking at a word and giving one-word clues to their partners. Clues should not use any of the words in the key word or phrase. Model: *My word is [mystery]. My clues are: [code, CIA, sculpture].* Have students play in pairs, or in teams against one another. You may want to set a time limit of 60 seconds for a list of 4–5 items, and award a point to each individual or team for each item guessed correctly within the time limit.

Writing and Spelling Games

Hangman
Choose a word or phrase (e.g., *Taos, New Mexico*) and write a line for each letter, any punctuation such as commas, and any spaces between the words, on the board. Elicit a letter from an individual. If the letter is in the word or phrase, write it on the correct line. If not, then start to draw a person, one part at a time. Explain that the word needs to be guessed before the person is fully drawn. Once students are comfortable with the game, you can invite an individual to choose a word and lead the game.

Memory Game
Use this game to review forms of verbs or vocabulary sets. Sit with the whole class in a circle. You start by saying a sentence like *I went to Mars and I took my camera.* The student on your right repeats your information and adds his/her own: *She went to Mars and she took her camera. I took my backpack.* Continue with the next student, in order, until a student can't remember the whole list. Start the game again with the next student.

Word Search Puzzles
Have students create word-search puzzles to preview or review vocabulary or to practice spelling. Model creating a simple word search puzzle on the board using some simple words (or use one that has already been created). Point out that words can be hidden horizontally, vertically, or diagonally. Have students work in pairs or groups to create their own word-search puzzles using a specific list of vocabulary terms. After they create the grid of 'hidden' words, have students fill in the other spaces in their grid with random letters. Finally, invite students to exchange puzzles and find the hidden words.

AUDIO SCRIPTS
Student's Book and Workbook

Welcome Unit, Welcome to Class!

Student's Book page c. Activity 5

Listen, read, and write. What's special about today for Lexie?

- **A:** Hi Jacob!
- **B:** Hey, Lexie! What's up?
- **A:** It's the first day at my new school.
- **B:** How are you feeling? Nervous?
- **A:** Yes, a bit! But, I think I have everything covered…
- **B:** OK, let's check then. You don't want to forget anything!
- **A:** OK, OK! You're just like my mom!
- **B:** So, do you have your lunchbox? I hope you have something healthy in there?
- **A:** Yes, yes, I got it… There's some fruit in there, and carrots, so don't worry!
- **B:** What about your pencil case? Have you packed it?
- **A:** It's in my backpack. I packed it last night.
- **B:** And what about your school schedule? You don't want to forget where to go!
- **A:** Got it! The principal emailed it through to Dad last week. He printed it out for me.
- **B:** Great, you should put it in your backpack you know. And do you know where to go first when you get to school?
- **A:** Yes, I need to go to the principal's office. She's called Mrs Goodwin. Then I have math and English. I have history in the afternoon – my favorite!
- **B:** Ok, so, what's left to do?
- **A:** Nothing, but I have to catch the bus! Wish me luck!
- **B:** Good luck! You'll be great!

Unit 1, All About School

Student's Book page 5. Activity 2

Listen and complete the questions. Then listen again and match the questions to the excuses.

1. **A:** Have you done your homework yet?
   B: Yes, I've already done it, but I lost it on the bus!
2. **A:** Have you studied for the test yet?
   B: No, I haven't studied yet. I tried to study last night, but I was playing with my baby sitter, so I didn't have time!
3. **A:** Has she done her book report yet?
   B: Yes, she's already finished it, but there's a problem. She forgot the report at home. She'll bring it in tomorrow.
4. **A:** Has he handed in his assignment yet?
   B: No, he hasn't handed it in yet. He left it on the kitchen table and there was an accident. His brother spilled orange juice on it. He has to write it again!
5. **A:** Have they finished their project yet?
   B: No, they haven't. They haven't *started* the project yet, they're watching TV!

Workbook page 3. Activity 3

Check the verbs you use with each phrase. Then listen and check your answers.

1. study for a test
   hand in a test
   finish a test
2. do an assignment
   hand in an assignment
   finish an assignment
3. do a book report
   hand in a book report
   finish a book report
4. do homework
   hand in homework
   finish homework
5. do a project
   hand in a project
   finish a project

Student's Book page 8. Activity 8

Listen and stick. Then complete the sentences. Use the correct form of the verb.

1. **A:** Oh, man!
   B: What's wrong, Marc?
   A: I need a ride back to school. I left the research for my writing assignment in my locker.
   B: Can't Mom take you?

A: She doesn't feel well so she's taking a nap. I don't want to bother her.
B: I can take you.
A: What? No, you can't. You haven't gotten your license yet.
B: What are you talking about? I got it yesterday.
A: Huh? Nobody told me that.
B: Wake up, man. That's the big news around here.
A: Well, take me, then. Let's go.

2 A: Pilar, I thought you had a book report to do. Why are you watching TV?
B: I'm just resting, Dad.
A: Resting? You haven't done anything yet today!
B: That's not true. I had breakfast.
A: I'll bet you haven't taken Buchi for his walk yet.
B: No, I haven't. How'd you guess?
A: Just look at him, the poor guy. And I'll bet you haven't started reading your book yet, right?
B: Umm… no, I haven't.
A: Pilar… ? TV, off.
B: OK. I'll go walk the dog.

3 A: Hi, Chetan. What's up?
B: I just met the new exchange student.
A: Really? I haven't seen him yet. Where's he from?
B: It's not a *he*, it's a *she*. She's from Finland. She's really nice!
A: Nice, huh? Is she smart, too?
B: Really smart. I've talked to her.
A: In English?
B: Of course, in English. I haven't thought of learning Finnish yet. Maybe I will.
A: You're crazy. You haven't even mastered English yet.
B: Because I haven't found my motivation to master English. Finnish is different. I'm sure I'll learn it fast.
A: Yeah, yeah, yeah.

4 A: Hey, Dawn. Have you seen that farm boy's music video on YouTube yet?
B: No, I haven't. What are you talking about?
A: This nine-year-old farm boy sings to "Call me maybe," but he's changed the words.
B: Oh, that song has had so many versions! I'm getting tired of it.
A: This one's totally adorable! It's all about his life on the farm. You have to watch it!
B: OK, I'll check it out.

A: I've learned a few farm words from that song, like "a heifer has no babies". And now I know what a silo is!
B: Nice way to learn new words.
A: I know.

Workbook page 5. Activity 9

Complete the dialogs. Circle the correct expressions. Then listen and check your answers.

1 A: I'm going to stop playing video games forever!
   B: You're crazy! You've played video games ever since I met you.

2 A: Jeffrey hasn't asked anyone to the dance yet.
   B: He hasn't, huh? I wonder who he'll ask.

3 A: This time I'm going to hand in my project on time.
   B: Yeah, yeah, yeah. That's what you always say!

Workbook page 8. Activity 14

Read and complete. Then listen and check.

Do you get enough sleep?

The American Academy of Sleep published a report in 2016. According to the report, teens 13–18 years old should sleep 8–10 hours a day. If teens don't get enough sleep, they can become depressed or have behavior problems. Studies show that, on average, teens don't get enough sleep.

Student's Book page 15. Activity 26

Listen to Lucas and Nina talking about their school. Take notes in the chart below.

A: Hey, Nina, have you studied for the test yet?
B: No, I haven't, I didn't have time. I just finished my book report.
A: Oh, yes, I handed in my book report yesterday. I'm doing my writing assignment today. I'll hand it in tomorrow.
B: Ugh. I hate writing assignments. But I finished mine on Wednesday. I forgot it at home yesterday, so I'll hand it in tomorrow, too. By the way, have you joined any of the after-school clubs yet? I haven't joined any yet, I've been too busy.
A: Yeah, I've already joined the art club. We've already started project with the science club.
B: Cool. Maybe I can join the project, it sounds fun! Anyway, I Have to go now. I haven't started the math homework yet. Have you?
A: Yeah, I started it last night. But it's really hard.
B: Why don't we ask Simone? I think she's already finished hers.
A: Good idea. Let's call her now!

Unit 2, Amazing Young People

Student's Book page 17. Activity 3

Listen. You will hear about some amazing young people and what they've achieved. As you listen, take notes to answer the questions.

1. Hou Yifan was born in Xinghua, Jiangsu, China, in 1994. Yifan has been playing chess since she was three years old. When she was ten years old, she won first place at the World Youth Championship. Since then, she has won several major international chess tournaments, including the 2010 World Chess Championship. Yifan, who has been called a chess genius, believes in having goals. She once said, "I believe you should have goals and reach them step by step."

2. William Kamkwamba was born in Malawi in 1987. He's lived in Malawi since he was born. When he was a young boy, his village had no electricity. When he was about fourteen years old, William built a windmill using materials from a junkyard. The windmill provided electricity, allowing William's family to irrigate their farm. Since then, he has built other things, like a solar-powered water pump that supplied the first drinking water in his village. William believes his life proves something: "With hard work, anything in life is possible."

Student's Book page 20. Activity 9

Listen and stick. Then complete the sentences. Use the correct form of the verb.

1. **A:** I'm so glad your family invited me to this!
   B: I'm glad you came. So you said you've never been to the ballet before, right?
   A: Never. This is my first time. I can't believe your sister is going to be on that stage.
   B: Amazing, right? She's amazing.
   A: How long has she been a dancer?
   B: Well, she's been dancing since she was about 5 years old. But she's been dancing professionally since she was 15.
   A: 15? That sounds young.
   B: I know. Oh, look! It's about to start!

2. **A:** Who's in this picture?
   B: Which one?
   A: The one on your dresser. The guy who's getting an award.
   B: Oh, that's my favorite uncle, Uncle Buddy.
   A: Buddy?
   B: His real name is Charles. He's pretty famous, actually.
   A: What does he do?
   B: He does medical research. A lot of his research has been published in medical journals.
   A: And he's famous for the research?
   B: Yeah, but he's also famous for how young he was when he started. He's been doing medical research for ten years, and he's only 25.
   A: He was only 15 when he started? Wow. Smart guy.

3. **A:** Felipe, what's your brother doing on his computer? I can see he's really getting into it.
   B: He's probably working on one of his computer programs.
   A: He designs computer programs? But he's only 12!
   B: I know. He started designing programs when he was about 9, so for the past 3 years.
   A: 9? That's incredible.
   B: He's in trouble with my parents, though. He wants to drop out of school and work on his programs all day.
   A: You're joking, right?
   B: Yeah, I'm just kidding. He's a good kid.

4. **A:** I hear music in your garage. Is your dad in there working?
   B: That's not the radio. That's my brother's band.
   A: What? They sound professional!
   B: Well, that's nice of you. He and his girlfriend have been playing in rock bands together for a long time. Since middle school. The rest of the band members are new.
   A: They're in high school now, right?
   B: Yeah. They're going to college next year.
   A: College! They should go on tour!
   B: I'm sure they'll keep playing while they're in college.

Workbook page 18. Activity 15

Read and complete with the words from 14. Then listen and check.

Gifted Children

Many children are talented, but some have exceptional abilities that make them famous throughout history. Here are just a few examples of gifted children who achieved amazing accomplishments when they were still young:

Wolfgang Amadeus Mozart composed a symphony at eight and an opera at fourteen – all by himself!

At two years old, Aelita Andre created beautiful paintings that art critics through the ages will admire.

Fourteen-year-old Nadia Comăneci scored a perfect 10 in gymnastics at the Olympic Games – an amazing accomplishment for such a young athlete. As a result, she has become a legend in the world of gymnastics!

Another talented child, twelve-year-old Louis Braille from France, changed the world of reading and writing forever when he invented the Braille code to help the blind read and write.

Mozart, Andre, Comăneci, and Braille are an inspiration for many people to try to achieve great things!

Unit 3, Dilemmas

Student's Book page 29. Activity 2 🎧 37

You'll hear three people talking about dilemmas or difficult situations they've experienced. Listen. Then read about their concerns.

Dilemma number 1
This afternoon, I was at the supermarket with my parents. I saw a man drop his wallet while he was shopping. He didn't know he'd dropped it. I picked up the wallet and guess what? It was full of money.

Dilemma number 2
My best friend lent me her favorite necklace. I wore it to a party last night. But when I got home, it wasn't on my neck. I've lost it! I'm so upset!

Dilemma number 3
Today, I was running to grab my cell phone when I bumped into a lamp. It fell over and broke. My dad came in and said, "Who did this?" I didn't know what to do!

Student's Book page 29. Activity 3 🎧 38

What's the right thing to do? Think of advice to give to Emily, Angela, and Al. Then listen and compare your answers.

1. **A:** If I keep the wallet, I'll feel guilty. What should I do?
   B: Emily, I think you should return the wallet and everything in it to the man.

2. **A:** If I tell my friend I lost her necklace, she'll be upset with me.
   B: Angela, I think you should tell your friend the truth and offer to buy her a new necklace.

3. **A:** If I confess that I was the one who broke the lamp, I'll get into trouble.
   B: Al, I think you should tell your dad it was you.

Student's Book page 32. Activity 9 🎧 42

Listen and stick. Then complete the sentences.

1. **A:** Oh no, Darren. Look! I think I broke this antique doll!
   B: No way! What happened?
   A: I don't know. All I did was pick it up and the arm came off.
   B: You should tell the shop owner.
   A: But he'll want me to pay for it. And it's really expensive. You know, I could just put it back and pretend it was already that way.
   B: If you want to do the right thing, you should tell the owner what happened.
   A: But I don't have the money to pay for it.
   B: How do you know he'll make you pay for it? Maybe the arm was already broken. If you tell him the truth, you'll feel better. Trust me.
   A: OK. I'll go tell him now.

2. **A:** Well, are you ready to go?
   B: Yeah, I think it's time. It looks like the fair is closing. Hey. What's that by your foot?
   A: I don't know. Hmm… it looks like… Wow! It's a gold necklace! It's beautiful.
   B: Someone must have lost it.
   A: Too bad. Well, finders, keepers. I found it, so I get to keep it!
   B: You can't be serious! If you keep it, you'll feel guilty every time you wear it, believe me.
   A: Yeah, you're probably right.
   B: The owner will probably go to the Lost and Found. We should take it there. If the owner comes to claim it, they'll give it back to her.
   A: But what if no one comes to claim it?
   B: Well, we can read their policy. Come on, let's go.

3. **A:** I don't think I can go to the concert with you, Emma.
   B: Why not, Ed? You finally saved up enough money for the ticket. What a disappointment!
   A: I know. I was really looking forward to it.
   B: So what's the problem?
   A: My older brother needs money. I overheard him talking to my mom. It's something important.
   B: But it's your money! And he's not asking you for it.
   A: I know, but…
   B: So what are you going to do? Oh man! If we don't go this time, we'll miss out. Who knows when they'll go on tour again.
   A: I'm really sorry about this, Emma. But I think my brother really needs it. If I go to the concert, I'll worry about my brother.
   B: Yeah, I get it. You should help him. I'm sure he'd do the same for you.

4. **A:** What's the matter, Chris?
   B: Nothing, Mom.
   A: Did something happen at school today?
   B: Well… yeah, but it's not important.
   A: Look. If you don't tell me what's wrong, I won't be able to help you. Please tell me what's going on.
   B: Well, a couple of guys at school are being kind of mean to me.
   A: They are? Did they hurt you?
   B: No, it's nothing like that. They're just calling me names once in a while.
   A: I'm glad you told me, Chris. Now we can tackle how to solve the problem…

Student's Book page 35. Activity 14

Read the passage quickly and put the proverbs a to d in the correct place. Then listen and check.

Proverbs From Around the World

Every culture has its own proverbs. Proverbs are short sayings about life that are passed on from generation to generation. They go back tens, hundreds, even thousands of years and sum up the practical experience of the people who use them. Because proverbs give sound advice, they help us make decisions. The Chinese proverb "One step in the wrong direction can cause a thousand years of regret" is a good example. Anyone who's about to make a hasty decision, without weighing the pros and cons first, is warned of the horrible consequences of a bad choice.

Sometimes proverbs can seem to have different meanings. The English proverb "A rolling stone gathers no moss" is one example. Some think that the proverb is a warning for people who keep moving and never settle down. If these people "gather no moss," then it means they haven't achieved anything. Others think that the proverb is a warning for people who never do anything. If you don't move and change with the times, you'll become like an old mossy piece of rock.

We often find that there are similar proverbs across cultures. Maybe this is because proverbs have traveled and have been translated from one language to another, or maybe it's because they're just common sense. An expression similar to "You'll reap what you sow" appears in many languages, and it means that you'll get what you give.

One proverb in Malaysia, where crocodiles are common, is "Don't think there are no crocodiles just because the water is calm."

Whatever advice they give, one thing that all proverbs teach us is that although societies are changing and becoming more advanced every day, there are some basic facts about life and human nature that'll never change.

Checkpoint, Units 1–3

Student's Book page 41. Activity 2

Get ready. A. Choose the correct word or phrase to complete the dialog. Then listen and check.

A: The school play is tomorrow night. Have you learned your lines yet?
B: I've learned most of them already. We've been practicing for two weeks.
A: Really? I didn't know that. Where have you been practicing?
B: We've been practicing every day at school, after lunch.
A: And have you studied for your math test tomorrow?
B: Yeah, I've studied a little.
A: You should study again after dinner tonight.
B: But, Mom, I need to practice my lines for the play! If I forget my lines on stage, I'll feel awful.
A: I know, Danny, but if you don't pass your math test, you'll feel even more awful, and then you won't enjoy your play! Listen – study math for an hour, then you can practice your lines again for an hour. You should try to get a good night's sleep, too.
B: OK, Mom. Thanks.

Unit 4, Dreams for the Future

Student's Book page 44. Activity 1

Read the predictions made by John E. Watkins in the year 1900. Say which predictions you think came true. Then listen to check.

A: I, John E. Watkins, an American civil engineer, predict that in one hundred years from now…

1 A: Trains will travel at speeds of up to 240 kilometers per hour.
   B: This is true. Exactly 100 years after Watkins predicted this, the first express train, the Acela, traveled from Boston to Washington, DC, at a speed of 240 kilometers per hour.

2 A: A man in the middle of the Atlantic Ocean will be talking to his family in Chicago. It'll be like his family is sitting next to him!
   B: This is true, thanks to cell phones.

3 A: People will be buying ready-cooked meals.
   B: This is true. Ready-cooked meals are commonly found in supermarkets and corner stores.

4 A: People will be sending pictures from anywhere in the world. Photographs of major events from another continent will be in newspapers in an hour and they'll have the colors of nature.
   B: This is true. Thanks to cell phones, email, and social media like Facebook, color photographs can be instantly transmitted from anywhere in the world.

5 A: People will be eating strawberries as big as apples. Raspberries and blackberries will also be big.
   B: This is *not* true. Although some fruits have gotten larger, we don't grow strawberries as big as apples yet.

6 A: Americans will be taller by three to five centimeters.
   B: This is true. The average American is now 4.4 centimeters taller than 100 years ago. This is almost *exactly* what he predicted!

Student's Book page 45. Activity 2

Look at the list as you listen to two boys discussing their dreams for the future. Which topics do you hear them talking about?

Dreams for the Future

- **A:** Hey, Jake. I heard your sister's going off to college soon.
- **B:** Yeah, she's planning to go to a college in Toronto.
- **A:** It's hard to imagine being in college. Life *after* college sounds *really* far away.
- **B:** I know. What do you think you'll be doing twenty years from now?
- **A:** Me? I hope I'll be living overseas, in another country. By then I'll be able to speak several languages.
- **B:** Which ones?
- **A:** Um… English, Spanish, and Arabic.
- **B:** Do you think you'll be living in Europe or Asia?
- **A:** Both. I think I'll probably live in one for a while, then the other. And you? What will you be doing twenty years from now?
- **B:** I'll definitely be working in my dream job.
- **A:** Which is?
- **B:** The music industry!
- **A:** Cool!
- **B:** So I'll be traveling a lot.
- **A:** Oh! So you can meet me overseas! We'll take adventurous vacations, like going hiking in the Himalayas and skydiving in England.
- **B:** That sounds great. But it seems like a hundred years from now.

Student's Book page 48. Activity 9

Listen and stick. Then complete the sentences. Use the correct form of the verb.

- **A:** Dad, what do you think the world will be like in a hundred years?
- **B:** I don't really know, Fábio. But I am sure it will be very different from our world now.
- **A:** Do you think people will be traveling to other planets by then?
- **B:** Yeah, probably. Things change so quickly now.
- **A:** What do you think life on another planet will be like?
- **B:** I don't know. But I don't think I want to go there. I like life here just fine.
- **A:** Me, too. But it might be fun to visit another planet. Maybe there are aliens and cool stuff like that.
- **B:** You can go first and tell me how it is!

2
- **A:** What're you doing?
- **B:** I'm writing in my diary.
- **A:** What're you writing about?
- **B:** The future.
- **A:** You mean about spaceships and stuff like that?
- **B:** No. I'm writing about *my* future – where I think I will be in twenty years. What I'll be doing. Stuff like that.
- **A:** Twenty years from now? So, where do you think you'll be?
- **B:** Promise you won't laugh.
- **A:** Promise.
- **B:** Well, for a start, I'll be living in Paris in a house with three dogs – all poodles! I'll be talking to my dogs in French.
- **A:** Do you think your dogs will understand French?
- **B:** Of course they will! They're French dogs!
- **A:** You know. I've always wondered about that. Do you think dogs can learn different languages?
- **B:** Hmm, I wonder.

3
- **A:** What do you think you'll be doing after you graduate from high school, Serena?
- **B:** College, I'm sure. How about you? What will you be doing in, say, fifteen years?
- **A:** I'll be working on a big movie!
- **B:** A movie? Are you planning to become a movie star?
- **A:** No, not a movie star. A movie *director*. I'll be working with all the big Hollywood stars.
- **B:** Really? And how will you do that?
- **A:** Well, I'm pretty good at making short movies on my computer right now. I just need one big break, and voilà! Meet the next Spielberg!
- **B:** Sure. I just hope you won't forget us once you're rich and famous.
- **A:** Of course, not! You and Mom will be walking on the red carpet with me!
- **B:** Oh, I like that idea!

4
- **A:** Hey, let's write to our future selves!
- **B:** What are you talking about?
- **A:** We should write something to ourselves in the future!
- **B:** And how do we do that?
- **A:** Through the website, FutureMe. Haven't you heard of it? You send an email to yourself and write about your future dreams and wishes. FutureMe will send this e-mail to you at a specific date, say 40 years from today.
- **B:** So, exactly forty years from now, we'll be reading our own emails that we wrote to ourselves. Right? That's kind of freaky.
- **A:** think it'll be awesome. We can see if any of our hopes and dreams came true.
- **B:** Hmm. Let's look at the website together.

Workbook page 40. Activity 14

Read and complete with the words in the box. Then listen and check.

Two Trends in Medicine

Futurists, whose job is to study the future and help people to prepare for the future, are talking about two important trends in the future of medicine. A trend is the way something is developing or changing, and these two trends in medicine may revolutionize the way illnesses and diseases are diagnosed and treated by doctors in the future.

One important trend in the future of medicine is nanotechnology. The word nano means billionth. That's really tiny! Scientists who are working in nanotechnology are studying particles that are so small that they are invisible to the human eye! In fact, they have to measure these particles with a new unit of measurement, called the nanometer. Do you see the word "meter" in nanometer? You know how long a meter is, don't you? Can you imagine something that is only 1/1,000,000,000 of a baseball bat? One example of this is the nanobot. These microscopic robots are made of the same material that we are made of: DNA. In the future, scientists will be using nanobots to treat diseases and illnesses. For example, when you become ill in the future, doctors will put a nanobot into your body. The robot will find the cause of your illness and give you the correct medicine to help it heal.

The second trend in the future is in virtual medicine. Thirty years from now, when you have a fever and feel ill, you won't have to leave the house and go to a doctor. You'll be using wireless technology to diagnose and treat your illness in your own home. In this futuristic scenario, you'll take 3-D pictures of your body using an object like a TV remote control.

You'll upload these images to a website. The doctor will download the images, review them, and upload medicine for you to download. If the doctor wants to talk to you, he or she will talk to you through a video call – or maybe he or she will "visit" you using 3-D technology. The doctor will look like he or she is in your house but it will just be a 3-D image. Wouldn't that be amazing?

Workbook page 41. Activity 16

Read and complete. Then listen and check.

Renewable energy

As the number of people in the world increases, the demand for energy increases. To meet this demand, many countries are turning to renewable energy. In Iceland, there are lots of active volcanoes which produce heat. Geothermal energy plants turn this heat into electricity and heating power.

In South America, they use water to produce electricity. The Itaipu Dam is a powerful hydroelectric dam.

In Morocco, they are building a large solar power plant which will use the powerful desert sun to get energy.

Unit 5, If I Could Fly…

Student's Book page 57. Activity 2

Some students are talking about things they could do if they had a super power. Listen and match.

If you could have one super power, what would it be?

1 If I had this super power, I could travel anywhere I wanted in the world without having to get on a plane.

2 I know what super power I'd want! I'm on my school's track team. If I had this super power, I'd easily win *all* of my races. Not only that, I could enter marathons around the world and win all of them, too!

3 There are so many things I could do with this super power. I could watch the Egyptians build the pyramids, I could meet Shakespeare, and I could watch Neil Armstrong take the first step on the moon. This would be the best super power ever!

4 I think I'd choose to be able to lift anything, no matter how heavy – a car, a bus, maybe even a building!

5 I'd want to have this power because then I could do anything I wanted without anyone seeing me, ever! How amazing is that?

Student's Book page 60. Activity 8

Listen and stick. Then make complete sentences about what each person would do.

1 **A:** Dad, do you think we'll ever be able to travel through time?

B: Wow, that's a hard one, Maya. A lot is possible today, but I really don't see how we'd manage time travel. Do you?

A: I'm not sure, but it would be fun if we could! If you could go back in time, where would you go?

B: Hmmm. Let me think… Maybe I'd go back to see my great-grandparents who lived in London. My great-grandfather was a shoemaker there – did I ever tell you that? I would love to talk with him. I've heard he was a real character. What would *you* do?

A: Me? Oh, I know already – that's easy. If I could travel through time, I'd go back to last weekend and spend more time studying. I don't feel ready for my math test.

2 **A:** You know what question I hate, Kelly?

B: What?

A: "What do you want to be when you grow up?" I have no idea.

B: Really? I know exactly what I want to be.

A: You do?

B: Yeah. If I could have any job, I'd be a doctor.

A: That's a pretty hard job.

B: I know. But I'd like to help sick people get better.

A: True. Go for it. I still don't know what I'd be.

3 **A:** Guess what I'm thinking right now, Logan.

B: Umm… you're thinking that if you were more quiet, I could get my homework done.

A: Wrong. Try again. I'm thinking about food.

B: Oh, don't talk about food. I'm so hungry right now.

A: So, if you could have anything to eat, what would you have?

B: I'd have ice cream.

A: I knew it! Look what Mom got us at the grocery store.

B: No way! That sounds *so good* right now!

4 **A:** What're you watching?

B: A TV show about a woman who says she can talk to animals.

A: Talk to animals? That's impossible.

B: I don't know. It looks like she really knows what they're thinking.

A: Hm. Actually, that'd be a nice talent to have. I know what I'd do if I had that talent.

B: What?

A: If we could talk to animals, I'd know what Kiku is saying all the time.

Student's Book page 62. Activity 11

Read and put sentences a to c in the correct place. Then listen and check your answers.

Super Power or Super Science?

People have always found super powers fascinating. We love watching movies about superheroes. They can do all the things that humans can't do. Or can we? Every year, engineers create new technologies that people couldn't even imagine in the past. Here are three surprising things that scientists are already working on.

Have you ever seen a gecko climb up a wall and wondered why it doesn't fall off? Geckos have very sticky feet, which stop them from slipping off the wall. If a human could climb like a gecko, it would seem like a super power. Scientists are experimenting with plastic to make an adhesive (a kind of glue) that will let humans climb up walls, and they're close to succeeding! Maybe we'll see skyscraper climbing as an Olympic sport one day!

How would you like to be able to tweet without using a keyboard? Believe it or not, there's a scientist who's trying to make this possible! His idea uses a cap with electrodes. While wearing the cap, he concentrates on one letter at a time, spelling out his message on a computer screen! He's able to tweet eight letters a minute. But in the future, who knows? It would certainly make texting in class easier!

Mark Rolston, a computer designer, thinks that computers as we know them – a monitor, a keyboard, and speakers – limit us. He believes that we need to start thinking that the computer is the room we're in and we interact with it using voice or gestures. Imagine, for example, being able to watch the news on the kitchen table, make a video call on your refrigerator, and read a recipe on the wall above your oven by activating the computer using voice or gestures. This would really be a digital world!

Unit 6, The Coolest School Subjects

Student's Book page 68. Activity 1

Read. Match what you learn to the school subject where you learn it. Listen to check.

1 We learn about Shakespeare in our literature class.
2 We study democracy in social studies.
3 We study animals and plants, like the sloth and the pitcher plant, in science class.
4 We exercise and play sports in P.E.
5 We learn English vocabulary and grammar in our English classes.
6 We learn about prime numbers in math.
7 We make murals in our art class.

Student's Book page 69. Activity 3

Listen. A group of students is putting on a game show. Complete the chart as you listen.

1 **A:** This is a social studies question. Ready? When and where were the earliest Olympic Games held?

B: Greece?

A: Yep. In a Greek village called Olympia, in 776 BC.

2 **A:** OK, this is a literature question. Here we go: Who is considered the greatest playwright of all time?

B: That's easy. Shakespeare!

A: Right.

3 **A:** This is another social studies question. Are you ready? Who were the first people to develop the earliest form of democracy?

B: I have no idea. Who?

A: The people of ancient Athens.

4 **A:** OK. Ready for a math question? What are the ten smallest prime numbers?

B: That's a difficult one! Uh, 2, 3, 5, 7, 11, 13 – that's all I know. What are the others?

A: 17, 19, 23, and 29.

5 **A:** Here's your first biology question. What's the slowest mammal in the world?

B: I don't know.

A: It's the sloth!

6 **A:** And here's another biology question. What's the biggest meat-eating plant in the world?

B: That's a trick question. Plants don't eat meat!
A: The pitcher plant does. It digests insects and can even digest rats!

7 A: Here's a third social studies question. Which country has the most speakers of English, the U.S.A., or China?
B: Not sure. I'd just be guessing. Is it the U.S.A.?
A: It's China. China has the largest population in the world and the highest number of people who can speak English.

8 A: And here's an art question for you! Who is Mexico's greatest mural artist?
B: I don't have a clue!
A: Diego Rivera!

Student's Book page 72. Activity 10

Listen and stick. Then complete the sentences. Include *most* or *least* and an adjective from the box.

1 A: Mom, can you help me with my homework?
B: Sure, Alejandro. What school subject is it this time?
A: Literature. It's about Shakespeare. First, I have to choose one of his plays, and I can't decide which one to choose.
B: Well, if I were you, I'd choose *Julius Caesar*. To me, it's his finest work, and it's very powerful.
A: Cool, we've been studying Julius Caesar in History class. Wasn't he a general in ancient Rome?
B: That's right. So what's the assignment about?
A: I have to adapt the play into a modern one.
B: That sounds like fun. First you need to read it, right?
A: Right. I need the least difficult version, though.
B: I think I actually have a simple version of the play on my computer already. See, here it is.
A: That's the least difficult version? It's so long!
B: I said the *least difficult* – not the shortest!

2 A: Have you studied for the math test yet?
B: Not yet. Hey, if all of us have to study for it, let's do it together. A study group!
C: Nice idea. So where are we going to hold it?
A: Well, Leo's place is the closest house to school. Leo, you think your parents will let us study at your house?
B: Sure, they will. My mom's good in math, so she can help us.
A: Great. The only thing I remember about prime numbers is that they're larger than 1.
C: Speaking of prime numbers, did you know you can do the most amazing thing with the numbers 379009? Type them on you calculator and read them upside down.
A: Seriously? Let me see… Whoa! It spells Google™!

3 A: So what are we going to do for Science Week?
B: I like Jasmine's idea.
C: Which one?
B: The one about endangered animals.
C: Oh, right. We could choose one of the most endangered animals on earth. If we do a public exhibit, we'll also be encouraging people in our community to help protect them.
A: Wow, Jasmine. It sounds like you've really been thinking about this.
C: I have been. I've already done a little research, actually. Here's one I think we could use: The kakapo from New Zealand. It's the most rare, the strangest, and the heaviest parrot in the world. And it's definitely one of the most endangered animals in the world. There are only about 100 of them left. Here's a picture.
A: I like this. Could you do some 3-D visuals on the computer, Juan Carlos?
B: Sure, no problem. And I'll add some sound effects, too. Especially for that parrot!

4 A: Hey, look at this. It's a list of origins for the names of the months. Do you know any of these?
B: Can't say that I do.
A: This one's interesting. July is named in honor of Julius Caesar. It's the month he was born.
B: It must be nice to have a month named after you.
A: I know. But a bunch of the months just come from numbers. Like October comes from "octo", which means "eight".
B: October. My least favorite month in the school year.
A: What do you mean? October's great. It has Halloween.
B: Yeah, but that's not a school holiday. There are no school holidays in October, so it's my least favorite month.
A: That's not true. We get Columbus Day off.
B: One day. Big deal. I like it when we get *a bunch* of days off!

Workbook page 57. Activity 8

Complete the dialog with the expressions in 7. Then listen and check your answers.

A: I was just chosen to be on a TV quiz program.
B: Seriously? Congratulations!
A: Yeah, they asked me what happens when you turn 01134 upside down. I said it spells "hello."
B: Let me see. Wow! You're right!
A: Speaking of numbers, let's make a study group for the math test tomorrow.
B: Good idea!

Workbook page 60. Activity 13 🎧 89

Read and complete. Then listen and check.

How to Take Care of a Pitcher Plant

Do you want to have a pet, but your parents won't let you? If your parents won't allow pets in your home, you could try growing a pitcher plant. It could be your perfect "pet plant!" You can take care of it and feed it just like a pet. But be careful. At mealtimes, these plants get very hungry!

Pitcher plants need lots of nutrients and protein. To be a good pitcher plant owner, you'll have to make sure that your plant gets lots of sunlight and water. These are important to keep your little carnivore happy and healthy. Water's especially important. It makes the top of the plant slippery so that insects can slip into the nectar. The plant is shaped like a cup, so insects are easily trapped in it. The sweet-smelling, sticky nectar helps the plant digest the food. The plant then uses chemicals to break down the proteins and nutrients in the food, and absorbs them.

Check your plant to make sure it's catching enough insects. Some days you'll have to feed it an extra insect or two if it looks hungry. Your pitcher plant will have the healthiest and happiest pet plant life of all if you love it and take good care of it.

Checkpoint, Units 4–6

Student's Book page 81. Activity 2 🎧 95

Get ready. A. Number the lines of the dialog in the correct order. Then listen and check.

A: What's for lunch tomorrow?
B: Let's see… Tomorrow's Friday. It looks like we'll be having pizza again.
A: Great! I love pizza! I wish I could eat pizza every day.
B: No, you don't. If you ate pizza every day, you'd get sick of it.
A: Yeah, maybe. But I'd like to try it and see. How about you? If you could have just one kind of food every day, what would it be?
B: Well, it wouldn't be pizza. I think I'd have a salad every day.
A: Yuck. If I only ate salad, I'd feel hungry all the time. It's too boring.
B: Salad isn't boring. You know, if I were you, I would try to eat more vegetables.
A: But I eat vegetables all the time – on pizza!

Unit 7, Mysteries!

Student's Book page 85. Activity 2 🎧 97

Look at the pictures. What's the mystery all about? Read and match the mysteries to the descriptions. Then listen to check.

1 A: Good evening and welcome to *Unsolved Mysteries Hour*. This is Stan the Mystery Man coming to you live from New York City. Let's take our first caller, Miguel. Miguel from Mexico – you're on the air. What is your question?

B: Yeah, hi, Stan. My name's Miguel. I have a couple of questions about the crop circles in England. What are they? And does anyone know how they were made and who made them?

A: Crop circles are perfect geometrical patterns that appear in crops of corn and other grain fields. They're best seen from high up, like from a plane. No one understands this phenomenon. There are some theories, but there are no scientific explanations. Maybe they're made by a cosmic force or by the wind. Or maybe crop circles are a hoax, and some very smart people are trying to trick us! There are no real answers yet. Good questions, Miguel.

2 A: Now, Chris from Norway. You're on the air. What's your question?

B: Thanks for taking my call, Stan. I have two questions. I was just wondering about the Bermuda Triangle. It's still an unsolved mystery, isn't it? And why don't ships and planes just stay away from the area?

A: You're right, this is still an unsolved mystery. No one can explain why ships and planes sometimes disappear there. The thing is, no one knows when or if a disappearance will occur so that's why ships and planes still travel there.

3 A: Now for our next caller. Ella from Sweden, you're on the air.

B: Hi, Stan. No one has discovered who built the Great Pyramids and why they were built, have they? It's amazing how well constructed they are.

A: That's very true, Ella. Scientists, like archeologists and geologists, have ideas about how they were built, but they're not really sure. To them, it seems almost impossible that the ancient Egyptians could have constructed these pyramids without modern tools. It's a real mystery.

4 A: Now, for a caller from Chicago, U.S.A. Go ahead with your question.

B: Hi, there. I'm Abby, and I'm a junior here at the University of Chicago. I agree with you 100% about the Great Pyramids, by the way. We've been studying them in my Ancient Civilizations class. My question is about the northern lights. Are scientists confident that they now have a good explanation for this phenomenon?

A: Very good question, Abby. The northern lights have been observed since ancient times. The scientists of long ago weren't sure what caused the brilliant colors, but the scientists of today now have a pretty clear idea, and they've been able to gather proof to support their theory. You should listen to this program next Wednesday night because we'll be talking all about the northern lights. That's all for tonight!

Workbook page 67. Activity 2 🎧98

Complete the dialogs. Then listen and check your answers.

A: Have you ever heard of the Northern Lights?
B: Yes, I think so. They're those bright, colorful lights in the night sky. They're caused by light reflecting off the ice caps in the Arctic.
A: No. That was just a theory. Now there's scientific proof. Gases in the air cause these nighttime fireworks.
C: The Great Pyramids in Egypt are incredible, aren't they?
D: They certainly are. Does anyone have an explanation of how they were built?
B: Well, some scientists have theories about it but the mystery is still unsolved.

Student's Book page 88. Activity 8 🎧102

Listen and stick. Then circle the correct ending to the question.

1 **A:** Mom, do you believe aliens exist?
   B: I have no idea, Tad.
   A: Me neither. There are a lot of mysterious phenomena in the world, but usually there are scientific explanations for them, aren't there?
   B: I agree with you one hundred percent. But you know, I just saw something the other day – a mystery about some ancient rocks.
   A: Oh, you mean the one about the stone spheres in Costa Rica?
   B: Yes… that's the one, Tad. But I can't remember… now where did I see those?
   A: You probably saw them in my textbook! We're reading about them in our social studies class. The mystery is that no one knows how they got to be so perfectly round. They are HUGE! Only a machine could do that! They say that ancient people made these, but ancient people didn't have machines back then, did they?
   B: No, that's true – they didn't. I'm just looking them up now. No one knows how those stones got so round. Wow – take a look. They're really amazing, aren't they?

2 **A:** Oh wow! These are so awesome!
   B: What are you watching?
   A: These videos on YouTube! Come, take a look.
   B: Oh yeah. I've seen those. They're called the Northern Lights, aren't they?
   A: Yep. Their other name is Aurora Borealis. We're studying them in science and English this week.
   B: You know what's also cool?
   A: What?
   B: Hang on a minute while I find it on my phone. Here, listen. It's music inspired by the Northern Lights. Listen to it while you're looking at those pictures.
   A: Wow. You're right. This is so neat.
   B: The lights look more beautiful when you look at them while listening to music, don't they?
   A: They really do!

3 **A:** I got you hooked on Kryptos, didn't I?
   B: You sure did. I found lots of cool stuff about Kryptos. Did you know the creator of the codes has given more clues recently?
   A: Seriously? What are the new clues?
   B: He gave six letters out of the 97 in that last phrase
   A: I bet the decoders got very excited, didn't they?
   B: Totally. On the sculpture, the letters are NYPVTT. When decoded, the letters read *BERLIN*.
   A: I can't imagine being a code breaker. I wouldn't be able to sleep because I'd be thinking about it all the time.
   B: That's exactly what's happening. Many people are obsessed with cracking the code, and that's all they think of and do every day.
   A: That's insane.

4 **A:** What's that?
   B: It's a comic book.
   A: I know it's a comic book. Duh. I mean, that picture It looks like a city, but it's under the sea, isn't it?
   B: Yeah. Well, they say it used to be a city. Don't you know the story of the Atlantis?
   A: I don't think so. If it used to be a city, why would it be under the sea?
   B: Well, if it ever existed, according to this story, an earthquake destroyed it.
   A: No way! An earthquake can't bury a whole city under the sea.
   B: Well, maybe there was also a tsunami.
   A: An earthquake and a tsunami – like in Japan.
   B: Exactly.
   A: Scary.
   B: I agree.

Workbook page 69. Activity 7 🎧104

Complete with the expressions in 6. Then listen and check.

1 **A:** Jennifer's always reading.
   B: I know. She's hooked on historical mysteries. She reads all day, every day!

A: Really? That's ridiculous.

2 **A:** There's a craft fair on Saturday. Let's go. They always have such cool stuff, don't they?

B: Absolutely. I could buy everything! Great idea!

Workbook page 72. Activity 12 🎧106

Read and complete the text with the words in the box. Then listen and check.

What Causes the Aurora Borealis?

The Aurora Borealis or "Northern Lights", whose colors light up the night sky, is one of the most beautiful phenomena on Earth. It is also one of the most mystifying since the display of shimmering colors, lines, and shapes is different every time it appears. In the past, there were various theories explaining the appearance of this beautiful swirling display. For example, long ago in Finland, people thought the lights came from a mystical fox flashing its tail in the sky. Over the years, different myths have been told to explain this extraordinary phenomenon that may be best seen during the winter months in the Arctic. The Aurora Borealis continues to inspire writers, artists, and musicians today.

However, in 2008, scientists developed a theory that everyone could agree on. The spectacular lights were caused by the solar wind blowing around ions, atoms, gases, and other things in the atmosphere and making them collide. When they collide, they produce the colorful displays of light. So, how does it actually happen?

The hot solar winds from the sun are blowing oxygen and nitrogen atoms around. There are two kinds of nitrogen atoms – the neutral and the ionic. The atoms are full of energy. When they collide, they give off colors. Oxygen produces a yellow-green to brownish red color. The neutral nitrogen atoms produce purple and red colors. The ionic nitrogen atoms produce blue colors.

Unit 8, Why Is It Famous?

Student's Book page 96. Activity 1 🎧112

Work with a partner. Match. Then listen and check.

1 St. Basil's Cathedral is located in Russia.
2 The City of Petra is located in Jordan.
3 The Forbidden City is located in Beijing, China.
4 Machu Picchu is located in Peru in South America.
5 The Sydney Opera House is located in Australia.
6 Stonehenge is located in the U.K.

Student's Book page 97. Activity 4 🎧113

Look at the pictures and read the information about each. Then listen and complete.

1 Big Ben (the Elizabeth Tower)
Big Ben (or the Elizabeth Tower) is located in London, U.K. It was completed in 1859.

2 Taj Mahal
The Taj Mahal is located in Agra, India. It was built between 1632 and 1654.

3 Great Sphinx of Giza
The Great Sphinx of Giza is located in Giza, Egypt. It was probably built between 2558 and 2532 BC.

4 Temple of Borobudur
The Temple of Borobudur is located in Central Java, in Indonesia. It was built in the eighth and ninth centuries.

5 Statue of Liberty
The Statue of Liberty is located in New York City Harbor, in the United States. It was dedicated in 1886.

6 Pyramid of Kukulcán (El Castillo) at Chichén Itzá
The Pyramid of Kukulcán (or El Castillo) at Chichén Itzá is located on the Yucatan Peninsula, in Mexico. It was built around ad 900.

Student's Book page 97. Activity 5 🎧114

Look at 4. Listen and match the descriptions to the places. Note down any new information you learn.

a This monument, which has the body of a lion and the head of a human, is located next to the Great Pyramids of Egypt. No one is exactly sure who built it or why it was built.

b This name is often used to refer to three things: the Great Clock at Westminster, the bell, and the tower. It's actually the name of the bell that hangs *inside* the famous clock tower. In 2012, the tower was renamed the Elizabeth Tower to recognize Queen Elizabeth's 60 years of dedication to her country.

c This temple, which has 504 statues of Buddha, is considered to be the largest Buddhist temple in the world. Some scholars say that the temple is actually a huge "textbook" of Buddhism.

d A gift from France to the United States, this structure was designed by the same person who built the Eiffel Tower. It symbolizes a new beginning for many immigrants to the U.S.A. in the late 19th and early 20th centuries.

e This is a famous temple that was built by the ancient Maya. It was constructed in a special way to reflect the 365 days of the year, the same number as on the ancient Mayan calendar.

f This mausoleum was built by Emperor Shah Jahan to remember and honor his wife, Mumtaz Mahal, who died during childbirth. The name of this mausoleum means "crown palace." Made of white marble, the inside of this structure is decorated with 28 different kinds of gemstones.

Workbook page 77. Activity 3

Listen and label the pictures with the words in the box.

1. This ancient pyramid was built by the Maya to honor their snake god, Kukulcán. The Pyramid of Kukulcán has 365 steps – one step for each day in the Mayan calendar.

2. This famous Buddhist temple is one of the largest Buddhist temples in the world. The Temple of Borobudur is sometimes listed as one of the Seven Wonders of the World.

3. This statue is known throughout the world as a symbol of hope and new beginnings. The Statue of Liberty was a gift from the French to the U.S.A. This famous statue stands on Liberty Island in the harbor of New York. But did you know that there are two other Statues of Liberty? An exact copy of the statue was offered by Americans living in Paris to the French in 1889. It's on the Allée des Cygnes in Paris. The third and original model of the Statue of Liberty, is in the Luxembourg Gardens in Paris.

4. A mausoleum is a building that holds the tombs of several people who have died. It's their burial place and a place to honor the dead. Probably the most famous and beautiful mausoleum in the world is the Taj Mahal.

5. The clock tower of the Palace of Westminster in London is often called Big Ben. The tower was built between 1843 and 1858 to hold the world's largest clock at that time. In 2012, the tower was officially renamed the Elizabeth Tower in honor of Queen Elizabeth the Second.

6. All countries have monuments to honor important events and the people who took part in those events. In downtown Mexico City, a famous monument has a golden angel on the very top representing victory, triumph, and freedom. This monument to independence is called "El Angel de la Independencia."

Student's Book page 100. Activity 11

Listen and stick. Then complete the sentences. Use the correct form of the verb.

1. **A:** Cool magazine!
   B: It's my mom's travel magazine. This issue is about famous tourist attractions. Look: here's one of the most photographed structures in the world.
   A: What is it? It looks like a huge sail that's just sitting on the water, doesn't it?
   B: Yeah, but it's not a sail – it's a hotel in Dubai – The Burj Al Arab Hotel. And you're right. It says here that the design was inspired by the sails of an Arabian trading ship.
   A: Nice! Was it built on an island?
   B: Yep. An island was created just for the hotel!
   A: Wow! I bet it took longer to construct the island than the hotel, don't you?
   B: Yeah, it says that it took three years to reclaim the land from the sea to make the island. And it took less time than that to actually build the hotel.
   A: See, I was right, wasn't I?
   B: Yep. And the hotel itself cost something like six hundred and fifty million dollars to build.
   A: Wow! I'd love to go there.

2. **A:** Have you heard of something called a bucket list?
   B: It's a wish list of things that people want to do before they die. Right?
   A: I think so. I heard my mom and her friend – the one who was just here – talking about it.
   B: Seriously? She did look pretty old, I guess. Old people like to talk about that kind of stuff.
   A: Hey! My mom isn't old!!
   B: Um… I have an idea. Let's make our own bucket lists!
   A: But… we're only twelve!
   B: I know. But it'll be fun. Number 1 on my list would be to see the pyramids in Mexico.
   A: The pyramids are in Egypt!
   B: There are pyramids in Egypt, but the ones that I want to see were built in Mexico.
   A: There are pyramids in Mexico? Where in Mexico?
   B: Let me get my history book. Here are some pictures. See, it says that these photographs of the pyramids were taken at Chichén Itzá and some other sites in Mexico. So what's on your bucket list?
   A: Hmm… let me think…

3. **A:** What do you think is the most generous thing a man can do for the woman that he loves?
   B: I don't know. Buy her a diamond ring? A big house? I give up. What?
   A: In Social Studies class today, we learned that the Taj Mahal in India was built by an emperor in honor of his wife who died in childbirth. She was buried there.
   B: Really? I didn't know that. I've seen pictures of it. It's so beautiful! I think it's made of marble, isn't it?
   A: Yes. And the marble is decorated with flowers and beautiful jewels. Inside is the tomb where the emperor's wife was buried.
   B: Wow!
   A: It took more than 22,000 people more than 20 years to build. And now, it's one of the most famous places in the world. To me, it's the best and most enduring tribute a man could give to the woman that he loved.
   B: That's a great love story! I don't know anyone who could top that!

4. **A:** Hey, Eric. You're from Australia, right?
   B: Yeah. I was born in Sydney, Tania. Why?

A: That's perfect! What do you know about the Sydney Opera House? I have to prepare a presentation about it for my art class.

B: Oh yeah, I had to do one, too. If it's for your art class, it'd be interesting to talk about its design. Did you know that the Opera House is known around the world for its design?

A: Oh yeah? That makes sense. I've seen some pictures of it. It's stunning, isn't it? Do you know who designed it?

B: Yeah, it's a work of art! Actually, I don't know who designed it, but I do know where the person was from. A design contest was held sometime in the 1950s, and the person who won was from Denmark.

A: Wow. The Sydney Opera House was designed by someone from Denmark? Now, that *is* interesting!

B: Yep.

A: You know, it looks like a big boat, doesn't it?

B: Yeah, I've heard other people say the same thing. It's awesome!

A: Thanks! I think you just did my homework for me.

Workbook page 79. Activity 8

Complete with three of the expressions in 7. Then listen and check.

1. **A:** My family is going to the city of Cambridge this weekend.
   B: Really? I've heard of it but I don't know much about it.
   A: It's known for its architecture and its university, of course. You should go!

2. **A:** How was your holiday in Paris?
   B: Great! We saw the Eiffel Tower. It's a phenomenal work of art!

3. **A:** I'm doing research on Machu Picchu since we're going there on our next vacation.
   B: That makes sense.

Workbook page 83. Activity 17

Read and complete using the words in the box. Then listen and check.

The New SEVEN Wonders of the World

Do you know what the seven wonders of the world are? Over the years, there have been several different lists and many people around the world think they know what the wonders are, but they are not always correct.

A Swiss adventurer, Bernard Weber, decided to create a new list of world wonders. He began the New 7 Wonders Foundation. This time, he wanted people from all around the world to choose the seven new wonders that exist today. He asked people to send in their votes for the new wonders. People voted by texting, voting online on the website, or calling in their votes. By 2007, more than 100 million people had voted.

Who were these voters? Most of the voters were not adults. Bernard Weber is proud of the fact that they were mostly children and young people. Weber and a group of people reviewed all the votes. They chose the new seven wonders based on these criteria:

- The places should each have a unique beauty.
- The places should come from all over the world and represent people from all over the world.
- The places should be from different environments, such as deserts and rainforests.
- The places should be important to people from different cultures.
- The places should be located on different continents.

Weber was delighted by the enthusiasm and love that people showed for their cultures and other cultures. This enthusiasm and love, he believes, creates a feeling of hope for the future.

Unit 9, That's Entertainment!

Student's Book page 108. Activity 1

Read about some performers, movies, and books from the world of entertainment. Guess the name of each one. Then listen carefully to check.

1. The first three movies in this series, *Twilight*, made almost 2 billion dollars at the box office and more than 450 million dollars in DVD sales. The fourth movie in this series was sold out in the theaters before it was even released.

2. The young singer-songwriter Justin Bieber has won many awards, including Artist of the Year and Best New Artist. This musician has more than 25 million followers on Twitter and has sold more than 15 million albums.

3. The *Harry Potter* series has sold 450 million copies, making it the best-selling book series in history. It has now been translated into sixty-seven languages. The last four books in this series have set records as the fastest-selling books ever.

4. Adele's second album alone has earned her seven Grammy awards, two Brit Awards, three American Music Awards, and at least fourteen other awards. She has sold more than 26 million albums and has written and sung an original song for *Skyfall*, the twenty-third James Bond film.

5. Taylor Lautner was recently named the highest-paid teenage actor in Hollywood. He has appeared in many TV shows and movies, but is best known for his role as Jacob Black.

Student's Book page 109. Activity 2

Listen. Complete Becky's plans for the year using the words from the box. Then match the events to the pictures below.

A: Next year is going to be so cool. I can't wait.
B: You've already planned next year? What are you going to do?
A: Well, there's something for every month. January the fourth's my birthday, so I'm going to an Adele concert.
B: Cool. I love Adele. *21* is my favorite album.
A: Mine, too. Then in February, my favorite author is having a book signing.
B: Who? Noah Carter?
A: Of course.
B: Can I come, too?
A: Of course. Let's try to take some pictures, too.
B: What about March?
A: In March, there's the comic book exhibit, which I'm definitely going to. Do you want to come?
B: Yeah, absolutely. I want to go to the Marvel Comics table and see what's new.
A: April is my official star-gazing month.
B: Star gazing?
A: Yes. I'm going to see how many celebs I can spot. To get started, I'm going to the premiere of the next James Bond movie in New York.
B: That's going to be crazy. You'll have to get there early to get a good seat.
A: I know. Then last of all, May is the month of music festivals. There's the Country music one, Creek Jam, in the park. I'm definitely going to that. I won free tickets with VIP passes to go backstage.
B: Tickets? You don't mean more than one of them, do you?
A: Yeah, two tickets – they just came today. Do you want to go with me?
B: Are you kidding? I'd love to!

Student's Book page 112. Activity 8

Listen and stick. Then complete the sentences. Use the correct words from the box.

1
A: Have you seen this?
B: What is it?
A: It's a review of the new bmx racing video game – *Time to Fly*.
B: What does it say?
A: Well, this reviewer said the animation was stunning and… it feels just like the real world… like you're riding a bmx.
B: Yeah, well I read a review of this old one. That one said that it was exciting and challenging, and guess what? It wasn't. It was so boring and so easy to figure out. Not challenging at all!
A: Well, this reviewer said the same thing about the old one. So I think we can trust what he says.

2
A: Mom? Um, could I possibly borrow ten dollars?
B: What for?
A: I want to go and see all the celebrities at the movie premiere with my friends. But I don't have enough money for the train.
B: What happened to your allowance?
A: I spent it to go to that concert last week. It was more expensive than I thought.
B: Well, I suppose I could give you next week's allowance in advance but that means you won't get anything next week.
A: OK. Deal.
B: What movie is it?
A: It's the new *Spider-man* movie.
B: Oh, I heard it's great.
A: Yeah. Luke said it was really good.
B: Well, have fun.
A: Thanks, Mom!

3
A: I'm thinking about getting the new Caleb Rivera CD. Have you heard anything about it?
B: Yes. I went online and read some of the reviews.
A: What did people say about it?
B: Well, one girl said that the new release was his best album yet. A boy said that it wasn't as good as his last album, but still impressive.
A: Great, thanks. I am definitely going to get it then.

4
A: What kind of movies do you like?
B: Oh, I like all kinds of movies. But I guess my favorite ones are action movies.
A: Really? Like what?
B: Well, I love all the Daniel Duke movies. They're great. Did you know Daniel Duke's biography is out?
A: His biography? I didn't know he had one. Have you read it yet?
B: No, not yet. But one of my friends read it already, and she said it was fantastic!
A: I'd like to get it.
B: I'm going to his book signing next week. You should come with me and get a copy of it.
A: Will Daniel Duke be there, or the author?
B: Oh, I guess just the author. But still. He *knows* Daniel Duke, so he's pretty cool.

Workbook page 89. Activity 8 🎧 136

Complete with two of the expressions in 6. Then listen and check.

A: Do you want to stop at the shopping mall on the way home?
B: What for?
A: I need some things for my science project.
B: OK. But only if we go to the pizza place in there first. I'm so hungry!
A: OK. Deal!

Workbook page 92. Activity 13 🎧 138

Read and complete the text with the words in the box. Then listen and check.

What's your dream job?

My dream job is to be a script writer for Hollywood movies. I love writing and watching movies. I joined the school newspaper last year. I write a movie review every week. There are so many different movies. I love finding a new movie to share with my friends. If you want to watch a great movie, you should read my reviews!

This year I want to start writing my own stories so I'm going to join the writing club. We're going to study books, plays, and movies to learn about the skills of being a writer. The first book I'm going to read is *Save the Cat!* By Blake Snyder. He's a famous script writer in Hollywood, so I'm sure the book will give me lots of great advice about the formula for writing my own movie script.

In ten years I'll probably be living in America. I might not be a successful script writer in ten years, but I will definitely be studying and writing everyday so I can achieve my goal! I don't want to be famous, but I want to work with famous actors and movie producers to make my stories into amazing movies for my friends to watch.

Workbook page 93. Activity 14 🎧 140

Read and complete the text with the words in the box. Then listen and check.

Unique Musical Instruments

Every culture has musical instruments that are unique to it. The instruments are often made from a variety of materials such as wood, steel, animal bones, and plastic. Many people are proud of the musical instruments that are associated with their cultures. Often these instruments make distinctive sounds, too – like no other sound that you've heard before. In Vienna, there's an orchestra that's really unique, because it plays instruments from the things your mother tells you to eat every day. The Vienna Vegetable Orchestra plays instruments made out of vegetables! Can you imagine the unique sounds they make?

The eleven musicians in the Vienna Vegetable Orchestra play carrot flutes, radish horns, pepper rattlers, carrot trumpets, eggplant clappers, pumpkin bongos, and cucumber phones. The orchestra plays contemporary, jazz, and electronic music, among other styles. They play concerts around the world. At the end of their concerts, the members of the audience receive a bowl of vegetable soup to enjoy. So, not only do you get to hear unusual music, but you get to taste something delicious, too! The third album of the Vienna Vegetable Orchestra is called *Onionoise* and includes songs entitled "Nightshades" and "Transplants". Can you think of any other suitable titles for their compositions?

Why did this group of visual artists, poets, designers, and writers choose vegetables to create music? They were fascinated by the challenge to produce musical sounds using natural foods. They constantly experiment with vegetables to create new and complex sounds. As part of their work, they give workshops on how to create instruments from vegetables. A morning TV program said it was, "…a highly unusual, tasty performance."

You knew vegetables were good for you. Now you know that they sound good, too! What's your favorite vegetable? Can you think of a musical instrument that you could make out of it?

Checkpoint, Units 7–9

Student's Book page 121. Activity 2 🎧 144

Get ready. A. Choose the correct word or phrase to complete the dialog. Then listen and check.

A: Hey, do you want to watch *Mystery Tour*?
B: I don't know. What's it about?
A: It's a new show about scientists who travel around the world and study mysterious places, like the Bermuda Triangle.
B: Oh, I've heard about that show! My friend at school said it was really good.
A: Oops, wait a minute, Kevin. It's not on until 9:00. Your mom said your bedtime was at 8:30, didn't she?
B: That's on weeknights. On Saturdays I'm allowed to stay up until 9:30.
A: Oh, lucky you. You can watch it, then.
B: So *Mystery Tour* is scary, isn't it?
A: Umm, not really. I think it's made for people who like science. But you're a science guy, aren't you?
B: Sort of. But I like scary shows better, like *Dark Corners*.
A: *Dark Corners*! That's a creepy show!
B: What's wrong with creepy? Anyway, it's not on anymore. It was canceled last month.
A: Probably because it was too creepy!

WORKBOOK Answer Key

Unit 1, All About School

1
1. e doing a project
2. a going on a field trip
3. c working on computers
4. d taking a test
5. b giving a presentation
6. f hand in an assignment

3
1. study for, hand in, finish
2. do, hand in, finish
3. do, hand in, finish
4. do, hand in, finish
5. do, hand in, finish

4 1 b 2 d 3 c 4 a

5 1 T 2 T 3 F 4 T

7
1. hasn't seen
2. has already talked
3. speaks

8 1 b 2 a 3 b

9
1. You're crazy!
2. huh?
3. Yeah, yeah, yeah.

10
1. Yes, they have. They've already gotten supplies for their project.
2. No, he hasn't. He's been playing video games.
3. Yes, he has.
4. Have Michael and Ted arrived in class yet?
5. Have Michael and Ted handed in their project yet?

11 1 made 2 has / made 3 started
4 has / started 5 hasn't finished 6 didn't finish

12
1. done / hasn't done
2. handed in / hasn't handed in
3. eaten / ate

13
1. finished / haven't handed
2. took / didn't study
3. haven't started / didn't have

14 1 published 2 According to 3 depressed
4 behavior 5 on average

15 1 N 2 Y 3 N 4 N

17 1 8-11 2 18 3 25 4 No 5 Yes

18 1 T 2 T 3 F 4 F 5 F

22
1. Has Anna done her social studies homework yet? / Yes, she has already done her social studies homework.
2. Has she studied for the math test yet? / No, she hasn't studied for her math test yet.

23 1 didn't study 2 didn't finish
3 hasn't handed in 4 hasn't done

Unit 2, Amazing Young People

1
1. d volunteer in Africa
2. c be a professional soccer player
3. b start my own band
4. f find a cure for diseases
5. e climb a mountain
6. a create a photography blog

4 1 F 2 T 3 T 4 F 5 T 6 F

5
1. was a contestant
2. invented something
3. speak 23 languages
4. published a book

6
1. She published a book of poetry that she co-wrote with her sister.
2. Her future goal is to win a Nobel Prize.

T154

3 People should trust children and expect that they will do great things at a young age.
4 Answers will vary.

7 1 T 2 F 3 T 4 F

8 1 d 2 c 3 b 4 a

10 **since:** I was born / he was little / he started reading about it / she started sixth grade; **for:** three days / seven years / two months

11
1 has danced / since
2 has read / since
3 has played / for
4 has worked / for

12
1 They have been working at Kids Biz since they were nine.
2 Jenny has been babysitting for six months.
3 Bobby has been volunteering for the animal shelter for two years.
4 Jenny has been collecting food for the homeless since she was eleven.
5 They have been blogging since they started sixth grade.

14 1 d 2 e 3 b 4 a 5 c

15
1 exceptional   2 gifted   3 composed
4 symphony   5 inspiration

16 1 an opera 2 two 3 gymnastics 4 France

17 Its purpose is to use music and dance to bring people and countries together for peace – especially countries taking sides against each other.

18 1 organization 2 neutral 3 conflict 4 peace

19
1 Where were you born?
2 What did you study in college?
3 What are some of your important memories?
4 What are some of your accomplishments?

21
1 have known	2 since	3 has played
4 for	5 has won	6 have tried
7 for	8 haven't had	9 have been
10 for	11 has played	12 since
13 has been	14 for	

22
1 Anthony has won a tournament.
2 Stella plays an instrument.
3 Anthony speaks another language.
4 Stella wants to invent something.
5 Anthony wants to write a book.

23
1 SpongeBob SquarePants has been playing on TV since 1999.
2 Seeds of Peace has been training students since 1993.

Unit 3, Dilemmas

1 1 b 2 a, c, d, f 3 e, g 4 e, g 5 d, f 6 b, c

3
1 be upset / tell the truth / return
2 get into trouble / feel good about

5 1 aren't 2 is 3 aren't 4 have to

7
1 If he should tell his problem to his mom.
2 She wants him to tell her what's the matter.
3 He doesn't want her to know what's wrong.

8 1 d 2 c 3 a 4 e 5 b

10
1 If I'm late for school
2 I will see my friend Jimmy
3 If I see my friend Jimmy
4 we will forget about going back to our classroom
5 The principal will yell at us
6 If he is in a bad mood

11 1 b 2 d 3 c 4 a

13
1 calls   2 should tell   3 says   4 should find
5 starts 6 should tell   7 stops 8 should give

15 "Character" is a person's traits and qualities taken together.

16
1 respectful   2 ethical   3 perspective
4 morally   5 acceptable   6 treat

17 1 c 2 a 3 b

18
Dilemma A: 2
Dilemma B: 3
Dilemma C: 1

19 caring, honest, serious, worried

23 1 e 2 c 3 a 4 f 5 d 6 b

24
1 If Maya tells her parents, her brother will be very upset with her.
2 If Maya apologizes to her mom, her mom will say she's disappointed.
3 If Ivy apologizes, the boy will probably say it's OK.

T155

Checkpoint, Units 1–3

1 School Activities

1 assignment 2 book report 3 test
4 homework 5 project

Reaching Goals

1 publish 2 become 3 play 4 meet 5 climb

Making Choices

1 cheat 2 feel 3 upset 4 tell 5 trouble

Unit 4, Dreams for the Future

1 1 e 2 b 3 a 4 d 5 c

3 **wallet photo** – earning a good salary, **man on the beach photo** – working in my dream job, **flower shop assistant photo** – running my own business, **family photo** – raising a family, **monuments photo** – living in another country

4 1 raising a family
2 working in my dream job
3 earning a good salary
4 running my own business
5 living in another country

5 1 I won't be running my own business; Answers will vary.
2 I won't be raising a family; Answers will vary.

6 1, 3, 8

8 1 b 2 b 3 a 4 b

10 1 I'll probably be living in Germany.
2 I'll definitely be driving a flying car.
3 I'll probably be taking vacations in Europe.
4 I'll definitely be living in a big city.
5 I'll probably be working in my dream job.

11 1 Yes, probably. She probably will be working in her dream job in 20 years.
2 Yes, probably. He probably will be living in Germany in 20 years.
3 No, definitely not. He definitely won't be taking vacations in Asia.
4 No, definitely not. She definitely won't be raising a family in 20 years.

14 1 nanotechnology
2 imagine

3 virtual
4 wireless
5 3-D

15 1 b 2 b 3 a

16 1 Geothermal 2 electricity 3 hydroelectric
4 solar 5 energy

18 1 informal 2 formal 3 informal
4 formal 5 formal 6 informal

20 1 will / be going 2 will be working
3 won't be living 4 will / be starting
5 will / be earning 6 won't be living
7 will be raising

Unit 5, If I Could Fly…

1 1 b has superhuman strength
2 c runs at lightning speed
3 a able to climb tall buildings
4 e saves the world from bad guys
5 d becomes invisible with the snap of a finger
6 f travels through time and space

3 1 c / C 2 d / D 3 b / A 4 a / B

4 1 travel through time
2 become invisible
3 run at lightning speed
4 have superhuman strength

6 1 T 2 F 3 F 4 T 5 T

7 1 Bulldog is making Duck give him money.
2 Because Bulldog is picking on someone smaller than him.
3 No, I don't think Duck will take good care of Bulldog.

8 1 b 2 a 3 a 4 b

9 1 d 2 a 3 b 4 c

11 1 were / would study
2 could fly / would visit
3 could run / would win
4 did / would be

12 could sing / would join / could travel / would meet / could drive / would take / could be / would be

14 1 where would you go
2 which language would you study

3 which animal would you be
  4 who would you be
  5 what would you play

15
  1 3 / Answers will vary.
  2 1 / Answers will vary.
  3 2 / Answers will vary.
  4 4 / Answers will vary.
  5 5 / Answers will vary.

17 1 D 2 A 3 E 4 B 5 C

18 1 F 2 T 3 T 4 F 5 T

19
  1 Darna   2 Meteorix
  3 Cat Girl Nuku Nuku

20 1 evil 2 senses 3 bolts 4 weapons

21 1, 4, 5, 6; **Missing information:** 2, 3, 7, 8

22
  7 – lived in the past and lives in the present, too
  8 – to make villains honest
  3 – in many stories she's an officer in the army
  2 – is tall / has long dark hair

24 1 b 2 a 3 c 4 d

26 1 b 2 a 3 a 4 b

Unit 6, The Coolest School Subjects

1
  1 d world history   2 f P.E.
  3 b music   4 c art history
  5 a geography   6 e science

3
  1 democracy   2 mammal   3 plant
  4 playwrights   5 prime number

4 1 c 2 e 3 b 4 a 5 d 6 f

5
  1 Because King Minos didn't want Daedalus or Icarus to share the secrets of the Labyrinth with anyone.
  2 Because he wanted to be free.
  3 Because he loved the feeling of freedom and flying.
  4 Answers will vary.
  5 Answers will vary.

6 1 b 2 a

7 1 c 2 a 3 b 4 d

8
  1 Seriously   2 Let me see
  3 Speaking of   4 let's make a study group

9 1 less 2 more 3 fewer 4 more 5 less 6 fewer

11
  1 It's the oldest tree alive.
  2 It has the most tourists of any city in Mexico.
  3 It is the heaviest parrot in the world.
  4 It has the least amount of rain a year of all deserts.
  5 It has the longest railway in the world.
  6 It is the lightest mammal in the world.

12
  1 Which species is one of the most endangered species in the Americas?
  2 Which species has the sharpest teeth of all fish?
  3 Which species has the most legs of any animal?
  4 Which land mammal has the fewest teeth?

13
  1 pitcher plant   2 nutrients   3 water
  4 slippery   5 nectar   6 absorbs
  7 insects

14
  1 Pitcher plants can grow up to one meter tall. A pitcher plant is like a pet because you can take care of it and feed it.
  2 To keep a pitcher plant healthy, you should make sure that it gets sunlight and water.
  3 Water is needed to make the top of the plant slippery.
  4 A pitcher plant eats insects.

15 1 The Greeks 2 The Incas 3 The Aztecs

16 1 T 2 T 3 T 4 F 5 T 6 F 7 F 8 F 9 F

17
  1 There are 3 characters in the story.
  2 Their names are Daedalus, Icarus, and King Minos.
  3 Daedalus is one of the greatest inventors and architects of that time, Icarus is his young son, and King Minos is the King of Crete.
  4 Daedalus and Icarus are put in prison so they don't share the secrets of The Labyrinth; Daedalus created wings so they could fly away and be free; Icarus flies too close to the sun and falls into the sea.
  5 King Minos thinks that Daedalus and Icarus will share the secrets of The Labyrinth; Daedalus wishes he was free; Icarus said that he would obey his father.

19 1 d 2 c 3 a 4 b

20
  1 more legs   2 fewer pets
  3 more people   4 fewer insects

21
1 do the least homework
2 has the most pet owners
3 has the fewest mammals
4 own the most dogs

Checkpoint, Units 4–6

1 **Dreams for the future:** live in another country, earn a good salary, work in my dream job, run my own business, raise a family; **Superpowers:** travel through time, climb tall buildings, run faster than the wind, save the world from the bad guys, super strong, be invisible; **School Interests:** prime numbers, democracy, mammal, plant, playwrights, artist

Unit 7, Mysteries!

1
1 Aliens from outer space created perfectly round sculptures in Costa Rica. / Answers will vary.
2 Giant pre-historic ape-like men still live in the Himalayas of Asia. / Answers will vary.
3 Large, heavy, rocks weighing up to 300 kilos move from place to place by themselves. / Answers will vary.
4 Aliens from outer space created perfectly round sculptures in Costa Rica. / Answers will vary.

2
1 Northern Lights   2 scientific proof
3 Great Pyramids   4 explanation
5 theories   6 unsolved

3
1 T
2 F / There is no scientific proof about how the Great Pyramids were built.
3 F / The Northern Lights appear in the night sky over the Arctic.

4
1 The Voynich Manuscript is 600 years old.
2 Scientists cannot figure out what the language or the plants are in the manuscript.

5 1 T 2 F 3 F

6 1 c 2 d 3 a 4 b

7
1 hooked on / That's ridiculous
2 cool stuff / Absolutely

8
1 isn't it   2 are they   3 can they
4 aren't they   5 is it   6 can't they

9 1 can they 2 aren't they 3 doesn't it 4 is there

10
1 Some people don't believe in the Bermuda Triangle, do they?

2 People love a mysterious phenomenon, don't they?
3 My classmates and I learned a lot about the Nazca lines, didn't we?
4 For a long time scientists didn't have a theory for the Sailing Stones, did they?
5 The city of Atlantis doesn't seem real, does it?

11 1 isn't it?   2 don't we?   3 do they?
4 were they? 5 didn't they? 6 wasn't he?

12 1 swirling   2 phenomenon   3 solar wind
4 oxygen   5 nitrogen

13 1 a 2 b 3 b 4 a

14 1 b 2 a 3 a 4 a

15 1 F 2 T 3 T 4 F

16 **Underline:** solar winds interact with the upper part of the atmosphere / As the atoms return to their normal state
Circle: atoms of oxygen and nitrogen to become charged / they give off colors.

18 1 a 2 a 3 b 4 b

19
1 The Aurora Borealis is a phenomenon in the northern hemisphere, isn't it?
2 The yeti lives in the Himalayas in Asia, doesn't it?
3 There's proof that the Sailing Stones are real, isn't there?
4 Anyone can read the Kryptos codes, can't they?

Unit 8, Why Is It Famous?

1
1 f Machu Picchu is a city high up in the Andes Mountains. / Answers will vary.
2 c Nobody is sure why Stonehenge was built the way it was. / Answers will vary.
3 d St. Basil's Cathedral is colorful on the inside and the outside. / Answers will vary.
4 e The Sydney Opera House was designed for all types of performances. / Answers will vary.
5 b The City of Petra stored water for use during droughts. / Answers will vary.
6 a The Forbidden City was built centuries ago. / Answers will vary.

3 1 pyramid   2 temple   3 statue
4 mausoleum 5 tower   6 monument

5
1 The Forbidden City was built in the early 1400s by Emperor Yongle as his imperial home.
2 It was called the Forbidden City because only people invited by the emperor were allowed into the palace.

T158

3 Answers will vary.
4 Answers will vary.

6 Yes, they do because they both say it's amazing.

7 1 c 2 d 3 b 4 a

8 1 known for 2 work of art 3 That makes sense

9 1 are known   2 is filled   3 is made
  4 are decorated 5 are painted 6 is located

10 1 P 2 P 3 P 4 A

11 1 The Pyramid at Kukulcán was called El Castillo.
   2 Some of the stones of Stonehenge were rebuilt in the early 20th century.
   3 The Statue of Liberty was given to the U.S.A. as a gift.

12 1 that 2 that 3 who 4 who 5 that

13 1 b 2 d 3 c 4 a

14 1 Machu Picchu is an ancient city that was built high in the Andes Mountains.
   2 Many tourists get to Machu Picchu by walking on paths that lead to the ancient city.
   3 Scientists don't know much about the Incas who lived in Machu Picchu long ago.
   4 Scientists know about the Spanish conquerors who invaded the city in the 1500s.

15 1 b 2 b 3 b 4 b

16 1 F 2 T 3 F 4 T 5 F

17 1 wonders 2 exist 3 children 4 cultures 5 hope

18 1 There are seven wonders of the world.
   2 Bernard Weber began the New 7 Wonders Foundation.
   3 More than 100 million people, mostly children and young people.
   4 People's enthusiasm and love for their cultures and other cultures.

19 **General Facts and Location:** 1, 3, 8; **Population, People and Languages:** 4, 5, 7; **Major Cities:** 2, 6

20 It's the seventh largest country in the world. / Hindi is its national language. / English is an important language, too.

22 1 b 2 a 3 b 4 b

23 1 was built 2 is located 3 is made 4 was discovered

24 1 The Rapa Nui are Polynesian people who lived on Easter Island.
   2 In the Cairo Museum in Egypt there are artifacts that belonged to King Tut.

Unit 9, That's Entertainment!

3 1 comic book exhibit
   2 video game launch
   3 concert
   4 movie premiere
   5 book signing
   6 festival

4 1 Jennifer 2 Nicky 3 Tim

5 1 Jennifer liked the adventures because they were like a puzzle – fun to figure out.
   2 Answers will vary.

6 1 Ann wants to borrow fifteen dollars from her mom.
   2 Ann won't get allowance next week because her mom is giving it to her in advance.

7 1 a 2 b 3 a

8 1 What for? 2 Deal!

9 1 He said he was going to a live show at Dragon's Den to see Ed Sheeran.
   2 She said she wasn't doing anything.
   3 He said the new Play to Win 2 video game was really challenging.
   4 She said it was much better than Play to Win 1.
   5 She said she wanted to go to the comic book exhibit.
   6 He said he was going to dress up as Mario.

10 1 said / didn't want
   2 said / was taking
   3 said / was
   4 said / was going with her friend

11 1 He said he was going to the movies with a friend.
   2 She said that her friend didn't want to go with her.
   3 She said she didn't want to go alone.
   4 She said she really wanted to see the new Bubble Sky movie.

12 1 a 2 a 3 a 4 b 5 a 6 b

13 1 script   2 review   3 movies
   4 formula 5 writing 6 producers

14 1 plastic 2 flutes 3 concerts 4 unusual 5 sounds

15 1 b 2 a 3 a 4 b

16 3, 1, 2

17 **The story:** 1
The hero and the characters: 2
The opinion (what you liked and didn't like): 3

19
1. book signing
2. comic book exhibit
3. festival
4. movie premiere
5. concert

20
1. She said she was tired.
2. He said he was going to be at the movie premiere.
3. She said she wanted to meet the author of the book.
4. He said he didn't really like sci-fi movies.

21
1. Paolo said, "I don't want to go to the festival today."
2. Lara said, "I am a pretty good singer."
3. Harry said, "I am excited about the comic book exhibit."

Checkpoint, Units 6–9

1 **Mysterious Events:**
1 Lights 2 crop 3 Triangle 4 Answers will vary.
Famous Places:
1 Temple 2 Statue 3 Pyramid 4 Answers will vary.
Special Events:
1 book 2 concert 3 premiere 4 Answers will vary.

Unit 1, Extra Grammar Practice

1
1. Has Julia gone to the museum yet? / Yes, she has. She has already gone to the museum.
2. Has Julia written her report yet? / No, she hasn't. She hasn't written her report yet.
3. Has Julia done her research yet? / Yes, she has. She has already done her research.
4. Has Julia created her presentation yet? / Yes, she has. She has already created her presentation.
5. Has Julia given her presentation yet? / No, she hasn't. She hasn't given her presentation yet.

Unit 2, Extra Grammar Practice

1
1. has been taking / since
2. has been playing / since
3. have been collecting / for
4. has been studying / for

2
1. How long has Rob collected coins? / He's collected coins for four years.
2. How long has Cynthia made jewelry? / She's made jewelry since she was nine.
3. How long has David drawn cartoon characters? / He's drawn cartoon characters for three years.
4. How long has Iris had dance lessons? / She's had dance lessons for six months.

Unit 3, Extra Grammar Practice

1 1 finish 2 will help 3 will call 4 asks / will do

3 1 b 2 c 3 a

4
1. If you are new, you should join clubs so that you meet people.
2. If some people are mean to you, you should stay away from those people.
3. If you don't speak the language well, you shouldn't worry about your mistakes. You should speak anyway.

Unit 4, Extra Grammar Practice

1 1 Emily 2 Al 3 Al 4 Al

2
1. a. I'll be working as a vet. / b. I'll be living in the country.
2. a. I'll be finishing medical school. / b. I won't be working as a chef.

Unit 5, Extra Grammar Practice

1
1. I'd have lots of singing lessons.
2. I'd start reading fun things like manga comics.
3. I'd join some clubs.
4. I'd start a blog.

2
1. got / wouldn't be
2. could have / would be
3. practiced / would play
4. won / would compete

3
1. If you could live anywhere / Answers will vary.
2. which would you choose / Answers will vary.

T160

Unit 6, Extra Grammar Practice

1 1 fewer 2 less 3 fewer 4 less

2 1 most people
2 most languages
3 the fewest species of mammals
4 fewest words
5 the least crime

3 1 the smallest bear
2 the tallest bird
3 the largest creature

Unit 7, Extra Grammar Practice

1 1 isn't 2 is 3 aren't 4 can

2 1 aren't they 2 are they 3 isn't it 4 can't you

3 1 Scientists found out about the Nazca Lines in the early 20th century, didn't they?
2 Scientists don't know why the Nazcans created the lines, do they?
3 The Nazcans drew animals and plant figures, didn't they?
4 You need to see the lines from a plane, don't you?
5 You didn't know the Nazca Lines, did you?

Unit 8, Extra Grammar Practice

1 1 was painted 2 was built 3 were designed

2 1 The Great Pyramids of Egypt were built by the people of Egypt.
2 The Moai statues of Easter Island were moved by someone.

3 1 The City of Petra, Jordan, was named one of the seven wonders of the world in 2007.
2 Spices, perfumes, and other things were traded in Petra.
3 The City of Petra was destroyed by an earthquake in 363 AD.

Unit 9, Extra Grammar Practice

1 1 said the acting was incredible.
2 said the music was really cool.
3 said it wasn't the director's best movie.
4 said it was definitely going to win an Oscar.
5 said it wasn't that entertaining.
6 said the plot was too predictable.

2 1 said (that) she was going to a Justin Bieber concert for her birthday.
2 said (that) he was going to a movie premiere to see Jennifer Lawrence.
3 said (that) he wanted to buy the new Cats video game.
4 said (that) she didn't like playing video games.
5 said (that) she wasn't going to the book signing.
6 said (that) he always goes to book signings.

WORDLIST

Welcome Unit

Other

assignment	a
classmate	a
due	a
essay	a
hand in (your homework)	a
have (everything) covered	b
improve	a
lastly	a
principal	b
print	b
schedule	a
sensation	a
top	a

Unit 1

School activities

apply for college	4
attend activities	4
be homeschooled	7
do a book report	5
do homework	4
finish a project	5
gather information	11
hand in an assignment	5
memorize facts	11
study for a test	5
take a test	4

Other

according to	10
allowance	8
alternative	4
anxious	12
barely	6
behave	11
behavior	10
body clock	10
curriculum	11
depressed	10
do chores	13
end up	6
excuse	5
flashlight	5
homeschooling	7
ideal	10
increase	8
license	8
look forward to	7
on average	10
pace	11
power cut	5
publish	10
punishment	6
quality time	12
rank (at the top)	4
reach	10
research	7
secondary school	4
standardized	4
stressful	6
strict	4
transfer	6
treat (n.)	4
workshop	11

Unit 2

Achievements

be a contestant on a game or a reality show	16
become a doctor	20
become a millionaire	16
climb a mountain	20
do research	20
meet a world leader	20
play an instrument	20
speak another language	20
start a company	20
take pictures	16
win a tournament	27
write and publish a book	16

T162

Other

achieve	16
age	22
award-winning	16
camper	23
co-found	22
compose	22
conflict	23
developing country	16
diagram	20
educator	23
eventually	18
exceptional talent	22
gifted	22
in-line skating	27
inspiration	22
issue	23
keep in touch	22
neutral	23
opera	22
participants	23
peace	23
reporter	23
running water	20
social media	22
succeed	23
symphony	22
windmill	20

Unit 3

Dilemmas

cheat/don't cheat in a test	28
return/don't return a wallet	29
tell/don't tell the truth	32

Results and consequences

apologize	37
be upset with	29
excuse	34
feel guilty	29
get into trouble	29
regret	35

Other

acceptable/unacceptable	34
according to	34
answer key	28
based on	34
be supposed to	28
be tempted to	39
character	34
common sense	35
compliment	37
cope with	29
dishonest	28

envelope	37
ethical behavior	34
ethics	34
fair/unfair	34
harmless	34
hasty	35
morally	34
moss	35
perspective	34
proverb	35
quality	34
rack	33
reap	35
respectful	34
saying	35
sound advice	35
sow	35
trait	34
treat	34
weigh the pros and cons	35

Unit 4

Dreams

be famous	45
earn a good salary	45
live in another country	45
raise a family	45
run a business	45
speak a foreign language	45
take adventurous vacations	45
work in my dream job	45
work in the music industry	45

Expressions of probability

definitely	49
probably	49

Other

appliances	50
climate change	51
dam	51
download	50
electricity	51
futurist	50
geothermal	51
hydroelectric	51
megawatt	51
microscopic	50
nanotechnology	50
power plant	51
renewable energy	51
revolutionize	50
solar	51
upload	50
wireless	50

Unit 5

Super powers

become invisible	57
fly	57
have superhuman strength	57
read people's minds	57
run at lightning speed	57
travel through time	57

Other

adhesive	62
android	63
bolt of lightning	63
computer designer	62
digital	62
electrodes	62
fascinating	62
gecko	62
gesture	62
industry	63
interact	62
meteorite	63
mischievious	63
native	63
originate	63
reflexes	63
skyscraper	62
spell out	62
tweet	62
work on	62

Unit 6

Areas of study

art	68
biology	68
English (school subject)	68
literature	68
math	68
music	77
P.E.	68
science	68
social studies	68

Things we learn about in school

artist	69
democracy	68
exercise	68
grammar	68
legend	72
mammal	69
mural	68
myth	70
plant	68
playwright	69

prime number	69
Shakespeare	68
sports	68
vocabulary	68

Other

absorb	74
adapt	74
article	75
blink	74
break down	74
civilization	75
contribution	75
cultivation	75
digest	74
give birth	74
herbal remedy	75
hippopotamus	74
infection	74
influence	75
injure	74
legacy	75
meat-eating	69
nectar	74
nutrients	74
pitcher plant	74
protein	74
rays	74
revolution	75
slippery	74
sloth	74
terraced farming	75

Unit 7

Mysteries

Atlantis	84
Aurora Borealis (Northern Lights)	85
Bermuda Triangle	84
crop circles	85
Great Pyramids	85
Kryptos	88
Nazca Lines	84
sailing stones	86

Mystery-related words

explanation	85
phenomenon	85
proof	85
scientific	85
theory	85
unsolved	84
altitude	90
artifact	91
cause	92
clapping	90

clearing	91
diameter	91
effect	92
estimate	91
evidence	91
interaction	90
nitrogen	90
observant	93
oxygen	90
phenomenon	90
pole	90
rapid	91
sighting	91
solar wind	90
stand out	90
swirling	90
ton	91

Unit 8

Famous places

Big Ben	97
Christ the Redeemer statue	101
City of Petra	96
Colosseum	103
Easter Island	98
Forbidden City	96
Great Sphinx of Giza	97
Great Wall of China	101
Machu Picchu	96
Pyramid of Kukulcán	97
St. Basil's Cathedral	96
Statue of Liberty	97
Stonehenge	96
Sydney Opera House	96
Taj Mahal	97
Temple of Borobudur	97

Other

cathedral	96
mausoleum	97
monument	96
palace	96
pyramid	97
stadium	105
statue	97
temple	97
tower	97
archeologist	102
architect	100
artifact	102
Brazil	103
carving	102
century	103
Chichén Itzá	103
compile	103
dig	102
emperor	97
emporer	103
gladiator	103
goddess	102
Incan	103
Jordan	103
landmark	103
pharaoh	102
remains	102
Rio de Janerio	103
sea level	103
tomb	102
treasure	102

Unit 9

Entertainment

book signing	109
comic book exhibit	109
concert	109
festival	109
movie premiere	109

Other

bagpipes	115
bandoneon	115
Carnival	115
climax	114
concertina	115
distinctive	115
formula	114
Hollywood	108
invent	115
notes	115
novel	114
play (n.)	114
plot	114
producer	114
script	114
squeezed	115
steel drums	115
structure	114
tango	115

INTERNATIONAL PHONETIC ALPHABET

IPA Symbols

Consonants

/b/	**b**a**b**y, clu**b**
/d/	**d**own, to**d**ay, sa**d**
/f/	**f**un, pre**f**er, lau**gh**
/g/	**g**ood, be**g**in, do**g**
/h/	**h**ome, be**h**ind
/k/	**k**ey, cho**c**olate, bla**ck**
/l/	**l**ate, po**l**ice, mai**l**
/m/	**m**ay, wo**m**an, swi**m**
/n/	**n**o, opi**n**io**n**
/ŋ/	a**ng**ry, lo**ng**
/p/	**p**a**p**er, ma**p**
/r/	**r**ain, pa**r**ent, doo**r**
/s/	**s**alt, medi**c**ine, bu**s**
/š/	**s**ugar, spe**c**ial, fi**sh**
/t/	**t**ea, ma**t**erial, da**t**e
/θ/	**th**ing, heal**th**y, ba**th**
/ð/	**th**is, mo**th**er, ba**th**e
/v/	**v**ery, tra**v**el, o**f**
/w/	**w**ay, any**o**ne
/y/	**y**es, on**i**on
/z/	**z**oo, cou**s**in, alway**s**
/ž/	mea**s**ure, gara**g**e
/č/	**ch**eck, pi**c**ture, wa**tch**
/ǰ/	**j**ob, re**f**ri**g**erator, oran**g**e

Vowels

/ɑ/	**o**n, h**o**t, f**a**ther
/æ/	**a**nd, c**a**sh
/ɛ/	**e**gg, s**ay**s, l**ea**ther
/ɪ/	**i**n, b**i**g
/ɔ/	**o**ff, d**augh**ter, dr**aw**
/e/	**A**pril, tr**ai**n, s**ay**
/i/	**e**ven, sp**ea**k, tr**ee**
/o/	**o**pen, cl**o**se, sh**ow**
/u/	b**oo**t, d**o**, thr**ough**
/ʌ/	**o**f, y**ou**ng, s**u**n
/ʊ/	p**u**t, c**oo**k, w**ou**ld
/ə/	**a**bout, penc**i**l, lem**o**n
/ɚ/	moth**er**, Sat**ur**day, doct**or**
/ɜ/	**ear**th, b**ur**n, h**er**

Diphthongs

/aɪ/	**i**ce, st**y**le, l**ie**
/au/	**ou**t, d**ow**n, h**ow**
/ɔɪ/	**oi**l, n**oi**se, b**oy**

The English Alphabet

Here is the pronunciation of the letters of the English alphabet, written in International Phonetic Alphabet Symbols.

a	/e/
b	/bi/
c	/si/
d	/di/
e	/i/
f	/ɛf/
g	/ǰi/
h	/eč/
i	/aɪ/
j	/ǰe/
k	/ke/
l	/ɛl/
m	/ɛm/
n	/ɛn/
o	/o/
p	/pi/
q	/kyu/
r	/ar/
s	/ɛs/
t	/ti/
u	/yu/
v	/vi/
w	/ˈdʌbəl̩ˌyu/
x	/ɛks/
y	/waɪ/
z	/zi/

Pearson Education Limited
KAO Two
KAO Park
Harlow
Essex
CM17 9NA
England
and Associated Companies throughout the world.

www.pearsonelt.com/bigenglish2

© Pearson Education Limited 2017

Authorised adaptation from the United States edition entitled Big English, 1st Edition, by Mario Herrera and Christopher Sol Cruz. Published by Pearson Education Inc. © 2013 by Pearson Education, Inc.

The right of Mario Herrera and Christopher Sol Cruz to be identified as the authors of this Work have been asserted by them in accordance with the Copyright, Designs and Patents Act 1988.

All rights reserved; no part of this publication may be reproduced, stored in a retrieval system, or transmitted in any form or by any means, electronic, mechanical, photocopying, recording, or otherwise without the prior written permission of the Publishers.

Third impression 2018

ISBN: 978-1-2922-0346-1

Set in Heinemann Roman.
Printed and bound by CPI Group (UK) Ltd, Croydon

Acknowledgements
The publisher would like to thank the following for their kind permission to reproduce photographs:

(Key: b-bottom; c-centre; l-left; r-right; t-top)

123RF.com: elnavegante 115bl, Goodluz 93tr, Ksenia Ragozina 74br, stockbroker Intro atl, Cathy Yeulet 23; **Alamy Stock Photo:** Aflo Co., Ltd. 22l, Sabena Jane Blackbird 91r, Blend Images 10, 27cl, blickwinkel 86tr, Cultura RM 25t, 27bl, Design Pics Inc 4, dieKleinert 85tr, Dpa Picture Alliance Archive 17cr, Larry Geddis 86tl, 86br, Ilya Genkin 96c, GL Archive 22r, Glow Asia RF 6t (boy1), 7 (boy1), 78bl, 97br, Hemis 85tl, Image Source 24, Image Source Plus 69br, imageBROKER 5lt, Interfoto 19, Jamie Pham Photography 109tc, Fredrick Kippe 108br, michel platini Fernandes Borges 6 (imsosmart), Mikko Mattila - Architecture, Finland, Helsinki 11r, Jeff Morgan 14 109tl, OJO Images Ltd 32tr, 112tr, David Pearson 31 (background), PhotoAlto sas 6 (citymouse1), Reuters / Youssef Boudlal 5lb, Marc Romanelli 100tr, RubberBall 29cl, Dmitriy Shironosov 72tr, Edd Westmacott 109tr, Andrew Woodley 115r, Xinhua 17tr, Lisa F. Young 16cr; **Fotolia.com:** ALCE 98, 99, AlienCat 84t, amfroey01 19, arekmalang 27br, biker3 6 (cookie), bst2012 29 (Al), chawalitpix 62tl, 80tr, Elenathewise 27t, faizzaki 74l, feferoni 85cl, Forewer 117, gavran333 29tr, grafikplusfoto 16tr, Jörg Hackemann 65, 93br, Eric Isselée 74tr, Iva 96tl, J_Foto 29tl, KaYann 16cl, Andrey Kiselev 56tr, 80-81b, lunamarina 66br, Magann 116t, Felix Mizioznikov 28r, Monteleone 7 (rainbowgirl), Notyouraveragebear 90, PiLensPhoto 85cr, Andres Rodriguez 46t, Sabphoto 16br, sellingpix 45tr, sjhuls 105b, Subbotina Anna 97cr; **Getty Images:** Anna_Om 109cl, 120cr; **Pearson Education Ltd:** Jon Barlow 57cl; **PunchStock:** 60tr; **Shutterstock.com:** AVAVA 15br, 45br, Galina Barskaya 5tr, Intro bbr, John David Bigl III 79, bikeriderlondon 66bl, 113t, Blend Images Intro ctl, Rob Byron 29bl, 55br, CandyBox Images 111, chungking 96tr, Costazzurra 56br, Creatista 57tc, Robert Crum 29 (Emily), Danomyte 64t, Dieter H 75bl, 115tl, Jaimie Duplass 17bl, 55bl, 106br, egd 109cr, erashov 113c, Hugo Felix 110, Tara Flake 5 (cute), 7 (cute), 78br, fotohunter 103l, Gelpi JM 57c, Goodluz Intro ctr, GuoZhongHua 47, Ruslan Guzov 97bl, holbox 29 (Angela), Hubis 50, Hurst Photo 37bc, jsouthby 113b, julia 102cl, Kamira 75tl, karelnoppe 62r, John Kershner 84cr, kouptsova 6 (34309843), 17br, 29br, 53tr, 94br, Pius Lee 97tr, R. Gino Santa Maria 5tl, 7 (techieboy), 118br, Intro bbl, michaeljung 69bl, Dudarev Mikhail 102 (background), milias1987 34, Monkey Business Images 5bl, 20tr, 45bl, 53tl, 68t, 116cl, 116cr, Intro abr, Nella 97tl, Nestor Noci 17c, Sergey Novikov 68b, Odua Images 53b, Oleg_Mit 54br, Oleksiy Mark 44, Edyta Pawlowska 28l, Pecold 96 (background), 96cr, Photobac 25b, photogl 16l, 40-41b, Phon Promwisate 97cl, Real Deal Photo 57tr, Julian Rovagnati 13, Ryan R Fox Intro acl, S-F 56cl, S.Borisov 46b, Sanmongkhol 14bl, Kirill Saveliev 104, 120tr, Serg64 18, Slazdi 105t, Somchai Som 97tc, 20br, James Steidl 108bc (background), Syda Productions 57bl, 85bl, 109bl, szefei 95tr, Shane W Thompson 75br, Aleksandar Todorovic 96tc, upthebanner 101, Kiselev Andrey Valerevich 5b, Jason Vandehey 27cr, Claudia Veja 108bl, Pippa West 103r, Tracy Whiteside 57tl, 57cr, WitR. 107, Ann Worthy 57br, 85br, 109br, Lisa F. Young 88tr, Zurijeta 53cl, 106bl; **SuperStock:** SOMOS 8t

Cover Images: *Front:* **Alamy Stock Photo:** Ronnie Chua

All other images © Pearson Education

Every effort has been made to trace the copyright holders and we apologise in advance for any unintentional omissions. We would be pleased to insert the appropriate acknowledgement in any subsequent edition of this publication.

Illustrated by
Valentina Belloni, Paula Franco, Anthony Lewis, Zaharias Papadopoulos (Hyphen), Rob Sharp, Christos Skaltsas (Hyphen),